# The
# Time-Life
# American
# Regional
# Cookbook

*Old-fashioned strawberry shortcake is one of America's most popular desserts.*

# The
# Time-Life
# American
# Regional
# Cookbook

*By the Editors of Time-Life Books*

Little, Brown and Company
Boston, Toronto

*T   06/78*

*Published simultaneously in Canada by Little, Brown & Company (Canada) Limited.*
*Library of Congress Cataloging in Publication Data*
*Main entry under title:*
*Time-Life American regional cookbook*
  *Includes index.*
    *1. Cookery, American regional. I. Time-Life Books.*
*II. Title: American regional*
*LOC 77–85391*
*ISBN 0–316–846–198*

*First Edition*

*Produced by Media Projects Incorporated.*

*Printed in the United States of America*

The TIME-LIFE American Regional Cookbook is a collection of tested recipes by leading authorities in the world of cooking that were originally published in the TIME-LIFE Books series Foods of the World and the Illustrated Library of Cooking. This volume contains recipes written by the experts listed below:

The late Michael Field, consulting editor for the Foods of the World series, was one of America's top-ranking experts and a contributor to leading magazines.

James A. Beard, a leading authority on American cuisine, is also an accomplished teacher and writer of the culinary arts.

The late Dione Lucas attended the famous Ecole du Cordon Bleu in Paris and received its diploma, Europe's highest award for fine cooking.

Ann Roe Robbins is the author of *How to Cook Well* and co-author of *The Dione Lucas Meat and Poultry Cook Book.*

The late Ruth Wakefield, who owned and managed the famous Toll House Restaurant at Whitman, Massachusetts, was the author of *Toll House Cook Book.*

Allison Williams is the author of *The Embassy Cookbook,* her collection of authentic recipes from various embassies in Washington.

# Contents

# *Introduction*

American home cooking—despite the temptations of convenience foods and fast food chains—remains rooted in regional tradition. It is shaped by a variety of factors, including history, population, climate, terrain and availability of ingredients, and is given further definition by the contributions of each successive immigrant group. From this great, diverse treasury of American recipes, we have chosen those that best reflect America's regions. Each recipe has been carefully tested, and many are accompanied by helpful step-by-step illustrations.

A culinary map of America would show regions based on geography and common traditions. We have identified six—New England, Eastern Heartland, the South, Creole-Acadian, the Northwest, the Far West —and one abstract "region" called the Melting Pot, which encompasses ethnic communities across the nation.

It was in New England, the northeasternmost region of America that ranges from Connecticut up through Rhode Island, Massachusetts, New Hampshire, Vermont and Maine (and including, for our purposes, Quebec and Nova Scotia), that the main traditions of American cooking got their start. Here the French and English colonists learned to adapt old-world kitchen techniques to such strange, new foods as wild turkey, corn, cranberries and pumpkins. They adapted well, and we are all beneficiaries of their skill and versatility.

West and south of New England is the region we have designated the Eastern Heartland: New York, New Jersey, Pennsylvania, Ohio, Michigan, Indiana and Illinois. These states enjoy a food heritage that originated with the Dutch, English and German colonists who made their homes in this lush agricultural region. Eastern Heartland cooking is stick-to-the-ribs stuff, more plain than fancy, given to substantial meat dishes, dumplings, breads, pies. It is hard to resist the seafood native to Long Island's waters; the corn-and-pork sturdiness of the Pennsylvania Dutch, Indiana and Illinois farm kitchens; the wonderful fish and game of Michigan's waterways and forests. It is a region where country cooking flourishes at its most impressive, but it is also the region that taught the entire country—through the influences of polyglot New York City —how to enjoy the finest sophistications of the table.

Of course, sophistication at the table is a hallmark, too, of the South, encompassing the Confederate states of Virginia, North and South Carolina, Georgia, Florida, Alabama, Mississippi, Tennessee and Arkansas, as well as southern Missouri, Kentucky, West Virginia, Maryland and Delaware, which are essentially southern in their cooking. The Deep South, home of soul food—grits, collard greens, cornbread, black-eyed peas, sweet-potato pie and countless ways of frying chicken—is equally famed for succulent Smithfield ham, lemony pickled shrimp, chocolate-rich black-bottom pie, piquant Key lime pie, coolly delicious peppermint stick ice cream and stuffed crabs.

New Orleans and southern Louisiana is a culinary world apart. The Creoles, descended from French and Spanish colonists, aspired to delicate blends and subtle combinations: *daube glacé,* chopped sliced meat cooked with herbs and covered with homemade meat jelly; chicken Rochambeau, chicken breasts masked with tarragon-flavored Béarnaise sauce and served over mushroom-coated ham slices; and pompano *en papillote,* fillets of pompano baked with shrimp and crab in parchment paper. In contrast, the later-arriving Acadians (or Cajuns) were French-speaking exiles from Nova Scotia whose food was—and is—peppery and pungent. Meats, fish and shellfish were sometimes fiercely spiced but then almost always calmed by a bed of gentle white rice. Among the Acadian specialties are seafood gumbo with crabs, shrimp and okra, and hotly spiced crawfish boil.

The sprawling, diverse region of the Northwest is edged on the east by Iowa, Minnesota and Wisconsin and on the west from Oregon through Washington and British Columbia to Alaska. In between are the mountain states of Idaho, Wyoming and Montana, and the plains states of Nebraska and North and South Dakota. The frontier past is much alive here, and the legacy of the pioneers ties the region together. Meals were, and are, simple, centering around the sportsfish and seafood of the Pacific Northwest, and plentiful game. Among the savory Northwestern specialties are tomato-cheese pie, venison mincemeat, trout in aspic, King crab salad ring, rhubarb custard pie and plum ketchup.

The cooking of America's Far West—California, Nevada, Utah, Arizona, Colorado, New Mexico, Kansas, Oklahoma, Texas and Hawaii— combines the hardiest traditions of campfire cookery with dishes learned from American Indians, Mexicans and the Spanish. The Far West kitchen culture is very new, and tolerates all that is good. The cooking is dominated by the profusion of fresh fruits and vegetables available all year round in California, "Tex-Mex" dishes such as tacos, tortillas and chili con carne, the Chinese stir-fry and the ubiquitous barbeque.

American cookery has also been shaped by the immigrants who settled in well-defined communities across the nation. The cooking of Central and Eastern Europe has flourished in enclaves in New Jersey, Chicago, Iowa and Nebraska; Basque sheepherders in Idaho retain their culinary heritage, as do the Greeks who settled in Florida, the Portuguese on Cape Cod, the Armenians in California, the Germans in Texas and the Japanese and Chinese who massed on the west and east coasts, the millions of Italians, Russians, Poles, Jews and Puerto Ricans who made their homes in New York and other metropolitan areas. These peoples transplanted their culture and their cooking, making spaghetti with meatballs, lasagne, shrimp chow mein, egg foo yung, pizza, fish teriyaki and blintzes part of the bubbling "melting pot" of America.

The recipes in this book, will allow you to sample the best cooking of these regions and of the nation. Some of the recipes are identified by region or ethnic heritage; the lack of identification points to the happy fact that a dish's popularity has gone beyond the confines of a particular region and can be considered an American favorite.

THE EDITORS

# Appetizers & First Courses

Having friends in to drinks can mean four or twenty-four, and the food on such relaxed, informal occasions may range from nuts and olives to finger foods so satisfying that dinner afterward becomes unnecessary. But when the drinks are meant to lead up to dinner, appetizers should be limited to a few attractively-presented, well-prepared foods intended to tease, not deaden, the palate.

Cocktails and cocktail parties seem to be an American invention. Americans do serve formal first courses on special occasions, and on the following pages are recipes for such elegant dishes as oysters Rockefeller and shad-roe pâté. For the most part, however, Americans tend to serve first courses informally, and this chapter features a wide variety of appetizers that are easy to eat without plates. Among the most popular are those that feature raw vegetables: there are few hors d'oeuvre more refreshing and less filling (as well as less fattening!) than a bowl of washed, neatly cut, crisp vegetables set in crushed ice and accompanied by a dip or spread.

The cheese tray has become another purely American tradition at cocktail time, and has the advantage of not requiring any preparation (unless you are inspired to make the spicy beer cheese recipe, following). American dairylands produce scores of good American interpretations of classic cheeses: superb cheddar, Swiss-type Emmenthaler, soft, silky Brie, and pungent blue cheese. An imported cheese tray might feature a small selection of cheeses varied in texture and flavor: perhaps a wedge of nutty Norwegian Jarlsberg, a slice of mellow Italian Fontina, and a dollop of creamy, herbed Boursin. Stay away from the very pungent cheeses that may have a stronger flavor than the dinner to follow, and from too-sweet dessert cheese, more appropriate with fruit after the meal. Be sure to take the cheese out of the refrigerator several hours before serving, or the cold will deaden its flavor and aroma.

OPPOSITE
*Shrimp-stuffed artichoke, displayed here in its most elegant form, is an attractive, delectable first course.*

11

To serve 4

4 large artichokes, each 4 to 5 inches
    in diameter at the base
1 lemon, cut in half crosswise
Salt
1 pound uncooked shrimp
½ pound plus 4 tablespoons
    butter, cut into ½-inch bits
6 cups soft fresh crumbs made from
    French- or Italian-type white
    bread, pulverized in a blender or
    finely shredded with a fork

1 cup finely chopped onions
4 teaspoons finely chopped garlic
2 cups freshly grated imported
    Romano or Parmesan cheese
½ cup finely chopped fresh
    parsley, preferably the flat-leaf
    Italian variety
2 teaspoons finely grated fresh
    lemon peel
½ cup Creole vinaigrette sauce*

With a small sharp knife, trim the bases of the artichokes flush and flat. Bend and snap off the small bottom leaves and any bruised outer leaves. Lay each artichoke on its side and slice about 1 inch off the top. With scissors, trim ¼ inch off the points of the rest of the leaves. To prevent discoloring, rub all the cut edges with lemon as you proceed.

In a 10- to 12-quart enameled pot, bring 5 quarts of water and 2 tablespoons of salt to a boil over high heat. Drop in the artichokes and one lemon half and return the water to a boil. Cook briskly, uncovered, for 15 to 20 minutes, or until the bases of the artichokes show no resistance when pierced with the point of a small sharp knife.

With tongs, invert the artichokes in a colander to drain. Discard the lemon and all but about 1 inch of the cooking liquid. Set the pot aside.

Meanwhile, shell the shrimp. Make a shallow incision down their backs with a small sharp knife and lift out the intestinal vein with the point of the knife. Wash the shrimp briefly in a colander set under cold running water. Then drop them into enough lightly salted boiling water to immerse the shrimp completely. Cook uncovered for 3 to 5 minutes, until they are pink and firm to the touch. Drain the shrimp and pat them dry with paper towels. Reserve four of the shrimp for garnish and chop the rest into fine bits. Set the shrimp aside.

Melt ½ pound of the butter bits in a heavy 12-inch skillet set over moderate heat, stirring so that the butter melts without browning. When the foam begins to subside, add the bread crumbs and stir over moderate heat until the crumbs are crisp and golden. With a rubber spatula, scrape the contents of the skillet into a bowl and set it aside.

In the same skillet, melt the remaining 4 tablespoons of butter bits over moderate heat. When the foam subsides, add the onions and garlic, and stir for about 5 minutes, until they are soft and translucent but not

* *See index.*

brown. Scrape the onion mixture over the bread crumbs, add the reserved shrimp, grated cheese, parsley and lemon peel, and toss the ingredients together gently but thoroughly with a spoon. Taste for seasoning.

Divide the shrimp mixture into four equal portions and stuff each artichoke in the following fashion: Starting near the base, gently ease the top of one leaf away from the artichoke and spoon about a teaspoonful of the shrimp mixture into the opening. Push the shrimp mixture down between the leaf and the artichoke, then press the leaf back into place.

Repeat until all of the large green outer leaves have been stuffed, then stand the artichoke upright on a large piece of heavy-duty aluminum foil. Fold the foil tightly up and around the artichoke, and twist the ends securely together at the top. To keep the stuffing in place, tie a short length of kitchen cord around the widest part of the foil package. Set aside. Stuff and wrap the remaining artichokes in the same way.

Stand the artichokes upright in the reserved pot and bring the liquid to a boil over high heat. Cover tightly and steam the artichokes for 20 minutes. With tongs, transfer the artichokes to a cutting board and remove the strings and foil. Arrange the artichokes attractively on a heated platter or four individual serving plates, and place one of the reserved whole shrimp on top of each one. Serve the Creole vinaigrette sauce separately as an accompaniment to the inner leaves and bottom of the artichokes.

## *Cheese-stuffed Mushroom Caps*  (*Italian-American*)

To make 18

1 cup ricotta cheese
¼ cup finely chopped parsley
¼ pound prosciutto (thinly sliced Italian cured ham), finely chopped
2 teaspoons salt

Freshly ground black pepper
1 tablespoon strained fresh lemon juice
4 tablespoons olive oil
18 medium-sized mushroom caps
2½ ounces mozzarella cheese, cut into ¼-inch bits (½ cup)

Preheat the oven to 400°. Place the ricotta in a large mixing bowl and, with a wooden spoon, beat in the parsley, prosciutto, salt, a few gratings of black pepper and the lemon juice. Beat vigorously until the ingredients are well combined and the mixture is smooth. Set aside.

In a 10- to 12-inch stainless-steel or enameled skillet, heat the oil until a light haze forms above it. Drop in the mushroom caps and fry over moderate heat for about 2 minutes, then turn them over and fry for another minute or two until they are lightly browned. Remove from the heat.

Fill the mushroom caps with the ricotta mixture and top each cap with bits of mozzarella. Arrange the caps side by side in a shallow baking dish or jelly-roll pan and bake in the center of the oven for 8 minutes, or until the filling begins to bubble. Slide the caps under a hot broiler for 30 seconds to brown the mozzarella topping. Serve at once as an accompaniment to drinks or as part of an antipasto.

## Marinated Mushrooms

To serve 6 as a first course

| | |
|---|---|
| 1 pound firm fresh mushroom caps, each about 1 inch in diameter | pepper |
| | 3 tablespoons finely chopped onions |
| 1 cup dry white wine | 1 tablespoon very finely chopped |
| 1 lemon | garlic |
| 1⅔ cups olive oil | 3 whole cloves |
| 1 teaspoon Tabasco sauce | 1 medium-sized bay leaf |
| 2 teaspoons salt | 3 tablespoons finely chopped fresh |
| ⅛ teapoon freshly ground black | parsley |

Make the marinated mushrooms at least 2 days before you intend to serve them. Wipe the mushroom caps with a dampened kitchen towel and drop them into a deep bowl. Pour in the wine and turn the mushrooms about with a spoon to coat them evenly. Cover with foil or plastic wrap and marinate in the refrigerator for about 1 hour.

With a small, sharp knife, score the lemon by cutting V-shaped grooves, about ⅛ inch wide and ⅛ inch deep, from one end of the lemon to the other and spaced about ½ inch apart. Then slice the lemon crosswise into ¼-inch-thick rounds.

In a mixing bowl, beat the olive oil, Tabasco sauce, salt and pepper together with a wire whisk. Add the onions and garlic and stir well, then drop in the lemon slices, cloves and bay leaf. Drain the wine from the mushroom caps and in its place add the oil mixture. Turn the caps about gently with a spoon until they are evenly coated.

Transfer the entire contents of the bowl to a wide-mouthed 1-quart jar or crock equipped with a tight-fitting lid. Cover and refrigerate for at least 2 days. Sprinkle with parsley before serving. The mushrooms can safely be kept in the refrigerator for 2 to 3 weeks.

OPPOSITE
*Either wild or cultivated mushroom caps can be used for marinated mushrooms.*

14

## Mushroom Caps Stuffed with Anchovy Cream Cheese

To make 3 dozen

36 small white mushrooms, each
about 1 inch in diameter (about 1
pound)
An 8-ounce package of cream cheese,

softened to room temperature
2 tablespoons anchovy paste
1 teaspoon lemon juice
1 teaspoon finely grated onion
2 tablespoons finely cut fresh chives

One at a time, remove the stems from the mushrooms by holding their caps securely, and gently bending back the stems until they snap free. With a small sharp knife, cut away any part of the stem that adheres to the center of the mushroom. It is not necessary to wash the mushrooms; merely wipe them clean with a damp cloth.

In a small mixing bowl, beat the cream cheese with a large spoon until smooth. Beat in the anchovy paste, lemon juice and grated onion. Taste for seasoning. Then spoon the mixture into a pastry bag fitted with a small star tip and pipe it into the mushroom caps. Or, if you prefer, use a small spoon to fill the mushrooms with the cheese mixture, mounding it slightly. Sprinkle lightly with the chives and refrigerate the mushrooms until ready to serve.

## Vegetables with Red Caviar Dip

To make 3 cups

VEGETABLES
4 cucumbers, peeled, seeded and cut
into 2-by-½-inch strips
4 carrots, peeled and cut into 2-by-
½-inch strips

2 green peppers, seeded and cut into
2-by-½-inch strips
4 celery stalks, cut into 2-by-½-inch
strips
1 bunch scallions, trimmed and cut
into 2-inch lengths
12 cherry tomatoes

Soak the vegetable strips in a bowl of ice water for an hour to crisp them. Pat dry with paper towels and arrange on a platter with the tomatoes. Cover with plastic wrap and refrigerate.

VEGETABLE DIP
1 pint sour cream
2 tablespoons finely chopped fresh
dill
2 tablespoons finely chopped

scallions, green stems only
½ teaspoon lemon juice
Pinch of cayenne pepper
8 ounces red caviar
1 tablespoon finely chopped parsley

Combine in a deep, attractive bowl the sour cream, dill, parsley, chopped scallions, lemon juice and cayenne. Gently fold in the caviar with a rubber spatula without crushing the fragile eggs. Taste for seasoning, then chill until ready to serve.

Serve cold, accompanied by the platter of cold vegetables.

## *Vegetables with Hot Butter-and-Anchovy Dip* *(Italian-American)*

To serve 4

VEGETABLES

1 large green pepper, halved, seeded, deribbed and cut into 2-by-½-inch strips
1 cucumber, peeled, cut in half lengthwise, seeded and cut into 2-by-½-inch strips
2 celery stalks, trimmed and cut into 2-by-½-inch strips
12 cherry tomatoes
¼ pound small mushrooms
12 red radishes, trimmed and washed

Place the strips of pepper, cucumber and celery in a bowl of ice water and soak them for about 1 hour, or until they are crisp. Drain, pat them dry with paper towels, and arrange them on a platter with the cherry tomatoes, mushrooms and radishes. Cover with plastic wrap and refrigerate.

SAUCE
¼ pound unsalted butter
¼ cup olive oil
6 cloves garlic, peeled and sliced
paper thin (3 tablespoons)
4 ounces anchovy fillets, drained, rinsed under cold running water and finely chopped

In a heavy 1-quart enameled or stainless-steel saucepan, combine the butter, oil and garlic. Cook over low heat, stirring frequently, for about 15 minutes, adjusting the heat if necessary to make sure that the butter does not burn. Stir in the chopped anchovies and, stirring constantly, cook for 10 minutes longer; do not let the mixture come to a boil.

Transfer the sauce to a 1- or 1½-cup flameproof container that fits over a candle warmer or spirit lamp, or set the container on an electric hot tray. Use as a dip for the cold vegetables.

The hot sauce may also be served with boiled fish or meat.

## Crab-Olive Spread *(Far West)*

To make about 2½ cups

½ cup homemade mayonnaise
  or substitute ½ cup
  unsweetened bottled
  mayonnaise
2 tablespoons finely chopped fresh
  parsley
2 teaspoons strained fresh lemon
  juice

2 teaspoons Worcestershire sauce
1 teaspoon bottled horseradish
2 hard-cooked eggs, finely chopped
½ cup finely chopped ripe olives
1 cup freshly cooked, canned or
  defrosted frozen crabmeat,
  drained and picked over to
  remove all bits of shell and
  cartilage

Combine the mayonnaise, parsley, lemon juice, Worcestershire sauce and horseradish in a deep bowl and mix well. Stir in the chopped eggs and olives and, when they are thoroughly incorporated, gently fold in the crabmeat. Serve at once as a spread for crackers, or cover the bowl with plastic wrap and refrigerate until ready to serve. Tightly covered, the crab-olive spread can safely be kept in the refrigerator for a day.

## Mussel, Herb and Caper Spread *(New England)*

To make about 3 cups

MAYONNAISE
2 egg yolks
1 tablespoon wine vinegar
1½ teaspoons dry mustard
1 teaspoon salt

⅛ teaspoon ground white pepper
1 cup vegetable oil
2 tablespoons strained fresh lemon
  juice
1 teaspoon finely chopped garlic

First, prepare the mayonnaise in the following fashion: Warm a small mixing bowl in hot water, dry it quickly but thoroughly, and drop in the egg yolks. With a wire whisk or a rotary or electric beater, beat the yolks vigorously for about 2 minutes until they thicken and cling to the beater when it is lifted from the bowl. Stir in the vinegar, mustard, salt and white pepper. Then beat in ½ cup of the oil, ½ teaspoon at a time; make sure each addition is absorbed before adding more. By the time the ½ cup of oil has been beaten in, the sauce should be the consistency of thick cream. Pour in the remaining oil in a slow, thin stream, beating constantly. Stir in the lemon juice and garlic and taste for seasoning. (There should be about 1 cup of mayonnaise.) Refrigerate until ready to use.

6 dozen large mussels in their shells
2 hard-cooked eggs, finely chopped
¼ cup capers, drained, rinsed
   thoroughly in a sieve under cold

running water and patted
   completely dry with paper towels
¼ cup finely cut fresh chives
¼ cup finely chopped fresh parsley

Scrub the mussels thoroughly under cold running water with a stiff brush or soapless steel-mesh scouring pad. With a small, sharp knife scrape or pull the black hairlike tufts off the shells and discard them.

Combine the mussels and 1 cup of water in a heavy 4- to 6-quart casserole and bring to a boil over high heat. Cover tightly, reduce the heat to low and let the mussels steam for 10 minutes, turning them about in the pot once or twice with a slotted spoon. When the mussels have steamed, all the shells should have opened; discard any that remain shut.

With tongs or a slotted spoon, transfer the mussels to a large platter. Remove and discard the shells. Then chop the mussels coarsely and let them cool to room temperature.

In a large bowl, combine the mussels, chopped hard-cooked eggs, capers, chives and parsley and toss them together gently but thoroughly. Add the mayonnaise and turn the mussel mixture about with a spoon until all the ingredients are well coated with the mayonnaise. Serve with toast points or toast triangles, as a first course or an accompaniment to drinks.

## Shad-Roe Pâté  *(Northwest)*

To make about 2½ cups

2 pairs shad roe (about 1½
   pounds)
½ cup plus 2 tablespoons flour
4 tablespoons butter
1 tablespoon vegetable oil
2 tablespoons finely chopped onions
1 cup heavy cream
2 tablespoons strained fresh lemon
   juice

½ teaspoon finely chopped garlic
¼ teaspoon celery seeds
¼ teaspoon crumbled dried
   marjoram
¼ teaspoon crumbled dried
   tarragon
⅛ teaspoon crumbled dried basil
1 teaspoon salt

Wash the roe under cold running water and pat them completely dry with paper towels. With scissors or a small, sharp knife, slit the membranes connecting the pairs of roe. Roll the roe gently in ½ cup of flour to coat them evenly, then shake gently to remove the excess flour.

In a heavy 8-inch skillet, melt the butter with the oil over moderate heat. When the foam begins to subside, add the roe and cook them for about 6 minutes on each side, turning them with a slotted spatula and regulating the heat so that they color richly without burning. Transfer the roe to a bowl and, with the back of a table fork, mash them to a smooth but granular paste.

Add the onions to the fat remaining in the skillet and, stirring frequently, cook for about 5 minutes, until they are soft and translucent but not brown. Stir in the remaining 2 tablespoons of flour and mix well. Then, stirring the mixture constantly with a wire whisk, pour in the cream in a slow, thin stream and cook over high heat until the sauce comes to a boil, thickens heavily and is smooth. Reduce the heat to low and simmer for about 3 minutes. Beat in the lemon juice, garlic, celery seeds, marjoram, tarragon, basil and salt, and taste for seasoning.

Add the sauce to the mashed roe and, with a wooden spoon, beat until the mixture is smooth. Cool to room temperature, cover tightly with foil or plastic wrap, and refrigerate for at least 3 hours, or until thoroughly chilled. Serve the shad-roe pâté as a first course, accompanied by crisp crackers or warm toast.

OPPOSITE
*Pickled shrimp get
their distinctive
tang from a
blend of lemons,
onions and spices.*

To make about 3 cups

1½ pounds raw shrimp, shelled and deveined (*see shrimp-stuffed artichokes**)

8 tablespoons unsalted butter, softened

2 tablespoons pale dry sherry

4 teaspoons strained fresh lemon juice

4 teaspoons finely grated onion

½ teaspoon ground mace

½ teaspoon dry mustard

½ teaspoon ground hot red pepper (cayenne)

2 teaspoons salt

½ teaspoon ground white pepper

Drop the shrimp into enough boiling water to immerse them completely and boil briskly, uncovered, for 3 minutes, or until they are firm and pink. Drain the shrimp, spread them on paper towels and pat them completely dry with fresh towels. Then put the shrimp through the finest blade of a food grinder. If you lack a food grinder, chop the shrimp as fine as possible and pound them to a smooth paste with a mortar and pestle or in a bowl with the back of a spoon.

In a deep bowl, cream the butter by beating and mashing it against the sides of the bowl with the back of a wooden spoon until it is light and fluffy. Beat in the sherry, lemon juice, onion, mace, mustard, red pepper, salt and white pepper. When thoroughly incorporated, add the shrimp and continue to beat until the mixture is smooth. Taste for seasoning.

Transfer the shrimp paste to a 3-cup serving bowl or mold, spreading it and smoothing the top with a spatula. Cover with foil or plastic wrap and refrigerate for at least 4 hours, or until the paste is firm to the touch.

Serve the paste directly from the bowl, or unmold it in the following fashion: Run a thin-bladed knife around the edges of the mold to loosen it and dip the bottom in hot water. Place an inverted serving plate over the bowl and, grasping plate and bowl together firmly, turn them over. Rap the plate on a table and the shrimp paste should slide out easily.

In Charleston, South Carolina, shrimp paste is traditionally served for breakfast, or with wafers or crackers as an accompaniment for drinks.

* *See index.*

To make 6 stuffed eggs

6 large hard-cooked eggs, shelled
A 4-ounce can Maine sardines,
  thoroughly drained
½ cup freshly made mayonnaise
  or substitute ½ cup
  commercial unsweetened
  mayonnaise

2 tablespoons strained fresh lemon
  juice
2 teaspoons dry mustard
¼ teaspoon ground hot red pepper
  (cayenne)
½ teaspoon salt
¼ cup finely chopped fresh parsley
¼ cup finely cut fresh chives

With a small, sharp knife, cut a ⅛-inch slice off the bottom of each egg so that it will stand upright. Then slice off the top third of each egg, chop the scraps of egg white finely and set them aside.

Gently squeeze the yolks out of the eggs, taking care not to break the white cases. Mash the yolks and sardines together with a fork or purée them through a food mill into a mixing bowl. Beat the mayonnaise into the purée and, when it is well incorporated, add the lemon juice, mustard, red pepper and salt. Taste for seasoning.

Spoon the filling into the egg-white cases, dividing it evenly among them and mounding it smoothly on top. Mix the reserved chopped egg whites, the parsley and chives together in a shallow bowl, then dip the filled eggs into the mixture, rolling them around to coat the tops thoroughly.

Stand the eggs on a chilled serving platter and serve at once, or cover the platter loosely with wax paper and refrigerate until ready to serve.

*Beer Cheese*  (*South*)

To make about 1½ cups

1½ teaspoons finely chopped
  garlic
1 tablespoon Worcestershire sauce
½ teaspoon Tabasco

½ teaspoon dry mustard
½ teaspoon salt
1 cup beer
4 cups (1 pound) freshly grated
  sharp natural Cheddar cheese

In a deep bowl, crush the garlic to a paste with a pestle or the back of a spoon. Beat in the Worcestershire, Tabasco, mustard and salt. Then, stirring the mixture constantly, pour in the beer in a slow, thin stream. When the ingredients are well blended, beat in the cheese, a cupful at a time, and continue to beat until the mixture is smooth.

Pack the beer cheese tightly into a 2-cup mold or an earthenware crock. Cover with a lid or foil and refrigerate for at least 24 hours before serving. Beer cheese is traditionally served with crisp crackers as a first course or as an accompaniment to drinks.

## Cheese Balls

To make about 2 dozen 1-inch balls

1 cup freshly grated Monterey Jack cheese plus 1 cup freshly grated Cheddar or longhorn cheese, or 2 cups any combination of these cheeses
2 tablespoons flour
1 cup fresh cracker crumbs, made from saltines pulverized in a blender or wrapped in wax paper and finely crushed with a rolling pin
3 egg whites
1½ teaspoons prepared mustard
Vegetable oil for deep frying
Salt

Combine the grated cheese and flour in a deep mixing bowl and toss them together with a spoon. Spread the cracker crumbs on a piece of wax paper and set aside.

With a wire whisk or a rotary or electric beater, beat the egg whites until they are stiff enough to stand in unwavering peaks on the whisk or beater when it is lifted from the bowl. Scoop the egg whites over the cheese mixture with a rubber spatula, add the mustard, and fold the ingredients together gently but thoroughly.

To make each cheese ball, scoop up a heaping tablespoonful of the cheese mixture and mold it into a ball by placing a second tablespoon on top. Slide the cheese ball off the spoon onto the cracker crumbs and roll it about to coat it evenly. Transfer the cheese ball to a piece of wax paper and set it aside while you proceed to shape and coat the remaining balls. (At this stage, the cheese balls can be draped with wax paper and refrigerated for up to 12 hours or overnight if you like.)

Pour vegetable oil into a deep fryer or large heavy saucepan to a depth of about 3 inches and heat the oil until it reaches a temperature of 375° on a deep-frying thermometer.

Deep-fry the cheese balls, four or five at a time, turning them about with a slotted spoon for about 3 minutes, or until they are crisp and golden brown. As they color, transfer them to paper towels to drain.

Arrange the cheese balls attractively on a heated platter, season them lightly with a sprinkling of salt, and serve them while they are still warm as an accompaniment to drinks.

To make 2½ to 3 cups

3 medium-sized firm ripe tomatoes
   or 1 cup chopped drained canned
   tomatoes
2 tablespoons butter
2 tablespoons flour
1 cup light cream
½ teaspoon finely chopped garlic
½ teaspoon salt

A 4-ounce can green chilies (not
   the *jalapeño* variety), drained,
   stemmed, seeded and finely
   chopped
2 cups (½ pound) freshly grated
   Monterey Jack cheese, or
   substitute 2 cups freshly grated
   Münster cheese

If you are using fresh rather than canned tomatoes, drop them into enough boiling water to immerse them completely. After 15 seconds, run the tomatoes under cold water and peel them with a small sharp knife. Then cut out the stems, slice the tomatoes in half crosswise and squeeze the halves gently to remove the seeds and juice. Chop the tomatoes coarsely.

In a heavy 1- to 1½-quart saucepan, melt the butter over moderate heat. When the foam begins to subside, add the flour and mix well. Stirring constantly with a wire whisk, pour in the cream in a slow, thin stream and cook over high heat until the sauce comes to a boil, thickens heavily and is smooth. Reduce the heat to low and simmer for 2 or 3 minutes to remove any taste of raw flour. Set the sauce aside off the heat.

Combine the tomatoes, garlic and salt in a heavy 10- to 12-inch skillet and, stirring frequently, cook briskly, uncovered, until the mixture is thick enough to hold its shape almost solidly in a spoon. Reduce the heat to low and stir in the cream sauce and chilies. Without letting the mixture boil, stir in the grated cheese a handful at a time.

To serve, light the burner under a fondue pot or chafing dish. If you are using a chafing dish, pour hot (not boiling) water into the bottom pan. Ladle the *chile con queso* into the fondue pot or chafing dish and serve at once, accompanied by *tostaditas*\* or crackers.

\* *See index.*

## Guacamole with Chilies *(Far West)*
AVOCADO DIP

To make about 2 cups

2 large ripe avocados
1 large firm ripe tomato, peeled,
  seeded and finely chopped *(see
  chile con queso* *)*
2 hard-cooked eggs, finely chopped
½ cup finely chopped onions
2 canned green chilies (not the
*jalapeño* variety), drained, seeded
  and finely chopped
1 tablespoon strained fresh lime
  juice
2 teaspoons salt
1 tablespoon finely chopped fresh
  coriander (optional)
*Tostaditas* *

Cut the avocados in half. With the tip of a small knife, loosen the seeds and lift them out. Remove any brown tissuelike fibers that cling to the flesh. Strip off the skins with your fingers or the knife, starting at the narrow or stem end. Chop the avocados coarsely; then, in a deep bowl, mash them to a rough purée. Add the tomato, half of the chopped eggs, the onions, chilies, lime juice and salt, and mix them together gently but thoroughly. Taste for seasoning.

Mound the *guacamole* in a serving bowl, scatter the remaining chopped eggs over it and, if you are using it, sprinkle the coriander on top. Serve at once, accompanied by the *tostaditas*.

## Cheese Pennies

To make about 3 dozen

8 tablespoons butter (1 quarter-
  pound stick), softened
½ pound Cheddar cheese, grated
  (about 2 cups)
¾ cup sifted flour
½ teaspoon salt
⅛ teaspoon cayenne
½ teaspoon powdered mustard

Cream the butter by beating it against the sides of a bowl with a wooden spoon until it is light and fluffy. Then beat in the cheese. Still beating, add the flour, ¼ cup at a time, then the salt, cayenne and mustard. (The entire process may be done more easily in an electric mixer equipped with a paddle or pastry arm attachment.) In either case, the mixture should be dense enough to be formed into a compact ball. If it is too soft to hold to-

* See index.

gether, beat in additional flour by the tablespoonful, testing the dough for density after each addition. On a lightly floured surface, shape the ball into a sausagelike roll about 10 inches long and 1¼ inches wide, wrap it in wax paper and refrigerate for at least an hour, until firm.

Preheat the oven to 350°. With a sharp, thin knife, carefully slice the chilled dough into ¼-inch rounds and arrange them ½ inch apart on an ungreased cookie sheet. Bake in the middle of the oven for 8 to 10 minutes, or until the pennies are firm and golden brown. Watch carefully; they burn easily. Transfer them with a metal spatula to a rack to cool. The cheese pennies may be served at once at room temperature, or stored in an airtight container or frozen for future use.

## Caraway Twists

To make about 4 dozen twists.

| | into ¼-inch bits |
|---|---|
| 1½ cups unsifted flour | 2 tablespoons vegetable shortening, |
| ½ cup freshly grated Swiss cheese | cut into ¼-inch bits |
| 1 tablespoon caraway seeds | 3 to 4 tablespoons ice water |
| ¼ teaspoon table salt | 1 egg, lightly beaten |
| 6 tablespoons butter, chilled and cut | 2 tablespoons coarse (kosher) salt |

Place the flour, cheese, caraway seeds and table salt in a deep mixing bowl. Add the butter and shortening bits and, with your fingertips, rub the flour and fat together until the mixture resembles flakes of coarse meal. Pour in 3 tablespoons of ice water all at once and mix with your fingers or a fork until the dough can be gathered into a compact ball. If the dough seems crumbly, add up to 1 tablespoon more ice water by drops until all the particles adhere. Divide the dough into two balls, wrap the balls in wax paper, and refrigerate for at least 1 hour.

Preheat the oven to 375°. On a lightly floured surface, roll out one ball of the dough into a 12-inch square about ¼ inch thick. With a ruler and a pastry wheel or sharp knife, cut the square in half crosswise and then lengthwise into ½-inch-wide strips to make about 4 dozen 6-by-½-inch strips. With a pastry brush, spread about half of the beaten egg lightly but evenly over the top of the strips, and sprinkle the entire surface with 1 tablespoon of the coarse salt. Repeat the entire process with the second ball of dough. When you finish you should have a total of 8 dozen strips of prepared dough.

To shape each caraway twist, press two strips of dough together, salt sides out. Pinch the strips tightly at one end and, with your fingers, gently wind the two strips together lengthwise to form a long loose spiral.

With a large metal spatula, carefully arrange the caraway twists on two ungreased baking sheets and bake them in the middle of the oven for 8 to 10 minutes, or until they are crisp and golden brown. Slide the twists onto wire racks to cool to room temperature before serving them. In a tightly covered jar or tin, they can safely be kept for a week or two.

## *Tostaditas*
DEEP-FRIED CORN CHIPS

| | |
|---|---|
| Vegetable oil for deep frying | thoroughly defrosted if frozen |
| Corn tortillas* | Salt |

Pour vegetable oil into a deep fryer or large heavy saucepan to a depth of about 3 inches and heat the oil until it reaches a temperature of 375° on a deep-frying thermometer.

Cut the tortillas into 1- or 2-inch pieces with a sharp knife, or tear them apart with your fingers.

Deep-fry the tortilla pieces, 5 or 10 at a time depending on their size, turning them about with a slotted spoon for about a minute, or until they are crisp and brown on all sides. As they are fried, transfer the *tostaditas* to paper towels to drain.

When all the *tostaditas* are deep-fried and drained, sprinkle them lightly with salt. Serve the *tostaditas* as a snack or as an accompaniment to *chile con queso*\* or *guacamole*.\* Tightly covered, the *tostaditas* can safely be kept for 2 or 3 weeks.

* *See index.*

*Dripping cheese and calories, a sizzling-hot square of juicy Sicilian pizza is lifted from its baking dish.*

## Ham Balls

To make 32 ham balls

1 cup fresh bread crumbs
3 tablespoons milk
1 pound fresh lean pork, finely
   ground, combined with ½ pound
   cooked smoked ham, finely ground
1 tablespoon prepared mustard

1 tablespoon finely chopped fresh
   parsley
1 egg, lightly beaten
Freshly ground black pepper
2 tablespoons butter
2 tablespoons vegetable oil
¾ cup dry red wine

Soak the bread crumbs in the milk for about 5 minutes, then combine them with the ground pork and ham in a large mixing bowl. Add the mustard, parsley, lightly beaten egg and a few grindings of black pepper, and with a large spoon mix them thoroughly together. Form the mixture into small balls about 1 inch in diameter and chill for at least ½ hour.

Preheat the oven to 350°. Over high heat, melt the butter with the oil in a large, heavy skillet. When the foam subsides, add the ham balls. To help keep their shape as they brown, roll the balls around in the hot fat by shaking the pan back and forth over the burner. When the ham balls are well browned on all sides (this should take about 5 minutes), transfer them with a slotted spoon to a 2-quart casserole. Pour off all but a thin film of fat from the skillet and pour in the wine. Bring it to a boil over high heat, scraping and stirring into it any brown bits clinging to the bottom and sides of the pan. Cook briskly for about a minute, then pour the wine into the casserole. Cover tightly and bake in the middle of the oven for about 30 minutes, basting the ham balls after 15 minutes with the wine. Serve either directly from the casserole or arrange the balls on a heated platter and pour the sauce over them. Or, place the ham balls and sauce in a chafing dish and serve, speared with decorative tooth picks, as an accompaniment to cocktails.

## Steak Tartare Balls

To make about 2 dozen

1 pound ground top round beef, free
   of all fat, and of the best quality
1 tablespoon Worcestershire sauce
½ teaspoon salt

Freshly ground black pepper
¼ cup finely chopped chives, or the
   green stems of scallions, finely
   chopped
2 tablespoons (1 ounce) black caviar

In a small mixing bowl, thoroughly combine the beef, Worcestershire sauce, ½ teaspoon of salt and a few grindings of pepper. Taste for seasoning, then shape the mixture into balls about 1 inch in diameter. Make a small indentation in each ball with the tip of a small spoon or your finger, and one by one, roll the balls in the chopped chives or scallions so that the herbs adhere to the surface of the meat. Fill the indentations of each ball with about ¼ teaspoon of caviar, arrange them caviar side up on an attractive platter and chill before serving.

More easily, if less impressively, the steak balls may be served without the caviar, in which case simply roll the balls in the herbs without indenting them.

## *Daube Glacé* (Creole-Acadian)
### MOLDED JELLIED BEEF

To make two 9-by-5-by-3-inch loaves

6 tablespoons vegetable oil
4 pounds beef shinbones, sawed into 1-inch lengths
4 pounds veal shinbones, sawed into 1-inch lengths
3 medium-sized onions, peeled and coarsely chopped
2 medium-sized celery stalks, including the green leaves, trimmed and coarsely chopped
2 large carrots, scraped and coarsely chopped, plus 3 medium-sized carrots, scraped and coarsely grated

2 pounds fresh pigs' feet
3 sprigs fresh parsley
5 quarts water
5 pounds bottom round beef, trimmed of excess fat and cut into 3 equal pieces
2 teaspoons finely chopped garlic
1 teaspoon ground hot red pepper (cayenne) or 1 teaspoon freshly ground black pepper
2 teaspoons salt
1 lemon, sliced crosswise into 6 thin rounds

In a heavy 12-inch skillet, heat 4 tablespoons of the oil over moderate heat until a light haze forms above it. Brown the beef and veal bones in the hot oil, eight or nine pieces at a time, turning them frequently with tongs and regulating the heat so that the bones color deeply and evenly on all sides without burning. As they brown, transfer the bones to a heavy 10- to 12-quart stock pot.

Pour off all but about 2 tablespoons of the fat remaining in the skillet and in its place add the onions, celery and chopped carrots. Stirring frequently, cook over moderate heat for 8 to 10 minutes, or until the vegetables are soft and delicately brown. Scrape the vegetable mixture into the stock pot and drop in the pigs' feet and parsley. Add the water,

31

bring to a boil over high heat, reduce the heat to low, and simmer partially covered for 4 hours.

With a slotted spoon, remove and discard the bones and pigs' feet. Strain the stock through a fine sieve into a large bowl, pressing down hard on the vegetables with the back of a spoon to extract all their juices before discarding the pulp. Set the stock aside.

Set the 12-inch skillet over moderate heat again and heat the remaining 2 tablespoons of oil. Brown the beef, one piece at a time, turning it with tongs and regulating the heat so that the meat colors richly and evenly on all sides without burning. As the pieces of beef brown, transfer them to a heavy 8- to 10-quart casserole.

Pour the reserved stock over the beef. The stock should cover the beef completely; add water if necessary. Bring to a boil over high heat, reduce the heat to low and cover the pot tightly. Simmer the beef for 3 to 3½ hours, or until it is very tender and shreds easily with a fork. Transfer the beef to a cutting board and strain the stock remaining in the casserole through a fine sieve lined with four layers of dampened cheesecloth and set over a large bowl.

When the beef is cool enough to handle, cut it into strips about ¼ inch wide and 2 inches long or, with the aid of two forks, pull the beef into 2-inch-long shreds. Drop the beef into a bowl, add the grated carrots, garlic, red or black pepper, and salt, and toss the ingredients together thoroughly with a fork. Refrigerate the beef mixture until you are ready to use it.

With a large spoon, skim the fat from the surface of the stock. Pour the stock into a 4- to 5-quart saucepan, cool to room temperature and refrigerate for at least 2 hours, or until the surface is covered with a layer of congealed fat. Carefully lift off the fat and discard it. Warm the stock over low heat and, when it liquefies, pour a ¼-inch layer of the stock into the bottoms of two 9-by-5-by-3-inch loaf pans. Refrigerate the pans until the stock has jelled and is firm to the touch.

(Keep the remaining stock at room temperature so that it remains liquid and ready to use. If it begins to set at any time, warm the stock briefly over low heat to soften it.)

Dip the lemon slices into the liquid stock and, when they are coated, arrange three of the slices in the bottom of each loaf pan. Chill until the lemon slices are anchored firmly.

Pour all the remaining liquid stock over the beef and mix well. Then ladle the mixture into the loaf pans, dividing it equally between them. Refrigerate the daube for at least 12 hours before serving.

Before unmolding the daube, scrape off any fat that has floated to the surface. Run a knife around the sides of one mold at a time and dip the bottom in hot water for a few seconds. Wipe the mold dry, place an inverted plate over it and, grasping plate and mold together firmly, turn them over. Rap the plate sharply on a table and the jellied beef should slide out easily. Refrigerate the *daube glacé* until ready to serve.

## *Tomato Cheese Croustades*

To make 12 *croustades*

1 tablespoon soft butter
12 thin slices fresh white bread
1 small tomato, peeled, seeded and
    coarsely chopped (about 2
    tablespoons)
1 teaspoon fresh basil, finely chopped

or ½ teaspoon dried, crumbled basil
½ teaspoon salt
Freshly ground black pepper
¼ cup grated Swiss cheese, preferably
    Gruyère
2 tablespoons butter, cut into ¼-inch
    bits

Preheat the oven to 400°. To make the little bread cases called *croustades*, you will need a muffin tin composed of 12 tiny cups, each about 2 inches in diameter. With a pastry brush, lightly coat each cup with the soft butter. Cut 2½-inch rounds from the centers of the bread slices using a cookie cutter or the rim of a wine glass. Fit the rounds in the tins, molding them gently to form little cups. Don't fuss with them too much. Bake the *croustades* in the middle of the oven for 10 to 12 minutes until golden brown, then remove them from the tin and cool. The *croustades* may be prepared as much as a day in advance, or a large supply may be frozen for later use.

Fill the *croustades* just before baking or hours earlier, if you wish. Preheat the oven to 400°. In a small bowl, combine the tomato, basil, salt and a few grindings of black pepper, and taste for seasoning. Fill each *croustade* with 1 teaspoon of grated cheese and spread about ½ teaspoon of the tomato mixture on top. Then dot with butter. Arrange the *croustades* on a cookie sheet or jelly-roll pan and bake for about 10 minutes. Slide under the broiler for a few seconds to brown the tops, and serve hot.

To make two 11-by-16-inch pizzas
(to serve 10 to 12)

DOUGH
3 cups lukewarm water (110° to
   115°)
2 packages active dry yeast
½ teaspoon sugar

8 to 10 cups all-purpose flour
1 tablespoon salt
4 tablespoons vegetable oil
1 tablespoon unsalted butter,
   softened

Pour ½ cup of the lukewarm water into a cup and sprinkle with the yeast and ½ teaspoon of sugar. Let the mixture rest for 2 or 3 minutes, then stir. Place the cup in a warm, draft-free place (such as an unlighted oven) for 5 to 8 minutes, until the yeast bubbles and the mixture almost doubles in volume.

Place 8 cups of flour and the 1 tablespoon of salt in a large mixing bowl and make a well in the center. Pour in the yeast mixture, the remaining lukewarm water and the vegetable oil and, with a large wooden spoon, gradually incorporate the dry ingredients into the liquid. Continue to stir until the ingredients are well combined and can be shaped into a ball. Transfer the ball to a floured surface and knead, pushing the dough down with the heel of your hand, pressing it forward and folding it back on itself. Continue to knead, incorporating up to 2 more cups of flour if necessary to make a smooth, elastic medium-firm dough.

With a pastry brush, coat the bottom and sides of a large bowl with the tablespoon of softened butter. Place the dough in the bowl, drape it with a kitchen towel and place in the warm, draft-free place for 1 to 1½ hours, or until the dough doubles in volume. Punch it down with a blow of your fist and replace it in the bowl to rise until it again doubles.

TOMATO SAUCE
4 tablespoons olive oil
1 cup finely chopped onions
1½ teaspoons finely chopped
   garlic
3 one-pound cans solid-packed
   tomatoes, and their liquid

1 tablespoon basil
1 tablespoon oregano
½ teaspoon sugar
½ teaspoon freshly ground black
   pepper
1½ teaspoons salt
A 6-ounce can tomato paste

Meanwhile, prepare the tomato sauce: In a 10- to 12-inch heavy skillet, heat the olive oil until a light haze forms above it. Add 1 cup of chopped onions and the garlic and, stirring frequently, cook over moderate heat until the onions are soft and translucent. Stir in the tomatoes and their liquid, the basil, oregano, ½ teaspoon of sugar, black pepper, 1½ teaspoons of salt and tomato paste. Bring to a boil over high heat, then lower the heat, partially cover the pan and simmer for 1 hour.

When the dough has risen the second time, punch it down with a blow of your fist and cut it in half. Roll out each half to fit into an 11-by-16-inch jelly-roll pan. Place the dough in the pans and stretch it with your fingers so that it fills the edges and corners. Drape with a towel and set aside again in the warm, draft-free place until the dough has risen almost to the top of the pans.

GARNISH
1 pound mozzarella cheese, coarsely grated
½ cup finely grated Parmesan cheese
¼ pound thinly sliced mushrooms (1 cup)
1 large green bell pepper, seeded, deribbed and thinly sliced
1 large red bell pepper, seeded, deribbed and thinly sliced
½ cup finely chopped onions
¼ cup olive oil

Preheat the oven to 500°. Divide the sauce in half and spread it over the top of the dough. Bake in the center of the oven for 30 minutes, then sprinkle the pizzas with the mozzarella and Parmesan, mushrooms, green and red pepper slices, and ½ cup of chopped onions. Dribble the ¼ cup of olive oil over the surface and bake for 10 minutes longer. Cut the pizzas into squares or rectangles and serve at once.

To serve 6

½ pound butter, cut into ½-inch bits and softened
1 tablespoon finely chopped fresh parsley
1 teaspoon finely chopped garlic
1 teaspoon Worcestershire sauce
½ teaspoon crumbled dried oregano
½ teaspoon salt
¼ teaspoon freshly ground black pepper

Rock salt
3 dozen small hard-shell clams shucked, with the deeper half shell of each reserved
¾ cup soft fresh crumbs made from homemade-type white bread, pulverized in a blender or finely shredded with a fork

Cream the butter by beating and mashing it against the sides of a bowl with the back of a spoon until it is light and fluffy. Beat in the parsley, garlic, Worcestershire, oregano, salt and pepper. With your hands, pat and shape the butter mixture into a cylinder 9 to 10 inches long and 1 inch in diameter. Wrap in wax paper and refrigerate the cylinder for at least 2 hours, or until it is firm.

Preheat the broiler to its highest setting. Spread the rock salt to a depth of about ½ inch in six individual shallow baking pans—each large enough to hold half a dozen clams comfortably. (Or spread a ½-inch layer of salt in the bottom of one or two shallow baking-serving dishes large enough to hold all the clams.) Arrange the pans on one or two large baking sheets and set them in the oven to heat the salt while you prepare the clams.

Scrub the reserved clam shells thoroughly under cold running water, then pat them dry and place a clam in each shell. With a small sharp knife, cut the cylinder of butter into ¼-inch-thick slices. Sprinkle each clam with 1 teaspoon of the bread crumbs and set a slice of seasoned butter on top. Then arrange the clams in one layer in the salt-lined pans.

Broil the clams about 4 inches from the heat for 3 minutes, or until the crumb topping is brown. Serve at once, directly from the baking dishes.

NOTE: The bed of salt is not indispensable to the success of this dish, but it will help keep the shells from tipping and, if heated beforehand, will keep the clams hot. You may, if you like, bake the clams in any shallow pan or pans large enough to hold the shells snugly in one layer, and serve them from a heated platter.

To serve 4 to 6

1 cup flour
½ teaspoon salt
1 tablespoon melted butter
1 egg, lightly beaten
½ cup beer

2 dozen fresh oysters, shucked, or 2
    dozen frozen oysters, thoroughly
    defrosted
1 egg white
Vegetable shortening or vegetable oil
    for deep-fat frying
Lemon wedges

Sift ½ cup of the flour and the salt into a mixing bowl. With a wooden spoon stir in the butter and the egg. Then pour in the beer gradually and mix only until the batter is fairly smooth. Don't overmix. Let the batter rest at room temperature for about an hour. When you are ready to fry the oysters, beat the egg white with a rotary beater or whisk until it is stiff enough to form unwavering peaks on the beater when it is lifted out of the bowl. Gently fold the beaten egg white into the batter and continue to fold until no streaks of white remain.

In a deep-fat fryer, heat the shortening or oil until it registers 375° on a deep-frying thermometer. The fat should be at least 3 inches deep. Dip the oysters in the remaining ½ cup of flour, shake off any excess and then dip in the batter. Let the excess batter drain off, then fry the oysters, 5 or 6 at a time, for 3 to 4 minutes until they are puffed and golden brown. Drain on paper towels and keep the fritters warm in a 200° oven until all the oysters have been fried. Serve at once with wedges of lemon.

## *Oysters en Brochette*

To make 1 brochette

4 oysters
Lemon juice
Salt
Pepper

3 to 4 mushroom caps
1 long strip of bacon
Melted butter
Chopped parsley
Lemon wedges

Sprinkle the oysters with lemon juice, salt and pepper. At the end of the skewer place a mushroom cap. Next put the end of the bacon strip, then an oyster, then loop the bacon around the oyster onto the brochette again, add another mushroom and another oyster, and continue until you have used 4 oysters. Brush with butter and broil over charcoal or under the broiler flame, turning several times. Sprinkle with parsley and serve with lemon wedges.

## Oysters Rockefeller *(Creole-Acadian)*
BAKED OYSTERS TOPPED WITH ANISE-FLAVORED GREEN SAUCE

To serve 4 as a first course

Rock salt

2 dozen large oysters, shucked, with all their liquor and the deeper halves of their shells reserved

Fresh or bottled clam broth

3 cups coarsely chopped scallions, including the green tops

3 cups coarsely chopped fresh parsley, preferably the flat-leaf Italian variety

1½ pounds fresh spinach, washed, trimmed, patted dry with paper towels and torn into 1-inch pieces

¾ pound unsalted butter, cut into ½-inch bits

4 teaspoons finely chopped garlic

¾ cup flour

3 tablespoons anchovy paste

¾ teaspoon ground hot red pepper (cayenne)

1½ teaspoons salt

¾ cup Herbsaint or Pernod

Preheat the oven to 400°. Spread the rock salt to a depth of about ½ inch in four 8- or 9-inch pie pans. Arrange the pans on baking sheets and set them in the oven to heat the salt while you prepare the oysters.

Drain the oysters and their liquor through a fine sieve lined with a double thickness of dampened cheesecloth and set over a bowl. Measure and reserve 3 cups of the oyster liquor. (If there is less than 3 cups, add fresh or bottled clam broth to make up that amount.) Transfer the oysters to a bowl. Scrub the oyster shells, then pat them dry with paper towels.

Put the scallions, parsley and spinach through the finest blade of a meat grinder, and set aside. In a 2- to 3-quart enameled or stainless-steel saucepan, melt the butter over moderate heat, stirring so that it melts evenly without browning. Add the garlic and stir for a minute or so, then add the flour and mix well. Stirring constantly with a wire whisk, pour in the 3 cups of oyster liquor in a slow, thin stream and cook over high heat until the sauce comes to a boil, thickens heavily and is smooth.

Stir in the anchovy paste, red pepper and salt. Then add the ground scallions, parsley and spinach, and reduce the heat to low. Stirring occasionally, simmer uncovered for 10 minutes, or until the sauce is thick enough to hold its shape almost solidly in the spoon. Remove the pan from the heat, stir in the Herbsaint or Pernod and taste for seasoning.

Arrange six oyster shells in each of the salt-lined pans and place an oyster in each shell. Spoon the sauce over the oysters, dividing it equally among them. Bake in the middle of the oven for 15 minutes, or until the sauce is delicately browned and the oysters begin to curl at the edges. Serve the oysters Rockefeller at once, directly from the baking pans.

NOTE: While the bed of salt helps to keep the shells from tipping and, if heated beforehand, will keep the oysters hot, it is not indispensable. You may, if you like, bake the oysters in any shallow pan large enough to hold the shells in one layer, and serve them from a heated platter.

## *Pickled Shrimp* *(South)*

To make about 2 quarts

2 pounds medium-sized raw shrimp
  (about 21 to 25 to the pound)
1 large onion, peeled, cut crosswise
  into ¼-inch-thick slices and
  separated into rings
2 lemons, cut crosswise into ⅛-
  inch-thick slices
A 1-inch piece of fresh ginger root,
  scraped and cut into paper-thin
  slices

¼ cup finely chopped fresh parsley
4 small bay leaves
2 cups cider vinegar
2 tablespoons mixed pickling spice
½ teaspoon dry mustard
¼ teaspoon ground mace
2 teaspoons salt
½ cup olive oil, combined with
  ½ cup vegetable oil

Shell the shrimp. Devein them by making a shallow incision down their backs with a small sharp knife and lifting out the black or white intestinal vein with the point of the knife. Drop the shrimp into enough lightly salted boiling water to immerse them completely and boil briskly, uncovered for about 3 minutes, or until they are firm and pink. Drain the shrimp, spread them on paper towels and pat them completely dry with fresh paper towels.

Place the shrimp in a deep bowl, add the onion rings, lemon slices, ginger root and parsley, and toss them together gently but thoroughly. Transfer the mixture to two wide-mouthed quart jars, dividing it evenly between them. Tuck 2 bay leaves down the sides of each jar.

Combine the vinegar, pickling spice, mustard, mace and salt in a 1- to 1½-quart enameled or stainless-steel saucepan and bring to a boil over high heat, stirring until the mustard and salt dissolve completely. At once pour the hot spiced liquid over the shrimp mixture by the tablespoonful. Allow each spoonful of liquid to flow completely through to the bottom of the jars before adding more.

To make the jars of pickled shrimp airtight, place a tablespoon upside down in the top of each jar and very slowly pour the olive-and-vegetable-oil mixture over the back of the spoon, letting it trickle off onto the top of the shrimp. Cover the jars with their lids and chill the shrimp for at least 24 hours before serving. (Tightly covered and refrigerated, the shrimp can safely be kept for about 1 month.)

## Pickled Mussels (New England)

To serve 6 to 8 as a first course

6 dozen large mussels in their shells
1½ cups water
1 large onion, peeled and cut
  crosswise into ⅛-inch-thick
  slices (about 1 cup)

4 medium-sized garlic cloves, peeled
  and bruised with the side of a
  cleaver or heavy knife
½ cup cider vinegar
2 teaspoons mixed pickling spice
1 teaspoon salt

Scrub the mussels thoroughly under cold running water with a stiff brush or soapless steel-mesh scouring pad. With a small, sharp knife scrape or pull the black, hairlike tufts from the shells and discard them.

Combine the mussels and water in a heavy 4- to 6-quart casserole and bring to a boil over high heat. Cover tightly, reduce the heat to low and let the mussels steam for 10 minutes, turning them about in the pot once or twice with a slotted spoon. When steamed, all the shells should have opened; discard any mussels that remain shut.

With tongs or a slotted spoon transfer the mussels to a platter and remove and discard the shells. Strain the broth remaining in the casserole and the liquid that has accumulated around the mussels through a fine sieve lined with a double thickness of dampened cheesecloth. Measure 1½ cups of the broth into a small saucepan and set the pan aside.

Place about ½ cup of the mussels in a 1-quart wide-mouthed jar, spread about ¼ of the onion slices over them, and set a garlic clove on top. Repeat three more times, alternating layers of mussels with onions and garlic until you have arranged them all in the jar.

Add the vinegar, pickling spice and salt to the reserved mussel broth and bring to a boil over high heat. Cook briskly, uncovered for 2 minutes, then pour the mixture slowly over the mussels and onions. Cool to room temperature, cover tightly and refrigerate for at least 3 days before serving.

Serve the mussels on chilled individual salad plates, mounded on fresh lettuce leaves if you like.

To serve 6 as a first course

1 tablespoon butter, softened, plus
    7 tablespoons butter, cut into
    ½-inch bits
2 cups plus 2 tablespoons soft fresh
    crumbs made from French- or
    Italian-type white bread,
    pulverized in a blender
¼ cup fish stock*, or ¼ cup
    fresh or bottled clam broth
¼ cup finely chopped onions
¾ pound fresh, frozen or canned

crabmeat, thoroughly drained and
    picked over to remove all bits of
    shell and cartilage
½ cup finely chopped scallions,
    including 3 inches of the green
    tops
2 tablespoons finely chopped fresh
    parsley, preferably the flat-leaf
    Italian variety
½ teaspoon ground hot red pepper
    (cayenne)
½ teaspoon salt

Preheat the oven to 400°. With a pastry brush, spread the tablespoon of softened butter evenly over the bottoms of six medium-sized natural or ceramic crab or scallop shells. Combine 2 cups of the bread crumbs with the fish stock or clam broth in a bowl, mix well and set aside.

In a heavy 10-inch skillet, melt 4 tablespoons of the butter bits over moderate heat. Add the onions and, stirring frequently, cook for about 5 minutes, or until they are soft and translucent but not brown. Remove the skillet from the heat and stir in the moistened bread crumbs, the crabmeat, scallions, parsley, red pepper and salt. Taste for seasoning.

Spoon the crabmeat mixture into the buttered shells, dividing it equally among them and slightly mounding the centers. Sprinkle the remaining 2 tablespoons of bread crumbs and the remaining 3 tablespoons of butter bits over the tops and arrange the crab or scallop shells side by side in a large shallow baking dish.

Bake the stuffed crabs in the upper third of the oven for 15 minutes, then slide them under the broiler for 30 seconds or so to brown the tops, if desired. Serve at once, directly from the shells.

* *See index.*

## Scallops Remoulade

To serve 4 to 6

1½ to 2 pounds fresh bay scallops

Only very fresh, tiny bay scallops can be served raw successfully. (Frozen and defrosted ones will not do.) Wash the scallops quickly under cold running water and dry them thoroughly with paper towels. Chill until ready to serve.

REMOULADE SAUCE
1 cup mayonnaise, freshly made or a good unsweetened commercial variety
1 teaspoon dry mustard
1 teaspoon lemon juice
¼ to ½ teaspoon garlic, finely chopped
1 tablespoon capers, drained, washed and finely chopped
1 tablespoon fresh tarragon, finely chopped, or 2 teaspoons finely crumbled dried tarragon
1 tablespoon finely chopped fresh parsley
1 hard-cooked egg, finely chopped
Salt
Cayenne or Tabasco

For the remoulade sauce, combine the mayonnaise, dry mustard and lemon juice in a small mixing bowl. Stir in the chopped garlic, capers, tarragon, parsley and hard-cooked egg. Mix together gently but thoroughly, and season to taste with salt and a few grains of cayenne pepper or drops of Tabasco. Arrange the scallops, pierced with decorative picks, on a chilled serving plate and pass the remoulade sauce separately.

## Melon and Prosciutto (Italian-American)

To serve 4

1 small cantaloupe, Spanish melon or honeydew melon
8 slices prosciutto
1 lemon, quartered

With a large heavy knife, cut the melon in half, then scoop out and discard the seeds. Cut each half into four wedges and, with a small knife, carefully cut away the rind.

Place two wedges of melon on each of four serving dishes and drape each with a prosciutto slice. Serve cold, accompanied by lemon quarters.

# Salads & Dressings

Americans enjoy salads composed of many elements as much as they savor a simple tossed green salad. Light composed salads, such as the Caesar, caviar-potato and orange-and-onion salads described on the following pages, accompany the main course. More substantial composed salads, such as Northwestern king crab salad ring or Southern chicken salad, become a meal in themselves. In recent years, green salads, too, have begun to fill different roles. In many homes, a green salad appears in its centuries-old place after the main course, as a kind of palate refresher before dessert. Other cooks present it with the main course, to complement its flavor and texture. And some cooks, especially in California, use a green salad as a first course, to whet the appetite for the main part of the meal.

Whatever its place in the progress of the meal, a successful salad usually depends on fresh, clean, cool greens for its main ingredient or garnish. To produce them, wash leaves separately in lukewarm water, shake off excess water, then pat the leaves dry with paper towels (moisture will dilute the dressing). You can also roll the moist leaves in towels, seal them in a plastic bag and refrigerate for as long as twenty-four hours.

Most of the salad recipes that follow are made with some variation of vinaigrette dressing: oil, vinegar, salt and pepper. Sometimes the dressing is enlivened with mustard; Creole vinaigrette is spiced with paprika and cayenne pepper as well. Several of the salads call for mayonnaise. Although ready-made mayonnaise will do, your taste buds will welcome a homemade version.

One class of salad not described in this chapter is the fruit concoction, usually served as a dessert. You do not need a recipe to concoct your own: simply toss together lightly, not bruising the fruit, grapes, berries and slices or chunks of firm ripe bananas, peaches, melons, apples or pears. Although it is sweet enough to serve plain, you can enhance its taste with an unusual honey and yoghurt dressing from the Far West.

## Green Salad

| | |
|---|---|
| Lettuce | Tender inside spinach leaves |
| Endive | Chinese cabbage |
| Watercress | Tender cabbage leaves |
| Romaine | Fennel |
| Chicory | Chervil |
| Escarole | 1 clove garlic (optional)· |
| Parsley | Salad dressing |
| Dandelion leaves | |

Select any or all of these salad greens. Wash them thoroughly. Shake off any excess water and wrap the greens in wax paper, a towel or cellophane. Place them in the refrigerator to chill and crisp. Just before serving time, tear the greens into bite-sized pieces. If you like the flavor of garlic, rub the salad bowl with the cut surface of a clove of garlic before adding the greens. Pour in a generous amount of salad dressing and toss the greens lightly with a large spoon and fork to coat them well. Serve at once.

## Caesar Salad

To serve 4 to 6

| | |
|---|---|
| | ⅛ teaspoon salt |
| 2 medium-sized heads romaine lettuce | ⅛ teaspoon freshly ground black |
| 10 to 12 croutons, preferably made | pepper |
| from French or Italian-style bread | ½ cup olive oil |
| 4 to 8 tablespoons vegetable oil | 4 tablespoons lemon juice |
| 1 teaspoon finely chopped garlic | 1 cup freshly grated Parmesan cheese |
| 2 eggs | 6 to 8 flat anchovies (optional) |

Separate the romaine lettuce and wash the leaves under cold running water. Dry each leaf thoroughly with paper towels. Then wrap the lettuce in a dry kitchen towel and chill while you assemble the other ingredients. Cut a loaf of bread into 1½-inch-thick slices. Trim the crusts and cut each slice into 1½-inch squares. In a heavy skillet, large enough to hold all the croutons in one layer, heat 4 tablespoons of the vegetable oil over high heat until a light haze forms above it. Add the croutons and brown them on all sides, turning them with tongs, and, if necessary, add up to another 4 tablespoons of oil. Remove the pan from the heat, then add the chopped garlic and toss the croutons about in the hot fat. Remove the croutons to paper towels to drain, cool and crisp.

Plunge the eggs into rapidly boiling water for 10 seconds, remove and set aside. Break the chilled romaine into serving-sized pieces and scatter them in the bottom of a large salad bowl, preferably glass or porcelain. Add the salt, pepper and olive oil, and toss the lettuce with two large spoons or, better still, with your hands. Then break the eggs on top of the salad, add the lemon juice and mix again until the lettuce is thoroughly coated with the dressing. Add the cheese and the anchovies, if you are using them, and mix once more. Scatter the croutons over the top and serve at once on chilled salad plates.

## *Waldorf Salad* (Eastern Heartland)

To serve 6 to 8

3 large firm ripe apples, cored and cut into ½-inch pieces (about 4 cups)
2 tablespoons strained fresh lemon juice
3 medium-sized celery stalks, trimmed and cut into ¼-inch dice (about 2 cups)

1 cup coarsely chopped walnuts
1 cup freshly made mayonnaise or substitute unsweetened bottled mayonnaise
½ cup heavy cream
1 or 2 heads Boston or bibb lettuce, separated into leaves, washed, patted dry and chilled

Combine the apples and lemon juice in a deep bowl and turn the apple pieces about gently with a spoon to moisten them evenly. Stir in the celery and walnuts. Then, in another bowl, mix the mayonnaise and cream and, when the mixture is smooth, pour it over the apples. Toss all the ingredients together gently but thoroughly.

Shape the lettuce leaves into cups on 6 or 8 chilled individual serving plates. Mound the Waldorf salad in the cups, dividing it evenly among them. Serve at once.

## Shaker Salad (Eastern Heartland)

To serve 4 to 6

½ pound green string beans,
  trimmed, washed and cut into
  1½-inch lengths
3 tablespoons tarragon vinegar
1 tablespoon finely chopped onions
½ teaspoon crumbled dried thyme
½ teaspoon crumbled dried savory
½ teaspoon dry mustard
1 teaspoon salt

Freshly ground black pepper
½ cup olive or vegetable oil or a
  combination of both
2 firm heads bibb or Boston lettuce,
  trimmed, washed, separated into
  leaves and cut into 1-inch pieces
  (about 3 cups)
2 tablespoons finely chopped
  scallions, including 1 inch of the
  green tops

Drop the string beans into enough lightly salted boiling water to cover them by at least 1 inch. Boil briskly, uncovered, for 4 to 5 minutes, or until the beans are tender but still somewhat crisp to the bite. Drain the beans in a sieve or colander and run cold water over them to cool them quickly and set their color. Spread the beans on paper towels to drain and pat them dry with fresh paper towels. Refrigerate until ready to serve.

Just before serving, combine the vinegar, onions, thyme, savory, dry mustard, salt and a few grindings of pepper in a serving bowl and mix well with a wire whisk. Whisking constantly, pour in the oil in a slow stream and stir until the dressing is smooth and thick. Add the beans, lettuce and scallions, and toss together gently but thoroughly. Serve at once.

## Spring Salad (Jewish-American)

To serve 6

2 medium-sized cucumbers, peeled
  and cut into ½-inch cubes
  (2 cups)
2 medium-sized firm ripe tomatoes,
  cut into ½-inch cubes (2 cups)
4 scallions, including 1 inch of the
  green stems, trimmed and sliced
  crosswise into ¼-inch-thick

rounds (¼ cup)
6 radishes, sliced crosswise into
  ¼-inch-thick rounds (¾ cup)
¾ pound cottage or pot cheese
1 teaspoon salt
Freshly ground black pepper
12 lettuce leaves, washed and
  thoroughly dried
1 pint sour cream

In a large mixing bowl, combine the cucumbers, tomatoes, scallions, radishes, cheese, salt and several grindings of black pepper. Toss together with a wooden spoon, then divide the salad into six equal portions.

Line each of six plates with two lettuce leaves, and mound the salad on top. Serve chilled, accompanied by a bowl of sour cream.

To serve 4 to 6

½ pound uncooked young spinach
1 large cucumber
1 teaspoon salt

4 medium-sized stalks celery
¼ cup coarsely chopped black olives
½ cup pine nuts

Wash the spinach under cold running water, drain and pat thoroughly dry with paper towels. Strip the leaves from the stems and discard the stems along with any tough or discolored leaves. Peel the cucumber and slice it in half lengthwise. Run the tip of a teaspoon down the center to scrape out the seeds. Cut the halves into strips ¼ inch wide and then cross-wise into ¼-inch dice. To rid the cucumber of excess moisture, in a small bowl mix the diced cucumber with 1 teaspoon of salt. Let it rest for 15 minutes to ½ hour, then drain the liquid that will accumulate and pat the cucumber dice dry with paper towels.

Trim the leaves and stems of the celery; wash the stalks under cold water and dry them thoroughly with paper towels. Cut each stalk in ¼-inch strips and then cut into ¼-inch dice. Toss the spinach, cucumber and celery in a salad bowl, preferably of glass, add the olives and nuts and toss again. Chill until ready to serve.

VINAIGRETTE DRESSING

2 tablespoons red wine vinegar
½ teaspoon salt
Freshly ground black pepper

½ teaspoon dry mustard
6 tablespoons vegetable oil

For the dressing, with a whisk beat the vinegar, salt, pepper and mustard together in a small bowl. Still whisking, gradually pour in the oil and beat until the dressing is smooth and thick. Pour over the salad, toss until all the ingredients are thoroughly coated with the dressing and serve at once on chilled salad plates.

To serve 4 to 6

POTATO SALAD
2 quarts water
2 pounds boiling potatoes (6 to 8)
2 medium-sized onions, finely
    chopped (¾ cup)
½ cup thinly sliced scallions

⅓ cup finely chopped parsley
6 tablespoons red wine vinegar
1 cup olive oil
2 teaspoons salt
1½ teaspoons freshly ground
    black pepper

POTATO SALAD: Bring the water to a boil in a 3- to 4-quart saucepan and drop in the potatoes. Boil uncovered for 30 minutes, or until they offer no resistance when pierced with the tip of a sharp knife. Drain the potatoes and let them cool to room temperature, then peel and cut them crosswise into ¼-inch-thick rounds.

Place the rounds of potatoes in a large mixing bowl, drop in the chopped onions, sliced scallions and chopped parsley and, with a rubber spatula, toss together lightly but thoroughly.

Pour the red wine vinegar into a small mixing bowl and, a tablespoon at a time, beat in the cup of olive oil. When it is well incorporated, beat in the salt and freshly ground black pepper, and pour the dressing over the potatoes. With a rubber spatula, toss the salad lightly until the dressing is evenly distributed.

GREEK SALAD
1 quart boiling water
6 medium-sized shrimp
1 large head romaine lettuce
12 leaves *roka (arugula),* or
    substitute 12 sprigs watercress
2 firm ripe tomatoes, each cut into
    6 wedges
1 medium-sized cucumber, peeled
    and cut lengthwise into 6 strips
1 avocado, peeled and cut into
    6 wedges

6 scallions, washed and trimmed
6 radishes, washed and trimmed
6 ounces *feta* cheese, cut into 4-by-
    4-by-½-inch slices
1 green pepper, cored, seeded and
    cut crosswise into ¼-inch-thick
    rings
6 slices canned beets
6 flat anchovy fillets, washed
12 black olives, preferably the
    Mediterranean variety
1 teaspoon oregano, crumbled

GREEK SALAD: Drop the shrimp into 1 quart of boiling water and let them boil briskly for 3 minutes. Drain and peel the shrimp, then devein them by making a shallow incision along their backs with a small sharp knife by lifting out the black or white intestinal vein with the tip of the knife. Set them aside.

Separate the head of romaine lettuce into individual leaves and wash the leaves thoroughly under cold running water. Spread the leaves out on paper towels, and pat them completely dry with additional towels. Line a large serving platter with the largest of the lettuce leaves, and mound the potato salad in the center. With a sharp heavy knife, cut the remaining lettuce leaves into shreds, and strew them and the sprigs of *roka* or watercress over and around the potato salad.

Surround the potato salad with alternating pieces of the tomatoes, cucumber, avocado, scallions and radishes. Lay the slices of *feta* cheese over the top of the potato salad and top them with the rings of green pepper. Set the beet slices on top of the green pepper rings and on each beet place a shrimp draped with an anchovy fillet. Scatter the olives over and around the salad, and sprinkle the whole with oregano. Chill the salad until ready to serve.

DRESSING
½ cup distilled white vinegar

¼ cup olive oil combined with
¼ cup vegetable oil

DRESSING: Just before serving, place the distilled white vinegar in a small bowl. Whisking constantly, pour in the olive-and-vegetable-oil mixture in a slow, thin stream. When it is well incorporated, pour the dressing over the salad and serve at once.

Greek salad may be served as a light luncheon or supper dish, accompanied by Greek bread.

## King Crab Salad Ring (Northwest)

To serve 8

2 cups water
¼ cup finely chopped shallots
2 cups fresh watercress leaves,
    tightly packed
½ cup finely chopped fresh parsley
2 teaspoons crumbled dried
    tarragon
4 teaspoons unflavored gelatin
3 egg yolks
4 teaspoons dry mustard
2 teaspoons salt
¼ teaspoon ground white pepper

1½ cups olive oil
2 tablespoons tarragon vinegar
2 tablespoons strained fresh lemon
    juice
1½ pounds freshly cooked king-
    crab meat, cut into 1-inch chunks,
    or substitute 1½ pounds
    thoroughly defrosted and drained
    frozen or canned king-crab meat,
    cut into 1-inch chunks
½ cup finely chopped celery
Bibb or Boston lettuce (garnish)
Watercress (garnish)

Bring 1½ cups of the water to a boil in a small saucepan, drop in the shallots, and cook briskly for 2 minutes. Stir in the watercress, parsley and tarragon, and boil for 1 minute longer. Drain the herbs through a fine sieve, pressing down hard with the back of a spoon to extract all their juices, and discard the juices and cooking water. Chop the drained herbs fine with a knife, then purée them through a food mill into a bowl.

Pour the remaining ½ cup of water into a heatproof measuring cup, sprinkle in the gelatin, and let it soften for 2 or 3 minutes. Then set the cup in a skillet of simmering water and, stirring constantly, cook over low heat until the gelatin dissolves completely. Remove the cup from the heat and let the gelatin cool to room temperature.

Warm a large mixing bowl in hot water, dry it quickly but thoroughly, and drop in the egg yolks. With a wire whisk or a rotary or electric beater, beat the yolks vigorously for about 2 minutes, until they thicken and cling to the beater. Stir in the mustard, salt and white pepper. Beat in ½ cup of the oil, ½ teaspoon at a time; make sure each addition is absorbed before adding more. By the time the ½ cup of oil has been beaten in, the mayonnaise should be the consistency of very thick cream. Beating constantly, pour in the remaining oil in a slow, thin stream. Stir in the vinegar and lemon juice, and taste for seasoning. Then incorporate the herb purée and mix in the cooled but still fluid gelatin.

Fold in the crabmeat and celery thoroughly, and ladle the mixture into a 1-quart ring mold, spreading it and smoothing the top with a spatula. Cover with foil or plastic wrap and refrigerate for at least 3 hours, or until the salad is thoroughly chilled and firm to the touch.

Just before serving, unmold the salad ring in the following fashion: Run a long, thin knife around the edges of the mold to loosen the sides and dip the bottom briefly in hot water. Invert a chilled serving plate on top of the mold and, grasping plate and mold together firmly, turn over. Rap the plate on a table and the mold should slide out easily.

Arrange lettuce leaves around the mold and fill the center of the ring with watercress. Serve at once. If you like, you may further garnish the salad with chunks of cold crabmeat.

To serve 6

1½ cups freshly made mayonnaise
   or substitute 1½ cups
   unsweetened bottled
   mayonnaise
¼ cup bottled chili sauce
3 tablespoons finely chopped
   scallions, including 2 inches of
   the green tops
3 tablespoons finely chopped sweet
   green bell peppers
1 tablespoon strained fresh lemon
   juice
1½ teaspoons Worcestershire
   sauce
4 drops Tabasco
½ teaspoon salt

1½ pounds (about 3 cups) freshly
   cooked or defrosted frozen
   crabmeat, preferably Dungeness,
   drained and thoroughly picked
   over to remove all bits of shell
   and cartilage, then cut into 1-inch
   pieces
3 large firm ripe avocados
2 heads bibb or Boston lettuce,
   separated into leaves, trimmed,
   washed and thoroughly chilled
2 medium-sized firm ripe tomatoes,
   washed, stemmed and each cut
   lengthwise into 6 wedges
3 hard-cooked eggs, cut lengthwise
   into quarters

Combine the mayonnaise, chili sauce, scallions, peppers, lemon juice, Worcestershire sauce, Tabasco and salt in a deep mixing bowl and stir with a wire whisk until the ingredients are well blended. Taste for seasoning, then add the crabmeat and toss it about gently with a spoon until the pieces are evenly coated.

Cut the avocados in half. With the tip of a small knife, loosen each seed and lift it out. Remove any brown tissuelike fibers clinging to the flesh. Strip off the skin with your fingers starting at the narrow stem end. (The dark-skinned variety does not peel easily; use a knife to pull the skin away, if necessary.)

To assemble the crab Louis, place the avocado halves on six individual serving plates and spoon the crab mixture into the cavities. Arrange the lettuce leaves in rings around the avocado, and garnish the leaves with the tomatoes and hard-cooked eggs. Serve at once.

To serve 6

1 pound medium-sized raw shrimp, shelled and deveined

Bring 1 quart of lightly salted water to a boil in an enameled or stainless-steel saucepan. Drop in the shrimp and boil them briskly for about 5 minutes, or until they turn pink and are firm to the touch. Do not over-cook. Drain them at once and plunge them into cold water to stop their cooking. Drain again on paper towels and chill.

PALACE COURT DRESSING

1¼ cups mayonnaise, freshly made, or a good, unsweetened commercial variety

¼ cup chili sauce, strained

1 tablespoon chopped fresh chives

2 tablespoons finely chopped fresh parsley

1 teaspoon fresh tarragon, finely chopped, or ½ teaspoon dried tarragon

Salt

White pepper

To make the dressing, in a small bowl combine the mayonnaise and the strained chili sauce, the chives, parsley and tarragon. Mix together thoroughly and taste. Season with salt and white pepper if necessary.

SALAD

1 teaspoon lemon juice

½ teaspoon salt

3 tablespoons mayonnaise

2 cups shredded iceberg lettuce

6 half-inch slices tomato, about 2½ inches in diameter

6 artichoke bottoms, canned or freshly cooked

3 hard-cooked eggs, finely chopped

6 strips pimiento (optional)

For the shrimp mixture, toss all but 6 of the shrimp (reserve them for the garnish) with the lemon juice and ½ teaspoon salt. Then add 3 table-spoons of mayonnaise to the shrimp and stir gently until they are well coated.

Construct the salad on individual chilled salad plates. Place a thin bed of shredded lettuce about 3 to 4 inches in diameter in the center of each plate. Put a tomato slice in the center of the lettuce, arrange an artichoke bottom on top of it and spoon equal amounts of the shrimp mixture into the slight hollow of each artichoke bottom. Sprinkle the chopped egg around the exposed circle of lettuce and garnish each mound of shrimp with the reserved shrimp. Top with a strip of pimiento if desired. Serve chilled and pass the dressing separately.

NOTE: This salad is often made with Dungeness crab and decorated with crab legs. Any crab meat may be substituted for the shrimp.

To serve 6 to 8

CHICKEN SALAD

| | 3 sprigs fresh parsley |
| Two 3- to 3½-pound chickens, | 2 tablespoons salt |
| each cut into 6 to 8 pieces | 10 whole black peppercorns |
| 1 small onion, peeled and cut into | 4 hard-cooked eggs, finely chopped |
| ¼-inch-thick slices | 1 cup finely chopped celery |
| 1 medium-sized carrot, scraped and | ½ cup finely chopped scallions, |
| cut into ¼-inch-thick slices | including 3 inches of the green |
| ½ cup coarsely chopped celery | tops |
| leaves | ¼ cup strained fresh lemon juice |

Combine the chicken, onion, carrot, celery leaves, parsley, 2 tablespoons of salt and the peppercorns in a heavy 4- to 5-quart casserole and pour in enough water to immerse the chicken completely. Bring to a boil over high heat, reduce the heat to low and simmer partially covered for 30 to 40 minutes, or until the chicken is tender but not falling apart.

With tongs or a slotted spoon, transfer the chicken to a platter or cutting board. (Strain the cooking liquid through a fine sieve, pressing down hard on the vegetables with the back of a spoon before discarding them. Reserve the stock for another use.) Remove the skin and bones from the chicken and discard them. Cut the meat into 1-inch pieces and place them in a serving bowl. Add the eggs, celery, scallions and lemon juice and with a wooden spoon toss together gently but thoroughly. Cover with foil or plastic wrap and refrigerate until ready to serve.

BOILED DRESSING

| 3 tablespoons sugar | ½ cup distilled white vinegar |
| 1 tablespoon flour | ½ cup water |
| 1 teaspoon dry mustard | 1 tablespoon butter |
| 1 teaspoon salt | 2 eggs, lightly beaten |

Meanwhile, prepare the boiled dressing in the following fashion: In a small enameled or stainless-steel saucepan, mix the sugar, flour, mustard and 1 teaspoon of salt together. With a wire whisk, stir in the vinegar, water and butter and cook over moderate heat, whisking constantly until the mixture comes to a boil and thickens lightly. Stir 1 or 2 tablespoonfuls of the simmering liquid into the beaten eggs, then pour the heated eggs into the saucepan and whisk until smooth. With a rubber spatula, transfer the dressing to a bowl and let it cool to room temperature.

Just before serving, pour the boiled dressing over the chicken mixture and stir until all the pieces of chicken and vegetables are evenly moistened.

## Chicken Salad

To serve 4 to 6

4 cups cooked chicken (see
Southern chicken salad*), cooled
and cut into ½-inch dice
1 teaspoon salt
Freshly ground black pepper
3 tablespoons finely chopped onion
or scallions

½ cup finely chopped celery,
including some of the leaves
3 tablespoons capers, washed, drained
and coarsely chopped
1 cup freshly made mayonnaise
or a good, unsweetened
commercial variety
1 cup sour cream
1 tablespoon finely chopped parsley

Combine the chicken, salt and a few grindings of black pepper in a large mixing bowl. Stir in the onion or scallions, the celery and the capers. Mix together the mayonnaise and sour cream, and carefully fold it into the chicken mixture. Taste for seasoning. The chicken salad will gain in flavor if it is allowed to rest for an hour or so in the refrigerator before serving. Serve on individual chilled plates on crisp lettuce, or arrange the salad on a large, lettuce-lined platter. In either case, sprinkle the salad with the chopped parsley before serving.

## Country-Style Potato Salad  (South)

To serve 6 to 8

3 pounds large boiling potatoes,
scrubbed under cold water and
left unpeeled
½ cup cider vinegar
1 cup finely diced celery
1 cup finely diced onions

½ cup finely diced green pepper
½ cup finely diced sweet mixed pickles
A pinch of ground cinnamon
2 teaspoons salt
⅛ teaspoon freshly ground black
pepper
2 cups mayonnaise, freshly made
or bottled

Drop the potatoes into enough boiling salted water to cover them by 1 inch. Cook uncovered over moderate heat until they are tender and offer only the slightest resistance when pierced deeply with a knife. Drain the potatoes in a colander and, as soon as they are cool enough to handle, peel and cut them into ½-inch dice. Transfer the dice to a large bowl, add the cider vinegar, and toss together gently but thoroughly with a rubber spatula.

In a separate mixing bowl, combine the celery, onions, green pepper, pickles, cinnamon, salt, pepper and mayonnaise. Add the diced potatoes and toss gently with the spatula. Taste for seasoning, then cover with plastic wrap or foil and set aside at room temperature for at least 3 hours before serving.

* See index.

To serve 6

| | |
|---|---|
| 6 medium-sized boiling potatoes (about 2 pounds) | unsweetened bottled mayonnaise |
| ¼ cup cider vinegar | ½ cup sour cream |
| ½ cup finely chopped onions | 2 tablespoons finely cut fresh dill |
| A 2-ounce jar of red caviar | 1 teaspoon salt |
| 1 cup freshly made mayonnaise or substitute 1 cup | ½ teaspoon freshly ground black pepper |
| | Sprigs of dill for garnish (optional) |

Drop the potatoes into enough boiling water to cover them completely. Cook briskly, uncovered, until the potatoes are tender and show no resistance when pierced deeply with the point of a small sharp knife. Drain the potatoes in a sieve or colander and, while they are still warm, peel and cut them into ½-inch-thick slices. Place the slices in a bowl, add the vinegar and onions, and toss together gently but thoroughly with a spoon.

Drain the caviar in a small strainer and run cold water over the grains to remove the excess salt. Spread the grains on paper towels and gently pat them dry with fresh paper towels. Reserve about 1 teaspoon of caviar to garnish the salad and place the rest in a bowl. With a rubber spatula, stir in the mayonnaise, sour cream, dill, salt and pepper, and taste for seasoning. Pour the mixture over the potatoes and with the spatula toss gently until the slices are evenly coated.

Mound the salad in a serving bowl, spread the reserved teaspoon of caviar on top and garnish it with sprigs of dill if desired. Serve at once.

## *Green Bean Salad* *(Northwest)*

To serve 4 to 6

| | |
|---|---|
| | Freshly ground black pepper |
| 1½ teaspoons salt | ½ cup olive oil |
| 1 pound fresh green string beans, trimmed and washed | 12 firm ripe cherry tomatoes |
| 3 tablespoons red wine vinegar | 1 large red onion, peeled and cut crosswise into ⅛-inch-thick |
| ½ teaspoon dry mustard | slices and separated into rings |

Bring 3 quarts of water and ½ teaspoon of salt to a boil in a large enameled or stainless-steel pan. Drop in the beans and boil briskly, uncovered, for about 10 minutes, or until they are tender but still slightly resistant to the bite. Drain the beans and transfer them to a serving bowl.

With a wire whisk, beat the vinegar, remaining salt, mustard and pepper together in a small bowl. Still whisking, slowly pour in the oil; continue to whisk until the mixture is smooth. Pour the dressing over the beans, and add the tomatoes and onions. Toss the ingredients together lightly with a wooden spoon, then cover the bowl with plastic wrap and refrigerate for at least 2 hours before serving.

## Three-Bean Salad

To serve 6 to 8

1 cup red kidney beans, freshly cooked or canned
1 cup white kidney beans, freshly cooked or canned
1 cup chick peas, freshly cooked or canned
3/4 cup finely chopped onion or scallions

1/2 teaspoon finely chopped garlic
2 tablespoons finely chopped parsley
1 small green pepper, seeded and coarsely chopped (optional)
1 teaspoon salt
Freshly ground black pepper
3 tablespoons wine vinegar
1/2 cup olive oil

If you plan to use canned cooked beans and chick peas, drain them of all their canning liquid, wash them thoroughly under cold running water, drain again and pat dry with paper towels. If you plan to cook the beans yourself, follow the initial soaking directions for beans in the recipe for Boston baked beans* and then cook them until tender. One half cup of dry uncooked beans yields approximately 1¼ cups cooked.

In a large bowl, combine the chick peas, red kidney beans and white kidney beans, the chopped onion or scallions, garlic, parsley and the chopped green pepper if you plan to use it.

Add the salt, a few grindings of pepper and the wine vinegar. Toss gently with a large spoon. Pour in the olive oil and toss again. This salad will be greatly improved if it is allowed to rest for at least an hour before serving it.

* See index.

To serve 8 to 10

½ cup cider vinegar
⅓ cup water
2 tablespoons sugar
2 tablespoons flour
2 teaspoons dry mustard

2 teaspoons salt
½ cup heavy cream
2 tablespoons butter
4 eggs, lightly beaten
2 pounds firm white cabbage
1 cup grated scraped carrots

In a 2- to 3-quart saucepan, combine the vinegar, water, sugar, flour, mustard and salt and beat vigorously with a wire whisk until the mixture is smooth. Place over moderate heat and, whisking constantly, add the cream and butter and cook until the butter melts and the sauce comes to a simmer. Stir 2 or 3 tablespoonfuls of the simmering liquid into the beaten eggs and, when they are well incorporated, pour the mixture into the sauce, whisking it constantly. Reduce the heat to low and continue to whisk until the sauce thickens heavily. With a rubber spatula, scrape the contents of the saucepan into a deep bowl and cool to room temperature.

Wash the head of cabbage under cold running water, remove the tough outer leaves, and cut the cabbage into quarters. To shred the cabbage, cut out the core and slice the quarters crosswise into ⅛-inch-wide strips.

Add the shredded cabbage and the carrots to the sauce, toss together gently but thoroughly and taste for seasoning. Cover with foil or plastic wrap and refrigerate for 2 or 3 hours before serving.

## *Bulghur Salad (Armenian-American)*

To serve 6 to 8

2 cups water
1 cup *bulghur* (cracked wheat)
1 small cucumber
1 medium-sized firm ripe tomato
1 small green bell pepper
1 bunch large scallions

¼ cup finely chopped parsley
2 teaspoons salt
½ teaspoon freshly ground black
   pepper
3 tablespoons strained fresh lemon
   juice
¼ cup olive oil

Bring the water to a boil in a 1½- to 2-quart saucepan and drop in the *bulghur* in a slow, thin stream so that the water continues to boil. Cover the pan, lower the heat and simmer the *bulghur* for 10 minutes, or until all of the water has been absorbed. Uncover the pan and, stirring frequently, cook over low heat for another 1 or 2 minutes to dry the grains.

Transfer the *bulghur* to a large mixing bowl and cool to room temperature. Then cover with plastic wrap and refrigerate for at least 30 minutes, or until it is thoroughly chilled.

With a small sharp knife or rotary peeler, peel the cucumber. Cut it crosswise into ½-inch slices, then cut each slice into ½-inch cubes. Cut the stem out of the tomato, then cut the tomato into ½-inch pieces. Halve the green pepper, cut out and discard the ribs and scoop out the seeds. Cut the pepper into ½-inch pieces. Trim the root ends from the scallions and wash them under cold running water. Cut them, including 2 inches of the green stems, crosswise into ⅛-inch-wide slices.

Add the cucumber, tomato, green pepper, scallions and parsley to the *bulghur*, and season with the salt and pepper. Just before serving, sprinkle the salad with the lemon juice and pour in the olive oil. With a rubber· spatula or wooden spoon, toss the salad together lightly but thoroughly. Taste for seasoning, and transfer the salad to a serving bowl or platter.

## *Oriental Salad* (*Northwest*)

To serve 4

½ cup raw long-grain white rice, boiled, drained and cooled
A 6-ounce can flat anchovy fillets, drained, rinsed under cold water and coarsely chopped
½ cup finely chopped scallions
½ cup finely chopped pimiento

1 firm ripe tomato, sliced ¼ inch thick and cut into ¼-inch dice
2 tablespoons red wine vinegar
½ teaspoon dry mustard
1 teaspoon salt
Freshly ground black pepper
6 tablespoons olive oil
Chilled crisp lettuce leaves

Place the rice, chopped anchovies, scallions, pimiento and tomato in a serving bowl and toss together thoroughly with a fork.

With a wire whisk, beat the vinegar, mustard, salt and a few grindings of pepper in a small bowl until the mustard has dissolved. Add the oil gradually and continue to beat until the dressing is smooth and thick. Taste for seasoning, pour the dressing over the rice mixture, and stir with a fork until the ingredients are well combined.

For each serving, arrange several lettuce leaves to form a cup on a chilled plate and spoon the salad into the lettuce cup.

If you prefer, you may pack the salad firmly into a 2-cup mold, cover tightly with plastic wrap, and refrigerate for 2 hours, or until thoroughly chilled. Just before serving, remove the plastic wrap and place an inverted plate over the mold. Grasping plate and mold together firmly, quickly turn them over. The molded salad should slide out easily. Surround with the lettuce and serve at once.

To serve 4 to 6

2 envelopes unflavored gelatin
½ cup cold beef stock, fresh or
   canned
2 tablespoons butter
¼ cup finely chopped onions
3 tablespoons tomato paste
4½ cups canned tomatoes with juice
   (2 one-pound, 3-ounce cans)
¾ teaspoon salt

¾ teaspoon sugar
½ teaspoon Worcestershire sauce
1 teaspoon finely chopped fresh
   tarragon or ½ teaspoon dried
   tarragon
1 teaspoon vegetable oil
1 cup mayonnaise combined with
   2 tablespoons finely cut chives, or
   1 cup sour cream combined with
   1 tablespoon red caviar

Soften the gelatin in the cold beef stock for about 5 minutes. In a heavy 2- to 3-quart saucepan, melt the butter over moderate heat. When the foam subsides, add the onions and cook, stirring, for 4 or 5 minutes until they are transparent but not brown. Stir in the tomato paste, the canned tomatoes and the softened gelatin, and mix together until the ingredients are thoroughly combined.

Then add the salt, the sugar, Worcestershire sauce and the tarragon, and bring to a boil, stirring constantly. Reduce the heat to its lowest point and simmer the mixture with the pan partially covered for about 30 minutes. Rub the mixture through a fine sieve or food mill into a mixing bowl.

With a pastry brush or paper towel, lightly coat the inside of a 1-quart mold with the vegetable oil. Pour in the tomato mixture, let it cool slightly and then refrigerate for 2 to 3 hours, or until the aspic is firm. To unmold, run a knife around the inside surfaces of the mold and place a serving plate upside down on top of the mold. Grasping the plate and the mold together firmly, invert the two. Rap the plate firmly on a table, and the aspic should slide out onto the plate. Serve the tomato aspic as a salad course with mayonnaise mixed with finely cut chives, or with sour cream mixed with red caviar.

## Orange and Onion Salad

To serve 6

2 tablespoons wine vinegar
½ teaspoon salt
Freshly ground black pepper
6 tablespoons olive oil

½ teaspoon lemon juice
4 navel oranges, peeled, and either
    thinly sliced or sectioned
2 red onions, peeled, thinly sliced
    and separated into rings

In a large mixing bowl beat the wine vinegar, salt, a few grindings of black pepper, the olive oil and lemon juice with a wire whisk or fork until they are all well combined. Add the oranges and onions, and toss them together gently. Taste for seasoning.

## Lime-Gelatin Salad

To serve 6 to 8

1 medium-sized firm ripe cucumber
1 teaspoon salt
1 tablespoon vegetable oil
2 packages lime-flavored gelatin
1 quart boiling water
2 eight-ounce packages cream
    cheese, cut into ½-inch bits and

softened
2 tablespoons strained fresh lime
    juice
2 teaspoons Worcestershire sauce
¼ teaspoon Tabasco sauce
1 cup finely chopped celery
¼ cup finely chopped onions
¼ cup finely cut fresh dill

With a small sharp knife, peel the cucumber and slice it lengthwise in half. Scoop out the seeds by running the tip of a teaspoon down the center of each half. Then cut the cucumber into ¼-inch dice. Place the dice in a fine sieve set over a bowl, add the salt and toss the cucumber about with a spoon to coat the dice evenly. Set aside to drain for at least 30 minutes, then pat the cucumber dice dry with paper towels.

Meanwhile, with a pastry brush, spread the vegetable oil evenly inside a 6-cup ring mold or eight individual 6-ounce molds. Invert the mold or molds on paper towels to allow the excess oil to drain off.

Place the powdered gelatin in a heatproof bowl, pour in the boiling water and mix well. Put the cream cheese in a large bowl, and with an electric mixer, beat it until it is light and fluffy. Beating the mixture constantly, pour in the gelatin in a slow thin stream and, when it is thoroughly incorporated, add the lime juice, Worcestershire sauce and Tabasco.

Set the bowl in a larger bowl half filled with crushed ice or ice cubes and cold water. Stir with a metal spoon until the gelatin mixture thickens enough to flow sluggishly off the spoon. Stir in the cucumber dice, the celery, onions and dill.

Pour the gelatin mixture into the oiled mold or molds, cover with plastic wrap and refrigerate for 4 hours, or until it is firm to the touch.

To unmold the salad, run a thin knife around the sides of the mold and dip the bottom briefly into hot water. Place an inverted serving plate on top of the mold and, grasping plate and mold together firmly, turn them over. Rap the plate on a table and the gelatin salad should slide out easily. Refrigerate until ready to serve.

*Blender Mayonnaise*

To make approximately 1 cup

1 egg
¼ teaspoon dry mustard
½ teaspoon salt

2 teaspoons lemon juice or wine
    vinegar
⅔ cup vegetable oil, or equal
    amounts of vegetable and olive oil

Combine the whole egg, mustard and salt in the container of an electric blender. Cover the jar and blend at top speed for 30 seconds. Pour in the lemon juice or wine vinegar and, still blending at high speed, pour in the oil as slowly as possible. If the mayonnaise thickens too much at any point, add a few more drops of lemon juice or vinegar.

## Homemade Mayonnaise

To make about 2 cups

| | |
|---|---|
| 3 egg yolks, at room temperature | ⅛ teaspoon ground white pepper |
| 1 to 3 teaspoons strained fresh lemon juice | 1½ cups vegetable or olive oil or a combination of both |
| ½ teaspoon dry mustard | 2 tablespoons boiling water |
| ½ teaspoon salt | (optional) |

Warm a small mixing bowl in hot water, dry it quickly but thoroughly, and drop in the egg yolks. With a wire whisk or a rotary or electric beater, beat the yolks vigorously for about 2 minutes, until they thicken and cling to the beater when it is lifted from the bowl. Stir in 1 teaspoon of the lemon juice, the mustard, salt and white pepper.

Beat in ½ cup of the oil, ½ teaspoon at a time; make sure each addition is absorbed before adding more. By the time ½ cup of the oil has been beaten in, the sauce should be the consistency of thick cream. Pour in the remaining oil in a thin stream, beating constantly. Taste for seasoning and add up to 2 more teaspoonfuls of lemon juice if desired.

To make the mayonnaise creamier and lessen the danger of separating, beat in the boiling water, 1 tablespoon at a time. Cover the mayonnaise tightly with foil or plastic wrap and refrigerate until ready to use. The mayonnaise can safely be kept in the refrigerator for up to one week.

## Blue-Cheese Salad Dressing

To make about ½ cup

| | |
|---|---|
| 3 tablespoons blue cheese, softened | 6 tablespoons olive oil or vegetable oil or a combination of both |
| 2 tablespoons heavy cream | 3 tablespoons red wine vinegar |
| 1 small garlic clove, peeled and finely chopped | ½ teaspoon salt |

Crumble the blue cheese into a small bowl, add the cream, and mash and stir the mixture into a smooth paste with a fork.

Drop the chopped garlic into a separate bowl and, with the back of a wooden spoon, crush it to a purée. Add the oil, vinegar and salt, and beat vigorously with a wire whisk until the mixture is smooth. Add the blue-cheese mixture, a tablespoon at a time. When the ingredients are thoroughly combined, taste for seasoning and serve.

To make about 1 cup

1 cup (8 ounces) plain unflavored
   yoghurt
2 tablespoons honey

1 tablespoon finely cut fresh mint
   leaves
1 to 2 teaspoons strained fresh
   lemon juice

Combine the yoghurt, honey and mint in a bowl and beat with a wire whisk until the mixture is smooth. Whisk in 1 teaspoon of the lemon juice, then taste the dressing and add up to 1 teaspoon more lemon juice if desired. Cover tightly with foil or plastic wrap and refrigerate until ready to serve.

   Yoghurt-and-honey dressing may be served with any fruit salad.

## *Creole Vinaigrette Sauce*

To make about ½ cup

2 tablespoons tarragon vinegar
1 teaspoon paprika
½ teaspoon Creole mustard or
   substitute any strong-flavored
   prepared brown mustard

¼ teaspoon ground hot red pepper
   (cayenne)
½ teaspoon salt
6 to 8 tablespoons olive oil

Combine the vinegar, paprika, mustard, red pepper and salt in a deep bowl and beat vigorously with a wire whisk to dissolve the salt. Whisking constantly, dribble in the oil a few drops at a time until no more oil is absorbed. When the sauce is thick and smooth, taste for seasoning.

   Creole vinaigrette may be served immediately or, if you prefer, cover the bowl tightly with foil or plastic wrap, and set the sauce aside at room temperature until you are ready to use it.

## Strawberry-and-Sour-Cream Dressing *(Far West)*

To make about 2 cups

A 10-ounce package frozen sliced
   sweetened strawberries,
   thoroughly defrosted, and their
   syrup

1½ cups sour cream
A pinch of salt
Confectioners' sugar (optional)

Place the strawberries and their syrup in a bowl and crush the berries slightly with the back of a large spoon. Add the sour cream and salt, and stir until the ingredients are thoroughly blended. Taste for sweetness and add up to 1 tablespoon of confectioners' sugar if desired. Cover with foil or plastic wrap and refrigerate the dressing for at least 1 hour before serving. Strawberry-and-sour-cream dressing may accompany any fruit salad.

## Poppy-Seed Dressing *(Far West)*

To make about 2½ cups

⅔ cup white distilled vinegar
2 teaspoons finely grated onion
1 cup sugar

2 teaspoons dry mustard
2 teaspoons salt
2 cups vegetable oil
3 tablespoons poppy seeds

Combine the vinegar, onion, sugar, mustard and salt in a bowl and stir vigorously with a wire whisk until the sugar, mustard and salt dissolve. Whisking constantly, pour in the oil in a slow, thin stream and continue to beat until the dressing is smooth and thick. Stir in the poppy seeds and taste for seasoning.

Serve the poppy-seed dressing at once with any fruit salad or cover tightly with plastic wrap and store in a cool place or the refrigerator until ready to serve. Tightly covered and refrigerated, the dressing can safely be kept for 6 to 10 days.

OPPOSITE
*No one can now identify the "Louis" of crab Louis, but he inspired a masterful salad, piled high in an avocado shell.*

# *Soups*

The Mock Turtle in *Alice's Adventures in Wonderland* sang the praises of "soup of the evening, beautiful soup!" Likewise, Americans think soup is beautiful—and not only in the evening. Soup has been an American favorite since Colonial days, when it sometimes appeared at the breakfast table. Hearty soups such as Mormon split pea or Southern okra stew, served with fresh bread and a crisp salad, provide a satisfying lunch or supper. And delicate soups such as Philadelphia's consommé Bellevue or a creamy cold cucumber bisque are appetizing introductions to elegant dinners.

Few foods have retained their regional natures as clearly as soups have: the tomato-rich clam chowder favored in New York would never be served by New Englanders, who prefer a creamy version. The seafood gumbos of the bayou country are a culinary continent apart from the oyster stew of the Pacific Coast, and the meat-and-vegetable-laden spiced meatball soup is as highly prized in the Far West as Virginia peanut soup is in the South.

Wherever it comes from, the basis of any good soup is stock, the broth made from cooking meat, fowl or seafood and seasonings in water. While you certainly can substitute canned versions, you can produce homemade chicken, beef or fish stock in just half an hour or so by simmering inexpensive chicken backs and gizzards, beef knuckles, or fish heads and trimmings with a few vegetables and herbs. Canned broths can be easily made richer and more nutritious. For chicken stock, combine a quart or so of undiluted chicken broth with chunks of onion and carrot, a few stalks of celery, parsley sprigs, a bay leaf and a bit of thyme. Simmer partially covered for about half an hour, then strain and taste for seasoning. For beef stock, combine undiluted canned beef broth with lightly browned onions and carrots, garlic cloves, parsley, celery leaves, a bay leaf and, if you like, some white wine. Simmer and strain, then taste for seasoning. Doctored or homemade, stock can be frozen in small batches, for use in sauces and stews as well as soups.

OPPOSITE
*Crab, shrimp and okra gumbo combines North American, African and European elements: it features Louisiana seafood thickened by an African vegetable, okra, and made with brown* roux, *a rich sauce base with French antecedents.*

67

## Consommé Bellevue *(Eastern Heartland)*

To serve 6 to 8

4 cups chicken stock, fresh or
    canned, thoroughly skimmed of
    all surface fat
2 cups fresh clam broth (*see
    steamed clams*\*) or substitute 2

cups bottled clam juice
A pinch of ground hot red pepper
    (cayenne)
¼ cup heavy cream, chilled

Combine the chicken stock, clam broth and red pepper in a heavy 2- to 3-quart saucepan and bring to a boil over high heat. Reduce the heat to low, cover partially, and simmer for 15 minutes.

Meanwhile, in a chilled bowl, whip the cream with a wire whisk or a rotary or electric beater until it is stiff enough to stand in unwavering peaks on the beater when it is lifted from the bowl.

Taste the consommé for seasoning, then ladle it into heated individual soup plates. Float a tablespoonful of whipped cream on the surface of each portion and serve at once.

## Cold Borscht *(Jewish-American)*
BEET SOUP WITH SOUR CREAM

To serve 8

3 pounds beets, trimmed, peeled
    and coarsely grated (4 cups)
1 medium-sized onion, peeled and
    halved
2½ quarts cold water
2 teaspoons salt
2 tablespoons sugar

½ teaspoon sour (citric) salt, or
    substitute 3 tablespoons strained
    fresh lemon juice plus 2
    teaspoons regular salt
4 eggs
1 pint sour cream

Combine the beets, onion, water and 2 teaspoons of salt in a 3- to 4-quart enameled or stainless-steel casserole. Bring to a boil over high heat, then reduce the heat and simmer, partially covered, for 1 hour. Skim the foam from the surface frequently with a slotted spoon.

Stir the sugar and sour salt (or lemon juice plus regular salt) into the soup. In a small bowl, beat the eggs together with a fork or wire whisk. Slowly beat in ½ cup of the simmering soup, then pour the warmed egg mixture slowly into the casserole, stirring constantly. Remove the casserole from the heat, discard the onion and set the soup aside to cool to

\* *See index.*

room temperature. When it is cool, taste for seasoning and refrigerate for at least 2 hours, or until thoroughly chilled. You may either stir the sour cream into the soup directly before serving it or present it in a separate bowl to be added to each serving at the table.

*Philadelphia Pepper Pot*

To serve 6

| | |
|---|---|
| 1 pound tripe, cut into ½-inch cubes | 1 cup finely chopped onions |
| A meaty veal shank (about 1 pound), sawed into 2 or 3 pieces | ½ cup finely chopped celery |
| | ½ cup finely chopped green pepper |
| 2 quarts water | 3 tablespoons flour |
| 4 to 6 whole black peppercorns | 2 medium-sized boiling potatoes, peeled and cut into ¼-inch dice |
| 1 teaspoon salt | Crushed dried hot red pepper |
| 4 tablespoons butter | Freshly ground black pepper |

Combine the tripe, veal shank and water in a heavy 4- to 5-quart casserole. The water should cover the meats by at least 2 inches; if necessary add more. Bring to a boil over high heat, meanwhile skimming off the foam and scum as they rise to the surface. Add the peppercorns and salt, reduce the heat to low, and simmer partially covered for 2 hours, or until the tripe is tender.

With a slotted spoon, transfer the tripe and pieces of veal shank to a platter or cutting board. Remove the veal from the shank, discard the bones and cut the meat into ½-inch pieces. Strain the cooking liquid through a fine sieve set over a bowl; measure and reserve 6 cups. If there is less, add enough water to make that amount.

In the same 4- to 5-quart casserole, melt the butter over moderate heat. When the foam subsides, add the onions, celery and green pepper and stir for about 5 minutes. When the vegetables are soft but not brown, add the flour and mix well. Stirring constantly, pour in the reserved cooking liquid in a slow, thin stream and cook over high heat until the soup thickens lightly, comes to a boil and is smooth. Add the potatoes, tripe and veal, reduce the heat to low, cover partially, and simmer for 1 hour.

Taste for seasoning. Add more salt if needed and enough crushed red pepper and freshly ground black pepper to give the soup a distinctly peppery flavor. Serve at once from the casserole or in individual soup plates.

To serve 6

CHICKEN SOUP
A 5- to 5½-pound stewing fowl,
    cut into 6 or 8 pieces, plus the
    neck, giblets and feet
3½ quarts cold water
2 medium-sized onions, peeled
2 medium-sized carrots, scraped and
    each cut crosswise into 3 pieces

1 celery stalk, including the green
    leaves, cut crosswise into 2 pieces
½ medium-sized parsnip
8 parsley sprigs
3 dill sprigs, or substitute
    1 teaspoon dried dill weed
1 tablespoon coarse (kosher) salt,
    or substitute 1 teaspoon regular
    salt

Place the pieces of fowl and the neck, giblets and feet in a heavy 8- to 10-quart pot and pour the cold water over it. The water should cover the pieces completely; if necessary, add more water. Bring to a boil over high heat, meanwhile skimming off the foam and scum as they rise to the surface. Add the onions, carrots, celery, parsnips, parsley, dill and 1 tablespoon of coarse salt. Return the soup to a boil, reduce the heat to low and simmer, partially covered, for 2½ to 3 hours, or until the fowl shows no resistance when a piece is pierced with the point of a small knife.

MATZO BALLS
6 egg yolks
8 tablespoons chicken stock, fresh
    or canned
2 teaspoons regular salt
Freshly ground black pepper

8 tablespoons chicken fat
1½ cups matzo meal
6 egg whites
2 tablespoons coarse (kosher) salt,
    or substitute 2 teaspoons regular
    salt

Meanwhile, make the matzo balls in the following fashion: With a whisk or a rotary or electric beater, beat the egg yolks until they are well blended. Whisk in the chicken stock, 2 teaspoons of regular salt, a few grindings of black pepper and the chicken fat. Whisking constantly, add the matzo meal, ¼ cup at a time. In a large bowl, beat the egg whites with a clean whisk or a rotary or electric beater until they are stiff enough to form firm, unwavering peaks on the beater when it is lifted from the bowl. With a wooden spoon or rubber spatula, lightly stir the whites into the matzo-meal mixture. Refrigerate the mixture for at least 30 minutes, until stiff enough so that a spoon will stand unsupported in the bowl.

OPPOSITE
*Philadelphia pepper pot is a stick-to-the-ribs tripe soup enlivened with both red and black pepper.*

In a 6- to 8-quart pot, bring about 4 quarts of water and 2 tablespoons of coarse salt (or 2 teaspoons of regular salt) to a boil over high heat. For each matzo ball, pinch off about a tablespoon of the dough and roll it between your hands. Drop the balls into the boiling water and stir gently once or twice so that they do not stick to one another or the bottom of the pot. Cook covered and undisturbed for 40 minutes. With a slotted spoon,

71

transfer the matzo balls to a bowl of cold water to prevent them from drying out. Set them aside.

When the soup has cooked its allotted time, remove the fowl and vegetables with tongs or a slotted spoon. Discard the vegetables, gizzard, neck and feet, and either reserve the pieces of fowl for later use or serve them, skinned, boned and sliced, with the soup.

Strain the soup through a fine sieve and return it to the pot. With a large spoon, skim as much fat as possible from the surface. Taste the soup for seasoning. Drain the matzo balls, add them to the soup and bring it to a simmer over moderate heat. Reduce the heat to low and cook gently, uncovered, for 15 minutes to heat the matzo balls through.

To serve the soup, place three matzo balls in each of six large soup plates and ladle the soup over them.

## Chicken-Corn Soup *(Eastern Heartland)*

To serve 8 to 12

| | |
|---|---|
| 2 pounds chicken backs and necks | |
| 10 cups water | Freshly ground black pepper |
| 2 medium-sized celery stalks | ½ pound egg noodles, ¼ inch |
| including the green leaves, cut | wide, preferably homemade, |
| into 3-inch lengths | broken into 3-inch pieces |
| 1 teaspoon whole black peppercorns | 2 cups fresh corn kernels, cut from |
| 3 teaspoons salt | about 4 large ears of corn, or |
| A 2½-pound chicken, cut into 6 | substitute 2 cups thoroughly |
| or 8 pieces | defrosted frozen corn |
| ½ cup finely chopped celery | A pinch of crumbled saffron threads |
| ¼ cup finely chopped fresh parsley | or ground saffron |

Combine the chicken backs and necks and the water in a 6- to 8-quart casserole and bring to a boil over high heat, meanwhile skimming off the foam and scum as they rise to the surface. Add the cut-up celery, the peppercorns and 2 teaspoons of the salt, reduce the heat to low, and simmer partially covered for 45 minutes.

With a slotted spoon or kitchen tongs, remove and discard the chicken backs and necks and the celery. Add the cut-up chicken to the stock and bring to a boil over high heat, skimming the surface of foam and scum until it remains clear. Reduce the heat to low and simmer partially covered for about 30 minutes.

When the chicken is tender but still intact, transfer it to a plate. With a small sharp knife, remove the skin from the chicken and cut the meat from the bones. Discard the skin and bones; cut the chicken meat into ½-inch pieces and set aside.

Strain the stock through a fine sieve and return it to the pot. Add the finely chopped celery, the parsley, the remaining 1 teaspoon of salt and a few grindings of black pepper, and bring to a boil over high heat.

Stir in the noodles, corn and saffron, and cook uncovered over moderate heat for about 15 minutes, or until the noodles show only slight resistance to the bite. Add the reserved chicken and cook for a minute or so to heat it through.

Taste the chicken-corn soup for seasoning and serve at once from a heated tureen or in individual bowls.

## Spiced Meatball Soup *(Far West)*

To serve 6 to 8

| | |
|---|---|
| 2 tablespoons vegetable oil | 1 pound ground lean beef |
| ½ cup finely chopped onions | 1 pound ground lean pork |
| 1 teaspoon finely chopped garlic | ½ cup raw long-grain white rice, not the converted variety |
| 2 quarts beef stock, fresh or canned | 1 egg, lightly beaten |
| ½ cup canned tomato purée | 4 teaspoons finely cut fresh mint leaves |
| 4 teaspoons finely chopped fresh hot green chilies (*caution: see appendix*) | 1½ teaspoons salt |
| 1 teaspoon ground cumin | ½ teaspoon freshly ground black pepper |
| 1 teaspoon ground coriander | |

In a heavy 4- to 6-quart casserole, heat the oil over moderate heat until a light haze forms above it. Add the onions and garlic and, stirring frequently, cook for about 5 minutes, or until they are soft and translucent but not brown. Stir in the beef stock, tomato purée, chilies, cumin and coriander, and bring to a boil over high heat. Reduce the heat to low and simmer partially covered for 20 minutes.

Meanwhile, combine the beef, pork, rice, egg, mint leaves, salt and pepper in a deep bowl and knead the ingredients together vigorously with both hands. Then beat with a large wooden spoon until the mixture is light and fluffy. To shape each meatball, scoop up about 2 teaspoons of the mixture and roll it into a ball about ½ inch in diameter.

Drop the meatballs into the simmering stock mixture and stir gently to prevent them from sticking to one another. Cover the casserole partially and simmer the soup for about 30 minutes longer.

Taste for seasoning. Serve at once.

## Minestrone *(Italian-American)*
### VEGETABLE SOUP WITH BEANS AND MACARONI

To serve 6 to 8

1 quart water
½ pound (1 cup) dried pea beans
    or Great Northern beans
½ pound salt pork, cut into
    ¼-inch dice (1 cup)
1½ cups finely chopped onions
1 teaspoon finely chopped garlic
¼ pound turnip, peeled and cut
    into ½-inch pieces (1 cup)
2 leeks, including 1 inch of the
    green leaves, washed and cut
    crosswise into ¼-inch-wide
    rounds (1½ cups)
2 tomatoes, peeled, seeded and
    coarsely chopped

2 medium-sized zucchini, scrubbed
    and cut into ½-inch pieces
    (1½ cups)
4 medium-sized carrots, scraped and
    thinly sliced (1 cup)
4 stalks celery, thinly sliced (1 cup)
2 medium-sized potatoes, peeled
    and cut into ½-inch pieces
    (1¼ cups)
½ small white cabbage, shredded
    (2 cups)
6 cups beef broth, fresh or canned
1 tablespoon tomato paste
½ cup elbow macaroni
2 teaspoons salt
⅛ teaspoon freshly ground black
    pepper

In a heavy 2- to 3-quart casserole, bring the water to a boil over high heat. Drop in the beans. The water should cover them by at least 2 inches; if necessary, add more water. Bring back to a boil and cook for about 2 minutes, then turn off the heat and let the beans soak for 1 hour.

Bring to a boil again, reduce the heat to low and simmer, partially covered, for 1 hour, or until the beans are tender. Drain them through a sieve set over a bowl, and set them and 2 cups of the cooking liquid aside separately.

Fry the salt-pork dice in a heavy 3- to 4-quart casserole over moderate heat, stirring the dice frequently with a slotted spoon until they are crisp and brown and have rendered all their fat. Transfer the dice to a paper towel to drain and pour the fat into a measuring cup. Pour 4 tablespoons of the fat back into the casserole and set the casserole over moderate heat. Stir in the onions and garlic and, stirring frequently, cook for 6 to 8 minutes, or until the onions are a light gold. Add the turnip, leeks, tomatoes, zucchini, carrots, celery, potatoes, cabbage, beef broth, the 2 cups of reserved bean liquid, tomato paste and macaroni. Bring to a boil over high heat, then reduce the heat, cover the casserole and simmer for 30 minutes, or until the vegetables are tender. Stir in the cooked beans and diced salt pork, sprinkle with the salt and black pepper, and serve directly from the casserole or from a large heated tureen.

To serve 8

2 quarts water
2 cups (1 pound) dried black beans
3 tablespoons butter
2 cups finely chopped onions
½ cup finely chopped scraped
   carrots
½ cup finely chopped celery
1½ teaspoons finely chopped
   garlic
1 to 2 quarts chicken stock, fresh or
   canned
1½ pounds smoked ham hocks

1 tablespoon distilled white vinegar
1 large bay leaf
1 teaspoon salt
1 tablespoon strained fresh lemon
   juice
Freshly ground black pepper
½ cup dry Madeira
1 lemon, cut crosswise into ⅛-inch-
   thick slices
2 hard-cooked eggs, finely chopped
1 tablespoon finely chopped fresh
   parsley

In a heavy 3- to 4-quart saucepan, bring the water to a boil over high heat. Drop in the beans, cook briskly, uncovered, for 2 minutes, then turn off the heat. Set aside to soak uncovered for about 1 hour.

Meanwhile, melt the butter in a heavy 4- to 5-quart casserole. When the foam begins to subside, add the onions, carrots, celery and garlic. Stirring frequently, cook over moderate heat for about 5 minutes, or until the vegetables are soft but not brown.

Drain the soaked beans through a sieve or colander set over a deep bowl and transfer them to the casserole. Measure the soaking liquid, add enough chicken stock to make 2½ quarts, and pour the mixture into the casserole. Stir in the ham hocks, vinegar, bay leaf and salt, and bring to a boil over high heat. Then reduce the heat to low, cover the casserole partially, and simmer for 2 hours, or until the beans are tender and can be easily mashed against the sides of the pan with a spoon.

Discard the ham hocks and bay leaf. Purée the soup through a food mill or rub it through a fine sieve with the back of a spoon.

Add the lemon juice and a few grindings of pepper, return the soup to the casserole and, stirring constantly, bring it to a simmer over moderate heat. Taste for seasoning and stir in the Madeira.

Ladle the soup into a heated tureen or individual heated soup plates and place the lemon slices on top. Sprinkle with the finely chopped hard-cooked eggs and the chopped parsley and serve at once.

## Virginia Peanut Soup

To serve 6 to 8

8 tablespoons (1 quarter-pound stick) unsalted butter, cut into bits
½ cup finely chopped onions
½ cup finely chopped celery
3 tablespoons flour
2 quarts chicken stock, freshly made or canned

2 cups smooth peanut butter, at room temperature
¼ teaspoon celery salt
1 teaspoon salt
1 tablespoon strained fresh lemon juice
½ cup ground peanuts

In a heavy 3- to 4-quart casserole, melt the butter bits over moderate heat. When the foam subsides, drop in the onions and celery and cook uncovered, stirring frequently, for 5 to 8 minutes, or until the vegetables are soft but have not yet begun to brown. Stir in the flour with a wooden spoon and, when it is thoroughly incorporated, pour in the chicken stock. Stirring constantly with a whisk, bring to a boil over high heat until the mixture thickens lightly and is smooth. Reduce the heat to low and simmer, partially covered, for 30 minutes, stirring occasionally. Pour the contents of the casserole into a fine sieve set over a bowl, pressing down hard on the vegetables with the back of a spoon before discarding the pulp.

Scrape the peanut butter into a large mixing bowl and whisk in the stock, ¼ cup at a time. After all of the liquid has been added and the soup is smooth, return it to the casserole. Stir in the celery salt, salt and lemon juice, and bring to a simmer over moderate heat. When the soup is hot (do not let it boil), pour it into a heated tureen or individual soup bowls. Present the ground peanuts in a small bowl, to be sprinkled on the soup by each diner.

## Cold Split Pea Soup with Mint

To serve 6 to 8

2 cups dry green split peas
2 quarts chicken stock, fresh or canned
1 cup coarsely chopped onion
1 stalk celery, coarsely chopped
⅛ teaspoon ground cloves

1 bay leaf
1 cup coarsely chopped fresh mint
1 teaspoon salt
Pinch white pepper
½ to 1 cup chilled heavy cream
Sprigs of fresh mint

*Encased in an ice-filled container, chilled, mint-flavored split pea soup is unusual for a summer buffet or picnic.*

Wash the split peas thoroughly under cold running water and continue to wash until the draining water runs clear. Pick over the peas and discard any discolored ones. In a heavy 4- to 5-quart saucepan or soup kettle, bring the chicken stock to a boil and drop in the peas slowly so that the stock does not stop boiling. Add the onions, celery, cloves, bay leaf and mint. Reduce the heat and simmer with the pan partially covered for 1½ hours or until the peas can be easily mashed with a spoon. Remove the bay leaf.

Purée the soup through a food mill or fine sieve into a large bowl, and then rub it through the sieve back into the saucepan or into another bowl. Add the salt and pepper, and chill the soup in the refrigerator. (If you wish to serve the soup immediately, place the soup in a bowl and set the bowl in a larger container filled with crushed ice or ice cubes. With a metal spoon, stir the soup until it is ice cold.) Before serving, stir in ½ to 1 cup of chilled heavy cream, thinning the soup as desired, and taste for seasoning. Garnish with sprigs of fresh mint.

## Mormon Split-Pea Soup (Far West)

To serve 6 to 8

| | |
|---|---|
| 2 tablespoons butter | coarsely grated |
| 1 cup finely chopped onions | ½ teaspoon crumbled dried |
| ½ cup finely chopped celery | marjoram |
| 2 cups (1 pound) dried green split | 3½ teaspoons salt |
|    peas, washed in a sieve under | ¼ teaspoon freshly ground black |
|    cold running water |    pepper |
| 3 quarts water | 1 pound lean ground pork |
| 3 medium-sized boiling potatoes | 1 teaspoon ground sage |
|    (about 1 pound), peeled and | ¼ teaspoon ground white pepper |

In a heavy 5- to 6-quart casserole, melt the butter over moderate heat. When the foam begins to subside, add the onions and celery and, stirring frequently, cook for about 5 minutes, until the vegetables are soft but not brown. Stir in the peas and water, then bring to a boil over high heat, meanwhile skimming off the foam and scum that rise to the surface. Add the potatoes, marjoram, 2 teaspoons of the salt and the black pepper, reduce the heat to low, and simmer partially covered for 1 hour.

Meanwhile, combine the ground pork, sage, the remaining 1½ teaspoons of salt and the white pepper in a bowl. Knead vigorously with both hands, then beat with a wooden spoon until the mixture is smooth. Moistening your hands in cold water occasionally, pinch off about 1 tablespoon of the pork mixture at a time and shape each piece into a ball about 1 inch in diameter.

When the soup has cooked its allotted time, drop in the pork balls and return the soup to a simmer. Cover the pot partially and continue to simmer for 30 minutes. To test the pork for doneness, lift one of the balls out of the water with a slotted spoon and pierce it deeply with the point of a small sharp knife. If the liquid that trickles out is clear yellow, the pork is done even though the meat itself appears somewhat pink; however, if the liquid is pink, simmer the soup for 5 to 10 minutes longer.

Taste for seasoning and serve the soup at once.

To serve 8 to 10

4 to 5 quarts water
2 cups (1 pound) dried pea beans
1 large onion, peeled and pierced
  with 3 whole cloves
4 sprigs fresh parsley and 1
  medium-sized bay leaf, tied
  together with kitchen string

2 teaspoons plus 1 tablespoon salt
2 one-pound smoked ham hocks
1½ cups finely chopped onions
1 cup finely chopped celery
¼ cup finely chopped fresh parsley
1 teaspoon finely chopped garlic
½ teaspoon freshly ground black
  pepper

In a heavy 5- to 6-quart casserole, bring 2 quarts of water to a boil over high heat. Drop in the dried beans and boil them for about 2 minutes. (The water should cover the beans by at least 2 inches; if necessary, add more.) Turn off the heat and let the beans soak for 1 hour.

Then add the clove-pierced onion, the parsley and bay leaf and 2 teaspoons of salt. Bring to a boil again, reduce the heat to low and simmer partially covered for about 1 hour, or until the beans are tender. (The beans should be covered with water throughout the cooking time. Keep a kettle of boiling water at hand and replenish the liquid in the casserole if necessary.) Pick out and discard the onion and the herb bouquet, then drain the beans through a sieve set over a bowl or pot.

Measure the cooking liquid and add enough fresh water to make 3 quarts. Return the liquid and the beans to the casserole, add the ham hocks and bring to a boil over high heat. Reduce the heat to low and simmer partially covered for 2 hours. Stir in the chopped onions, celery, chopped parsley, garlic, the remaining tablespoon of salt and the black pepper and continue to simmer, still partially covered, for 45 minutes.

Transfer the ham hocks to a plate and, with a small knife, remove and discard the skin and bones. Cut the meat into ½-inch pieces. Return the ham to the soup, taste for seasoning, and serve at once from a heated tureen or in individual deep soup bowls.

## Shaker Herb Soup  *(Eastern Heartland)*

To serve 4 to 6

| | |
|---|---|
| 4 tablespoons butter | 1 teaspoon crumbled dried tarragon |
| 1 cup finely chopped celery | 1 quart chicken stock, fresh or |
| 3 tablespoons finely cut fresh chives |    canned |
| 4 tablespoons finely cut fresh sorrel, | Freshly ground black pepper |
|    or substitute 2 tablespoons | Ground nutmeg, preferably freshly |
|    bottled or canned sorrel |    grated |
| 1 tablespoon crumbled dried chervil | 1 cup freshly grated Cheddar cheese |

In a heavy 2- to 3-quart saucepan, melt the butter over moderate heat. When the foam begins to subside, add the celery and chives and, stirring frequently, cook for about 5 minutes, until they are soft but not brown. Stir in the sorrel, chervil and tarragon and cook for a minute. Then add the chicken stock and a few grindings of pepper and bring the soup to a boil over high heat. Reduce the heat to low and simmer partially covered for 20 minutes.

Taste for seasoning, ladle the soup into individual heated bowls, and sprinkle each portion with a little nutmeg. Serve at once, accompanied by a bowl of grated cheese.

## Cheddar Cheese Soup

To serve 6 to 8

| | |
|---|---|
| 2 tablespoons butter | 5 cups chicken stock, fresh or canned |
| ¼ cup finely chopped onion | ½ pound Cheddar cheese, coarsely |
| ¼ cup finely chopped carrot |    grated (about 2 cups) |
| ¼ cup finely chopped green pepper | 1½ cups milk |
| ¼ cup finely chopped celery | Salt |
| 3 tablespoons flour | White pepper |

In a 2- to 3-quart saucepan melt the butter over moderate heat. When the foam subsides add the onion, carrot, green pepper and the celery, and cook for 6 to 8 minutes or until the vegetables are soft but not brown. Mix in the flour and pour in the stock. Bring to a boil over moderate heat, beating constantly with a whisk until it thickens slightly. Then reduce the heat to low and simmer the soup, partially covered, for about 10 minutes, stirring occasionally. Now, a handful at a time, beat in the cheese and cook until it dissolves, then pour in 1 cup of the milk, adding up to ½ cup more if the soup is too thick. It should have the consistency of heavy cream. Bring almost to a boil, then strain through a fine sieve into another saucepan. Taste for seasoning, and add as much salt and white pepper as you think is needed. Heat once more almost to the boiling point and serve. Cheddar soup is equally good cold. Chill it thoroughly and serve it in chilled cups or soup plates.

## Cucumber Bisque

To serve 4

6 tablespoons butter

2 medium onions, finely chopped (1 cup)

2 large cucumbers, peeled and finely chopped (2 cups)

3 cups chicken stock, fresh or canned

2 tablespoons flour

2 egg yolks

½ cup heavy cream

1 medium-sized cucumber, peeled and diced into ¼-inch pieces

Salt

White pepper

2 tablespoons finely chopped fresh parsley or chives

In a heavy 2- to 3-quart saucepan, melt 4 tablespoons of the butter over moderate heat. When the foam subsides, stir in the chopped onions and the chopped cucumbers and, stirring occasionally, cook them for about 5 minutes until the onions are transparent but not brown.

Add the chicken stock and bring to a boil. Lower the heat and simmer, uncovered, for 20 to 30 minutes, or until the vegetables are tender. Pour the soup into a sieve set over a large bowl and force the vegetables through with the back of a wooden spoon.

Melt the remaining 2 tablespoons of butter in the saucepan. Remove the pan from the heat and stir in the flour. Pour in the puréed soup, beating vigorously with a wire whisk. Return to moderate heat and cook about 3 to 5 minutes, whisking constantly, until the soup has thickened slightly.

In a small bowl, combine the egg yolks and heavy cream. Beating constantly with a whisk, pour into it 1 cup of the hot soup, 2 tablespoons at a time. Then reverse the process. Slowly pour this warmed mixture back into the remaining soup, still beating with the whisk. Simmer over very low heat for 5 minutes but do not let the soup come to a boil. Just before serving, stir in the diced raw cucumber, season with salt and white pepper, and sprinkle with the chopped parsley or chives.

To serve the soup cold, let it cool to room temperature, then cover and refrigerate for at least 3 hours. Add the diced raw cucumbers, seasonings and chopped herbs just before serving. If you like, you may serve the cold soup with a spoonful of slightly salted, stiffly whipped cream in each portion, or a spoonful of sour cream may be used.

## Cream of Leek Soup *(Rumanian-American)*

To serve 6 to 8

6 medium-sized leeks
4 tablespoons butter
3 medium-sized onions, finely
  chopped
6 cups chicken stock, fresh or
  canned

1 pound potatoes, peeled and cut
  into ½-inch cubes
1 cup dry white wine
½ teaspoon white pepper
1 cup heavy cream
2 tablespoons finely chopped parsley
2 tablespoons finely cut chives

Wash the leeks well under cold running water and pat them dry with paper towels. Cut off the green leaves and discard the very tough or damaged leaves. Chop the leaves fine and set them aside. Slice the white part of the leeks crosswise into ¼-inch-thick rounds.

In a 2½- to 3-quart enameled or stainless-steel casserole, melt the butter over moderate heat. When the foam begins to subside, add the leek rounds and onions; stirring frequently, cook for 5 to 8 minutes, or until they are translucent. Stir in the chopped leaves and cook for 2 or 3 minutes. Add the stock, potato and wine, and bring to a boil over high heat. Partially cover the casserole, lower the heat and simmer for 1 hour.

Purée the soup through a food mill or fine sieve set over a mixing bowl, and again through a fine sieve back into the pan. Stir in the white pepper and bring to a simmer over moderate heat. Stir in the heavy cream, sprinkle with the parsley and chives, and taste for seasoning. Ladle the soup into a heated tureen or individual soup plates.

## Bowl of the Wife of Kit Carson *(Far West)*
### TURKEY, CHICK-PEA AND GREEN CHILI SOUP

To serve 6 to 8

1 cup (½ pound) dried chick-peas
  (*garbanzos*)
2 quarts water
Two 1½- to 2-pound turkey legs,
  thoroughly defrosted if frozen
2 medium-sized onions, peeled and
  coarsely chopped
1 medium-sized bay leaf, crumbled
1 tablespoon salt
8 whole black peppercorns
3 tablespoons uncooked long-grain
  white rice (not the converted
  variety)
1½ teaspoons crumbled dried

oregano
3 tablespoons finely chopped
  seeded canned green chilies (not
  the *jalapeño* variety; (*caution:
  see note, appendix*)
½ pound Monterey Jack cheese,
  cut into ¼-inch dice, or
  substitute ½ pound diced
  Münster cheese
2 tablespoons finely chopped fresh
  parsley
1 large firm ripe avocado, halved,
  seeded, peeled and cut lengthwise
  into thin slices

Starting a day ahead, wash the chick-peas in a sieve under cold running water, place them in a large bowl or pan, and pour in enough cold water to cover them by 2 inches. Soak at room temperature for at least 12 hours.

Drain the peas in a sieve or colander and discard the soaking water. Then place the peas in a heavy 4- to 5-quart casserole, add the 2 quarts of water, and bring to a boil over high heat. Reduce the heat to low and simmer partially covered for about 1 hour, or until the chick-peas are tender. With a slotted spoon, transfer them to a bowl and set aside.

Add the turkey legs to the chick-pea cooking liquid. The liquid should cover the turkey completely; if necessary, add water. Bring to a boil over high heat, meanwhile skimming off the foam and scum that rise to the surface. Add the onions, bay leaf, salt and peppercorns, reduce the heat to low, and simmer partially covered for about 45 minutes, or until the turkey legs show no resistance when pierced deeply with the point of a small sharp knife.

Transfer the turkey legs to a plate. Then strain the stock through a fine sieve set over a bowl, and return it to the pot. Remove the skin from the turkey legs with a small knife or your fingers. Cut or pull the meat away from the bones and discard the skin and bones. Cut the meat into 1-inch cubes and set them aside.

Over high heat, bring the stock in the casserole to a boil. Add the rice and oregano, stir well and reduce the heat to low. Cover tightly and simmer for 20 minutes, or until the rice is tender. Stir in the chick-peas, cubed turkey and chilies, and simmer for 4 or 5 minutes longer to heat all the ingredients through.

Taste for seasoning and ladle the soup into a heated tureen or serving bowl. Scatter the diced cheese and the parsley over the soup, arrange the avocado slices on top, and serve at once.

## Clam Bisque *(Eastern Heartland)*

To serve 6

3 dozen hard-shell clams
  each about 3 inches in
  diameter, shucked (about 3
  cups), with their liquor reserved
4 tablespoons butter

¼ cup flour
¼ teaspoon crumbled dried thyme
¼ teaspoon freshly ground black
  pepper
2 cups light cream

Put the clams through the finest blade of a meat grinder, or purée them in an electric blender. Strain the clam liquor through a fine sieve lined with a double thickness of dampened cheesecloth and set over a bowl. Measure and reserve 2 cups of the liquor.

In a heavy 2- to 3-quart saucepan, melt the butter over moderate heat. When the foam begins to subside, add the flour and stir well. Then, stirring the mixture constantly with a wire whisk, pour in the clam liquor in a slow, thin stream and cook over high heat until the mixture comes to a boil, thickens lightly and is smooth. Reduce the heat to low, stir in the clams, thyme and pepper, and simmer partially covered for 15 minutes.

Stirring constantly, pour in the cream and simmer for a few minutes longer to heat the clam bisque through. Taste for seasoning, ladle the bisque into individual heated soup plates and serve at once.

## Dungeness Crabmeat Bisque *(Northwest)*

To serve 6

4 tablespoons butter
½ cup finely chopped onions
½ cup finely chopped celery
2 tablespoons flour
½ teaspoon paprika
1 teaspoon salt
⅛ teaspoon ground white pepper
2 cups milk

2 cups heavy cream
1 pound (about 2 cups) freshly
  cooked or frozen Dungeness
  crabmeat, defrosted if frozen,
  drained and picked over to
  remove all bits of shell and
  cartilage
¼ cup pale dry sherry

In a heavy 2- to 3-quart saucepan, melt the butter over moderate heat. When the foam begins to subside, add the onions and celery and, stirring frequently, cook for about 5 minutes, until they are soft but not brown. Add the flour, paprika, salt and pepper, and mix well. Then, stirring the mixture constantly with a wire whisk, pour in the milk and cream in a slow, thin stream and cook briskly until the mixture comes to a boil and is smooth. Reduce the heat to low and simmer for about 3 minutes to remove any taste of raw flour.

Stir in the crabmeat and simmer for 2 or 3 minutes longer to heat it through. Add 1 tablespoon of the sherry, taste and add as much of the remaining sherry as you like. Serve the bisque at once from a heated tureen or in individual soup plates.

## Cold Shrimp-and-Tomato Bisque *(Creole-Acadian)*

To serve 4 to 6

| | |
|---|---|
| 1 pound raw shrimp | 1 cup light cream |
| 3 cups water | 1½ teaspoons salt |
| 2 tablespoons butter | ¼ teaspoon ground hot red pepper |
| ¼ cup finely chopped onions | (cayenne) |
| 3 tablespoons flour | 1 large firm ripe tomato, washed, |
| 1 tablespoon canned tomato purée | stemmed, and sliced crosswise |
| 2 teaspoons curry powder | into ¼-inch-thick rounds |
| | 2 hard-cooked eggs, finely chopped |

Shell the shrimp. Devein them by making a shallow incision down their backs with a small sharp knife and lifting out the black or white intestinal vein with the point of the knife. Wash the shrimp briefly in a sieve or colander set under cold running water.

Bring the 3 cups of water to a boil over high heat, drop in the shrimp and cook briskly, uncovered, for 3 to 5 minutes, or until they are pink and firm to the touch. With a slotted spoon, transfer the shrimp to a bowl and put them through the finest blade of a food grinder. Set the shrimp aside and reserve the cooking liquid.

In a heavy 2- to 3-quart saucepan, melt the butter over moderate heat. When the foam begins to subside, add the onions and, stirring frequently, cook for about 5 minutes, or until they are soft and translucent but not brown. Add the flour, tomato purée and curry powder, and mix well. Stirring constantly with a wire whisk, pour in the reserved cooking liquid in a slow, thin stream and cook over high heat until the sauce comes to a boil, thickens lightly and is smooth.

Reduce the heat to low and simmer for 3 or 4 minutes to remove the raw taste of flour. Add the ground shrimp, cream, salt and red pepper, and stir over moderate heat until the soup comes to a boil. Taste for seasoning, pour the soup into a bowl, and let it cool to room temperature. Cover the bowl tightly with foil or plastic wrap and refrigerate the soup for at least 4 hours, until it is thoroughly chilled.

To serve, ladle the soup into chilled individual bowls and garnish each portion with the sliced tomato and chopped eggs.

To serve 8 to 10

5 pounds live crawfish

4 quarts water

2 cups coarsely chopped onion

Herb bouquet of 3 sprigs parsley, 1 bay leaf, ¼ teaspoon thyme, 6 peppercorns tied together in cheesecloth

8 tablespoons butter

1 cup finely chopped onion

½ cup finely diced carrot

½ cup finely diced celery

1 teaspoon finely chopped garlic

2 tablespoons finely chopped parsley

¾ teaspoon thyme

8 tablespoons flour

2 teaspoons salt

2 tablespoons paprika

Wash the crawfish under cold running water, then soak in water for at least 10 minutes. In a heavy 8- to 10-quart pot, bring 4 quarts of water to a rapid boil. Add the chopped onion and the herb bouquet. Then drop in all the crawfish a handful at a time and boil uncovered for about 5 minutes. Remove the crawfish and set aside. Strain the cooking liquid through cheesecloth, then return it to the thoroughly washed pot.

In a heavy skillet, melt the butter over moderate heat. When the foam subsides, add the onion, carrot, celery, garlic, parsley and thyme. Cook for about 5 minutes, until the vegetables are limp but not brown, then stir in the flour. Stir this mixture over low heat for about 10 minutes. With a rubber spatula, scrape it into the crawfish stock. Bring to a boil, mixing with a whisk until the stock thickens slightly. Turn the heat to low and simmer gently while you shell the crawfish.

Break the heads from the crawfish and pick the meat from the tails, adding the tail shells to the simmering stock as you proceed. Discard the vein in the tail meat, chop the meat fine and reserve in a bowl. In another bowl, shake the yellow fat from the crawfish heads by gently tapping them against the sides of the bowl. With a small knife, scrape the heads clean of any black matter and set aside 35 to 40 of them to be stuffed. Add the remaining heads to the stock, and stir in the 2 teaspoons of salt and the paprika. Simmer partially covered for 45 minutes.

STUFFING (for about 40 heads)

2 tablespoons butter

3 tablespoons minced onion

½ teaspoon finely chopped garlic

1½ cups fresh bread crumbs

1 egg yolk, lightly beaten

3 tablespoons chopped parsley

2 tablespoons sherry

½ teaspoon salt

Pinch of cayenne

While the bisque is simmering, make the stuffing. In a small skillet, melt 2 tablespoons of butter over moderate heat. When the foam subsides, add the minced onion and garlic and cook for about 4 minutes, or until they are transparent but not brown. Scrape them into a mixing bowl. Add half the reserved crawfish meat, the bread crumbs, egg yolk, parsley, sherry, salt and cayenne, mix and taste for seasoning. Pack each head with stuffing, then place in one layer in a shallow baking dish. Dot with soft butter and bake for about 10 minutes in a preheated 350° oven.

Before serving, strain the bisque through a fine sieve and discard the crawfish shells. Bring the bisque to a simmer once more, and add the remaining crawfish meat. Divide the stuffed heads among individual soup plates, pour the hot bisque over them and serve.

## Clam Chowder *(New England)*

To serve 4

3 dozen hard-shell or littleneck clams, each about 3 inches in diameter, shucked (about 3 cups), with their liquor or juices reserved

2 medium-sized boiling potatoes, peeled, sliced ½ inch thick and cut into ½-inch dice (about 2 cups)

2 ounces lean slab bacon with rind removed, sliced ¼ inch thick and cut into ¼-inch dice

1 tablespoon plus 4 teaspoons butter

1 cup finely chopped onions

2 cups milk

½ cup light cream

½ teaspoon crumbled dried thyme

½ teaspoon salt

Freshly ground black pepper

With a sharp knife, chop the tough meat surrounding the soft centers, or stomachs, of the clams and set aside. Cut the soft centers in half and reserve separately on a plate. Strain the clam liquor through a fine sieve lined with a double thickness of dampened cheesecloth and set over a bowl. Measure and set aside 1 cup of the liquor.

Drop the potato dice into enough boiling water to cover them completely and cook briskly until they are tender but still somewhat resistant to the bite. Drain the potatoes in a sieve set over a bowl or pan, and reserve ½ cup of the cooking liquid.

Meanwhile, drop the bacon dice into enough boiling water to cover them completely and boil for 2 minutes. Drain the dice and pat them completely dry with paper towels.

In a heavy 2- to 3-quart saucepan, fry the bacon and 1 tablespoon of butter over moderate heat, stirring frequently until the dice are crisp and brown and have rendered all their fat. With a slotted spoon transfer the dice to paper towels to drain.

Add the onions to the fat remaining in the pan and, stirring frequently, cook for about 5 minutes over moderate heat until they are soft and translucent but not brown. Watch carefully for any sign of burning and regulate the heat accordingly.

Stir in the reserved cup of clam liquor, the ½ cup of potato cooking liquid and the finely chopped clams. Reduce the heat to low, cover tightly

87

and simmer for 10 minutes. Stir in the halved clam centers and the reserved potatoes and continue to simmer covered for 3 minutes longer.

Meanwhile, in a separate saucepan, warm the milk and cream over moderate heat until small bubbles appear around the edge of the pan.

Pour the hot milk and cream into the simmering clam mixture and mix well. Then stir in the thyme, salt, a few grindings of pepper and the drained bacon dice. Taste the chowder and add more salt if needed.

Ladle the chowder into 4 heated soup plates, place a teaspoon of butter on top of each serving, and serve at once.

## Manhattan Clam Chowder

To serve 6

| | |
|---|---|
| 4 large firm ripe tomatoes, or substitute 4 cups chopped drained canned tomatoes | ¼ cup finely chopped carrots |
| | ¼ cup finely chopped celery |
| | 3 cups water |
| | 1 medium-sized bay leaf |
| 2 dozen large hard-shell clams , shucked and drained, and their liquor | ½ teaspoon crumbled dried thyme |
| | Freshly ground black pepper |
| | 3 medium-sized boiling potatoes, peeled and cut into ¼-inch dice (about 2 cups) |
| 3 tablespoons butter | |
| 1 cup finely chopped onions | |

If you are using fresh tomatoes, drop them into boiling water for 15 seconds, then peel off the skins with a small sharp knife. Cut out the stems and cut the tomatoes in half crosswise. Squeeze the halves to remove the juice and seeds, then coarsely chop the pulp. Canned tomatoes need only to be drained thoroughly and chopped.

Chop the clams fine and reserve them. Strain the clam liquor through a fine sieve lined with a double thickness of dampened cheesecloth; measure and save 3 cups of the liquor. (If there is less than 3 cups of liquor, add enough water to make that amount.)

In a heavy 3- to 4-quart saucepan, melt the butter over moderate heat. When the foam begins to subside, add the onions, carrots and celery and, stirring frequently, cook for about 5 minutes, or until the vegetables are soft but not brown. Add the chopped tomatoes, clam liquor, 3 cups of water, bay leaf, thyme and a few grindings of pepper, and bring to a boil over high heat. Reduce the heat to low, cover the pan partially and simmer for 45 minutes.

Stir in the potatoes and continue to simmer partially covered for about 12 minutes longer. Then add the chopped clams and cook the chowder for 2 to 3 minutes more. Pick out and discard the bay leaf.

Taste the chowder for seasoning and serve at once from a heated tureen or in individual soup plates.

## Corn Chowder *(New England)*

To serve 4 to 6

2 cups fresh corn kernels, cut from about 4 large ears of corn, or substitute 2 cups frozen corn kernels, thoroughly defrosted
3 ounces lean salt pork, rind removed and the pork cut into ¼-inch dice
4 medium-sized onions, peeled and

cut crosswise into ⅛-inch-thick slices
3 medium-sized boiling potatoes, peeled and cut into ¼-inch dice (about 2½ cups)
2 cups water
1 cup milk
1 cup light cream

Place 1 cup of the corn in the jar of an electric blender and blend at high speed for 30 seconds. Turn off the machine, scrape down the sides of the jar with a rubber spatula, and blend again until the corn is a smooth purée. Set aside.

In a heavy 3- to 4-quart casserole, fry the salt pork over moderate heat, turning the bits frequently with a slotted spoon until they are crisp and brown and have rendered all their fat. Transfer the pork bits to paper towels to drain thoroughly.

Add the onions to the fat remaining in the casserole and, stirring frequently, cook for 8 to 10 minutes until they are soft and golden brown. Watch carefully for any sign of burning and regulate the heat accordingly. Stir in the corn purée, the remaining cup of corn kernels, the potatoes, and the water and bring to a boil over high heat. Reduce the heat to low and simmer partially covered until the potato dice are soft but still intact. Add the milk and cream and, stirring constantly, cook for 5 or 6 minutes to heat them through. Stir in the reserved pork bits and taste the chowder for seasoning.

Ladle the corn chowder into a heated tureen or individual soup plates and serve at once.

# Fish Chowder *(New England)*

To serve 6

¼ pound lean salt pork with rind
    removed, the pork cut into
    ½-inch dice
1 tablespoon butter plus
    2 tablespoons butter, cut into
    ½-inch bits
1 cup coarsely chopped onions
A 3- to 3½-pound haddock or
    cod, cleaned, with head and tail
    removed but reserved and the

    body cut into 3-inch-thick steaks
2 cups water
2 medium-sized boiling potatoes,
    peeled and cut into ½-inch dice
    (about 2 cups)
2 teaspoons salt
Freshly ground black pepper
1 quart milk
⅛ teaspoon crumbled dried thyme

In a heavy 4- to 5-quart enameled or stainless-steel casserole, brown the salt-pork dice in 1 tablespoon of butter over moderate heat, turning them about with a slotted spoon until they are crisp and have rendered all their fat. Add the onions and, stirring frequently, cook for about 5 minutes until they are soft and golden brown.

Place the haddock or cod head and tail in the casserole, pour in the water and bring to a boil over moderate heat, meanwhile skimming off the foam and scum that rise to the surface. Add the potatoes, 1 teaspoon of salt and a few grindings of pepper, reduce the heat to low and simmer partially covered for 15 minutes. Add the steaks and continue to simmer partially covered for 10 minutes longer, or until the fish flakes easily when prodded gently with a fork. (Skim off any foam or scum that rises to the surface.)

Remove and discard the fish head and tail. With tongs or a slotted spoon, transfer the steaks to a platter. Remove the skin and bones from the steaks with a small knife and discard them. Cut the meat into 1-inch pieces and return them to the casserole.

Add the milk, the 2 tablespoons of butter bits, the thyme, the remaining teaspoon of salt and a few grindings of pepper to the casserole. Stirring gently, bring the chowder to a simmer over moderate heat and taste for seasoning.

Ladle the chowder into a heated tureen or individual soup plates, or, following New England custom, let it rest at room temperature for no longer than an hour, and reheat it briefly before serving.

To serve 4

5 tablespoons plus 4 teaspoons
   butter
2 medium-sized onions, peeled and
   cut crosswise into ¼-inch-thick
   slices
1 quart milk, or substitute 2 cups
   milk and 2 cups light cream
1 medium-sized boiling potato,

peeled and cut into ½-inch dice
   (about 1 cup)
Salt
1 pound sea scallops, thoroughly
   defrosted if frozen, cut against
   the grain into ¼-inch-thick
   slices
Paprika

In a heavy 2- to 3-quart saucepan, melt 3 tablespoons of butter over moderate heat. When the foam begins to subside, add the onions and, stirring frequently, cook for about 5 minutes, or until they are soft and translucent but not brown.

Pour in the milk (or milk and light cream) and bring the mixture to a simmer over moderate heat. Reduce the heat to low and simmer partially covered for 15 minutes.

Meanwhile, drop the potato dice into enough lightly salted boiling water to cover them by at least 1 inch and cook briskly until tender. Drain thoroughly and set aside in a bowl.

Melt 2 tablespoons of butter in a heavy 10- to 12-inch skillet. Drop in the scallops and, turning them about almost constantly with a slotted spoon, fry over high heat for 2 or 3 minutes until they are opaque on all sides. Set the scallops aside with the potato dice.

Strain the onion-and-milk mixture through a fine sieve into a bowl; discard the onions and return the liquid to the saucepan. Add the scallops and potato dice and simmer for 2 or 3 minutes to heat them through.

Taste for seasoning and ladle the chowder into heated individual soup bowls. Place one of the remaining 4 teaspoons of butter in each bowl, sprinkle the chowder with a little paprika and serve at once.

## *Pacific Oyster Stew*

To serve 4

4 tablespoons soft butter
1½ pints light or heavy cream
1½ pints Pacific oysters, or other

oysters, and their liquor
Salt
Freshly ground black pepper
Paprika (optional)

Warm 4 deep soup bowls in a shallow baking pan that is half filled with boiling water. Add 1 tablespoon of soft butter to each bowl. In a small saucepan, bring the cream almost but not quite to a boil over moderate heat. When small bubbles appear around the edge of the pan, reduce the heat to its lowest point and keep the cream barely simmering.

Pour the oysters and all their liquor into a 12-inch enameled or stainless-steel skillet. Set it over moderate heat and poach the oysters, turning them gently about in their liquor with a wooden spoon for 2 or 3 minutes, or until the oysters plump up and their edges begin to curl. Immediately pour the simmering cream into the skillet, add salt and pepper to taste, and simmer a moment longer. Ladle the stew into heated soup bowls, sprinkle with a little paprika if you like and serve at once accompanied by crackers or, less traditionally, hot French or Italian bread.

## Shrimp-and-Oyster Gumbo  *(South)*

To serve 10 to 12

8 tablespoons butter
1 pound fresh okra, thinly sliced, or substitute two 10-ounce packages of frozen okra, thoroughly defrosted and thinly sliced
1 cup finely chopped onions
½ cup finely chopped green pepper
1 teaspoon finely chopped garlic
2 tablespoons flour
4 cups chicken stock, fresh or canned
6 medium-sized firm ripe tomatoes, washed, cored and coarsely chopped
6 fresh parsley sprigs and 1 large

bay leaf, tied together with kitchen cord
½ teaspoon crumbled dried thyme
2 teaspoons salt
Freshly ground black pepper
1½ pounds small raw shrimp (about 30 to the pound)
24 shucked oysters, thoroughly defrosted if frozen
2 teaspoons strained fresh lemon juice
2 teaspoons Worcestershire sauce
½ teaspoon ground hot red pepper (cayenne)
2 cups freshly cooked Southern dry rice

In a heavy 10- to 12-inch skillet, melt 4 tablespoons of the butter over moderate heat. When the foam begins to subside, add the okra. Stirring constantly, cook until the okra stops "roping," that is, until the white threads the vegetable produces disappear. Remove the pan from the heat and set aside.

Over moderate heat, melt the remaining 4 tablespoons of butter in a heavy 3- to 4-quart soup pot or casserole. When the foam subsides, add the onions, green pepper and garlic, and cook for about 5 minutes, or until the vegetables are soft but not brown. Add the flour and cook for 2 or 3 minutes, stirring constantly with a wire whisk. Still whisking, pour in the chicken stock in a slow, thin stream. Then add the okra, the tomatoes, parsley and bay leaf, thyme, salt and a few grindings of black pepper. Bring to a boil, reduce the heat to low, and simmer partially covered for 30 minutes.

Meanwhile, shell the shrimp. Devein them by making a shallow incision down their backs with a small sharp knife and lifting out the black or white intestinal vein with the point of the knife.

Drop the shrimp into the gumbo and simmer for 5 minutes; add the oysters and continue to simmer for 2 or 3 minutes longer, until they plump up and their edges begin to curl. Pick out and discard the parsley and bay leaf, stir the lemon juice, Worcestershire sauce and red pepper into the gumbo and taste for seasoning.

Serve in 10 or 12 heated soup plates, heaping up a small mound of dry rice in the bottom of each plate and ladling the shrimp-and-oyster gumbo over the rice.

## Crab, Shrimp and Okra Gumbo *(Creole-Acadian)*

To serve 4

1 pound uncooked medium-sized shrimp (about 20 to 24 to the pound)
7 quarts water
5 dried hot red chilies, each about 2 inches long *(caution: see note, appendix)*
1 lemon, cut crosswise into ¼-inch-thick slices
3 large bay leaves
1½ teaspoons crumbled, dried thyme
1 tablespoon plus 1 teaspoon salt
10 live blue crabs, each about 8 ounces
4 tablespoons brown *roux*
½ cup coarsely chopped onions
1½ teaspoons finely chopped garlic
½ pound fresh okra, trimmed, washed and cut into 1-inch chunks
¾ cup coarsely chopped green pepper
1 teaspoon ground hot red pepper (cayenne)
½ teaspoon Tabasco sauce
4 to 6 cups freshly cooked long-grain white rice

Shell the shrimp. Devein them by making a shallow incision down their backs with a small knife and lifting out the intestinal vein with the point of the knife. Wash the shrimp briefly and set them aside.

In a 10- to 12-quart pot, bring the water, chilies, lemon slices, 2 bay leaves, 1 teaspoon of thyme and 1 tablespoon of salt to a boil over high heat. Drop in the crabs and boil briskly, uncovered, for 5 minutes. Remove the crabs from the stock with tongs, and set them aside to cool.

Drop the shrimp into the stock remaining in the pot and cook uncovered for 3 to 5 minutes, or until they are pink and firm to the touch. With tongs, transfer the shrimp to a plate. Then boil the stock, uncovered, until it is reduced to 3 quarts. Strain the stock through a fine sieve set over a large pot, and discard the seasonings. Cover the pot to keep the stock warm until you are ready to use it.

When the crabs are cool enough to handle, shell them in the following fashion: Grasping the body of the crab firmly in one hand, break off the large claws and legs close to the body. With the point of a small sharp knife, pry off the pointed shell, or apron, and loosen the large bottom shell from around the meat and cartilage, cutting near the edges where the legs are joined to the shell. Lift the body of the crab, break it in half lengthwise, then with the knife pick out the firm white pieces of meat. Discard the gray featherlike gills and tough bits of cartilage but save the morsels of yellow liver and "fat" as well as any pieces of orange roe. Leave the large claws in their shells, but crack the legs lengthwise with a cleaver and pick out the meat. Reserve the meat, claws and roe (if any).

In a heavy 5- to 6-quart casserole, warm the *roux* over low heat, stirring constantly. Add the onions and garlic and stir for about 5 minutes, or until they are soft. Add the okra and green peppers and mix well.

Stirring constantly, pour in the reserved warm stock in a slow, thin stream and bring to a boil over high heat. (If the stock has cooled, reheat before adding it.) Add the red pepper, Tabasco, the remaining bay leaf, ½ teaspoon of thyme and 1 teaspoon of salt. Stir in the crabmeat and claws, reduce the heat to low and simmer, partially covered, for 1 hour.

Add the shrimp and simmer a few minutes longer, then taste for seasoning. The gumbo may require more Tabasco or red pepper.

Ladle the gumbo into a heated tureen and serve at once, accompanied by the rice in a separate bowl. Traditionally, a cupful of rice is mounded in a heated soup plate and the gumbo spooned around it. Give each diner a nutcracker so that the claws can be cracked easily at the table.


BROWN ROUX
To make about 11 tablespoons

| 8 tablespoons unsifted all-purpose flour | 8 tablespoons vegetable oil |
|---|---|

Combine the flour and oil in a heavy 10-inch skillet (preferably cast-iron or enameled iron) and, with a large metal spatula, stir them to a smooth paste. Place the skillet over the lowest possible heat and, stirring constantly, simmer the *roux* slowly for 45 minutes to an hour.

After 5 minutes or so the mixture will begin to foam and this foaming may continue for as long as 10 minutes. After about half an hour, the *roux* will begin to darken and have a faintly nutty aroma. Continue to cook slowly, stirring with the spatula, until the *roux* is a dark rich brown. (During the last 5 minutes or so of cooking, the *roux* darkens quickly and you may want to lift the pan from the heat periodically to let it cool. Should the *roux* burn, discard it and make another batch.)

Immediately scrape the contents of the skillet into a small bowl. Let the *roux* cool to room temperature, then cover with foil or plastic wrap and refrigerate it until ready to use. (It can safely be kept for weeks.)

When it cools the *roux* will separate and the fat will rise to the surface. Before using the *roux,* stir it briefly to recombine it. Measure the desired amount into the pan and warm the *roux* slowly over low heat, stirring constantly. Whether added immediately or not, any liquid that is to be incorporated with the brown *roux* must be at least lukewarm or the mixture may separate. If it does, beat it together again with a whisk.

## Seafood Gumbo (South)

To serve 8 to 10

8 tablespoons butter
2 ten-ounce packages of frozen okra, thoroughly defrosted and thinly sliced, or 1 pound fresh okra, thinly sliced
½ cup finely chopped onion
½ cup finely chopped green pepper
½ teaspoon finely chopped garlic.
2 tablespoons flour
4 cups chicken stock, fresh or canned
2 cups coarsely chopped fresh ripe tomatoes, or an equivalent amount of drained canned tomatoes

Herb bouquet of 6 sprigs parsley and a large bay leaf, tied with cord
½ teaspoon thyme
2 teaspoons salt
Freshly ground black pepper
1 pound of small raw shrimp, shelled and deveined
½ pound of lump crab meat, fresh or canned
16 oysters, shucked
2 teaspoons lemon juice
2 teaspoons Worcestershire sauce
¼ teaspoon Tabasco
2 cups hot steamed rice (optional)

In a 10- to 12-inch frying pan, melt 4 tablespoons of the butter over moderate heat. Add the fresh or frozen okra and, stirring constantly, cook until the okra stops "roping," that is, until the white threads the vegetable produces disappear. Over moderate heat, melt the remaining 4 tablespoons of butter in a heavy 2- or 3-quart soup pot or casserole. When the foam subsides, add the onion, green pepper and garlic, and cook without browning for about 5 minutes. Stir in the 2 tablespoons of flour, and when it has been absorbed by the vegetables, cook 2 to 3 minutes longer, stirring constantly. Pour in the chicken stock and stir with a whisk to dissolve the flour. Then add the okra, the tomatoes, the herb bouquet, thyme, salt and a few grindings of black pepper. Bring to a boil, turn the heat to its lowest point and simmer, partially covered, for ½ hour. Then drop in the shrimp, simmer for 5 minutes and add the crab meat and oysters. Simmer for 2 or 3 minutes, or only until the oysters curl around the edges and the crab meat is heated through. Season with the lemon juice, Worcestershire sauce and the ¼ teaspoon Tabasco, or more to taste.

To serve, it is customary to ladle the gumbo over small mounds of hot rice in deep soup plates. However, the rice may be omitted if you prefer.

## Fish Stock

To make about 1 quart

1½ pounds fish trimmings: the heads, tails and bones of any firm white fish
1 quart cold water
½ cup coarsely chopped onions
¼ cup coarsely chopped celery, including the leaves
1 small bay leaf
¼ teaspoon crumbled dried thyme
½ teaspoon salt
3 whole black peppercorns

Wash the fish trimmings in a deep bowl set under cold running water. Drain, then mash the pieces of fish with the back of a large spoon.

Place the mashed fish in a 3- to 4-quart enameled or stainless-steel saucepan and pour in the water. Bring slowly to a simmer over moderate heat and cook uncovered for 5 minutes, skimming off the foam and scum as they rise to the surface. Add the onions, celery, bay leaf, thyme, salt and peppercorns, and reduce the heat to low. Simmer partially covered for 30 minutes, skimming the surface from time to time.

Remove the pan from the heat and, with a slotted spoon, lift out and discard the fish and vegetables. Strain the stock into a deep bowl through a fine sieve lined with a double thickness of dampened cheesecloth. The stock will keep refrigerated for 2 or 3 days or it can be cooled to room temperature, covered tightly and frozen.

# Eggs & Cheese

Although they play supporting roles in most recipes, eggs or cheese become the featured attraction in such succulent dishes as Creole creamed eggs Chartres, Chinese-American egg foo yung, and a zesty version of Welsh rabbit from Cape Breton. As with any ingredient, cooking eggs successfully requires attention to basic details. The size of the egg, for example, becomes critical in soufflé recipes, which assume you are using two-ounce, or "large," eggs. Two of these measure about half a cup; it would take three medium eggs to measure that much. The age of an egg, too, is important. Newly laid eggs are essential for poaching, as in eggs Sardou. Eggs more than two or three days old develop thin, watery whites; these detach from their yolks as soon as they touch the hot poaching water, rather than swirl around the yolks in gossamer veils. Happily for city dwellers, older eggs have their virtues: their whites can be beaten to a greater volume, and they are preferable for hardcooking. Hardcooked fresh eggs are impossible to peel perfectly.

Age is important, too, in cheeses used in cooking. Young cheeses do not have a fully developed flavor, and do not melt as well as aged cheeses. Hard cheeses—those that retain less than thirty per cent moisture after aging—are the most successful cooking cheeses. Some examples are Cheddar, Gruyère, Provolone, Swiss, Parmesan and Romano, any of which can be grated—by hand or in the blender—and used in rabbits, soufflés or omelets, or sprinkled over salads, vegetables or noodles.

In cooking, fresh, uncured cheeses such as cottage, pot, farmer and ricotta have their place as fillings for pancakes (as in Jewish-American blintzes), vegetables (cheese-stuffed mushrooms*) or even pastry (*cannoli**). All but ricotta are made from skim milk; all are salted except pot cheese. The four cheeses can be used interchangeably, as only their textures, and calories, vary.

97

* *See index.*

## Scrambled Eggs on Anchovy Toast

To serve 4

4 eggs
3 tablespoons heavy cream
⅛ teaspoon salt
Freshly ground black pepper

3 tablespoons butter
4 slices hot buttered toast
2 tablespoons anchovy paste
8 flat anchovy fillets, thoroughly
   drained

In a small bowl, beat the eggs with a fork or whisk until they are well blended, then beat in the cream, salt and a few grindings of pepper. Place the skillet over low heat, and in it melt the 3 tablespoons of butter. Do not let the butter brown. Pour in the eggs and cook them over the lowest possible heat, stirring with the flat of a table fork or a rubber spatula, until they form soft, creamy curds. Do not overcook; the finished eggs should be moist. Quickly spread the toast with anchovy paste, arrange the slices on individual serving plates, and spread a layer of the scrambled eggs on top. Crisscross two anchovy fillets over each portion, and serve at once.

## Kentucky Scramble

To serve 4

6 slices lean bacon
1 tablespoon butter
1 cup fresh corn kernels, cut from 3
   medium-sized ears of corn, or
   substitute 1 cup canned or
   defrosted frozen corn kernels,

   thoroughly drained
½ cup finely chopped green pepper
¼ cup finely chopped pimiento
1½ teaspoons salt
⅛ teaspoon freshly ground black
   pepper
6 eggs

In a heavy 10- to 12-inch ungreased skillet, fry the bacon over moderate heat. Turn the slices with tongs until they are crisp and brown, then transfer them to paper towels to drain.

Pour off all but 3 tablespoons of the fat remaining in the skillet and in its place add the butter. Drop in the corn and stir over moderate heat for 1 or 2 minutes until the kernels glisten. Then add the green pepper, pimiento, salt and black pepper and cook uncovered, stirring frequently, for 5 minutes, or until the vegetables are soft but not brown.

Break the eggs into a bowl, beat them lightly with a table fork, and pour them into the skillet. Stirring with the flat of the fork or a rubber spatula, cook over low heat until the eggs begin to form soft, creamy curds. Mound the eggs on a heated platter, arrange the bacon slices attractively on top and serve at once.

To serve 2 to 4

4 eggs
6 cups water
1 tablespoon white vinegar
4 three-inch rounds of white bread,

½ inch thick, or 2 English muffins
4 teaspoons soft butter
Four ¼-inch-thick slices cooked
   ham, cut into rounds 3 inches in
   diameter

To poach eggs successfully they must be very fresh or the whites will come away from their yolks during the poaching process. Pour 6 cups of water into a 10-inch enameled or stainless-steel skillet. Add 1 tablespoon of white vinegar and, over high heat, bring the water to a boil. Reduce the heat to low and, when the water is barely simmering, gently drop the eggs in one at a time, carefully turning the whites over the yolks with a wooden spoon. Let the eggs poach undisturbed for 3 to 4 minutes, or until the whites are set and the yolks still fluid. Remove them with a slotted spoon and keep them warm in a bowl of warm water.

Preheat the oven to 250°. Toast the rounds of bread or the split English muffins, spread each half with about a teaspoon of soft butter and top with a slice of hot or cold ham. Arrange them on a heatproof serving platter or individual plates and keep them warm in the oven while you make the hollandaise sauce.

BLENDER HOLLANDAISE

¼-pound stick of butter, cut into
   ½-inch pieces
3 egg yolks

1 teaspoon lemon juice
¼ teaspoon salt
Pinch of white pepper

Melt the butter without browning it and keep it warm over very low heat. Combine the egg yolks, lemon juice, salt and pepper in the container of an electric blender. Cover the jar and blend at high speed for about 2 seconds. Then remove the cover and, still blending at high speed, slowly pour in the hot butter. For a finer sauce do not pour in the whey or milky solids on the bottom of the pan, although it will not be disastrous if you do. Taste for seasoning.

Working quickly, remove poached eggs from the bowl of water and drain them on a kitchen towel. Place an egg atop each slice of ham, pour hollandaise sauce over each of them and serve at once.

To serve 6

1 pair veal sweetbreads (about
    ½ pound)
Distilled white vinegar
3 cups water
1 cup coarsely diced celery
¼ cup finely chopped onions
2½ teaspoons salt
Freshly ground black pepper
6 tablespoons plus 1 cup heavy
    cream
1 tablespoon butter, softened, plus
    4 tablespoons butter
6 hard-cooked eggs
3 ounces cooked ham, preferably
    country ham, finely ground or

very finely chopped (about ⅓
    cup)
1 teaspoon dry mustard
¼ teaspoon ground white pepper
½ pound firm fresh mushrooms,
    trimmed, wiped with a dampened
    cloth and cut into ½-inch pieces
    including the stems
4 tablespoons flour
3 tablespoons pale dry sherry
¼ cup freshly grated imported
    Parmesan cheese combined with
    ¼ cup freshly grated sharp
    natural Cheddar cheese
½ cup slivered blanched almonds

Soak the sweetbreads for 2 hours in enough cold water to cover them by at least 1 inch, changing the water every 30 minutes or so; then soak them for another hour in acidulated cold water, using 1 tablespoon of white vinegar for each quart of water. Gently pull off as much of the outside membrane as possible without tearing the sweetbreads, and cut the two lobes from the tube between them with a small sharp knife; discard the tube.

Place the sweetbreads in a small enameled saucepan and add 3 cups of water, the celery, onions, 1 teaspoon of salt and a few grindings of black pepper. Bring to a boil over high heat, then reduce the heat to its lowest point and simmer uncovered for 15 to 20 minutes. Remove the sweetbreads with a slotted spoon, cut them into ¼-inch bits and set them aside in a small bowl. Strain the cooking liquid through a fine sieve set over a bowl and reserve 1 cup.

Meanwhile, preheat the oven to 350°. With a pastry brush, spread the tablespoon of softened butter evenly over the bottom and sides of an 8- or 9-inch baking-serving dish about 2 to 3 inches deep.

Peel the hard-cooked eggs and cut them lengthwise in half. Set the egg whites aside. Drop the yolks into a small bowl and, with the back of a fork, mash them to a smooth purée. Stir in the ground ham, mustard, ½ teaspoon of salt, ⅛ teaspoon of the white pepper and the 6 tablespoons of cream. Taste for seasoning. Spoon the egg-yolk mixture into the egg-white halves, dividing it evenly and mounding the stuffing slightly. Arrange the eggs in one layer in the baking dish and set aside.

In a heavy 10- to 12-inch skillet, melt the 4 tablespoons of butter over moderate heat. When the foam begins to subside, add the mushrooms and, stirring frequently, cook for 8 to 10 minutes, or until the liquid that accumulates in the pan has evaporated completely. Do not let the mushrooms brown. Stir in the flour and, when it is completely absorbed, pour in the remaining cup of cream and the reserved cup of sweetbread cooking liquid. Stirring the mixture constantly with a whisk, bring to a boil, reduce the heat to low, and simmer for 3 or 4 minutes to remove any taste of raw flour. Then stir in the sweetbreads, sherry, the remaining teaspoon of salt and ⅛ teaspoon of white pepper. Taste for seasoning.

Ladle the sweetbreads-and-mushroom mixture over the stuffed eggs and sprinkle with the cheese and almonds. Bake in the upper third of the oven for 20 to 25 minutes, or until the sauce bubbles and the cheese is delicately browned. Serve at once directly from the baking dish.

### *Eggs Sardou* *(Creole-Acadian)*
POACHED EGGS WITH ARTICHOKE BOTTOMS AND CREAMED SPINACH

To serve 4 or 8

| | |
|---|---|
| 6 tablespoons butter | 1 teaspoon salt |
| 2 tablespoons flour | ¼ teaspoon ground white pepper |
| 1 cup milk | 8 canned artichoke bottoms, drained |
| 1½ pounds fresh spinach, cooked, drained, squeezed dry and finely chopped (about 2 cups) | 8 very fresh eggs |
| | 1 cup freshly made hollandaise sauce* |

In a heavy 1- to 2-quart saucepan, melt 2 tablespoons of the butter over moderate heat. When the foam begins to subside, add the flour and mix well. Stirring constantly with a wire whisk, pour in the milk in a slow, thin stream and cook over high heat until the sauce comes to a boil, thickens lightly and is smooth. Reduce the heat to low and simmer for about 3 minutes to remove any raw taste of the flour. Then stir in the spinach, ½ teaspoon of the salt and the white pepper. Taste for seasoning, remove the pan from the heat and cover tightly.

Melt the remaining 4 tablespoons of butter in a heavy 10- to 12-inch skillet. Add the artichoke bottoms, concave side down, and baste them with the hot butter. Sprinkle them with the remaining ½ teaspoon of salt, reduce the heat to the lowest possible point, cover tightly and cook for several minutes until the artichoke bottoms are heated through. Do not let them brown. Remove the skillet from the heat and cover tightly to keep the artichoke bottoms warm.

To poach the eggs, pour cold water into a 12-inch skillet to a depth of about 2 inches. Bring to a simmer, then reduce the heat so that the surface of the liquid barely shimmers. Break the eggs into individual saucers.

* *See index.*

Gently slide one of the eggs from its saucer into the water, and with a large spoon, lift the white over the yolk. Repeat once or twice more to enclose the yolk completely in the white.

One at a time, slide the seven other eggs into the pan, enclosing them in their whites and spacing them about an inch apart. Poach the eggs for 3 or 4 minutes, until the whites are set and the yolks feel soft when prodded gently. With a slotted spatula, transfer the poached eggs to a large bowl half-filled with lukewarm water and set them aside while you prepare the hollandaise sauce.

Before assembling the eggs Sardou, transfer the poached eggs to a linen towel with a slotted spatula to drain briefly. If the creamed spinach and artichoke bottoms have cooled, warm them over low heat.

Spread the creamed spinach smoothly on a heated serving platter to make a bed about ¼ inch deep. Arrange the artichoke bottoms, concave sides up, on the spinach and place an egg in each one. Spoon the hollandaise sauce over the eggs and serve at once.

## Creamed Egg Chartres (Creole-Acadian)

To serve 8

1 tablespoon butter, softened, plus 8 tablespoons butter, cut into ½-inch bits
5 medium-sized onions, peeled and cut crosswise into ⅛-inch-thick rounds
¾ cup flour
3 egg yolks, plus 12 hard-cooked eggs, cut crosswise into ¼-inch-thick slices
6 cups milk
1½ teaspoons salt
1 teaspoon ground hot red pepper (cayenne)
1 cup freshly grated imported Parmesan cheese
3 tablespoons paprika

Preheat the oven to 350°. With a pastry brush, spread the tablespoon of softened butter evenly over the bottom and sides of a 14-by-9-by-2-inch baking-serving dish. Set the dish aside.

In a heavy 12-inch skillet, melt the 8 tablespoons of butter bits over moderate heat. When the foam begins to subside, add the onions and, stirring frequently, cook for about 8 minutes, or until they are soft and translucent but not brown. Add the flour and mix well, then reduce the heat to low and simmer for 3 or 4 minutes to remove the raw taste of the flour.

Meanwhile, in a deep bowl, beat the egg yolks with a wire whisk or a rotary or electric beater until they are smooth. Beat in the milk, salt and red pepper, and set aside. Mix the Parmesan cheese and paprika together in a bowl and reserve them.

Stirring the onion mixture constantly with a wire whisk, pour in the egg yolks and milk in a slow, thin stream and cook over high heat until the sauce comes to a boil, thickens heavily and is smooth. Taste the sauce for seasoning, remove the skillet from the heat and gently stir in nine of the sliced hard-cooked eggs.

Pour the eggs and sauce into the buttered dish and scatter the Parmesan cheese mixture evenly over the top. Bake in the middle of the oven for about 15 minutes, or until the top is browned and the sauce begins to bubble. Garnish the top with the remaining hard-cooked egg slices and serve at once, directly from the baking dish.

*Egg Croquettes*

To make 12 croquettes

3 tablespoons butter
1¼ cups flour
1 cup milk
7 hard-cooked eggs, finely chopped
1 small onion, peeled and finely
  grated
¼ cup finely chopped fresh parsley
1 teaspoon dry mustard

¼ teaspoon ground hot red pepper
  (cayenne)
1½ teaspoons celery salt
1 cup soft fresh crumbs made from
  homemade-type white bread,
  pulverized in a blender or finely
  shredded with a fork
1 egg
Vegetable oil for deep frying

In a heavy 8- to 10-inch skillet, melt the butter over moderate heat. When the foam begins to subside, mix in ¼ cup of the flour. Then, stirring the mixture constantly with a wire whisk, pour in the milk in a slow, thin stream. Cook over high heat until the sauce comes to a boil, thickens heavily and is smooth. Reduce the heat to low and simmer for about 3 minutes to remove any taste of flour. Remove the skillet from the heat and stir the chopped eggs, grated onion and parsley into the sauce. Add the mustard, red pepper and celery salt, and taste for seasoning.

With a rubber spatula, scrape the contents of the skillet onto a large platter and spread it about ½ inch thick. Cover with plastic wrap and refrigerate for about 3 hours, or until the croquette mixture is firm.

Divide the mixture into 12 equal parts and, with your hands, shape each one into a cylinder about 3 inches long and 1 inch in diameter, or into 2-inch balls or cones. Spread the remaining cup of flour on one plate and the bread crumbs on another. Beat the egg lightly in a shallow bowl. Bread the croquettes one at a time by lightly coating them with the flour, immersing them in the egg, then rolling them in the crumbs. Arrange the croquettes side by side on wax paper and refrigerate them for about 20 minutes to firm the coating.

Pour vegetable oil into a deep fryer or large heavy saucepan to a depth of 2 to 3 inches and heat the oil until it reaches a temperature of 350° on a deep-frying thermometer. Deep-fry the croquettes, 3 or 4 at a time, turning them with a slotted spoon for about 4 minutes, or until they are golden brown on all sides. As they brown, transfer the croquettes to paper towels to drain while you deep-fry the rest. Serve at once.

## Creole Shrimp Omelets

To make 4 omelets

SAUCE
¼ cup olive oil
1 cup finely chopped onions
1 cup finely chopped celery
½ cup finely chopped green peppers
2 teaspoons finely chopped garlic
A 1-pound can tomatoes, drained and coarsely chopped, with their

liquid reserved
2 tablespoons finely chopped fresh parsley, preferably the flat-leaf Italian variety
1 medium-sized bay leaf
¼ teaspoon crumbled dried thyme
¼ teaspoon ground hot red pepper (cayenne)
1 teaspoon salt

First prepare the sauce in the following manner: In a heavy 10- to 12-inch skillet, heat the olive oil over moderate heat until a light haze forms above it. Add the onions, celery, green peppers and garlic and, stirring frequently, cook for about 5 minutes, or until they are soft but not brown. Stir in the coarsely chopped tomatoes and their liquid, 2 tablespoons of parsley, the bay leaf, thyme, red pepper and 1 teaspoon of salt. Bring to a boil over high heat, reduce the heat to low and simmer, tightly covered, for 20 minutes. Remove the skillet from the heat and discard the bay leaf. Taste for seasoning, then set the sauce aside in the skillet.

FILLING
½ pound uncooked shrimp
4 tablespoons butter
½ cup finely chopped scallions, including 3 inches of the green tops
½ cup finely chopped drained

canned tomatoes
2 tablespoons finely chopped fresh parsley, preferably the flat-leaf Italian variety
⅛ teaspoon ground white pepper
1 teaspoon salt

Meanwhile, shell the shrimp. Devein them by making a shallow incision down their backs with a small sharp knife and lifting out the black or white intestinal vein with the point of the knife. Wash the shrimp briefly in a colander set under cold running water and pat them completely dry with paper towels. Chop the shrimp into small bits.

To make the filling, melt 4 tablespoons of butter in a heavy 1- to 1½-quart saucepan set over moderate heat. When the foam begins to subside, add the shrimp and scallions and stir for 2 to 3 minutes, or until the shrimp are pink and the scallions are soft. Add the finely chopped tomatoes, 2 tablespoons of parsley, the white pepper and 1 teaspoon of salt. Stirring constantly, cook briskly over high heat until all of the liquid in the pan has evaporated. Taste the filling for seasoning and set the pan aside off the heat.

OMELETS

| 12 eggs | Freshly ground black pepper |
| Salt | 4 tablespoons butter |

For each omelet, break three eggs into a small bowl, season with a little salt and a few grindings of black pepper, and stir briskly with a table fork for 20 to 30 seconds, or until the whites and yolks are blended together. Heat an ungreased 7- to 8-inch omelet pan until it is very hot, drop in 1 tablespoon of butter and swirl it in the pan so that it melts quickly and coats the bottom and sides. When the foam begins to subside but before the butter browns, pour in the eggs.

Working quickly, stir the eggs with the flat of the fork, at the same time shaking the pan back and forth vigorously to prevent the eggs from sticking. In a few seconds, the eggs will form a film on the bottom of the pan and the top will thicken to a light, curded custard. Still shaking the pan with one hand, gently stir through the top custard to spread the still-liquid eggs into the firmer areas; try not to pierce the bottom film.

Spoon about ¼ cup of the filling in a band down the center of the omelet. Then lift the edge closest to you with the fork and gently fold the omelet in half. Let it rest for a moment on the lip of the pan, then tilt the pan and roll the omelet out onto a heated plate. Immediately wipe the pan clean and prepare three more omelets in the same fashion.

Reheat the reserved sauce briefly and ladle it over the filled omelets, dividing the sauce equally among them. Serve at once.

## *Tortilla de Patatas* (Basque-American)
### POTATO-AND-ONION OMELET

| To serve 4 | ⅛-inch-thick slices |
| 4 to 5 tablespoons olive oil | 1 teaspoon salt |
| 1 medium-sized onion, thinly sliced | ¼ teaspoon freshly ground black |
| 3 medium-sized potatoes (1 pound), | pepper |
| peeled and cut crosswise into | 4 eggs |

Heat 4 tablespoons of the olive oil in a heavy 10- to 12-inch skillet (preferably one with a nonstick surface) until a light haze forms above it. Stir in the sliced onions and potatoes and, tossing them about gently with a spatula, cook them over moderate heat until they have colored lightly.

Cover the skillet tightly and cook over low heat for 12 to 15 minutes, or until the potatoes are tender and offer no resistance when pierced with the tip of a small sharp knife.

Sprinkle the potatoes with the salt and pepper. In a small bowl, beat the eggs vigorously with a table fork or whisk until they are frothy. Pour into the skillet and cook uncovered for 3 to 4 minutes, or until the eggs are set. Place an inverted plate over the pan and, grasping plate and skillet together firmly, turn them over. Add an additional tablespoon of oil to the pan if necessary, then slide the omelet back into the skillet, browned side up. Cook the omelet over moderate heat for another 3 or 4 minutes.

Traditionally, *tortilla de patatas* is served in wedges, directly from the skillet. It is also popular at room temperature, and is a favorite picnic staple served sandwich-style on French bread.

## Corn and Clam Soufflé *(Northwest)*

To serve 6

| | |
|---|---|
| 1 cup freshly shucked or canned minced clams, drained, with liquor reserved | pimiento |
| | 1 teaspoon salt |
| | ⅛ teaspoon cayenne |
| ½ to ¾ cup milk | 6 egg whites |
| 4 tablespoons unsalted butter | 1½ cups corn kernels, cut from |
| ¼ cup finely chopped onions | about 3 large ears, or substitute |
| 5 tablespoons all-purpose flour | 1½ cups canned or frozen |
| 5 egg yolks | kernels, drained and thoroughly |
| 2 tablespoons finely chopped | defrosted if frozen |

With a large, sharp knife, chop the clams as fine as possible and set them aside. Strain the clam liquor through a fine sieve lined with a double thickness of cheesecloth. Measure the liquor, add enough milk to make 1 cup, then pour into a small saucepan and place over moderate heat. When bubbles appear around the edge of the pan, remove from the heat.

Preheat the oven to 400°. With a pastry brush, coat the bottom and sides of a 2-quart soufflé dish with 1 tablespoon of the butter. Melt the remaining butter in a heavy 1½- to 2-quart saucepan, add the onions, and cook over moderate heat for about 3 minutes, until the onions are soft but not brown. Off the heat, mix in 4 tablespoons of the flour and stir the mixture to a smooth paste. Add the lukewarm milk-and-clam-liquor mixture all at once and beat vigorously with a whisk. Cook over moderate heat, whisking constantly, until the sauce is smooth and very thick. Remove the pan from the heat and, one at a time, beat in the egg yolks. Stir in the pimiento, salt, cayenne and chopped clams, and taste for seasoning.

In a separate bowl, preferably one of unlined copper, beat the egg whites with a large whisk or a rotary or electric beater until they are stiff enough to form unwavering peaks on the beater when it is lifted out of the bowl. Stir 3 heaping tablespoons of the whites into the clam sauce. Toss the corn with the remaining tablespoon of flour and stir it into the sauce. With a rubber spatula, gently but thoroughly fold in the remaining egg whites until no white streaks show. Be careful not to overfold.

Pour the mixture into the soufflé dish and smooth the top with a spatula. Reduce the oven heat to 375° and bake the soufflé undisturbed in the center of the oven for 35 to 40 minutes, or until it is puffed and lightly brown on top. Serve at once.

### Dilled Salmon Soufflé

To serve 6

4 tablespoons butter
4 tablespoons finely chopped onion
4 tablespoons flour
1 cup milk
5 egg yolks
1 tablespoon tomato paste
1½ cups canned salmon, thoroughly

drained and flaked (2 seven-ounce cans)
3 tablespoons finely cut fresh dill
1½ teaspoons lemon juice
1½ teaspoons salt
⅛ teaspoon cayenne
6 egg whites
Hollandaise sauce (optional)

Preheat the oven to 400°. Coat the bottom and sides of a 2-quart soufflé dish with a tablespoon of the butter and melt the remaining butter in a heavy saucepan. When the foam subsides add the onion and cook over moderate heat for about 3 minutes. Do not let the onions brown. Off the heat, mix in the flour and stir it to a smooth paste. Add the milk all at once and beat with a whisk to partially dissolve the flour. Then cook over moderate heat, whisking constantly, until the sauce is smooth and very thick. Remove the pan from the heat and beat into it, one at a time, the 5 egg yolks, then stir in the tomato paste, salmon, dill, lemon juice, salt and cayenne. Cool slightly. Meanwhile, with a large whisk or rotary beater, beat the egg whites, preferably in an unlined copper bowl, until they are stiff enough to form unwavering peaks on the beater when it is lifted out of the bowl. Stir a heaping tablespoon of the whites into the salmon mixture, then with a rubber spatula, fold in the remaining egg whites gently but thoroughly until no white streaks show; be careful not to overfold. Pour the mixture into the soufflé dish, reduce the heat to 375° and bake the soufflé undisturbed in the center of the oven for 35 to 40 minutes, or until it has puffed and is lightly brown on top. Serve, if you like, with hollandaise sauce.

To make 12 pancakes (to serve
4 to 6)

PANCAKES
1½ cups canned bean sprouts
1 medium-sized onion, halved and
cut lengthwise into 1/16-inch-
wide strips (¾ cup)
1 stalk celery, trimmed, cut into
2-inch lengths, then cut
lengthwise into 1/16-inch-wide
strips (¼ cup)
½ pound thinly sliced boiled ham,
cut into 2-by-1/16-inch strips
(1½ cups)
8 eggs
¾ teaspoon salt
½ teaspoon freshly ground black
pepper

PANCAKES: Spread the bean sprouts to drain on a layer of paper towels
and cover them with additional towels. Combine the strips of onion, celery
and ham in a bowl, and set aside. In a large mixing bowl, beat the
eggs lightly and stir in the salt and pepper.

SAUCE
2 tablespoons vegetable oil
¼ pound mushrooms, thinly sliced
(1 cup)
2 cups boiling chicken stock, fresh
or canned
1 tablespoon soy sauce
1 tablespoon tomato ketchup
2 tablespoons cornstarch, dissolved
in 2 tablespoons cold water

Vegetable oil for deep frying

SAUCE: In an 8- to 10-inch skillet, heat the 2 tablespoons of vegetable
oil until a light haze forms above it. Stir in the mushrooms and cook over
moderate heat until they are soft and lightly colored. Stir in the hot chicken
stock, the soy sauce and ketchup, and bring to a boil over high heat.
Stir the cornstarch-and-water mixture to recombine it, then stir into the
boiling sauce. Lower the heat and simmer the sauce for 2 or 3 minutes, or
until it is clear and has thickened enough to coat a spoon lightly. Partially
cover the pan and keep the sauce warm over the lowest possible heat.

Pour vegetable oil into a heavy 10- to 12-inch skillet to a depth of 2
inches; place over high heat until it registers 350° on a deep-frying
thermometer. Stir the bean sprouts, onions, celery and ham into the beaten
eggs and, using ¼ cup of the batter per pancake, cook three pancakes at
a time over high heat. Turn the pancakes with a slotted spatula after 30
seconds, and fry for 30 seconds longer, until they are puffy and golden
brown. Serve at once, accompanied by a bowl or sauceboat of the hot
mushroom sauce.

## Dunvegan Welsh Rabbit *(New England)*

To serve 4

3 tablespoons butter
4 cups freshly grated sharp Cheddar
   cheese (1 pound)
½ cup ale
1 teaspoon Worcestershire sauce
1 teaspoon dry mustard

½ teaspoon paprika
¼ teaspoon ground hot red pepper
  (cayenne)
¼ teaspoon salt
2 eggs, lightly beaten
4 slices homemade-type white bread,
   trimmed of crusts, toasted and
   each cut diagonally into four triangles

In a heavy 2- to 3-quart saucepan, melt the butter over moderate heat. When the foam begins to subside, add the cheese, ale, Worcestershire sauce, mustard, paprika, red pepper and salt. Stirring constantly with a fork, cook until the cheese melts completely and the mixture is smooth.

Remove the pan from the heat and beat in the eggs. Then return the pan to low heat and stir for about 5 minutes until the mixture is thick and creamy. Taste for seasoning.

Arrange the toast triangles attractively on four heated individual serving plates, ladle the Welsh rabbit over them and serve at once.

## Grits and Cheddar Cheese Casserole *(South)*

To serve 4 to 6

2 tablespoons butter
¼ cup finely chopped onion
2 cups water
½ teaspoon salt

½ cup quick grits
1 teaspoon Tabasco
Freshly ground black pepper
1¾ cups grated Cheddar cheese
3 tablespoons soft butter
2 egg whites

In a small skillet, melt 2 tablespoons of butter over moderate heat. When the foam subsides add the ¼ cup of onion and cook for 4 or 5 minutes until translucent but not brown. Meanwhile, bring the 2 cups of water to a bubbling boil in a 1-quart saucepan. Add the salt and pour in the grits slowly without allowing the water to stop boiling. Boil for about a minute, stirring constantly, then reduce the heat to medium and cook for another 2 minutes. With a rubber spatula, scrape into the saucepan the onions and add the Tabasco, a few grindings of black pepper and 1½ cups of the grated Cheddar cheese combined with the 3 tablespoons of soft butter.

Preheat the oven to 400°. Lightly butter a 1-quart casserole or soufflé dish. With a wire whisk or rotary beater, beat the egg whites until they form stiff peaks on the beater when it is lifted from the bowl. With a rubber spatula, thoroughly fold the egg whites into the grits mixture. Pour into the casserole and sprinkle the top with the remaining grated Cheddar cheese. Bake in the middle of the oven for about 30 minutes, or until the mixture has puffed and browned. Serve at once as an accompaniment for any meat or poultry dish.

## *Blintzes (Jewish-American)*
ROLLED PANCAKES FILLED WITH COTTAGE CHEESE

To make 10 blintzes

COTTAGE-CHEESE FILLING
1 pound dry cottage cheese, or
    substitute 1 pound creamed
    cottage cheese, wrapped in
    cheesecloth and squeezed dry

2 tablespoons sour cream
1 egg yolk
2 tablespoons sugar
½ teaspoon vanilla extract
¼ teaspoon salt

To prepare the filling: With the back of a large wooden spoon, force the cottage cheese through a fine sieve into a deep bowl, or put the cheese through a food mill set over a bowl. Add 2 tablespoons of sour cream, the egg yolk, sugar, vanilla extract and ¼ teaspoon of salt. Stirring and mashing vigorously, beat with a large spoon until the ingredients are well blended and the mixture smooth. Set aside.

BLINTZES
3 eggs
½ cup water
¾ cup sifted all-purpose flour
¼ teaspoon salt
2 tablespoons butter, melted and

cooled
4 tablespoons melted butter,
    combined with 1 tablespoon
    flavorless vegetable oil

1 cup sour cream

To make the batter for the blintzes: Combine the eggs, water, flour, ¼ teaspoon of salt and 2 tablespoons of cooled melted butter in the jar of an electric blender and blend them at high speed for a few seconds. Turn the machine off, scrape down the sides of the jar with a rubber spatula and blend again for 40 seconds.

To make the batter by hand, stir the flour and eggs together in a mixing bowl and gradually stir in the water and ¼ teaspoon of salt. Beat with a whisk or a rotary or electric beater until the flour lumps disappear, then force the batter through a fine sieve into another bowl and stir in the 2 tablespoons of cooled melted butter.

However you make it, the batter should have the consistency of heavy cream; dilute it if necessary by beating in cold water a teaspoon at a time.

To cook the blintzes, heat a 6-inch crêpe pan or skillet over high heat until a drop of water flicked onto it evaporates instantly. With a pastry brush or crumpled paper towels, lightly grease the bottom and sides of the pan with a little of the combined melted butter and oil.

Pour about 3 tablespoons of batter into the pan and tip the pan so that the batter quickly covers the bottom; the batter should cling to the pan and begin to firm up almost immediately. Cook the blintz for a minute or so, until a rim of brown shows around the edge. Then, without turning it over, slide the blintz onto a plate. Brush the combined butter and oil on the skillet again and proceed with the rest of the blintzes. As they are cooked, stack the blintzes one on top of the other.

When all the blintzes have been browned on one side, fill and roll each of them in the following fashion: Place about 3 tablespoons of filling on the cooked side of the blintz an inch or so from the top edge. With a knife or metal spatula, smooth the filling into a strip about 3 inches long and 1 inch deep. Fold the sides of the blintz toward the center, covering the ends of the filling. Then turn the top edge over the filling and roll the blintz into a cylinder about 3 inches long and 1 inch wide.

Pour the remaining butter-and-oil mixture into a heavy 10- to 12-inch skillet and set over moderate heat. Place four or five blintzes, seam side down, in the pan, and fry them for 3 to 5 minutes on each side, turning them with a metal spatula and regulating the heat so they color quickly and evenly without burning. As they are browned, transfer them to a heated serving platter.

Serve the blintzes hot, accompanied by the cup of sour cream, presented separately in a bowl.

# Fish & Shellfish

Each region of the United States has its own characteristic seafoods and its own way of cooking them. New England's bounty includes the Maine lobster, preferred as simply boiled or broiled, and the sacred cod. Generally, the cookery becomes more complex as you move south. Maryland's crabs, for example, range from basic crab cakes, fried a golden brown, to deviled crab. The shrimp of the Carolinas and the Gulf go into a broad spectrum of dishes—the most famous, perhaps, being pilau, a savory rice-and-tomato concoction. On the West Coast, the pleasures of fish range from huge Dungeness crabs to the fantastic salmon of the Northwest. Between the coasts, commercial and sport fishermen seek scores of fish in lakes, rivers and streams.

The key to perfectly cooked fish is perfectly fresh fish. Ideally, it should be eaten as soon as it is caught; nonfishermen can delay as long as twenty-four hours. When buying a fish, dare to look it in the eye: the pupil should be bright and clear. Then poke it with a finger: it should be firm to the touch. The oldest test of freshness remains the surest—smell the fish. If it is truly fresh, there will be very little odor. When fresh fish is not available, frozen often is, and thanks to the new flash-freezing techniques, it is often of high caliber.

Almost as important as the freshness of the fish is how long it is cooked. Unlike almost all meat, fish is tender to begin with, and gets tough and dry the longer it is cooked. There is—thanks to the Canadian Department of Fisheries—a nearly foolproof rule for cooking fish perfectly: measure it through its thickest part and then give it about ten minutes to the inch, however you are cooking it. For undefrosted frozen fish, the same system applies, except that the cooking time is doubled to twenty minutes per inch.

All fish have a different taste, but if the one called for in a recipe is not available, you can usually make substitutions. The ingredients list and directions will alert you to what size and type of fish is needed.

To serve 4

STUFFING:
2 tablespoons butter
2 tablespoons finely chopped
   scallions, including part of the
   green stem

2 tablespoons finely chopped green
   pepper
1 medium tomato, peeled, seeded and
   coarsely chopped
1 tablespoon finely chopped fresh parsley
Salt
Freshly ground black pepper

For the stuffing, melt the 2 tablespoons of butter in a small skillet over moderate heat. When the foam subsides, add the chopped scallions and green pepper and cook, stirring constantly, for 2 to 3 minutes until the vegetables are wilted but not brown. Scrape into a small mixing bowl. Add the chopped tomato, parsley, salt and a few grindings of black pepper. Mix thoroughly.

A 2½- to 3-pound striped bass,
   eviscerated but head and tail left
   on (or other firm white-meat fish
   such as red snapper, pompano,
   haddock, cod, pollack, rockfish,
   whitefish or lake trout)
4 tablespoons melted butter
1 medium onion, peeled and thinly
   sliced

1 small green pepper, seeded and
   thinly sliced
6 sprigs fresh dill
½ cup dry vermouth
1 tablespoon lemon juice
Salt
Freshly ground black pepper

Preheat the oven to 375°. Wash the fish inside and out under cold running water, and dry it thoroughly with paper towels. Fill the fish with the stuffing, sew the opening with thread or close it with small skewers and crisscross kitchen string around the skewers to secure them. Brush 2 tablespoons of the melted butter on the bottom of a shallow, flameproof baking dish attractive enough to serve from, and place the fish in it, surrounding it with the sliced onion, the green pepper and sprigs of fresh dill.

Combine the vermouth with the lemon juice and the rest of the melted butter, pour it over the fish and vegetables and bring it to a boil on top of the stove. Sprinkle the fish with salt and a few grindings of black pepper, and immediately transfer the baking dish to the middle of the oven. Bake uncovered for about 30 minutes, basting the fish every 8 minutes or so with the pan juices. The fish is done when it is firm to the touch and flakes easily when prodded gently with a fork. Serve directly from the baking dish.

113

## Broiled Bluefish Fillets *(Eastern Heartland)*

To serve 4

4 eight-ounce bluefish fillets, with
    skin left on
2 tablespoons strained fresh lemon
    juice

1 teaspoon salt
1 tablespoon vegetable oil
4 tablespoons butter, melted
¼ cup sesame seeds

Set the broiler pan and its grid 4 inches from the heat and preheat the broiler to its highest point. Wash the fillets briefly under cold running water and pat them completely dry with paper towels. Season the fish on both sides with the lemon juice and salt.

With a pastry brush, spread the vegetable oil over the grid of the broiler pan and arrange the bluefish fillets on it, skin side down. Brush the fillets with 2 tablespoons of the melted butter and broil about 4 inches from the heat for 4 to 5 minutes. Baste the fish once or twice with the remaining butter. The fillets are done when the flesh is lightly brown and flakes easily if prodded gently with a fork.

Sprinkle the sesame seeds evenly over the fillets and broil for a minute or so longer to brown the seeds. Serve at once.

## Braised Carp Fillets

To serve 4

2 medium onions, coarsely chopped
Olive oil
4 carp fillets
Flour
2 cloves garlic, chopped
½ cup chopped parsley

Dried thyme
1 teaspoon salt
1 teaspoon ground black pepper
1 cup red wine
1 cup tomato purée
20 ripe olives
Steamed rice

Place the chopped onions on a well oiled baking pan. Dip the fillets in flour and arrange them on the bed of onions. Sprinkle with the chopped garlic and parsley, thyme, salt and pepper. Add the red wine to the pan, and then drizzle olive oil all over the fish. Top each fillet with 3 tablespoons of the tomato purée. Bake at 425° for 15 to 18 minutes, basting often with the sauce in the pan. Remove the fish to a hot serving platter. Blend the sauce in the pan with the remaining tomato purée and add the ripe olives. Pour the sauce around the fish and serve with steamed rice.

To make about 30 two-inch balls

1 pound salt cod
6 medium-sized boiling potatoes
    (about 2 pounds), peeled and
    quartered
8 tablespoons butter, softened and

cut into ½-inch bits
3 egg yolks
1½ teaspoon Worcestershire
    sauce
1 teaspoon dry English mustard
½ teaspoon ground white pepper
Vegetable oil for deep frying

Starting a day ahead, place the cod in a glass, enameled or stainless-steel pan or bowl. Cover it with cold water and soak for at least 12 hours, changing the water 3 or 4 times.

Drain the cod, rinse it under cold running water, place it in a saucepan and add enough fresh water to cover the fish by 1 inch. Bring to a boil over high heat. (Taste the water. If it seems very salty, drain, cover with fresh water and bring to a boil again.) Reduce the heat to low and simmer partially covered for about 20 minutes, or until the fish flakes easily when prodded gently with a fork. Drain the cod, remove and discard any skin and bones, and shred the fish into fine flakes with a fork.

Meanwhile, drop the potatoes into enough boiling water to cover them completely. Boil briskly uncovered until the potatoes are soft and crumble easily when pierced with a fork. Drain off the water and return the pan of potatoes to low heat. Slide the pan back and forth over the heat for a minute or so until the potatoes are completely dry.

Purée the potatoes through a food ricer set over a deep bowl, or place them in the bowl and mash them to a smooth purée with a potato masher or electric mixer. Add the flaked cod, butter bits and egg yolks to the purée and beat them vigorously together with a wooden spoon. Beat in the Worcestershire sauce, mustard and pepper. Taste for seasoning.

Preheat the oven to its lowest setting. Line a large shallow baking dish with paper towels and place it in the center of the oven.

Pour vegetable oil into a deep fryer or large, heavy saucepan to a depth of 3 inches and heat the oil to a temperature of 375° on a deep-frying thermometer. To make each codfish ball, drop a heaping tablespoon of the cod mixture into the hot oil. Fry the balls 5 or 6 at a time for about 4 minutes, or until they are golden on all sides. As they brown, transfer them to the lined pan and keep them warm in the oven while you fry the rest.

Serve the codfish balls hot, mounded attractively on a heated platter and accompanied if you wish by cole slaw, presented in a separate bowl.

To serve 4 to 6

8 fillets of white firm-fleshed fish, such as pike, perch or sole
6 tablespoons unsalted butter, plus
  1 tablespoon butter, softened, and
  1 tablespoon butter, cut into
  ¼-inch bits

4 to 6 slices white bread, trimmed and cut into ¼-inch dice (2½ cups)
3 tablespoons finely cut chives
¼ teaspoon thyme
½ teaspoon tarragon
½ teaspoon salt
¼ teaspoon white pepper

Wash the fish fillets under cold running water and pat them thoroughly dry with paper towels. Place the fillets side by side on a flat surface and trim them evenly to 8- or 9-inch lengths. Gather all the fish you have trimmed from the fillets and chop it fine.

In a 10- to 12-inch skillet, melt 2 tablespoons of the butter over moderate heat. Stir in the chopped fish and, stirring it constantly, cook over moderate heat for 4 or 5 minutes, until the flesh becomes opaque. Transfer to a bowl and set aside.

Add 4 tablespoons of butter to the skillet and drop in the bread cubes. Toss them constantly with a wooden spoon until they are a light gold, then add them to the bowl of fish. Sprinkle the fish and bread cubes with the chives, thyme, tarragon, ½ teaspoon of salt and the pepper, and toss together lightly but thoroughly.

Preheat the oven to 400°. With a pastry brush, lightly coat the bottom and sides of a 9-by-12-inch flameproof baking dish with the tablespoon of softened butter. Place 2 tablespoons of the herbed stuffing on the narrow end of each fillet and gently roll up the fillets. Arrange them seam side down in the baking dish, and dot with the tablespoon of butter bits. Bake in the center of the oven for 12 to 15 minutes, or until the fish feels firm when prodded gently with a finger. With a spatula, transfer the fish rolls to a heated platter and keep them warm in the turned-off oven while you make the sauce.

SAUCE

½ cup sour cream
1 tablespoon flour
1 teaspoon strained fresh lemon

juice
½ teaspoon salt
1 tablespoon tomato purée

In a small bowl, combine the ½ cup of sour cream with the 1 tablespoon of flour. Place the flameproof baking dish over moderate heat and, with a wire whisk, gradually beat in the sour-cream-and-flour mixture, the lemon juice and ½ teaspoon of salt. Stir in the tomato purée and taste for seasoning.

Spoon the sauce over the fish rolls. Or, if you prefer, present the sauce separately in a heated sauceboat.

OPPOSITE

*A neatly trimmed fillet of sole is filled with golden-brown bread cubes, herbs and bits of the trimmed fish itself. Starting from one of the narrow ends, the fillet is loosely rolled up, laid seam side down and baked. At the table the fish rolls are bathed in a tomato-accented sour cream sauce.*

116

To serve 4

1½ pounds uncooked shrimp

10 tablespoons butter, cut into ½-inch bits, plus 3 tablespoons butter, melted

1½ cups soft fresh crumbs made from French- or Italian-type white bread, pulverized in a blender

⅓ cup finely chopped onions

⅓ cup finely chopped green peppers

⅓ cup finely chopped celery

⅓ cup finely chopped scallions, including 3 inches of the green tops

2 teaspoons finely chopped garlic

⅓ cup finely chopped drained canned tomatoes

4 teaspoons Worcestershire sauce

1½ teaspoons Creole mustard, or substitute any strong-flavored, prepared brown mustard

½ teaspoon ground hot red pepper

2 teaspoons salt

1 pound (2 cups) fresh, frozen or canned crabmeat, thoroughly drained and picked over to remove all bits of shell or cartilage

3 tablespoons finely chopped fresh parsley, preferably the flat-leaf Italian variety

Four 1½-pound flounders, cleaned and with the heads removed but the tails intact

¼ teaspoon freshly ground black pepper

Shell the shrimp. Devein them by making a shallow incision down their backs with a small sharp knife and lifting out the black or white intestinal vein with the point of the knife. Wash the shrimp briefly in a colander set under cold running water.

Drop the shrimp into enough lightly salted boiling water to immerse them completely and boil briskly, uncovered, for 3 to 5 minutes, or until they are firm and pink. Drain the shrimp, spread them on paper towels, and pat them completely dry with fresh towels. Then chop the shrimp coarsely and reserve them.

In a heavy 10- to 12-inch skillet, melt 6 tablespoons of the butter bits over moderate heat. When the foam begins to subside, add the bread crumbs and stir until they are crisp and golden. With a rubber spatula, scrape the entire contents of the skillet into a deep bowl and set aside.

Add the remaining 4 tablespoons of butter bits to the skillet and melt them over moderate heat. Drop in the onions, green peppers, celery, scallions and garlic and, stirring frequently, cook for about 5 minutes, or until the vegetables are soft but not brown. Stir in the tomatoes, Worcestershire sauce, Creole mustard, red pepper and 1 teaspoon of the salt. Then scrape the mixture into the bowl with the bread crumbs. Add the reserved shrimp, the crabmeat and the parsley, and toss all the stuffing ingredients together gently but thoroughly. Taste for seasoning.

Preheat the oven to 400°. With a pastry brush, spread 1 tablespoon of the melted butter over the bottom and sides of a shallow baking-serving dish large enough to hold the flounders in one layer. Set aside.

Wash the fish under cold running water and pat them dry with paper towels. To prepare the flounders for stuffing, place one at a time on its belly (light-colored side) on the cutting board. With a small sharp knife, make a 4- to 5-inch-long slit completely through the skin and top surface of flesh to the backbone of the fish, cutting from about 1 inch behind the head to within about 1 inch of the tail.

With your fingers or the point of the knife, gently lift the top surface of the flesh away from the rows of small bones radiating from the backbone, to create pockets on both sides of the slit.

Sprinkle the remaining teaspoon of salt and the black pepper inside the pockets formed in the flounders. Then fill the pockets and the space between them with the shrimp-and-crab stuffing, dividing it equally among the four fish and mounding the stuffing in the centers.

Arrange the flounders side by side in the buttered dish and brush the tops with the remaining 2 tablespoons of melted butter. Bake on the middle shelf of the oven for about 20 minutes, or until the fish feel firm when prodded gently with a finger. Serve the shrimp-and-crab-stuffed flounder at once, directly from the baking dish.

## Sole Baked in Cheese Sauce

To serve 6

1 teaspoon butter, softened, plus 4 tablespoons butter, cut into ¼-inch bits
6 six-ounce sole fillets, skinned, or substitute 6 six-ounce fillets of flounder or other firm, white-fleshed fish
1 teaspoon salt

¼ teaspoon ground white pepper
½ cup finely chopped onions
2 tablespoons flour
1 cup light cream or ½ cup heavy cream combined with ½ cup milk
1 cup freshly grated sharp cheddar cheese
1 teaspoon strained fresh lemon juice

Preheat the oven to 350°. With a pastry brush, spread the teaspoon of softened butter evenly over the bottom and sides of a shallow baking and serving dish about 10 inches in diameter.

Pat the fillets completely dry with paper towels and sprinkle them evenly with ½ teaspoon of the salt and ⅛ teaspoon of the pepper. Starting at the narrower tapered end, roll each fillet lengthwise into a thick cylinder and stand the fillets side by side in the buttered dish.

In a heavy 8- to 10-inch skillet, melt 2 tablespoons of butter bits over moderate heat. When the foam begins to subside, add the onions and, stirring frequently, cook for about 5 minutes until they are soft and translucent but not brown. Stir in the flour and blend well. Then, stirring the mixture constantly with a wire whisk, pour in the light cream or the combined heavy cream and milk in a slow, thin stream and cook over high heat until the sauce comes to a boil, thickens heavily and is smooth. Add ¾ cup of the grated cheese and, when it has melted completely, slowly stir in the lemon juice and the remaining ½ teaspoon of salt and ⅛ teaspoon of pepper.

Taste for seasoning, pour the sauce over the fish fillets and dot the top with 1 tablespoon of the butter bits. Bake in the middle of the oven for 20 minutes. Then sprinkle the remaining ¼ cup of grated cheese and the tablespoon of butter bits over the fish and slide the dish under the broiler for about 30 seconds until the top is lightly browned. Serve at once.

## Southern Fried Fish

To serve 4

3 pounds catfish, porgy or
    butterfish, filleted but with skins
    left on
2 teaspoons salt

¼ teaspoon freshly ground black
    pepper
1 cup white cornmeal, preferably
    water-ground
Lard for deep frying

Pat the fish completely dry with paper towels. To keep the fish from curling up as they fry score the flesh side of each fillet with a small sharp knife, making three diagonal slashes about 2 inches long and ⅛ inch deep spaced an inch or so apart. Season the fillets on both sides with the salt and pepper. Then dip them in the cornmeal to coat them evenly, and gently shake off any excess meal.

In a heavy 12-inch skillet at least 2 inches deep, melt enough lard to fill the pan to a depth of about ½ inch. Heat the fat until it is very hot but not smoking, then add the fish. Fry the fillets for 4 minutes, turn them with a slotted spatula and fry for 3 or 4 minutes longer, or until they are richly and evenly browned. Arrange the fillets attractively on a heated platter and serve at once. Traditionally, Southern fried fish is accompanied by coleslaw and hush puppies.

To serve 4

DIPPING SAUCE

¼ cup dry sherry
¼ cup Japanese soy sauce

¼ cup chicken stock, fresh or
canned

DIPPING SAUCE: Heat the sherry in a small skillet over moderate heat until it is lukewarm. Ignite the sherry with a match, turn off the heat and shake the pan gently until the flames die out. Add the soy sauce and chicken stock, and bring to a boil over high heat. Pour the sauce into four small bowls and cool to room temperature.

SHRIMP AND VEGETABLES

2 pounds shrimp, peeled and
    deveined (*see shrimp-stuffed
    artichokes\**)
¼ pound string beans, trimmed
    and cut in half crosswise

1 small eggplant, peeled, cut in half
    lengthwise, then cut crosswise
    into ¼-inch-wide semicircles
¼ pound small mushrooms, cut in
    half

SHRIMP AND VEGETABLES: Butterfly the shrimp by cutting them three quarters of the way through along their inner curves and gently spreading them open. Flatten them slightly with the side of a knife.

Divide the shrimp, string beans, eggplant and mushrooms into four individual portions, and place them near the stove on separate dishes or sheets of wax paper.

BATTER

2 cups all-purpose flour
1 egg

2 to 2½ cups ice water

Vegetable oil for deep frying

BATTER: Place the 2 cups of flour in a large mixing bowl and make a well in the center. Drop in the egg and 2 cups of the ice water. With a large wooden spoon, gradually stir the flour into the liquid. Continue to stir vigorously until the batter is very smooth, using up to ½ cup of the traditional ice water if necessary to make a somewhat thin batter that will coat a spoon lightly.

Preheat the oven to 250°. Pour vegetable oil into a deep-fat fryer or heavy 3- to 4-quart saucepan to a depth of 3 inches. Heat the oil until it registers 375° on a deep-frying thermometer.

Dip the shrimp and pieces of vegetable one at a time in the batter, twirling each piece around to coat it evenly, then drop it into the hot oil. Fry six or eight pieces at a time for 3 to 4 minutes, or until they are a light gold. Drain on paper towels, arrange a serving of food on an individual plate or in a basket and keep warm in the oven.

\* *See index.*

With a mesh skimmer or slotted metal spoon or spatula, skim any food particles from the surface of the oil. Check the temperature of the oil to make sure that it remains at 375° and fry the remaining portions as described above.

Serve each portion of *tempura* with its own bowl of dipping sauce.

## Fish Teriyaki (Japanese-American)
BROILED FISH FILLETS WITH SWEET SOY-SEASONED GLAZE

To serve 4

1 tablespoon powdered mustard
¼ cup Japanese soy sauce
¼ cup dry sherry
½ cup chicken stock, fresh or
  canned
1 tablespoon sugar

2 teaspoons cornstarch dissolved in
  1 tablespoon water
4 eight-ounce firm-fleshed fish
  fillets, such as red snapper, porgy
  or striped bass
1 tablespoon vegetable oil
4 sprigs parsley

Preheat the broiler to its highest setting. In a small bowl, mix the powdered mustard with just enough hot water to make a thick paste. Set aside for 15 minutes.

Combine the soy sauce, sherry, chicken stock and sugar in a small saucepan, and bring to a simmer over moderate heat. Stir the combined cornstarch and water into the sauce, and cook over low heat, stirring constantly, until the mixture thickens to a clear syrupy glaze. Immediately pour into a dish and set aside.

Pat the fish fillets completely dry with paper towels. With a pastry brush, spread the tablespoon of oil over the rack of the broiler pan. Place the fillets on the rack, skin side down, and brush them with about 2 tablespoons of the glaze. Broil 4 inches from the heat for 6 to 8 minutes, brushing the fillets three or four times with the remaining glaze, until the fish feels firm when prodded gently with a finger.

Mix the reserved mustard paste into the remaining glaze and spoon a little over each serving of fish. Garnish each fish fillet with a sprig of parsley and serve at once.

NOTE: *Teriyaki* glaze is easily adaptable to broiled steak or chicken. For steak, slice 1 pound of lean boneless beef (preferably tenderloin or sirloin) into ¼-inch-thick slices, or cut the meat into ½-inch cubes and string the cubes on skewers. Broil 2 inches from the heat for 1 or 2 minutes on each side. For chicken, use four whole chicken breasts, boned but with their skin intact; or cut the boned chicken breasts into 1-inch pieces and alternate them on skewers with 1-inch lengths of scallions. Broil 3 inches from the heat for 3 to 4 minutes on each side.

To serve 4

24 pairs baby frogs' legs (if frozen, thoroughly defrosted)
2 cups milk

½ teaspoon salt
4 tablespoons paprika
1½ cups flour
Vegetable oil or shortening for deep frying

Gently split the frogs' legs apart and wash them under cold running water. Pat them thoroughly dry with paper towels. In a small bowl, mix together the milk, salt and 2 tablespoons of the paprika, and soak the frogs' legs in the mixture for about 5 minutes. Combine the flour and the remaining paprika, and place on a sheet of wax paper.

In a heavy 12-inch skillet, heat the oil (which should be about 2 inches deep) over high heat until a light haze forms above it. Dip the frogs' legs in the flour, shake loose any excess and fry them in the hot oil for about 5 minutes, turning them frequently with tongs. Regulate the heat so the legs brown quickly without burning. When they are golden brown, arrange them on paper towels to drain. Serve hot with tartar sauce.

## *Deviled Finnan Haddie* (New England)

To serve 6

1 medium-sized onion, peeled and cut into ¼-inch-thick slices
1½ pounds smoked haddock
3 cups milk
4 tablespoons butter
2 tablespoons finely chopped scallions, white part only
½ cup finely chopped red bell pepper
¼ cup finely chopped green bell pepper

½ teaspoon dry mustard
½ teaspoon paprika
¼ teaspoon ground hot red pepper (cayenne)
1 teaspoon salt
¼ cup flour
1 cup light cream
1 tablespoon pale dry sherry
2 teaspoons Worcestershire sauce
6 slices white bread, trimmed of crusts, toasted and each cut diagonally into 4 triangles

Place the onion slices in a heavy 10-inch skillet, set the smoked haddock on top and pour in 2 cups of the milk. The milk should cover the fish completely; add more if necessary. Bring to a boil over high heat, reduce the heat to low and cover the skillet tightly. Simmer undisturbed for 10 to 15 minutes, or until the fish flakes easily when prodded with a fork. Do not overcook. With a slotted spatula, transfer the smoked haddock to a plate. Then break the fish into large flakes with a fork, picking out and discarding any bones you find. Discard the milk and onions.

123

In a heavy 10- to 12-inch skillet, melt the butter over moderate heat. When the foam begins to subside, add the scallions and stir for a minute or so until they are soft but not brown. Add the chopped red and green pepper, the mustard, paprika, ground red pepper and salt, and cook, until the vegetables are soft. Add the flour and mix well.

Then, stirring the mixture constantly with a wire whisk, pour in the cream and the remaining 1 cup of milk in a slow, thin stream. Cook over high heat until the sauce comes to a boil and thickens heavily. Reduce the heat to low and simmer for 3 minutes, then stir in the haddock, sherry and Worcestershire sauce and simmer until the fish is heated through.

To serve, arrange the toast triangles attractively on six heated plates and ladle the deviled finnan haddie over them.

## Mushroom-stuffed Halibut Steak *(Eastern Heartland)*

To serve 4 to 6

| | |
|---|---|
| 1 tablespoon butter, softened, plus 5 tablespoons butter, cut into ¼-inch bits, plus 2 tablespoons butter, melted | ½ cup soft fresh crumbs made from homemade-type white bread, pulverized in a blender or finely shredded with a fork |
| 2 two-pound halibut steaks, cut about 1½ inches thick | ⅓ cup heavy cream |
| ½ teaspoon salt | ¼ cup finely chopped fresh parsley |
| ½ cup finely chopped onions | ⅛ teaspoon crumbled dried thyme |
| ½ cup finely chopped fresh mushrooms | 1 teaspoon strained fresh lemon juice |
| | Freshly ground black pepper |

Preheat the oven to 425°. With a pastry brush, spread the tablespoon of softened butter evenly over the bottom of a baking-serving dish at least 2 inches deep and wide enough to hold one of the halibut steaks comfortably. Pat the halibut steaks completely dry with paper towels and season them on both sides with the salt. Set the steaks aside while you prepare the mushroom stuffing.

In a heavy 8- to 10-inch skillet, melt 4 tablespoons of the butter bits over moderate heat. When the foam begins to subside, add the onions and, stirring frequently, cook for about 5 minutes, until they are soft and translucent but not brown.

Add the mushrooms and, still stirring from time to time, cook for 5 to 10 minutes but do not let them brown. When the moisture in the pan has evaporated, add the crumbs and stir until golden. Then stir in the cream, parsley, thyme, lemon juice and a few grindings of pepper, and remove the pan from the heat. Taste for seasoning.

Place one of the halibut steaks in the buttered baking dish and spread the mushroom mixture evenly over it. Set the second steak on top and dot it with the remaining tablespoon of butter bits.

Bake in the middle of the oven for about 30 minutes, basting the steaks every 10 minutes or so with the 2 tablespoons of melted butter and the liquids that accumulate in the dish. The halibut is done when it feels firm to the touch. Serve at once, directly from the baking dish.

## Shrimp-stuffed Baked Pike *(Northwest)*

To serve 4

7 tablespoons butter, plus 4
    tablespoons butter, softened and
    cut into ¼-inch bits
¼ cup vegetable oil
½ pound uncooked shrimp
1 cup soft fresh crumbs made from
    homemade-type white bread,
    pulverized in a blender or finely
    shredded with a fork

1 tablespoon very finely chopped
    fresh parsley
⅛ teaspoon ground mace
½ teaspoon salt
Freshly ground black pepper
1 egg yolk
A 2½- to 3-pound pike, cleaned
    but with head and tail left on

Preheat the oven to 375°. In a small pan, melt 4 tablespoons of the butter with the oil over moderate heat. Remove the pan from the heat and, with a pastry brush, spread about 1 tablespoon of the mixture evenly over the bottom of a baking-serving dish large enough to hold the fish comfortably. Set the remaining butter-and-oil mixture aside.

Shell the shrimp. Devein them by making a shallow incision down their backs with a small, sharp knife and lifting out the black or white intestinal vein with the point of the knife. Chop the shrimp as fine as possible and place them in a mixing bowl.

Melt 3 tablespoons of butter in a 6- to 8-inch skillet and brown the bread crumbs, stirring them frequently until they are golden. With a rubber spatula, scrape the entire contents of the skillet over the shrimp. Add the parsley, mace, salt and a few grindings of pepper, and beat vigorously with a wooden spoon until the mixture is a thick, smooth paste. Beat in the egg yolk and the 4 tablespoons of butter bits.

Wash the fish inside and out under cold running water and dry it thoroughly with paper towels. Loosely fill the cavity of the fish with the shrimp stuffing, then close the opening with small skewers, crisscrossing them with kitchen cord as if lacing a turkey. Place the fish in the prepared baking dish and brush the top with 1 or 2 tablespoons of the butter-oil mixture. Bake uncovered in the middle of the oven for 30 minutes, basting every 10 minutes with the remaining butter-and-oil mixture. Serve at once, directly from the baking dish.

## Pompano en Papillote *(Creole-Acadian)*

POMPANO FILLETS WITH SHRIMP AND CRAB BAKED IN PARCHMENT PAPER

To serve 4

1 pound fish trimmings: the heads, tails and bones of any firm white fish

3 cups water

2 medium-sized onions, peeled and coarsely chopped

1 medium-sized bay leaf, crumbled

6 whole black peppercorns

2 teaspoons salt

3 tablespoons butter, softened, plus 5 tablespoons butter, cut into small bits, plus 4 teaspoons butter, melted

4 eight-ounce pompano fillets, or substitute 4 eight-ounce sole or flounder fillets

½ cup dry white wine

½ pound uncooked small shrimp

¼ cup finely chopped scallions, including 3 inches of the green tops

2 tablespoons finely chopped fresh parsley, preferably the flat-leaf Italian variety

¼ cup flour

3 tablespoons heavy cream

¼ teaspoon ground hot red pepper (cayenne)

¼ pound freshly cooked, frozen or canned crabmeat, thoroughly drained and picked over to remove all bits of shell and cartilage

Combine the fish trimmings and water in a 3- to 4-quart enameled saucepan and bring to a boil over high heat, skimming off the foam and scum as they rise to the surface. Add the onions, bay leaf, peppercorns and salt, reduce the heat to low, and simmer, partially covered, for 30 minutes. Then strain the fish stock through a fine sieve set over a bowl, pressing the trimmings and seasonings with the back of a spoon to extract all their juices before discarding the bones and pulp. Set the stock aside.

Preheat the oven to 350°. With a pastry brush, spread 1 tablespoon of the softened butter evenly over the bottom and sides of a 13-by-9-by-2-inch baking dish. Cut a piece of wax paper to fit over the dish and brush one side of the paper with 1 tablespoon of softened butter.

Place the fish fillets in the buttered dish and pour the reserved stock and the wine over them. Cover the dish loosely with the buttered paper and bake in the middle of the oven for 5 minutes, or until the fillets feel firm when prodded gently with a finger. With a large metal spatula, transfer the fish to a platter. Measure the stock remaining in the baking dish and reserve 1½ cups. Increase the oven temperature to 450°.

Meanwhile, shell the shrimp. Unless you are using tiny river shrimp, devein the shrimp by making a shallow incision down their backs with a small sharp knife and lifting out the intestinal vein with the point of the knife. If the shrimp are over 1 inch long, cut them into pieces. Wash the shrimp briefly in a colander and pat them dry with paper towels.

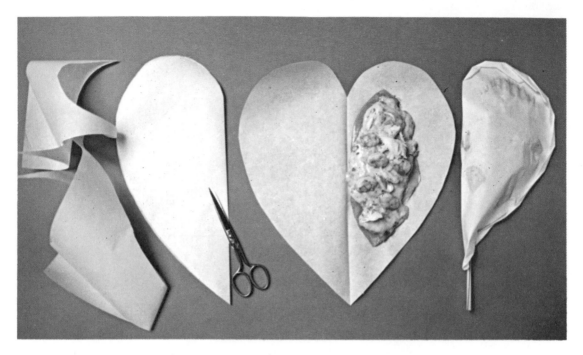

To prepare pompano en papillote, cut an 11-by-15-inch parchment-paper heart. Place the fish and sauce on one side, fold the heart, and crimp the edges shut. Before sealing the tip, blow air into the papillote with a paper straw.

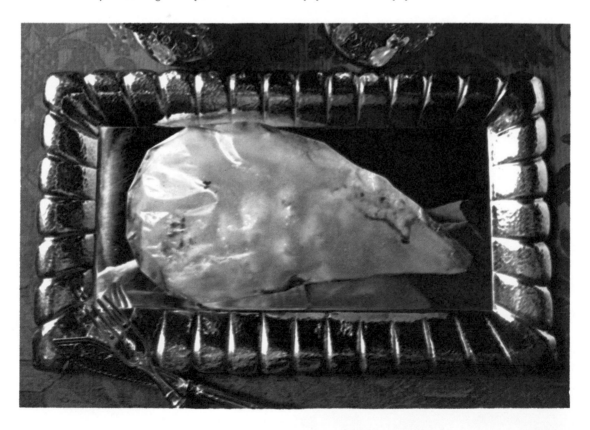

Melt 2 tablespoons of the butter bits in a small skillet set over moderate heat. When the foam begins to subside, add the shrimp and stir for 2 to 3 minutes, until they are pink and firm to the touch. Set the shrimp aside off the heat.

Cut out four paper hearts about 11 inches long and 15 inches wide and brush one side with melted butter. Set the hearts aside.

In a heavy 1- to 1½-quart saucepan, melt the remaining 3 tablespoons of butter bits over moderate heat. Add the scallions and parsley and, stirring frequently, cook for about 5 minutes, until they are soft but not brown. Add the flour and mix well. Then, stirring constantly with a wire whisk, pour in the reserved 1½ cups of stock in a slow, thin stream and cook over high heat until the sauce comes to a boil, thickens and is smooth. Reduce the heat to low and simmer the sauce uncovered for 3 minutes. Stir in the cream and red pepper, and taste for seasoning.

To assemble each pompano en papillote, place a fish fillet on one side of a paper heart and cover the fillet with about ¼ cup of shrimp and ¼ cup of crabmeat. Spoon the sauce over the top, dividing it equally among the four portions. Fold over the exposed side of the paper so that the edges of paper meet. Starting at the upper end of the fold, seal the edges by crimping them at about ½-inch intervals. Before crimping the bottom point of the heart, open the seam slightly and blow through the hole to inflate the papillote. Then quickly crimp the bottom point closed.

Brush a large baking sheet with the remaining tablespoon of softened butter and place the papillotes on it. Bake in the middle of the preheated 450° oven for 8 to 10 minutes. The paper should turn a golden brown. Serve the papillotes at once, opening the paper at the table.

## Broiled Spanish Mackerel *(Creole-Acadian)*

To serve 4

| | |
|---|---|
| 4 tablespoons butter | ½ teaspoon salt |
| 1 tablespoon strained fresh lime juice | 4 six-ounce Spanish mackerel fillets, skinned |
| ½ teaspoon anchovy paste | 1 tablespoon vegetable oil |
| ⅛ teaspoon ground hot red pepper (cayenne) | 1 lime, cut lengthwise into 4 or 8 wedges |

Preheat the broiler to its highest setting. Melt the butter over moderate heat in a small saucepan. Remove the pan from the heat and stir in the lime juice, anchovy paste, red pepper and salt. Set the butter sauce aside.

Pat the mackerel fillets completely dry with paper towels. Then, with a pastry brush, spread the vegetable oil evenly over the grid of the broiling pan. Arrange the fillets side by side on the grid, and brush them with about 2 tablespoons of the butter sauce. Broil 4 inches from the heat for 4 to 5 minutes, brushing the fillets once or twice more with the remaining sauce. The mackerel is done when the tops are golden brown and the fish feel firm to the touch.

With a wide metal spatula, transfer the fillets to a heated platter. Arrange the lime wedges around the fish and serve at once.

## Red Snapper with Vegetable Sauce  (Greek-American)

To serve 4 to 6

| | |
|---|---|
| 6 tablespoons vegetable oil | 2 one-pound cans solid-pack |
| 1 cup finely chopped onions | tomatoes and 1 cup of their liquid |
| 1 teaspoon finely chopped garlic | 1 cup dry white wine |
| ½ cup finely chopped celery | A 5½- to 6-pound red snapper, |
| 1 green pepper, halved, deribbed, | cleaned and scaled but with head |
| seeded and finely chopped | and tail left on |
| (½ cup) | 1 teaspoon salt |
| ½ cup thinly sliced carrots | ¼ cup strained fresh lemon juice |
| 2 tablespoons finely chopped dill | Freshly ground black pepper |
| 1 tablespoon finely chopped parsley | 1 tablespoon butter, softened |

Heat the oil in a heavy 10- to 12-inch enameled or stainless-steel skillet until a light haze forms above it. Drop in the onions and garlic and, stirring frequently, cook until the onions are soft and translucent. Stir in the celery, green pepper, carrots, dill and parsley, and cook for 3 to 5 minutes more, or until the vegetables are soft. Add the tomatoes, 1 cup of tomato liquid and the wine, and bring to a boil over high heat. Reduce the heat and simmer, partially covered, for 15 minutes. Pour the vegetable sauce into a flameproof baking dish just large enough to hold the fish comfortably, and set it aside.

Preheat the oven to 400°. Wash the fish under cold running water and pat it thoroughly dry with paper towels. Sprinkle the fish inside and out with the salt, lemon juice and several grindings of black pepper. Lay the fish on top of the vegetable sauce. Cut a piece of wax paper just large enough to fit the baking dish and coat it with the softened butter. Set it buttered side down on top of the fish.

Bake the snapper in the center of the oven for 35 to 40 minutes, or until it feels firm when prodded gently with a finger. Transfer the fish to a heated serving platter and place in the turned-off oven to keep warm while you complete the sauce.

Set the flameproof baking dish on top of the stove and bring the sauce to a boil over high heat. Boil briskly, uncovered, until the sauce has thickened to the consistency of heavy cream. Spoon the sauce over the fish or, if you prefer, serve it separately in a heated bowl or sauceboat.

## Red Snapper Citrus (South)

To serve 4

| | |
|---|---|
| ½ cup finely chopped onions | Four 8- to 10-ounce red snapper |
| ¼ cup strained fresh orange juice | fillets, with the skin left on |
| 2 teaspoons finely grated fresh | A pinch of ground nutmeg, |
| orange peel | preferably freshly grated |
| 1 teaspoon salt | Freshly ground black pepper |

Mix the onions, orange juice, orange peel and salt together in a shallow baking-serving dish large enough to hold the red snapper fillets in one layer. Add the fillets, turn them about in the orange mixture to moisten them evenly, then place them skin side up and set aside to marinate at room temperature for about 30 minutes.

Preheat the oven to 400°. Turn the fillets flesh side up and sprinkle them with a pinch of nutmeg and a few grindings of pepper. Basting the fish with the marinade from time to time, bake in the middle of the oven for 10 to 12 minutes, or until the fillets flake easily when prodded gently with a fork. Do not overcook. Serve the fish at once directly from the baking dish.

NOTE: Red snapper citrus can also be served chilled. If you prefer to present the fish cold, add 1 more teaspoon of salt to the marinade ingredients and follow the directions above for marinating and baking the fillets. Then cool them to room temperature, cover the dish tightly with foil or plastic wrap and refrigerate for 5 to 6 hours. The marinade will become a delicate jelly when it is chilled.

## *Poached Salmon Steaks with Mousseline Sauce* (Eastern Heartland)

To serve 6

POACHING LIQUID
2 quarts water
1 cup dry white wine
½ cup coarsely chopped onions
½ cup coarsely chopped leeks,
    including the green tops,
    thoroughly washed to remove any
    sand
¼ cup coarsely chopped celery,
    including the leaves
1 medium-sized carrot, scraped and
    coarsely chopped
2 tablespoons finely chopped fresh
    parsley
1 small bay leaf, crumbled
¼ teaspoon crumbled dried thyme
1 tablespoon salt
1 teaspoon whole black peppercorns

First prepare the poaching liquid in the following fashion: Combine the water, wine, onions, leeks, celery, carrot, parsley, bay leaf, thyme, 1 table-spoon of salt and the peppercorns in a 4- to 5-quart enameled pot and bring to a boil over high heat. Reduce the heat to low, cover partially and simmer for 30 minutes. Strain the poaching liquid through a fine sieve into a heavy skillet at least 12 inches in diameter and 2½ inches deep.

SALMON
6 salmon steaks, cut 1 inch
thick and each weighing about
¾ pound

Arrange the salmon steaks side by side in the poaching liquid. Cover the skillet tightly and bring to a simmer over moderate heat. Immediately reduce the heat to low and simmer gently for about 10 minutes, or until the fish flakes easily when prodded gently with a fork. With a slotted spoon, transfer the salmon steaks to a heated platter.

MOUSSELINE SAUCE
½ pound unsalted butter, cut into
    ¼-inch bits
3 egg yolks
2 tablespoons cold water
3 tablespoons strained fresh lemon
juice
1 teaspoon salt
A pinch of ground hot red pepper
    (cayenne)
½ cup heavy cream, chilled

Meanwhile, make the hollandaise base for the mousseline sauce. In a small heavy saucepan, melt the butter over low heat, being careful not to let it brown.

In a heavy 2-quart enameled saucepan, beat the egg yolks and water vigorously together with a wire whisk until they are foamy. Place the egg mixture over the lowest possible heat and continue whisking until it thickens to the consistency of heavy cream. Do not let the eggs come any-where near a boil or they will curdle.

Still whisking constantly, pour in the clear hot butter as slowly as pos-sible, discarding the milky solids that will settle at the bottom of the pan. Continue to beat until the sauce thickens heavily, then add the lemon juice, the teaspoon of salt and the red pepper, and taste for seasoning. Set the hollandaise sauce aside to cool to lukewarm.

Just before serving, pour the cream into a chilled bowl. With a wire whisk or a rotary or electric beater, whip the cream until it is stiff enough to stand in unwavering peaks on the beater when it is lifted from the bowl. With a rubber spatula, scoop the whipped cream over the cooled hollandaise sauce and fold them toegther gently but thoroughly. Pour the mousseline sauce into a sauceboat or serving bowl and present it separately with the salmon.

## Molded Salmon with Cucumber Sauce (Northwest)

To serve 4

MOLDED SALMON

| | |
|---|---|
| 1 pound fresh salmon | 2 teaspoons unflavored gelatin |
| ¼ cup distilled white vinegar | ¼ cup wine vinegar |
| 1 medium-sized bay leaf | 1½ teaspoons dry mustard |
| ¼ teaspoon crumbled dried thyme | 1 teaspoon sugar |
| 2 tablespoons plus 1 teaspoon salt | 2 egg yolks |
| 6 whole black peppercorns | 2 tablespoons unsalted butter, cut |
| 1 tablespoon vegetable oil | into ¼-inch bits |
| ¼ cup plus 1 tablespoon cold | ¾ cup milk |
| water | |

Place the salmon in an enameled or stainless-steel casserole just large enough to hold it and pour in enough cold water to cover the fish completely. Add the distilled white vinegar, bay leaf, thyme, 2 tablespoons of the salt and the 6 peppercorns, and bring to a boil over high heat. Reduce the heat to low and simmer partially covered for about 25 minutes, or until the salmon flakes easily when prodded gently with a fork.

With a slotted spatula, transfer the fish to a plate; discard the cooking liquid and seasonings. Remove the skin and discard it, then break the salmon into large flakes with a fork, discarding any bones you find. Cover the fish with foil or plastic wrap and set aside.

With a pastry brush, spread the vegetable oil evenly over the bottom and sides of four 6-ounce individual molds. Invert the molds over paper towels to drain.

Pour ¼ cup of the cold water into a small bowl, sprinkle in the gelatin and let it soften for a few minutes. Meanwhile, combine the wine vinegar, the dry mustard, the sugar and the remaining teaspoon of salt in a 1-quart enameled or stainless-steel saucepan. Stir until the dry ingredients are completely dissolved, then boil briskly to reduce the mixture to about 3 tablespoons. Remove the pan from the heat and stir in the remaining tablespoon of cold water.

Stirring the vinegar mixture constantly with a wire whisk, add the egg yolks one at a time. Still whisking, cook over the lowest possible heat for 1 minute, or until it thickens lightly. Do not let the mixture get too hot or it will curdle. Immediately remove the pan from the heat and whisk in the butter bits.

In a separate small saucepan, heat the milk over moderate heat until bubbles begin to appear around the edges. Add the gelatin to the milk and stir until it dissolves completely. Stirring the vinegar mixture with the whisk, pour in the milk and gelatin in a slow, thin stream, then stir in the flaked salmon. Taste for seasoning. Pour the mixture into the oiled molds, spreading it and smoothing the top with a spatula. Refrigerate for at least 4 hours, or until the molded salmon is very firm.

CUCUMBER SAUCE

| | |
|---|---|
| 1 large firm cucumber | 1 teaspoon salt |
| ½ cup heavy cream, chilled | 1 tablespoon finely cut fresh dill |
| 1 tablespoon wine vinegar |    leaves, or substitute 1 teaspoon |
| ⅛ teaspoon ground hot red pepper |    dried dill weed |
|    (cayenne) | |

Just before serving, prepare the cucumber sauce in the following fashion: With a small, sharp knife, peel the cucumber and slice it lengthwise in half. Scoop out the seeds by running the tip of a teaspoon down the center of each half. Chop the cucumber fine and squeeze it handful by handful to remove the excess liquid. Spread the cucumber on a paper towel to drain completely.

In a chilled bowl, beat the cream with a wire whisk or a rotary or electric beater until it is stiff enough to stand in firm peaks on the beater when it is lifted from the bowl. Beat in the wine vinegar, red pepper and 1 teaspoon of salt. Add the cucumber and dill, and fold them into the cream mixture gently but thoroughly.

To unmold and serve the salmon, dip the bottom of the molds briefly into hot water and run a thin knife around the edges. Place an inverted serving plate over each mold and, grasping plate and mold together firmly, turn them over. Rap the plate on a table and the salmon should slide out easily. Serve the cucumber sauce separately in a bowl or sauceboat.

*This tempting broiled stuffed coho salmon was caught in nearby Lake Michigan. The coho, a native of the Pacific Northwest, was introduced into the Great Lakes in 1966 and is a protected sport fish, barred to commercial fishermen.*

*Shad roe on a bed of sorrel is the ultimate spring treat for seafood lovers on the Atlantic Coast. The fresh roe is available from April through June, a time, happily, when sorrel is young and tender. Traditionally, roe is served on the sorrel, with lemon and boiled new potatoes.*

To serve 6 to 8

1½ cups dry white wine
½ cup strained fresh lemon juice
½ cup plus 1 tablespoon vegetable oil
1 medium-sized onion, peeled and thinly sliced
3 medium-sized garlic cloves, crushed with the side of a cleaver or a large heavy knife
3 sprigs fresh parsley
1 teaspoon ground ginger
½ teaspoon crumbled dried thyme
¼ teaspoon Tabasco sauce
1 teaspoon salt
¼ teaspoon freshly ground black pepper

A 5- to 5½-pound coho or other salmon, cleaned and with head and tail removed
1 cup freshly cooked rice, made from ½ cup long-grain white rice, not the converted variety
¼ cup finely chopped scallions, including 2 inches of the green tops
¼ cup finely chopped fresh parsley
The peel of ½ lemon, cut into matchlike strips
1 lemon, cut crosswise into ¼-inch-thick rounds

First prepare the marinade in the following manner: Combine the wine, lemon juice, ½ cup of the oil, the onion, garlic, parsley sprigs, ginger, thyme, Tabasco, salt and pepper in a small enameled saucepan and, stirring occasionally, bring to a boil over high heat. Pour the marinade into an enameled casserole or roasting pan large enough to hold the salmon comfortably, and set it aside to cool to room temperature.

Wash the salmon inside and out under cold running water and pat it dry with paper towels. With a sharp knife, score both sides of the fish by making four or five evenly spaced diagonal slits about 4 inches long and ¼ inch deep. Place the salmon in the cooled marinade and turn it over to moisten it evenly.

Cover the pan tightly with foil or plastic wrap and marinate at room temperature for about 3 hours, or in the refrigerator for about 6 hours, turning the fish occasionally.

Light a layer of briquettes in a charcoal broiler and let them burn until a white ash appears on the surface, or preheat the broiler of your stove to its highest setting.

Transfer the salmon to paper towels and pat it completely dry with more paper towels. Strain the marinade through a fine sieve set over a bowl. To prepare the stuffing, combine the rice, scallions, chopped parsley and lemon strips in a small bowl. Pour in ¼ cup of the strained marinade and mix well. Set the remaining marinade aside.

Loosely fill the salmon with the stuffing, then close the opening with small skewers and kitchen cord. With a pastry brush, spread the remaining tablespoon of oil over the hot grill or the broiler rack. Place the salmon on top and brush it with a few spoonfuls of the reserved marinade.

Broil 3 or 4 inches from the heat, basting the salmon frequently with the remaining marinade. The salmon should be broiled for about 15 minutes on each side, or until it is evenly and delicately browned and feels firm when prodded gently with a finger.

Serve the salmon at once from a heated platter, with the lemon slices arranged attractively in a row along the top of the fish. Garnish it further, if you like, with red and green pepper strips and onion rings.

## Scrod Broiled in Lemon Butter *(New England)*

To serve 4

| | |
|---|---|
| 6 tablespoons butter, melted | 2 pounds skinless fresh scrod (young cod or haddock) fillets |
| 2 tablespoons strained fresh lemon juice | 2 tablespoons soft fresh crumbs made from homemade-type white |
| 1 teaspoon salt | bread, pulverized in a blender or |
| Freshly ground black pepper | finely shredded with a fork |

Preheat the broiler to its highest setting. In a 13-by-8-by-2-inch baking-serving dish, mix the melted butter, lemon juice, salt and a few grindings of pepper. Dip the scrod fillets in the mixture and when they are evenly coated on both sides arrange them in one layer in the dish.

Broil the fish 3 to 4 inches from the heat for 5 minutes. Then, with a spoon or bulb baster, baste the fillets with the lemon-and-butter mixture.

Scatter the bread crumbs over the fillets and broil for 5 minutes longer, or until the fish flakes easily when prodded gently with a fork. Serve at once, from the baking dish, or arrange the scrod attractively on a heated platter and moisten it with some of the lemon-and-butter mixture.

## Shad Roe on a Bed of Sorrel *(Eastern Heartland)*

To serve 4

| | |
|---|---|
| 1 pound fresh sorrel | A pinch of sugar |
| 10 tablespoons unsalted butter, cut into ¼-inch bits | Salt |
| | Freshly ground black pepper |
| 3 egg yolks | 2 pairs shad roe |
| ¼ cup heavy cream | ½ cup flour |
| | 1 lemon, cut into 4 wedges |

Wash the sorrel under cold running water. With a sharp knife, trim away any blemished spots and cut off the white stems. Stack the leaves together a handful at a time, roll them into a tight cylinder and cut it crosswise into fine shreds. Drop the sorrel into enough lightly salted boiling water to cover it by at least 1 inch and boil briskly for 2 or 3 minutes, until the shreds have wilted. Drain the sorrel thoroughly in a sieve.

Melt 4 tablespoons of the butter bits over moderate heat in a heavy 8- to 10-inch skillet. When the foam subsides, add the sorrel and stir it about to coat the shreds evenly. Then reduce the heat to low. Beat the egg yolks and cream together with a wire whisk and pour the mixture slowly over the sorrel, stirring continuously. Add the sugar, 1 teaspoon of salt and a liberal grinding of pepper and stir for 1 to 2 minutes. Do not let the mixture come anywhere near a boil or the egg yolks will curdle. Remove the pan from the heat and cover to keep the sorrel warm.

With scissors or a small sharp knife, slit the membrane connecting each pair of roe. Sprinkle the roe with salt and a few grindings of pepper, dip them in the flour to coat both sides and shake off the excess. Melt the remaining 6 tablespoons of butter in a heavy 8- to 10-inch skillet. When the foam subsides, add the roe and fry them for 5 to 6 minutes on each side, regulating the heat so that they brown evenly without burning.

Spoon the sorrel onto 4 individual heated plates, dividing it evenly among them, and place the roe on top of each portion. Garnish with lemon and serve at once, accompanied if you like by boiled potatoes.

## Planked Shad with Potatoes Duchesse *(Eastern Heartland)*

To serve 6

9 medium-sized boiling potatoes (about 3 pounds), peeled and quartered
Salt
3 egg yolks, lightly beaten
12 tablespoons butter, melted

½ teaspoon ground white pepper
A 2½- to 3-pound shad fillet, with the skin left on
2 tablespoons vegetable oil
Fresh parsley sprigs
2 lemons, each cut lengthwise into 6 or 8 wedges

Drop the potatoes into enough lightly salted boiling water to cover them by at least 1 inch. Boil briskly, uncovered, until a potato quarter is soft enough to be easily mashed against the sides of the pan with the back of a spoon. Drain the potatoes in a sieve or colander, and pat them dry with paper towels.

Purée the potatoes through a food mill or ricer set into a deep bowl or place them in the bowl and mash them to a smooth purée with the back of a fork. Beat in the egg yolks and, when they are completely incorporated, add 6 tablespoons of the melted butter, 1½ teaspoons of salt and ½ teaspoon of white pepper. Cover the bowl tightly with foil to keep the purée warm.

Meanwhile, set the broiler pan and its rack 4 inches from the heat and preheat the broiler to its highest point. Wash the shad briefly under cold running water and pat it completely dry with paper towels. With a pastry

138

brush, spread the vegetable oil evenly over the broiler pan rack and place the fish on top of it, skin side down. Brush the shad with 2 tablespoons of the remaining melted butter and broil about 4 inches from the heat for 6 to 8 minutes, basting the fish once or twice with 2 more tablespoons of the butter. The shad is done when its flesh is delicately browned and flakes easily when prodded gently with a table fork.

With the aid of two large metal spatulas, carefully transfer the shad to the center of an oak plank large enough to hold it comfortably. Using a pastry bag fitted with a large star tip, pipe the potato purée around the shad. Brush the shad with the remaining 2 tablespoons of melted butter and place the plank under the broiler for 2 or 3 minutes to brown the potatoes lightly.

Garnish the planked shad with the parsley sprigs and serve at once. Present the lemon wedges separately in a small bowl.

*In the home version of a shad bake, the fillet is butter-basted and broiled. It is then planked on a hardwood board, ringed with a piping of potatoes* duchesse *and briefly put under the broiler again.*

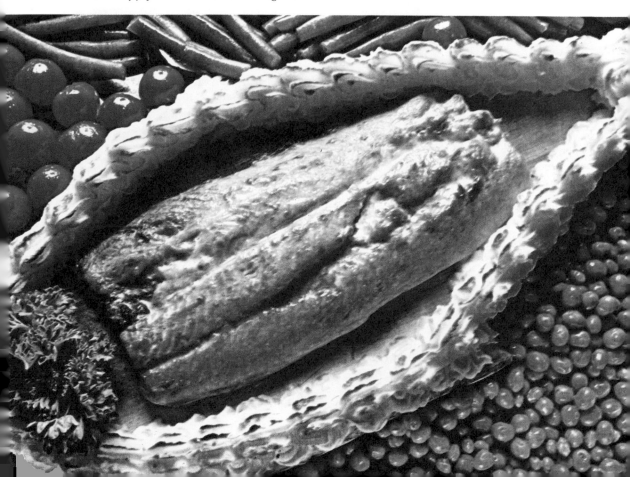

To serve 4

4 pounds fish trimmings: the heads, tail and bones of any firm white-fleshed fish

2 quarts water

2 medium-sized onions, peeled and coarsely chopped

1 medium-sized bay leaf, crumbled

½ teaspoon crumbled dried tarragon

2 teaspoons salt

4 ten-ounce brook trout, cleaned but with heads and tails left on, thoroughly defrosted if frozen

4 envelopes unflavored gelatin

2 cups dry white wine

4 egg whites

4 egg shells, finely crushed

Combine the fish trimmings and water in a 5- to 6-quart enameled or stainless-steel pot. The water should cover the trimmings completely; add more if necessary. Bring to a boil over high heat, skimming off the foam as it rises to the surface. Add the onions, bay leaf, tarragon and salt, reduce the heat, and simmer partially covered for 20 minutes.

Strain the contents of the pot through a fine sieve into a heavy 12-inch skillet, pressing down hard on the fish trimmings to extract all their juices before discarding them. Set the pot aside.

Let the stock cool to lukewarm, then wash the trout inside and out under cold running water and place them in the skillet. Bring to a simmer over moderate heat, reduce the heat, and simmer uncovered for 5 minutes, or until the fish feel firm when prodded gently with a finger.

With a slotted spatula, arrange the trout side by side on a flat platter or jelly-roll pan. While they are still warm, skin each of the fish in the following fashion: With a small, sharp knife, cut the skin crosswise about an inch above the base of the tail and about an inch below the gill. Gently pull off the skin in strips from tail to gill, then turn the fish over and peel the upturned side. Drape a dampened kitchen towel over the trout and refrigerate them while you prepare the aspic.

Measure 6 cups of the fish stock remaining in the skillet into the reserved pot and let it cool to room temperature. Sprinkle the gelatin evenly over it and let it soften for a few minutes. Add the wine, egg whites and egg shells and, stirring constantly, bring to a boil over moderate heat. When the mixture begins to froth and rise, remove the pot from the heat and let the stock rest for 10 minutes. Then pour the entire contents of the pot into a fine sieve lined with a double thickness of dampened cheese-cloth and set over a shallow enameled or stainless-steel pan. Allow the liquid to drain through undisturbed. Season with more salt if needed.

Set the pan in a large bowl half filled with crushed ice or ice cubes and water, and stir the aspic with a metal spoon until it thickens enough to flow sluggishly off the spoon. Pour aspic to a depth of about ¼ inch into a chilled serving platter large enough to hold the four trout attractively, and refrigerate the platter until the aspic is firm.

Keep the remaining aspic at room temperature so that it remains liquid and ready to use; if it begins to set, warm briefly over low heat to soften it, then stir it over ice again until it is thick but still fluid.

GARNISH

| | |
|---|---|
| 1 or 2 large green leaves from the top of a leek or scallion | sliced into ¼-inch-thick rounds |
| 1 medium-sized carrot, scraped and | The white of 1 hard-cooked egg |
| | 4 sprigs of watercress |

Meanwhile, prepare the garnish. Drop the leek or scallion leaves into boiling water for 1 or 2 minutes. Transfer them to a sieve, run cold water over them, then spread them on paper towels and pat them dry. Cut the leaves into a dozen or more long, thin strips to use as stems.

Boil the carrot rounds briskly in the same water for about 5 minutes, until they are barely tender. Drain, run cold water over them, then spread the rounds on paper towels and pat them dry. With a lily-of-the-valley truffle cutter or with the tip of a sharp knife, make carrot flowers. Slice a ¼-inch-thick round from the egg white and cut out four small circles from the round to cover the eyes of the trout.

Set stems, flower and egg-white circles aside, covered with wax paper.

Arrange the trout on the aspic-coated platter and glaze them with a few tablespoonfuls of the liquid aspic. Refrigerate until the glaze is firm. Dip the carrot flowers and green leaf stems into the aspic and arrange them fancifully on top of the fish. Dip the egg-white circles in the aspic and place them over the eyes. Chill again until the decorations are anchored firmly. Then carefully spoon aspic over the trout two more times, chilling the fish after each coating to set the glaze.

Melt the aspic remaining in the pan over low heat, and pour it into a small loaf pan. Refrigerate until the aspic has set firm. Run a thin knife around the edges to loosen them and dip the bottom into hot water.

Place an inverted plate over the pan and, grasping pan and plate together firmly, turn them over. The aspic should slide out easily. Cut the aspic into paper-thin slices, and then into fine dice. Scatter the dice around the edge of the fish platter. Garnish the top with sprigs of watercress and refrigerate the trout in the aspic until ready to serve.

*Usually fried, trout of the Northwest make a formal meal when simmered in stock, chilled and served in wine-flavored aspic.*

## Barbecued Swordfish

To serve 4 to 6

MARINADE
2 tablespoons lemon juice
4 tablespoons orange juice
4 tablespoons soy sauce
2 tablespoons tomato paste
1 teaspoon minced garlic
1 teaspoon oregano

2 tablespoons finely chopped
  fresh parsley
½ teaspoon salt
Freshly ground black pepper

2 pounds swordfish, cut about 1 inch
  thick
1 tablespoon soft butter

Combine the lemon and orange juice, soy sauce, tomato paste, garlic, oregano, parsley, salt and a few grindings of black pepper in a large, shallow baking dish. Stir until all the ingredients are well combined. Place the swordfish in the dish, baste thoroughly and marinate for about 2 hours at room temperature, turning the fish over after the first hour.

Preheat the broiler to its highest point for at least 10 minutes. Then, with a pastry brush, grease the broiler rack with the tablespoon of soft butter. Lay the swordfish on the rack, brush heavily with the marinade and broil the fish 3 inches from the heat for about 5 minutes, brushing it once or twice with the marinade. When the surface of the fish is lightly browned, turn it over with a large spatula and broil on the other side for 5 minutes, brushing on the remaining marinade once or twice more to keep the surface of the fish well moistened. When the swordfish is done it should be a golden brown and firm to the touch. Be careful not to overcook. Transfer the fish to a heated platter, pour the broiling pan juices over it and serve at once, cut into appropriate portions.

## San Francisco Fried Trout

To serve 4

| | |
|---|---|
| Four 10- to 12-ounce trout, cleaned but with heads and tails left on, thoroughly defrosted if frozen | 2 eggs |
| | 1 cup vegetable oil |
| | 8 tablespoons butter, cut into bits |
| 2 teaspoons salt | ¼ cup strained fresh lime juice |
| Freshly ground black pepper | 2 tablespoons finely cut fresh chives |
| 1 cup unsifted flour | 2 tablespoons finely chopped fresh |
| 1 cup yellow cornmeal | parsley |

Wash the trout under cold running water, pat them dry and season them inside and out with the salt and a few grindings of pepper. Spread the flour on one piece of wax paper and the cornmeal on a separate piece; break the eggs into a shallow bowl and beat them to a froth with a fork.

In a heavy 12-inch skillet, heat the oil over moderate heat until a light haze forms above it. Roll each trout in the flour, immerse it in the egg and then turn it about in the cornmeal to coat it evenly. Fry the trout in the hot oil, two at a time, for 4 to 5 minutes on each side, or until they are golden brown. Drain the trout briefly on paper towels, then place them on a heated platter.

Melt the butter over moderate heat in a separate skillet, stirring so that the bits melt without browning. Remove the pan from the heat, stir in the lime juice, chives and parsley, and taste for seasoning. Pour over the trout and serve at once.

## Speckled Trout Amandine *(Creole-Acadian)*

To serve 6

Vegetable oil for deep frying
2 eggs
1 cup unsifted flour
6 four-ounce speckled trout or
weakfish fillets, skinned
1 teaspoon salt
¼ teaspoon ground white pepper
½ pound butter, cut into ½-inch

bits
1 cup finely chopped blanched
almonds
¼ cup strained fresh lemon juice
2 tablespoons finely chopped fresh
parsley, preferably the flat-leaf
Italian variety
1 teaspoon Worcestershire sauce

Preheat the oven to its lowest setting. At the same time, line a large shallow baking dish with a double thickness of paper towels and place it on the middle shelf of the oven.

Pour vegetable oil into a deep fryer or large heavy saucepan to a depth of 2 to 3 inches and heat the oil until it reaches a temperature of 360° on a deep-frying thermometer.

Meanwhile, break the eggs into a shallow bowl and beat them to a froth with a fork or wire whisk. Spread the flour out on wax paper.

Pat the fish fillets completely dry with paper towels and season them with the salt and white pepper. Roll one fillet at a time in the flour, immerse it in the beaten eggs, then roll it in the flour again to coat it evenly. Shake the fillet to remove the excess flour and set it aside on a plate.

Deep-fry the fillets, two or three at a time, for about 6 minutes, or until they are crisp and golden on both sides. As they brown, transfer the fillets to the paper-lined pan and keep them warm in the oven while you deep-fry the rest.

When all the fillets are cooked, prepare the sauce in the following manner: In a heavy 10- to 12-inch skillet, melt the butter bits over moderate heat, stirring frequently so that the butter melts completely without burning. As soon as the butter begins to brown, add the almonds and toss them about with a spoon to moisten them evenly. Stir in the lemon juice, parsley and Worcestershire sauce, and taste the sauce for seasoning.

To serve, arrange the fillets attractively on a heated platter or individual serving plates and pour the sauce over them.

To serve 8

FISH STOCK

2 pounds fish trimmings: the heads, tails and bones of any firm white-fleshed fish

6 cups water

1 large onion, peeled and coarsely chopped

1 medium-sized bay leaf, crumbled

6 whole black peppercorns

1 teaspoon salt

To prepare the fish stock, combine the fish trimmings and water in a 4- to 5-quart enameled or stainless-steel pot and bring to a boil over high heat, skimming off the foam and scum that rise to the surface. Add the coarsely chopped onion and the bay leaf, peppercorns and 1 teaspoon of salt, reduce the heat to low, and simmer partially covered for 20 minutes.

Strain the contents of the pot through a fine sieve into a bowl, pressing down hard on the fish trimmings with the back of a spoon to extract all their juices. Measure and reserve 4 cups of the fish stock.

FISH STEW

¼ cup olive or vegetable oil

1 cup coarsely chopped onions

1 tablespoon finely chopped garlic

3 medium-sized firm ripe tomatoes, washed, coarsely chopped and puréed in a food mill, or substitute 1 cup canned puréed tomatoes

1 cup dry white wine

2 tablespoons finely chopped fresh parsley

Two 1½-pound precooked Dungeness crabs, thoroughly defrosted if frozen

3 dozen large mussels in their shells

2 dozen small hard-shell clams in their shells

2 pounds fresh cod steaks, cut into 8 equal portions

½ teaspoon salt

Wash the pot, add the oil and heat it over moderate heat until a light haze forms above it. Add the cup of coarsely chopped onions and the garlic, and, stirring frequently, cook for about 5 minutes, until the onions are soft and translucent but not brown. Stir in the reserved stock, the tomato purée, wine and parsley, and bring to a boil over high heat. Reduce the heat and simmer partially covered for 15 minutes.

Meanwhile, prepare the crabs. Holding a crab tightly in one hand, lift off the top shell and discard it. Pull out the spongy gray lungs, or "dead man's fingers," from each side and scrape out the intestines in the center. Place the crab on its back and, with the point of a small sharp knife, pry off the pointed flap or apron. Cut away the head just behind the eyes. With a cleaver or heavy knife, cut the crab into quarters. Shell, clean and quarter the second crab in the same manner and set both aside on a plate.

Under cold running water, scrub the mussels and clams thoroughly with a stiff brush or soapless steel-mesh scouring pad, and remove the

*Cioppino, a highly seasoned seafood stew, is at its best when made with a mixture of both finned- and shellfish. The version shown here includes crabs, mussels, clams and cod steaks. White wine adds flavor to the broth, but cioppino is normally served with a red wine.*

black ropelike tufts from the mussels. Season the cod on both sides with ½ teaspoon of salt. Set the mussels and clams and the cod aside on wax paper or plates.

To assemble the cioppino, arrange the pieces of crab in the bottom of a 6- to 8-quart enameled casserole. Lay the mussels and clams on top and pour in the tomato mixture. Bring to a boil over high heat, reduce the heat to low, cover tightly and cook for 10 minutes. Add the pieces of cod, cover the casserole again and continue to cook for 8 to 10 minutes longer. The cioppino is done when the mussel and clam shells have opened and the cod flakes easily when prodded gently with a fork. Discard any mussels or clams that remain closed.

Serve at once, directly from the casserole, or spoon the cod and shellfish into a large heated tureen and pour the broth over them.

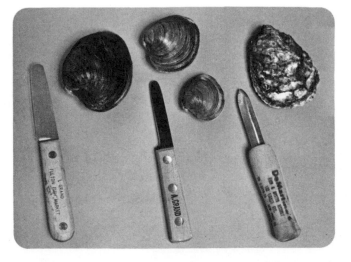

## How to Shuck Oysters and Quahogs

*Live hard-shell clams and oysters are shut so tightly that you need special knives to pry them open. At far left is a sturdy clam knife designed for shucking the large quahog, or chowder clam, efficiently. The more slender-bladed knife at center is for opening the smaller quahogs, the cherrystone (top) and littleneck (bottom), which are most often served on the half-shell. The oyster knife shown at near left has a sharp curved tip and a distinctive round handle.*

*To shuck an oyster: (1) grip the narrow end between thumb and fingers, rounded half against your palm. Hold the oyster knife near its point, curved tip down, and insert it near the narrow end. (2) Pressing the knife firmly against the top shell half, cut through to the muscle attached to the center of the shell and then around the rim, holding the shell slightly open with your thumb. (3) Turn the blade, curved tip up, and free the meat and membrane or veil from the top shell half. (4) Open the shell and cut the meat from the other shell half.*

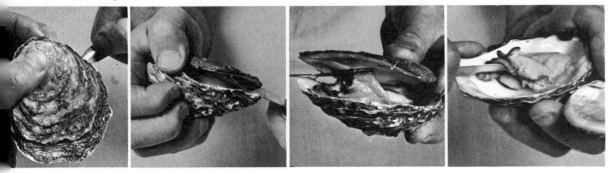

*To shuck a quahog: (1) hold the shell lengthwise along your palm with the hinged side away from the clam knife. Insert the knife blade into the shell under the hinge. (2) Keeping the knife blade firmly pressed against the top half, cut toward the hinge to sever the muscle there. Next cut around the rim, with the knife blade penetrating about ½ inch inside, holding the shell slightly open with your thumb. (3) Now open the clam and free the meat completely from the membrane on the top half. (4) Free the meat from the other shell half.*

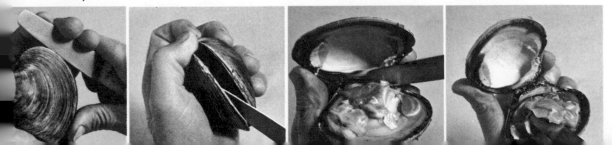

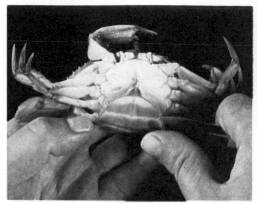

*To clean a live soft-shell crab, first
freeze the crab briefly to numb it,
then peel back the triangular apron.*

*With a small sharp knife,
scrape out the stomach and the intestines,
which lie beneath the apron.*

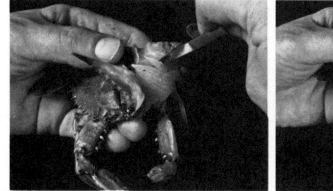

*Turn over the crab, lift the shell at
the tapering points on each end
and insert knife into the grayish lungs.*

*Clean out the spongy lungs,
or "dead man's fingers," until the
cartilage is completely exposed.*

*With a pair of sharp scissors,
cut off and discard the head
of the crab, just behind the eyes.*

*Squeeze the body and the sand
sac will pop out of the head opening.
Wash the crab in cold water.*

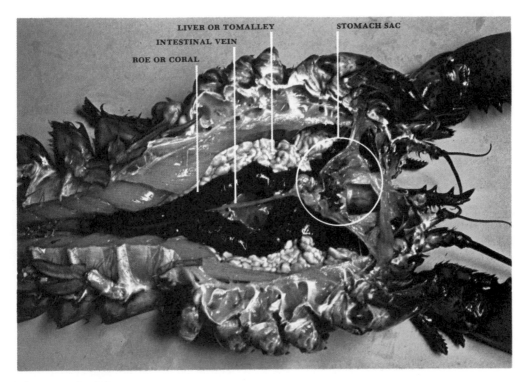

LIVER OR TOMALLEY

INTESTINAL VEIN

ROE OR CORAL

STOMACH SAC

*Anatomy of a lobster.*

*Shellfish Boil* (Creole-Acadian)

*In Louisiana, a "boil" is a mixture of dried spices used to flavor the stock in which crawfish, shrimp or blue crabs are boiled.*

**To make about 1 cup**

¼ cup mustard seeds
¼ cup coriander seeds
2 tablespoons dill seeds
2 tablespoons whole allspice
1 tablespoon ground cloves

4 dried hot red chilies, each about
  1½ inches long, washed,
  stemmed and coarsely crumbled
  (*caution: see note, appendix*)
3 medium-sized bay leaves, finely
  crumbled

Mix the mustard, coriander, dill, allspice, cloves, chilies and bay leaves together in a jar, cover tightly and store the boil at room temperature.

## Fried Ipswich Clams (New England)

To serve 6

Vegetable oil for deep frying  
3 eggs  
1 cup milk  
1 cup flour  
3 cups drained, shucked Ipswich clams, or substitute 3 cups any other drained, shucked soft-shell or long-neck clams  
Salt  
Lemon wedges

Preheat the oven to its lowest setting. Line a large jelly-roll pan with a double thickness of paper towels and place it in the middle of the oven.

Pour vegetable oil into a deep fryer or large, heavy saucepan to a depth of about 3 inches and heat until the oil reaches a temperature of 375° on a deep-frying thermometer.

In a bowl, beat the eggs with a whisk or fork until well blended, then stir in the milk. Spread the flour on a long strip of wax paper.

Drop the clams into the egg-milk mixture and let them soak for a minute. Pick up a handful of the soaked clams, roll them quickly in the flour until well coated, then place them in a large sieve and shake vigorously to remove the excess flour.

Immediately drop the floured clams into the hot oil. Separating them with a slotted spoon or spatula, deep-fry the clams for 1 or 2 minutes until they are a delicate golden color. As they brown, transfer them to the paper-lined pan and keep them warm in the oven while you flour and deep-fry the remaining clams in similar fashion.

Serve the clams hot, salted and accompanied by wedges of lemon.

## Steamed Clams (New England)

To serve 4

8 dozen steamer or small soft-shell or long-neck clams  
4 tablespoons butter, cut into ½-inch bits, plus ½ pound butter, melted  
½ cup finely chopped onions  
2 tablespoons finely chopped fresh parsley  
3 cups water

Wash the clams thoroughly under cold running water, discarding any with broken shells as well as those whose necks do not retract when prodded gently with a finger.

In an 8- to 10-quart steamer or casserole, melt the 4 tablespoons of butter bits over moderate heat. When the foam begins to subside, add the onions and, stirring frequently, cook for about 5 minutes. When the onions are soft and translucent, stir in the parsley and 3 cups of water and bring to a boil over high heat. Add the clams, cover tightly, and steam for 5 to 8 minutes, turning them about in the pot once or twice with a slotted spoon. All the shells should open; discard any clams that remain shut.

With tongs or a slotted spoon, transfer the clams to a deep heated platter or serving bowl. Strain the broth remaining in the steamer through a sieve lined with a double thickness of damp cheesecloth and set over a bowl. Pour the broth into 4 heated soup cups and serve the melted butter separately in individual bowls.

To eat a steamed clam, remove it from the shell with a small fork or your fingers, dip it into the broth to moisten the clam and remove any trace of sand, and then immerse it in the melted butter.

NOTE: Though steamers taste best when fresh, they can be safely kept in the refrigerator for 2 or 3 days. Place them in a bowl or pan and store them uncovered so that the clams can breathe. Do not wash them until you are ready to steam them.

### Tartar Sauce (South)

To make about 1 cup

2 tablespoons tarragon vinegar
1 teaspoon dry mustard
⅛ teaspoon ground hot red pepper (cayenne)
½ teaspoon salt
¼ cup finely chopped dill pickles
2 tablespoons finely chopped onions

1 tablespoon finely cut fresh chives
1 tablespoon finely chopped fresh parsley
1 teaspoon finely chopped capers
1 cup freshly made mayonnaise or substitute unsweetened bottled mayonnaise

Combine the vinegar, mustard, red pepper and salt in a bowl and beat with a wire whisk until the spices are dissolved. Stir in the pickles, onions, chives, parsley and capers. Then beat in the mayonnaise and taste for seasoning. Cover with foil or plastic wrap and refrigerate for at least 2 hours before serving.

Tartar sauce is traditionally served as an accompaniment to deep-fried fish or crab cakes.* Tightly covered and refrigerated, it can safely be kept for 1 or 2 days.

* See index.

To serve 4

2 teaspoons butter, softened, plus 4
   tablespoons butter
6 tablespoons soft fresh crumbs
   made from homemade-type white
   bread, pulverized in a blender or
   finely shredded with a fork
2 tablespoons flour
¾ cup milk
2 hard-cooked eggs, the yolks
   rubbed through a fine sieve with
   the back of a spoon, and the
   whites finely chopped

2 teaspoons strained fresh lemon juice
1 teaspoon Worcestershire sauce
¼ teaspoon Tabasco
½ teaspoon dry mustard
¼ teaspoon ground hot red pepper
   (cayenne)
1 teaspoon salt
Freshly ground black pepper
1 pound fresh, frozen or canned
   lump crabmeat, thoroughly
   drained and picked over to
   remove all bits of cartilage
3 tablespoons finely chopped green
   pepper

Preheat the oven to 375°. With a pastry brush, spread the 2 teaspoons of softened butter over the bottoms of 4 medium-sized natural or ceramic crab or scallop shells.

In a heavy 8- to 10-inch skillet, melt 2 tablespoons of butter over moderate heat. Drop in the bread crumbs and stir until they are crisp and golden. With a rubber spatula, scrape the entire contents of the pan into a small bowl and set aside.

In the same skillet, melt the remaining 2 tablespoons of butter over moderate heat. When the foam begins to subside, add the flour and mix well. Stirring the mixture constantly with a wire whisk, pour in the milk in a slow stream and cook over high heat until the sauce comes to a boil, thickens and is smooth. Then reduce the heat to low and simmer the sauce for 2 or 3 minutes.

Remove the skillet from the heat and stir the sieved egg yolks into the sauce. When they are well incorporated, beat in the lemon juice, Worcestershire sauce, Tabasco, dry mustard, red pepper, salt and a few grindings of black pepper. Now add the crabmeat, chopped green pepper and chopped egg whites and toss the mixture together gently but thoroughly with a table fork. Taste for seasoning.

Spoon the crab mixture into the buttered shells, dividing it evenly among them and slightly mounding the centers. Sprinkle the reserved crumbs over the tops.

Bake the deviled crab in the upper third of the oven for 15 to 20 minutes, then slide them under the broiler for 30 seconds to brown the tops, if desired. Serve at once, directly from the shells.

To serve 4

1 egg
2 tablespoons freshly made
   mayonnaise, or substitute
   bottled mayonnaise
½ teaspoon dry mustard
⅛ teaspoon ground hot red pepper
   (cayenne)
⅛ teaspoon Tabasco
½ teaspoon salt
½ teaspoon ground white pepper
1 pound fresh, frozen or canned

crabmeat, drained and picked
   over to remove all cartilage
3 tablespoons finely chopped fresh
   parsley
1½ tablespoons fresh crumbs
   made from unsalted soda
   crackers, pulverized in a blender
   or with a rolling pin
Vegetable oil for deep frying
1 lemon, cut into 8 wedges
Tartar sauce

In a deep bowl, beat the egg lightly with a wire whisk. Add the mayonnaise, mustard, red pepper, Tabasco, salt and white pepper and whisk until the mixture is smooth. Then add the crabmeat, parsley and cracker crumbs and toss together all the ingredients with a fork. Divide the mixture into 8 equal portions, and shape each of these into a ball about 2 inches in diameter. Wrap in wax paper and chill the cakes for 30 minutes.

Pour oil into a deep fryer or large heavy saucepan to a depth of 3 inches and heat the oil to a temperature of 375° on a deep-frying thermometer.

Deep-fry the crab cakes 4 at a time, turning them with a slotted spoon for 2 or 3 minutes until they are golden on all sides. As they brown, transfer them to paper towels to drain. Arrange the crab cakes with the lemon wedges on a heated platter. Serve at once, accompanied by the tartar sauce in a separate bowl.

## *Fried Soft-Shell Crabs* (*South*)

To serve 4

12 soft-shell crabs, cleaned
1 tablespoon salt
1 cup flour
11 tablespoons butter

3 to 6 tablespoons vegetable oil
6 tablespoons finely chopped fresh
   parsley
3 tablespoons strained fresh lemon
   juice

Preheat the oven to its lowest setting. Then line a large shallow baking dish with a double thickness of paper towels and place it on the middle shelf of the oven.

Wash the crabs under cold running water, pat them completely dry with paper towels and season them evenly with the salt. One at a time, dip the crabs in the flour to coat both sides and shake vigorously to remove the excess flour.

153

## How to Eat a Lobster

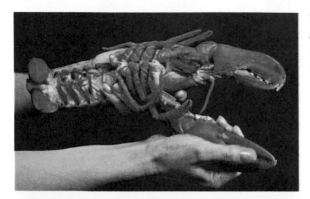

The lobster is a delicious but tantalizingly difficult food to enjoy. Yet with a lobster cracker and picks, and the proper approach, the last tender morsel can be efficiently extracted.

1 *Twist off the large claws (top of page)* and crack them *(above)* with cracker, pliers or hammer.

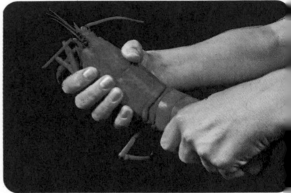

2 *Grip the lobster and separate the tail from the body by bending it up or down until it cracks.*

3 *Break off the fan-shaped flippers from the tail by bending them back until they snap free.*

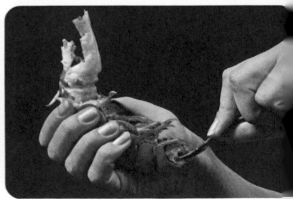

4 *Hold the tail; insert a pick or fork in the flipper end and push meat out of the opposite end.*

In a heavy 10- to 12-inch skillet, melt 3 tablespoons of the butter with 3 tablespoons of the oil over moderate heat until the foam begins to subside. Fry the crabs, 2 or 3 at a time, for about 5 minutes, turning them frequently with tongs and regulating the heat so that they color richly and evenly without burning. As they brown, transfer the crabs to the lined dish to drain and keep them warm in the oven while you fry the rest. Add the remaining 3 tablespoons of oil to the skillet, a spoonful at a time, if necessary.

Just before serving, melt the remaining 8 tablespoons of butter over moderate heat in a 6- to 8-inch skillet, regulating the heat and stirring to prevent the butter from browning. Remove the pan from the heat and stir in the chopped parsley and lemon juice.

Arrange the crabs attractively on a heated platter and dribble a few tablespoonfuls of the butter sauce over them. Present the rest of the butter separately in a small bowl or sauceboat.

## Boiled Lobster *(New England)*

To serve 2 to 4

| Two 1- to 3-pound live lobsters | ½ pound butter, melted |
|---|---|

Pour enough water into a 12- to 14-quart pot to fill it halfway and bring the water to a boil over high heat. Plunge the lobsters head first into the pot. They should be entirely submerged; if not add more boiling water.

Cover the pot tightly, return the water to a boil, then reduce the heat to moderate. Regulate the heat as needed to prevent the water from boiling

Pull off the shell. The body contains the *malley*, or liver, and, in some females, the roe.

6 Eat the small claws by sucking out the meat and juices as though you were sucking on a straw.

over, but keep the liquid at a boil throughout the cooking. Do not over-cook the lobsters. Allow about 12 minutes cooking time for 1-pound lob-sters; 15 to 18 minutes for 1½ pounds; 20 to 22 minutes for 2 pounds; and 30 to 35 minutes for 3-pound lobsters. (The shell may turn red be-fore the water even returns to a boil, therefore color is not a reliable test for doneness.) A better test is to remove one of the lobsters from the pot and grasp the end of one of the small legs at either side of the body. Jerk the lobster sharply. If the leg pulls away from the body, the lobster is done. If the leg remains attached to the body, boil the lobster for 2 or 3 minutes longer.

With tongs or a slotted spoon, transfer the lobsters to a heated platter or individual plates and serve at once. Pour the melted butter into small bowls and present it separately with the lobsters.

*Locke-Ober's lobster Savannah must be prepared in a special way. Tie the live lobster firmly to a long wooden spoon with kitchen string (left), to keep the shell flat and the tail from curling up. After cooking, cut a long oval-shaped opening in the back of the shell (center), using a sharp boning knife or kitchen scissors. Cut an oval about 1½ to 2 inches wide from the base of the head to within ½ inch of the fan-shaped tail. Pick out the meat with a seafood fork, then remove and discard the stomach sac and intestinal vein, but save the tomalley and any roe. After boiling you may cut or twist off the claws and antennae.*

To serve 4

Four 1½-pound live lobsters
3 tablespoons butter
½ cup thinly sliced fresh
   mushroom caps
¼ cup finely chopped green pepper
2 tablespoons flour
1 cup milk
¼ cup cognac, or substitute ¼ cup
   dry sherry

1 teaspoon paprika
1 teaspoon salt
Freshly ground black pepper
2 tablespoons canned pimiento,
   drained and finely chopped
¼ cup soft fresh crumbs made
   from homemade-type white
   bread, pulverized in a blender or
   finely shredded with a fork
3 tablespoons freshly grated
   imported Parmesan cheese

In an 8-quart fish poacher or stock pot, bring 5 quarts of water to a boil over high heat. Meanwhile, with short lengths of kitchen string, tie the head, midsection and tail of each lobster to a long wooden spoon. The spoons will hold the shells flat and prevent the tails from curling when the lobsters are boiled.

Plunge 2 lobsters into the pot and return the water to a boil. (The water should cover the lobsters by at least 1 inch; if necessary, add more boiling water.) Set the lid on the pot and cook briskly for 15 to 18 minutes. To test for doneness, remove one of the lobsters from the pot and grasp the end of one of the small legs at either side of the body. Jerk the lobster sharply. If the body drops away from the leg, the lobster is done. If the body remains attached to the leg, boil the lobster for 2 or 3 minutes longer. With tongs, transfer the cooked lobsters to a platter to drain, and boil the remaining 2 lobsters similarly in the same water.

Cut off all the strings and transfer the lobsters to a cutting board. Then cut or twist off the antennae and discard them. Twist off the claws of each lobster at the point where they meet the body, crack each claw in two or three places with a cleaver, and pick out all the meat. Cut the lobster meat into ½-inch pieces and reserve it; discard the claw shells.

One at a time place the lobsters on the board. With a sharp boning knife or heavy kitchen scissors, carefully cut a long oval-shaped opening out of the back of the shell. Start cutting at the base of the head and finish cutting just before the fan-shaped tail; depending on the size of the lobster, make the oval 2 to 2½ inches wide. Reaching through the opening, pick out all the meat from the body and tail. Remove and discard the gelatinous sac (stomach) in the head and the long white intestinal vein attached to it. Scoop out the greenish tomalley (liver) and reserve it. Discard the red coral (roe), if there is any. Cut the meat into ½-inch pieces and set the meat and shell aside. (At this point the lobster meat and body shells may be covered tightly with foil or plastic wrap and safely kept in the refrigerator for up to a day.)

Half an hour before you plan to serve the lobsters, preheat the oven to 400°. In a heavy 10- to 12-inch skillet, melt the butter over moderate heat. When the foam begins to subside, add the mushroom caps and green pepper and, stirring frequently, cook for 8 to 10 minutes until the liquid that has accumulated in the pan has almost completely evaporated. Do not let the mushrooms or peppers brown; watch carefully and regulate the heat as necessary.

Stir in the flour and mix well. Then pour in the milk and, stirring constantly with a whisk, cook over high heat until the sauce comes to a boil, thickens lightly and is smooth. Reduce the heat to low and stir in the reserved tomalley, the cognac (or sherry), paprika, salt and a few grindings of pepper. Simmer for about 5 minutes, then add the lobster meat and pimiento and turn them about with a spoon until they are coated with sauce. Taste for seasoning.

Spoon the lobster mixture into the shells, dividing it evenly among them and mounding it attractively. Mix the bread crumbs and grated Parmesan together in a bowl and sprinkle them over the filling. Arrange the shells side by side on a jelly-roll pan and bake in the middle of the oven for 15 minutes, or until the sauce is bubbling and the tops lightly browned. If you like, slide the lobsters under a preheated broiler for 30 seconds or so to brown the tops further. Serve at once.

## Lobster Newburg

| | |
|---|---|
| To serve 4 to 6 | ¾ teaspoon salt |
| 6 tablespoons butter | ⅛ teaspoon cayenne |
| 3 cups cooked lobster, fresh or canned, cut into 2-inch pieces | ½ teaspoon lemon juice |
| ⅓ cup Madeira or dry sherry | 6 patty shells, or 2 to 3 cups of steamed rice, or 8 to 12 buttered toast points |
| 1½ cups heavy cream | |
| 5 egg yolks | Paprika (optional) |

In a large enameled or stainless-steel skillet, melt the butter over moderate heat. When the foam subsides, add the lobster meat and, stirring constantly, cook for about a minute. Pour in the Madeira or sherry and 1 cup of the heavy cream and, stirring, bring it to a boil. Reduce the heat to its lowest point and, still stirring, cook for about 2 minutes. In a small bowl, beat the egg yolks into the remaining ½ cup of cream. Beat into them 4 tablespoons of the simmering lobster sauce, and then, in a slow stream, pour the mixture back into the skillet, stirring constantly. Cook over moderate heat until the sauce thickens, but under no circumstances let it come to a boil or it will curdle. Season with the salt, cayenne and lemon juice. Serve immediately in patty shells, on beds of steamed rice, or on hot buttered toast points, and sprinkle the lobster Newburg lightly with paprika if you like.

## Boiled Crawfish *(Creole-Acadian)*

To serve 4 to 6

6 to 8 quarts water
2 lemons, cut in half crosswise
4 medium-sized onions, with skins intact
2 celery stalks, including the leaves, cut into 3-inch lengths
1 dried hot red chili *(caution: see note, appendix)*

4 garlic cloves, peeled and bruised with the flat of a cleaver or large heavy knife
1 cup shellfish boil, or substitute 1 cup commercial shrimp spice or crab boil
2 tablespoons salt
20 pounds live crawfish

Combine the water, lemons, onions, celery, chili, garlic, shellfish boil and salt in a 10- to 12-quart enameled pot, and bring to a boil over high heat. Cover tightly, reduce the heat to low, and cook for 20 minutes.

Meanwhile, soak the live crawfish in a sinkful of cold water for at least 10 minutes, then wash them thoroughly—a small batch at a time —in a colander set under cold running water.

With tongs, drop about 5 pounds of the live crawfish into the pot and boil briskly, uncovered, for 5 minutes. Transfer the boiled crawfish to a heated platter, then drop about 5 more pounds of live crawfish into the stock remaining in the pot and boil them for 5 minutes. Repeat the entire procedure two more times and, when all of the crawfish have been boiled, serve them at once in their shells (directions on how to crack and eat crawfish, opposite). Because they are so highly spiced, they are eaten without any accompaniment except cold beer.

NOTE: In Louisiana, crabs and shrimp are boiled and served in the same fashion as crawfish. Substitute three dozen live blue crabs or 4 pounds of large shrimp in their shells for the crawfish, and boil them in one batch. Boil the crabs for 10 to 15 minutes, the shrimp 5 minutes.

## *Moules Marinière* ( New England )
### MUSSELS STEAMED IN WINE BROTH

To serve 4 as a first course

| | |
|---|---|
| 4 dozen large mussels in their shells | 1½ cups dry white wine |
| 4 tablespoons butter cut into small bits, plus ½ pound butter, melted | 1 cup water |
| | 2 tablespoons finely chopped fresh parsley |
| ½ cup finely chopped onions | ⅛ teaspoon crumbled dried thyme |

Scrub the mussels thoroughly under cold running water with a stiff brush or soapless steel-mesh scouring pad. With a small, sharp knife scrape or pull the black hairlike tufts off the shells and discard them.

In a 6- to 8-quart enameled or stainless-steel casserole, melt the butter bits over moderate heat. When the foam begins to subside, add the onions and, stirring frequently, cook for about 5 minutes until they are soft and translucent but not brown. Stir in the wine, water, parsley and thyme. Drop in the mussels and bring to a boil over high heat. Cover tightly, reduce the heat to low and let the mussels steam for about 10 minutes, turning the mussels about once or twice with a slotted spoon. When the mussels have steamed the allotted time, all the shells should have opened; discard any that remain shut.

With a slotted spoon, transfer the mussels to a large, heated platter or individual serving plates. Strain the broth into a bowl, using a fine sieve lined with a double thickness of dampened cheesecloth. Pour the broth into 4 heated soup cups and serve the melted butter separately in individual bowls on the side.

To eat a steamed mussel, remove it from the shell with a small fork, dip it into the broth to moisten the mussel and remove any traces of sand, and then immerse it in the melted butter.


## *Fried Scallops, Portuguese Style* (New England)

To serve 2

| | |
|---|---|
| 1 pound (1 pint) fresh bay scallops or frozen scallops, thoroughly defrosted | 1 cup flour |
| | 1 teaspoon finely chopped garlic |
| 8 tablespoons butter, cut into ½-inch bits | 3 tablespoons finely chopped fresh parsley |
| | ¼ teaspoon salt |
| | Freshly ground black pepper |

Wash the scallops quickly under cold running water, then spread them in one layer on a jelly-roll pan covered with a linen towel. Drape a second towel over the scallops and place them in the refrigerator for about 4 hours to drain thoroughly.

In a small, heavy saucepan or skillet, melt the butter over low heat, turning the bits about with a wooden spoon to melt them slowly and completely without letting the butter brown. Remove the pan from the heat and let the butter rest for a minute or so. Then skim off the foam from the surface and discard it.

Tipping the pan at a slight angle, spoon the clear butter on top into a heavy 12-inch skillet (preferably a slope-sided one with a non-stick cooking surface). Leave behind all of the milky solids that will have settled at the bottom of the pan.

Place the flour in a large bowl and drop the scallops into it. With a slotted spoon or your fingers toss the scallops about gently until they are coated on all sides with the flour. Then turn them out into a sieve and shake them vigorously to remove the excess flour.

Warm the clear butter in the skillet over high heat for 10 seconds. Add the scallops and, sliding the pan back and forth to turn them about, fry them for 2 or 3 minutes until they are firm but not brown. Do not overcook the scallops.

Add the chopped garlic and parsley to the skillet and slide the pan vigorously back and forth for about 30 seconds longer.

Mound the scallops attractively on a heated platter, season with the salt and a few grindings of pepper, and serve at once.

## Skewered Sea Scallops *(New England)*

To serve 4

1 medium-sized onion, peeled
¼ cup strained fresh lemon juice
½ teaspoon salt
Freshly ground black pepper
1½ pounds sea scallops,
   thoroughly defrosted if frozen,

and cut into halves lengthwise if
   they are larger than
   1½ inches in diameter
4 tablespoons butter, melted
1 firm ripe tomato, cut into 8
   wedges
1 lemon, cut into 4 or 8 wedges

Using the second smallest holes of a four-sided grater, grate the onion into a deep bowl. Stir in the lemon juice, salt and a few grindings of pepper. Add the scallops and turn them about with a spoon until evenly coated. Cover the bowl with foil or plastic wrap and marinate the scallops at room temperature for at least 1 hour, or in the refrigerator for 2 hours, turning the scallops over from time to time.

Light a layer of briquettes in a charcoal broiler and let them burn until a white ash appears on the surface, or preheat the broiler of your stove to its highest setting.

161

Remove the scallops from the marinade and, dividing the pieces evenly, thread them onto 4 long skewers and push the scallops compactly together so that there are no spaces between them. With a pastry brush, thoroughly coat the scallops with the melted butter. Broil about 4 inches from the heat for 8 to 10 minutes, turning the skewers from time to time and basting the scallops frequently with the remaining melted butter. The scallops are done when they are opaque, firm to the touch and flecked all over with brown.

With the side of a knife, slide the scallops off the skewers onto a heated platter or individual plates. Arrange the tomato and lemon wedges attractively around the scallops and serve at once.

## Shrimp Pilau *(South)*

To serve 4 to 6

| | |
|---|---|
| 6 medium-sized firm ripe tomatoes, or substitute 2 cups chopped drained canned tomatoes | 3 cups chicken stock, fresh or canned |
| 2 cups uncooked long-grain white rice, not the converted variety | 2 teaspoons Worcestershire sauce |
| 2 pounds medium-sized raw shrimp (about 21 to 25 to the pound) | 1 teaspoon ground mace |
| 8 slices bacon, cut into ¼-inch dice | ½ teaspoon ground hot red pepper (cayenne) |
| 2 cups finely chopped onions | 2 teaspoons salt |
| | 2 tablespoons finely chopped fresh parsley |

If you are using fresh tomatoes, prepare them in the following fashion: Drop 2 or 3 at a time into a pan of boiling water for 15 seconds. Run them under cold water and peel them with a small sharp knife. Cut out the stems, then slice each tomato in half crosswise. Squeeze the halves gently to remove the seeds and juice, then finely chop the tomatoes.

Place the rice in a sieve and wash it under cold running water, stirring the grains with a fork until the draining water runs clear. Set aside.

Peel the shrimp. Devein them by making a shallow incision down their backs with a small sharp knife and lifting out the black or white intestinal vein with the point of the knife. Wash the shrimp, then refrigerate until ready to use.

Preheat the oven to 350°. In a heavy 3- to 4-quart casserole, fry the bacon dice over moderate heat, stirring until they are crisp and brown and have rendered all their fat. With a slotted spoon, transfer the bacon to paper towels to drain.

Pour off all but about 3 tablespoons of the fat remaining in the casserole and drop in the onions. Stirring frequently, cook the onions over moderate heat for about 5 minutes, or until they are soft and translucent but not brown. Add the rice and stir until the grains glisten with the fat, then mix in the chicken stock or water, the tomatoes, Worcestershire, mace, red pepper and salt.

Bring to a boil over high heat, cover the casserole tightly and place it in the middle of the oven. Bake for 30 minutes, then add the shrimp and bacon and toss together gently but thoroughly. Cover tightly and continue to bake 10 minutes longer, or until the liquid in the pan has been absorbed and the shrimp are pink and tender.

Remove the casserole from the oven and set it aside without removing the cover for 10 minutes. Fluff the shrimp pilau with a fork, strew the parsley over the top and serve at once, directly from the casserole.

## *Shrimp-and-Ham Jambalaya* (Creole-Acadian)

To serve 6 to 8

2 cups water
2 teaspoons salt
1 cup short-grain white rice
2 pounds uncooked medium-sized
    shrimp (about 20 to 24 to the
    pound)
6 tablespoons butter
1½ cups finely chopped onions
2 tablespoons finely chopped garlic
A 1-pound can tomatoes, drained
    and finely chopped, with all their
    liquid
3 tablespoons canned tomato paste
½ cup finely chopped celery

¼ cup finely chopped green pepper
1 tablespoon finely chopped fresh
    parsley, preferably the flat-leaf
    Italian variety
3 whole cloves, pulverized with a
    mortar and pestle or finely
    crushed with a kitchen mallet or
    the flat of a heavy cleaver
½ teaspoon crumbled dried thyme
½ teaspoon ground hot red pepper
    (cayenne)
¼ teaspoon freshly ground black
    pepper
1 pound cooked lean smoked ham,
    trimmed of excess fat and cut into
    ½-inch cubes

Bring the water and 1 teaspoon of the salt to a boil in a small saucepan set over high heat. Add the rice, stir once or twice, and immediately cover the pan. Reduce the heat to low and simmer for about 20 minutes, or until the rice is tender and the grains have absorbed all of the liquid in the pan. Fluff the rice with a fork, cover, and set it aside.

Meanwhile, shell the shrimp. Devein them by making a shallow incision down their backs with a small sharp knife and lifting out the black or white intestinal vein with the point of the knife. Wash the shrimp briefly in a colander set under cold running water. Drop the shrimp into enough boiling salted water to cover them completely and cook briskly, uncovered, for 4 to 5 minutes, or until they are pink and firm. With a slotted spoon, transfer the shrimp to a bowl and set aside.

In a heavy 5- to 6-quart casserole, melt the butter over moderate heat. When the foam begins to subside, add the onions and garlic and, stirring frequently, cook for about 5 minutes, or until they are soft and translucent but not brown. Add the tomatoes, the tomato liquid and the tomato paste, and stir over moderate heat for 5 minutes. Then add the celery, green pepper, parsley, cloves, thyme, red pepper, black pepper and the remaining teaspoon of salt. Stirring frequently, cook uncovered over moderate heat until the vegetables are tender and the mixture is thick enough to hold its shape lightly in the spoon.

Add the ham and, stirring frequently, cook for 5 minutes. Then stir in the shrimp and, when they are heated through, add the reserved rice. Stir over moderate heat until the mixture is hot and the rice has absorbed any liquid in the pan.

Taste for seasoning and serve the shrimp-and-ham jambalaya at once, directly from the casserole or mounded in a heated bowl.

## Shrimp Creole

To serve 6

| | |
|---|---|
| 12 medium-sized firm ripe tomatoes or 4 cups coarsely chopped drained canned tomatoes | 2 teaspoons finely chopped garlic |
| | 1 cup water |
| | 2 medium-sized bay leaves |
| 3 pounds uncooked medium-sized shrimp (about 20 to 24 to the pound) | 1 tablespoon paprika |
| | ½ teaspoon ground hot red pepper (cayenne) |
| ½ cup vegetable oil | 1 tablespoon salt |
| 2 cups coarsely chopped onions | 2 tablespoons cornstarch mixed with ¼ cup cold water |
| 1 cup coarsely chopped green peppers | 6 to 8 cups freshly cooked long-grain white rice |
| 1 cup coarsely chopped celery | |

If you are using fresh tomatoes, drop them three or four at a time into a pan of boiling water and remove them after 15 seconds. Run cold water over them and peel them with a small sharp knife. Cut out the stems, then slice the tomatoes in half crosswise, and squeeze the halves gently to remove the seeds and juice. Chop the tomatoes coarsely. (Canned tomatoes need only be thoroughly drained and chopped.)

Shell the shrimp. Devein them by making a shallow incision down the back with a small sharp knife and lifting out the black or white intestinal vein with the point of the knife. Wash the shrimp in a colander set under cold running water and spread them on paper towels to drain.

In a heavy 4- to 5-quart casserole, heat the oil over moderate heat until a light haze forms above it. Add the onions, green peppers, celery and garlic and, stirring frequently, cook for about 5 minutes, or until the vegetables are soft and translucent but not brown.

Stir in the tomatoes, water, bay leaves, paprika, red pepper and salt, and bring to a boil over high heat. Reduce the heat to low, cover the casserole partially and, stirring occasionally, simmer the mixture for 20 to 25 minutes, or until it is thick enough to hold its shape almost solidly in a spoon. Stir in the shrimp and continue to simmer, partially covered, for about 5 minutes longer, or until they are pink and firm to the touch.

Stir the cornstarch-and-water mixture once or twice to recombine it, and pour it into the casserole. Stir over low heat for 2 or 3 minutes, until the sauce thickens slightly. Pick out and discard the bay leaves, then taste the sauce for seasoning.

Serve the shrimp Creole at once, directly from the casserole, accompanied by the rice in a separate bowl. Or, if you prefer, mound the rice on a deep heated platter and ladle the shrimp Creole around it.

## Shrimp de Jonghe

| To serve 6 to 8 | Salt |
|---|---|
| 2 cloves garlic | A pinch of nutmeg |
| ¼ pound butter | 1 pinch of mace |
| 1 teaspoon chopped parsley | Freshly ground black pepper |
| 1 teaspoon chopped chervil | ⅔ cup bread crumbs |
| 1 teaspoon chopped shallots | ½ cup dry sherry |
| 1 teaspoon chopped tarragon | 2 pounds shrimp |

Preheat the oven to 400°. Crush the garlic with a fork and gradually work it into the butter along with the parsley, chervil, shallots, tarragon, salt, nutmeg, mace and pepper. Work in the crumbs and sherry.

Shell and clean the shrimp and cook them in boiling salted water for 3 minutes. Butter 6 to 8 ramekins or individual baking dishes. Arrange layers of the shrimp and the herbed crumb mixture alternately in the ramekins. Top with butter crumbs and bake for 10 to 15 minutes.

## Shrimp Chow Mein *(Chinese-American)*
### SHRIMP WITH CHINESE VEGETABLES

To serve 4

6 tablespoons peanut or other vegetable oil

2 pounds shrimp, shelled and deveined (*see shrimp-stuffed artichokes\**), then split in half lengthwise and cut lengthwise into ¼-inch wide strips

2 teaspoons finely chopped garlic

1 medium-sized onion, cut in half lengthwise, then crosswise into ¼-inch-wide semicircles (1 cup)

2 stalks celery, cut crosswise into 4-inch lengths, then cut lengthwise into ⅛-inch-wide strips (1 cup)

1 cup finely shredded *bok choy*

(Chinese cabbage) or white cabbage

1 cup snow peas, thoroughly defrosted if frozen, and cut in half diagonally

½ cup canned water chestnuts, drained and thinly sliced

½ pound fresh mushrooms, cut lengthwise into ⅛-inch-wide slices (2 cups)

1½ cups canned bean sprouts, drained

1 teaspoon salt

3 tablespoons soy sauce

1¾ cups chicken stock, fresh or canned

2 tablespoons cornstarch

½ cup toasted slivered almonds

Heat the oil in a 12-inch *wok* or in a 10- to 12-inch heavy skillet until it is very hot but not smoking. Add the shrimp and toss them over moderately high heat for 1 minute, or until they turn pink. Transfer the shrimp to a plate and add the garlic, onion, celery, cabbage, snow peas, water chestnuts, mushrooms and bean sprouts to the skillet. Stirring constantly, cook the vegetables for 2 or 3 minutes, then sprinkle with the salt, pour in the soy sauce and 1¼ cups of the chicken stock, and cover the pan. Cook over moderate heat for 6 to 8 minutes, or until the vegetables are tender but still slightly resistant to the bite.

Replace the shrimp in the skillet and, in a small mixing bowl, combine the cornstarch and the remaining ½ cup of chicken stock. Stir to dissolve the cornstarch, then pour into the chow mein. When the sauce has thickened and become clear—about 30 seconds—remove the pan from the heat. Transfer the chow mein to a heated platter and sprinkle with the almonds. Serve at once, with Chinese noodles or boiled rice.

*\* See index.*

# *Poultry*

At the turn of the century, chickens were Sunday-best fare that cost a walloping twenty cents a pound—much more than roast beef. Since then, American farmers have perfected techniques for mass producing chickens more economically, if not more flavorfully, and cooks can afford to serve chicken any day of the week. A versatile bird, chicken can be fried Southern-style, with or without gravy; batter-fried in the manner of the Eastern Heartland; roasted; stewed; combined with pineapples in a Hawaiian sauce; cut up in pies; layered with noodles; or the breasts boned and lightly sauced.

Nearly as popular as chicken, turkey was once a holiday luxury but has now become a year-round staple. Scholars think it unlikely that the Pilgrims feasted on wild turkey at the first Thanksgiving, but it is hard to imagine Thanksgiving today without a richly browned turkey, stuffed with cornbread and pecans in the Southern style, or with a New England oyster-and-bread-cube mélange. Curiously, although most Americans prefer white breast meat (and, indeed, large-breasted birds have been specially bred for this purpose), most cooks roast turkeys until the dark leg meat is no longer pink—meaning that the breast meat is dried out. One solution is to cut off the legs and thighs and cook them longer than the breast. A simpler solution is to roast the whole bird for a shorter time, thus discovering how deliciously juicy dark meat with a bit of pink can taste.

Delightful and festive as ducks may be, they have a high proportion of bone and fat compared to chicken or turkey. A lovely four-pound duck will only serve two hungry—or four polite—persons. Most commercially grown ducks are not bred from the wild native variety, but from a Chinese strain brought to New York in the late nineteenth century and popularized as Long Island duckling. Whether simply broiled Long Island-style or enhanced with grapefruit juice, honey and soy sauce in the Far West, the Chinese bird has become all-American.

## Batter-fried Chicken (Eastern Heartland)

To serve 4

| | |
|---|---|
| 1 egg | 1½ teaspoons salt |
| ½ cup milk | Vegetable oil for deep frying |
| 1 cup unsifted flour | A 3- to 3½-pound chicken, cut |
| 1 teaspoon double-acting baking | into 8 serving pieces |
| powder | 2 teaspoons paprika |

In a deep bowl, beat the egg and milk lightly together with a wire whisk. Combine the flour, baking powder and ½ teaspoon of the salt, and add them to the egg mixture a few tablespoonfuls at a time, stirring gently after each addition. Stir until the batter is smooth, but do not beat or over-mix. Set the batter aside at room temperature for about 30 minutes.

Preheat the oven to its lowest setting. Then line a large shallow baking dish with a double thickness of paper towels and place it in the middle of the oven.

Pour vegetable oil into a deep fryer or large heavy saucepan to a depth of 2 to 3 inches and heat the oil until it reaches a temperature of 360° on a deep-frying thermometer.

Meanwhile, pat the pieces of chicken completely dry with paper towels and season them evenly on both sides with the paprika and the remaining teaspoon of salt.

Dip the chicken drumsticks and thighs into the batter, one at a time, and when they are thoroughly coated place them in a deep-frying basket. Lower the basket into the hot oil and deep-fry the chicken for 12 to 15 minutes, turning the drumsticks and thighs frequently with kitchen tongs so that they color richly and evenly.

To test for doneness, after 12 minutes lift a thigh out of the oil and pierce it deeply with the point of a small skewer or sharp knife. The juice that trickles out should be pale yellow; if it is still tinged with pink, deep-fry the chicken for 1 or 2 minutes longer. Transfer the drumsticks and thighs to the paper-lined dish to drain, and keep them warm in the oven.

Then dip the wings and breasts into the batter, place them in the deep-frying basket, and lower it into the oil. Fry the white-meat pieces for about 7 or 8 minutes, then drain them on the paper-lined dish.

Arrange the chicken attractively on a heated platter and serve at once.

To serve 4

A 2½-pound frying chicken, cut into
   serving pieces
Salt

1 cup flour
1 cup lard, or ½ cup vegetable
   shortening combined with
   ½ cup lard

Wash the chicken pieces under cold running water and pat them thoroughly dry with paper towels. Sprinkle the pieces with salt on all sides. Put the cup of flour in a sturdy paper bag. Drop the chicken into the bag a few pieces at a time and shake the bag until each piece is thoroughly coated with flour. Remove the chicken pieces from the bag and vigorously shake them free of all excess flour. Lay them side by side on a sheet of wax paper. Preheat the oven to 200° and in the middle of the oven place a shallow baking dish.

Over high heat melt the lard or combined lard and shortening in a 10- or 12-inch heavy skillet. The fat should be ¼ inch deep. If it is not, add a little more. When a light haze forms above it, add the chicken pieces, starting them skin side down. It is preferable to begin frying the legs and thighs first, since they will take longer to cook than the breasts and wings. Cover the pan and fry the chicken over moderate heat for about 6 to 8 minutes, checking every now and then to make sure the chicken does not burn. When the pieces are deep brown on one side, turn them over and cover the pan again. Transfer the finished chicken to the baking dish in the oven and continue frying until all the pieces are cooked. Keep the chicken warm in the oven while you make the gravy.

CREAM GRAVY
2 tablespoons flour
¾ cup chicken stock, fresh or canned

½ to ¾ cup light cream
Salt
White pepper

Pour off all but 2 tablespoons of fat in the frying pan. Add 2 tablespoons of flour, and stir until the fat and flour are well combined. Pour in the chicken stock and ½ cup of the light cream, and cook over moderate heat, beating with a whisk until the gravy is smooth and thick. If it is too thick for your taste, stir in the remaining cream to thin it. Strain it through a fine sieve if you wish. Taste for seasoning, then pour into a heated gravy boat and serve with the fried chicken arranged attractively on a heated serving platter.

## Oven-fried Chicken (South)

To serve 12 to 16

Four 2½- to 3-pound chickens,
    each cut into 8 pieces
2 tablespoons salt

2 tablespoons paprika
Freshly ground black pepper
8 tablespoons (1 quarter-pound
    stick) unsalted butter, cut into bits

Preheat the oven to 400°. Wash the chicken pieces under cold running water and pat them thoroughly dry with paper towels. Sprinkle the pieces on all sides with the salt, paprika and several grindings of black pepper. Spread the pieces out in one layer in one or more shallow baking pans. Scatter half of the butter bits evenly over the chicken and cover the pan or pans securely with a large sheet of aluminum foil. Bake in the center of the oven for 20 minutes, then remove the foil, raise the oven temperature to 450°, and bake undisturbed for 30 minutes longer. Turn over the chicken pieces with tongs, sprinkle with the remaining butter bits, and bake uncovered for an additional 30 minutes. Serve the chicken either hot or at room temperature, accompanied, if you like, by potato salad or cole slaw with boiled dressing.*

## Chicken à la King

To serve 4 to 6

A 4- to 4½-pound cooked chicken
    or 3 cups cooked chicken or
    turkey
4 tablespoons butter
½ pound mushrooms, thinly sliced
½ green pepper, shredded
2 tablespoons flour
1 cup chicken stock

Salt
White pepper
2 egg yolks
½ teaspoon paprika
1 cup cream
2 to 3 tablespoons sherry
1 piece pimiento, shredded
Patty shells or thin toast (optional)

Cut the meat into thin strips.

Melt the butter. Add the sliced mushrooms and green pepper and sauté for 5 minutes. Blend in the flour, off the fire. Add the chicken stock and stir over the fire until the sauce comes to a boil. Season with salt and a little white pepper. Beat the egg yolks and paprika lightly with a fork. Slowly beat in the cream. Add the egg-and-cream mixture to the sauce and cook until the sauce is thickened but do not let it boil again. Add the chicken and heat thoroughly. Just before serving add the sherry and pimiento. Chicken à la King can be served in patty shells or in a hot serving dish or chafing dish, garnished with triangles of thin toast.

* See index.

To serve 4

| | |
|---|---|
| 1 lemon | ½ teaspoon paprika |
| 1½ teaspoons salt | ½ cup vegetable oil |
| A 2½- to 3-pound chicken, cut | 1 cup chicken stock, fresh or canned |
| into 8 serving pieces | 2 tablespoons dark brown sugar |
| ½ cup flour | ½ teaspoon Angostura bitters |

Preheat the oven to 375°. With a sharp knife, cut the lemon in half cross-wise and slice one half into paper-thin rounds. Set the lemon slices aside and squeeze the juice of the remaining lemon half into a deep bowl. Stir the salt into the lemon juice.

Pat the pieces of chicken completely dry, drop them into the bowl with the lemon juice and salt, and turn the pieces about with a spoon to moist-en them evenly. Combine the flour and paprika in a large paper bag, add two or three pieces of chicken at a time to the bag, and shake them until they are lightly covered with the flour mixture. Remove the chicken from the bag and shake off the excess flour.

In a heavy 10- to 12-inch skillet, heat the oil over moderate heat until a light haze forms above it. Brown three or four pieces of chicken at a time in the hot oil, starting the pieces skin side down and turning them fre-quently with tongs so that they color richly and evenly all over without burning. As they brown, arrange the pieces of chicken in one layer in a large baking dish equipped with a tight-fitting cover.

Pour off the fat remaining in the skillet and in its place add the chick-en stock. Bring to a boil over high heat, meanwhile scraping in the browned particles that cling to the bottom and sides of the pan. Stir in the brown sugar and, when it is dissolved, remove the skillet from the heat and add the bitters. Pour the stock mixture over the chicken and ar-range the lemon slices on top.

Cover the dish tightly and bake the chicken in the middle of the oven for about 30 minutes, or until it is tender and shows no resistance when pierced deeply with the point of a small sharp knife. With tongs, trans-fer the chicken to a heated platter. Discard the lemon slices and strain the gravy remaining in the baking dish through a fine sieve into a bowl. With a spoon, skim as much fat as possible from the surface of the gravy. Taste for seasoning, pour the gravy over the chicken and serve at once.

171

To serve 4

A 2½- to 3-pound chicken, cut
into 8 serving pieces
½ teaspoon salt
½ teaspoon ground hot red pepper
(cayenne)
½ cup vegetable oil
4 tablespoons butter
¾ pound fresh mushrooms,
trimmed, wiped with a dampened
cloth, and finely chopped (about
4 cups)
¼ cup flour
2 cups chicken stock, fresh or
canned
¼ cup thinly sliced pitted green
olives
¼ cup dry sherry
A 10-ounce package frozen
artichoke hearts, freshly cooked

Pat the pieces of chicken completely dry with paper towels and season
them on all sides with the salt and red pepper. In a heavy 12-inch skillet,
heat the oil over moderate heat until a light haze forms above it. Fry the
chicken in the hot oil, starting the pieces skin side down and turning
them frequently with tongs for about 20 minutes, or until they brown richly and evenly. To be sure that the bird is cooked to the proper degree of
doneness, lift a thigh from the pan and pierce it deeply with the point of
a small skewer or sharp knife. The juice that trickles out should be clear
yellow; if it is still tinged with pink, fry the chicken for 2 or 3 minutes
more. As they are cooked, drain the pieces of chicken briefly on paper towels. Then arrange them on a heated platter and drape them with foil to
keep them warm.

Meanwhile, in another large heavy skillet, melt the butter over moderate heat. When the foam subsides, add the mushrooms and, stirring occasionally, cook for 5 minutes, or until the mushrooms are tender and the
liquid that accumulates in the pan has evaporated. Do not let the mushrooms brown. Remove the pan from the heat and reserve the mushrooms.

When the chicken has cooked its allotted time and been transferred to
the platter, pour off all but about 4 tablespoons of the fat remaining in
the skillet and in its place add the flour; mix well. Stirring constantly
with a wire whisk, pour in the chicken stock in a slow, thin stream and
cook over high heat until the sauce comes to a boil, thickens heavily and
is smooth. Reduce the heat to low and simmer for 2 or 3 minutes to remove the raw taste of the flour.

Stir in the mushrooms, olives, sherry and artichoke hearts, and simmer
for a minute or so longer to heat them through. Taste for seasoning, then
ladle the sauce and vegetables over the chicken and serve at once.

To serve 6 to 8

Two 2½- to 3-pound chickens,
  each cut into 8 pieces, or
  substitute 5 to 6 pounds rabbit,
  cut into serving pieces and
  thoroughly defrosted if frozen
2 pounds boneless chuck or
  shoulder of veal in 1 piece,
  trimmed of excess fat
1 teaspoon salt
Freshly ground black pepper
4 tablespoons vegetable oil
2 cups thinly sliced onions
2 cups coarsely chopped celery,
  including 2 inches of the green
  tops
1 ham bone (about 2 pounds),
  preferably from baked Smithfield
  or country ham sawed into
  2-inch pieces (optional)
1 medium-sized bay leaf
1 teaspoon basil

3 sprigs parsley
1 fresh hot red chili, washed, seeded
  and crushed *(caution: see note,*
  *appendix)*
3 pounds (about 9) tomatoes,
  peeled, seeded and coarsely
  chopped
1 pound fresh butter beans or wax
  beans (4 cups), washed and
  trimmed
8 tablespoons (1 quarter-pound
  stick) unsalted butter, cut into
  bits
4 cups fresh corn kernels, cut from
  about 8 large ears of corn, or
  substitute 4 cups thoroughly
  defrosted frozen corn kernels
1½ pounds (about 4) medium-
  sized boiling potatoes, peeled,
  boiled and coarsely mashed
  (about 4 cups)
¼ cup finely chopped parsley

Sprinkle the chicken and chuck (or veal) with the salt and several grind-ings of black pepper. In an 8- to 10-quart casserole, heat the vegetable oil until very hot but not smoking. Add the chicken a few pieces at a time, and fry over moderately high heat, turning the pieces frequently, until golden brown. Transfer the chicken to a platter. In the remaining fat, sim-ilarly brown the chuck (or veal) on all sides, then transfer it to the plat-ter of chicken. Pour off all but a thin film of the oil from the casserole, add the onions and celery and, stirring constantly, cook over moderate heat until the vegetables are soft but not brown. Return the chicken and meat to the casserole, and add the ham bone (if you are using it), bay leaf, basil, parsley sprigs, chili and tomatoes. Pour in enough cold water to cover the ingredients by 1 inch and bring to a boil over high heat. Then lower the heat and simmer tightly covered for 35 to 45 minutes, or until the chicken is tender. With tongs or a slotted spoon, transfer the chicken to a platter or cutting board, leaving the other meat in the pot.

Cover the casserole again and simmer for about 1 hour longer, or until the meat shows no resistance when pierced deeply with the prongs of a large fork. Transfer the meat and ham bone to the platter with the chicken.

Add the beans to the casserole and cook uncovered over high heat for 10 to 15 minutes, or until they are tender but still resistant to the bite.

With a small knife, remove the skin and bones from the chicken and discard them. Cut off any meat from the ham bone if you have used it, and cut the chicken meat and beef or veal into 1-inch pieces. Return all the pieces to the casserole along with any juices that may have accumulated on the platter. Stir in the butter and the corn. Simmer the stew uncovered for 5 minutes, and stir in the mashed potatoes. Stirring frequently, cook for an additional 10 minutes, until the potatoes have been absorbed by the liquid and have thickened the stew. Add the chopped parsley and taste for seasoning.

Serve the stew directly from the casserole, or from a heated bowl. Brunswick stew is often served over Southern dry rice .

## Chicken alla Cacciatora (Italian-American)

To serve 4

A 3- to 3½-pound chicken, cut into 8 pieces
1 teaspoon salt
Freshly ground black pepper
Flour
½ cup olive oil

1 cup finely chopped onions
1 teaspoon finely chopped garlic
¼ pound fresh mushrooms, trimmed, wiped clean and thinly sliced
A 1-pound can solid-pack tomatoes, drained and coarsely chopped
½ cup dry red wine
1 cup chicken stock, fresh or canned

Wash the chicken pieces under cold running water and pat them dry with paper towels. Season the chicken with the salt and a few grindings of black pepper, then dip the pieces in flour and shake off the excess flour.

In a heavy 10- to 12-inch skillet, heat the olive oil until a light haze forms above it. Brown the chicken a few pieces at a time, starting them skin side down and turning them with tongs. Transfer the browned pieces to a plate. Add the onions, garlic and mushrooms to the skillet and, stirring frequently, cook over moderate heat for 3 or 4 minutes, until the vegetables have softened and colored lightly. Transfer to the plate with the chicken and pour off all but a thin layer of fat. Add the tomatoes, wine, chicken stock and several grindings of black pepper to the skillet. Bring to a boil, scraping in any browned bits that may be clinging to the bottom of the pan, then return the chicken and vegetables to the pan. Bring back to a boil, then partially cover the skillet, reduce the heat and simmer for 20 to 30 minutes. To test the chicken for doneness, pierce a thigh with the tip of a sharp knife. The juice that runs out should be clear yellow; if it is tinged with pink, cook for 5 to 10 minutes longer.

To serve, arrange the chicken on a heated platter. Taste the sauce for seasoning and pour over the chicken.

To serve 4

2 medium-sized pineapples, or
    substitute 4 cups canned
    unsweetened pineapple chunks,
    drained
½ cup chicken stock, fresh or
    canned
1 cup water-chestnut flour, or
    substitute ½ cup cornstarch

combined with ½ cup all-
    purpose flour
2 teaspoons salt
2 eggs, lightly beaten
2 whole chicken breasts (about
    1 pound each), skinned, boned
    and cut into
    ½-inch cubes
Vegetable oil for deep frying

Cut the fresh pineapple in half lengthwise and, with a small sharp knife, cut the fruit away from the sides and bottom of the skin. Remove the fruit from the shells, leaving the pineapple shells intact. Slice the fruit into ½-inch pieces, and set the fruit and shells aside.

In a large mixing bowl, combine ½ cup of chicken stock, the water-chestnut flour (or combined cornstarch and flour), salt and eggs. Beat vigorously with a fork or wire whisk until the batter is well combined.

Preheat the oven to 250°. Pour vegetable oil into a 10- to 12-inch skillet or *wok* to a depth of 1 inch. Set over high heat until the oil almost begins to smoke, or reaches 375° on a deep-frying thermometer. Drop the chicken and pineapple pieces into the batter and stir until they are thoroughly coated. Lower half of the coated pieces into the hot fat, a few at a time. Fry for 4 to 6 minutes, stirring from time to time to prevent the chicken and pineapple from sticking together. When they are crisp and golden brown, transfer them with a slotted spoon to paper towels to drain and keep them warm in the low oven while you fry the remaining pieces. Add these to the first batch in the oven.

SAUCE

2 tablespoons vegetable oil
1 teaspoon finely chopped garlic
2 large green bell peppers, seeded,
    deribbed and cut into ½-inch
    squares
2 carrots, scraped and sliced into
    2-inch strips ¼ inch wide and

¼ inch thick
1 cup chicken stock, fresh or canned
½ cup red wine vinegar
½ cup sugar
2 tablespoons soy sauce
2 tablespoons cornstarch dissolved
    in ¼ cup chicken stock or water

SAUCE: Pour off any oil remaining in the pan and, in its place, pour in the 2 tablespoons of fresh oil. Stir in the garlic, then add the green-pepper squares and carrot strips. Stirring constantly, cook over moderate heat for 3 or 4 minutes. Do not overcook; the vegetables should remain crisp and brightly colored. Pour in 1 cup of chicken stock and the wine vinegar, sugar and soy sauce, and bring to a boil. Boil rapidly for about 1 minute,

175

or until the sugar has thoroughly dissolved. Quickly stir the cornstarch mixture to recombine it and stir it into the pan. Cook for a minute more, stirring constantly, until the sauce is thick and clear.

Place each of the pineapple shells on a serving plate and fill them evenly with the fried chicken and pineapple. Pour the vegetable sauce over the shells and serve. Or, if you have used canned pineapple, arrange the chicken and pineapple on a heated platter, and cover with the sauce.

## *Chicken-and-Shrimp Casserole* (*Basque-American*)

To serve 4

| | |
|---|---|
| A 2½- to 3-pound chicken, cut into 8 pieces | garlic |
| | 3 tablespoons all-purpose flour |
| ½ teaspoon salt | ½ pound boiled ham, cut into |
| ¼ teaspoon freshly ground black pepper | ¼-inch dice (1 cup) |
| | ¼ teaspoon sweet Hungarian paprika |
| ½ cup olive oil | 1 cup dry white wine |
| ¾ cup finely chopped onions | ½ pound medium-sized shrimp |
| 1½ teaspoons finely chopped | 2 tablespoons finely chopped parsley |

Wash the pieces of chicken under cold running water and pat them thoroughly dry with paper towels. Sprinkle the pieces of chicken with the salt and pepper. In a heavy 10- to 12-inch stainless-steel or enameled skillet, heat the olive oil over moderate heat until a light haze forms above it. Add the pieces of chicken to the skillet and cook for 4 or 5 minutes on each side, or until the chicken is golden brown. Transfer the chicken to a 2½- to 3-quart casserole and set aside.

Drop the onions and garlic into the skillet and cook over moderate heat until the onions are golden brown. Mix in the flour and, stirring constantly, cook for another 1 or 2 minutes.

Stir in the ham and paprika, pour in the wine and bring to a boil over high heat. Pour the contents of the skillet over the chicken and set the casserole over high heat. Bring to a boil, then cover the casserole tightly, lower the heat and simmer for 30 minutes.

Shell the shrimp. Devein them by making a shallow incision down their backs with a small sharp knife and lifting out the black or white intestinal vein with the point of the knife. Wash the shrimp under cold running water and set them aside.

To test the chicken for doneness, pierce a thigh with the tip of a small sharp knife. The juice that spurts out should be clear yellow; if it is tinged with pink, cook the chicken for 5 minutes longer. Arrange the shrimp on top of the chicken, cover the casserole again and cook for 5 minutes longer, until the shrimp are pink.

Arrange the pieces of chicken and the shrimp attractively on a heated serving platter and ladle the sauce in the casserole over them. Sprinkle with parsley and serve at once.

## *Chicken Chop Suey (Chinese-American)*
### CHICKEN WITH CHINESE VEGETABLES

**To serve 4**

1 whole chicken breast (about 1 pound), skinned, boned and cut into narrow strips (1¾ cups)
1 teaspoon salt
4 tablespoons peanut or other vegetable oil
1 large onion, thinly sliced (2 cups)
¼ pound mushrooms, left whole if small or quartered if medium-sized or large (2 cups)
3 stalks celery, cut into ¼-inch dice (1 cup)
½ cup canned water chestnuts, drained and cut into ½-inch dice

¼ pound green peas, shelled (¼ cup)
½ cup canned bamboo shoots, drained and cut into ½-inch pieces
½ small green pepper, seeded, deribbed and cut into ½-inch dice (¼ cup)
2 pimientos, cut into ½-inch dice (¼ cup)
3 tablespoons soy sauce
1 cup chicken stock, fresh or canned
2 cups canned bean sprouts, drained
1 tablespoon cornstarch, dissolved in ¼ cup water

Sprinkle the strips of chicken with the salt. Place 3 tablespoons of the oil in a 10- to 12-inch skillet or *wok* and set over moderate heat. When the oil is very hot but not smoking, add the chicken. Stirring constantly, cook for about 2 minutes, or until the pieces are firm and white. Add the remaining tablespoon of oil and the onion, mushrooms, celery, water chestnuts, green peas, bamboo shoots, green pepper and pimientos. Cook, stirring constantly, for 2 minutes. Pour in the soy sauce and chicken stock, add the bean sprouts, and bring to a boil over high heat. Cover the pan and boil briskly for 2 to 3 minutes. Quickly stir the cornstarch mixture to recombine it, add it to the pan and cook, stirring constantly, for a few seconds, until the ingredients are coated with a light, clear glaze. Transfer the contents of the pan to a heated platter and serve at once.

To serve 4

A 3½- to 4-pound chicken, cut into 8 serving pieces
¼ cup flour
⅓ cup vegetable oil
1 large onion, peeled and sliced crosswise into ¼-inch-thick rounds
6 cups chicken stock, fresh or canned
¼ cup cider vinegar
1 celery stalk, including the green leaves, cut crosswise into 4 pieces
1 medium-sized bay leaf
¼ teaspoon crumbled dried sage leaves
2 teaspoons salt
Freshly ground black pepper

Pat the chicken dry with paper towels. Place the flour in a paper bag, add the chicken, and shake vigorously to coat the pieces evenly.

In a heavy 4- to 5-quart casserole or Dutch oven at least 10 inches in diameter, heat the oil over moderate heat until a light haze forms above it. Brown 3 or 4 pieces of chicken at a time, starting them skin side down, and turning them frequently with tongs. Regulate the heat so that the pieces color richly and evenly without burning. As they brown, transfer the pieces to a plate.

Drop the onion slices into the fat remaining in the casserole and, stirring frequently, cook for about 5 minutes. When the onions are soft and translucent but not brown, return the chicken and the liquid that has accumulated around it to the casserole. Add the chicken stock, vinegar, celery, bay leaf, sage, 2 teaspoons of salt and a few grindings of pepper, and bring to a boil over high heat. Reduce the heat to low, cover partially and simmer for 45 minutes, or until the bird is almost tender and its thigh shows only the slightest resistance when pierced deeply with the point of a small sharp knife. Pick out and discard the celery and bay leaf.

DUMPLINGS

2 cups unsifted flour
4 teaspoons double-acting baking powder
1 teaspoon salt
¼ cup finely chopped fresh parsley
2 tablespoons vegetable shortening, cut into ½-inch bits
1 cup milk

Meanwhile, prepare the dumpling batter in the following fashion: Combine the flour, baking powder, 1 teaspoon of salt and the parsley in a deep bowl. Add the vegetable shortening and, with your fingertips, rub the flour and fat together until they look like flakes of coarse meal. Add the milk and beat vigorously with a spoon until the batter is smooth.

When the chicken has cooked its allotted time, drop the dumpling mixture on top by the tablespoonful. Cover the casserole tightly and simmer undisturbed for about 10 minutes longer. The dumplings are done when they are puffed and fluffy and a cake tester inserted in the center of a dumpling comes out clean.

With a slotted spoon remove the dumplings and place them on a plate. Transfer the stewed chicken to a heated bowl or a deep platter, then arrange the dumplings on top. Serve at once.

## *Roast Chicken with Chicken-Liver Stuffing* (*Polish-American*)

To serve 4

2 tablespoons butter, plus
  2 tablespoons butter, softened
2 tablespoons finely chopped onions
3 chicken livers, washed under cold
  running water and patted dry
  with paper towels
2 tablespoons finely chopped parsley

1 tablespoon finely cut fresh dill
  leaves
1 cup bread crumbs
1 egg, lightly beaten
A 2½- to 3-pound chicken
1½ teaspoons salt
Freshly ground black pepper

In a 10- to 12-inch skillet, melt 2 tablespoons of butter over moderate heat. When the foam begins to subside, stir in the onions and cook, stirring frequently, for 3 to 5 minutes, or until they are soft and translucent. Add the livers and, tossing them about constantly, cook for 3 to 5 minutes, until they are a rich brown. Remove from the heat, chop the livers coarsely and place them in a mixing bowl with the onions. Toss with the parsley, dill, bread crumbs and egg, taste for seasoning and set aside.

Preheat the oven to 450°. Wash the chicken quickly under cold running water and dry it thoroughly, inside and out, with paper towels. Spread the 2 tablespoons of softened butter over the chicken, and sprinkle the bird with the salt and several grindings of black pepper. Stuff the body cavities with the chicken-liver mixture and secure the openings with skewers, or sew them closed with kitchen string. Truss the chicken securely and place it on its back on a rack in a shallow roasting pan. Place the pan in the middle of the oven for 10 minutes, then reduce the heat to 350° and continue to roast for 50 minutes. With a bulb baster or large spoon, baste the chicken from time to time with the pan juices. To test the bird for doneness, pierce a thigh with the point of a small sharp knife. The juice that spurts out should be yellow; if it is pink, roast for 5 to 10 minutes more.

Remove the chicken to a heated serving platter and let it stand for 10 minutes before carving.

To serve 4 to 6

A 4½- to 5-pound roasting chicken
3 large onions, peeled and cut
    crosswise into ¼-inch-thick slices
1 cup coarsely chopped celery,
    including the green leaves
4 sprigs fresh parsley and 1 small
    bay leaf tied together with

kitchen string
¼ teaspoon crumbled dried thyme
1½ teaspoons salt
Freshly ground black pepper
1 quart plus 2 tablespoons water
2 tablespoons butter
6 tablespoons flour
½ teaspoon ground white pepper

Remove the chunks of fat from the cavity of the chicken, cut them into small bits and reserve them. Truss the bird securely and place it in a heavy 7- to 8-quart (preferably oval-shaped) casserole. Scatter the onions, celery, parsley and bay leaf, thyme, 1 teaspoon of salt and a few grindings of pepper around the chicken and pour in 1 quart of water.

Bring to a boil over high heat, reduce the heat to low and place the lid on the casserole. Poach the chicken for about 1 hour and 15 minutes. To test for doneness, pierce the thigh of the bird with the point of a small, sharp knife. The juice that trickles out should be a clear yellow; if it is slightly pink, poach the bird for another 5 to 10 minutes.

Transfer the chicken to a platter and strain the cooking stock through a fine sieve into a bowl, pressing down hard on the vegetables and herbs with the back of a spoon to extract all their juices before discarding them. Measure and reserve 2½ cups of the stock. When the chicken is cool enough to handle, remove the skin and pull the meat from the bones with your fingers or a small knife. Discard the skin and bones and cut the meat into 1-inch pieces.

Drop the reserved bits of chicken fat into a heavy 10- to 12-inch skillet, add 2 tablespoons of water and cook over moderate heat, stirring frequently. When the bits have rendered all their fat, remove them from the skillet with a slotted spoon and discard them.

Add 2 tablespoons of butter to the chicken fat and melt over moderate heat. When the foam begins to subside, stir in 6 tablespoons of flour and mix to a smooth paste. Pour in the 2½ cups of reserved chicken stock and, stirring constantly with a wire whisk, cook over high heat until the sauce comes to a boil, thickens heavily and is smooth. Reduce the heat to low and simmer, uncovered, for about 5 minutes.

Stir in ½ teaspoon of salt and the white pepper and taste for seasoning. Remove the skillet from the heat, add the chicken pieces and toss together gently but thoroughly. Pour the entire contents of the pan into a 7-by-7-by-2-inch baking-serving dish and spread the pieces of chicken evenly over the bottom of the dish.

2 to 2¼ cups all-purpose flour

1 tablespoon double-acting baking
    powder

1 teaspoon salt

2 tablespoons butter, chilled and cut

into ¼-inch bits plus ¼ cup
    butter, melted

2 tablespoons lard, chilled and cut
    into ¼-inch bits

½ cup cold milk

To prepare the biscuits, preheat the oven to 450°. Combine 2 cups of flour, the baking powder and 1 teaspoon of salt and sift them into a large chilled bowl. Add the butter bits and lard and, with your fingertips, rub the flour and fat together until they look like flakes of coarse meal. Pour in the milk and beat with a wooden spoon until the dough is smooth and can be gathered into a fairly dry, compact ball. If the dough remains moist and sticky, beat in up to ¼ cup more flour by the tablespoonful.

Place the dough on a lightly floured surface and roll it out into a rough rectangle about ⅓ inch thick. With a cookie cutter or the rim of a glass, cut the dough into 2-inch round biscuits. Gather the scraps together, roll them out again and cut out as many more rounds as you can. Ideally you should have about 12 biscuits.

Place the biscuits side by side over the chicken in the baking dish, arranging them so that they cover the top completely. Brush the biscuits with the melted butter and bake in the middle of the oven for about 25 minutes, or until the biscuits have puffed and are golden brown. Serve at once, directly from the baking dish.

## Chicken Potpie *(Eastern Heartland)*

To serve 6 to 8

A 5- to 6-pound roasting chicken,
    cut into 6 or 8 pieces

4 quarts water

2 medium-sized celery stalks,
    including the green leaves, cut
    into 3-inch pieces

¼ teaspoon crumbled dried saffron
    threads or ¼ teaspoon ground
    saffron

1 tablespoon plus 2 teaspoons salt

6 whole black peppercorns

½ cup coarsely chopped celery

2 medium-sized boiling potatoes,
    peeled and coarsely chopped

½ pound potpie squares *(see
    homemade egg noodles)* *

2 tablespoons finely chopped fresh
    parsley

Freshly ground black pepper

*In Pennsylvania Dutch cooking, potpies are pieces of noodle or baking-powder dough. They are boiled with meat and often potatoes to make rib-sticking potpie stews that are named for the kind of meat used. Thus,*

181

* See index.

*the following recipe made with chicken is called "chicken potpie" though it bears no resemblance to the pastry-encased potpies typical of other parts of the United States.*

Combine the chicken and water in a heavy 6- to 8-quart casserole and bring to a boil over high heat, meanwhile skimming off the foam and scum as they rise to the surface. Add the pieces of celery, saffron, 1 tablespoon of salt and the peppercorns, and reduce the heat to low. Simmer partially covered for about 1 hour, or until the chicken shows no resistance when a thigh is pierced deeply with a small sharp knife.

With a slotted spoon, transfer the chicken to a plate. Strain the stock through a fine sieve and return 2 quarts to the casserole. (Reserve the remaining stock for another use.) With a small sharp knife, remove the skin from the chicken and cut the meat from the bones. Discard the skin and bones; slice the meat into 1-inch pieces and set aside.

Add the chopped celery, potatoes and the remaining 2 teaspoons of salt to the casserole and bring to a boil over high heat. Drop in the potpie squares and stir briefly, then cook briskly, uncovered, for about 15 minutes, until the noodles are tender. Stir in the reserved chicken and parsley and cook for a minute or so to heat them through. Taste and season with more salt if desired and a few grindings of pepper.

To serve, ladle the chicken potpie into heated individual bowls.


## *Chicken Tetrazzini* (Italian-American)
CHICKEN CASSEROLE WITH NOODLES AND MUSHROOMS

To serve 8

| CHICKEN | |
| --- | --- |
| A 3- to 3½-pound chicken, cut into 6 or 8 pieces | 2 stalks celery, including the leaves |
| | 1 tablespoon salt |
| 1 small onion, peeled and halved | 1 small bay leaf |
| 2 whole cloves | 1 medium-sized carrot |
| | 6 cups water |

CHICKEN: Combine the chicken, onion, cloves, celery, salt, bay leaf, carrot and water in a 3- to 4-quart casserole, and bring to a boil over high heat. Reduce the heat to low and simmer, partially covered, for 30 to 40 minutes, or until the chicken is tender but not falling apart.

With tongs or a slotted spoon, transfer the chicken to a platter or cutting board. Strain the cooking liquid through a fine sieve set over a large bowl, pressing down hard on the vegetables with the back of a spoon before discarding them. With a large spoon, skim off and discard the fat from the stock, and set the stock aside.

Remove the skin and bones from the chicken, and discard them. Cut the chicken into 1-inch pieces and place the pieces in a serving bowl.

NOODLES AND MUSHROOMS
1 pound broad egg noodles
6 tablespoons butter
½ pound mushrooms, thinly sliced

NOODLES AND MUSHROOMS: Bring about 4 quarts of water to a boil in a 6- to 8-quart pot and drop in the noodles. Boil briskly, stirring from time to time for about 9 minutes, or until the noodles are *al dente*—that is, tender but still slightly resistant to the bite. Drain the noodles in a colander and cool them under cold running water. Set aside.

In an 8- to 10-inch skillet, melt 6 tablespoons of butter over moderate heat. Stir in the mushrooms and cook, stirring frequently, for about 5 minutes, or until they are soft and lightly colored. Set aside off the heat.

SAUCE
6 tablespoons butter
6 tablespoons flour
½ cup heavy cream
½ cup sherry

2 egg yolks
⅛ teaspoon Tabasco

2 tablespoons butter, softened
1 cup grated Parmesan cheese

SAUCE: In a 1½- to 2-quart enameled or stainless-steel saucepan, melt 6 tablespoons of butter over moderate heat. Stir in the flour and mix together thoroughly. Stirring the mixture constantly with a wire whisk, gradually pour in 2 cups of the reserved chicken stock, the cream and the sherry. Cook over high heat until the sauce comes to a boil, then reduce the heat to moderate. In a small bowl, beat the egg yolks with a wire whisk. Whisking constantly, slowly pour in about ½ cup of the hot liquid, then stir this egg mixture into the saucepan. Cook for 1 or 2 minutes more, then stir in the Tabasco and remove the pan from the heat.

TO ASSEMBLE AND BAKE: Preheat the oven to 350°. With a pastry brush, coat the bottom and sides of a 9-by-13-by-2-inch baking dish with the 2 tablespoons of softened butter. Pour in 1 cup of the sauce and arrange half of the noodles over the bottom of the dish. Spread the noodles with half of the mushrooms, and top these with half of the chicken. Repeat the layers—using 1 cup of sauce and the remaining noodles, mushrooms and chicken—and top with the remaining sauce. Sprinkle the sauce with the grated Parmesan cheese and bake in the center of the oven for 30 minutes. Serve at once, directly from the baking dish.

## Chicken Rochambeau *(Creole-Acadian)*
### CHICKEN AND HAM ON RUSKS WITH MUSHROOM AND BÉARNAISE SAUCES

To serve 4

MUSHROOM SAUCE
2 tablespoons butter
1 cup finely chopped scallions, including 3 inches of the green tops
1 teaspoon finely chopped garlic
2 tablespoons flour
2 cups chicken stock, fresh or canned
½ cup finely chopped fresh mushrooms (¼ pound)
½ cup dry red wine
1 tablespoon Worcestershire sauce
⅛ teaspoon ground hot red pepper (cayenne)
½ teaspoon salt

First prepare the mushroom sauce in the following fashion: In a heavy 1- to 1½-quart saucepan, melt the 2 tablespoons of butter over moderate heat. When the foam begins to subside, add the cup of scallions and the garlic and stir for about 5 minutes, or until they are soft but not brown. Add 2 tablespoons of flour and mix well. Stirring constantly with a wire whisk, pour in the chicken stock in a slow, thin stream and cook over high heat until the sauce comes to a boil, thickens lightly and is smooth.

Stir in the mushrooms, reduce the heat to low and simmer partially covered for about 15 minutes, until the mushrooms are tender but still intact. Then add the wine, Worcestershire, ⅛ teaspoon of red pepper and ½ teaspoon of salt, and stir over low heat for 2 or 3 minutes. Taste for seasoning, remove from the heat and cover tightly to keep the sauce warm.

CHICKEN
2 one-pound chicken breasts, boned and halved but with the skin intact
1 teaspoon salt
½ teaspoon freshly ground black pepper
½ cup flour
12 tablespoons butter, cut into ½-inch bits

Pat the chicken breasts completely dry with paper towels and season them on all sides with the teaspoon of salt and the black pepper. Roll one piece of chicken breast at a time in the ½ cup of flour and, when evenly coated, shake vigorously to remove the excess flour.

Melt 12 tablespoons of butter bits in a heavy 10- to 12-inch skillet set over moderate heat. Do not let the butter brown. When the foam subsides, add the chicken breasts skin side down and, turning the pieces occasionally with tongs, cook over moderate heat until they are lightly brown on all sides. Reduce the heat to low, cover the skillet tightly and simmer the chicken for about 20 minutes, until it is tender and shows no resistance when pierced deeply with the point of a small sharp knife. As it simmers use a bulb baster or a large spoon to baste the chicken every 7 or 8 minutes with the pan juices.

HAM
1 teaspoon butter
Four ¼-inch-thick slices Canadian
bacon or lean cooked smoked
ham
4 Holland rusks

Meanwhile preheat the oven to its lowest setting. In another large skillet, melt 1 teaspoon of butter over moderate heat and brown the ham. Turn the slices with tongs and regulate the heat so that they color richly and evenly on both sides without burning. When they brown, arrange the ham slices in one layer on a large baking sheet, drape loosely with foil and keep them warm in the oven. Place the Holland rusks side by side on another baking sheet and put them in the oven to warm.

BÉARNAISE SAUCE
⅔ cup tarragon vinegar
¼ cup finely chopped scallions
1 teaspoon crumbled dried tarragon
4 sprigs fresh parsley
¼ teaspoon whole peppercorns
12 tablespoons butter, cut into
   ½-inch bits
4 egg yolks
1 tablespoon water
2 tablespoons strained fresh lemon
   juice
¼ teaspoon ground hot red pepper
   (cayenne)
½ teaspoon salt

About 10 minutes before the chicken is done, make the béarnaise sauce. Combine the vinegar, ¼ cup of scallions, tarragon, parsley and peppercorns in a small enameled or stainless-steel saucepan. Bring to a boil over high heat and cook briskly, uncovered, until reduced to about 2 tablespoons. Strain the liquid through a fine sieve into a small bowl, pressing down hard on the seasonings with the back of a spoon to extract all their juices before discarding the pulp. Set the strained liquid aside.

In a heavy 8- to 10-inch skillet, melt the 12 tablespoons of butter bits over low heat, stirring so that the butter melts evenly without browning. Remove the pan from the heat and cover to keep the melted butter warm.

Working quickly, combine the egg yolks and water in a 1½- to 2-quart enameled or stainless-steel saucepan, and beat with a wire whisk until the mixture is foamy. Then place the pan over the lowest possible heat and continue whisking until the mixture thickens and almost doubles in volume. Do not let it come anywhere near a boil or the yolks will curdle; if necessary, lift the pan off the heat from time to time to cool it.

Still whisking constantly, pour in the reserved hot melted butter as slowly as possible and beat over low heat until the sauce thickens heavily. Beat in the reserved strained liquid, the lemon juice, ¼ teaspoon of red pepper and the salt, and taste for seasoning. Set it aside off the heat.

Before assembling the chicken Rochambeau, stir the mushroom sauce briefly and warm it over low heat if necessary. Arrange the rusks on a large heated platter or four individual serving plates. Place a slice of ham

185

on each rusk and spoon the mushroom sauce over the slices, dividing it equally among them. Set a chicken breast on top of each ham slice and ladle 2 or 3 tablespoons of béarnaise over it. Pour the remaining béarnaise into a sauceboat and serve it at once with the chicken Rochambeau.

## Chicken Breasts and Ham with Sherried Cream Sauce (Eastern Heartland)

To serve 6

| | |
|---|---|
| 9 tablespoons butter | ½ cup heavy cream |
| 2 tablespoons finely chopped shallots | 2 tablespoons dry sherry |
| | 1 tablespoon finely chopped parsley |
| 3 one-pound chicken breasts, halved, skinned and boned | ½ teaspoon salt |
| | A pinch of ground white pepper |
| 1½ cups chicken stock, fresh or canned | 6 thin slices cooked country ham, plus 1 thin slice country ham cut |
| ¼ cup flour | in matchlike strips |

In a heavy 10- to 12-inch skillet, melt 2 tablespoons of the butter over moderate heat. When the foam begins to subside, add the shallots and, stirring frequently, cook for 2 or 3 minutes, until they are soft and translucent but not brown. Add the chicken breasts and stock, and bring to a boil over high heat, meanwhile skimming off the foam and scum as they rise to the surface. Reduce the heat to low and simmer partially covered for about 10 minutes, or until the chicken feels firm to the touch. With a slotted spoon, transfer the chicken to a plate and drape it with foil to keep it warm. Set the stock aside.

Melt 3 tablespoons of the remaining butter in a 1- to 2-quart saucepan over moderate heat. Add the flour and mix to a paste. Then, stirring the mixture constantly with a wire whisk, pour in the reserved chicken stock and shallots, and cook over high heat until the sauce comes to a boil, thickens heavily and is smooth.

Whisking constantly, add the cream, sherry, parsley, salt and white pepper. Reduce the heat to low and simmer uncovered for 3 minutes to remove any taste of raw flour. Taste for seasoning.

While the sauce is simmering, melt the remaining 4 tablespoons of butter in a heavy 12-inch skillet over high heat. Add the ham slices and, turning them over frequently with kitchen tongs, cook for a few minutes to heat the ham through.

To serve, place the ham slices on six heated individual serving plates and set a chicken breast half on each slice. Pour the sauce over the chicken and ham, dividing it evenly among the portions. Garnish the top with the strips of ham and serve at once.

186

To serve 4 to 6

3 quarts water
4 teaspoons salt
2 medium-sized eggplants (about 1
    pound each), peeled and cut into
    1½- to 2-inch cubes (8 cups)
4 tablespoons butter plus 1
    tablespoon butter, cut into bits
½ pound chicken livers
1 pound mushrooms, thinly sliced

2 eggs
½ cup heavy cream
¼ teaspoon ground nutmeg
Freshly ground black pepper
½ cup soft fresh crumbs, made
    from homemade-type white
    bread, pulverized in a blender or
    finely shredded with a fork
½ cup grated Parmesan cheese

Preheat the oven to 350°. In a 6- to 8-quart casserole, combine 3 quarts of water and 3 teaspoons of the salt, and bring to a boil over high heat. Drop in the eggplant, reduce the heat to moderate, and cook uncovered for 15 to 20 minutes, or until the eggplant is tender enough to offer no resistance when pierced with the tip of a sharp knife. Drain the eggplant in a colander and place the cubes in a large mixing bowl. Then, with a potato masher or fork, mash them to a smooth purée and set aside.

Melt the 4 tablespoons of butter in a heavy 10- to 12-inch skillet set over moderate heat. When the foam begins to subside, add the chicken livers and fry them for 3 or 4 minutes on each side, tossing and turning them with a wooden spoon or spatula. When they are a light golden brown, remove the livers from the pan with a slotted spoon and chop them as fine as possible. Add them to the bowl of puréed eggplant.

In the fat remaining in the skillet, fry the mushrooms for 4 or 5 minutes over moderate heat, stirring frequently. When they are lightly colored, transfer the mushrooms to the purée and chicken livers.

In a small mixing bowl, beat the eggs lightly with a wire whisk or fork, then beat in the heavy cream, nutmeg, the remaining teaspoon of salt and several grindings of black pepper. Pour the contents of the bowl over the eggplant, livers and mushrooms. Toss with a large spoon until the ingredients are thoroughly combined. Taste for seasoning, and spoon the mixture into a 1-quart baking-and-serving casserole, smoothing the surface with a rubber spatula. Combine the bread crumbs and grated cheese and sprinkle them evenly over the top. Dot with the tablespoon of butter bits and bake the casserole in the center of the oven for 25 to 30 minutes, or until the crust is golden brown. Serve at once, directly from the casserole.

To serve 8

A 12-pound turkey, thoroughly defrosted if frozen

2 teaspoons plus 1 tablespoon salt

The neck, gizzard, heart and liver of the turkey

1 medium-sized carrot, scraped and cut into 1-inch lengths

1 small onion, peeled and quartered

4 sprigs fresh parsley

1 small bay leaf

4 cups water

2 one-pound loaves of day-old homemade-type white bread, trimmed of crusts and torn into

½-inch pieces (about 10 cups)

¾ cup finely chopped fresh parsley

2 tablespoons finely grated fresh lemon peel

1 tablespoon crumbled dried sage leaves

½ teaspoon freshly ground black pepper

½ pound butter, cut into ½-inch bits plus 8 tablespoons butter, softened

3 cups finely chopped onions

2 cups finely chopped celery

1½ pints shucked oysters (3 cups) drained

1 egg, lightly beaten

3 tablespoons flour

Pat the turkey completely dry inside and out with paper towels. Rub the cavity with 1 teaspoon of the salt and set the bird aside.

Before making the stuffing, combine the turkey neck, gizzard, heart and liver, the carrot, quartered onion, parsley sprigs, bay leaf, 1 teaspoon of salt and the water in a 3- to 4-quart saucepan. Bring to a boil over high heat, reduce the heat to low and simmer partially covered for 1½ hours.

Strain the liquid through a fine sieve into a bowl and reserve it. (There should be about 2 cups of turkey stock; if necessary, add enough fresh or canned chicken stock for the required amount.) Remove the liver, chop it into ¼-inch dice and reserve. Discard the rest of the turkey pieces as well as the vegetables and herbs.

Meanwhile preheat the oven to 400°. Combine the bread, chopped parsley, lemon peel, sage, 1 tablespoon of salt and the pepper in a large deep bowl and toss with a spoon until well mixed.

In a heavy 10- to 12-inch skillet, melt the ½ pound of butter bits over moderate heat. When the foam begins to subside, add the chopped onions. Stirring frequently, cook for about 5 minutes until they are soft and translucent but not brown.

Stir in the celery and cook for a minute or so; then, with a rubber spatula, scrape the entire contents of the skillet into the bread mixture. Add the oysters and egg and stir the ingredients gently but thoroughly together. Taste the oyster stuffing for seasoning.

Fill both the breast and the neck cavity of the turkey with the stuffing and close the openings by lacing them with small skewers and kitchen cord, or sewing them with heavy, white thread. Truss the bird securely. With a pastry brush, spread the 8 tablespoons of softened butter evenly over its entire outside surface.

Place the bird on its side on a rack set in a large, shallow roasting pan and roast it in the middle of the oven for 15 minutes. Turn it on its other side and roast 15 minutes longer. Then reduce the oven temperature to 325°, place the turkey breast side down and roast for 1 hour. Now turn it breast side up and roast it for about 1 hour longer, basting it every 15 minutes or so with the juices that have accumulated in the bottom of the pan.

To test for doneness, pierce the thigh of the turkey with the tip of a small, sharp knife. The juice that trickles out should be a clear yellow; if it is slightly pink, return the bird to the oven and roast for another 5 to 10 minutes. Transfer it to a heated platter and let it rest for 10 minutes or so for easier carving.

Meanwhile, skim off and discard all but a thin film of fat from the roasting pan. Stir the flour into the fat and cook over moderate heat for 2 to 3 minutes, meanwhile scraping in the brown particles clinging to the pan.

Pour in the reserved turkey stock (first skimming it of all surface fat) and, stirring constantly with a wire whisk, cook over high heat until the sauce comes to a boil, thickens and is smooth. Reduce the heat to low and simmer uncovered for about 5 minutes, then strain the gravy through a fine sieve into a serving bowl or sauceboat. Taste for seasoning and stir in the reserved chopped liver. Carve the turkey at the table, and present the gravy separately.

### *Roast Turkey with Cornbread, Sausage and Pecan Stuffing* (South)

To serve 8 to 12

A 12- to 14-pound oven-ready
  turkey, thoroughly defrosted if
  frozen, and the turkey liver,
  finely chopped
1½ teaspoons salt
Freshly ground black pepper
1 pound breakfast-type sausage
  meat
1½ cups finely chopped onions
½ cup finely chopped celery
5 cups coarsely crumbled, cooled
  cornbread
1½ cups (about ½ pound)

  coarsely chopped pecans
¼ cup pale dry sherry
¼ cup milk
¼ cup finely chopped fresh parsley
½ teaspoon crumbled dried thyme
¼ teaspoon ground nutmeg,
  preferably freshly grated
12 tablespoons butter, melted
½ cup coarsely chopped onions
3 tablespoons flour
1½ cups turkey stock (*see note,*
  *below*), or substitute fresh or
  canned chicken stock

Preheat the oven to 400°. Pat the turkey completely dry inside and out with paper towels. Rub the cavity with 1 teaspoon of the salt and a few grindings of pepper, and set the bird aside.

In a heavy 10- to 12-inch ungreased skillet, fry the sausage meat over moderate heat, stirring frequently and mashing the meat with the back of a fork to break up any lumps as they form. When no trace of pink remains, scoop up the sausage meat with a slotted spoon and transfer it to a fine sieve to drain.

Pour off all but a few tablespoonfuls of the sausage fat remaining in the skillet and add the finely chopped onions and celery. Stirring frequently, cook over moderate heat for about 5 minutes, or until the vegetables are soft but not brown. With a slotted spoon, transfer them to a deep bowl. Add the drained sausage meat, the cornbread, pecans, sherry, milk, turkey liver, parsley, thyme, nutmeg, the remaining ½ teaspoon of salt and a few grindings of pepper, and toss together gently but thoroughly. Taste for seasoning and let the stuffing cool to room temperature.

Fill both the breast and the neck cavity of the turkey with the stuffing and close the openings by lacing them with small skewers and kitchen cord or sewing them with heavy white thread. Truss the bird securely.

With a pastry brush, spread the melted butter evenly over the entire surface of the turkey. Place the bird on its side on a rack set in a large shallow roasting pan and roast in the middle of the oven for 15 minutes. Turn the turkey on its other side, and roast for 15 minutes more.

Then reduce the oven temperature to 325°, place the turkey breast side down and roast for 1 hour, basting it every 15 minutes or so with the juices that have accumulated in the pan. Turn the bird breast side up and scatter the coarsely chopped onions around it. Roast for about 1 hour longer, basting the turkey every 15 minutes or so with the pan juices.

To test for doneness, pierce the thigh of the turkey with the tip of a small sharp knife. The juice that trickles out should be a clear yellow; if it is slightly pink, return the bird to the oven and roast for another 5 to 10 minutes. Transfer the turkey to a heated platter and let it rest for 10 minutes or so for easier carving.

Meanwhile, skim off and discard all but a thin film of fat from the roasting pan. Stir the flour into the fat and cook over moderate heat for 2 or 3 minutes, meanwhile scraping in the brown particles clinging to the bottom and sides of the pan.

Pour in the turkey or chicken stock and, stirring constantly with a wire whisk, cook over high heat until the sauce comes to a boil, thickens and is smooth. Reduce the heat to low and simmer uncovered for about 5 minutes, then strain the gravy through a fine sieve into a serving bowl or sauceboat. Taste for seasoning. Carve the turkey at the table and present the gravy separately.

NOTE: If you would like to prepare turkey stock, start about 2 hours before you prepare the stuffing. Combine the turkey neck, gizzard, and heart, 1 scraped chopped carrot, 1 peeled and quartered onion, 4 fresh parsley sprigs, 1 small bay leaf, 1 teaspoon of salt and 4 cups of water in a saucepan. Bring to a boil over high heat, reduce the heat to low and simmer partially covered for 1½ hours. Strain the liquid through a fine sieve into a bowl and skim as much fat as possible from the surface. There should be about 2 cups of stock.

## Individual Turkey Hash Ovals *(Northwest)*

To serve 4

| | |
|---|---|
| 1 large boiling potato, peeled and quartered | ¼ cup heavy cream |
| 8 tablespoons butter, cut into bits | 1½ teaspoons salt |
| 2 cups coarsely chopped cooked turkey | ½ teaspoon freshly ground black pepper |
| ½ cup finely chopped onions | ½ cup flour |
| ¼ cup finely chopped celery | 1½ cups soft fresh crumbs made |
| ¼ cup coarsely chopped fresh parsley | from homemade-type white bread, pulverized in a blender or finely shredded with a fork |
| 1 egg plus 2 lightly beaten eggs | 4 tablespoons vegetable oil |

Drop the potato quarters into enough boiling water to cover them by 1 inch and boil briskly until they are tender and show no resistance when pierced deeply with the point of a small skewer or sharp knife. Drain off the water, return the pan to low heat and slide it back and forth for a minute or so to dry the potato quarters completely. Mash them to a smooth purée with a table fork, add 4 tablespoons of the butter bits, and beat until the butter is completely absorbed.

Put the turkey, onions, celery and parsley through the medium blade of a food grinder into a deep bowl. Add one egg and stir with a wooden spoon until well blended. Add the potatoes, cream, salt and pepper, and beat vigorously until the mixture is smooth and fluffy. Cover the bowl with wax paper and chill the mixture for about 30 minutes.

To shape the turkey hash, divide the mixture into eight equal parts and pat each one into a somewhat flattened oval cake about 4 inches long and 1 inch wide. One at a time, dip each cake in the flour to coat it evenly on all sides and shake off the excess. Immerse the cake in the beaten eggs, then roll it in the bread crumbs. Set the cakes side by side on a plate or piece of wax paper and refrigerate them for at least 30 minutes to firm the coating.

In a heavy 10- to 12-inch skillet, melt the remaining 4 tablespoons of butter bits with the oil over moderate heat. Add the turkey-hash cakes and fry them for 2 or 3 minutes on each side, or until they are golden brown. Serve at once.

To serve 4

2 cups water
2 teaspoons salt
1 cup long-grain white rice, not the
   converted variety
24 dried apricots (about 1½ cups),
   quartered
Freshly ground black pepper
A 5- to 6-pound duck

2 cups chicken stock, fresh or
   canned
½ cup finely chopped onions
½ teaspoon finely chopped garlic
⅛ teaspoon crumbled dried thyme
2 tablespoons apricot preserves
2 tablespoons cornstarch combined
   with 2 tablespoons cold water

Preheat the oven to 425°. To prepare the stuffing, bring the 2 cups of water and 1 teaspoon of the salt to a boil over high heat in a small saucepan. Pour in the rice, stir once or twice, and reduce the heat to low. Cover the pan tightly and simmer for 10 minutes. Drain the rice in a sieve and transfer it to a bowl. Add the apricots and a liberal grinding of black pepper and mix well.

Wash the duck quickly under cold running water and pat it dry inside and out with paper towels. Rub the inside of the duck with the remaining teaspoon of salt and a few grindings of black pepper. For a crisper skin, prick the surface around the thighs, the back and the lower part of the breast with the tip of a sharp knife.

Fill the cavity of the duck loosely with the stuffing and close the opening by lacing it with small skewers and cord or sewing it with heavy white thread. Fasten the neck skin to the back of the duck with a skewer and truss the bird neatly.

Place the duck breast side up on a rack set in a large shallow pan and roast it in the middle of the oven for 20 minutes. Pour off the fat from the roasting pan or draw it off with a bulb baster. Then reduce the heat to 350° and roast for about 1 hour longer.

To test for doneness pierce the thigh of the bird deeply with the point of a small skewer or a sharp knife. The juice that trickles out should be a clear yellow; if it is still slightly tinged with pink, roast the duck for another 5 to 10 minutes. Transfer the bird to a heated serving platter and discard the string and skewers. Let the roast duck rest for about 10 minutes for easier carving.

Meanwhile, prepare the sauce in the following way: Pour off all but about 3 tablespoons of the fat remaining in the roasting pan and add the chicken stock, onions, garlic and thyme. Bring to a boil over high heat, stirring constantly and scraping in the brown particles that cling to the bottom and sides of the pan. Reduce the heat to low and simmer uncovered for about 5 minutes.

Add the apricot preserve and the cornstarch-water mixture and, still stirring, cook over low heat until the sauce comes to a boil and thickens lightly. Strain the sauce through a fine sieve into a sauceboat or gravy bowl, pressing down hard on the onions with the back of a spoon to extract all their juices before discarding the pulp. Taste for seasoning.

Serve the duck at once, accompanied by the sauce. If you like, you may garnish the duck with dried apricots that have been simmered in water to cover for 30 minutes, or until tender, and thoroughly drained.

*The South's famous fried chicken comes with cream gravy that may be poured over the bird or served separately.*

Chicken Rochambeau, a dish to try a cook's mettle, occupies a place of honor on the menus of fine New Orleans restaurants—but it can also be prepared at home.

*Tender morsels of ham and shrimp add their flavors to golden-brown chicken in this chicken and shrimp casserole, a subtle Basque specialty.*

## Grapefruit Duck   *(Far West)*

To serve 4 to 6

| | |
|---|---|
| A 4½- to 5-pound duck | quartered |
| ½ teaspoon salt | ¼ cup strained fresh grapefruit |
| ¼ teaspoon freshly ground black | juice |
|   pepper | ¼ cup honey |
| 1 medium-sized onion, peeled and | 2 tablespoons soy sauce |

Preheat the oven to 450°. Wash the duck under cold running water and cut off the wing tips at the first joint. Pat the duck dry inside and out with paper towels. Rub the cavity of the duck with the salt and pepper and insert the onion quarters. Then truss the bird securely. For a crisper skin, prick the surface around the thighs, the back and the lower part of the breast with the point of a sharp knife.

Place the duck breast up on a rack set in a large shallow pan and roast for 20 minutes. Reduce the oven temperature to 350° and draw off the accumulated fat from the pan with a bulb baster or a large spoon. Turn the duck on one side and roast it for 30 minutes, then turn it on the other side and roast for 30 minutes longer.

Combine the grapefruit juice, honey and soy sauce in a bowl and mix well. Turn the duck breast up and, with a pastry brush, spread 2 or 3 tablespoons of the grapefruit mixture evenly over the bird. Roast the duck for 30 minutes longer, basting it twice more with about 3 tablespoons of the grapefruit mixture. Pierce the thigh of the bird with the point of a small sharp knife to make sure it is cooked through. The juice that trickles out should be clear yellow; if it is slightly tinged with pink, roast the bird for another 5 to 10 minutes.

Transfer the duck to a heated platter and let it rest for about 10 minutes for easier carving.

## Duck in Orange Aspic

To serve 6

A 5- to 6-pound duck, cut into
   quarters
Duck giblets
4 cups orange juice, fresh or frozen
4 cups chicken stock, fresh or canned

1 cup thinly sliced onion
½ cup thinly sliced carrot
¾ cup celery, cut into 2-inch pieces
Herb bouquet of 6 sprigs parsley and
   1 bay leaf, tied together
½ teaspoon thyme

In a 4- or 5-quart casserole combine the duck, giblets, orange juice and chicken stock. Bring to a boil, skim off all the surface scum and froth, then add the onion, carrot, celery, herb bouquet and thyme. Season with salt if you think it necessary. Half cover the casserole, reduce the heat to its lowest point and simmer the duck for about 1½ hours, or until tender. Then cut the skin and duck meat away from the bones and return the skin and bones to the casserole. Simmer the broth about ½ hour longer. Cut the duck meat into ½- by ¾-inch pieces and refrigerate.

ASPIC
2 envelopes unflavored gelatin
½ cup cold chicken stock or water
10 whole peppercorns
Peel of 2 oranges, coarsely chopped

2 teaspoons lemon juice
2 egg whites
Peel of 2 navel oranges cut into tiny
   slivers and blanched

THE ASPIC: Strain the entire contents of the casserole broth through a fine sieve, pressing down on the vegetables and duck parts to extract all

*Duck in aspic forms a jewellike salad ringed by orange slices and filled with onion rings and orange sections.*

their liquid before throwing them away. Measure the broth. You should have 4 cups. If less, add chicken stock; if more, boil down rapidly to 4 cups. Skim the surface of the broth of every bit of fat you can (this is easier if you chill the broth first until the fat rises and congeals on the surface), then return the broth to a 3- or 4-quart saucepan. Soften the gelatin in the ½ cup of cold stock or water for 5 minutes, then stir it into the broth. To clarify the aspic, add the peppercorns, the coarsely chopped orange peel and the lemon juice, then beat the egg whites to a froth with a wire whisk and whisk them into the broth. Bring to a boil over moderate heat, whisking constantly. When the aspic begins to froth and rise, remove the pan from the heat. Let it rest 5 minutes, then strain it into a deep bowl through a fine sieve lined with a dampened kitchen towel. Allow all the aspic to drain through without disturbing it at any point. The aspic should now be brilliantly clear. Taste for seasoning and add salt if necessary. Pour the aspic into a 1½-quart ring mold and set the mold in a bowl in crushed ice. Stir with a metal spoon until it becomes thick and syrupy (don't allow it to set), then mix into it the duck meat and slivers of orange peel. Refrigerate at least 2 hours, or until firmly set.

When you are ready to serve it, run a thin, sharp knife around the insides of the mold (including the cone), and dip the bottom in hot water for a few seconds. Then wipe the outside of the mold dry, place a large, chilled, circular serving plate upside down over the mold and, grasping both firmly, quickly turn plate and mold over. Rap them sharply on the table and the aspic should slide out. If it doesn't, repeat the process.

Fill the center of the aspic ring with orange and onion salad * and arrange extra orange slices around the ring if you wish.

* See index.

To serve 4

One 5- to 6-pound Long Island
duckling, cut into quarters

MARINADE

¾ cup vegetable oil

½ cup red-wine vinegar

1 teaspoon salt

Freshly ground black pepper

1 cup thinly sliced onion

3 large garlic cloves, thinly sliced

2 large bay leaves, coarsely crumbled

Salt, preferably the coarse (kosher)
variety

Wash the duck under cold running water and pat thoroughly dry. With poultry shears or a sharp knife, trim the quarters, cutting away all exposed fat. In a shallow glass, porcelain or stainless-steel pan large enough to hold the duck quarters in one layer, mix the oil, vinegar, salt and a few grindings of pepper. Add the onion, garlic and bay leaves. Lay the duck in this marinade, baste thoroughly and marinate at room temperature at least 3 hours, turning the pieces every half hour.

When you are ready to broil the duck, remove it from the marinade. Strain the marinade through a fine sieve and discard the vegetables. Preheat the broiler to its highest point. Arrange the duck, skin side down, on the broiler rack, sprinkle lightly with salt and broil 4 inches from the heat for about 35 minutes, regulating the heat or lowering the rack so the duck browns slowly without burning. Baste every 10 minutes or so with the marinade. Turn the pieces over with tongs, sprinkle with salt and broil 10 to 15 minutes longer, basting 2 or 3 times with the marinade. When the duck is tender and a deep golden brown, arrange it on a heated serving platter. Moisten with a tablespoon or so of the pan drippings if you wish and serve at once.

To serve 4

2 duck breasts, halved
3 tablespoons butter
3 tablespoons Marsala
1 clove garlic, crushed
½ cup sliced mushrooms
1 teaspoon meat extract

2 teaspoons potato flour
1 cup stock
Salt
Pepper
1 cup pitted black cherries
1 tablespoon red currant jelly
¾ cup hollandaise sauce

Skin the duck breasts and trim off the bone and any excess fat. Brown them quickly in 1 tablespoon of hot butter. Heat the Marsala in a small pan, ignite it and pour it over the duck. Remove the duck fom the pan.

Put 1 tablespoon of butter and the garlic in the pan, lower the heat and cook for 2 minutes. Add the remaining tablespoon of butter and sauté the mushrooms until they are lightly browned. Off the heat, blend in the meat extract and the flour. Pour on the stock and stir over the heat until the sauce comes to a boil. Season with salt and pepper. Return the duck to the pan and simmer it for 20 to 30 minutes, or until it is tender.

Arrange the duck on an ovenproof serving dish. Add the cherries to the sauce in the pan, then the currant jelly and the hollandaise sauce. Spoon this mixture over the duck and brown it quickly under the broiler.

# Game & Game Birds

At the turn of the century, venison and quail were nearly as common a sight in American markets and on American tables as beef and chicken are today. Even now, although housing developments have swallowed up many forests and fields, some unspoiled areas still survive, abounding in wildlife and open at specified times for hunting. Venison remains the favorite game meat in the United States. The most popular game bird nationwide is now the ring-necked pheasant, which is not a native American species at all but a late-nineteenth century import from China.

Venison is a red meat, somewhat sweet-flavored. Because a deer is such a large animal, hunters have learned to use the meat in a variety of ways, roasting a leg or haunch or marinating it first in a tenderizing red-wine bath as in the Northwest; baking loin chops to serve with a tangy bar-becue sauce, Eastern Heartland fashion; and even grinding up the meat for a fruit-flavored mincemeat, used in the Northwest as a pie filling.

Pheasant is an elegant bird with delicately gamey dark meat. Hunters roast young pheasants—as in the recipe for filbert-stuffed pheasant from the Eastern Heartland, but wisely braise the older birds, as in a succulent Northwestern dish of pheasant and apples with sour-cream sauce. Among other popular game birds today is the quail, whose gentle flavor can be enlivened by braising the bird, Southern style, or by roasting it filled with a wild rice stuffing, then bathing it with a rich cream-and-morel sauce from the Northwest.

Nonhunters, too, can enjoy game and game birds. All the animals specified in the recipes in this chapter can be purchased fresh in season, but often frozen at other times of the year, through gourmet and butcher shops. But whether you shoot and field dress your bird or animal your-self, or buy it oven-ready, you will have to prepare and cook it carefully. Since four-legged and winged game have little fat—and what there is should be removed, as it carries much of the "gamey" flavor many people object to—the meat can become unappetizingly dry. You can ensure juicy meat by barding or larding the meat before cooking, or basting it frequently during cooking, and by cooking it to the slightly rare stage, so as to keep it moist.

201

To serve 10 to 12

| | |
|---|---|
| 2 tablespoons butter | 1 medium-sized bay leaf, crumbled |
| 1½ cups finely chopped onions | 6 whole juniper berries and 10 |
| 1 medium-sized carrot, scraped and | whole black peppercorns, |
| finely chopped | wrapped in a towel and coarsely |
| ¼ cup finely chopped celery | crushed with a rolling pin |
| 1 teaspoon finely chopped garlic | 1 tablespoon salt |
| 3 cups dry red wine | A 10- to 11-pound leg of venison |
| 1 cup plus 1 tablespoon cold water | 1 tablespoon cornstarch |

In a 3- to 4-quart enameled or stainless-steel saucepan, melt the butter over moderate heat. When the foam begins to subside, add the onions, carrot, celery and garlic and, stirring frequently, cook for about 5 minutes, until the vegetables are soft but not brown. Stir in the wine, 1 cup of the water, the bay leaf, the juniper berries and peppercorns, and the salt, and bring to a boil over high heat. Remove the pan from the heat and let the marinade cool to room temperature.

Place the venison in a roasting pan large enough to hold it comfortably, pour the marinade over it, and turn the meat in the marinade to moisten it on all sides. Cover tightly with foil or plastic wrap and refrigerate for at least 12 hours, turning the meat two or three times.

Preheat the oven to 425°. Insert the tip of a meat thermometer at least 2 inches into the thickest part of the meat, and roast the venison on the middle shelf of the oven for 15 minutes. Reduce the heat to 375° and continue roasting for 1 hour and 15 minutes longer, basting the venison every 15 minutes with the liquids in the bottom of the pan. When done, the meat thermometer should register 140° to 150°, and the roast should be slightly pink. Transfer it to a large heated platter and let it rest for 10 minutes or so for easier carving.

Meanwhile, prepare the sauce. Strain the cooking liquid through a fine sieve set over a bowl, pressing down hard on the vegetables to extract all their juice before discarding them. Measure the liquid, pour it into a small saucepan and skim the fat from the surface. You will need 2 cups of liquid for the sauce. If you have more, boil it briskly until it is reduced to that amount; if you have less, add as much water as you need to make the required amount. Make a smooth paste of the cornstarch and the remaining tablespoon of cold water.

Bring the cooking liquid to a simmer over moderate heat and, stirring constantly with a wire whisk, pour in the cornstarch mixture. Continue to simmer until the sauce thickens lightly and is smooth. Taste for seasoning, pour the sauce into a bowl or sauceboat, and serve at once with the roast venison.

*Roasted venison with a German accent is marinated in tart red wine before cooking and served with spiced plums and spaetzle.*

## Venison Mincemeat (Northwest)

To make about 2½ quarts

2 pounds boneless venison
½ pound beef suet, finely chopped
1½ pounds apples, peeled, cored
  and coarsely chopped (4 cups)
2 pints sour cherries, pitted
1½ cups seedless raisins
½ cup finely chopped citron
¼ cup candied orange peel
¼ cup candied lemon peel
¼ cup lemon juice
2 teaspoons grated lemon rind
½ cup orange juice

4 teaspoons grated orange rind
½ teaspoon salt
¼ teaspoon freshly ground black
  pepper
2 cups sugar
2 teaspoons ground allspice
1 teaspoon ground mace
2 teaspoons ground cinnamon
1 teaspoon grated nutmeg
1 teaspoon ground cloves
1 quart apple cider
1 cup brandy

Place the venison in an 8- to 10-quart pot or casserole and add enough water to cover the meat by 1 inch. Bring to a boil over high heat, then reduce the heat and simmer, partially covered, for 2 hours, or until the meat offers only the slightest resistance when pierced with the tip of a small, sharp knife. Drain the venison, pat it dry with paper towels, and cut it into 1-inch chunks. Mince the meat by putting it through the medium blade of a food grinder, or chop it fine with a sharp knife.

Transfer the ground venison to a 3- to 4-quart casserole and add all the remaining ingredients except the brandy. Bring to a boil over high heat, then lower the heat, and simmer partially covered for 1½ hours, stirring frequently to prevent the mixture from sticking to the pan. Remove from the heat and stir in the brandy, then ladle the mincemeat into hot, sterilized jars following the directions for canning and sealing in the appendix. Store at room temperature for at least 2 weeks before using as a filling for pies or tarts.

## Barbecued Venison Chops *(Eastern Heartland)*

To serve 6

¼ cup vegetable oil
6 six-ounce venison loin chops, cut about 1 inch thick
½ cup finely chopped onions
1 teaspoon finely chopped garlic
3 medium-sized firm ripe tomatoes, coarsely chopped and puréed

through a food mill or rubbed through a fine sieve with the back of a spoon
¼ cup strained fresh lemon juice
¼ cup Worcestershire sauce
1 teaspoon crumbled dried basil
1 teaspoon salt
Freshly ground black pepper

Preheat the oven to 400°. In a heavy 10- to 12-inch skillet, heat the oil over moderate heat until a light haze forms above it. Pat the venison chops completely dry with paper towels. Then brown them in the oil, 2 or 3 at a time, turning the chops frequently with tongs and regulating the heat so that they color richly and evenly without burning. As they brown, arrange the chops side by side in a shallow baking-serving dish large enough to hold them in one layer.

To prepare the barbecue sauce, add the onions and garlic to the fat remaining in the skillet. Stirring frequently, cook over moderate heat for about 5 minutes, until the onions are soft and translucent but not brown. Stir in the puréed tomatoes, lemon juice, Worcestershire, basil, salt and a few grindings of pepper.

Bring the sauce to a boil over high heat, stirring constantly and scraping in any brown particles clinging to the bottom and sides of the skillet. Taste for seasoning and pour the sauce evenly over the chops.

Bake uncovered in the middle of the oven for about 20 minutes, or until the chops show no resistance when pierced deeply with the point of a small sharp knife. Serve at once, directly from the baking dish.

OPPOSITE
*A hunter's well-earned reward lies in a hearty casserole of pigeon enhanced by onions, celery, carrots, mushrooms and Lima beans in a red-wine sauce.*

To serve 4 to 6

A 3- to 3½-pound rabbit,
thoroughly defrosted if frozen,
cut into 12 serving pieces

1 teaspoon salt

¼ teaspoon ground white pepper

¾ cup flour

½ cup vegetable oil

1¾ cups chicken stock, fresh or
canned

1 cup heavy cream

1 teaspoon crumbled dried tarragon

Pat the pieces of rabbit dry with paper towels and season them on all sides with the salt and white pepper. Roll the pieces in ½ cup of the flour to coat them evenly, and vigorously shake off the excess flour.

In a heavy 6- to 8-quart casserole, heat the oil over high heat until a light haze forms above it. Brown four or five pieces of rabbit at a time, starting them skin side down and turning them frequently with tongs. Regulate the heat so that the meat colors richly and evenly on all sides. As the pieces of rabbit brown, transfer them to a plate.

Pour off all but about 4 tablespoons of the fat remaining in the casserole, then add the remaining ¼ cup of flour and mix well. Stirring constantly with a wire whisk, pour in the chicken stock in a slow, thin stream and cook over high heat until the sauce comes to a boil, thickens and is smooth. Whisk in the cream and tarragon and return the rabbit and the juices that have accumulated around it to the casserole. Reduce the heat to low, cover tightly and simmer for about 1 hour, or until the rabbit is tender but not falling apart.

Taste for seasoning and serve the rabbit at once, directly from the casserole. Or, if you prefer, arrange the pieces of rabbit in a deep heated platter and ladle the tarragon cream gravy over them.

## *Roast Pheasant with Filbert Stuffing and Currant Sauce* (*Eastern Heartland*)

To serve 4

9 tablespoons butter, plus
6 tablespoons butter, softened

4 to 5 slices homemade-type white
bread, trimmed of all crusts and
cut into ¼-inch cubes (about
2 cups)

½ cup finely chopped celery

1 cup finely chopped onions

½ cup filberts, pulverized in a
blender or with a nut grinder

¼ teaspoon ground sage

1 teaspoon salt

Freshly ground black pepper

A 3- to 3½-pound oven-ready
pheasant

2 tablespoons thin strips orange
peel, each cut about ⅛ inch wide and
1 inch long

1 tablespoon thin strips lemon peel,
each cut about ⅛ inch wide and
1 inch long

1¼ cups chicken stock, fresh or
canned

2 tablespoons currant jelly

2 tablespoons port

1 tablespoon cornstarch

Preheat the oven to 400°. To make the stuffing, melt 8 tablespoons of the butter over moderate heat in a heavy 8- to 10-inch skillet. When the foam begins to subside, add the bread cubes and stir until they are crisp and brown. With a slotted spoon, transfer the cubes to a deep bowl.

Add 1 tablespoon of butter to that remaining in the skillet and drop in the celery and ½ cup of the onions. Stirring frequently, cook over moderate heat for about 5 minutes, or until the vegetables are soft but not brown. With a rubber spatula, scrape the entire contents of the skillet over the bread cubes. Add the filberts, sage, salt and a few grindings of pepper, and toss together gently but thoroughly.

Wash the pheasant quickly under cold running water and pat it dry inside and out with paper towels. Fill the cavity loosely with the stuffing and close the opening by lacing it with small skewers and cord or sewing it with heavy white thread. Fasten the neck skin to the back of the pheasant with a skewer and truss the bird neatly. With a pastry brush, spread 4 tablespoons of the softened butter evenly over the surface of the bird.

Lay the bird on its side on a rack set in a shallow roasting pan. Roast the pheasant in the middle of the oven for 10 minutes. Turn it over, brush it with the remaining 2 tablespoons of softened butter, and roast it for 10 minutes longer. Then turn the bird breast side up and baste it with the fat that has accumulated in the pan. Continue roasting for 20 to 30 minutes, or until it is golden brown, basting the bird with its pan juices every 10 minutes. To test for doneness, pierce a thigh with the point of a small skewer or with a sharp knife; the juices that trickle out should be clear yellow. If they are still tinged with pink, roast the pheasant for about 5 minutes longer.

Meanwhile drop the strips of the orange and lemon peel into enough boiling water to immerse them completely and cook briskly, uncovered, for 5 minutes. Drain in a sieve and run cold water over the peel to set the color. Reserve the peel.

When the pheasant has roasted for its allotted time, transfer it to a heated platter. Remove the trussing string and drape the platter loosely with foil to keep the bird warm while you prepare the sauce.

With a large spoon, skim as much fat as possible from the surface of the liquid remaining in the roasting pan. Add 1 cup of the chicken stock, the remaining ½ cup of onions, the currant jelly and port. Bring to a boil over high heat, stirring constantly and scraping in the brown particles that cling to the bottom and sides of the pan. Reduce the heat to low and simmer uncovered for about 5 minutes.

Dissolve the cornstarch in the remaining ¼ cup of chicken stock and stir it into the simmering sauce. Cook, still stirring, until the sauce comes to a boil, thickens and clears. Strain the sauce through a fine sieve into a sauceboat or gravy bowl and stir in the reserved orange and lemon peel. Taste for seasoning. Serve at once, accompanied by sauce.

## *Pheasant and Apples with Sour-Cream Sauce* (Northwest)

To serve 4

| | |
|---|---|
| 2 one-pound oven-ready pheasants, split lengthwise into halves | ½ cup finely chopped onions |
| 1 teaspoon salt | The livers, hearts and gizzards of the pheasants, finely chopped |
| ¼ teaspoon freshly ground black pepper | 1 cup chicken stock, fresh or canned |
| ½ cup plus 2 teaspoons flour | 2 firm unpeeled cooking apples, cored and quartered |
| 4 slices bacon | 2 tablespoons brandy |
| 3 tablespoons butter | ½ cup sour cream |

Pat the pheasant halves dry with paper towels and sprinkle them with the salt and pepper. One at a time, dip each half in ½ cup of the flour, turning it to coat both sides, and vigorously shake off the excess flour.

In a heavy 12-inch skillet, fry the bacon over moderate heat until the slices are crisp and brown and have rendered all their fat. Set the bacon slices aside on paper towels to drain, then crumble them into bits.

Pour off all but about 2 tablespoons of the fat remaining in the skillet and add the butter. Melt the butter in the fat and then brown the pheasant halves, one or two at a time. Turn the pheasant frequently and regulate the heat so that it colors richly and evenly without burning. As each half browns, set it aside on a plate.

Add the onions to the fat remaining in the skillet and, stirring frequently, cook for about 5 minutes, until they are soft and translucent but not brown. Add the pheasant livers, hearts and gizzards, and stir for 2 to 3 minutes. Stir in the stock and return the birds and the liquid that has accumulated around them to the skillet. Bring to a boil over high heat, reduce the heat to low, and simmer partially covered for 20 minutes.

Place the apple quarters in the skillet and spoon the cooking liquid over them. Then simmer partially covered for about 10 minutes longer. To test for doneness, pierce the thigh of a pheasant with the point of a small, sharp knife. The juice that trickles out should be clear yellow; if it is tinged with pink, simmer the birds for a few minutes more. Arrange the pheasants and apples attractively on a heated platter and drape foil over them to keep them warm while you prepare the sauce.

Skim the fat from the surface of the cooking liquid, pour in the brandy and bring to a simmer over moderate heat. Reduce the heat to low and cook for 1 to 2 minutes. Meanwhile, with a wire whisk, beat the remaining 2 teaspoons of flour into the sour cream. Stirring the sauce with the whisk, pour in the sour-cream mixture and simmer slowly for 4 to 5 minutes, until it is smooth and slightly thickened. Taste for seasoning, then pour the sauce over the pheasants. Sprinkle the pheasants with the reserved bacon bits and serve at once.

OPPOSITE
*Roast pheasant is more than than fair game when laden with filbert stuffing, moistened by currant-and-fruit-peel sauce and served with Brussels sprouts.*

209

## Barbecued Quail (South)

To serve 4

1 cup finely chopped onions
¼ cup dark brown sugar
¼ cup distilled white vinegar
¼ cup Worcestershire sauce
1 teaspoon dry mustard

¼ teaspoon Tabasco
½ cup catsup, preferably freshly
   made
3 tablespoons vegetable oil or lard
4 oven-ready quail

To prepare the barbecue sauce, combine the onions, sugar, vinegar, Worcestershire, mustard, Tabasco and catsup in a 1- to 1½-quart enameled or stainless-steel saucepan. Stirring constantly with a wooden spoon, bring the sauce to a boil over high heat. Reduce the heat to low and simmer uncovered for 5 to 8 minutes, until the onions are soft.

Heat the oil or lard in a heavy 10- to 12-inch enameled or stainless-steel skillet set over high heat. When the fat is very hot but not smoking, add the quail and fry for 2 to 3 minutes on each side, turning the birds with tongs. When they are golden brown, remove the skillet from the heat.

With a bulb baster, remove and discard all the fat in the pan. Pour the barbecue sauce over the quail and partially cover the skillet. Simmer the quail for 15 to 20 minutes over low heat, basting them with the sauce every 5 minutes or so. To test the quail for doneness, pierce a thigh with the point of a small sharp knife. The juice that trickles out should be pale yellow; if pink, cook for 5 to 10 minutes more. Transfer the quail to a heated platter, pour the sauce over them, and serve at once, accompanied, if you like, by Southern dry rice.*

## Grouse with Brandied Orange Stuffing (Northwest)

To serve 6

6 one-pound oven-ready grouse
2 teaspoons salt
Freshly ground black pepper
1 large navel orange
12 tablespoons butter, plus 4
   tablespoons butter, melted
8 to 10 slices homemade-type white
   bread, cut into ¼-inch cubes
   (4 cups)
2 cups finely chopped celery

½ cup finely chopped onions
6 grouse livers, finely chopped
¼ cup brandy
1 teaspoon crumbled dried sage
   leaves
½ teaspoon crumbled dried
   rosemary
⅛ teaspoon crumbled dried chervil
⅛ teaspoon crumbled dried
   marjoram
½ cup strained fresh orange juice

210

* See index.

Preheat the oven to 425°. Wash the grouse quickly under cold running water and pat them dry inside and out with paper towels. Season the cavities of the birds with 1 teaspoon of the salt and a few grindings of pepper, and set aside.

Grate the peel of the orange fine, taking care not to include any of the bitter white pith underneath; measure and set aside 2 tablespoons of grated peel. With a small, sharp knife, remove all the remaining peel, the pith and white membrane from the orange. Chop the orange pulp fine and squeeze it between your hands to remove the excess juice. Reserve the orange pulp.

In a heavy 12-inch skillet, melt 6 tablespoons of the butter over moderate heat. Drop in the bread cubes and stir until they are delicately browned. Transfer the cubes to a deep bowl, add 6 tablespoons of butter to the skillet and melt it as before. When the foam begins to subside, add the celery, onions and grouse livers and, stirring frequently, cook for about 5 minutes, or until the vegetables are soft but not brown. Pour in the brandy, bring to a boil over high heat, and cook briskly for 30 seconds.

With a rubber spatula, scrape the contents of the skillet over the bread cubes. Add the chopped orange pulp, the reserved orange peel, the sage, rosemary, chervil, marjoram, the remaining teaspoon of salt and a few grindings of pepper. Mix well, taste for seasoning, then spoon the stuffing into the cavities of the grouse. Close the openings by lacing them with skewers and kitchen cord or sewing them with heavy white thread.

Truss the birds neatly and lay them on their backs on a rack in a large, shallow roasting pan. Combine the 4 tablespoons of melted butter with the orange juice and, with a pastry brush, spread a few tablespoons of the mixture over the breasts and legs of the birds.

Roast in the middle of the oven for 15 minutes, then reduce the temperature to 375° and brush the grouse again with the butter and orange juice. Continue roasting for 25 to 30 minutes longer, basting the birds every 10 minutes. To test for doneness, pierce the thigh of a bird with the point of a small, sharp knife. The juice that trickles out should be clear yellow; if it is slightly tinged with pink, roast the grouse for another 5 to 10 minutes.

Transfer the grouse to a heated platter and let them rest about 10 minutes before serving.

To serve 4 or 8

½ ounce dried morels, or substitute any type dried mushrooms
¾ cup water

Place the morels (or other dried mushrooms) in a small bowl, pour the water over them, and let stand at room temperature for at least 2 hours. Drain the morels, reserving the soaking liquid, and chop them coarsely.

WILD-RICE STUFFING
2 tablespoons butter
¼ cup finely chopped onions
½ cup wild rice, thoroughly rinsed

1 to 1½ cups boiling chicken stock, fresh or canned
¼ teaspoon salt
Freshly ground black pepper

Meanwhile, prepare the wild-rice stuffing in the following fashion: In a heavy 8- to 10-inch skillet, melt 2 tablespoons of butter over moderate heat. When the foam begins to subside, add ¼ cup of chopped onions and, stirring frequently, cook for about 5 minutes, until they are soft and translucent but not brown. Add the wild rice and stir for 2 or 3 minutes to coat the grains evenly with butter. Then pour in 1 cup of the boiling chicken stock, add ¼ teaspoon of salt and a few grindings of pepper, and bring to a boil again over high heat. Reduce the heat to low, cover tightly, and simmer for about 30 to 45 minutes, or until the grains are tender and have absorbed all the stock. (Check the skillet from time to time; if the wild rice is too dry add up to ½ cup more boiling chicken stock, a tablespoon at a time.) Remove the skillet from the heat, taste for seasoning, and cover to keep the stuffing warm.

QUAIL
8 six-ounce oven-ready quail
2 teaspoons salt
½ teaspoon freshly ground black pepper

4 slices bacon, each cut crosswise in half
6 tablespoons butter, melted

Preheat the oven to 475°. Wash the quail under cold running water and dry them thoroughly with paper towels. Rub 2 teaspoons of salt and ½ teaspoon of black pepper into the cavities of the birds. Then fill them loosely with the wild-rice stuffing, dividing it evenly among them, and close the opening of each bird by sewing it with heavy white thread.

Arrange the quail on their backs on a rack in a large shallow roasting pan. Drape a piece of bacon across the breasts and thighs of each bird, pressing the bacon snugly against the bird to keep it in place. Roast in the middle of the oven for 15 to 20 minutes, basting the quail every 5 minutes or so with 6 tablespoons of melted butter and the liquid that has accumulated in the bottom of the pan. The birds are done when they are golden brown and the drumsticks feel tender to the touch.

SAUCE

| | |
|---|---|
| ½ cup finely chopped onions | 2 tablespoons brandy |
| 2 tablespoons flour | ⅛ teaspoon crumbled dried thyme |
| ½ cup chicken stock, fresh or canned | 2 tablespoons heavy cream |

Discard the bacon, transfer the quail to a heated platter, and drape foil over them to keep them warm while you prepare the sauce. Pour off all but about 2 tablespoons of the fat from the roasting pan and in its place add ½ cup of chopped onions. Stirring frequently, cook over moderate heat for about 5 minutes, or until the onions are soft and translucent but not brown. Add the flour and mix well. Stirring the mixture constantly with a wire whisk or large spoon, add ½ cup of chicken stock, the reserved soaking liquid from the mushrooms, the brandy and thyme, and cook over high heat until the sauce comes to a boil, thickens lightly and is smooth. Reduce the heat to low and simmer for 2 or 3 minutes to remove the taste of flour.

Stir in the cream, then strain the sauce through a fine sieve into a small saucepan, pressing down hard on the onions with the back of a spoon to extract all their juice before discarding the pulp. Add the reserved mushrooms and simmer the sauce for a minute or so to heat it through. Taste for seasoning, pour into a bowl or sauceboat and serve at once with the stuffed quail.

*Hearst Ranch Squab* (Far West)

To serve 4

| | |
|---|---|
| 6 tablespoons butter, cut into bits, plus 6 tablespoons butter, melted | Parmesan cheese |
| 7 or 8 slices homemade-type white bread, trimmed of all crusts and cut into ¼-inch cubes (about 3 cups) | 1 tablespoon finely chopped fresh parsley |
| | ¼ teaspoon crumbled dried marjoram |
| ½ cup finely chopped onions | 1½ teaspoons salt |
| 1½ teaspoons finely chopped garlic | ⅛ teaspoon ground white pepper |
| | 4 one-pound oven-ready squab |
| ¾ cup freshly grated imported | Parsley sprigs or watercress for garnish |

First prepare the stuffing in the following manner: Preheat the oven to 400°. In a heavy 8- to 10-inch skillet, melt 4 tablespoons of the butter bits over moderate heat. When the foam begins to subside, drop in the bread cubes and, stirring frequently, fry them until they are golden brown on all sides. Transfer the bread cubes to a mixing bowl. In the skillet melt the remaining 2 tablespoons of butter bits. When the foam subsides, add the onions and garlic, and stir over moderate heat for 5 minutes, or until the onions are soft and translucent but not brown.

With a rubber spatula, scrape the entire contents of the skillet over the bread cubes. Mix well, then stir in the grated cheese, chopped parsley, marjoram, ½ teaspoon of the salt and the white pepper. Taste the stuffing for seasoning.

Wash the squab briefly under cold running water and pat them completely dry inside and out with paper towels. Season the cavities of the birds with the remaining teaspoon of salt, and fill the cavities with the stuffing, dividing it equally among them. Sew the openings securely with white thread, then truss the bird securely.

Place the birds side by side on a rack set in a shallow roasting pan and, using a pastry brush, coat the squab evenly with 2 tablespoons of the melted butter. Roast in the middle of the oven for about 40 minutes, brushing the birds from time to time with the remaining melted butter and the fat that will accumulate in the bottom of the pan.

To test for doneness, pierce the thighs of the birds with the point of a small sharp knife. The juice that trickles out should be a clear yellow; if it is tinged with pink, roast the squab for 5 or 10 minutes longer.

Arrange the squab attractively on a heated platter, garnish them with parsley or watercress and serve at once.

## Pigeon Casserole *(Creole-Acadian)*

**To serve 2**

2 one-pound oven-ready squab
    pigeons
½ teaspoon ground hot red pepper
    (cayenne)
1 teaspoon salt
2 tablespoons butter
2 tablespoons vegetable oil
½ cup finely chopped onions
½ cup finely chopped celery
2 medium-sized carrots, scraped and
    thinly sliced
¼ cup finely chopped scallions,
    including 3 inches of the green
    tops

¼ cup flour
2 cups chicken stock, fresh or
    canned
½ cup dry red wine
¼ pound firm fresh mushrooms,
    trimmed, wiped with a dampened
    towel and cut lengthwise,
    including the stems, into ¼-inch-
    thick slices
½ cup fresh or thoroughly
    defrosted frozen Lima beans
2 tablespoons finely chopped fresh
    parsley, preferably the flat-leaf
    Italian variety

Wash the pigeons briefly under cold running water and pat them completely dry, inside and out, with paper towels. Season the cavities and skin of the birds with ¼ teaspoon of the red pepper and ½ teaspoon of the salt, then truss them neatly.

In a heavy 4- to 5-quart casserole, melt the butter with the oil over moderate heat. When the foam begins to subside, place the pigeons in the casserole and brown them, turning the birds about with a spoon and regulating the heat so that they color richly and evenly on all sides without burning. Transfer the birds to a plate and set them aside.

Add the onions, celery, carrots and scallions to the fat remaining in the casserole and, stirring frequently, cook for 8 to 10 minutes, or until the vegetables are soft and delicately browned. Add the flour and mix well. Stirring constantly, pour in the chicken stock and the red wine in a slow, thin stream and cook over high heat until the sauce mixture comes to a boil and thickens lightly.

Stir in the mushrooms, Lima beans and the remaining ¼ teaspoon of red pepper and ½ teaspoon of salt. Return the pigeons and the liquid that has accumulated around them to the casserole and turn the birds about with a spoon to coat them evenly with the sauce and vegetables.

Reduce the heat to low and partially cover the casserole. Turning the birds from time to time, simmer for about 45 minutes, or until they are tender and a thigh shows no resistance when pierced deeply with the point of a small sharp knife.

Taste for seasoning, add the parsley and serve at once, directly from the casserole or from a large heated bowl.

## Roast Rock Cornish Game Hens with Pine-Nut Stuffing

To serve 4

STUFFING
5 tablespoons butter
1 cup long-grain rice
2 cups chicken stock, fresh or canned
1 teaspoon salt
1 cup finely chopped onion
½ cup pine nuts

6 tablespoons finely chopped fresh parsley

4 Rock Cornish game hens, about 1 pound each
2 teaspoons salt
4 tablespoons melted butter
Watercress

For the stuffing, melt 3 tablespoons of the butter in a 2-quart heavy casserole or saucepan over moderate heat. Add the rice and stir constantly for 2 to 3 minutes, or until most of the rice has turned milky and opaque. Do not let it brown. Then pour in the chicken stock, add the salt and bring the stock to a boil, stirring occasionally. Cover the pan tightly, reduce the heat to its lowest point and simmer for 18 to 20 minutes, or until the rice has absorbed all the liquid. Meanwhile, in a small skillet melt the remaining 2 tablespoons of butter and when the foam subsides add the onion. Cook over moderate heat for 8 to 10 minutes, then add the pine nuts. Cook 2 or 3 minutes longer, stirring, until the nuts are lightly browned. In a small mixing bowl combine the cooked rice, the onion, pine nuts and the parsley. Mix gently but thoroughly. Taste for seasoning.

Preheat the oven to 400°. Wash the birds under cold running water, then dry them inside and out with paper towels. Sprinkle the inside of each bird with ½ teaspoon of salt, then pack the cavities loosely with the stuffing; they should be no more than ¾ full. Skewer or sew the openings with thread, truss the birds securely and brush them with the melted butter. Place them on their sides on a rack set in a shallow roasting pan just large enough to hold them. Roast them in the middle of the oven for 15 minutes, then turn them on the other side and brush them with butter again. Roast for another 15 minutes. Turn them breast side up, brush with the remaining butter and salt each bird lightly. Roast, basting occasionally with the drippings in the bottom of the pan, for 15 to 20 minutes longer, or until the birds are golden brown all over and tender. Test for doneness by piercing the fleshy part of the thigh with the point of a sharp knife. The juice that spurts out should be yellow. If it is pink, roast a few minutes longer. Transfer the birds to a warm serving platter, pour the pan juices over them and serve, garnished with watercress.

# Pork & Ham

Barring game, pork is America's oldest meat. Pigs came to the United States with the earliest settlers, and were set loose to fatten in the woods. Pork has been a staple of the American diet ever since. Most pork comes from pigs less than one year old, so the meat is naturally tender. Nonetheless, pork rarely comes to the table at its best. Too many cooks over-react to the fear of trichinosis, and roast or fry the meat so long that it turns gray-brown and becomes stringy. Trichina are a real danger, but they are destroyed at 137°F., making the internal temperature of 170°F. —which results in succulently moist, white meat—absolutely safe to eat. Pork's mild flavor can be further enhanced by adding a piquant herb stuffing, as in the Ukranian-American recipe for pork chops found on the following pages, or by braising in a vegetable-rich stock, accented by white wine and paprika (a recipe for loin prepared this way also follows). Fresh pork can also be ground and prepared as the spicy stuffing for an elegant crown roast of pork chops, or for Creole-Acadian sausages.

In addition to supplying fresh pork, pigs also find their way to the table in the form of processed ham. Smoked hams may be fully cooked, ready-to-cook or country-style. The fully cooked ham can be simply heated and served—perhaps broiled with melon, as in the Far West. Ready-to-cook ham may be baked with cheese, as described below—or glazed with a bourbon glaze so popular in the South. Ready-to-cook hams are generally cured by injecting brine into the blood vessels, then are smoked over sawdust; fully cooked hams may be similarly prepared, then boiled.

Country hams, from Pennsylvania and New York State as well as from Virginia, Kentucky and Tennessee, have a strong, smoky taste. The best-known are the Smithfield, Virginia, hams, bred on acorns, nuts, peanuts and corn. The hams are dry-salted until cured, then covered with black pepper and slowly smoked over hickory fires. They are then aged for a year or longer, intensifying their unique flavor as they shrink. The mold-and salt-encrusted hams need to be scrubbed, soaked and boiled before being glazed and baked like their ready-to-cook cousins. Or for an unusual treat, the prepared ham may be stuffed Southern style, with greens, baked, then sliced wafer-thin so that each pink morsel is flecked with green.

*In the South, Smithfield and other types of country ham are never served as a main meat course; instead, paper-thin slivers of the smoked, salty hams are presented as a first course or as an accompaniment to chicken or other fowl. They are also a traditional part of buffet tables. All of these hams are available baked and ready to serve—but at a higher price than the uncooked ones command. If you would like to prepare your own ham, the following recipe describes the basic procedures.*

| | |
|---|---|
| A 12- to 16-pound Smithfield ham or a 12- to 16-pound Virginia, Kentucky, Tennessee or Georgia country ham | ½ to ¾ cup fine dry bread crumbs<br>1 cup dark brown sugar<br>¼ cup whole cloves (optional) |

Starting a day ahead, place the ham in a pot large enough to hold it comfortably and pour in enough water to cover the ham by at least 1 inch. Let the ham soak for at least 12 hours (for 24 hours if possible), changing the water 2 or 3 times. Remove the ham from the pot and discard the soaking water. Then, under lukewarm running water, scrub the ham vigorously with a stiff brush to remove any traces of pepper or mold.

With a dampened kitchen towel wipe the ham and return it to the pot. Pour in enough water to cover the ham by at least 1 inch and bring to a simmer over high heat. Reduce the heat to low and simmer partially covered for 3 to 4 hours, allowing 15 to 20 minutes to the pound. When the ham is fully cooked, you should be able to move and easily pull out the small bone near the shank.

Transfer the ham to a platter and, if you wish, set the cooking water aside to be used for cooking greens. When the ham is cool enough to handle remove the rind with a small sharp knife, leaving only a ⅛-inch-thick layer of fat. If you intend to stud the ham with cloves, make crisscrossing cuts about 1 inch apart on the fatty side, slicing down through the fat to the meat.

Preheat the oven to 400°. With your fingers, press enough of the bread crumbs into the fatty side of the ham to coat it thoroughly. Then sift the brown sugar evenly over the crumbs. If you are using cloves, insert them where the scoring lines intersect. Place the ham on a rack set in a shallow roasting pan and bake it uncovered in the middle of the oven for about 20 minutes, or until the glaze is richly browned.

Set the ham on a large platter and let it cool to room temperature before serving. Smithfield or country ham is carved into paper-thin slices. Tightly covered with foil or plastic wrap, the ham can safely be kept in the refrigerator for at least 1 month.

To serve 12 to 14

A 12- to 14-pound smoked ham, processed, precooked variety

¾ cup bourbon whiskey

2 cups dark brown sugar

1 tablespoon dry mustard

¾ cup whole cloves

2 navel oranges, peeled and sectioned

Preheat the oven to 325°. Place the ham fat side up on a rack set in a shallow roasting pan large enough to hold the ham comfortably. Bake in the middle of the oven, without basting, for two hours, or until the meat can be easily pierced with a fork. For greater cooking certainty, insert a meat thermometer in the fleshiest part of the ham before baking it. It should register between 130° and 140° when the ham is done.

When the ham is cool enough to handle comfortably, cut away the rind with a large, sharp knife. Then score the ham by cutting deeply through the fat until you reach the meat, making the incisions ½ inch apart lengthwise and crosswise. Return the ham to the rack in the pan and raise the oven heat to 450°. With a pastry brush, paint the ham on all sides with ½ cup of the whiskey. Then combine the sugar and mustard and ¼ cup of whiskey, and pat the mixture firmly into the scored fat. Stud the fat at the intersections or in the center of each diamond with a whole clove, and arrange the orange sections as decoratively as you can on the top of the ham with toothpicks or small skewers to secure them. Baste lightly with the drippings on the bottom of the pan and bake the ham undisturbed in the hot oven for 15 to 20 minutes, or until the sugar has melted and formed a brilliant glaze.

## *Ham Baked with Cheese*

To serve 4

4 slices cooked ham, cut ½ inch thick

½ cup light cream

½ pound American cheese, diced

2 tablespoons lemon juice

½ teaspoon Worcestershire sauce

½ teaspoon French mustard

Cayenne pepper

Paprika

Preheat the oven to 350°. Place the slices of ham in a baking dish and put them aside. Heat the cream in the top of a double boiler. Add the diced cheese, lemon juice, Worcestershire sauce, mustard and a few grains of cayenne and paprika. Cook, stirring constantly, until the cheese is melted. Cover the ham slices with the cheese sauce and bake in the oven until the cheese is lightly browned.

## Stuffed Fresh Ham *(Eastern Heartland)*

To serve 8 to 10

| | |
|---|---|
| 1 cup soft fresh crumbs made from homemade-type white bread, pulverized in a blender or finely shredded with a fork | ½ teaspoon finely chopped garlic |
| | ¼ teaspoon ground sage |
| | ½ teaspoon salt |
| | Freshly ground black pepper |
| ½ pound lean pork, finely ground | A 7- to 8-pound shank half of fresh ham, boned and trimmed of excess fat |
| 1 egg | |
| ½ cup finely chopped onions | |
| ¼ cup finely chopped fresh parsley | 1 cup apple butter |

Preheat the oven to 300°. First prepare the stuffing in the following fashion: Place the bread crumbs, ground pork, egg, onions, parsley, garlic, sage, salt and a few grindings of pepper in a deep bowl. Knead vigorously with both hands to combine the ingredients, then beat with a wooden spoon until the mixture is smooth and fluffy.

Spoon the stuffing into the cavity of the ham, packing it in as tightly as you can. To keep the stuffing in place, close the openings at both ends of the ham with small skewers and cord as if you were lacing a turkey or sew them tightly shut with heavy white thread. For the most predictable results, insert a meat thermometer at least 2 inches into the fleshiest part of the ham.

Place the ham, fat side up, on a rack in a shallow roasting pan and roast it uncovered in the middle of the oven for 4 hours, or until the juices run clear when the ham is pierced deeply with the point of a small skewer or sharp knife. A meat thermometer will register 165° to 170° when the ham is done.

Remove the thermometer if you have used one and, with a pastry brush, spread the apple butter evenly over the surface of the ham. Roast the ham for 30 minutes longer, or until the apple butter has formed a glaze. Then transfer the ham to a heated platter, remove the skewers or thread, and let the ham rest for 15 minutes for easier carving.

Meanwhile, skim as much fat as possible from the surface of the juices remaining in the pan. Taste for seasoning and pour the juices into a small bowl or sauceboat.

To serve, carve the ham vertically into ⅛-inch-thick slices and arrange the slices attractively on another heated platter. Present the gravy separately with the ham.

A 12- to 16-pound country ham
3 tablespoons butter
¼ cup finely chopped scallions,
    including 2 inches of the green
    tops
½ cup finely chopped celery
½ pound fresh mustard greens,
    trimmed, washed and coarsely

chopped (about 4 cups)
½ pound fresh spinach, trimmed,
    washed and coarsely chopped
    (about 4 cups)
1 teaspoon crushed dried hot red
    pepper
½ teaspoon salt
Freshly ground black pepper

Starting a day ahead, place the ham in a pot large enough to hold it comfortably and pour in enough cold water to cover the ham by at least 1 inch. Let the ham soak at room temperature for at least 12 hours.

When you are ready to cook the ham drain off the soaking water and replace it with fresh cold water to cover the ham by 1 inch. Bring to a boil over high heat, then reduce the heat to low and simmer the ham partially covered for 1 hour. Transfer the ham to cool on a large platter or cutting board. Discard the cooking liquid, wash the pot and set it aside.

With a large sharp knife, cut the rind off the ham and discard it. Then remove the excess fat from the entire outside surface of the ham, leaving a layer no more than ⅛ inch thick all around. Set the ham aside.

In a heavy 4- to 5-quart saucepan, melt the butter over moderate heat. When the foam begins to subside, add the scallions and celery and, stirring frequently, cook for about 5 minutes until they are soft and transparent but not brown. Stir in the mustard greens, spinach, red pepper, salt and a few grindings of black pepper. Reduce the heat to the lowest possible setting, cover the pan tightly, and cook for 15 minutes, or until all the vegetables are tender.

Cut 6 to 8 incisions in the ham and stuff them with the mustard-green-and-spinach mixture. Wrap the ham in cheesecloth.

Return the ham to the original pot and add enough water to cover by at least 1 inch. Bring to a boil over high heat, reduce the heat to low and partially cover the pot. Simmer for 3 to 4 hours, allowing about 15 minutes to the pound, or until the ham is tender and shows no resistance when pierced deeply with the point of a small skewer or sharp knife. (The ham should be kept constantly immersed in water. Check the pot from time to time and add more boiling water if necessary.) The cooking liquid can be saved, if you like, for cooking greens.

Transfer the ham to a large platter and, without removing the cheesecloth, cool to room temperature and refrigerate for at least 12 hours. Just before serving, unwrap the ham and with a large sharp knife, carve it into paper-thin slices as shown opposite.

221

To serve 4

½ pound butter, cut into ½-inch
    bits
½ cup finely chopped bottled
    chutney
2 teaspoons curry powder
1 tablespoon vegetable oil

A 2-pound center-cut ham steak, cut
    about ¾ inch thick and trimmed
    of all but ⅛ inch of fat
1 large firm ripe cantaloupe, cut
    lengthwise into 8 equal wedges
    and peeled

Light a layer of briquettes in a charcoal grill and let them burn until white ash appears on the surface. Or preheat the broiler of your stove to its highest setting.

Meanwhile, in a small saucepan, melt the butter over moderate heat, stirring so that it melts evenly without browning. Remove the pan from the heat, add the chutney and curry powder, and mix well.

With a pastry brush, spread the vegetable oil evenly over the grill of the barbecue or the rack of the broiling pan. Place the ham steak on the grill or rack, and brush the top with about ⅓ cup of the chutney mixture. Broil the ham steak for about 15 minutes, turning it over every 5 minutes with kitchen tongs and brushing it each time with about ⅓ cup of the chutney mixture. When the ham steak is richly browned on both sides, transfer it to a heated platter.

Arrange the wedges of cantaloupe in one layer on the grill or broiling-pan rack, brush them with about half of the remaining chutney mixture and broil them for 1 or 2 minutes. Turn the wedges over, coat them with the rest of the mixture and broil for about 1 minute longer, or until they are richly colored.

Serve the ham steak at once, surrounded on the platter by the broiled cantaloupe wedges.

## Homesteaders' Ham Loaf   (South)

To serve 6 to 8

HAM LOAF

1 tablespoon vegetable oil
1 pound (about 3 cups) ground
    cooked ham (leftover from baked
    country ham)
½ pound ground lean fresh pork

1 cup dry bread crumbs
2 tablespoons prepared mustard
1 egg, lightly beaten
½ cup grated onions
½ cup milk

Preheat the oven to 350°. With a pastry brush, spread the tablespoon of oil evenly over the bottom of a shallow roasting pan. Set aside.

In a large mixing bowl, combine the ground ham, fresh pork, bread crumbs, prepared mustard, egg, onions and milk. Knead briefly with your hands to mix the ingredients thoroughly, then transfer the mixture to the roasting pan and pat and shape it into a loaf about 8 inches long, 4 inches wide and 3 inches high.

SAUCE
¼ cup dark brown sugar
½ teaspoon dry mustard

2 tablespoons cold water
2 tablespoons distilled white
 vinegar

To make the sauce, beat the sugar, dry mustard, water and vinegar together in a small mixing bowl. Spoon 2 tablespoons of the sauce over the ham loaf, then place the loaf in the middle of the oven and bake for 1 hour, basting every 10 minutes or so until you have used all the remaining sauce.

Serve the ham loaf at once, from a heated platter. Or, if you prefer the ham loaf cold, let it cool to room temperature, cover with foil or plastic wrap, and refrigerate for several hours.

## Ham Hocks and Black-eyed Peas   (South)

To serve 6 to 8

2 one-pound smoked ham hocks, or
 substitute a meaty ham bone or
 pieces of slab bacon with the rind on
2 cups (1 pound) dried black-eyed
 peas
1 cup coarsely chopped onions
2 medium-sized celery stalks,

trimmed of all leaves and coarsely
 chopped
1 fresh hot red chili, about 3 inches
 long, washed, stemmed, seeded if
 desired, and coarsely chopped
 (caution: see note, appendix)
Freshly ground black pepper

Place the ham hocks in a heavy 4- to 6-quart pot and add enough water to cover the meat by at least 1 inch. Bring to a boil over high heat, reduce the heat to low and simmer partially covered for 2 hours, or until the ham hocks are tender and show no resistance when pierced deeply with the point of a small skewer or sharp knife.

In a sieve or colander, wash the black-eyed peas under cold running water until the draining water is clear. Add the peas, onions, celery, chili and a few grindings of black pepper to the pot, mix well, and bring to a boil over high heat. Reduce the heat to low and simmer partially covered for 1 to 1½ hours, or until the peas are tender. Check the pot from time to time and add more boiling water if necessary. When the peas are fully cooked, they should have absorbed almost all of the pan liquid.

Taste for seasoning and serve at once from a heated platter or bowl.

To serve 6

| | |
|---|---|
| 2 cups dried apples (½ pound) | 6 cups chicken stock, fresh or canned |
| 3 pounds smoked ham butt | 2 tablespoons dark brown sugar |

Place the dried apples in a small bowl and pour in enough water to cover them by at least 1 inch. Set the apples aside at room temperature to soak for at least 8 hours, or overnight. Drain the apples in a sieve or colander and discard the soaking water.

Place the ham butt in a heavy 5- to 6-quart casserole at least 12 inches in diameter and pour in enough water to cover the ham by 2 inches. Bring to a boil over high heat, reduce the heat to low, and simmer partially covered for 1½ hours, or until the ham shows no resistance when pierced deeply with the point of a small skewer or sharp knife. Transfer the ham to a plate and discard the cooking liquid.

With a sharp knife, cut the ham into ¼-inch-thick slices and then into ¼-inch cubes. Return the ham to the casserole and add the apples, chicken stock and brown sugar.

Bring to a boil over high heat, stirring until the sugar dissolves. Reduce the heat to low and simmer partially covered for 15 minutes. Taste for seasoning.

DUMPLINGS

| | |
|---|---|
| 2 cups unsifted flour | ¼ teaspoon salt |
| 1 tablespoon double-acting baking powder | 2 tablespoons butter, cut into ¼-inch bits and softened |
| | 1½ cups milk |

While the stew is simmering, prepare the dumpling dough: Combine the flour, baking powder and salt, and sift them into a deep bowl. Add the butter bits and, with your fingers, rub the flour and fat together until they look like flakes of coarse meal. Add the milk and beat vigorously with a spoon until the dough is smooth.

Drop the dumplings on top of the simmering stew by the heaping tablespoon. Cover the casserole tightly, and simmer undisturbed for about 10 minutes longer. The dumplings are done when they are puffed and fluffy and a cake tester or toothpick inserted in the center of a dumpling comes out clean.

Remove the dumplings with a slotted spoon and pour the ham-and-apple mixture into a preheated bowl or deep platter. Arrange the dumplings on top and serve at once.

To serve 4

2 medium-sized eggplants (each
  about 1 pound)
⅓ cup olive oil
8 tablespoons butter, cut into
  ½-inch bits, plus 4 teaspoons
  butter, melted
½ cup finely chopped onions
½ cup finely chopped scallions,
  including 3 inches of the green
  tops
1½ teaspoons finely chopped
  garlic
1 cup coarsely chopped drained
  canned tomatoes

1 teaspoon crumbled dried thyme
½ teaspoon ground hot red pepper
  (cayenne)
¼ teaspoon freshly ground black
  pepper
½ teaspoon salt
½ pound lean smoked ham, finely
  ground
2¼ cups soft fresh crumbs made
  from French- or Italian-type
  white bread, trimmed of all crusts
  and pulverized in a blender
¼ cup finely chopped fresh
  parsley, preferably the flat-leaf
  Italian variety

Cut the eggplants in half lengthwise and, with a spoon, hollow out the center of each half to make a boatlike shell about ¼ inch thick. Finely chop the eggplant pulp and set it aside.

In a heavy 12-inch skillet, heat the olive oil over moderate heat until a light haze forms above it. Add the eggplant shells and turn them about with tongs or a spoon until they are moistened on all sides. Then cover the skillet tightly and cook over moderate heat for 5 or 6 minutes. Turn the shells over and continue to cook, still tightly covered, for 5 minutes longer, or until they are somewhat soft to the touch. Invert the shells on paper towels to drain briefly and arrange them cut side up in a baking dish large enough to hold them snugly in one layer.

Preheat the oven to 400°. Drain off the oil remaining in the skillet, add the 8 tablespoons of butter bits and melt them over moderate heat. When the foam subsides, add the onions, scallions and garlic and, stirring frequently, cook for 5 minutes, or until they are soft but not brown.

Add the reserved chopped eggplant pulp, the tomatoes, thyme, red and black pepper, and salt and, stirring frequently, cook briskly until most of the liquid in the pan evaporates and the mixture is thick enough to hold its shape almost solidly in a spoon. Remove the skillet from the heat and stir in the ground ham, 2 cups of the bread crumbs and the parsley. Taste for seasoning.

Spoon the filling into the eggplant shells, dividing it equally among them and mounding it slightly in the centers. Sprinkle each shell with 1 tablespoon of the remaining bread crumbs and dribble 1 teaspoon of the melted butter on top. Bake in the middle of the oven for 15 minutes, or until the shells are tender and the filling lightly browned. Arrange the ham-stuffed eggplant attractively on a large heated platter or individual plates and serve at once.

## Pot-roasted Loin of Pork

To serve 6 to 8

A 5-pound pork loin in one piece, with the excess fat removed, finely chopped and reserved, and with the backbone (chine) sawed through at ½-inch intervals, but left attached and tied to the loin in 2 or 3 places

3 tablespoons flour

2 large onions, peeled and cut crosswise into ¼-inch-thick slices

1 teaspoon finely chopped garlic

3 medium-sized carrots, scraped and finely chopped

1 cup dry white wine

½ cup chicken stock, fresh or canned

½ teaspoon crumbled dried thyme

½ teaspoon paprika

2 teaspoons salt

Freshly ground black pepper

Preheat the oven to 350°. Pat the pork loin completely dry with paper towels, then sprinkle it on all sides with the flour and spread the flour evenly with your fingers.

In a heavy 6- to 8-quart casserole, fry the reserved pork fat over moderate heat, turning the bits about frequently with a slotted spoon until they are crisp and have rendered all their fat. Remove and discard the bits. Brown the pork loin in the fat, turning it over frequently and regulating the heat so that it colors richly and evenly without burning.

Transfer the pork loin to a plate and add the onions and garlic to the fat remaining in the casserole. Stirring frequently, cook over moderate heat for about 5 minutes, or until the onions are soft and translucent but not brown. Add the carrots and cook for a minute or so longer.

Stir in the wine, chicken stock, thyme, paprika, salt and a few grindings of pepper, and bring to a boil over high heat, meanwhile scraping in any brown particles that cling to the bottom and sides of the casserole. Return the pork loin and the liquid that has accumulated around it and cover the casserole tightly. Braise in the middle of the oven for about 1½ hours, or until the pork shows no resistance when pierced deeply with the point of a small skewer or sharp knife.

Place the pork loin on a heated platter. With a slotted spoon, skim as much fat as possible from the surface of the cooking liquid. Then strain the liquid through a fine sieve into a bowl, pressing down hard on the vegetables with the back of a spoon to extract all their juices before discarding the pulp. Moisten the pork with a little of the gravy, pour the rest into a sauceboat and serve at once.

To serve 10 to 12

STUFFING

3 tablespoons butter
3/4 cup finely chopped onion
1/4 cup finely chopped celery
1/2 cup peeled, cored and coarsely
    diced tart apples
1/2 cup fresh bread crumbs
1 pound ground pork (the crown
    roast trimmings plus extra pork, if
    necessary)

1/2 pound well-seasoned sausage
    meat
1/2 cup finely chopped parsley
1/2 teaspoon sage
1 1/2 teaspoons salt
Freshly ground black pepper

A crown roast of pork, consisting of
    22 chops and weighing 8 to 9
    pounds

Preheat the oven to 350°. For the stuffing, melt the butter over moderate heat in an 8- to 10-inch skillet. When the foam subsides, add the onion and cook, stirring frequently, for about 5 minutes, then add the celery and apples. Cook without browning about 5 minutes longer. Scrape the contents of the pan into a large mixing bowl. Add the bread crumbs, ground pork, sausage meat, parsley, sage, salt and a few grindings of black pepper. With a large spoon, mix all the ingredients gently but thoroughly together. Do not taste the uncooked stuffing, for it contains raw pork; instead, fry a small ball of the stuffing in the skillet. Then season the rest of the mixture with more salt and pepper if necessary.

Fill the center of the crown with the stuffing, mounding it slightly. Cover it with a round of foil and wrap the ends of the chop bones in strips of foil to prevent them from charring and snapping off. Place the crown on a rack in a shallow roasting pan just about large enough to hold it comfortably, and roast it in the center of the oven, undisturbed, for about 3 hours, or until a meat thermometer, if you have used one, reads 170° to 175°. One half hour before the pork is done, remove the circle of foil from the top of the stuffing to allow the top to brown.

Carefully transfer the crown to a large, heated, circular platter, strip the foil from the ends of the chops and replace it with paper frills. Let the crown rest for about 10 minutes before carving and serving.

To carve the pork, insert a large fork in the side of the crown to steady it and, with a large, sharp knife, cut down through each rib to detach the chops. Two chops per person is a customary portion, accompanied by a generous serving of the stuffing. Buttered peas would make a fine and colorful accompaniment.

## Smoked Pork Chops and Lentils *(Eastern Heartland)*

To serve 6

¼ cup vegetable oil

1 teaspoon finely chopped garlic

2½ cups chicken stock, fresh or canned

2½ cups dried lentils

1 cup finely chopped scallions, including 2 inches of the green tops

¼ cup finely chopped fresh parsley

6 six-ounce smoked loin pork chops, each cut about 1 inch thick

In a heavy 4- to 5-quart casserole, heat the vegetable oil over moderate heat until a light haze forms above it. Add the garlic and stir for a minute or so, then pour in the chicken stock and bring to a boil over high heat. Stir in the lentils, scallions and parsley and, when the mixture returns to a boil, add the pork chops and turn them about with kitchen tongs to moisten them evenly.

Cover the casserole tightly, reduce the heat to low and simmer for about 45 minutes, or until the lentils are tender but not falling apart. Taste for seasoning and serve at once, directly from the casserole or, if you prefer, mound the lentils on a heated platter and arrange the pork chops attractively around them.

## Pork Chops with Paprika and Dill

To serve 4 to 6

8 pork chops, ¾ inch thick (trimmed)

Salt

Freshly ground black pepper

Flour

3 tablespoons lard

1½ cups finely chopped onions

¼ teaspoon finely chopped garlic

3 tablespoons sweet Hungarian paprika

1 cup chicken stock, fresh or canned, or water

⅓ cup heavy sweet cream

⅓ cup sour cream

2 tablespoons flour

3 tablespoons finely chopped fresh dill

Sprinkle the chops generously with salt and a few grindings of pepper, then dip them in the flour and shake off the excess. In a 12-inch skillet, heat the lard over high heat until a light haze forms over it. Add the pork chops to the skillet and cook them 3 to 4 minutes on each side. Transfer the chops to a platter.

Add the onions and garlic to the fat remaining in the pan, and cook them for 8 to 10 minutes, or until the onions are lightly colored. Off the heat, stir in the paprika, continuing to stir until the onions are well coated. Return the skillet to the heat, pour in the stock or water and bring it to a boil, stirring in any brown bits that cling to the pan.

Return the chops to the skillet, reduce the heat to its lowest point, cover tightly and simmer the chops for 1 hour, or until they are tender, then arrange them on a heated platter. Combine the sweet cream and the sour cream in a mixing bowl, then with a wire whisk, beat in the flour. While still beating, pour this mixture into the skillet. Stirring constantly, simmer for 2 to 3 minutes, or until the sauce is thick and smooth. Add the chopped dill and taste for seasoning.

## *Stuffed Pork Kotlety* (*Ukrainian-American*)
### HERB-STUFFED PORK CHOPS

To serve 4

| | |
|---|---|
| 4 center-cut loin pork chops, cut 1 inch thick | ¼ cup finely chopped parsley |
| | ¼ cup finely chopped celery |
| ¼ cup strained fresh lemon juice | ½ teaspoon salt |
| 5 tablespoons unsalted butter | ¼ teaspoon freshly ground black |
| 1 cup fine dry bread crumbs | pepper |
| ¼ cup finely cut chives | 2 tablespoons vegetable oil |

With a small knife, slit each chop through its side to create a pocket about 3 inches deep. Sprinkle the pocket and outside of the chops with the lemon juice and set aside.

In a small skillet, melt 2 tablespoons of the butter over moderate heat. Stir in the bread crumbs and, stirring constantly, brown the crumbs lightly. Transfer to a mixing bowl and toss with the chives, ¼ cup of parsley, the celery, ½ teaspoon of salt and the pepper. Taste for seasoning. With a small spoon, pack the stuffing evenly into the pork-chop pockets and secure the openings with toothpicks or small skewers.

Combine the remaining 3 tablespoons of butter with 2 tablespoons of oil in a heavy 10- to 12-inch skillet. Place over high heat until a light haze forms above it, then add the chops and cook them for about 3 minutes on each side until golden brown. Lower the heat, cover the skillet and simmer for 10 minutes. Then turn the chops over and cook, covered, for 10 more minutes. Transfer the chops to a heated platter, cover with foil, and keep warm in a low oven.

| | |
|---|---|
| SAUCE | preferably Dijon-style |
| 2 tablespoons butter | ¼ cup heavy cream |
| ½ cup sour cream | ½ teaspoon salt |
| 1 tablespoon all-purpose flour | 4 thin lemon slices |
| 1 tablespoon prepared mustard, | 2 tablespoons finely chopped parsley |

229

Pour off the fat remaining in the skillet, replace it with 2 tablespoons of butter and set over low heat. In a small bowl, beat together the sour cream, flour and mustard and, with a wire whisk, beat the mixture into the melted butter. Stir in the heavy cream and ½ teaspoon of salt and, whisking constantly, bring to a boil. Pour the sauce over the pork chops, garnish the chops with the lemon slices and chopped parsley, and serve at once.

## *Chaurice* *(Creole-Acadian)*
### SPICY PORK SAUSAGE

To make 3 sausages, each about 30 inches long

3 three-foot lengths of hog sausage casing

4 pounds lean boneless pork, trimmed of excess fat and cut into 1½-inch chunks

2 pounds fresh pork fat

2 cups finely chopped onions

1 cup finely chopped fresh parsley, preferably the flat-leaf Italian variety

2 tablespoons finely chopped garlic

2 tablespoons finely chopped fresh hot red chilies *(caution: see note, appendix)*

2 teaspoons crushed dried hot red pepper

2 teaspoons ground hot red pepper (cayenne)

2 teaspoons freshly ground black pepper

2 teaspoons ground thyme

½ teaspoon ground allspice

¼ teaspoon saltpeter

1 tablespoon salt

Place the sausage casing in a large bowl, pour in enough warm water to cover it by at least 1 inch, and soak for 2 or 3 hours, until the casing is soft and pliable.

Put the pork and the pork fat through the medium blade of a food grinder and place the mixture in a deep bowl. Add the onions, parsley, garlic, chilies, crushed red pepper, ground red pepper, black pepper, thyme, allspice, saltpeter and salt. Beat vigorously with a wooden spoon until the mixture is smooth and fluffy.

Wash the sausage casing thoroughly but gently under cold, slowly running water to remove all traces of the salt in which it was preserved. Hold one end securely around the faucet and let the cold water run through to clean the inside of the casing.

To make each sausage, tie a knot about 3 inches from one end of a length of the casing. Fit the open end snugly over the funnel (or "horn") on the sausage-making attachment of a meat grinder. Then ease the rest of the casing up onto the funnel, gently squeezing it together like the folds of an accordion.

Spoon the meat mixture into the mouth of the grinder and, with a wooden pestle, push it through into the casing. As you fill it, the sausage casing will inflate and gradually ease away from the funnel in a ropelike coil. Fill the casing to within an inch or so of the funnel end but do not try to stuff it too tightly, or it may burst. Slip the casing off the funnel and knot the open end of the sausage.

You may cook the sausages immediately, or, if you prefer, you may refrigerate them safely for 5 or 6 days.

Before cooking a sausage, prick the casing in five or six places with a skewer or the point of a small sharp knife. Coil the sausage in concentric circles in a heavy 10- to 12-inch skillet and pour in enough water to cover it completely. Then bring to a simmer over moderate heat. Cook uncovered for 30 to 45 minutes, until the liquid in the pan has evaporated and only the fat given up by the sausage remains. Reduce the heat to low and, turning the sausage once or twice with tongs, continue frying for about 10 minutes longer, or until it is brown on both sides.

NOTE: If you do not have a food grinder with a sausage-stuffing attachment, you can prepare sausage meat as a dish in itself. Ask the butcher to grind the pork and the pork fat. Combine the mixture with the seasonings as described above. Then pat and shape the sausage meat into equal cylinders each about 2 inches in diameter. Wrap tightly with foil or plastic wrap and refrigerate for up to 5 or 6 days, or until ready to use.

To cook, slice the sausage into rounds about ½ inch thick, and fry them in a little hot vegetable oil. Test for doneness by piercing the sausage with the point of a knife; the sausage is done when no trace of pink shows in the meat.

## *Barbecued Spareribs* (*South*)

To serve 4 to 6

| | |
|---|---|
| 1 cup finely chopped onions | ¼ cup Worcestershire sauce |
| 1 cup freshly made ketchup | 1 teaspoon dry mustard |
| or 1 cup peach preserves | ¼ teaspoon Tabasco |
| (depending on whether you | 4 pounds spareribs, in 2 or 3 pieces, |
| prefer a very spicy or slightly | trimmed of excess fat |
| sweet sauce) | 2 teaspoons salt |
| ¼ cup dark brown sugar | Freshly ground black pepper |
| ¼ cup distilled white vinegar | 2 lemons, cut crosswise into ¼- |
| | inch-thick slices |

Preheat the oven to 400°. While it is heating, prepare the barbecue basting sauce: combine the onions, catsup or peach preserves, brown sugar, vinegar, Worcestershire, mustard and Tabasco in a 1- to 1½-quart enameled or stainless-steel saucepan. Stirring constantly with a wooden spoon, bring the sauce to a boil over high heat. Reduce the heat to low and simmer for 4 or 5 minutes until the onions are soft.

Arrange the spareribs, flesh side up, side by side on a rack set in a large shallow roasting pan and sprinkle them with the salt and a few grindings of pepper. With a pastry brush, spread about ½ cup of the basting sauce evenly over the ribs and lay the lemon slices on top. Bake uncovered in the middle of the oven for about 1½ hours, brushing the ribs 3 or 4 more times with the remaining sauce. The ribs are done if the meat shows no resistance when pierced deeply with the point of a small skewer or sharp knife.

Arrange the barbecued spareribs on a heated platter and serve at once.

## *Stuffed Spareribs* (*Northwest*)

To serve 4

| | |
|---|---|
| 2 strips of spareribs, each about 10 inches long, trimmed of excess fat (about 3 to 3½ pounds in all) | (about 2 cups) |
| | 4 large firm apples, preferably green cooking apples, peeled, cored and |
| 3 teaspoons salt | cut into ½-inch-thick slices |
| Freshly ground black pepper | ¼ cup light-brown sugar |
| 1 pound pitted dried prunes, halved | 1 tablespoon ground cinnamon |

Preheat the oven to 350°. Sprinkle the meaty sides of the spareribs with 2 teaspoons of the salt and a few grindings of pepper. Place one strip of ribs meat side down and spread it evenly with all the prunes and apples. Sprinkle with the brown sugar, the remaining salt and the cinnamon, and cover with the other strip of spareribs, meat side up. Tie the two together, crosswise and lengthwise, securely enclosing the stuffing. Place the ribs on a rack set in a shallow roasting pan and bake in the middle of the oven for 1½ hours, or until the ribs show no resistance when pierced with the tip of a knife. Cut away the strings and serve the spareribs.

# Beef

To most Americans, meat means beef—and if there is a food this country can be proud of, it is surely its beef. Nowhere in the world do farmers produce so much affordable beef with so fine a texture and so rich a flavor. American beef is generally of such excellence, in fact, that it is tempting—if expensive—to make a diet of broiled steaks or roasted standing ribs. Succulent as these premium cuts are, however, the recipes in this chapter also demonstrate other more reasonably priced cuts you can choose from, and describe the many kinds of flavorings and cooking methods that characterize beef dishes throughout regional America. The repertoire here ranges from a corned beef brisket, used for a New England boiled beef and vegetable dinner, Eastern Heartland deviled short ribs, Southern spiced beef round and Texas chili con carne. And, too, it suggests appetizing ways of utilizing ground beef for a Northwestern meat loaf with bacon or to stuff Shaker flank steak, Michigan-style pasties, tacos or cabbage leaves.

The best way to be sure of getting a fine piece of beef—hopefully, one that has been aged, for greater flavor and tenderness—is to find a butcher you trust. Wherever you buy your beef, though, you can make visual tests of quality: the flesh should be a uniform, bright cherry color and have white fat, called marbling, distributed through it. The fat surrounding the lean portions should be creamy white.

Keep in mind that the muscle fibers of the beef are bound together by connective tissues (the flesh); the more a muscle is used, the more connective tissue builds up and toughens the meat. Muscles along the backbone of an animal get little excercise; these areas produce tender loin cuts and rib roasts and chops, which can be dry roasted, broiled or sautéed. Muscles in other areas such as the flank, shoulders, legs and breast are used more, so the cuts from these areas tend to be tough and need slow cooking with moisture, as in braising, stewing or pot roasting.

There are two American methods for cooking a rib roast successfully, and each one has its partisans. The first is the searing method, in which the roast is seared in a 450° oven for 20 to 30 minutes, the oven then turned down to 325° and the roast cooked to the desired degree of doneness. The second is the low-, constant-temperature method, in which the roast is cooked in a 300° to 325° oven. In either of these procedures the following points should be kept in mind.

1. Salt and pepper may be sprinkled over the roast before, during or after the roasting period.

2. It is unnecessary to use a rack for a standing rib roast, since the ribs of the roast form a natural rack. Roast the ribs, fat side up, in a shallow roasting pan a little larger than the roast itself.

3. No water or any other liquid should be added to the roast during the cooking period. Nor should it be covered or basted at any time.

4. For predictable results, a good meat thermometer (preferably a professional cook's thermometer, which begins at 0° rather than 140°) is imperative. How long the beef has been aged, the width of the so-called "eye" (the meaty heart of the rib) and the accuracy of the oven are factors which cause unpredictable variations in cooking times. Insert the meat thermometer so that its tip is directly in the center of the roast. It should not touch bone or rest in fat. The roasting-time chart which follows is at best only an approximate gauge.

TIMETABLES FOR ROASTING A STANDING RIB ROAST

WEIGHT: 6 TO 8 POUNDS                    OVEN TEMPERATURE: 300° TO 325°

| INTERNAL TEMPERATURE WHEN DONE | COOKING TIME MINUTES PER POUND |
|---|---|
| 130° to 140° (rare) | 20 |
| 150° to 160° (medium) | 25 |
| 160° to 170° (well done) | 30 |

Ideally, a standing rib roast (or, for that matter, any other roast) should be allowed to rest outside the oven for at least 10 minutes before carving. Since the meat will continue to cook internally as it stands, remove it from the oven when the meat thermometer reads 10° lower than the temperature you desire. As the roast rests, the surface juices will retreat back into the meat, carving will be easier, and the beef juicier and better textured. To carve, first remove a thin slice of beef from the large end of the roast so that it will stand firmly on this end. Insert a large fork below the top rib and carve slices of beef from the top, separating each slice as you proceed down along the rib bone.

1 cup dark brown sugar
1 cup salt
1 tablespoon ground allspice
1 tablespoon freshly ground black
  pepper
2 teaspoons ground ginger
1 teaspoon ground nutmeg
1 teaspoon ground cinnamon

1 teaspoon ground hot red pepper
  (cayenne)
A 4- to 5-pound beef round roast
  about 3 inches thick, tied securely
  in 3 or 4 places
¼ pound beef suet, cut into 8 or
  9 strips each 3 inches long and
  ¼ inch wide

Starting about 2 weeks ahead, combine the brown sugar, salt, allspice, black pepper, ginger, nutmeg, cinnamon and red pepper in a large bowl. Mix thoroughly, then place the beef in the bowl and, with your fingers, rub the sugar-and-spice mixture into all sides of the meat. Cover the bowl tightly with foil or plastic wrap and marinate in the refrigerator for 2 weeks, turning the meat over every day and basting it with the liquid that will accumulate in the bowl.

Preheat the oven to 275°. Transfer the meat to a plate and reserve the marinade. With a larding needle or sharp skewer, make 8 or 9 evenly spaced holes through the beef roast from top to bottom and insert a strip of suet in each one. Place the beef on a rack in a large heavy casserole equipped with a tightly fitting lid. Pour ¾ cup of the marinade down the sides of the casserole. Then cover tightly with the lid and braise in the middle of the oven for 3½ hours, or until the beef is tender and shows no resistance when pierced deeply with a large two-pronged fork.

Transfer the beef to a platter and cool to room temperature. Cover with foil or plastic wrap, and refrigerate the beef for at least 8 hours, or until it is thoroughly chilled and firm.

Spiced beef round is a traditional Christmas dish in Virginia and Tennessee. This version, from Virginia, is served sliced paper-thin and accompanied by beaten biscuits.*

235

*\* See index.*

To serve 4

| | |
|---|---|
| A 2½- to 3-pound porterhouse steak | 4 sautéed chopped chicken livers |
| 1 clove garlic, crushed | ½ pound cooked ham, ground |
| 7 tablespoons butter | 1 teaspoon chopped parsley |
| Salt | 3 tablespoons sour cream |
| Pepper | 2 tablespoons grated Parmesan cheese |
| 4 tomatoes | 6 medium-sized old potatoes |
| 8 large mushrooms | 2 eggs |
| 1 cup finely chopped onion | ½ cup hot milk |

Rub the steak with 1 clove of crushed garlic, brush with 2 tablespoons of melted butter and season with salt and pepper. Broil on one side only. Place on a large wooden plank that has been rubbed with oil, uncooked side up.

Prepare the following stuffing for the tomatoes and mushroom caps. Chop the mushroom stems and sauté in 1 tablespoon of butter with 1 cup of finely chopped onion until soft and lightly browned. Blend with 4 sautéed chopped chicken livers, ½ pound of ground cooked ham, 1 teaspoon of chopped parsely, 3 tablespoons of sour cream; salt and pepper.

Cut the tops off 4 tomatoes and scoop out the seedy pulp with a spoon. Fill with the stuffing, top with 2 tablespoons of grated Parmesan cheese and 2 tablespoons of melted butter. Fill 4 mushroom caps with the same mixture, cover with the other 4 caps and sprinkle with the remaining butter.

Peel 6 potatoes and cook for about 20 minutes in boiling salted water, or until tender. Drain and dry for a minute or so over a slow fire. Put through a ricer or strainer, beat in 1 egg, ½ cup of hot creamy milk, salt and pepper.

Place the mushrooms and tomatoes alternately around the steak. Pipe the potatoes all around the edge, using a pastry bag with a large rose tube. Brush the potatoes with a slightly beaten egg. Place under the broiler, 3 to 4 inches away from the flame, for 8 to 10 minutes. Serve on the plank.

NOTE: Four *filets mignons* may be used instead of a porterhouse steak to simplify carving. Or the steak may be boned before it is cooked.

To serve 6 to 8

A 2- to 2½-pound flank steak, thoroughly trimmed
8 tablespoons butter
4 or 5 slices homemade-type white bread, cut into ¼-inch cubes (2 cups)
1 cup finely chopped onions
1 cup finely chopped celery
¼ pound lean ground beef
¼ pound lean ground veal
¼ pound lean ground pork
1 egg
¼ cup finely chopped fresh parsley
¼ teaspoon crumbled dried rosemary
½ teaspoon crumbled dried basil
½ teaspoon crumbled dried savory
¼ teaspoon ground sage
1½ teaspoons salt
¼ teaspoon freshly ground black pepper
2 tablespoons vegetable oil
2 medium-sized celery stalks, trimmed, leaves removed, cut crosswise into ¼-inch-thick slices
1 medium-sized onion, peeled and cut crosswise into ¼-inch-thick slices
1 medium-sized carrot, scraped and coarsely chopped
1 cup beef stock, fresh or canned, or 1 cup water or a combination of the two

Ask your butcher to cut a pocket in the steak, or do it yourself in the following manner: With a long, very sharp knife, slit the steak horizontally from one of the long sides, cutting through the steak to within about ½ inch of the other long side and to within about 1 inch of each short end.

Preheat the oven to 350°. In a heavy 8- to 10-inch skillet, melt 4 tablespoons of the butter over moderate heat. Add the bread cubes and, stirring frequently, fry them until they are crisp and golden brown. With a slotted spoon, transfer the cubes to a deep bowl.

Melt 2 more tablespoons of butter in the skillet, add the chopped onions and chopped celery and stir for about 5 minutes, until they are soft but not brown. With a rubber spatula, scrape the onions and celery over the bread cubes. Add the ground beef, veal, pork, egg, parsley, rosemary, basil, savory, sage, salt and pepper. Knead vigorously with both hands, then beat with a wooden spoon until all the ingredients are well blended.

Holding the steak upright on its long closed side, pack the stuffing tightly into the pocket, a handful at a time. Then lay the steak flat and close the open side by sewing it with a large needle and white thread.

Melt the remaining 2 tablespoons of butter with the oil in a heavy casserole large enough to hold the steak comfortably. Brown the steak in the hot fat, turning it with two spoons and regulating the heat so that the meat colors richly and evenly on both sides without burning. Transfer the steak to a plate and add the sliced celery, sliced onion and carrot to the fat remaining in the casserole. Stirring frequently, cook for 8 to 10 minutes, or until the vegetables are soft and delicately browned.

237

Pour in the stock or water or stock-and-water combination and bring to a boil over high heat, meanwhile scraping in the brown particles clinging to the bottom and sides of the pan. Return the steak to the casserole together with any juices that have accumulated around it. Cover tightly and braise in the middle of the oven for 1 hour, or until the steak shows no resistance when pierced deeply with the point of a small sharp knife. Place the steak on a heated platter. Remove the thread.

Skim off the surface fat and strain the cooking liquid through a fine sieve into a sauceboat or bowl, pressing down hard on the vegetables with the back of a spoon to extract all their juices before discarding the pulp. Taste for seasoning, and serve the gravy separately with the steak.

## Swedish Pot Roast *(Northwest)*

| To serve 6 to 8 | 1 medium-sized carrot, scraped and finely chopped |
|---|---|
| ¼ cup vegetable oil | 10 flat anchovy fillets, drained and |
| A 4- to 4½-pound boneless beef roast, preferably bottom round, rump, brisket or chuck, trimmed of excess fat and tied securely in 3 or 4 places | rinsed thoroughly in a sieve under cold running water |
| | 1 teaspoon whole black peppercorns, bruised with the side of a cleaver or heavy knife, |
| 1½ cups finely chopped onions | 1 large bay leaf and 2 sprigs fresh |
| 3 tablespoons flour | parsley, wrapped together in |
| 1 tablespoon dark-brown sugar | cheesecloth and tied with a string |
| 2 cups beef stock, fresh or canned | Salt |
| ¼ cup distilled white vinegar | Freshly ground black pepper |

Preheat the oven to 350°. In a heavy 5- to 6-quart casserole equipped with a tight-fitting lid, warm the oil over moderate heat until a light haze forms above it. Pat the beef completely dry with paper towels and brown it in the hot oil, turning the roast with two spoons and regulating the heat so that it colors richly and evenly on all sides without burning. Set the beef aside on a plate.

Pour off all but a thin film of fat from the casserole and add the onions. Stirring frequently, cook over moderate heat for 8 to 10 minutes, until they are soft and delicately browned. Stir in the flour and brown sugar and, when they are thoroughly absorbed, pour in the beef stock and vinegar. Bring to a boil over high heat, stirring constantly with a whisk until the mixture is smooth and fairly thick.

Add the carrot, anchovy fillets, and the wrapped peppercorns, bay leaf, and parsley. Return the roast and the liquid that has accumulated around it to the casserole, and bring to a boil over high heat.

Cover the casserole tightly and roast the beef in the lower third of the oven for about 3 hours. Check from time to time and lower the heat if necessary to keep the liquid in the casserole at a slow simmer. When the beef is done, it should be tender and offer no resistance when pierced with the tines of a long-handled fork.

Transfer the pot roast to a heated platter and drape it loosely with foil to keep it warm while you prepare the gravy. Discard the wrapped peppercorns, bay leaf and parsley, and skim as much fat as possible from the surface of the gravy. Then boil briskly, uncovered, over high heat until it reaches the thickness and intensity of flavor you prefer. Taste and add salt and a few grindings of pepper if needed. Pour the gravy into a heated sauceboat and serve it separately with the pot roast.

### *New England Boiled Dinner*

| | |
|---|---|
| To serve 6 | inches in diameter, peeled |
| | 6 small carrots, scraped |
| 4 pounds corned beef | 12 small white onions, about 1 inch |
| 2 pounds green cabbage, cored and | in diameter, peeled and trimmed |
| quartered | 6 medium-sized beets |
| 12 to 16 new potatoes, about 1½ | 2 tablespoons finely chopped parsley |

Before cooking the corned beef, ask your butcher whether it should be soaked in water to remove some of the salt. If it has been mildly cured, soaking will not be necessary.

Place the corned beef in a 5- or 6-quart pot and cover it with enough cold water to rise at least 2 inches above the top of the meat. Bring to a boil, skimming off any scum that rises to the surface. Half cover the pot, turn the heat to its lowest point (the liquid should barely simmer) and cook the beef from 4 to 6 hours, or until tender. If necessary, add more hot water to the pot from time to time to keep the meat constantly covered.

Cook the cabbage separately in boiling salted water for about 15 minutes. The potatoes, carrots and onions may be cooked together in a pot of salted boiling water of their own. The beets, however, require different treatment. Scrub them thoroughly, then cut off their tops, leaving 1 inch of stem. Cover them with boiling water and bring to a boil. Simmer the beets from ½ to 1½ hours, or until they are tender. Let them cool a bit, then slip off their skins.

To serve the dinner in the traditional way, slice the corned beef and arrange it along the center of a large heated platter. Surround the meat with the vegetables and sprinkle the vegetables with chopped parsley. Horseradish, mustard and a variety of pickles make excellent accompaniments to this hearty meal.

NOTE: In New England the vegetables, other than the beets, are often added to the simmering corned beef during the last half hour or so of cooking. For some tastes, however, the briny flavor imparted to the vegetables by the corned beef detracts from their natural flavors.

## Home-cured Corned Beef (Jewish-American)

To serve 12 to 14

| | |
|---|---|
| 4 quarts water | 8 large bay leaves |
| 1½ cups salt | A 5-pound brisket of beef in one |
| 1 tablespoon sugar | piece |
| 2 tablespoons pickling spice | 8 cloves garlic, peeled |
| ½ ounce saltpeter or potassium | 2 onions, peeled |
| nitrate, available through | 2 stalks celery |
| pharmacies | |

In a 6- to 8-quart pot, prepare a brine by combining the water, salt, sugar, pickling spice, saltpeter and bay leaves. Bring to a boil over high heat and boil briskly for 5 minutes. Remove from the heat and cool the brine to room temperature.

Place the beef in an enameled or earthenware crock or casserole and pour in the brine. Drop in the garlic, set a heavy pan or board on top of the meat to keep it immersed in liquid, and cover the crock or casserole with cheesecloth. Set aside in a cool—not cold—place for 12 days.

Remove the meat from the brine and discard the brine. Wash the meat thoroughly under cold running water and place it in a 4- to 6-quart casserole. Pour in enough cold water to cover the meat by at least 1 inch and bring to a boil over high heat. Taste the water; if it seems excessively salty, pour it off and add fresh cold water to the casserole. Bring back to a boil, meanwhile skimming the foam and scum that rise to the surface. Add the onions and celery, reduce the heat to low, and simmer partially covered for 3 hours, or until the meat is tender and offers no resistance when pierced with the point of a sharp knife.

To serve Jewish-style corned-beef sandwiches, transfer the beef to a cutting board and, while it is still warm, slice it crosswise into ⅛-inch-thick slices. Serve on rye bread spread with spicy mustard, and accompany with sour pickles or sauerkraut. The meat can also be served sliced, as part of a main course or cold-cuts platter.

OPPOSITE
*Shaker cookery made superb use of herbs. This meat-stuffed flank steak boasts rosemary, basil, savory and sage.*

To serve 4 to 6

BEEF

2 pounds lean beef chuck, trimmed
    of excess fat and cut into 1-inch
    cubes
2 teaspoons salt
¼ teaspoon freshly ground black
    pepper
½ cup flour
¼ cup vegetable oil
½ cup finely chopped onions

1 teaspoon finely chopped garlic
1 quart water
1 medium-sized bay leaf
3 medium-sized boiling potatoes,
    peeled and cut into 1-inch cubes
    (about 3 cups)
4 medium-sized carrots, scraped and
    cut crosswise into ¼-inch-thick
    rounds
¼ cup finely chopped fresh parsley

Pat the cubes of beef completely dry with paper towels and sprinkle them on all sides with the salt and pepper. Dip them in the flour to coat them lightly and shake off the excess flour.

In a heavy 3- to 4-quart casserole, heat the oil over moderate heat until a light haze forms above it. Brown the beef cubes in the oil, 4 or 5 at a time, turning them about with a slotted spatula and regulating the heat so that they color richly and evenly without burning. As they brown, transfer the beef cubes to a plate.

Add the onions and garlic to the fat remaining in the casserole and, stirring frequently, cook for about 5 minutes, until they are soft and translucent but not brown. Pour in the water and bring to a boil over high heat, meanwhile scraping in the brown particles clinging to the bottom and sides of the pan. Return the beef and the liquid that has accumulated around it to the pan, add the bay leaf, and reduce the heat to low.

Simmer partially covered for 1 hour, then add the potatoes, carrots and parsley. Partially cover the pan again and simmer for 20 to 30 minutes longer, or until the vegetables are tender but still intact. (As the beef and vegetables simmer, check the casserole from time to time. If the liquid seems to be cooking away too rapidly, reduce the heat and add a little more water.) Remove the casserole from the heat, uncover the beef mixture and set aside to cool to room temperature.

TOPPING

Nonsweet short-crust pastry for a
    piecrust top*

1 egg lightly beaten with
    1 tablespoon milk

Meanwhile, preheat the oven to 375°. On a lightly floured surface, pat the pastry dough into a rough circle about 1 inch thick. Dust a little flour over and under it and roll it out from the center to within an inch of the far edge. Lift the dough and turn it 2 inches; then roll again from the

* *See index.*

center to within an inch or so of the far edge. Repeat—lifting, turning, rolling—until the circle is 12 inches in diameter and about ⅛ inch thick.

When the meat mixture has completely cooled, drape the dough over the rolling pin, lift it up and unroll it carefully over the casserole. Trim off the excess dough with scissors or a small knife, leaving a 1-inch over-hang all around the rim. Fold the overhang underneath the edges of the pastry and secure the dough to the rim by crimping it tightly with your fingers or the tines of a fork.

Cut three 2-inch-long diagonal slashes, spaced about 1 inch apart, in the top of the pie and brush the surface with the egg-and-milk mixture. Bake the pie in the middle of the oven for 45 to 50 minutes, or until the crust is golden brown. Serve at once directly from the baking dish.

## Beef Stroganoff *(Russian-American)*
### SLICED BEEF AND MUSHROOMS IN SOUR-CREAM SAUCE

| To serve 4 to 6 | 1 tablespoon flour |
|---|---|
| 5 tablespoons butter | ½ cup dry white wine |
| 1 tablespoon oil | ½ cup sour cream |
| 2 pounds fillet of beef, trimmed of all fat and cut across the grain into ¼-inch-thick slices | 1 tablespoon tomato paste |
| | 2 to 3 drops Worcestershire sauce |
| | 1 tablespoon salt |
| ½ cup thinly sliced scallion rounds | Freshly ground black pepper |
| ¼ pound mushrooms, thinly sliced | 1 tablespoon finely chopped parsley |

*Beef stroganoff is a simple but elegant Russian dish that has become a stan-dard main course in many American homes. Along the way, it has also been altered: the scallions, tomato paste and Worcestershire sauce in this recipe are New World additions.*

Place 3 tablespoons of the butter and the tablespoon of oil in a heavy 10- to 12-inch skillet, and set over moderate heat. When the foam subsides, drop in the slices of beef and fry for 2 minutes on each side, or until the meat is lightly browned. With tongs or a slotted spoon, transfer the meat to a plate. Add the remaining 2 tablespoons of butter to the skillet and stir in the scallions and mushrooms. Cook, stirring frequently, for 3 to 4 minutes, or until they are soft and lightly browned. Add the flour and mix thoroughly with the vegetables, then pour in the white wine and add the sour cream, a tablespoon at a time. Stir in the tomato paste, Worcester-shire sauce, salt and a few grindings of pepper. Return the beef to the pan, together with any juices that may have accumulated on the plate. Coat the meat thoroughly with the sauce, cover the pan, and simmer for 2 to 3 minutes, or until the sauce is heated through. Taste for seasoning and transfer the beef stroganoff to a large heated platter. Sprinkle with the parsley and serve at once, with noodles or rice.

To serve 4

½ cup flour
2 tablespoons dry mustard
1½ teaspoons salt
½ teaspoon freshly ground black
    pepper
2 pounds round steak in a 1-inch-
    thick slice, trimmed of excess fat
3 tablespoons vegetable oil
6 medium-sized firm ripe tomatoes,
    peeled, seeded and finely chopped,

or substitute 2 cups
    chopped drained canned
    tomatoes
2 medium-sized onions, peeled and
    cut crosswise into ¼-inch-thick
    slices
½ cup finely chopped celery
2 tablespoons Worcestershire sauce
1 tablespoon dark-brown sugar
½ cup sour cream

Preheat the oven to 350°. Combine the flour, mustard, salt and pepper, and sift them together into a deep platter. Coat the round steak on both sides with the flour mixture, then pound the seasoning into the meat with a kitchen mallet or the side of your fist. Cut the steak into four or eight equal pieces.

In a heavy 10- to 12-inch skillet at least 3 inches deep, or in a Dutch oven, heat the oil over moderate heat until a light haze forms above it. Brown the steak in the hot oil, in two batches if necessary to avoid over-crowding the pan. Turn the steak with tongs or a spatula and regulate the heat so that the meat colors richly and evenly without burning. As the steak pieces brown, transfer them to a plate.

Add the tomatoes, onions, celery, Worcestershire sauce and brown sugar to the fat remaining in the skillet and bring to a boil over high heat, stirring and scraping in any brown particles that cling to the bottom and sides of the pan. Return the steak to the pan along with the liquid that has accumulated around it and turn it about in the vegetable mixture until evenly coated.

Cover tightly and braise in the middle of the oven for 1½ hours, or until the steak is tender and shows no resistance when pierced with the point of a small, sharp knife. Transfer the steak to a platter and drape with foil to keep it warm while you prepare the sauce.

Skim as much fat as possible from the surface of the vegetable mixture remaining in the skillet. Bring to a simmer over moderate heat, stir in the sour cream, and cook for a minute or so to warm it through. Taste for seasoning and ladle the sauce over the steak.

To serve 6

STEW

½ pound lean salt pork, cut into
  ¼-inch dice
4 medium-sized onions, peeled and
  cut crosswise into ¼-inch slices
  (about 1½ cups)
2 pounds lean beef chuck, trimmed
  of excess fat and cut into 1-inch
  cubes
¼ cup flour
6 cups water
4 sprigs fresh parsley and 1 small

bay leaf tied together with
  kitchen string
⅛ teaspoon crumbled dried thyme
2 teaspoons salt
Freshly ground black pepper
2 medium-sized boiling potatoes,
  peeled and cut into ½-inch
  cubes (about 2 cups)
12 medium-sized carrots, scraped
  and cut into ½-inch pieces
  (about 2 cups)
1 medium-sized white rutabaga,
  peeled and cut into ½-inch
  cubes (about 1 cup)

In a heavy 12-inch skillet at least 3 inches deep, fry the salt pork dice over moderate heat, turning them about frequently with a slotted spoon until they are crisp and brown and have rendered all their fat. Remove the pork bits and discard them.

Add the onions to the fat in the skillet and, stirring frequently, cook for 8 to 10 minutes, or until they are soft and delicately brown. With a slotted spoon, transfer the onions to a bowl and set aside.

Pat the beef cubes completely dry with paper towels, roll them in ¼ cup of flour to coat them on all sides and shake off the excess flour. Brown 6 or 7 cubes at a time in the hot fat remaining in the skillet, turning them with a slotted spoon and regulating the heat so that they color evenly without burning. As they brown, add the cubes to the onions.

Pour 1 cup of water into the skillet and bring to a boil over high heat, stirring constantly and scraping in the brown particles that cling to the bottom and sides of the pan. Return the onions and beef and the liquid that has accumulated around them to the skillet. Add the remaining 5 cups of water, the parsley and bay leaf, the thyme, salt and a liberal grinding of pepper. Bring to a boil over high heat, reduce the heat to low, cover tightly and simmer for 1 hour. Stir in the potatoes, carrots and rutabaga, cover again and simmer for 30 minutes longer.

PARSLEY DUMPLINGS

2 cups flour
1 tablespoon double-acting baking
  powder
½ teaspoon salt

2 tablespoons butter, cut into
  ½-inch bits and softened
1⅓ cups milk
¼ cup finely chopped fresh parsley

Meanwhile prepare the parsley dumplings in the following fashion: Combine the 2 cups of flour, baking powder and ½ teaspoon of salt and sift them into a deep bowl. Add the butter bits and, with your fingers, rub the flour and fat together until they look like flakes of coarse meal. Add the milk and chopped parsley and beat vigorously with a spoon until the dumpling mixture is smooth.

*Joe Booker stew makes a robust meal of beef simmered with rutabagas, potatoes and carrots and topped with parsley-flavored dumplings.*

Remove the parsley and bay leaf from the simmering stew, and drop the dumpling mixture on top by the heaping tablespoon. Cover tightly and simmer undisturbed for about 10 minutes longer. The dumplings are done when they are puffed and fluffy, and a cake tester inserted in the center of a dumpling comes out clean.

Remove the dumplings and transfer the stew to a preheated bowl or deep platter. Arrange the dumplings on top and serve at once.

To serve 6 to 8

2 pounds boneless beef shank,
   trimmed of excess fat
1½ pounds beef bones
½ pound lean boneless lamb,
   trimmed of excess fat
A 2- to 2½-pound chicken, cut
   into 6 or 8 pieces
A 1-inch piece fresh hot red chili,
   seeded (*caution: see note,
   appendix*)
1 tablespoon salt
Freshly ground black pepper
3 quarts water
2 medium-sized potatoes, peeled
   and diced (2 cups)
2 cups finely chopped onions
2 cups fresh kernels cut from about
   4 large ears of corn, or substitute
   2 cups frozen corn kernels,
   thoroughly defrosted

3 or 4 medium-sized carrots, scraped
   and cut crosswise into ¼-inch-
   thick slices (about 2 cups)
6 medium-sized ripe tomatoes, cored
   and coarsely chopped
¼ pound butter beans or wax
   beans, washed, trimmed and cut
   crosswise into halves (about
   1 cup)
1 medium-sized green pepper,
   halved, seeded, deribbed and cut
   into ½-inch pieces
½ pound fresh okra, washed,
   trimmed and cut into 1-inch dice
   (about 1 cup), or substitute
   frozen okra, thoroughly defrosted
   and cut into 1-inch dice
1 teaspoon finely chopped garlic
1 cup finely chopped fresh parsley

Combine the beef shank, beef bones, lamb, chicken, chili, salt, a liberal grinding of black pepper and the water in a heavy 6- to 8-quart casserole. Bring to a boil over high heat, meanwhile skimming off the foam and scum as they rise to the surface.

Reduce the heat to low and simmer partially covered for 30 to 40 minutes, or until the chicken is tender. Remove the chicken pieces with tongs or a slotted spoon, and place them on a plate.

Cover the casserole partially again and simmer for about 1½ hours longer, or until the beef and lamb are tender and show no resistance when pierced deeply with the point of a small skewer or sharp knife. Add the beef and lamb to the plate with the chicken. Remove the beef bones and chili and discard them.

Drop the potatoes, onions, corn, carrots, tomatoes, beans, green pepper, okra and garlic into the stock remaining in the casserole. Stirring from time to time, bring to a boil over high heat. Reduce the heat to low and simmer uncovered for 1½ hours. Check the pot from time to time and add up to 2 cups more water, if the stew seems too thick.

With a small knife, remove the skin and bones from the chicken and discard them. Cut the chicken meat, beef shank and lamb into 1-inch pieces and return them to the casserole. Stirring frequently, simmer the burgoo until the meat is heated through. Then stir in the parsley and taste for seasoning. Serve from the casserole or from a heated bowl.

To serve 6 to 8

6 dried *ancho* chilies, plus 8 dried
hot red chilies, each about 2
inches long (*caution: see note,
appendix*)
3½ cups boiling water
½ pound beef suet, preferably
kidney suet, cut into ½-inch bits
3 pounds lean boneless venison or
beef chuck, trimmed of excess
fat, sliced ½ inch thick and cut
into ½-inch cubes
3 medium-sized bay leaves, finely
crumbled

1 tablespoon cumin seeds
2 tablespoons coarsely chopped
garlic
4 teaspoons dried oregano
3 tablespoons paprika
1 tablespoon sugar
1 tablespoon salt
3 tablespoons yellow cornmeal
1 teaspoon ground hot red pepper
(cayenne; optional)
Freshly cooked pinto beans
9 cups freshly cooked rice made
from 3 cups long-grain white rice

Under cold running water, pull the stems off the *ancho* and red chilies.
Tear the chilies in half and brush out their seeds. With a small sharp
knife, cut away any large ribs. Chop the chilies coarsely, drop them into
a bowl, and pour the boiling water over them. Let them soak for at least
30 minutes, then strain the soaking liquid through a sieve set over a bowl
and reserve it. Set the chilies aside.

In a heavy 5- to 6-quart casserole, cook the beef suet over moderate
heat, stirring frequently until it has rendered all its fat. With a slotted
spoon, remove and discard the suet bits. Pour off all but about ¼ cup of
the fat remaining in the pot.

Add the venison or beef cubes to the casserole and, stirring constantly,
cook over moderate heat until the pieces of meat are firm but not brown.
Add 2½ cups of the reserved chili-soaking liquid and bring it to a boil
over high heat. Drop in the bay leaves and reduce the heat to low. Simmer
partially covered for 1 hour, stirring the mixture from time to time.

Meanwhile, place the cumin seeds in a small ungreased skillet and, sliding the pan back and forth frequently, toast the seeds over low heat for
10 minutes. Drop the seeds into the jar of an electric blender and blend
at high speed for 30 seconds. Turn off the machine, add the *ancho* and
red chilies, the remaining chili-soaking liquid, the garlic, oregano, paprika,
sugar and salt, and blend again at high speed until all of the ingredients
are reduced to a smooth purée.

When the meat has cooked its allotted time, stir in the chili purée.
Simmer partially covered for 30 minutes. Then, stirring constantly, pour
in the cornmeal in a slow stream and cook over high heat until the chili
comes to a boil and thickens lightly. Taste the chili for seasoning and add
the ground hot red pepper if desired.

*A Texas version of chili con carne is free of tomatoes or chili powder, and accompanied by separate bowls of beans and rice.*

Serve the chili con carne directly from the casserole, or from a heated tureen or serving bowl. Mound the pinto beans and the rice in separate bowls and present them with the chili.

## *Beef Tacos (Far West)*

### DEEP-FRIED FOLDED TORTILLAS WITH BEEF FILLING

To make 8 tacos

Vegetable oil for deep frying
8 corn tortillas each
   5 to 6 inches across, thoroughly
   defrosted if frozen
3 tablespoons lard
1 pound lean ground beef

1 cup finely chopped onions
1 teaspoon salt
1 cup *ancho* sauce (*see below*)
1 cup finely shredded iceberg lettuce
1 cup (about 4 ounces) coarsely
   shredded Cheddar or longhorn
   cheese

Pour vegetable oil into a deep fryer or large heavy saucepan to a depth of about 4 inches and heat the oil until it reaches a temperature of 350° on a deep-frying thermometer. At the same time, preheat the oven to its lowest setting. Line a jelly-roll pan with a double thickness of paper towels and place it in the middle of the oven.

Meanwhile, soften and warm the tortillas one at a time in an ungreased 10-inch skillet set over moderate heat. Turn the tortillas over and back with kitchen tongs for about 30 seconds, until they are soft but not browned. Stack them on a plate as you proceed.

To shape and fry the tortillas to make taco shells, fold two tortillas around the outside of the holders of a taco fryer and set the holders into place in the fryer. Lower the holders into the hot oil by a wire and deep-fry the tortillas for 2 minutes, or until they are brown and crisp. As they are fried, transfer the completed taco shells to the lined pan and keep them warm in the oven.

In a heavy 10- to 12-inch skillet, melt the lard over moderate heat. Add the beef and fry it for 8 to 10 minutes, stirring frequently and mashing the meat with the back of a spoon to prevent lumps from forming. When no trace of pink remains, stir in ½ cup of the onions and the salt. Remove the pan from the heat, add ½ cup of the *ancho* sauce, and taste the beef mixture for seasoning.

Spoon the beef filling into the taco shells, dividing it evenly among them. Then arrange the tacos attractively on a heated platter and serve at once, accompanied by the shredded lettuce and cheese and the remaining chopped onions and *ancho* sauce in four separate bowls.

NOTE: Lacking a taco fryer, pour vegetable oil into a heavy 10- to 12-inch skillet to a depth of about 1 inch and heat the oil until it is very hot but not smoking. To shape each taco shell, fold a tortilla in half and carefully place it in the hot oil. As it fries, hold the tortilla slightly open with kitchen tongs or two forks so that there is about ½ inch of space between the halves. Fry the taco shell for 2 to 3 minutes, turning it over so that it is crisp and brown on both sides. As they brown, transfer the taco shells to the paper-lined pan and keep them warm in the oven while you fold and fry the rest.

## Ancho Sauce *(Far West)*

To make about 2 cups

| | |
|---|---|
| 12 dried *ancho* chilies (*caution: see note, appendix*) | 1 teaspoon finely chopped garlic |
| | 1 teaspoon crumbled dried oregano |
| 2 cups boiling water | ½ teaspoon ground cumin |
| ¼ cup tomato paste | ½ teaspoon sugar |
| | 1½ teaspoons salt |

Under cold running water, pull the stems off the *ancho* chilies, tear them in half and brush out their seeds. Tear the chilies into pieces, place them in a bowl and pour in the boiling water. The water should cover the chilies by at least 1 inch; if necessary, add more boiling water. Let the chilies soak for about 1 hour, then drain the soaking liquid into a bowl and reserve it. Force the chilies through a food mill set over a small heavy saucepan or rub them through a fine sieve with the back of a spoon.

Pour 1½ cups of the reserved soaking liquid into the chilies and mix well. Add the tomato paste, garlic, oregano, cumin, sugar and salt and, stirring constantly, bring to a boil over high heat. Reduce the heat to low and, stirring occasionally, simmer uncovered for 10 minutes, or until the sauce thickens enough to hold its shape lightly in a spoon. Taste for seasoning. Serve the sauce with tortillas, tacos or *tostadas*. Or transfer the sauce to a bowl, cool it to room temperature. Covered tightly and refrigerated, the sauce can safely be kept for about a week. Reheat it briefly before serving.

## *Carne Santa Fe*
### SPICED BRAISED BEEF

To serve 4 to 6

2 pounds lean top round of beef, cut ½ inch thick and trimmed of excess fat
½ cup flour
3 tablespoons vegetable oil
1 medium-sized onion, peeled and sliced crosswise into ¼-inch-thick rounds
A 1-pound can tomatoes, drained and coarsely chopped, with the liquid reserved

A 4-ounce can green chilies (not the *jalapeño* variety), drained and coarsely chopped
½ cup dry red wine
1 tablespoon dark brown sugar
1 teaspoon crumbled dried mint
½ teaspoon fennel seeds, crushed with a mortar and pestle or wrapped in a kitchen towel and crushed with a kitchen mallet or the side of a cleaver
½ teaspoon salt

Pat the beef completely dry with paper towels and sprinkle it evenly on both sides with the flour. With a kitchen mallet or the flat of a cleaver, pound the beef to a uniform thickness of about ¼ inch, turning the meat over from time to time. Then shake the beef vigorously to remove the excess flour.

In a heavy 12-inch skillet, heat the oil over moderate heat until a light haze forms above it. Brown the beef in the hot oil, turning it occasionally with tongs and regulating the heat so that the meat colors richly and evenly without burning. Transfer the beef to a platter and set it aside.

Add the onion slices to the fat remaining in the skillet and, stirring frequently, cook for about 5 minutes, until they are soft and translucent but not brown. Stir in the tomatoes, chilies, wine, brown sugar, mint, fennel and salt, and bring to a boil over high heat. Return the beef and the liquid that has accumulated around it to the skillet and spoon the tomato mixture over it. Reduce the heat to low, cover the pan partially and simmer for about 1 hour, or until the beef shows no resistance when pierced deeply with the point of a small sharp knife.

Transfer the beef to a heated platter and taste the braising sauce for seasoning. If the sauce seems thin, boil it briskly over high heat, stirring all the while. When the sauce reaches the consistency you desire, pour it over the beef. Serve the *carne Santa Fe* at once.

## Pasties, Michigan Style

To make six 9-inch pasties

4 cups unsifted flour
2 teaspoons plus 1 tablespoon salt
1½ cups lard (¾ pound), chilled and cut into ¼-inch bits
10 to 12 tablespoons ice water
2 pounds top round steak, trimmed of fat and cut into ¼-inch cubes
5 medium-sized boiling potatoes

(about 1½ pounds), peeled and coarsely chopped
3 medium-sized turnips, scraped and cut into ¼-inch cubes (about 1½ cups)
1½ cups finely chopped onions
1 teaspoon freshly ground black pepper

In a large chilled bowl combine the flour, 2 teaspoons of the salt and the lard. Working quickly, rub the flour and fat together with your fingertips until it looks like flakes of coarse meal. Pour in 10 tablespoons of ice water, toss together, and gather the dough into a ball. If the dough crumbles, add up to 2 tablespoons more water, a teaspoonful at a time, until the particles adhere. Divide the dough into 6 equal balls, dust them with flour and wrap in wax paper. Refrigerate for at least 1 hour.

Preheat the oven to 400°. Combine the beef, potatoes, turnips, onions, the tablespoon of salt and the pepper in a bowl and stir them together.

## PUTTING A PASTY TOGETHER

*Roll out all of the pasty dough and cut it into 9-inch rounds. For each pasty, spread 1½ cups of the filling in a strip across the center of the round. Fold one side of the round up over the filling. Then turn up the other side of the round and press the edges of the dough together snugly at one end. Starting from the sealed end, press the two edges of the round together to encase the filling securely and form a double-thick band of dough about ½ inch wide along the seam. With your fingers, crimp the band into a decorative rope or scalloped fluting; it is ready for baking.*

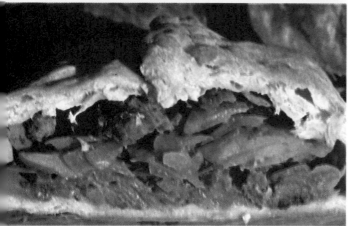

On a lightly floured surface, roll out one ball of dough at a time into a rough circle about ¼ inch thick. Using a plate or pot lid about 9 inches in diameter as a guide, cut the dough into a round with a pastry wheel or sharp knife. Place about 1½ cups of the filling mixture on the round, and fold and shape the pasty as shown below. With a large spatula, carefully transfer the pasty to an ungreased baking sheet. Then repeat the procedure to roll, fill and shape the remaining pasties.

Bake in the middle of the oven for 45 minutes, or until the pasties are golden brown. Serve them hot, or at room temperature.

Hamburgers should be made from ground chuck or top round that has not been trimmed of all its fat before grinding. Most people handle the meat too much while forming it into patties; this makes it too tough. To make sure the hamburgers are moist and juicy, put a small piece of ice in with each patty. Searing the hamburgers also helps keep them from becoming hard and dry. Outdoors, sear them by grilling over a very hot fire. Indoors, pan-broil them in a heavy skillet. First, heat enough fat or vegetable oil in the skillet to coat the bottom thinly; then, on high heat, brown the hamburgers quickly on both sides to give them a light, tasty crust. Reduce the heat to medium and cook, uncovered, to the desired degree of doneness. (Well-done hamburgers must be turned two or three times during cooking.) Hamburgers may be sprinkled with salt and pepper at any point after they have been browned. If you prefer cheeseburgers, try grating the cheese of your choice and mixing it with the meat instead of placing a slice of cheese on top of the hamburgers.

## *Meat Loaf with Bacon* (Northwest)

To serve 6

2 pounds lean ground beef chuck
1 pound lean ground pork
2 cups finely chopped onions
1 cup soft fresh crumbs made from
   homemade-type white bread,
pulverized in a blender or finely
   shredded with a fork
1 tablespoon finely chopped garlic
½ teaspoon crumbled dried thyme
1 egg
6 slices lean bacon

Preheat the oven to 350°. Combine the beef, pork, onions, bread crumbs, garlic, thyme and egg in a deep bowl and knead them vigorously with your hands. Then, with a large wooden spoon, beat until the mixture is smooth and fluffy.

Arrange 4 of the bacon slices side by side in a large shallow roasting pan. Pat the meat mixture into a rectangular loaf about 9 inches long, 5 inches wide, and 3 or 4 inches high. Place the loaf in the pan on top of the bacon and drape the remaining bacon lengthwise over the loaf.

Bake in the middle of the oven for about 1½ hours. To test for doneness, pierce the loaf deeply with the point of a small skewer or sharp knife. The juices that trickle out should be clear yellow; if they are still tinged with pink, bake the meat loaf until the juices are clear.

Using a wide metal spatula, transfer the meat loaf to a heated platter and serve at once.

To make 18 small rolls

A 3-pound head of white cabbage

2 cups water

¼ cup long-grain unconverted rice

1 pound ground chuck

1 egg

2 medium-sized onions, grated
 (¼ cup)

1 medium-sized carrot, scraped and
 grated (¼ cup)

1 small potato (about ¼ pound),
 peeled and grated (⅓ cup)

1½ teaspoons salt

Freshly ground black pepper

1 large onion, sliced

¼ cup seedless white raisins

⅓ to ½ cup light brown sugar

2 cups canned whole tomatoes,
 drained and chopped

¾ cup tomato purée

½ to ¾ teaspoon citric (sour)
 salt or substitute

¼ cup strained fresh lemon juice

Drop the cabbage into a large pot of boiling water and let it cook briskly for about 10 minutes. Remove the cabbage (letting the water continue to boil), carefully detach as many of the outer leaves as you can and reserve them. Return the rest of the cabbage to the boiling water and cook for a few minutes longer. Remove and again detach as many more leaves as you can. Repeat this process until you have separated 18 individual leaves; discard the smallest inner leaves.

Bring the 2 cups of water to a boil in a 1-quart saucepan, add the rice and boil briskly, uncovered, for about 12 minutes. Drain the rice in a sieve and set it aside.

In a large mixing bowl, combine the ground chuck, egg, grated onions, carrot, potato, 1 teaspoon of the salt and a few grindings of black pepper. Add the rice and mix together until the ingredients are well combined.

Lay the cabbage leaves side by side and, with a small knife, trim the tough rib end from the base of each leaf. Place 2 heaping tablespoons of meat filling in the center of each leaf and roll up all of the leaves tightly, tucking in the ends as if you were wrapping a package. Line the bottom of a 2- to 2½-quart casserole with the onion slices and arrange the cabbage rolls over them, seam side down, in one or more layers.

In a large bowl, mix the raisins, ⅓ cup of brown sugar, the chopped tomatoes, tomato purée, the remaining ½ teaspoon of salt and ½ teaspoon sour salt or ¼ cup of lemon juice. Bring the sauce to a boil. When the sour salt has thoroughly dissolved, taste the sauce for seasoning; add up to ¼ teaspoon more of sour salt or up to 3 tablespoons more of brown sugar, depending on whether you prefer a more pronounced sweet or sour flavor. Bring the sauce to a boil again, and pour this mixture over the stuffed cabbage rolls. Cover the casserole tightly and simmer for 1 to 1½ hours, or until the cabbage is tender. Serve hot, as either a main or first course.

255

To serve 4 to 6

¼ pound lean salt pork with rind removed, the pork cut into ¼-inch dice
½ cup finely chopped onions
3 cups coarsely chopped boiled potatoes
2 cups (about 1 pound) finely chopped boiled corned beef (*see*

*New England boiled dinner\**)
1 cup diced boiled beets, fresh or canned
¼ cup heavy cream
4 tablespoons finely chopped fresh parsley
Salt
Freshly ground black pepper

In a heavy 10- to 12-inch skillet, preferably one with a nonstick cooking surface, fry the salt pork dice over moderate heat until they are lightly browned and crisp and have rendered all their fat. With a slotted spoon transfer them to paper towels to drain. Pour all but 2 tablespoons of the fat remaining in the skillet into a cup and reserve. Add the onions to the skillet and, stirring frequently, cook for about 5 minutes until they are soft and translucent but not brown.

With a rubber spatula, transfer the entire contents of the skillet to a deep bowl. Add the salt pork bits, potatoes, corned beef, beets, cream and 2 tablespoons of the parsley. Toss gently but thoroughly together, taste the hash for seasoning and add salt and pepper if desired.

Pour the reserved pork fat into the original skillet and warm over moderate heat until a drop of water flicked into it splutters and evaporates instantly. Add the hash, spreading it evenly and smoothing the top with a spatula, and reduce the heat to low. Shaking the pan occasionally to prevent the hash from sticking, cook uncovered for 35 to 40 minutes. With a bulb baster or a spoon, remove any fat that accumulates around the edges of the hash as it cooks.

When the bottom is a crusty brown, loosen the hash from the pan by sliding a thin flexible spatula under the edges. Then place a heated platter upside down over the skillet and, grasping platter and skillet firmly together, invert them. The hash should slide out onto the platter. If any of the hash sticks to the pan, lift it out with a spatula and patch it in place.

Sprinkle the top with the remaining chopped parsley and serve at once.

*\* See index.*

To serve 4

| | |
|---|---|
| ¼ cup finely chopped onions | 1 teaspoon finely chopped garlic |
| ¼ cup strained fresh lemon juice | 2 teaspoons salt |
| ¼ cup vegetable oil | Freshly ground black pepper |
| 3 tablespoons prepared mustard | 3 pounds lean short ribs of beef, each 4 to 5 inches long |

Combine the onions, lemon juice, oil, mustard, garlic, salt and a liberal grinding of pepper in a deep bowl and mix them well. Add the short ribs and turn them about with a spoon until they are evenly coated. Then let the ribs marinate at room temperature for about 2 hours, turning them from time to time.

Preheat the oven to 400°. Arrange the ribs fat side up in a single layer on a rack set in a shallow roasting pan. (Discard the remaining marinade.) Roast the ribs uncovered in the middle of the oven for 20 minutes. Then reduce the heat to 350° and continue to roast for 1 hour and 15 minutes longer, or until the meat is tender and shows no resistance when pierced with the point of a small skewer or sharp knife. Arrange the ribs attractively on a heated platter and serve at once.

## *Beef Birds with Pea Purée*

To serve 4

BEEF BIRDS

| | |
|---|---|
| 8 thin slices round of beef | 3 tablespoons brandy |
| 6 chicken livers | 1 teaspoon meat extract |
| 3 tablespoons butter | ½ teaspoon tomato paste |
| ¼ pound mushrooms, sliced | 2 teaspoons potato flour |
| Salt | 1¼ cups beef stock |
| Pepper | ¼ cup red wine |
| 8 thin slices cooked ham or tongue | 1 bay leaf |

Put the slices of beef between 2 pieces of wax paper and beat until very thin with a wooden mallet. Brown 6 chicken livers quickly in 1 tablespoon of melted butter. Remove them from the pan. Put another tablespoon of butter into the pan and sauté ¼ pound sliced mushrooms until lightly browned. Shred the chicken livers and mix with the mushrooms, salt and pepper. Put a thin slice of ham or tongue on each piece of beef with a spoonful of the mushroom mixture on top. Press down carefully. Roll each slice of beef and bind each end with string. Brown these beef birds quickly all over in 1 tablespoon of melted butter. Heat

3 tablespoons of brandy in a small pan, ignite and pour over the beef birds. Remove them from the pan.

Blend in, off the fire, 1 teaspoon of meat extract, ½ teaspoon of tomato paste and 2 teaspoons of potato flour. Pour on 1¼ cups of stock and ¼ cup of red wine and stir over the fire until the mixture comes to a boil. Taste for seasoning. Put back the beef birds with a bay leaf. Cover and cook gently until the beef is tender, about 45 minutes. While the beef is simmering prepare a pea purée.

PEA PURÉE

| | |
|---|---|
| 3 cups fresh or frozen peas | 2 tablespoons flour |
| Salt | Pepper |
| 2 tablespoons butter | 3 tablespoons sour cream |

Cook 3 cups of shelled fresh or frozen peas in boiling salted water until very tender. Drain well and put through a strainer. Melt 2 tablespoons of butter in a small pan. Stir in 2 tablespoons of flour, salt and pepper, and brown very slowly. Add the strained peas, 3 tablespoons of sour cream and a little more seasoning. Keep warm in a double boiler until ready for use.

TO SERVE: Make a bed of pea purée on a hot serving dish. Remove the beef birds, cut off the strings and arrange the beef birds on top of the pea purée. Strain the sauce over all.

## Beef Tongue in Sweet-and-Sour Sauce *(Jewish-American)*

To serve 4 to 6

| | |
|---|---|
| A 5-pound fresh beef tongue | 2 tablespoons slivered blanched |
| 4 tablespoons vegetable oil | almonds |
| 2 cups finely chopped onions | 7 tablespoons cider vinegar |
| 10 gingersnaps, pulverized in a | ¼ cup seedless raisins |
| blender or wrapped in a kitchen | 2 teaspoons salt |
| towel and crushed with a rolling | 5 tablespoons brown sugar |
| pin (½ cup) | ½ lemon, thinly sliced |

Place the tongue in a large pot or casserole and pour in enough cold water to cover it by at least 2 inches. Bring to a boil over high heat, then partially cover the pot and simmer for 3 to 3½ hours, or until the tongue is tender and offers no resistance when pierced with a fork.

Remove the tongue from the water and transfer it to a cutting board. Do not discard the water. When the tongue is just cool enough to handle, skin it with a small sharp knife, cutting away the fat, bones and gristle at its base. Cut the tongue crosswise into ½-inch-thick slices. Strain the tongue broth through a fine sieve and set 4 cups aside.

In a heavy 10- to 12-inch enameled or stainless-steel skillet, heat the oil until a light haze forms above it. Stir in the onions and cook, stirring frequently, for 5 to 8 minutes, or until they are soft and lightly colored. Now stir in the gingersnaps, the reserved 4 cups of tongue broth, and the almonds, vinegar, raisins, salt and brown sugar, and bring to a boil. Place the tongue slices in the sauce and turn them about to coat them thoroughly. Top with the slices of lemon, cover the skillet, and simmer the tongue for 15 to 20 minutes, or until it is heated through and the sauce is thick and smooth. Taste for seasoning, then transfer to a deep heated platter and serve at once.

# Lamb

Lamb has been the most unpopular meat in America, probably because it usually is cooked for hours as though it were mutton that needed to have all the fat rendered out of it. But fortunately, in recent years there has been an upsurge of interest in lamb, and a new appreciation of its mild, distinctive flavor. Today's lamb is classified by age: genuine spring lamb, lamb and yearling mutton. Spring lamb, also called baby or hothouse lamb, is never more than four months old. It usually appears on the market in April or May. The cuts are small (a leg may weigh only four pounds) and expensive, and the meat is pale red in color and delicate in flavor. Lamb is from an animal five months to just under a year old. The untrimmed leg may weigh over eight pounds; the meat is red and has a sweet, rich taste. Yearling mutton, more available in Europe than in America, is between one and two years old. The meat is dark red, tougher and somewhat gamey in flavor.

At any age, the best lamb is characterized by finely grained lean portions which are well-marbled. Such lamb is delicious when cooked simply, either by broiling or roasting, depending on its cut and size. The recipes in this chapter for roast mint-stuffed leg of lamb and a crown roast of lamb and the Far Western specialty, lamb chops with pine nuts, are delectable representatives of these simple, satisfying techniques. But even lesser cuts or grades of lamb can reach culinary heights when broiled Far Western-style with a spicy chili sauce, boiled New England-style with capers, combined with broccoli in a richly sauced stew or stuffed with spinach and breadcrumbs and braised in a New England recipe for shoulder of lamb.

To serve 6 to 8

A 5- to 6-pound leg of lamb,
   trimmed of excess fat and with
   the fell (the parchmentlike
   covering) removed
2 medium-sized garlic cloves, peeled
   and cut lengthwise into paper-
   thin slivers

1 cup brandy
1 teaspoon ground cumin
1½ tablespoons salt
2 teaspoons freshly ground black
   pepper
¼ cup dry sherry
¼ cup dry white wine
Sprigs of watercress for garnish

With the point of a small sharp knife, cut a dozen or more 1-inch-deep slits all over the surface of the leg of lamb and insert a sliver of garlic into each slit. Cut a double thickness of cheesecloth about 16 inches wide and 18 to 20 inches long and drench it thoroughly with ½ cup of the brandy. Wrap the cheesecloth around the leg of lamb and cover it tightly with plastic wrap to prevent the brandy from evaporating. Set the lamb aside to marinate at room temperature for about 2 hours.

Preheat the oven to 450°. Mix the cumin, salt and pepper together in a small bowl, and combine the sherry and white wine in another bowl. Unwrap the lamb and place the leg, fat side up, on a rack in a shallow roasting pan. Press the cumin mixture into the surface of the lamb, coating the meat with the spices as evenly as possible. For the most predictable results, insert a meat thermometer 2 inches into the thickest part of the leg, being careful not to touch the bone.

Roast the lamb in the middle of the oven for 20 minutes. Then reduce the heat to 350° and baste with a tablespoon or so of the wine mixture. Continue to roast 40 to 60 minutes longer, or until the leg is cooked to your taste, basting two or three more times with the remaining wine mixture. A meat thermometer will register 130° when the lamb is rare, 140° when medium and 150° when well done.

Transfer the lamb to a heated platter and let the roast rest for 15 minutes for easier carving. Just before serving, warm the remaining ½ cup of brandy in a small saucepan. Ignite the brandy with a match and pour it flaming over the lamb. When the flame dies, garnish the platter with sprigs of watercress and serve at once.

To serve 8 to 10

A 6-pound leg of lamb, boned
4 slices bacon, cut into ½-inch
    pieces
1 cup coarsely chopped fresh mint
1 teaspoon finely chopped garlic
½ teaspoon salt
Freshly ground black pepper

4 tablespoons vegetable oil
2 large onions, thinly sliced
2 large carrots, thinly sliced
4 stalks celery, coarsely chopped
Salt
1½ cups beef or chicken stock, fresh
    or canned (optional)

Have the butcher bone a leg of lamb by removing the rump and leg bone, which will create a deep pocket for the stuffing. Ask him to leave the shank bone in. Although the effect will not be quite as impressive, the leg may be cut open and boned entirely. Do not remove the parchmentlike covering called the fell from the outside of the lamb.

For the stuffing, combine in a mixing bowl the bacon, chopped mint and garlic and stir into it ½ teaspoon of salt and a few grindings of black pepper. Fill the pocket with the stuffing and either sew the openings together or tightly skewer them. Or, if the leg has been cut open, lay it out flat, skin side down, and spread the stuffing over it. Roll the meat so as to enclose the stuffing completely, sew or skewer it, then tie it at 2-inch intervals so that it will hold its shape while cooking.

Preheat the oven to 475°. With a pastry brush or paper towel coat the lamb with the vegetable oil and place it fat side up on a rack set in a roasting pan just about large enough to hold it comfortably. Roast the lamb uncovered in the center of the oven for about 25 minutes. Then turn the heat down to 375° and scatter the onions, carrots and celery in the bottom of the pan. Sprinkle the lamb generously with salt and a few grindings of black pepper, and roast for about an hour for medium-rare lamb (140° to 150° on a meat thermometer) or up to ½ hour longer for well-done lamb (165° to 170°).

A simple pan gravy may be made by removing the lamb to a heated platter (the meat will be easier to carve if it rests for about 10 minutes) and pouring the 1½ cups of stock into the roasting pan. Bring it to a boil on top of the stove for about 3 minutes, meanwhile scraping into it any brown particles clinging to the bottom and sides of the pan. Strain it, discard the vegetables, and then skim the gravy of all its surface fat. Taste for seasoning and serve in a gravy boat with the carved lamb.

To serve 8

2 pairs calf's sweetbreads (about
1½ pounds)
A 7-pound leg of lamb, boned but
not split, with shank meat cut off
1½ teaspoons salt
Freshly ground black pepper
4 tablespoons butter, melted, plus 4
tablespoons butter, cut into ½-
inch bits, plus 4 tablespoons
butter, softened
1 tablespoon anchovy paste
4 tablespoons finely chopped fresh
parsley
2 teaspoons capers, finely chopped
½ teaspoon crumbled dried thyme
¼ teaspoon finely grated fresh
lemon peel
¼ teaspoon crumbled dried
marjoram
1 cup soft fresh crumbs made from

homemade-type white bread,
pulverized in a blender or finely
shredded with a fork
1 cup finely chopped onions
½ cup dry white wine
1½ to 2½ cups chicken stock,
fresh or canned
12 breakfast-type pork sausages
(about 1 pound)
¼ cup water
2 lamb kidneys, peeled and trimmed
of fat
2 tablespoons strained fresh lemon
juice
The yolks of 4 hard-cooked eggs
⅛ teaspoon ground white pepper
8 thin slices homemade-type white
bread, cut into 3-inch rounds and
fried in 4 tablespoons of butter
8 capers
16 flat anchovy fillets

Starting 6 hours or more ahead, soak the sweetbreads in several changes
of cold water for 3 hours. Place them in a 4-quart enameled or stainless-
steel pan and pour in 2 quarts of fresh cold water. Bring to a simmer slowly over moderate heat and blanch the sweetbreads by simmering them for
3 minutes. With tongs or a slotted spoon, transfer the sweetbreads to a
bowl of cold water to rest for 1 or 2 minutes. Pat them dry with paper towels, and gently pull off as much of the outside membrane as possible.

Cut the two lobes from the tube between each pair of sweetbreads with
a small sharp knife. Discard the tubes. Put the sweetbreads on a large flat
platter. Cover them with a towel and weight them with a casserole
or skillet weighing about 5 pounds to flatten and remove excess moisture
from the sweetbreads. Refrigerate the sweetbreads for at least 2 hours.

Preheat the oven to 450°. Season the lamb on all sides with ½ teaspoon of salt and a few grindings of pepper. To prepare the stuffing, combine the 4 tablespoons of melted butter and 1 tablespoon of anchovy
paste in a bowl and mix well. Add 2 tablespoons of parsley, the chopped
capers, thyme, lemon peel and marjoram. Then stir in the bread crumbs.

Close the opening at the shank end of the leg of lamb by sewing it
with a large needle and heavy white thread. Then fill the pocket in the
lamb with the stuffing, and sew up the opening securely. Tie the leg of

263

lamb crosswise in 5 or 6 places and lengthwise 2 or 3 times to hold it in a neat cylindrical shape. For the most predictable results, insert the tip of a meat thermometer at least 2 inches into the roast.

Set the lamb on a rack in a shallow roasting pan and roast it in the middle of the oven for 20 minutes. Reduce the oven temperature to 350°. Sprinkle the chopped onions around the lamb, roast 15 minutes more, and pour the wine and 1½ cups of chicken stock over the onions. Continue roasting for about 1 hour longer, or until the lamb is cooked to your taste. A meat thermometer will register 130° to 140° when the lamb is rare, 140° to 150° when medium, and 150° to 160° when well done. Ideally the lamb should be medium rare.

Half an hour or so before the lamb is ready to be served, prepare the garnishes: Combine the pork sausages and ¼ cup of water in a heavy 10- to 12-inch skillet and bring to a boil over high heat. Reduce the heat to low, cover tightly and simmer for 5 minutes. Then uncover the pan and, turning the sausages occasionally with a spatula, cook over moderate heat for about 5 minutes to brown them on all sides. Drain the sausages on paper towels, transfer them to a heated plate and cover with foil.

With a sharp knife, cut the sweetbreads crosswise into ½-inch-thick slices. Cut the kidneys crosswise into ¼-inch-thick slices and then cut the slices into ¼-inch-wide strips. In a heavy 10- to 12-inch skillet, melt 4 tablespoons of butter bits over moderate heat. When the foam begins to subside, add the sweetbreads and kidneys and, stirring frequently, fry for 6 to 8 minutes, or until the pieces are lightly browned. Add 2 tablespoons of lemon juice, ½ teaspoon of the salt and a few grindings of black pepper, and taste for seasoning. Remove the skillet from the heat and cover to keep the sweetbreads and kidneys warm.

Force the hard-cooked egg yolks through a fine sieve with the back of a spoon, then beat in the 4 tablespoons of softened butter. Add the remaining ½ teaspoon of salt and ⅛ teaspoon of white pepper, and taste for seasoning. Spoon the mixture into a pastry bag fitted with a star tube and pipe an egg-yolk rosette onto the center of each bread round. Set a caper on each rosette and arrange 2 anchovy fillets around it. Set aside.

When the leg of lamb has roasted its allotted time, transfer it to a large heated platter, and let it rest while you prepare the anchovy sauce.

ANCHOVY SAUCE
2 egg yolks
2 tablespoons flour

1 tablespoon anchovy paste
2 to 3 teaspoons strained fresh
 lemon juice

Strain the contents of the roasting pan through a fine sieve set over a 1-quart measuring cup, pressing down hard on the onions with the back of a spoon to extract all their juices. Pour the liquid into a small saucepan and add enough chicken stock to make 2 cups in all. Bring to a simmer over low heat. In a small bowl, beat the egg yolks, flour and 1 tablespoon of anchovy paste with a wire whisk until smooth. Ladle 2 or 3 tablespoons of simmering stock into the egg yolks and mix well. Whisking constantly, pour the yolks into the pan and cook over low heat until the sauce thickens lightly. Do not let the sauce come near a boil or the yolks will curdle. Taste and add 2 to 3 teaspoons of lemon juice.

To serve, mound the sweetbreads and kidneys at both the ends and sides of the leg of lamb and sprinkle them with the remaining 2 tablespoons of parsley. Arrange the sausages and bread rounds attractively on the platter, and present the anchovy sauce in a bowl or sauceboat.

*Martha Washington's "grand leg of lamb" is served with sweetbreads, kidneys, sausages and richly garnished bread rounds.*

To serve 7 or 8

A 6- to 8-pound leg of lamb
1 sliced medium-sized onion
1 sliced carrot
¼ teaspoon dried oregano

½ cup olive oil
1 cup red wine vinegar
Peppercorns
1 garlic clove (optional)
Salt

Have the leg of lamb boned, then place it in a large bowl. Sprinkle the onion, carrot and oregano over the lamb. Blend together the oil and vinegar and pour this mixture over the meat. Add a few peppercorns and, if you wish, a clove of garlic. Let the meat stand in the marinade in a cool place for several hours or overnight, turning it occasionally.

Preheat the broiling unit and pan. Remove the meat from the marinade but do not dry it. Spread it out flat and put it in the broiler pan about 2½ to 3 inches away from the fire. Broil the lamb for 20 minutes, brush the top side with a little of the marinade, season it with salt and turn the meat over. Brush the top with the marinade and cook for 20 minutes more. Sprinkle the top side with salt and serve the meat on a heated platter.

## Crown Roast of Lamb with Peas and New Potatoes

To serve 6 to 8

A crown roast of lamb, consisting of
16 to 18 chops and weighing about
4½ pounds
1 clove garlic, cut into tiny slivers
(optional)
2 teaspoons salt
1 teaspoon freshly ground black

pepper
1 teaspoon crushed dried rosemary
16 to 18 peeled new potatoes, all
about 1½ inches in diameter
3 cups cooked fresh or frozen peas
2 tablespoons melted butter
6 to 8 sprigs of fresh mint

Preheat the oven to 475°. With the point of a small, sharp knife make small incisions a few inches apart in the meaty portions of the lamb, and insert in them the slivers of garlic, if you are using it. Combine the salt, pepper and rosemary, and with your fingers pat the mixture all over the bottom and sides of the crown. To help keep its shape, stuff the crown with a crumpled sheet of foil and wrap the ends of the chop bones in strips of foil to prevent them from charring and snapping off. Place the crown of lamb on a small rack set in a shallow roasting pan just large enough to hold it comfortably and roast it in the center of the oven for about 20 minutes. Then turn down the heat to 400° and surround the crown with the new potatoes, basting them with the pan drippings and sprinkling them lightly with salt. Continue to roast the lamb (basting the lamb is unnecessary, but baste the potatoes every 15 minutes or so) for about an hour to an hour and 15 minutes, depending upon how well done you prefer your lamb. Ideally, it should be served when it is still somewhat pink, and should register 140° to 150° on a meat thermometer.

When the crown is done, carefully transfer it to a large circular platter, remove the foil and let the lamb rest about 10 minutes to make carving easier. Meanwhile, combine the peas with the melted butter and season them with as much salt as is necessary. Fill the hollow of the crown with as many of the peas as it will hold and serve any remaining peas separately. Put a paper frill on the end of each chop bone and surround the crown with the roasted potatoes. Garnish with mint and serve at once.

To carve the lamb, insert a large fork in the side of the crown to steady it and with a large, sharp knife cut down through each rib to detach the chops. Two rib chops per person is a customary portion.

*A crown roast of lamb, gaily decorated with paper frills, is a dish fit for a king. Whole new potatoes and sprigs of mint embellish this regal dish, whose hollow is filled with fresh peas.*

## Braised Stuffed Shoulder of Lamb  (New England)

To serve 4 to 6

11 tablespoons butter

5 tablespoons vegetable oil

1 cup finely chopped onions plus, 1 small onion, peeled and sliced into ⅛-inch-thick rounds

1½ teaspoons finely chopped garlic plus 1 garlic clove, peeled and crushed with the side of a cleaver or heavy knife

1 pound fresh spinach, cooked, drained, squeezed completely dry and finely chopped, or substitute 2 cups thoroughly defrosted frozen chopped spinach, squeezed completely dry and finely chopped

½ cup finely chopped green bell pepper

3 cups soft fresh crumbs made from homemade-type white bread, pulverized in a blender or finely shredded with a fork

¼ cup finely chopped celery, plus 1 small celery stalk, coarsely chopped

¼ teaspoon ground nutmeg, preferably freshly grated

1½ teaspoons salt

Freshly ground black pepper

A 6- to 7-pound lamb shoulder, boned and flattened, with the bones sawed into small pieces and reserved

1 medium-sized carrot, scraped and cut into ⅛-inch-thick slices

2 cups water

4 sprigs fresh parsley and 1 medium-sized bay leaf tied with kitchen string

2 teaspoons arrowroot dissolved in ¼ cup cold water

1 tablespoon prepared mustard

In a heavy 12-inch skillet, melt 2 tablespoons of butter in 2 tablespoons of oil over moderate heat. When the foam begins to subside, add the chopped onions and chopped garlic and, stirring frequently, cook for about 5 minutes until they are soft but not brown. Add the spinach and green pepper and stir until most of the liquid in the pan has evaporated. With a rubber spatula, scrape the spinach mixture into a deep bowl.

Melt 6 tablespoons of the remaining butter in the same skillet. Add the bread crumbs and fry them over moderate heat, stirring frequently until they are a delicate golden color. Add the contents of the skillet to the spinach mixture, then stir in the finely chopped celery, nutmeg, 1 teaspoon of the salt and a few grindings of pepper. Taste for seasoning.

Lay the lamb flat, cut side up, on a work surface and sprinkle it with the remaining ½ teaspoon of salt and a few grindings of pepper. Spread the spinach stuffing mixture evenly over the lamb. Starting at one long side, carefully roll the lamb into a tight cylinder. Wrap one end of a 10-foot length of cord around the lamb about 1 inch from the end of the roll and knot it securely. Then, in spiral fashion, loop the cord around the length of the roll to within about 1 inch of the opposite end. Wrap the end of the spiral tightly around the lamb and knot it securely.

Preheat the oven to 325°. In a heavy casserole large enough to hold the lamb comfortably, melt the remaining 3 tablespoons of butter over moderate heat. When the foam begins to subside, add the sliced onion, carrot, coarsely chopped celery, and crushed garlic and, stirring frequently, cook for about 5 minutes until the vegetables are soft but not brown. Set the casserole aside off the heat.

Meanwhile, warm the remaining 3 tablespoons of oil in the reserved skillet until a light haze forms above it. Brown the rolled lamb in the hot oil, turning it frequently with tongs or a slotted spatula and regulating the heat so that it colors richly and evenly on all sides without burning. Transfer the lamb roll to the casserole. Then brown the lamb bones in the fat remaining in the skillet and add them to the casserole.

Pour off the fat from the skillet and in its place add the water. Bring to a boil over high heat, stirring constantly and scraping in the brown particles that cling to the bottom and sides of the pan. Pour the mixture over the lamb and drop in the tied parsley and bay leaf.

Cover the casserole tightly and braise the lamb in the middle of the oven for 1½ hours, or until it is tender and shows no resistance when pierced deeply with the point of a skewer or small, sharp knife.

Transfer the lamb to a heated platter and drape foil over it to keep it warm while you prepare the sauce. With tongs, remove the bones from the casserole and discard them. Then strain the liquid remaining in the casserole through a fine sieve into a small saucepan, pressing down hard on the vegetables and herbs with the back of a spoon to extract all their juices before discarding them.

Skim as much fat as possible from the surface of the stock and bring to a simmer over moderate heat. Stirring the stock constantly, pour in the arrowroot mixture and cook until the sauce comes to a boil, thickens lightly and is smooth. Remove from the heat, add the mustard and taste for seasoning. Pour the sauce into a bowl and serve at once with the lamb.

## Boiled Lamb with Caper Sauce *(New England)*

To serve 6

A 5- to 6-pound leg of lamb, trimmed of excess fat, but with the fell (the parchmentlike covering) left on
2 medium-sized garlic cloves, each peeled and cut lengthwise into 6

thin slivers
1 teaspoon crumbled dried rosemary
3 to 4 quarts water
1 medium-sized onion, peeled
4 sprigs fresh parsley
1 medium-sized bay leaf
1 tablespoon salt

With the tip of a small, sharp knife, make 12 half-inch-deep incisions on the fat side of the lamb and insert a sliver of garlic and a pinch of rosemary deeply into each cut. Place the leg in a heavy casserole just large enough to hold it comfortably and pour in 3 quarts of water. The water should cover the lamb by at least 1 inch; add more if necessary.

Bring to a boil over high heat, meanwhile skimming off the foam and scum as they rise to the surface. Add the onion, parsley, bay leaf and 1 tablespoon of salt, reduce the heat to low and simmer partially covered for about 2½ hours, or until the lamb is tender and shows no resistance when pierced deeply with the point of a small skewer or sharp knife. Transfer the lamb to a heated platter and drape loosely with foil to keep it warm while you prepare the caper sauce.

CAPER SAUCE
2 tablespoons butter
2 tablespoons flour
½ cup capers, rinsed in a sieve under cold running water, and

patted dry with paper towels
1 teaspoon strained fresh lemon juice
¼ teaspoon salt
⅛ teaspoon ground white pepper

Strain the lamb stock through a fine sieve into a deep bowl or saucepan and set aside. In a heavy 8- to 10-inch skillet, melt the butter over moderate heat. When the foam begins to subside, add the flour and blend well. Then, stirring the mixture constantly with a wire whisk, pour in 1½ cups of the reserved lamb stock (thoroughly degreased) in a slow, thin stream and cook over high heat until the sauce comes to a boil, thickens lightly and is smooth. Reduce the heat to low and simmer for about 3 minutes, then stir in the capers, lemon juice, ¼ teaspoon salt and white pepper. Taste for seasoning and serve at once with the boiled lamb.

## Lamb Chops with Pine Nuts  *(Far West)*

To serve 4

½ cup pine nuts *(pignolia)*
3 large garlic cloves, peeled and coarsely chopped
2 dried hot red chilies, each about 1 inch long, stemmed, seeded and coarsely crumbled *(caution: see note, appendix)*

½ teaspoon salt
2 tablespoons distilled white vinegar
1 teaspoon sugar
A 6-ounce can tomato paste
¾ cup plus 1 tablespoon olive oil
4 lean shoulder lamb chops, each cut about 1 inch thick

Place the pine nuts in a small ungreased skillet and, stirring frequently, toast them over moderate heat for 5 to 10 minutes, or until they are golden brown. Transfer ¼ cup of the nuts to a large mortar or small heavy bowl and set the rest aside.

With a pestle or the back of a spoon, pulverize the ¼ cup of pine nuts. Add the garlic, chilies and salt and pound the mixture to a smooth paste. Stir in the vinegar and sugar, then add the tomato paste and, when it is well incorporated, beat in ¾ cup of the olive oil, 2 tablespoons at a time. Set the tomato sauce aside.

Set the broiler pan and rack 4 inches from the heat and preheat the broiler to its highest setting. With a pastry brush, spread the remaining tablespoon of olive oil over the broiler pan rack. Place the lamb chops on the rack and brush each one with a heaping tablespoon of the sauce. Broil the chops for 5 to 6 minutes, turn them over, and coat the top of each one with another heaping tablespoon of sauce. Broil for 5 to 6 minutes longer, or until the lamb chops are done to your taste.

Arrange the lamb chops attractively on a heated platter and scatter the reserved whole pine nuts over them. Warm the tomato sauce briefly over low heat and present it separately in a small bowl.

### *Lamb and Broccoli St. Francis* (Far West)

---

To serve 4 to 6

| | |
|---|---|
| 3 pounds lean boneless lamb, trimmed of excess fat and cut into 1-inch cubes | 1 teaspoon finely chopped garlic |
| 1 teaspoon salt | 2 cups water |
| ½ teaspoon freshly ground black pepper | 1 pound firm fresh brocolli, stemmed, washed and separated into small flowerets |
| 6 tablespoons vegetable oil | 3 egg yolks |
| 2 cups finely chopped onions | 3 tablespoons flour |
| | ½ cup strained fresh lemon juice |

Pat the lamb cubes completely dry with paper towels and season them with the salt and pepper.

In a heavy 5- to 6-quart casserole, heat 4 tablespoons of the oil over moderate heat until a light haze forms above it. Brown the lamb, seven or eight pieces at a time, turning the cubes about frequently with tongs and regulating the heat so that they color richly and evenly on all sides without burning. As they brown, transfer the cubes of lamb to a plate.

Add the remaining 2 tablespoons of oil to the casserole, then drop in the onions and garlic. Stirring frequently, cook over moderate heat for about 5 minutes, or until the onions are soft and translucent but not brown. Pour in the water and bring the mixture to a boil over high heat, meanwhile scraping in the brown particles clinging to the bottom and sides of the pot.

Return the lamb and the liquid that has accumulated around it to the casserole. Stir well, reduce the heat to low and simmer partially covered for 45 minutes. Stir in the broccoli, cover the casserole partially again and simmer for 15 minutes more, or until the lamb shows no resistance when pierced deeply with the point of a small sharp knife. Reduce the heat to its lowest setting.

Combine the egg yolks and flour in a small bowl and beat with a wire whisk until the mixture is smooth. Whisk in the lemon juice, then beat in about ½ cup of the lamb-braising liquid. Stirring the lamb and broccoli constantly with a wooden spoon, pour in the egg-yolk mixture in a slow, thin stream and cook for 2 or 3 minutes, until the sauce thickens heavily and is smooth. Do not let the sauce come anywhere near a boil or the egg yolks will curdle.

Taste for seasoning and serve at once, directly from the casserole or from a deep heated platter.

*Piping-hot lamb shanks and lentils make a simple but sustaining winter meal.*

To serve 4

2 cloves garlic cut into paper-thin
    slivers
4 meaty lamb shanks (about 1 pound
    each)
Salt
Freshly ground black pepper
3 tablespoons vegetable oil

2 tablespoons butter
½ cup finely chopped onion
2½ cups beef stock, fresh or canned
2½ cups lentils, thoroughly washed
    and drained
1 bay leaf
½ cup chopped scallions
¼ cup chopped fresh parsley

Preheat the oven to 350°. With the point of a small, sharp knife, insert 2
or 3 garlic slivers into the meaty portion of each lamb shank. Then sprinkle the shanks generously with salt and a few grindings of black pepper.
In a 12-inch heavy skillet, heat the oil over high heat until a light haze
forms over it. Add the shanks, and then, over moderate heat, cook them
on all sides for about 10 minutes, turning them with tongs. When the
shanks are a deep golden brown, transfer them to a rack set in a shallow
roasting pan. Roast them in the middle of the oven for about an hour, or
until the shanks are tender. Basting is unnecessary.

While the shanks are roasting, melt 2 tablespoons of butter over moderate heat in a 2- to 4-quart saucepan. When the foam subsides add the
onions and cook them for about 6 minutes, stirring frequently until they
are transparent but not brown. Pour in the stock and add the lentils, bay
leaf, salt and a few grindings of black pepper. Bring to a boil. Cover the
pot and reduce the heat to its lowest point. Simmer the lentils, stirring occasionally, for about 30 minutes, or until they have absorbed all the stock
and are very tender.

To serve, stir into the lentils 2 tablespoons of drippings from the roasting pan and ½ cup of chopped scallions. Taste for seasoning. Arrange
the lamb shanks and the lentils on a large, heated platter and sprinkle
with parsley.

## *Shepherd's Pie*

To serve 6

Flank of lamb
1 onion, sliced
3 potatoes, peeled and diced

2 carrots, scraped and diced
1 tablespoon of flour
Salt
Pepper

Cover the lamb with cold water and cook until tender. Remove the bones
and the fat and cut the meat into small pieces. Let the broth cool and
remove the fat. Add the onion to the broth and bring to a boil. Add

273

the potatoes and carrots and cook until the vegetables are nearly done, about 12 minutes. Then add the lamb. When the potatoes are cooked thoroughly, thicken the broth with a thin paste of the flour mixed with a little water. Season with salt and pepper.

PASTRY

| | |
|---|---|
| 1 cup flour | ⅓ cup shortening |
| ⅛ teaspoon salt | 2 tablespoons ice water |

Sift together the flour and salt. Add half the shortening and chop fine, using two knives. Add the remaining shortening and chop, leaving quite large lumps, which make flakes when rolled out. Add about two tablespoons of ice water to hold the mixture together. Turn out on lightly floured board and roll thin.

Preheat the oven to 450°. Turn the lamb stew into a 9-inch casserole, cover with the pastry and bake about 12 minutes or until well browned.


## Lamb Pilau

To serve 4 to 6

| | |
|---|---|
| 3 tablespoons butter | Salt |
| 1½ pounds shoulder or leg of | Pepper |
| lamb, cut into ¾-inch cubes | ¼ teaspoon dried oregano |
| 1 large yellow onion, thinly sliced | 2 tablespoons finely chopped |
| 1½ cups raw rice | parsley |
| 3 cups water | 1 lemon, cut in wedges |

Heat 1 tablespoon of butter in a heavy casserole. When it is just turning color, add the lamb and quickly brown it all over. Have only a single layer of meat in the pan at one time. You will need 1 additional tablespoon of butter to brown it all. Remove the meat from the pan. Put the remaining tablespoon of butter into the pan. Add the sliced onion and cook it over a moderate fire until golden brown. Add 1½ cups of raw rice and stir over the fire for about 2 minutes. Pour on 3 cups of water; there will be enough glaze in the pan to flavor and color the water so that stock is not needed. Season with salt, pepper and ¼ teaspoon of dried oregano. Put the meat back into the pan. Cover and cook in a moderate oven at 350° for 1 hour.

Serve in the casserole and sprinkle 2 tablespoons of chopped parsley over the top. Serve lemon wedges separately.

To serve 4 to 6

2½ pounds boneless lamb
    shoulder, trimmed of excess fat
    and cut into 1½-inch cubes
1 teaspoon salt
Freshly ground black pepper
4 tablespoons vegetable oil
2 cups finely chopped onions
1 teaspoon finely chopped garlic
2 tablespoons flour
2 cups water
1 medium-sized firm, ripe tomato,

peeled, seeded and finely chopped
    (*see chile con queso**), or substitute
    ½ cup chopped drained, canned
    tomatoes
6 medium-sized carrots, scraped
6 white onions, each about 1½
    inches in diameter, peeled
½ cup fresh shelled lima beans, or
    substitute ½ cup frozen lima
    beans, not defrosted
2 tablespoons finely chopped fresh
    parsley

Pat the pieces of lamb completely dry with paper towels and sprinkle them evenly with the salt and a few grindings of pepper. In a heavy 10- to 12-inch skillet, warm the oil over moderate heat. When it is very hot but not smoking, brown the lamb in the oil, 5 or 6 pieces at a time, turning them frequently with a slotted spoon and regulating the heat so that they color deeply and evenly without burning. As they brown, transfer the pieces of lamb to a heavy 4- to 5-quart flameproof casserole.

Add the chopped onions and garlic to the fat remaining in the skillet and, stirring frequently, cook for about 5 minutes until they are soft and translucent but not brown. With a slotted spoon, transfer the onion mixture to the casserole.

Add the flour to the skillet and stir for a minute or so. When it is delicately colored, pour in the water, add the tomato and continue to stir until the sauce comes to a boil, thickens lightly and is smooth. Pour the sauce over the lamb and onions and bring to a boil over high heat. Reduce the heat to low and simmer partially covered for 20 minutes.

Drop the carrots, whole white onions and beans into the casserole, turning them about with a spoon until they are evenly coated with the sauce. Cover partially and simmer for about 20 minutes longer, or until the lamb and vegetables are tender and show no resistance when pierced deeply with the tip of a small, sharp knife.

Taste for seasoning, sprinkle the top with parsley and serve at once directly from the casserole.

* *See index.*

## The Somerset Club's Lamb Kidneys Pepperell (New England)

To serve 4

12 lamb kidneys, split lengthwise
    in half, trimmed of all fat, then
    each half cut crosswise into 4 pieces
½ teaspoon salt
Freshly ground black pepper
4 tablespoons butter

1 tablespoon vegetable oil
1 tablespoon curry powder
2 teaspoons Worcestershire sauce
¼ cup flour
⅔ cup pale dry sherry
4 slices hot toast made from
    homemade-type white bread
    trimmed of all crusts

Pat the kidneys completely dry with paper towels and sprinkle the pieces with the salt and a few grindings of pepper.

In a heavy 10- to 12-inch skillet, melt the butter in the oil over moderate heat. Drop in the kidneys and fry them for about 3 minutes, turning them about with a large spoon and regulating the heat so that they color delicately on all sides without burning. Stir in the curry powder, Worcestershire sauce and flour. Then, stirring constantly, pour in the sherry in a slow stream and cook for 1 or 2 minutes longer until the sauce comes to a boil, thickens heavily and is smooth. Taste for seasoning.

Arrange the slices of toast on heated individual plates and ladle the kidneys and sauce over them. Serve at once.

# *Veal*

A mild-flavored meat, veal is the flesh of calves five to twelve weeks old. The best quality veal, as scarce and expensive as it is young, is milk-fed, with firm, smooth and fine-grained meat that is a delicate mother-of-pearl white in color. Most of the veal marketed in America, however, is baby beef, fed on grass or grain. The meat has already darkened to pink and is no longer as smooth or fine in texture as milk-fed veal. Since it is so young, veal is generally tender, but it cannot be as casually broiled or pan-fried as you might suspect. There is very little natural fat covering the outer surfaces, and no marbling of fat within the meat, so unless veal is given moist, gentle cooking, it toughens.

Americans are not familiar with veal for good reason. Land is plentiful here, and calves grow to full size, ending up as milk-producers or beef. In Italy and other parts of the world where pasturage is limited, the calves are slaughtered young. Where veal *is* consumed in America, it tends to reflect definite regional and ethnic preferences: veal is a great favorite, for example, among the Creoles and Acadians of Louisiana. They combine a European fondness for braised veal with a Southern taste for hominy grits. The most popular ethnic veal dish in America is undoubtedly Italian veal *parmigiana,* which layers the veal with cheese and tomato sauce. The scallops, or *scallopini,* for this dish are cut from the leg, across the grain, in slices less than three-quarters of an inch thick. Then the slices are pounded even thinner. Such scallops are marvelously adaptable, either quickly sautéed and sauced as in *parmigiana* or rolled around a stuffing, as in the Creole specialty, veal rolls and olives.

## Veal Loaf

To serve 8

| | |
|---|---|
| 2 pounds ground lean veal | 1 cup light cream |
| ¼ pound ground salt pork | 2 tablespoons chopped parsley |
| 1 cup soft bread crumbs | Salt |
| 1 tablespoon finely chopped onion | Pepper |
| 1 tablespoon lemon juice | Nutmeg |
| 1 egg, lightly beaten | 2 tablespoons melted butter |

Preheat the oven to 350°. In a large bowl mix together the veal, salt pork, bread crumbs, chopped onion, lemon juice, egg, cream and parsley. Add salt, pepper and nutmeg to taste. Place the mixture in a greased loaf pan. Brush the top well with the melted butter. Bake in the oven for 1½ hours. Remove, let stand for 5 minutes, then turn it out onto a heated dish and serve immediately.

## Veal Steaks with Apple Rings in Cream  (Northwest)

To serve 6

| | |
|---|---|
| 4 tablespoons butter | 2 teaspoons salt |
| 2 medium-sized apples, cored but not peeled, and cut crosswise into ¼-inch rings | ¼ teaspoon freshly ground black pepper |
| | ½ cup flour |
| 6 five- to six-ounce boneless veal round steaks, sliced ½ inch thick and trimmed of excess fat | ¼ cup vegetable oil |
| | ½ cup heavy cream |
| | 1 teaspoon strained fresh lemon juice |

In a heavy 10- to 12-inch skillet, melt 2 tablespoons of the butter over moderate heat. When the foam begins to subside, add the apple rings and cook, turning them frequently with a slotted spatula, until they are tender and delicately browned. Remove the skillet from the heat and cover to keep the apple rings warm.

Pat the veal steaks completely dry with paper towels and season them with the salt and pepper. One at a time, dip the steaks in the flour to coat both sides, then shake off the excess flour.

Melt the remaining 2 tablespoons of butter with the oil in a heavy 12-inch skillet. Fry the steaks for about 4 minutes on each side, or until they are tender and show no resistance when pierced with the point of a small, sharp knife. Regulate the heat so that the steaks brown richly and evenly without burning.

Transfer them to a heated platter and drape foil over them to keep them warm while you prepare the sauce. Pour off the fat remaining in the skillet and in its place add the cream. Bring to a simmer over moderate heat, meanwhile scraping in the browned particles that cling to the bottom and sides of the pan. Reduce the heat to low and stir until the cream thickens slightly. Stir in the lemon juice and taste for seasoning.

To serve, arrange the apple rings on top of the veal steaks and pour the sauce over them.

## *Grillades and Grits* (*Creole-Acadian*)
### BRAISED VEAL STEAKS WITH HOMINY GRITS

To serve 4

Four 5- to 6-ounce boneless veal round steaks, sliced ½ inch thick and trimmed of excess fat
2 teaspoons salt
¼ teaspoon freshly ground black pepper
½ cup flour
3 tablespoons lard
4 tablespoons butter
2 large onions, peeled and coarsely chopped
1½ cups coarsely chopped green peppers

½ cup coarsely chopped celery
1 tablespoon finely chopped garlic
2 cups chicken stock, fresh or canned
1½ cups coarsely chopped drained canned tomatoes
1 medium-sized bay leaf
1 tablespoon cornstarch combined with 1 tablespoon cold water
5 cups water
1 cup regular yellow or white hominy grits, not the quick-cooking variety

Pat the veal steaks completely dry with paper towels and season them with 1 teaspoon of the salt and the black pepper. One at a time, dip the steaks in the flour to coat them evenly. Then shake off the excess flour.

In a heavy 12-inch skillet, melt the lard over moderate heat until it is very hot but not smoking. Brown the veal steaks, two at a time, turning them with tongs and regulating the heat so that they color richly on both sides without burning. As they brown, transfer the steak to a plate.

Pour off the fat remaining in the skillet, add the butter, and melt it over moderate heat. When the foam begins to subside, add the onions, green peppers, celery and garlic and, stirring frequently, cook for about 5 minutes, or until the vegetables are soft but not brown. Stir in the stock, tomatoes and bay leaf, and bring to a boil over high heat. Reduce the heat to low, partially cover the skillet, and simmer for 20 minutes.

Return the steaks and the liquid that has accumulated around them to the skillet and turn to coat them with the vegetable mixture. Simmer partially covered for about 1 hour, or until the veal is tender and shows no resistance when pierced with the point of a small sharp knife. Pour the cornstarch-and-water mixture over the simmering veal and stir for 2 or 3 minutes, until the gravy thickens slightly. Taste for seasoning.

About half an hour before the veal is done, bring the water and the remaining teaspoon of salt to a boil in a heavy 1½- to 2-quart saucepan. Pour in the hominy grits slowly enough so that the boiling continues at a rapid rate, stirring all the while with a wooden spoon to keep the mixture smooth. Reduce the heat to low and, stirring occasionally, simmer the grits tightly covered for 30 minutes.

Mound the grits on heated individual plates or a deep platter and place the veal steaks on the top. Pour the gravy over the grits and steaks and serve at once. (If allowed to cool, the grits will be undesirably firm.)

## Veal Rolls and Olives *(Creole-Acadian)*

To serve 4 or 8

| | |
|---|---|
| 8 tablespoons butter | (cayenne) |
| 1 cup soft fresh crumbs made from French- or Italian-type white bread, pulverized in a blender | ½ teaspoon salt |
| | Eight 6-by-4-inch veal scallops (about 4 ounces each), cut about ⅜ inch thick and pounded ¼ inch thick |
| ½ cup finely chopped onions | |
| ½ pound lean cooked smoked ham, sliced ⅛ inch thick and finely chopped | ¼ cup flour |
| | 2 tablespoons vegetable oil |
| 1 hard-cooked egg, finely chopped | 1 cup chicken stock, fresh or canned |
| ¼ teaspoon crumbled dried thyme | ½ cup pitted green olives, coarsely chopped |
| ⅛ teaspoon ground hot red pepper | |

In a heavy 12-inch skillet, melt 4 tablespoons of the butter over moderate heat. When the foam begins to subside, add the bread crumbs and stir until they are crisp and golden brown. With a slotted spoon, transfer the crumbs to a bowl.

Melt 2 tablespoons of the remaining butter in the same skillet and, when the foam subsides, drop in the onions. Stirring frequently, cook over moderate heat for about 5 minutes, or until they are soft and translucent but not brown. With a rubber spatula, scrape the entire contents of the skillet over the bread crumbs. Add the ham, egg, thyme, red pepper and salt, and toss all the stuffing ingredients together gently but thoroughly. Set the skillet aside.

Pat the veal scallops dry with paper towels. To make each veal roll, spread about ¼ cup of the stuffing mixture on each scallop in a band about 1 inch from one narrow end of the scallop. Fold the end over the stuffing and roll up the scallop into a tight cylinder. Tie the roll securely in shape with two or three short lengths of kitchen cord and turn it about in the flour to coat the surface lightly.

Place the reserved skillet over moderate heat and in it melt the remaining 2 tablespoons of butter with the oil. Add the veal rolls and brown them on all sides, turning them with tongs or a spatula and regulating the heat so that they color richly and evenly without burning. As they brown, transfer the veal rolls to a plate.

Pour the chicken stock into the fat remaining in the skillet and bring to a boil over high heat, meanwhile scraping in the brown particles that cling to the bottom and sides of the pan. Stir in the olives, then return the veal rolls and the liquid that has accumulated around them to the skillet. Cover tightly, reduce the heat to low and simmer for about 1 hour, or until the veal is tender and shows no resistance when pierced deeply with the point of a small sharp knife.

With a slotted spatula, transfer the veal rolls to a heated platter. Taste the olive sauce for seasoning, pour it over the veal and serve at once.

### *Veal Parmigiana* (Italian-American)
VEAL SCALLOPS WITH CHEESE-AND-TOMATO SAUCE

To serve 4

| | |
|---|---|
| 1½ pounds veal scallops, cut ¾ inch thick and pounded ¼ inch thick | 2 cups bread crumbs |
| Salt | ½ cup olive oil |
| Freshly ground black pepper | ¼ pound mozzarella cheese, thinly sliced |
| Flour | ½ cup tomato and meat sauce (*see below*) |
| 1 egg, combined with 1 cup milk | ¼ cup freshly grated Parmesan cheese |

Preheat the oven to 400°. Sprinkle the veal scallops lightly with salt and pepper, dredge them in flour and vigorously shake off any excess flour. Immerse the scallops in the egg-and-milk mixture, then coat them on both sides with the bread crumbs.

In a heavy 10- to 12-inch skillet, heat the olive oil until a light haze forms above it. Add the veal scallops, four or five at a time, and brown them quickly on both sides. With tongs, transfer the scallops to a baking dish just large enough to hold them in one layer.

Top the scallops with the slices of mozzarella, and cover with the tomato sauce. Scatter the grated Parmesan over the top and bake in the center of the oven for 10 minutes, or until the sauce bubbles. Serve at once, directly from the baking dish.

To make about 5 cups

4 tablespoons olive oil
½ pound boneless pork, in 1 piece
½ pound chuck, in 1 piece
1 cup finely chopped onions
1½ teaspoons finely chopped
   garlic
3 one-pound cans solid-pack

tomatoes and their liquid
1 six-ounce can tomato paste
2 cups water
1 teaspoon oregano
1 tablespoon basil
1½ teaspoons salt
½ teaspoon freshly ground black
   pepper

In a heavy 10- to 12-inch skillet, heat the oil until it is very hot but not smoking. Add the pork and chuck, and brown them over moderate heat, turning them with tongs and regulating the heat so that the meats color richly without burning. Add the onions and garlic and, stirring frequently, cook until the onions are soft and translucent. Stir in the tomatoes and their liquid, the tomato paste, water, oregano, basil, salt and pepper, and bring to a boil over high heat. Partially cover the pan, lower the heat and simmer for 2 to 2½ hours, or until the meat offers no resistance when pierced with the tip of a sharp knife.

Remove the meat from the sauce and set it aside. The sauce may be used at once. Or the sauce may be cooled to room temperature, tightly covered, and refrigerated or frozen. The meat may be served as a main course with pasta.

NOTE: To make a meatless tomato sauce, prepare the sauce as described but omit the pork and chuck and simmer the sauce for only 1 hour.

## *Veal Paprikash* (*Hungarian-American*)
### VEAL AND MUSHROOMS IN SOUR-CREAM SAUCE

To serve 6
8 tablespoons lard
3 pounds boneless veal, cut into
   1 ½-inch cubes
2 cups finely chopped onions
2 tablespoons sweet Hungarian

   paprika
2 teaspoons salt
Freshly ground black pepper
1 pound mushrooms, sliced
1 cup sour cream

Preheat the oven to 350°. In a 1½- to 2-quart casserole, heat the lard over high heat until a light haze forms above it. Add as many cubes of veal as will fit without crowding the pan and, tossing them constantly with a wooden spoon, cook for 2 or 3 minutes. As they brown lightly on all sides, transfer to a plate and replace them with the remaining cubes.

When all the veal has been browned and removed from the casserole, stir in the onions and cook over moderate heat for 6 to 8 minutes, or until they are soft and a light gold. Return the veal to the casserole. Off the heat, stir in the paprika, salt and several grindings of pepper, and toss the meat about with a spoon until the cubes are well coated. Cover the casserole tightly and place in the center of the oven. Cook for 30 minutes, then add the mushrooms, re-cover the casserole and cook the veal and mushrooms for 30 minutes more.

Remove the casserole from the oven and stir in the sour cream. Transfer the veal *paprikash* to a large heated platter and serve at once, accompanied by boiled rice or noodles.

### Veal Stew with Dumplings  *(Northwest)*

To serve 8 to 10

| | |
|---|---|
| VEAL STEW | 3 tablespoons vegetable oil |
| 6 pounds boneless breast of veal, | 6½ cups chicken stock, fresh or |
|     trimmed of excess fat and |     canned |
|     cartilage and cut into 2½-by- | 1 cup finely chopped onions |
|     1½-inch strips | ⅓ cup flour |
| 1 teaspoon salt | 3 sprigs fresh parsley |
| Freshly ground black pepper | 1 medium-sized bay leaf |
| 6 to 10 tablespoons butter | ¼ teaspoon crumbled dried thyme |

Pat the strips of veal completely dry with paper towels. Place the meat in a bowl. Add 1 teaspoon of salt and a few grindings of black pepper, and toss about with a spoon to season the meat evenly. In a heavy 10- to 12-inch skillet, melt 2 tablespoons of the butter with the oil over high heat. When the foam subsides, add 5 or 6 pieces of veal and, turning frequently, cook only until they are no longer pink. Do not let them brown. Transfer the veal to a bowl and repeat the entire procedure with the remaining pieces, cooking them 5 or 6 at a time over high heat and adding up to 4 tablespoons more butter to the skillet if necessary.

Pour off all the fat remaining in the skillet and in its place add ½ cup of the chicken stock. Bring to a boil over high heat, meanwhile scraping in any brown particles that cling to the bottom and sides of the pan. Pour the stock over the veal and set aside.

In a heavy 6- to 8-quart casserole, melt 4 tablespoons of butter over moderate heat. Add the onions and, stirring frequently, cook for about 5 minutes, until they are soft and translucent but not brown. Add the flour and mix well. Stirring the mixture constantly with a wire whisk, pour in the remaining 6 cups of chicken stock in a slow, thin stream and cook until the liquid comes to a boil, thickens slightly and is smooth.

Stir in the veal and the stock from the bowl and add the parsley, bay leaf and thyme. Reduce the heat to low and simmer partially covered for 1½ hours, or until the veal is tender and shows no resistance when pierced with the point of a small, sharp knife.

| | |
|---|---|
| DUMPLINGS | ½ cup farina |
| 2 cups milk | 1 egg, lightly beaten |
| 2 tablespoons butter | 6 tablespoons finely chopped fresh parsley |
| ½ teaspoon salt | ⅛ teaspoon white pepper |

About 10 minutes before the veal is done, prepare the dumplings in the following fashion: In a small, heavy saucepan, combine the milk, 2 tablespoons of butter and ½ teaspoon of salt, and bring to a boil over moderate heat. Stirring constantly, pour in the farina in a thin stream and cook until the mixture is thick enough to draw away from the sides of the pan in a solid mass. Remove the pan from the heat and beat in the egg, parsley and white pepper.

| | |
|---|---|
| ½ cup heavy cream | 1 tablespoon strained fresh lemon juice |

With a slotted spoon, transfer the veal strips to a plate. Strain the entire contents of the casserole through a fine sieve, pressing down hard on the onions and herbs to extract all their juices before discarding them. Return the liquid to the casserole, add the cream and bring to a simmer over moderate heat. Stir in the lemon juice and taste for seasoning. Return the veal to the casserole and mix well with the sauce. Then drop the dumplings into the simmering sauce by the teaspoonful. Cover tightly and cook for 5 or 6 minutes, or until the dumplings are tender. Serve at once, directly from the casserole.

## Veal Stew (Creole-Acadian)

| | |
|---|---|
| To serve 8 to 10 | ½ pound lean cooked smoked ham, sliced ½ inch thick and cut into ½-inch cubes |
| 4 pounds lean boneless veal shoulder, trimmed of excess fat and cut into 1½-inch cubes | 2 one-pound cans tomatoes, drained and coarsely chopped, with all their liquid reserved |
| 2 teaspoons salt | |
| ¼ teaspoon freshly ground black pepper | 3 medium-sized yams (1 pound), peeled and cut into 1-inch chunks |
| ½ cup flour | 4 fresh parsley sprigs and 1 large bay leaf, tied together |
| 4 tablespoons butter | |
| ¼ to ½ cup vegetable oil | ¼ teaspoon ground hot red pepper (cayenne) |
| 2 cups finely chopped onions | |
| ½ cup finely chopped green pepper | 1 pound fresh okra, washed, trimmed and cut crosswise into 1-inch-thick rounds |
| 1 tablespoon finely chopped garlic | |
| 2 cups chicken stock, fresh or canned | |

Pat the cubes of veal dry with paper towels and season them on all sides with 1 teaspoon of the salt and the black pepper. Roll one piece at a time in the flour to coat it lightly and shake off the excess flour.

In a heavy 12-inch skillet, melt the butter with ¼ cup of oil over moderate heat. When the foam begins to subside, add about half the veal and brown it, turning the pieces frequently with tongs and regulating the heat so that they color richly and evenly without burning. When the first batch of veal is browned, transfer it to a heavy 8-quart casserole and brown the remaining pieces in the same fashion, adding up to ¼ cup more oil to the skillet if necessary.

Pour off all but a thin film of fat from the skillet and add the onions, green pepper and garlic. Stirring frequently, cook over moderate heat for about 5 minutes, or until the vegetables are soft but not brown. Transfer the vegetables to the casserole with the veal, pour the chicken stock into the skillet and bring it to a boil over high heat, meanwhile scraping in any brown particles that cling to the bottom and sides of the pan. Pour the stock mixture over the veal.

Stir the ham, tomatoes, yams, parsley sprigs and bay leaf, the red pepper and the remaining teaspoon of salt into the veal mixture and bring to a boil over high heat. Reduce the heat to low, cover the casserole partially, and simmer for 1½ hours. Stir in the okra and simmer, partially covered, for about 30 minutes longer, until the veal is tender and shows no resistance when pierced with the point of a small sharp knife.

Pick out and discard the parsley sprigs and bay leaf, and taste the stew for seasoning. Serve at once, directly from the casserole or from a large heated bowl.

## Sweetbreads en Coquille

To serve 4

2 pairs calf's sweetbreads (about 1½ pounds)
1 tablespoon strained fresh lemon juice
3 teaspoons salt
1 tablespoon butter, softened, plus 9 tablespoons butter, cut into ½-inch bits

1 cup finely chopped fresh mushrooms
6 tablespoons flour
2 cups light cream
⅛ teaspoon ground hot red pepper (cayenne)
¼ cup freshly grated imported Parmesan cheese

Soak the sweetbreads in several changes of cold water for 3 hours. Gently pull off as much of the outside membrane as possible without tearing the sweetbreads. Cut the two lobes of each pair from the tube between them with a small sharp knife. Discard both tubes.

Place the sweetbreads in an enameled saucepan with enough water to cover them by 2 inches, add the lemon juice and 2 teaspoons of the salt, and bring to a boil over high heat. Reduce the heat to its lowest point and simmer uncovered for about 15 minutes, or until the sweetbreads feel firm to the touch. Place the sweetbreads on paper towels to drain and pat them completely dry with fresh towels. Then cut them into ½-inch dice and set them aside on a plate.

Preheat the oven to 375°. With a pastry brush, spread the tablespoon of softened butter evenly over the bottoms and sides of four large scallop shells or four shallow individual baking dishes.

In a heavy 8- to 10-inch skillet, melt 3 tablespoons of the butter bits over moderate heat. When the foam begins to subside, add the mushrooms and, stirring occasionally, cook uncovered for 5 to 10 minutes but do not let them brown. When the moisture in the pan has evaporated completely, transfer the mushrooms to a bowl with a slotted spoon.

Add the remaining 6 tablespoons of butter bits to the skillet and melt over moderate heat. Then add the flour and mix well. Stirring the mixture constantly with a wire whisk, pour in the cream in a slow, thin stream and cook over high heat until the sauce comes to a boil, thickens heavily and is smooth. Reduce the heat to low and simmer for 2 to 3 minutes to remove any taste of raw flour.

Stir in the reserved sweetbreads and mushrooms, the remaining teaspoon of salt and the red pepper. Taste for seasoning and spoon the mixture into the buttered shells or baking dishes, dividing it evenly among them. Sprinkle the tops with the grated cheese.

Arrange the shells or dishes on a jelly-roll pan and bake in the upper third of the oven for 15 to 20 minutes, or until the sauce has begun to bubble and the top is lightly browned. If you like, slide the pan under a hot broiler for 30 seconds or so to brown the tops further. Serve at once.

# Grains & Pasta

The starch that accompanies an entree can be varied countless ways to make a change from potatoes and add interest to a meal. The most familiar alternative is rice, at its simple best in Southern dry (never gummy!) rice, or flavored with fine bits of chicken gizzard and liver, onions and vegetables in the unusual Creole-Acadian dish known as dirty rice. Other variations include wild rice—not really a true rice but rather a brownish-white grain of a tall, aquatic grass—from the Northwest, and Southern hominy grits, made from coarsely ground hulled kernels of corn. Coarsely ground cracked grains—oats, barley, wheat or buck-wheat—are known as groats, and buckwheat groats (or kasha), popular in Jewish, Russian and Polish cookery, have a distinctive, nutty flavor and texture. Middle Eastern cracked wheat, or bulghur, is an Armenian-American food, which is often combined with herbs and vegetables, tossed with a dressing and served cold as a salad.*

Noodles are another menu choice, served simply, as in the Pennsylvania Dutch recipe for homemade egg noodles, or in a pudding, Jewish style, with the additions of raisins and dried fruit.

Certainly pasta (noodlelike pastes, or doughs, made from hard wheat called semolina) has become the most universally accepted of all the melting pot foods. And it is certainly versatile! Pasta is available in more than five hundred forms: sea shells, macaronis of all sizes, spirals, bow-ties, alphabets, thin spaghettis, wide lasagna noodles, tubes for stuffing. Pasta can be light enough to serve as a side dish when tossed with butter and freshly grated Parmesan cheese. Or, as described in detail on the following pages, pasta can become a meal in itself.

* See index.

To serve 4

1 cup uncooked long-grain white
  rice, not the converted variety
1½ cups cold water

2 tablespoons unsalted butter
1 teaspoon strained fresh lemon
  juice
1 teaspoon salt

Place the rice in a sieve or colander and wash it under cold running water, stirring the grains with a fork until the draining water runs clear.

In a heavy 2- to 3-quart saucepan, bring the water, butter, lemon juice and salt to a boil over high heat. Pour in the rice, stir well and reduce the heat to low. Cover the pan tightly and simmer for about 20 minutes, or until the rice is tender and the grains have absorbed all the liquid. Remove the pan from the heat and, without removing the cover, set the rice aside for 10 minutes.

To serve, transfer the rice to a heated bowl and fluff it with a fork. Southern dry rice often accompanies fried chicken* and when it does, the chicken gravy is poured over the rice before serving.

## *Dirty Rice* *(Creole-Acadian)*

To serve 6 to 8

½ pound chicken gizzards,
  thoroughly defrosted if frozen,
  trimmed of excess fat and
  coarsely chopped
½ pound chicken livers,
  thoroughly defrosted if frozen,
  and coarsely chopped
2 medium-sized onions, peeled and
  coarsely chopped
1 large green pepper, stemmed,

  seeded, deribbed and coarsely
  chopped
½ cup coarsely chopped celery
2 tablespoons olive oil
1½ teaspoons salt
½ teaspoon freshly ground black
  pepper
1 cup uncooked long-grain white
  rice, not the converted variety
2 cups water
½ cup finely chopped fresh parsley

*The term dirty rice may be a jocular reference to the appearance of the finished dish, since the bits of chicken gizzard and liver that are tossed with the rice give it a brown, or "dirty," look.*

Put the chicken gizzards, chicken livers, onions, green pepper and celery through the finest blade of a food grinder. In a heavy 4- to 5-quart casserole, heat the olive oil over moderate heat until a light haze forms above it. Add the ground chicken mixture, stir in the salt and black pepper, and reduce the heat to low. Stirring occasionally, cook uncovered for about 1 hour, or until the bits of chicken are richly browned.

*\* See index.*

Meanwhile, place the rice in a heavy 1-quart pot, stir in the water and bring to a boil over high heat. Reduce the heat to low, cover tightly, and simmer for 20 to 25 minutes, or until the rice has absorbed all the liquid in the pan and the grains are tender. Remove the pan from the heat and let the rice rest, still tightly covered, for 10 minutes or so.

When the chicken mixture has cooked its allotted time, fluff the rice with a fork and add it to the casserole. With the fork, toss the rice and the chicken mixture together gently but thoroughly.

Taste for seasoning and stir in the parsley. Mound the dirty rice on a heated platter or in a heated serving bowl and serve at once.

## Wild Rice with Mushrooms and Almonds *(Northwest)*

To serve 4 to 6

| | |
|---|---|
| 5 tablespoons butter | ¼ cup slivered blanched almonds |
| 4 tablespoons finely chopped onions | ½ pound firm fresh mushrooms, |
| 1 cup wild rice | wiped with a dampened towel, |
| 2 cups chicken stock, fresh or | trimmed, and cut lengthwise, |
| canned | including the stems, into ⅛- |
| 1 teaspoon salt | inch-thick slices |
| | Freshly ground black pepper |

Preheat the oven to 350°. In a heavy 2-quart casserole equipped with a tightly fitting lid, melt 2 tablespoons of the butter over moderate heat. When the foam begins to subside, add 2 tablespoons of the onions and, stirring frequently, cook for about 5 minutes, until they are soft and translucent but not brown.

Add the wild rice and stir until the grains glisten with butter. Then pour in the chicken stock and ½ teaspoon of the salt, and stir until the mixture comes to a boil.

Cover the casserole with a double thickness of aluminum foil and set the lid in place. Bake in the middle of the oven for 1 hour, remove the casserole from the oven, and let the rice rest at room temperature for 15 minutes before removing the lid and foil.

Meanwhile, melt 1 tablespoon of butter in a heavy 10-inch skillet and brown the almonds for a minute or so, stirring constantly so that they color delicately and evenly. With a slotted spoon, transfer the almonds to paper towels to drain.

Add the remaining 2 tablespoons of butter to the skillet and melt over moderate heat. When the foam begins to subside, add the remaining 2 tablespoons of onions and stir for about 5 minutes, until they are soft and translucent but not brown.

Add the mushrooms and, stirring frequently, cook for 10 to 15 minutes, until the moisture they give off has evaporated. Do not let the mushrooms brown. Season with the remaining ½ teaspoon of salt and a few grindings of pepper and set aside.

To serve, combine the wild rice and mushrooms in a heated bowl and toss them together gently but thoroughly. Scatter the almonds on top and serve at once.

## Hominy Grits Soufflé (South)

To serve 4 to 6

| | |
|---|---|
| 2 cups water | 1 tablespoon strained bacon fat, or |
| 1 teaspoon salt | substitute 1 tablespoon lard |
| ½ cup white hominy grits | 4 egg yolks, beaten |
| 1 tablespoon butter, softened, plus | Freshly ground black pepper |
| 8 tablespoons (1 quarter-pound | 4 egg whites |
| stick) unsalted butter, cut into bits | ¼ cup dry bread crumbs |

Preheat the oven to 350°. Pour the water and salt into a heavy 1½- to 2-quart saucepan and bring to a boil over high heat. Slowly pour in the grits, stirring constantly and pouring slowly enough so that the boiling continues at a rapid rate. Stir constantly with a wooden spoon to keep the mixture smooth. Cover the pan tightly, reduce the heat to low and, stirring occasionally, simmer 15 minutes.

Meanwhile, lightly coat the bottom and sides of a 1½- to 2-quart casserole with the tablespoon of softened butter. Set aside.

Remove the saucepan from the heat and with a wooden spoon, beat into the grits the butter bits, bacon fat, egg yolks and several grindings of black pepper.

In a large mixing bowl, beat the egg whites with a whisk or a rotary or electric beater until they are stiff enough to form firm, unwavering peaks on the beater when it is lifted from the bowl. With a rubber spatula, fold the egg whites into the hominy grits mixture, then pour it into the casserole, smoothing the top with the spatula. Sprinkle evenly with the bread crumbs and bake in the middle of the oven for 45 minutes, until the soufflé has puffed and the top is golden brown. Serve at once, directly from the casserole.

## Homemade Egg Noodles (Eastern Heartland)

To make about 1 pound

| | |
|---|---|
| 2 to 2½ cups unsifted flour | 3 eggs |
| ½ teaspoon salt | 1 tablespoon cold water |

Combine 2 cups of the flour and the salt in a deep bowl or in a heap on a pastry board. Make a well in the center and add the eggs and water. With your fingers or a spoon, gradually mix the dry ingredients into the liquid ones. When the mixture is well blended, gather it into a ball.

Knead the dough on a board, or in the bowl, by pushing it down with the heels of your hands, pressing it forward and folding it back on itself. As you knead, incorporate up to ½ cup more flour, sprinkling it over the ball by the tablespoonful and adding only enough to make a firm dough. Knead for about 10 minutes in all.

Gather the dough into a ball, place it on a floured board or table and, with the heel of your hand, press it into a circle about 1 inch thick. Dust a little flour over and under it and roll it out from the center to within an inch of the far edge. Lift the dough and turn it about 2 inches; roll again from the center to the far edge.

Repeat—lifting, turning, rolling—until the circle is almost paper thin. If the dough sticks to the board or table, lift it gently with a metal spatula and sprinkle a little flour under it.

To make potpie squares, cut the dough into 2-inch squares with a small sharp knife or a pastry wheel. Place the squares in one layer on a piece of wax paper. To make egg noodles, slice the dough into ¼-inch-wide strips with a pastry wheel or a long sharp knife.

The freshly made potpies or noodles may be cooked at once or covered tightly with plastic wrap and kept in the refrigerator for a day or so or in the freezer for several months.

*How to make homemade egg noodles.*

1 *Make a well in a mound of flour, break in three eggs and add the water.*

2 *Push the flour in from the edges and gradually incorporate it into the eggs.*

3 *Collect the particles of flour with a scraper and gather the dough into a ball.*

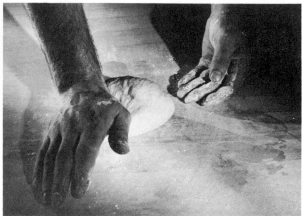

4 *Knead the dough for 10 minutes: push it down, forward, and then back on itself.*

5 *Whisk away any excess flour from the surface of the dough with a pastry brush.*

6 *Roll the dough out almost paper thin, turning it about 2 inches after each roll.*

7 *Trim the edges and cut 2-inch potpie squares with a pastry wheel or small knife.*

8 *Or trim the edges and cut the dough into long noodles each about 1/4 inch wide.*

## Lukshen Kugel *(Jewish-American)*
### NOODLE CASSEROLE WITH APPLES, RAISINS AND APRICOTS

To serve 6 to 8

6 to 8 quarts water
4 teaspoons salt
½ pound broad egg noodles
4 eggs, beaten
6 tablespoons sugar
9 tablespoons vegetable oil or
   melted shortening

2 medium-sized apples, peeled,
   cored and cut into ¼-inch dice
   (about 2 cups)
⅓ cup seedless white raisins
½ cup dried apricots, cut into
   ¼-inch dice
¼ teaspoon cinnamon combined
   with ¾ teaspoon sugar

In a large kettle or pot, bring the water and 3 teaspoons of the salt to a boil over high heat. Drop in the noodles, stir briefly with a wooden spoon or fork, and boil briskly for 15 minutes, or until they are tender. Drain the noodles thoroughly in a colander and place them in a large bowl.

Preheat the oven to 350°. Toss the noodles with the eggs, sugar, 8 tablespoons of the vegetable oil or shortening, the remaining teaspoon of salt, and the apples, raisins and apricots.

Coat the bottom and sides of a 2-quart casserole with the remaining tablespoon of oil or shortening and pour in the noodle mixture. Sprinkle the top with the cinnamon-sugar mixture and bake in the center of the oven for 40 minutes. Serve hot as an accompaniment to meat or poultry.

## Green Noodles with Red Clam Sauce *(Italian-American)*

To serve 2 or 3

1 quart clams in shell
1 medium-sized onion
1 stalk celery
1 carrot
1 cup white wine or vermouth
½ cup olive oil
3 cloves garlic, finely chopped

½ cup chopped parsley
1½ tablespoons chopped basil
Salt
Pepper
½ cup tomato purée
8 ounces green noodles
Grated Gruyère cheese

Wash the clams well. Cut the onion, celery and carrot into fine strips, and put them in a large kettle. Add the wine and the clams. Cover tightly and steam until the clams open. Remove the clams from their shells and strain the broth. Heat the olive oil and the garlic, add the parsley, basil, and salt and pepper to taste. Reduce the clam broth by half, add it to the olive mixture and let it come to a boil. Add the tomato purée and cook until well blended. Thin with a dash of white wine or vermouth. Taste for seasoning. Add the clams, chopped.

Cook the noodles and drain. Pour the clam mixture over the noodles and top with grated cheese.

To serve 8

SAUCE

4 tablespoons olive oil
1 pound ground veal
1 pound ground chuck
¼ pound *peperoni* (Italian
  sausage), sliced crosswise into
  ¼-inch-thick rounds
1 cup finely chopped onions
1½ teaspoons finely chopped
  garlic

3 one-pound cans solid-pack
  tomatoes and their liquid
A 6-ounce can tomato paste
2 cups water
1 teaspoon oregano
1 tablespoon basil
1½ teaspoons salt
½ teaspoon freshly ground black
  pepper

In a heavy 10- to 12-inch skillet, heat 4 tablespoons of olive oil until it is very hot but not smoking. Stir in the veal, chuck and sliced *peperoni* and, stirring constantly, cook for 6 to 8 minutes, or until there is no longer any trace of pink in the meat. Stir in the onions and garlic, and cook for 4 to 6 minutes longer, or until the onions are soft and translucent. Add the tomatoes and their liquid, the tomato paste, 2 cups of water, oregano, basil, 1½ teaspoons of salt and ½ teaspoon of pepper, and bring to a boil over high heat. Partially cover the pan, reduce the heat to low, and simmer the sauce for 2 hours.

LASAGNA
6 to 8 quarts water
2 teaspoons olive oil
2 teaspoons salt
½ pound *lasagna* noodles

1½ cups freshly grated Parmesan
  cheese

1 pound mozzarella cheese, thinly
  sliced

Preheat the oven to 375°. In a large soup pot or kettle, bring 6 to 8 quarts of water, 2 teaspoons of olive oil and 2 teaspoons of salt to a boil over high heat. Add the *lasagna* noodles, one at a time, and stir gently with a wooden fork or spoon for a few minutes to make sure the strips do not stick to one another. Boil over high heat, stirring occasionally, for about 15 minutes, until the noodles are tender but still *al dente*—somewhat resistant to the bite. Place the pot under cold running water to cool the noodles quickly, and let them remain in the cold water until you are ready to assemble the casserole.

Spread the bottom of a 9-by-12-by-3-inch baking dish with a thin layer of the meat sauce. Lay one third of the noodles on top of the sauce, overlapping the strips slightly. Sprinkle with ½ cup of the grated Parmesan, then repeat the layers of meat sauce, noodles, and Parmesan two more times. Spread the sliced mozzarella over the top and cover the dish tightly with aluminum foil. Bake in the center of the oven for 45 minutes, or until the cheese has melted and the sauce is bubbling. Remove from the oven and set aside for 10 minutes before serving, directly from the dish.

## Spaghetti with Meatballs in Tomato Sauce *(Italian-American)*

To serve 8

MEATBALLS
1½ pounds ground chuck
½ cup finely chopped onions
½ cup finely chopped green pepper
1½ teaspoons finely chopped
  garlic
1½ teaspoons salt
¼ teaspoon freshly ground black
  pepper
1 egg

1½ cups bread crumbs
¼ cup finely chopped parsley
¼ cup freshly grated Parmesan cheese
½ cup olive oil
6 cups tomato and meat sauce
  (*see veal parmigiana**)
6 to 8 quarts water
1 tablespoon salt
2 pounds spaghetti
Freshly grated Parmesan cheese

Place the ground chuck in a large mixing bowl and add the onions, green pepper, garlic, 1½ teaspoons salt, pepper, egg, bread crumbs, parsley and ¼ cup of Parmesan cheese. Knead with both hands until the ingredients are well combined, then beat vigorously with a wooden spoon until the mixture is smooth and fluffy. Shape the mixture into small balls about 1½ inches in diameter (there should be about 32 meatballs), and lay them out in one layer on a baking sheet.

Heat the olive oil in a heavy 10- to 12-inch skillet until a light haze forms above it. Fry the meatballs five or six at a time over moderately high heat, shaking the pan constantly to roll the balls and help keep their shape. When they are browned on all sides, transfer to a 3- to 4-quart saucepan. Pour in the tomato sauce, bring to a boil, then cover the pan and simmer over low heat for 30 minutes.

Bring the water and 1 tablespoon of salt to a boil in a large kettle or pot and drop in the spaghetti. Stir it gently with a wooden fork or spoon for a few minutes to prevent the strands from sticking to one another, then boil briskly, stirring occasionally, for 7 to 9 minutes, or until the pasta is tender but still *al dente*—slightly resistant to the bite. Immediately drain the spaghetti in a large colander, lifting the strands with a fork to be sure it is thoroughly drained.

Transfer the spaghetti to a large heated serving bowl and toss with the meatballs and tomato sauce. Serve at once, accompanied by a small bowl of grated Parmesan cheese.

* *See index.*

To serve 4 to 6

3 quarts water

1 tablespoon salt

2 cups elbow macaroni

4 tablespoons butter

4 tablespoons flour

2 cups milk

1 teaspoon salt

⅛ teaspoon cayenne

2 cups cooked ham, cut into ¼-inch dice

1¾ cups grated sharp Cheddar cheese

1 tablespoon grated onion

2 tablespoons dry bread crumbs

2 tablespoons melted butter

In a 4- to 5-quart pot, bring the water and the salt to a boil over high heat. Pour the macaroni in slowly so that the water never stops boiling. Cook briskly, uncovered, for about 20 minutes, or until the macaroni is tender. Then drain it thoroughly in a colander.

Melt the butter over moderate heat in a small saucepan. Add the flour and cook, stirring until the mixture froths and foams. Add the milk all at once and stir with a wire whisk until the sauce thickens into a smooth cream. Add the salt and cayenne, and simmer over very low heat for about 2 minutes. Pour the sauce into a large mixing bowl, and stir in the macaroni, diced ham, 1½ cups of the cheese and the grated onion. Taste for seasoning.

Preheat the oven to 375°. Lightly butter a 2½- or 3-quart casserole. Spoon in the macaroni mixture and spread the bread crumbs, mixed with the remaining cheese and melted butter, evenly over the top. Bake in the middle of the oven for 30 to 40 minutes, or until the cheese and bread crumb topping is lightly brown. Serve directly from the casserole.

## *Spaetzle* (German-American)
TINY DUMPLINGS WITH FRIED CROUTONS

To serve 4 to 6

3 cups flour

1 teaspoon salt

¼ teaspoon ground nutmeg, preferably freshly grated

4 eggs, lightly beaten

1 cup milk

2 quarts water

2 tablespoons butter

1 cup ¼-inch cubes white bread, preferably cut from day-old French or Italian bread

2 tablespoons finely chopped parsley

To make the dumplings, combine the flour, ½ teaspoon of the salt and the nutmeg in a large mixing bowl. Make a well in the center and drop in the eggs and milk. With a large spoon, stir the flour into the liquid ingredients and continue to stir until the dough is smooth.

Bring 2 quarts of water and the remaining ½ teaspoon of salt to a boil in a heavy 4- to 5-quart saucepan. Set a colander, preferably one with large openings, over the saucepan and, with a spoon, press the dough a few tablespoons at a time through the colander into the boiling water. Stir the dumplings gently to prevent them from sticking to each other, then boil briskly 5 to 8 minutes, or until they are tender. Drain through a sieve or colander and transfer to a large heated serving bowl. Cover the bowl with foil to keep the dumplings hot while you prepare the croutons.

Melt the butter in a heavy 10- to 12-inch skillet and add the bread cubes. Turn the cubes about in the butter for 2 to 3 minutes, or until golden brown on all sides, then add them to the bowl of dumplings. Toss the croutons and dumplings together lightly with a spoon, sprinkle with parsley, and serve at once.

### *Kasha Varnishkes* (Jewish-American)
#### EGG NOODLES WITH BUCKWHEAT GROATS

To serve 6 to 8

KASHA

| | |
|---|---|
| 4 tablespoons rendered chicken fat | (buckwheat groats) |
| 1 cup finely chopped onions | 1 egg, lightly beaten |
| 1 cup medium-grain *kasha* | 1 teaspoon salt |
| | 2 cups water |

KASHA: Melt the chicken fat in a 10- to 12-inch skillet and stir in the onions. Stirring frequently, cook for 6 to 8 minutes, or until the onions are soft and translucent. Off the heat, stir in the *kasha,* the beaten egg and 1 teaspoon of salt. Pour in 2 cups of water, cover the pan tightly, and bring to a boil over high heat. Reduce the heat to low and cook undisturbed for 20 to 25 minutes, or until all of the water has been absorbed and the grains of *kasha* are separate and fluffy.

NOODLES

| | |
|---|---|
| 6 to 8 quarts water | ½ pound broad egg noodles |
| 2 teaspoons salt | Freshly ground black pepper |

NOODLES: Bring 6 to 8 quarts of water and 2 teaspoons of salt to a boil in a large kettle or pot. Drop in the noodles and stir them briefly with a wooden spoon or fork. Boil briskly for 15 to 20 minutes, or until they are tender. Drain in a colander and transfer to a large heated bowl.

With wooden spoons, toss the *kasha* and noodles together until they are well combined. Sprinkle with freshly-ground black pepper. Serve at once.

To serve 4 to 6

| | |
|---|---|
| ½ cup imported dried mushrooms | 2 tablespoons finely chopped onion |
| 1 cup water | ¼ teaspoon freshly ground black |
| ½ cup pearl barley |    pepper |
| 1½ teaspoons salt | ¼ teaspoon marjoram |
| ½ teaspoon finely chopped garlic | 2 tablespoons melted lard or butter |

Soak the dried mushrooms in the water for about 30 minutes, or until they are soft. Drain them in a fine sieve set over a measuring cup. Remove them from the sieve, chop fine, and set aside. Add enough cold water to the mushroom liquid to make 3 cups, and combine the liquid, chopped mushrooms and barley in a 1½- to 2-quart casserole. Sprinkle with the salt and bring to a boil over high heat, then reduce the heat to low and simmer uncovered for 45 minutes to 1 hour, until the barley is tender and almost all of the water has been absorbed.

Preheat the oven to 350°. Stir the garlic, onion, pepper, marjoram and melted lard or butter into the casserole, cover tightly and bake in the center of the oven for 30 minutes. If the casserole becomes too dry while baking, add up to ½ cup more water.

# Vegetables

Fresh produce is more nutritious, tastier and often more economical than the packaged varieties, and preparing it takes only slightly more effort. Most vegetables are at their absolute best when quickly steamed, boiled or stir-fried, then tossed with butter or lemon juice and seasonings. In fact, America's favorite summertime vegetable, corn on the cob, need only be husked, dropped into boiling unsalted water (salt will toughen the kernels), and after the water returns to a boil, cooked for no more than five minutes.

As a rule, the younger the vegetable, the sweeter and more tender it will be. Since freshness is so important to flavor and quality, buy only enough vegetables for a few days at a time, and refrigerate them unwashed and untrimmed.

Many of the recipes in this chapter suggest simple ways of enhancing the flavor of vegetables—dusting carrots with mint, as they do in Kentucky; introducing nutmeg to a broccoli purée, as in the Eastern Heartland; scattering buttered crumbs over cauliflower; dribbling Vermont maple syrup over acorn squash. Other, more elaborate vegetable dishes, such as an eoxtic eggplant-banana casserole from the Far West, a Northwestern spinach ring with cheese sauce or Italian-American light, crisply fried vegetables, could complement a simple main course at dinner or take center stage at lunch or a light supper.

## Fresh Asparagus with Lemon Cream Sauce, Shaker Style *(Eastern Heartland)*

To serve 4

| | |
|---|---|
| 2 pounds fresh asparagus | 1 egg yolk, lightly beaten |
| 1¼ teaspoons salt | 1 teaspoon strained fresh lemon |
| 1 cup light cream | juice |
| 2 tablespoons butter | ½ teaspoon ground nutmeg, |
| 1 teaspoon finely cut fresh mint | preferably freshly grated |

Line up the asparagus tips on a chopping board and cut off the ends so that the spears are the same length. With a small sharp knife, peel off the tough outer skin of each spear. At the end, the peel may be as thick as ⅛ inch but it will become paper-thin toward the tip. Divide the spears into four equal bundles and tie each bundle at both ends with string.

In a 4- to 5-quart enameled or stainless-steel casserole, bring 2 quarts of water and 1 teaspoon of the salt to a boil over high heat. Drop in the asparagus and cook briskly, uncovered, for 8 to 10 minutes, or until the stalks are barely tender and show slight resistance when pierced with the point of a small, sharp knife.

With two kitchen forks, lift the bundles out of the water by their strings. Cut off the strings, spread the asparagus on paper towels to drain, then transfer them to a heated platter. Drape loosely with foil to keep the asparagus warm while you prepare the sauce.

In a heavy 6- to 8-inch skillet, combine the cream, butter, mint and the remaining ¼ teaspoon of salt. Bring to a boil over high heat and, stirring frequently, boil for 5 minutes, or until the cream has reduced to about ¾ of a cup. Then reduce the heat to low. Add about 2 tablespoons of the cream to the egg yolk and mix well. Stirring constantly, gradually pour the mixture into the cream and simmer gently for a minute or so. Do not let the sauce come anywhere near a boil or it will curdle. Stir in the lemon juice, taste for seasoning, and pour the sauce over the asparagus. Sprinkle with nutmeg and serve at once.

## Plantation String Beans *(South)*

To serve 4

| | |
|---|---|
| 4 slices lean bacon, cut into | 1 teaspoon salt |
| ½-inch dice | ¼ teaspoon freshly ground black |
| ½ cup thinly sliced scallion rounds | pepper |
| 1 pound green beans, washed and | 1½ teaspoons red wine vinegar |
| trimmed | 2 tablespoons finely cut fresh mint |
| 1 tablespoon cold water | leaves (optional) |

Fry the bacon dice in a 10- to 12-inch enameled or stainless-steel skillet, turning them frequently with a wooden spoon until they are brown and crisp and have rendered all their fat. With a slotted spoon, transfer the dice to paper towels to drain.

Drop the scallions into the fat and, stirring occasionally, cook over moderate heat for 3 to 4 minutes, until they are soft but not brown. Now add the beans, stirring them about until they glisten with the fat. Add the tablespoon of water and cover the pan tightly. Cook over low heat for 5 minutes, then uncover the pan and continue to cook until the beans are tender but still slightly resistant to the bite. Sprinkle with the salt and pepper, stir in the vinegar, and remove from the heat. Serve from a heated dish, garnished with the bacon bits and, if you like, with the cut mint leaves.

## Boston Baked Beans

To serve 6 to 8

| | |
|---|---|
| 4 cups dried pea or Great Northern beans | ½ cup molasses |
| | 1 cup brown sugar |
| 2 teaspoons salt | 2 teaspoons dry mustard |
| 2 medium-sized whole onions, peeled | 1 teaspoon black pepper |
| 4 cloves | 2 cups water |
| | ½ pound salt pork, scored |

Put the beans in a large saucepan and pour in enough cold water to cover them by at least 2 inches. Bring to a boil, let boil for 2 minutes, then let the beans soak in the water off the heat for about 1 hour. Bring them to a boil again, add 1 teaspoon of the salt, half cover the pan and simmer the beans as slowly as possible for about 30 minutes, or until they are partially done. Drain the beans and discard the bean water.

Preheat the oven to 250°. To bake the beans, choose a traditional 4-quart bean pot or a heavy casserole with a tight-fitting cover. Place 2 onions, each stuck with 2 cloves, in the bottom of the bean pot or casserole and cover with the beans. In a small mixing bowl, combine the molasses, ¾ cup of the brown sugar, mustard, and 1 teaspoon each of salt and black pepper. Slowly stirring with a large spoon, pour in the 2 cups of water.

Pour this mixture over the beans and push the salt pork slightly beneath the surface. Cover tightly and bake in the center of the oven for 4½ to 5 hours. Then remove the cover and sprinkle with the remaining ¼ cup of brown sugar. Bake the beans uncovered for another ½ hour and serve.

*Pinto Beans* (*Far West*)

To serve 6 to 8
2 cups (1 pound) dried pinto beans
6 cups water
1 medium-sized onion, peeled
1 medium-sized bay leaf
1 teaspoon salt

In a large sieve or colander, wash the pinto beans under running water until the draining water runs clear. Pick out and discard any beans that are broken or blemished. Drop the beans into a heavy 3- to 4-quart saucepan, add the water, onion and bay leaf, and bring to a boil over high heat. Reduce the heat to low, cover partially and simmer for 4 hours. Add the salt and continue to simmer for 30 minutes longer, or until the beans are tender but still intact.

Drain the beans in the sieve or colander, transfer them to a heated bowl and serve at once.

*Refried Beans* (*Far West*)

To serve 4 to 6

2 cups (1 pound) dried pinto or
    kidney beans
6 cups water
1 cup coarsely chopped onions
2 medium-sized firm ripe tomatoes,
    peeled, seeded and coarsely
chopped or ⅔ cup chopped,
    drained canned tomatoes
1½ teaspoons finely chopped
    garlic
8 tablespoons lard
1 teaspoon salt
Sour cream (optional)

Under cold running water, wash the beans in a sieve or colander until the draining water runs clear. Pick out and discard any black or shriveled beans. Combine the beans, the 6 cups of water, ½ cup of the onions, ¼ cup of the tomatoes, the garlic and 1 tablespoon of lard in a heavy 3- to 4-quart saucepan. Bring to a boil over high heat, reduce the heat to low, cover the pan partially, and simmer for 1½ hours. Stir in the salt and continue to simmer partially covered for 30 to 40 minutes, or until a bean can be easily mashed against the side of the pan with the back of a spoon. (Check the pot from time to time and stir the beans gently. If the water seems to be boiling away, add more boiling water by the ¼ cup. When fully cooked, however, the beans should have absorbed most of the liquid.) Drain the beans in a sieve or colander set over a bowl and reserve the cooking liquid.

In a heavy 12-inch skillet, melt 2 tablespoons of the lard over moderate heat until a light haze forms above it. Add the remaining ½ cup of onions and, stirring frequently, cook for about 5 minutes, until they are soft and translucent but not brown. Add the remaining chopped tomatoes and stir for 2 to 3 minutes. Reduce the heat to low.

Fry the beans in the following manner: Add about ½ cup of the beans to the skillet, mash them flat with a table fork and stir in 1 tablespoon of the remaining lard. Repeat, alternating about 1 cup of the beans with 1 tablespoon of the lard until all the beans and lard have been mashed together. The bean mixture should be moist and creamy. If it appears dry, beat in the reserved cooking liquid by the tablespoonful, adding only enough to achieve the texture you desire.

Mound the refried beans in a heated bowl or individual dishes and serve at once, accompanied if you like by a bowl of sour cream.

## Red Beans and Rice *(Creole-Acadian)*

To serve 4 to 6

6 cups water
1 pound dried small red beans or 1 pound dried red kidney beans
4 tablespoons butter
1 cup finely chopped scallions, including 3 inches of the green tops

½ cup finely chopped onions
1 teaspoon finely chopped garlic
2 one-pound smoked ham hocks
1 teaspoon salt
½ teaspoon freshly ground black pepper
6 to 8 cups freshly cooked long-grain rice

In a heavy 3- to 4-quart saucepan, bring the water to a boil over high heat. Drop in the beans and boil briskly, uncovered, for 2 minutes. Then turn off the heat and let the beans soak for 1 hour. Drain the beans in a sieve set over a large bowl; measure the soaking liquid and, if necessary, add more water to make 4 cups. Set the beans and liquid aside.

Melt the butter in a heavy 4- to 5-quart casserole set over moderate heat. When the foam begins to subside, add ½ cup of the scallions, the onions and the garlic and, stirring frequently, cook for about 5 minutes, or until they are soft and translucent but not brown.

Stir in the beans and their liquid, the ham hocks, salt and pepper. Bring the mixture to a boil over high heat, reduce the heat to low and simmer partially covered for about 3 hours, or until the beans are very soft. Check the pot from time to time and, if the beans seem dry, add up to 1 cup more water, a few tablespoonfuls at a time. During the last 30 minutes or so of cooking, stir frequently and mash the softest beans against the sides of the pan to form a thick sauce for the remaining beans.

With tongs or a slotted spoon, transfer the ham hocks to a plate. Cut the meat away from the bones and remove and discard the skin, fat and gristle. Cut the meat into ¼-inch dice and return it to the beans.

Taste the red beans for seasoning and serve at once, directly from the casserole or from a large heated tureen. Place the rice and the remaining ½ cup of scallions in separate bowls and present them with the beans.

NOTE: In Louisiana, red beans and rice are traditionally made with a leftover ham bone, and you may substitute a ham bone for the ham hocks in this recipe. Without trimming off the meat, cut the bone into 2- or 3-inch pieces with a hacksaw, so that the marrow inside the pieces will melt and flavor the beans. Add the pieces of bone to the soaked bean mixture and pour in enough additional water to cover them completely. When the beans are cooked, remove the bones from the pot, trim off and dice the meat, and return it to the beans. Discard the bones.

## Hopping John  (South)

To serve 8 to 10

| | |
|---|---|
| 2 cups (1 pound) dried black-eyed peas | and ½ inch wide |
| 6 cups cold water | 1 cup finely chopped onions |
| 1 pound salt pork (rind removed), cut into strips about 2 inches long | 2½ cups uncooked long-grain white rice, not the converted variety |

Place the black-eyed peas in a sieve or colander and run cold water over them until the draining water is clear. Transfer the peas to a 3- to 4-quart casserole, add 6 cups of cold water, and bring to a boil over high heat. Then lower the heat and simmer, partially covered, for 30 minutes.

Meanwhile, drop the salt pork strips into a pot of boiling water and bring the water back to a boil. Immediately drain the strips, pat them dry with paper towels, then place them in a 10- to 12-inch skillet. Fry uncovered over moderately high heat for 10 to 12 minutes, turning the strips frequently with a large spoon and adjusting the heat if necessary to prevent the pork from burning. When the strips are brown and crisp and have rendered all their fat, transfer them with tongs to paper towels to drain, and set aside.

Add the chopped onions to the fat remaining in the skillet and cook over moderate heat for 3 to 5 minutes, stirring frequently, until the onions are soft but not yet browned. Remove from the heat and set aside.

In a fine sieve, wash the rice under cold running water until the draining water is clear.

After the peas have cooked their allotted time, stir in the salt pork, on-ions and the rice and brink back to a boil. Cover the casserole tightly, re-duce the heat to low, and simmer 20 to 30 minutes, or until the peas are tender and the rice is dry and fluffy. Taste for seasoning and serve at once.

## *Harvard Beets* (New England)

To serve 6 to 8

12 medium-sized firm young beets
⅓ cup sugar
1½ teaspoons cornstarch

½ teaspoon salt
⅓ cup red wine vinegar
2 tablespoons butter, cut into ½-
    inch bits

With a small, sharp knife cut the tops from the beets, leaving about 1 inch of stem on each. Scrub the beets under cold running water and place them in a 4- to 5-quart saucepan. Pour in enough cold water to cover them by 2 inches, bring to a boil over high heat and cover the pan tightly. Reduce the heat to low and simmer until the beets show no resistance when pierced deeply with the point of a small skewer or knife. This may take from 30 minutes for young beets to as long as 2 hours for older ones. The beets should be kept constantly covered with water; add boil-ing water if necessary.

Drain the beets in a colander set over a bowl and reserve ½ cup of the cooking liquid. Slip off the skins, cut the beets crosswise into ¼-inch-thick slices and set them aside. Combine the sugar, cornstarch, salt and vinegar in a 2- to 3-quart enameled or stainless-steel saucepan and stir until the mixture is smooth. Add the reserved beet liquid and, stirring con-stantly, cook over moderate heat until the sauce comes to a boil and thickens. Swirl in the butter bits and then add the beets. Turning the slices about with a spoon to coat them evenly with the sauce, simmer for 2 or 3 minutes to heat the beets through. Taste for seasoning and serve at once from a heated bowl.

## Broccoli Purée *(Eastern Heartland)*

To serve 6 to 8

3 pounds firm fresh broccoli
8 tablespoons butter, cut into
    ½-inch bits and softened
¼ teaspoon ground nutmeg,

preferably freshly grated
1 teaspoon salt
Freshly ground black pepper
1 hard-cooked egg, finely chopped

With a small sharp knife, cut the broccoli flowerets from their stalks. Trim off and discard the tough woody ends of the stalks, then peel each of them deeply enough with the knife to expose the pale green flesh. Slice the stalks into 2-inch lengths.

Drop the stalks and flowerets into enough lightly salted boiling water to cover them by at least 2 inches. Boil briskly, uncovered, for 8 to 10 minutes, or until a piece of the stalk can be easily mashed against the side of the pan with the back of a fork. Thoroughly drain the broccoli in a large sieve or colander, shaking it from side to side to remove any clinging water. Then purée the broccoli through the coarse blade of a food mill or rub it through a coarse sieve with the back of a spoon.

Return the purée to the saucepan and, stirring constantly, cook over low heat until almost all of its moisture has evaporated. Stir in the softened butter bits, the nutmeg, salt and a few grindings of pepper. Taste for seasoning. Mound the broccoli purée in a heated serving dish, garnish the top with the chopped egg and serve at once.

## Cabbage in White Wine

To serve 6 to 8

8 tablespoons (1 quarter-pound stick)
    butter
3 pounds green cabbage, cored and
    coarsely chopped

1 cup dry white wine
1 teaspoon fresh tarragon or
    ½ teaspoon dried
1 teaspoon salt
Freshly ground black pepper

In a heavy 10- or 12-inch skillet, melt the butter over moderate heat. When the foam subsides, add the cabbage and, with a fork, toss it in the melted butter until it is well coated. Cook uncovered, stirring occasionally, for 10 minutes, then add the wine, tarragon, salt and a few grindings of pepper.

Bring to a boil, cover tightly and reduce the heat to low. Simmer for 5 to 10 minutes, or until the cabbage is tender. With a slotted spoon, remove the cabbage from the pan to a heated vegetable dish or platter. Boil the liquid in the pan rapidly, uncovered, for a few minutes to concentrate its flavor before pouring it over the cabbage.

To serve 4

1 pound (about 8 to 10) medium-
sized carrots, trimmed, washed,
scraped and cut diagonally into
¼-inch lengths
1 cup water

1 teaspoon salt
3 tablespoons unsalted butter, cut
into bits
Freshly ground black pepper
2 tablespoons coarsely cut fresh
mint leaves

Place the carrots in a 1-quart saucepan and add the water and salt. Cover
the pan tightly and bring to a boil over high heat, then reduce the heat to
moderate and cook the carrots for about 15 minutes, or until the water is
almost completely evaporated and the carrots are tender but still slightly
resistant to the bite. Stir in the butter and several grindings of pepper,
then remove the pan from the heat. Toss the carrots lightly with the
mint, taste for seasoning and serve at once, in a heated vegetable dish.

*Celery Victor* (*Far West*)

To serve 6

3 bunches celery, about 2 inches in
diameter
1½ cups chicken stock, fresh or
canned
An herb bouquet of 4 sprigs parsley,
1 bay leaf and celery leaves tied
together
Salt

Freshly ground black pepper
3 tablespoons white-wine vinegar
½ cup olive oil
12 flat anchovy fillets
12 strips pimiento
6 slices tomato (optional)
6 slices hard-cooked eggs (optional)
1½ teaspoons finely chopped fresh
parsley

Remove the outer stalks of the celery, leaving a heart about 1 inch wide
and 6 inches long. Cut each celery heart in half lengthwise. Cut away all
but the small leaves and trim the root ends (do not cut too deep; the celery halves should hold together). Use the cut-away leaves for the herb
bouquet. With a sharp knife, scrape the outer stalks if they seem coarse.
    Arrange the celery halves side by side in a 10- or 12-inch skillet, prefer-
ably enameled or stainless steel, and pour in the stock, using more stock
or water if the celery is not completely covered. Add the herb bouquet,
with as much salt and pepper as suits your taste, and bring to a boil. Reduce the heat to its lowest point, cover tightly and simmer the celery for
about 15 minutes, or until it shows no resistance when pierced with the
tip of a sharp knife. With tongs or a slotted spoon, transfer the celery
halves to a deep platter that will hold them in a single layer.

With a whisk, beat the vinegar and the oil together and pour over the celery while it is still warm. Refrigerate for at least an hour before serving. To serve, arrange the celery halves on individual chilled plates and criss-cross 2 anchovy fillets and 2 strips of pimiento over each serving. Or instead, if you prefer, garnish the celery with a slice of tomato and a slice of hard-cooked egg. In either case, moisten the celery with a spoonful or so of the vinegar-olive oil sauce and sprinkle with chopped parsley.

## Cauliflower with Buttered Crumbs

To serve 6

A 1½- to 2-pound firm unblemished cauliflower
8 tablespoons butter, cut into ½-inch bits

½ cup soft fresh crumbs made from homemade-type white bread, pulverized in a blender or finely shredded with a fork

Cut away the thick stem at the base of the cauliflower and break off the green leaves. Wash the cauliflower thoroughly under cold running water. Then drop the cauliflower into enough lightly salted boiling water to cover it completely and boil uncovered for about 20 minutes, or until the core shows only the slightest resistance when pierced deeply with the point of a small sharp knife. Drain the cauliflower in a colander and place it on a heated platter.

In a heavy 6- to 8-inch skillet, melt the butter bits over moderate heat. When the foam begins to subside add the crumbs and, stirring frequently, fry them until they are crisp and golden brown. Dribble the crumbs and butter over the cauliflower and serve at once.

## Corn Oysters (New England)

To make about 20

1 cup grated fresh corn (from 3 to 4 medium-sized cobs)
1 egg yolk, beaten
2 tablespoons flour

¼ teaspoon salt
Freshly ground black pepper
1 egg white
¼ to ½ cup vegetable shortening
Salt

In a small mixing bowl, combine the grated corn, egg yolk, flour, salt and a few grindings of black pepper. With a whisk or rotary beater, beat the egg white until it forms unwavering peaks on the beater when it is lifted out of the bowl. Gently but thoroughly fold it into the corn mixture.

In an 8- to 10-inch heavy skillet, heat 2 tablespoons of shortening over high heat until a light haze forms over it. Drop the batter by teaspoonfuls into the fat (the corn oysters should be about the size of silver dollars) and fry them for a minute or two on each side, watching them carefully for any sign of burning and regulating the heat accordingly. Drain the corn oysters on paper towels, batch by batch as you proceed, and add more shortening to the pan as needed. There should be a thin film of fat on the bottom of the pan at all times. Before serving on a heated platter, sprinkle the corn oysters liberally with salt. These make good accompaniments to meat and chicken dishes.

## Corn Pudding *(New England)*

| | |
|---|---|
| To serve 6 | ¼ teaspoon ground white pepper |
| | 3 eggs |
| 1 tablespoon butter, softened, plus | 3 cups fresh corn kernels, cut from |
| 4 tablespoons butter, melted and | about 6 large ears of corn, or |
| cooled | substitute 3 cups frozen corn |
| ¼ cup flour | kernels, thoroughly defrosted |
| 1 teaspoon salt | 2 cups light cream |

Preheat the oven to 325°. Brush the tablespoon of softened butter evenly over the bottom and sides of a 1½-quart baking-serving dish.

Combine the flour, salt and pepper and set aside. In a deep bowl, beat the eggs with a wire whisk or rotary beater until they are frothy. Stir in the corn and then, stirring constantly, sift in the combined flour, salt and pepper. Add the melted butter and cream and stir well for 2 to 3 minutes.

Pour the mixture into the baking dish and place it in a large shallow pan set on the middle shelf of the oven. Then pour enough boiling water into the pan to rise at least 1 inch up the sides of the dish. Bake the pudding for 2 hours, or until the top is a delicate brown and a knife inserted in the center comes out clean. (Keep a kettle of boiling water handy, and replenish the water in the pan if it boils away.)

Serve at once, directly from the baking dish.

## Summer Succotash (New England)

To serve 6

1 tablespoon plus 1 teaspoon salt
2 cups fresh corn kernels, cut from
  about 4 large ears of corn
1 pound fresh green string beans,
  trimmed, washed and cut
  diagonally into 1-inch lengths

( 2½ to 3 cups )
4 tablespoons butter
1 teaspoon sugar
¼ teaspoon freshly ground black
  pepper
1 cup heavy cream

In a heavy 3- to 4-quart saucepan, bring 1 quart of water and 1 tablespoon of salt to a boil over high heat. Drop in the corn and beans and cook briskly, uncovered, until they are tender but still somewhat crisp to the bite. Drain the vegetables in a sieve or colander, then plunge them into a pot of cold water and let them cool for about 5 minutes. Drain again and spread the vegetables on paper towels to dry them completely.

In a heavy 10-inch skillet, melt the butter over moderate heat. When the foam begins to subside, add the corn and beans and, stirring constantly, cook for 1 or 2 minutes to heat them through. Add the remaining teaspoon of salt, the sugar and pepper, then pour in ¼ cup of the cream and stir over moderate heat until it has almost but not quite cooked away. Pour in and boil down the remaining cream, ¼ cup at a time, in similar fashion. Taste for seasoning and serve the succotash from a heated bowl.

## Indian-style Stewed Corn and Tomatoes (Creole-Acadian)

To serve 4 to 6

¼ cup bacon drippings
2 medium-sized onions, peeled and
  coarsely chopped
1 teaspoon finely chopped garlic
4 cups fresh corn kernels, cut from
  5 or 6 large ears of corn, or
  substitute 4 cups frozen corn
  kernels, thoroughly defrosted
1 medium-sized green pepper,

stemmed, quartered, seeded,
  deribbed and coarsely chopped
A 1-pound 12-ounce can whole
  tomatoes, drained and coarsely
  chopped, with all the liquid
  reserved
1 cup water
½ teaspoon ground hot red pepper
  (cayenne)
1½ teaspoons salt

In a heavy 4- to 5-quart casserole, melt the bacon drippings over moderate heat. Add the onions and garlic and, stirring frequently, cook for about 5 minutes, or until the onions are soft and translucent but not brown. Stir in the corn, green pepper, tomatoes and tomato liquid, water, red pepper and salt, and bring to a boil over high heat. Reduce the heat to low, cover the casserole partially, and simmer for about 10 minutes, or until the corn is tender. Taste for seasoning and serve at once, directly from the casserole or from a heated bowl.

To serve 4

| | |
|---|---|
| 1 medium-sized eggplant (about 1 pound), cut lengthwise into ¼-inch-thick slices | 1 tablespoon butter, softened, plus 4 tablespoons butter, cut into ½-inch bits |
| 2 teaspoons salt | 3 large ripe bananas, peeled and cut lengthwise into halves |
| 1 teaspoon crumbled dried thyme | |
| ½ teaspoon freshly ground black pepper | ¾ teaspoon ground nutmeg, preferably freshly grated |
| ½ to 1 cup vegetable oil | 3 large firm ripe tomatoes |

Sprinkle the eggplant slices lightly with 1 teaspoon of the salt, lay them side by side between two layers of paper towels and weight them down with a large heavy platter or casserole. Let them rest for 20 to 30 minutes, then pat them dry with fresh paper towels. Season the eggplant slices on both sides with the thyme and black pepper.

In a heavy 12-inch skillet, bring ½ cup of the vegetable oil almost to the smoking point over high heat. Add a few slices of the eggplant and cook them for a minute or two on each side, regulating the heat so that they color quickly without burning. Transfer them to paper towels to drain and brown the remaining eggplant, a few slices at a time, adding up to ½ cup more oil to the skillet as necessary.

Meanwhile, preheat the oven to 350°. With a pastry brush, spread the tablespoon of softened butter evenly over the bottom and sides of a 1½-quart baking dish at least 2 inches deep, and set it aside.

Melt the 4 tablespoons of butter bits over moderate heat in a heavy 12-inch skillet. When the foam begins to subside, add the banana halves and, turning them once with tongs, fry for about 2 minutes on each side, or until they are golden brown. Remove the pan from the heat and sprinkle the bananas with the nutmeg.

Drop the tomatoes into enough boiling water to cover them completely. After 15 seconds remove the tomatoes and run them under cold water. With a small sharp knife, remove the stems, peel the tomatoes and slice them into ¼-inch-thick rounds. Season the tomatoes with the remaining teaspoon of salt.

Before assembling the casserole, spread the eggplant slices on paper towels and set aside the two most attractive slices. Arrange about half of the remaining slices in the bottom of the buttered dish, set three banana halves side by side over them and cover with half of the tomato slices. Repeat the layers with the rest of the eggplant, bananas and tomatoes, and place the two reserved eggplant slices on top.

Bake in the middle of the oven for 30 minutes, or until the top has begun to bubble. Serve at once, directly from the baking dish.

## Boiled Greens  (South)

To serve 6

3 pounds fresh young turnip,
   collard or mustard greens
1½ pounds salt pork, with rind
   removed, cut into 1-inch dice

1½ cups water
1 cup coarsely chopped onions
1 teaspoon sugar
Salt
Freshly ground black pepper

With a sharp knife trim away any bruised or blemished spots on the greens and strip the leaves from their stems. Wash the leaves in several changes of cold running water to remove all traces of dirt or sand.

In a heavy 10- to 12-inch skillet, fry the salt pork over moderate heat, stirring the dice frequently with a slotted spoon until they are crisp and brown and have rendered all their fat. Transfer the dice and liquid fat to a bowl and pour the water into the skillet. Bring to a boil over high heat, meanwhile scraping in any brown particles that cling to the bottom and sides of the pan. Remove from the heat and set aside.

Place the greens in a heavy 4- to 6-quart pot and set over high heat. Cover tightly and cook for 3 to 4 minutes, or until the greens begin to wilt. Stir in the pork fat and dice, the skillet liquid, and the onions and sugar. Cover the pot again and continue to cook over moderate heat for about 45 minutes, or until the greens are tender.

Drain off the cooking liquid and reserve it as "pot likker" for soups, or as a dunking sauce for cornbread. Taste the boiled greens, season them with as much salt and pepper as you think they need and serve at once.


## Leeks Vinaigrette  (Creole-Acadian)

To serve 4 as a salad

8 firm fresh leeks, each 1 to 1½
   inches in diameter

½ cup Creole vinaigrette sauce *

With a sharp knife, cut off the roots of the leeks and strip away any withered leaves. Line up the leeks in a row and cut off enough of their green tops to make each leek 6 or 7 inches long. Then slit the green parts in half lengthwise, stopping within about ½ inch of the root ends. Carefully spread the leaves apart and wash the leeks under cold running water to rid them of all sand.

Lay the leeks in one or two layers in a heavy stainless-steel or enameled skillet or casserole just large enough to hold them flat. Pour in enough cold water to cover them by about 1 inch and bring to a boil over high

312

* See index.

heat. Reduce the heat to low, cover the pan partially, and simmer for 10 minutes, or until the leeks show only the slightest resistance when their bases are pierced with a fork.

With tongs or a slotted spoon, transfer the leeks to a double thickness of paper towels and let them drain for a minute or two. Arrange the leeks attractively in a serving dish or deep platter and pour the Creole vinaigrette sauce over them. Cool to room temperature, then refrigerate the leeks for at least 1 hour to chill them thoroughly before serving.

## *Batter-fried Mushrooms* (Eastern Heartland)

To serve 4 to 6 as a first course

| | |
|---|---|
| 1 cup unsifted flour | 2 dozen firm fresh mushrooms, each |
| 1 cup beer, at room temperature | about 2 inches in diameter |
| Vegetable oil for deep frying | Salt |

Sift the flour into a deep bowl and make a well in the center. Slowly pour in the beer and, stirring gently, gradually incorporate the flour. Stir until the mixture is smooth, but do not beat or overmix. Set the batter aside uncovered to rest at room temperature for 3 hours before using.

Preheat the oven to its lowest setting. Meanwhile, line a large shallow baking dish or jelly-roll pan with a double thickness of paper towels and place it in the middle of the oven. Pour vegetable oil into a deep fryer or large heavy saucepan to a depth of about 3 inches and heat the oil until it reaches a temperature of 375° on a deep-frying thermometer.

Trim off the ends of the mushroom stems with a small sharp knife and wipe the caps and stems with a dampened kitchen towel. One at a time, pick up a mushroom with tongs or a slotted spoon, immerse it in the batter and, when it is well coated on all sides, drop it into the hot oil. Deep-fry 4 or 5 mushrooms at a time for about 4 minutes, turning them occasionally until they are delicately and evenly browned. As they are fried, transfer the mushrooms to the paper-lined pan and keep them warm in the oven while you coat and deep-fry the rest.

Arrange the mushrooms on a heated platter and sprinkle them lightly with salt just before serving.

## Mushrooms and Onions in Sour Cream

To serve 4 to 6

4 tablespoons butter
2 medium onions, thinly sliced
1 pound fresh mushrooms, 1 to 1½
   inches in diameter

1 cup sour cream
1 teaspoon lemon juice
1 teaspoon salt
Freshly ground black pepper
2 teaspoons finely chopped fresh
   parsley

In a heavy 10-inch skillet, melt the butter over medium heat. When the foam subsides, add the onions and cook for 6 to 8 minutes until they are lightly colored. Stir in the mushrooms, cover the pan and cook, still over moderate heat, for about 7 minutes. Add the sour cream, lemon juice, salt and a few grindings of pepper; simmer, stirring, until the cream is heated through. Don't let it boil. Taste for seasoning and sprinkle with chopped parsley. Serve as a first course over pieces of freshly made buttered toast, as a vegetable to accompany a main dish, or as a luncheon or supper dish in the center of or around a molded spinach ring.*

## Buttermilk Fried Onions

To serve 4 to 6

3 egg yolks
1½ cups flour
½ teaspoon baking soda
1½ teaspoons salt
2 cups buttermilk

Vegetable oil or shortening for deep
   frying
4 large yellow onions, 3 to 4 inches
   in diameter, peeled and cut in ¼-
   inch-thick slices
Salt

In a mixing bowl, combine the egg yolks, flour, baking soda and salt, and beat them together with a large spoon. Pour in the buttermilk slowly, beating until the mixture forms a fairly smooth paste. Heat the shortening in a deep-fat fryer—the fat should be at least 3 inches deep—until it registers 375° on a deep-fat thermometer.

Separate the onion slices into rings, drop them in the batter and then, 7 or 8 rings at a time, fry them in the fat for 4 to 5 minutes until lightly browned. Transfer them to paper towels while you proceed with the next batch. When all the onion rings are done, fry them again in the hot fat for a minute or two to heat them through and crisp them. Drain on paper towels and serve sprinkled with salt.

* See index.

To serve 4

1 pound fresh okra, or substitute
 two 10-ounce packages frozen
 okra, thoroughly defrosted
4 lean slices bacon, cut crosswise
 into halves
1 medium-sized onion, peeled and

coarsely chopped
1½ teaspoons salt
3 medium-sized firm ripe tomatoes,
 peeled and coarsely chopped
1 teaspoon finely chopped fresh hot
 red chili *(caution: see note,
 appendix)*

Wash the fresh okra under cold running water, and with a small sharp knife scrape the skin lightly to remove any surface fuzz. (Frozen okra needs only to be thoroughly defrosted and drained.) Pat the okra completely dry with paper towels, cut off the stems and slice the okra crosswise into ¼-inch-thick rounds.

In a heavy 10-inch skillet, fry the bacon over moderate heat, turning the pieces frequently with tongs until they are crisp and brown and have rendered all their fat. Transfer the bacon to paper towels to drain.

Add the okra, onion and salt to the fat remaining in the skillet and, stirring constantly, cook over moderate heat for 10 minutes. Watch carefully and regulate the heat so that the vegetables do not burn. Add the tomatoes and chili and cook over high heat for 2 minutes, still stirring constantly. Reduce the heat to low and, stirring the mixture occasionally, simmer uncovered for about 15 minutes, or until the okra and tomatoes are soft. Taste for seasoning.

To serve, transfer the entire contents of the skillet to a heated bowl and arrange the bacon on top.

## *Basque Potatoes* (Northwest)

To serve 4

6 medium-sized boiling potatoes,
 peeled
6 slices bacon
½ cup finely chopped onions

4 eggs
1 teaspoon salt
¼ teaspoon freshly ground black
 pepper

Drop the potatoes into enough lightly salted boiling water to cover them by at least 1 inch, and boil briskly until they are almost tender and show only slight resistance when pierced deeply with the point of a small skewer or sharp knife. Drain off the water, return the pan to low heat, and slide it back and forth for a minute or so to dry the potatoes completely. Cut the potatoes crosswise into ⅛-inch-thick slices and set aside.

In a heavy 12-inch skillet, preferably one with a nonstick cooking surface, fry the bacon over moderate heat, turning the slices frequently until they are crisp and brown and have rendered all their fat. Transfer the slices to paper towels to drain, then crumble them into bits.

Pour all but about 4 tablespoons of the bacon fat into a heatproof cup or bowl; set aside. Add the onions to the fat remaining in the skillet and, stirring frequently, cook over moderate heat for about 5 minutes, until they are soft and translucent but not brown. Carefully add the potatoes and mix them with the onions, using a wooden spoon. Slide the pan back and forth until the potato slices lie flat. Then cook over moderate heat until the bottom side of the potatoes is golden brown.

Slide the spatula around the edges of the skillet and as far under the potatoes as you can without crumbling them. Place an inverted plate over the pan and, grasping plate and skillet together firmly, turn them over. Slide the potatoes back into the skillet, browned side up, first adding a few spoonfuls of the reserved fat to the pan if it is not the nonstick type.

Cook over moderate heat for 2 or 3 minutes to brown the bottom, then reduce the heat to low. Meanwhile beat the eggs, salt and pepper with a wire whisk or rotary beater until they are well combined. Pour the eggs over the potatoes and sprinkle the reserved bacon bits on top. Cover the skillet and cook for 5 or 6 minutes, or until the eggs are set and firm to the touch. Serve at once, directly from the skillet.

## Stuffed Baked Potatoes with Sour Cream

To serve 8

3 tablespoons butter, softened, plus
   6 tablespoons butter, melted and
   cooled
10 six-ounce baking potatoes,
   thoroughly scrubbed and patted

   dry with paper towels
1 teaspoon salt
¼ teaspoon ground white pepper
½ cup sour cream
2 egg yolks

Preheat the oven to 350°. With a pastry brush, spread 2 tablespoons of the softened butter over the skins of the potatoes. Bake the potatoes on a rack in the middle of the oven for about 45 minutes, until they feel soft when squeezed gently between your thumb and forefinger.

Cut a ¼-inch-thick slice lengthwise off the top of each baked potato. With a spoon, scoop the potato pulp into a bowl, leaving a boatlike shell about ¼ inch thick. Reserve the eight most uniform potato shells and discard the other two shells but retain their pulp.

Mash the potato pulp to a smooth purée with the back of a fork, or force the pulp through a ricer into a deep bowl. Add 4 tablespoons of the melted butter and the salt and pepper. In a small bowl, mix the sour cream and egg yolks together and beat the mixture into the potato purée. Taste for seasoning. Spoon the potato mixture into a pastry bag fitted with a No. 5B decorative tip, filling the bag no more than one third full, and pipe the mixture into the shells. Or spoon the mixture into the potato shells, mounding it slightly in the center. Brush a jelly-roll pan with the remaining tablespoon of softened butter and arrange the shells side by side in the pan.

If you wish to serve the potatoes at once, preheat the broiler to its highest setting. Brush the potatoes with the remaining 2 tablespoons of melted butter and slide them under the broiler for a minute or so to brown them.

If you prefer, the stuffed potatoes may be kept at room temperature for 2 or 3 hours before serving. In that event, preheat the oven to 400°, brush the potatoes with 2 tablespoons of melted butter and bake them in the middle of the oven for 15 or 20 minutes, or until they are golden brown and crusty.

## Hashed Brown Potatoes

To serve 4 to 6

6 medium-sized boiling potatoes (about 2 pounds), peeled and cut into quarters

¼ pound sliced bacon
2 tablespoons butter
1 teaspoon salt
Freshly ground black pepper

Bring 2 quarts of lightly salted water to a boil in a 4- to 5-quart pot and boil the potatoes uncovered until they can be easily pierced with the tip of a small, sharp knife. Drain the potatoes in a colander, return to the pan in which they were cooked or put them in a large, dry skillet and shake over moderate heat until they are dry.

Let the potatoes cool, then cut them into small dice. In a heavy 10- to 12-inch skillet, preferably one with a good nonstick surface, cook the bacon until it has rendered all of its fat and is crisp and brown. Remove the bacon with a slotted spoon and drain on paper towels. Add the butter to the bacon fat and place over moderate heat until the butter melts. Add the potatoes, and sprinkle them with the salt and a few grindings of black pepper. Then press the potatoes down firmly into the pan with a spatula. Cook over moderate heat, shaking the pan occasionally to prevent the potatoes from sticking. A brown crust should form on the bottom surface of the potatoes in about 20 minutes. Check by gently lifting the edge of the potatoes with a spatula. Cook a few minutes longer, raising the heat if necessary to achieve the proper color. They should be golden brown and crusty. To serve, cover the skillet with a heated platter and, grasping skillet and plate together, turn them upside down. The potatoes should fall out easily. Serve at once, sprinkled with the crumbled reserved bacon if desired.

## Gnocchi di Patate (Italian-American)
### POTATO DUMPLINGS WITH BUTTER AND CHEESE

To serve 8

| | |
|---|---|
| 3 medium-sized potatoes | 6 to 8 quarts water |
| 2 egg yolks, lightly beaten | 4 tablespoons melted butter |
| 4 teaspoons salt | ¼ cup freshly grated Parmesan |
| 1 to 1½ cups all-purpose flour | cheese |

Drop the potatoes into enough boiling water to cover them by at least 1 inch. Bring back to a boil and cook uncovered until the potatoes are tender and offer no resistance when pierced deeply with a sharp knife. Drain the potatoes in a sieve or colander, peel them, and put them through a ricer or mash them in a large mixing bowl with a fork. Set aside to cool to room temperature.

Beat the egg yolks and 1 teaspoon of the salt thoroughly into the mashed potatoes and transfer the mixture to a lightly floured board. Knead in flour, a little at a time, using only enough so that the dough no longer sticks to your hands.

Divide the dough in half and, with your hands, roll each half into a rope about 1 inch in diameter and 12 inches long. Cut the rope crosswise into ½-inch-thick rounds and, with your thumb, press each round gently so that the edges curl toward the center.

In a large kettle or pot, bring the water and the remaining 3 teaspoons of salt to a boil. Drop in the curled rounds and simmer uncovered for 5 to 8 minutes, or until they rise to the top and are firm to the touch.

With a slotted spoon, transfer the *gnocchi* to a large serving bowl or dish and dribble the melted butter over them. Sprinkle with the grated cheese and serve at once.

## Sautéed Potato Balls

To serve 4 to 6

| | |
|---|---|
| ½ pound unsalted butter, cut into ½-inch bits | 9 medium-sized boiling potatoes (about 3 pounds) |

First clarify the butter in the following fashion: In a small heavy saucepan, melt the butter over low heat, turning the bits about with a spoon so that they melt slowly and completely without browning. Remove the pan from the heat and let the butter rest for a minute or so. Then skim off and discard the foam. Tipping the pan slightly, spoon the clear butter into a bowl. (There will be about 12 tablespoons.) Discard the milky solids left in the pan.

Peel the potatoes and, with a melon baller or small knife, cut them into balls about 1 inch in diameter. Spread the potato balls on paper towels, and pat them completely dry with fresh towels.

In a heavy 10- to 12-inch skillet, warm 8 tablespoons of the clarified butter over moderate heat. When the butter is hot, drop in the potatoes and brown them lightly. Slide the pan back and forth occasionally to roll the balls around and regulate the heat so that they color evenly without burning. Add more clarified butter by the tablespoonful if necessary.

Reduce the heat to low, cover the skillet tightly and cook for 12 to 15 minutes, still sliding the pan back and forth from time to time. The potatoes are done when they are golden brown and show no resistance when pierced deeply with the point of a small sharp knife. Serve at once.

## Sweet Potatoes in Orange Baskets *(South)*

To serve 4

| | |
|---|---|
| 4 large navel oranges | 1 egg |
| 2 tablespoons unsalted butter, softened, plus 2 teaspoons unsalted butter, cut into bits | 4 teaspoons salt |
| | ½ teaspoon white pepper |
| | ¼ teaspoon grated lemon rind |
| 4 large sweet potatoes, boiled, peeled and mashed (1½ cups) | 2 tablespoons finely chopped walnuts |

Preheat the oven to 350°. With a sharp heavy knife, cut off and discard a 1-inch-deep slice from the stem end of each orange. Squeeze the oranges and use the juice for some other purpose. With a small sharp knife, scrape and cut away the pulp and membranes from the orange shells, keeping the shells intact and as regular in shape as possible. Set the shells side by side in a baking dish just large enough to hold them.

In a large mixing bowl, beat the softened butter into the mashed sweet potatoes, then beat in the egg, salt, white pepper and lemon rind. Taste for seasoning. Fill each orange basket with the potato mixture, swirling the tops attractively with a rubber spatula. Sprinkle the filling with the walnuts, and dot with the butter bits, dividing the bits equally among the baskets. Bake in the center of the oven for 45 minutes, until the tops are lightly browned. Serve at once, with roast ham or chicken.

## Sherried Yams with Pecans *(South)*

To serve 6

| | |
|---|---|
| 6 medium-sized yams or sweet potatoes | 1 tablespoon grated orange rind |
| ½ cup brown sugar | ⅓ cup sherry |
| 1 cup orange juice | 1 cup pecans, coarsely chopped |
| | 2 tablespoons butter |

Boil the yams or sweet potatoes in salted water until they are tender. Peel them and cut them in thick slices.

Preheat the oven to 350°. In a bowl, combine the sugar, orange juice, orange rind and sherry. Place a layer of yams in a baking dish, cover it with some of the sherry mixture, and sprinkle generously with pecans. Repeat layers of yams, liquid and pecans until the casserole is filled. Pour the remaining juice over the top, sprinkle with nuts, and dot with the butter. Cover and bake for 30 minutes, or until the juice has been absorbed by the yams and the top is browned.

## Squash Soufflé *(New England)*

To serve 4 to 6

| | |
|---|---|
| 2½ pounds acorn, Hubbard or butternut squash, peeled, seeded and cut into 2-inch chunks | ¾ cup milk |
| | ¼ cup heavy cream |
| | 4 egg yolks |
| 2 teaspoons butter, softened, plus 3 tablespoons butter | 2 teaspoons sugar |
| | ½ teaspoon ground nutmeg, preferably freshly grated |
| 1 tablespoon vegetable oil | 1½ teaspoons salt |
| ¼ cup flour | ¼ teaspoon ground white pepper |
| | 5 egg whites |

Pour boiling water into the lower part of a steamer to within about 1 inch of the top pan. Return the water to a boil, place the squash in the top pan and set it in place. Immediately cover the pan and steam over high heat for 30 minutes, or until the squash can be pierced easily with a fork.

(Lacking a steamer, you can improvise one by using a large pot equipped with a tightly fitting cover and a collapsible steaming basket on legs, or a standing colander. Pour boiling water into the pot to within about 1 inch of the perforated container and return it to a boil. Place the squash in the basket or colander, set it in place and cover the pot. Steam over high heat for about 30 minutes, or until the squash is soft.)

Purée the squash through a food mill or fine sieve set over a bowl lined with dampened cheesecloth. Wrap the cloth around the squash, and, holding the ends in both hands, squeeze vigorously to remove as much of the moisture from the squash as possible. There should be about 2 cups of purée. Set it aside in a bowl.

Meanwhile, preheat the oven to 375°. With a pastry brush, spread the 2 teaspoons of softened butter evenly over the bottom and sides of a 2-quart soufflé dish and set it aside.

In a heavy 2- to 3-quart saucepan, melt the remaining 3 tablespoons of butter over moderate heat. When the foam begins to subside, stir in the flour and mix to a paste. Stirring constantly with a wire whisk, pour in the milk and cream and cook over high heat until the mixture comes to a boil, thickens heavily and is smooth. Reduce the heat to low and simmer for 2 or 3 minutes. Remove the pan from the heat and stir in the squash. Then beat in the egg yolks, one at a time, stir in the sugar, nutmeg, salt and pepper and taste for seasoning.

With a whisk or a rotary or electric beater—and in an unlined copper bowl, if possible—beat the egg whites until they are stiff enough to stand in firm peaks on the beater when it is lifted from the bowl. Stir 2 or 3 large spoonfuls of the whites into the squash mixture, then gently but thoroughly fold in the remaining whites.

Pour the soufflé mixture into the buttered dish and smooth the top with a rubber spatula. Bake in the middle of the oven for 40 minutes or until the soufflé puffs up well above the rim of the dish and the top is lightly browned. Serve at once.

*Maple Baked Acorn Squash*  *(New England)*

To serve 4

| | |
|---|---|
| 2 one-pound acorn squash | 8 teaspoons pure maple syrup |
| 4 tablespoons unsalted butter | 1 teaspoon salt |
| | Freshly ground black pepper |

Preheat the oven to 375°. With a sharp knife, cut each squash in half lengthwise. Scoop out all the seeds and cut away any stringy filaments.

Arrange the squash halves side by side, hollow surfaces up, in a baking dish just large enough to hold them comfortably. Put 1 tablespoon of butter and 2 teaspoons of maple syrup in each half and sprinkle the insides of the squash evenly with the salt and a few grindings of pepper.

Pour enough boiling water down the sides of the dish to rise to about 1 inch around the squash. Then bake in the middle of the oven for about 1 hour, or until the squash are tender and show no resistance when pierced deeply with the point of a small, sharp knife. (Keep a kettle of boiling water at hand and replenish the water in the baking dish if it cooks away.) Serve at once, arranged attractively on a heated platter.

To serve 6

2 teaspoons butter, softened, plus 3
   tablespoons butter
2 tablespoons soft fresh crumbs
   made from homemade-type white
   bread, pulverized in a blender or
   finely shredded with a fork
4 tablespoons flour
2 cups milk
1 cup heavy cream
1 teaspoon salt
¼ teaspoon ground white pepper
Freshly grated nutmeg

¼ pound sliced bacon
½ cup finely chopped onions
2 pounds fresh spinach, washed,
   cooked, drained, squeezed and
   finely chopped, or 4 ten-ounce
   packages frozen chopped spinach,
   thoroughly defrosted and
   squeezed dry
Freshly ground black pepper
3 egg yolks
3 egg whites
¼ cup freshly grated imported
   Parmesan or Gruyère cheese

Preheat the oven to 375°. With a pastry brush, coat all the inner surfaces of a 1-quart ring mold with the 2 teaspoons of softened butter. Add the bread crumbs and tip the pan from side to side to spread them as evenly as you can. Then invert the pan and rap it lightly on a table to remove any excess crumbs. Set aside.

In a 2- or 3-quart saucepan melt the 3 tablespoons of butter but do not let it brown. Remove the pan from the heat, and stir in the 4 tablespoons of flour. Then pour in the milk and cream, and stir with a whisk until the flour mixture is partially dissolved. Return the pan to medium heat and cook, whisking constantly, until the sauce comes to a boil and is thick and smooth. Stir in ½ teaspoon of the salt, the white pepper and a pinch of nutmeg. Set aside.

In a 10-inch skillet, fry the bacon over moderate heat, turning the slices from time to time until they have rendered all their fat and are golden brown and crisp. Transfer them to paper towels to drain, then crumble the bacon into small bits and set them aside. Meanwhile, pour off and discard all but about ¼ cup of the bacon fat from the pan and add the ½ cup of onions. Stirring occasionally, cook over moderate heat for about 5 minutes, until the onions are soft but not brown.

Add the spinach to the skillet and raise the heat to high. Stirring constantly, fry the mixture until all the moisture has evaporated and the spinach begins to stick lightly to the pan. Watch carefully for any sign of burning and regulate the heat accordingly. With a rubber spatula, scrape the contents of the skillet into a large mixing bowl and mix in the remaining ½ teaspoon of the salt, a pinch of nutmeg, and as much freshly ground black pepper as you like. Then pour in about half of the reserved sauce (leaving the rest in the pan), and stir vigorously with a wooden spoon until the ingredients are well combined. Beat in the egg yolks one at a time and stir in the crumbled bacon.

Beat the egg whites with a wire whisk or rotary beater—in an unlined copper bowl, if possible—until they are stiff enough to form unwavering peaks on the beater when it is lifted from the bowl. Stir 2 or 3 large spoonfuls of the whites into the spinach mixture to lighten it, then gently fold in the remaining whites. Ladle the mixture into the prepared mold and smooth the top with a rubber spatula. Bake undisturbed in the center of the oven for about 30 minutes, or until the ring has puffed and the top is lightly browned.

While the spinach ring is baking, bring the reserved pan of sauce to a simmer over moderate heat. Then stir in the cheese and simmer for 2 or 3 minutes, until the cheese is melted. Taste for seasoning; it will probably need more salt. To keep the sauce warm, cover and set aside off the heat while you unmold the ring.

Place a large plate upside down over the top of the mold, and firmly grasping plate and mold together, invert the two. Rap them sharply on a table and the spinach ring should slide out easily onto the plate. Pour the hot cheese sauce (reheated, if necessary) over the ring, masking it as completely as you can. Serve at once.

### Fresh Spinach and Herbs, Shaker Style *(Eastern Heartland)*

To serve 4

| | |
|---|---|
| 2 pounds fresh spinach | ½ teaspoon crumbled dried rosemary |
| 4 tablespoons butter | 1 tablespoon finely chopped fresh parsley |
| ¼ cup finely cut scallions, including 2 inches of the green tops | 1 teaspoon salt |
| | Freshly ground black pepper |

With a small sharp knife, cut away the ends of the spinach, the tough stems and any bruised or yellow leaves. Pile the leaves in small stacks and chop them fine. Then wash the spinach in a sieve or colander set under cold running water.

Drop the spinach into a 4- to 5-quart enameled saucepan, cover tightly and cook over moderate heat for about 8 minutes. Drain the spinach in a colander and, a handful at a time, squeeze the leaves vigorously until they are completely dry. Set aside.

In a heavy 8- to 10-inch skillet, melt the butter over moderate heat. When the foam begins to subside, add the scallions and rosemary and, stirring frequently, cook for about 5 minutes, until the scallions are soft and translucent but not brown. Add the spinach, parsley, salt and pepper and stir over low heat for a minute or so to heat the spinach through. Taste for seasoning and serve at once.

To make one 9-inch pie

LATTICE PASTRY TOPPING
1 cup flour
1½ teaspoons double-acting
   baking powder

½ teaspoon salt
½ cup freshly grated Cheddar cheese
1 tablespoon butter, softened
1 tablespoon lard, softened
¼ cup milk

Combine the flour, baking powder and ½ teaspoon of salt, and sift them into a deep bowl. Add the cheese, 1 tablespoon of softened butter and the lard and, with your fingertips, rub the flour and fat together until they look like flakes of coarse meal.

Pour in the milk, toss together lightly, and knead until the dough is smooth and can be gathered into a compact ball. Wrap the dough in wax paper and refrigerate for at least 1 hour.

TOMATO FILLING
1 tablespoon butter, softened, plus
   2 tablespoons butter
¼ cup finely chopped shallots
1 cup soft fresh crumbs made from
   homemade-type white bread,
   pulverized in a blender or finely
   shredded with a fork

¼ cup finely chopped fresh parsley
1 teaspoon crumbled dried basil
⅛ teaspoon sugar
⅛ teaspoon salt
Freshly ground black pepper
9 medium-sized firm ripe tomatoes
   (about 3 pounds)

When you are ready to make the pie, preheat the oven to 350°. With a pastry brush, spread 1 tablespoon of softened butter evenly over the bottom and sides of a 9-inch pie pan.

In a heavy 8- to 10-inch skillet, melt the remaining 2 tablespoons of butter over moderate heat. Add the shallots and, stirring constantly, cook for 4 or 5 minutes, until they are soft and translucent but not brown. Add the bread crumbs and continue to stir until they are golden. Remove the skillet from the heat and stir in the parsley, basil, sugar, ⅛ teaspoon of salt and a few grindings of pepper.

Drop the tomatoes into a pan of boiling water, remove them after 15 seconds, and run them under cold water. Peel the tomatoes with a small, sharp knife, cut out the stems, then slice the tomatoes crosswise into ½-inch-thick rounds.

Place half of the tomato slices in the buttered pie pan and sprinkle them with half of the shallot-and-crumb mixture. Add the rest of the tomatoes and scatter the remaining shallot-and-crumb mixture on top.

On a lightly floured surface, roll the pastry dough out into a rough rectangle 12 inches long and 9 inches wide and about ⅓ inch thick. With a ruler and a pastry wheel or sharp knife, cut the dough into eighteen 12-inch strips, each ½ inch wide.

To make the lattice topping, center one strip across the middle of the pie. Arrange four strips on each side of it, laying them all parallel and spacing them about ½ inch apart. Turn the pie and, in a similar fashion, arrange 9 more strips at right angles to the 9 strips.

With scissors or a small, sharp knife, trim off the excess dough, leaving a 1-inch overhang all around. Fold the overhang under the ends of each strip and crimp the dough to the rim of the pie pan with your fingers or the tines of a fork.

Bake in the middle of the oven for 30 to 35 minutes, or until the crust is golden brown. Serve at once, directly from the pie pan.

## Creole Tomatoes

To serve 8

| | |
|---|---|
| 1 tablespoon butter, softened, plus | Italian variety |
| 4 tablespoons butter, plus | 4 large firm ripe tomatoes, washed, |
| 2 tablespoons butter, cut into | stemmed and sliced crosswise in |
| ¼-inch bits | half |
| ½ cup finely chopped onions | 1½ teaspoons salt |
| ½ cup finely chopped green pepper | Freshly ground black pepper |
| 1½ teaspoons finely chopped garlic | 2 tablespoons flour |
| 1 tablespoon finely chopped fresh | 1 cup light cream |
| parsley, preferably the flat-leaf | ⅛ teaspoon Tabasco sauce |

Preheat the oven to 350°. With a pastry brush, spread the tablespoon of softened butter evenly over the bottom and sides of a 13-by-9-by-2-inch baking dish. Set the dish aside.

In a heavy 8- to 10-inch skillet, melt 2 tablespoons of butter over moderate heat. When the foam subsides, add the onions, green pepper and garlic and, stirring frequently, cook for 5 minutes, until the vegetables are soft but not brown. Remove the pan from the heat and stir in the parsley.

Arrange the tomato halves, cut side up, in one layer in the buttered dish and sprinkle them with 1 teaspoon of the salt and a few grindings of black pepper. Spoon the onion mixture over the tomatoes, dividing it evenly among them, and scatter the 2 tablespoons of butter bits over the tops. Bake in the middle of the oven for 30 minutes, or until the tomatoes are tender but not limp.

Meanwhile, prepare the sauce in the following manner: Melt the remaining 2 tablespoons of butter in a small, heavy saucepan set over moderate heat. Add the flour and mix well.

Stirring constantly with a wire whisk, pour in the cream in a slow, thin stream and cook over high heat until the sauce comes to a boil, thickens lightly and is smooth. Reduce the heat to low and simmer for 2 or 3 minutes to remove the raw taste of the flour. Stir in the remaining ½ teaspoon of salt and the Tabasco, and taste the sauce for seasoning.

With a metal spatula transfer the baked Creole tomatoes to a heated platter. Pour the sauce over the tomatoes, masking each of them completely, and serve at once.

## Pennsylvania Dutch Fried Tomatoes

To serve 4 to 6

| | |
|---|---|
| 4 to 5 large firm ripe tomatoes, 3 to 4 inches in diameter, thickly sliced | 4 to 6 tablespoons butter |
| 2 teaspoons salt | 2 tablespoons sieved brown sugar |
| Freshly ground black pepper | 1 cup heavy cream |
| ½ cup flour | 1 tablespoon finely chopped fresh parsley |

Sprinkle the tomatoes on both sides with salt and a few grindings of black pepper. Then dip the tomato slices in the flour, coating each side thoroughly and very gently shaking off any excess. In a 12-inch heavy skillet, preferably of the nonstick variety, melt the butter over moderate heat.

When the foam subsides, add the tomato slices and cook them for about 5 minutes, or until they are lightly browned. Sprinkle the tops with half the brown sugar, carefully turn the tomatoes over with a spatula and sprinkle with the rest of the brown sugar. Cook for 3 to 4 minutes, then transfer the slices to a heated serving platter.

Pour the cream into the pan, raise the heat to high and bring the cream to a boil, stirring constantly. Boil briskly for 2 to 3 minutes, or until the cream thickens. Taste for seasoning, then pour over the tomatoes. Sprinkle with the finely chopped parsley.

NOTE: Traditionally, this recipe is made with green tomatoes; however, they are not easily available. If you can find them, cook them somewhat more slowly and for a few minutes longer on each side.

## Zucchini in Cheese Sauce

| | |
|---|---|
| 3 small zucchini | 1 egg |
| Salt | ⅔ cup grated cheese |
| ¼ cup milk | 4 tablespoons butter |

Wash the zucchini and cut it crosswise into ½-inch slices. Cook them in a small amount of salted water until they are soft.

Preheat the oven to 400°. In a small bowl, beat the egg. Add the milk and grated cheese and mix well. Place the zucchini in a casserole and pour the cheese sauce over it. Dot the top with the butter. Bake, uncovered, until the cheese is melted and the top is nicely browned.

## *Deep-fried Mixed Vegetables* (*Italian-American*)

To serve 4

BATTER

| | |
|---|---|
| 2 cups sifted all-purpose flour | 1½ cups lukewarm water |
| 1¾ teaspoons salt | ⅓ cup vegetable oil |
| ¼ teaspoon white pepper | 3 egg whites |

BATTER: Combine the flour, 1¾ teaspoons of salt, the pepper and water in a large mixing bowl and stir in ⅓ cup of vegetable oil. Continue to stir until the ingredients form a fairly smooth cream, then set aside to rest at room temperature for 1½ to 2 hours. Just before using the batter, beat the egg whites in a large mixing bowl with a wire whisk or a rotary or electric beater. When they are stiff enough to form firm, unwavering peaks on the beater when it is lifted from the bowl, fold them into the batter with a rubber spatula.

VEGETABLES

| | |
|---|---|
| 8 spears asparagus | rounds |
| 2 zucchini, scrubbed under cold running water and cut crosswise into ½-inch-thick rounds | 1 small cauliflower (about ½ pound), separated into small flowerets |
| 16 medium-sized mushrooms, halved | Salt |
| ½ pound eggplant, peeled and cut crosswise into ½-inch-thick | Vegetable oil for deep frying |
| | Lemon quarters |

VEGETABLES: Lay the asparagus spears side by side on a board and trim their bases with a sharp knife. With the knife, peel each spear, starting at the base. At the base end the peeling may be as thick as 1/16 inch, but it should gradually become paper thin as the knife slides toward the tip. When all the spears are peeled, wash them under cold running water.

Drop the asparagus into boiling water and bring back to a boil over high heat. Boil briskly for 2 or 3 minutes, then drain the asparagus and plunge them into a bowl of cold water.

Place the asparagus, zucchini, mushrooms, eggplant and cauliflower on a large platter and sprinkle them lightly with salt. Pour vegetable oil into a deep fryer or heavy saucepan to a depth of 3 inches, and heat it to a temperature of 375° on a deep-frying thermometer. Preheat the oven to its lowest setting and line a baking sheet with paper towels.

Dip five or six pieces of vegetable at a time into the batter and, when they are well coated, lift them out with tongs or a slotted spoon. Deep-fry the vegetables, turning them once or twice, for 3 to 4 minutes, or until the batter is golden brown. With tongs, transfer the vegetables to the lined baking sheet to drain, and keep them warm in the low oven while you similarly coat and deep-fry the remaining pieces. When all of the vegetables are browned, arrange on a napkin-lined platter and serve garnished with the lemon quarters.

# Relishes, Pickles & Preserves

America's early homemakers preserved the harvest's fruits and vegetables as a way of providing for the long, hard winters. Today, preserving is a creative pastime that makes these staples of the larder—vegetable pickles and relishes, fruit butters and sauces, jellies, conserves and preserves—always available to add last-minute zest, sweetness and color to a meal. Hearty pot roasts can be perked up with homemade chowchow or bread and butter pickles from the farm kitchens of the Eastern Heartland, and simple roast meat or bird can be sweetened with a side dish of pickled watermelon rind or sparked by a New England cranberry-orange relish. And you will definitely want to throw out your store-bought ketchup after tasting homemade tomato ketchup and Northwestern plum ketchup. Desserts, too, can be transformed by preserves: try a dollop of Southern summer fruit conserve or Northwestern trapper's fruit over a scoop of ice cream.

As American cooks return to natural ingredients, eschewing preservatives and artificial flavorings, the beauty of rows of glass jars glowing with jewellike colors becomes increasingly appealing. Gardeners, too, appreciate having a new use for the end-of-the-season bounty from the garden. "Putting up" food in any quantity requires some special equipment and calls for care in preparation. The techniques for home canning set forth in the Appendix will ensure bacteria-free results.

To make 7 to 8 quarts

6 quarts water
1 cup dried navy beans
1 cup dried red kidney beans
2 pounds shelled fresh Lima beans
1 pound fresh green string beans, trimmed, washed and cut into 1-inch pieces
1½ pounds fresh yellow wax beans, trimmed, washed and cut into 1-inch pieces
A 1- to 1¼-pound head fresh cauliflower, trimmed, washed and broken into small flowerets
A 1- to 1¼-pound bunch celery, trimmed, leaves removed, washed and cut into 1-inch pieces

1 pound green bell peppers, halved, seeded, deribbed and cut into 2-by-¼-inch strips
1 pound red bell peppers, halved, seeded, deribbed and cut into 2-by-¼-inch strips
6 cups fresh corn kernels, cut from 10 to 12 large ears of corn
1 cup sugar
2 quarts distilled white vinegar
¼ cup mustard seeds
2 teaspoons celery seeds
1 teaspoon turmeric
2 two-inch pieces stick cinnamon and 1 tablespoon whole cloves, wrapped together in cheesecloth

*Traditionally, Pennsylvania Dutch housewives cook the vegetables for chowchow separately. Though this may seem tedious, the technique ensures that each vegetable keeps its shape and color and is properly crunchy. You may want to combine vegetables to speed the process, but, if you do, keep a close eye on the pot to prevent overcooking them.*

In a heavy 3- to 4-quart saucepan, bring 2 quarts of the water to a boil over high heat. Drop in the dried navy and kidney beans, and boil them briskly, uncovered, for about 2 minutes. (The water should cover the beans by at least 2 inches; if necessary, add more water.)

Turn off the heat and let the beans soak for 1 hour. Then bring to a boil again and reduce the heat to low. Simmer partially covered for about 1 hour, or until the beans are tender. Check the pan from time to time and add more boiling water if needed. Drain the beans through a fine sieve, discarding the cooking liquid, and set them aside.

Meanwhile, bring 4 quarts of water to a boil in an 8- to 10-quart enameled pot. Drop in the Lima beans. When the water returns to a boil, cook the beans briskly for 20 to 30 minutes, or until they are tender but still crisp to the bite. With a slotted spoon, scoop the beans out of the water into a colander or sieve and run cold water over them for a minute or so to set their color and stop their cooking. Drain well and set the Limas aside in a 10- to 12-quart pot.

Return the water in the pot to a boil over high heat. Then drop in the string beans and wax beans, a handful at a time so that the boiling never stops. Cook briskly, uncovered, for 8 to 10 minutes, or until the beans are barely tender. With a slotted spoon, transfer them to a colander or sieve and run cold water over them briefly. Let them drain for a minute or so, then add them to the Lima beans. Return the cooking water to a boil again and in similar fashion boil the cauliflower, the celery, the green and red peppers, and the corn separately, running cold water over each vegetable and adding it to the Lima beans as soon as it is cooked. Allow about 8 to 10 minutes for the cauliflower, 5 to 6 minutes for the celery, 5 minutes for the green and red peppers, and 4 to 5 minutes for the corn.

Add the cooked navy and kidney beans to the vegetable mixture and, with a wooden spoon, toss gently but thoroughly together. Pack the vegetables into sterilized jars, dividing them evenly, according to the directions for home canning in the appendix.

Combine the sugar, vinegar, mustard seeds, celery seeds, turmeric, and the wrapped cinnamon and cloves in a 5- to 6-quart enameled saucepan and bring to a boil over high heat, stirring until the sugar dissolves. Cook briskly for 5 minutes.

Remove the pan from the heat and discard the bag of cinnamon and cloves. Ladle the hot syrup over the vegetables, a few tablespoonfuls at a time, allowing the liquid and spices to flow through to the bottom of the jars before adding more, and filling the jars to within ¼ inch of the top. Following the directions for home canning in the appendix, process the jars 15 minutes in a boiling-water bath.

*Hot Mustard Pickle*

To make about 3 quarts

1 medium-sized cauliflower (about 1 pound), trimmed and separated into individual flowerets with approximately 1-inch stems
2 small green (unripe) tomatoes (about ½ pound), cut into 1-inch chunks
1 pound small white onions, about 1 inch in diameter, peeled
2 medium-sized yellow onions (about ½ pound), peeled and cut into ¼-inch slices

1 cup plus 1 teaspoon salt
2 small cucumbers (about 1 pound), peeled and cut into ¼-inch slices
1 tablespoon capers, drained and rinsed in cold water
½ teaspoon celery seed
¼ pound butter
¼ cup all-purpose flour
2 cups malt vinegar
½ cup sugar
1 tablespoon turmeric
¼ cup dry English mustard

In a 10- to 12-quart enameled or stainless-steel pot, combine the cauliflower, green tomatoes, white onions and sliced yellow onions. Dissolve 1 cup of the salt in 4 quarts of water, pour it over the vegetables, and stir until they are thoroughly moistened. Set aside in a cool place (not the refrigerator) for 12 to 18 hours.

Drain off the liquid, and add the cucumbers, capers, celery seed, the remaining teaspoon of salt and 1 quart of fresh water to the pot. Bring to a boil over high heat, stirring occasionally. Then reduce the heat to moderate and cook, uncovered, for about 10 minutes, or until the vegetables are tender but still slightly resistant when pierced with the tip of a small knife. Drain through a colander, discard the liquid and place the vegetables in a large stainless-steel, glass or enameled bowl.

Melt the butter in a heavy 1½- to 2-quart saucepan over moderate heat. When the foam begins to subside, stir in the flour, and mix thoroughly. Pour in the vinegar and cook, stirring constantly, until the sauce thickens and comes to a boil. Reduce the heat to low and simmer for about 3 minutes, then beat in the sugar, turmeric and mustard. Pour half the sauce over the vegetables, turning them about to coat them evenly. Set the remaining sauce aside covered with plastic wrap. (Do not refrigerate.) Marinate the vegetables at room temperature for 24 hours, then stir in the reserved mustard sauce. The pickles may be served at once, or packed into jars and stored, tightly covered, in the refrigerator for up to 3 months. Mustard pickle is traditionally served with cold meats or bread and cheese.

## Bread-and-Butter Pickles *(Eastern Heartland)*

To make 3 to 4 quarts

5 pounds firm ripe cucumbers (about 10 medium-sized cucumbers), scrubbed, trimmed of ends and cut crosswise into ¼-inch-thick rounds

3 medium-sized onions, peeled and cut crosswise into ¼-inch-thick slices

1 large green bell pepper, washed, halved, seeded, deribbed and cut into 2-by-¼-inch strips

1 large red bell pepper, washed, halved, seeded, deribbed and cut into 2-by-¼-inch strips

1 cup salt

6 cups sugar

3 cups distilled white vinegar

1 tablespoon celery seeds

1 tablespoon celery salt

Combine the cucumbers, onions, and green and red peppers in a large colander set over a bowl. Sprinkle with the salt, turning the vegetables about with a wooden spoon to coat them evenly. Let the vegetable mixture stand at room temperature for 2 to 3 hours to allow the excess liquid to drain. Then place the colander under cold running water and wash off the salt, tossing the vegetables about with the spoon. Set the colander aside and let the vegetables drain.

In a 6- to 8-quart enameled casserole, bring the sugar, vinegar, celery seeds and celery salt to a boil over high heat, stirring with a wooden spoon until the sugar dissolves. Add the vegetables handful by handful, and return the liquid to the boil. Boil the vegetables briskly, uncovered and undisturbed, for about 2 minutes.

Remove the pan from the heat and ladle the pickle mixture immediately into hot sterilized jars, filling them to within ¼ inch of the top. Following the directions for home canning in the appendix, process the jars 15 minutes in a boiling-water bath.

## Mixed Vegetable Pickles  *(South)*

To make about 5 quarts

6 large firm ripe cucumbers
1 pound white cabbage, halved lengthwise, cored and cut into 1-inch chunks (about 5 cups)
4 medium-sized onions, peeled and cut into 1-inch chunks (about 3 cups)
2 large green bell peppers, halved lengthwise, seeded, deribbed and cut into 1-inch squares (about 2 cups)
1 cup salt
3 medium-sized celery ribs, trimmed of all leaves, halved lengthwise and cut crosswise into 1-inch strips (about 2 cups)
5 medium-sized carrots, scraped and sliced into ⅛-inch-thick rounds (about 2 cups)
1 pound cauliflower, trimmed, washed and broken into small flowerets (about 3 cups)
1 pound (2 cups) dark brown sugar
¼ cup celery seeds
¼ cup mustard seeds
1 cup dry mustard
1 tablespoon turmeric
6 cups cider vinegar

With a small sharp knife, peel the cucumbers and cut them lengthwise into halves. Scoop out the seeds by running the tip of a teaspoon down the center of each half. Then cut each half lengthwise into 3 strips and slice the strips crosswise into 1-inch lengths.

Place the cucumbers, cabbage, onions and peppers in a large colander. Add the salt and toss the vegetables about with a spoon to coat them evenly. Set aside at room temperature for about 2 hours to let the excess moisture drain from the vegetables, then transfer them to a large pot or casserole. Add the celery, carrots and cauliflower, and turn the vegetables about with a spoon until they are well mixed.

In a 4- to 5-quart enameled or stainless-steel saucepan, stir the brown sugar, celery seeds, mustard seeds, dry mustard, turmeric and 1 cup of the vinegar together with a wooden spoon until the sugar and dry mustard dissolve. Stir in the remaining 5 cups of vinegar, add the vegetables and, stirring occasionally, bring to a boil over high heat. Cook briskly, uncovered, for 5 minutes.

Immediately, with a slotted spoon, transfer the vegetables to hot sterilized jars, dividing the pieces evenly among them. Ladle the hot liquid over the vegetables, a few tablespoonfuls at a time, allowing the liquid and spices to flow through to the bottom of the jars before adding more, and filling the jars to within ⅛ inch of the top. Follow the directions for canning and sealing, and process the jars 10 minutes in a hot-water bath as described in the appendix.

## Pickled Onions

To make 2 quarts

5 pounds small white onions, each about 1 inch in diameter
1 cup salt
¼ cup mixed pickling spice
1 quart cider vinegar
1½ cups sugar
Alum

Drop the onions into a 3- to 4-quart saucepan filled with boiling water, bring back to a boil, and cook uncovered for 2 to 3 minutes. Pour off the water and with a small, sharp knife peel the onions.

Place the hot onions in a large mixing bowl, sprinkle with the salt, and add enough ice water to cover them by about an inch. Soak undisturbed for 30 minutes, then drain and discard the soaking liquid. Place the onions in hot sterilized jars, sprinkling each layer of onions with the pickling spice as you proceed.

In a 2- to 3-quart enameled or stainless-steel saucepan, bring the vinegar and sugar to a boil over high heat, stirring constantly until the sugar dissolves. Ladle the mixture over the onions a few tablespoons at a time, letting it flow through to the bottom before adding more. Add a 1-by-½-inch piece of alum to each jar, and seal following the directions in the appendix. Store for at least 2 weeks before serving.

## Pickled Watermelon Rind (South)

To make about 3 quarts

A 15- to 16-pound firm ripe watermelon
½ cup salt
2 quarts plus 2½ quarts cold water
1¾ cups distilled white vinegar
7 cups sugar
1 teaspoon ground mace
3 one-inch-long pieces of stick

cinnamon
1 tablespoon whole allspice and 1 tablespoon whole cloves, wrapped together in cheesecloth and tied securely
2 medium-sized lemons, cut crosswise into ¼-inch-thick slices (about 1 cup)
3 drops green food coloring

334

Prepare the pickled watermelon rind at least 2 weeks before you plan to serve it. With a large sharp knife, cut the watermelon crosswise in half and then cut each half lengthwise into quarters. Scrape out all the watermelon pulp with the knife or a large spoon; refrigerate the pulp for another use if you wish.

Then, with a small sharp knife or rotary vegetable peeler, cut off and discard the green skin of the watermelon, leaving only the white inner rind. Cut the rind into 1- to 1½-inch chunks and drop them into a large deep crock or enameled pot. Add the salt and 2 quarts of the water and stir until the salt dissolves. The brine should cover the rind completely; if necessary, add more water. Set the rind aside in the brine at room temperature for about 12 hours.

Pour off the brine and transfer the rind to a large colander. Rinse the chunks under cold running water, tossing them about with a spoon, until the draining water runs clear.

In an 8- to 10-quart enameled or stainless-steel pot, combine 2½ quarts of water, the vinegar, sugar, mace, cinnamon, and the wrapped allspice and cloves. Bring to a boil over high heat, stirring until the sugar dissolves. Drop in the watermelon rind and, when the mixture returns to a boil, reduce the heat to moderate. Boil gently, uncovered, for about 45 minutes, or until the rind is tender but not too soft.

Turn off the heat and pick out and discard the cheesecloth bag of spices. Add the lemon slices and food coloring to the pot and stir gently for a moment or two with a long wooden spoon.

Ladle the watermelon rind and lemon slices immediately into hot sterilized jars. Then ladle the hot liquid over the rind and lemon slices, a small amount at a time, allowing it to flow through to the bottom of the jars before adding more, and filling the jars to within ⅛ inch of the top. Follow the directions for canning and sealing, and process the jars for 5 minutes in a hot-water bath as described in the appendix. Let the pickled watermelon rind stand in a cool, dark place (not the refrigerator) for at least 2 weeks before serving.

### Plum Ketchup *(Northwest)*

To make 3 cups

| | |
|---|---|
| 3 pounds firm ripe tart plums | ½ teaspoon ground mace |
| 1½ pounds (3¾ cups) sugar | ¾ teaspoon ground cloves |
| 1 cup cider vinegar | ⅛ teaspoon freshly ground black |
| 2 teaspoons ground cinnamon |     pepper |
| | ½ teaspoon ground nutmeg |

With a small, sharp knife, slit the plums open and remove and discard the pits. Wash the plums under cold running water, then place them in a heavy 2- to 3-quart enameled or stainless-steel saucepan. Add the sugar and vinegar and, with a wooden spoon, stir until the sugar has almost dissolved. Bring to a boil over high heat, lower the heat, and simmer the plums, stirring occasionally, until the fruit is tender enough to be easily mashed against the side of the pan with a wooden spoon. Now stir in the cinnamon, mace, cloves, pepper and nutmeg, and raise the heat to high. Boil briskly, stirring frequently to prevent the mixture from sticking to the pan, for about 45 minutes, or until the ketchup has reached 215° on a candy thermometer. With a slotted spoon, skim off and discard any foam that may appear on the surface of the ketchup and ladle the ketchup at once into hot, sterilized jars or glasses, following the directions for canning and sealing in the appendix. The ketchup provides an excellent accompaniment to wild game, other meats and poultry.

## Tomato Ketchup *(South)*

To make about 1 quart

12 medium-sized firm ripe tomatoes (about 4 pounds), washed, cored and quartered
2 cups finely chopped onions
1½ cups light brown sugar
1½ cups distilled white vinegar
5 tablespoons mixed pickling spice
1 tablespoon finely chopped fresh hot red chili
   *(caution: see note, appendix)*
1½ teaspoons salt

Combine all the ingredients in a 5- to 6-quart enameled or stainless-steel pot. Bring to a boil over high heat, stirring constantly with a wooden spoon until the brown sugar dissolves. Reduce the heat to low and simmer partially covered until the mixture is thick enough to hold its shape almost solidly in the spoon. As the ketchup begins to thicken, stir from time to time (especially around the corners) to prevent it from scorching.

Rub the ketchup through a fine sieve into a bowl, pressing down hard on the vegetables with the back of the spoon to extract all their juices before discarding the pulp. (Or purée the ketchup through the finest blade of a food mill.) Cool to room temperature, cover with foil or plastic wrap, and chill until ready to serve. Tightly covered and refrigerated, the ketchup can safely be kept for one month.

## Corn Relish

To make 3 quarts

1 pound white cabbage, cored and finely chopped
8 cups fresh corn kernels, cut from about 12 large ears of corn
¾ cup finely chopped onions
1 cup finely chopped green bell peppers
1 cup finely chopped red bell peppers
1 cup sugar
1 tablespoon salt
4 teaspoons celery seed
2½ cups cider vinegar

In a 6- to 8-quart enameled or stainless-steel casserole, combine the cabbage, corn, onions, peppers, sugar, salt and celery seed. Pour in the vinegar and, with a wooden spoon, stir the ingredients together. Bring to a boil over high heat, stirring the mixture frequently, then reduce the heat to low and simmer uncovered for 20 minutes. Taste for seasoning, then immediately ladle the relish into hot sterilized jars, following the directions for canning and sealing in the appendix.

### *Green Tomato Relish* (*New England*)

To make about 3 quarts

20 medium-sized firm green tomatoes (about 6 pounds), washed, stemmed, cut in half and cut crosswise into ½-inch-thick slices

¼ cup plus 2 tablespoons salt

6 medium-sized onions (about 2 pounds), peeled and cut crosswise into ¼-inch-thick slices

6 medium-sized red bell peppers, seeded, deribbed and cut lengthwise into ½-inch-wide strips

1 cup sugar

2 teaspoons celery seed

1 teaspoon dry mustard

1 teaspoon ground cinnamon

½ teaspoon ground allspice

¼ teaspoon ground cloves

4 to 6 cups cider vinegar

Spread the tomato slices in layers on a large, deep platter, sprinkling each layer with salt as you proceed and using ¼ cup salt in all. Cover the platter with foil or plastic wrap and set it aside at room temperature for at least 12 hours.

Pour off the liquid that has accumulated around the slices and transfer the tomatoes to a 5- to 6-quart enameled casserole. Add the onions, peppers, sugar, celery seed, dry mustard, cinnamon, allspice, cloves and the remaining 2 tablespoons of salt. Pour in the vinegar; it should cover the vegetables completely. If necessary add more. Stirring gently but constantly, bring the mixture to a boil over high heat. Reduce the heat to low and simmer partially covered for about 5 minutes, or until the vegetables are barely tender.

At once ladle the relish into hot sterilized jars, filling them to ⅛ inch of the tops and following the directions for canning and sealing given in the appendix.

*Preserves of all descriptions are staples of the Southern larder. These include citrus marmalade, pickled watermelon rind, mixed vegetable pickles and summer fruit conserve.*

## Summer Fruit Conserve *(South)*

To make about 3½ quarts

16 medium-sized firm ripe peaches
  (about 4 pounds)
¾ pound medium-sized firm ripe
  apricots
1 pound firm ripe cherries
1 large grapefruit

1 large orange
3 lemons
6 cups sugar
2 cups (½ pound) seedless raisins
2 cups (½ pound) shelled pecan
  halves
1 cup bourbon

Drop the peaches and apricots into enough boiling water to cover them completely and boil briskly for 2 to 3 minutes. Drain in a sieve or colander, then remove the skins with a small sharp knife. Cut the peaches and apricots in half, discard the pits, chop the fruits coarsely and combine them in a 6- to 8-quart enameled or stainless-steel pot.

Wash, stem and pit the cherries and add them to the pot. Slice the unpeeled grapefruit, orange and lemons into ¼-inch-thick rounds and pick out the seeds with the point of a small knife. Put the slices through the coarsest blade of a food grinder and add all the pulp and juices to the peach-and-cherry mixture. Stir in the sugar, cover the pot with foil or plastic wrap and set aside at room temperature for at least 12 hours.

Stirring constantly with a wooden spoon, bring the fruit mixture to a boil over high heat. Reduce the heat to low and simmer uncovered for 1 to 1½ hours, or until the mixture is thick enough to hold its shape almost solidly in a spoon. As the conserve begins to thicken, stir deeply from time to time to prevent it from sticking to the bottom of the pot.

Add the raisins and, stirring frequently, continue to simmer for 15 minutes. Stir in the pecans and the bourbon and mix well. Immediately ladle the conserve into hot sterilized jars. Fill the jars to within ⅛ inch of the top and follow the directions for canning and sealing in the appendix.

Summer fruit conserve is used as a topping for ice cream and is also served as an accompaniment to game and roast meats.

## Trappers' Fruit *(Far West)*

To make about 5 cups

3 cups (about 12 ounces) coarsely
  chopped dried apples
1 cup canned puréed pumpkin
½ cup dark brown sugar

¼ cup roasted sunflower seeds
¼ cup seedless raisins
¼ teaspoon coriander seeds
1 teaspoon salt
1 quart water

Combine the dried apples, pumpkin, brown sugar, sunflower seeds, raisins, coriander, salt and water in a heavy 3- to 4-quart casserole and mix well. Bring to a boil over high heat, reduce the heat to low, cover tightly and simmer for about 1½ hours, or until the apples are tender. Check the pan occasionally and, if the fruit seems dry, add more water ¼ cup at a time. Transfer the fruit to a bowl and cool to room temperature before serving. Trappers' fruit, so called because it was easy for Colorado fur trappers of the mid-19th Century to prepare, is served as an accompaniment to roasted and broiled meats.

## Ginger Fruit Kabobs *(Far West)*

To make 8 kabobs

8 tablespoons butter, cut into
  ½-inch bits
2 tablespoons sugar
1 teaspoon ground ginger
2 half-inch-thick orange slices, each
cut crosswise into quarters
1 large firm apple, cored and cut
  lengthwise into 8 wedges
1 large banana, peeled and cut
  crosswise into 8 chunks
8 one-inch cubes fresh pineapple

Immerse eight individual Oriental bamboo skewers in water and soak them for at least an hour. Then light a layer of briquettes in a hibachi or charcoal broiler and let them burn until a white ash appears on the surface. Or preheat the broiler of the oven to its highest setting.

To prepare the basting syrup, combine the butter, sugar and ginger in a small pan and cook over low heat, stirring constantly until the butter melts and the sugar dissolves. Set the pan aside off the heat.

Thread an orange quarter, apple wedge, banana chunk and pineapple cube on each skewer, pushing the pieces of fruit close together. With a pastry brush, spread about 1 teaspoon of the basting syrup evenly over each fruit kabob.

Broil the kabobs about 3 inches from the heat for 2 minutes, turn them over and baste them with the remaining syrup. Continue to broil for 1 or 2 minutes longer, or until the kabobs are golden brown on all sides.

Arrange the kabobs attractively on a heated platter and serve them at once as an accompaniment to broiled steak or any roasted meat.

To make about 1 quart

2 cups sugar

6½ to 7 pounds firm ripe pears,
peeled and cut in half lengthwise

4 teaspoons finely grated fresh
lemon peel

With a small, sharp knife, cut out and discard the cores of the pears. Grate the pears on the finest blades of a standing four-sided grater. Combine the pear pulp and the sugar in a 3-quart enameled or stainless-steel saucepan and, stirring constantly, bring to a boil over high heat. Then reduce the heat to low and simmer uncovered for about 45 minutes, or until the mixture is thick enough to hold its shape in a spoon. (As it simmers, with a large spoon skim off any foam that rises to the surface, and stir the purée frequently to prevent it from sticking to the pan.)

Stir in the lemon peel and simmer for 2 minutes longer, then remove from the heat and pour into hot sterilized jars, following the directions for canning and sealing in the appendix.

## *Apple Butter* *(Eastern Heartland)*

To make about 3 pints

5 pounds tart cooking apples,
peeled, quartered and cored

3 cups apple cider
4 cups sugar

Combine the apples and cider in a 4- to 5-quart enameled or stainless-steel pot and bring to a boil over high heat. Reduce the heat to low. Simmer partially covered for 20 to 25 minutes, or until an apple quarter can be easily mashed against the side of the pot with a fork.

Preheat the oven to 300°. Purée the apples through the finest blade of a food mill set over a deep bowl, or rub them through a fine sieve with the back of a spoon. Add the sugar and mix well.

Pour the apple purée into a shallow 14-by-8-inch baking dish, spreading it evenly and smoothing the top with a rubber spatula. Bake in the middle of the oven for about 2 hours, or until the apple butter is thick enough to hold its shape solidly in a spoon.

The traditional test for doneness is to dab a spoonful of the apple butter on a plate and turn the plate upside down. The apple butter should be thick enough to adhere to the inverted plate.

At once ladle the apple butter into hot sterilized jars, filling them to within ⅛ inch of the top. Seal the jars immediately, following the directions for home canning in the appendix.

To make 3 pints

| | |
|---|---|
| 2 pounds rhubarb, coarsely chopped | sectioned |
| ¼ cup orange juice | 1 lemon, peeled, seeded and sectioned |
| ¼ cup lemon juice | Grated rind of 1 orange |
| 2 pounds sugar | Grated rind of 1 lemon |
| 2 oranges, peeled, seeded and | 1½ cups walnuts, halved |

Combine the rhubarb, orange juice and lemon juice in an enameled or stainless-steel saucepan. Bring to a boil, cover, reduce the heat and simmer for about an hour, or until the rhubarb is soft. Stir in the sugar and, stirring constantly, boil rapidly for about 5 minutes, or until the mixture is translucent and lightly holds its shape in a spoon. Turn off the heat, stir in the orange and lemon sections and rinds, and the walnuts. Still stirring occasionally, let the marmalade cool to room temperature, then pour it into sterilized glasses and seal with paraffin.

*Citrus Marmalade* *(South)*

To make about 3 pints

| | |
|---|---|
| 9 medium-sized oranges | 4 lemons |
| 1 medium-sized grapefruit | 5 to 6 cups sugar |

Wash the oranges, grapefruit and lemons and pat them dry with paper towels. With a swivel-bladed vegetable parer, remove the peel without cutting into the bitter white pith and cut it into strips one inch long and ⅛ inch wide. Cut away the white outer pith of the fruit.

Slice the fruit in half crosswise. Wrap the halves one at a time in a double thickness of damp cheesecloth and twist the cloth to squeeze all of the juice into a bowl. Wrap all the squeezed pulp into the cloth and tie the cloth securely into a bag. Measure the juice; then add enough cold water to make 3½ quarts of liquid. Drop in the bag of pulp and the strips of peel and set aside at room temperature for at least 12 hours.

Pour the contents of the bowl—the juice and water, peel and bag of pulp—into an 8- to 10-quart enameled casserole and bring to a boil over high heat. Reduce the heat to low and, stirring frequently, simmer uncovered for 2 hours. Remove the pulp bag and extract its liquid by pressing it against the side of the casserole with the back of a spoon. Now measure the mixture and add 1 cup of sugar for each cup of the mixture. Bring to a boil, stirring constantly. When the sugar has dissolved, increase the heat to high and boil briskly for 20 to 30 minutes undisturbed, until the marmalade reaches a temperature of 220° on a jelly, candy or deep-frying thermometer.

Remove from the heat. With a large spoon skim off the surface foam. Ladle the marmalade into hot sterilized jars or jelly glasses following the instructions in the appendix. To prevent the peel from floating to the top gently shake the jars occasionally as they cool.

## Apricot and Pineapple Jam  *(Northwest)*

| To make 3 pints | 2½ pounds sugar ( 6¼ cups ) |
| 3 pounds unpeeled firm ripe | 1 cup cold water |
|    apricots | 2 cups finely diced fresh pineapple |

Wash the apricots under cold running water. With a small, sharp knife, cut them in half, remove the pits, and set the pits aside. Place the halved apricots in a deep mixing bowl, add the sugar and, with a wooden spoon, toss the fruit to distribute the sugar evenly.

With a nutcracker or the flat side of a heavy knife or cleaver, split as many of the apricot pits as you need to obtain ½ cup of the kernels. Discard the cracked shells and the remaining pits.

In a 2- to 3-quart enameled or stainless-steel saucepan, combine the sugared apricots with the water and mix them together thoroughly with a wooden spoon. Bring to a boil over high heat, stirring constantly, then lower the heat and, stirring frequently, simmer the mixture uncovered for about 45 minutes, or until the jam is thick enough to hold its shape loosely in the spoon. Stir in the reserved apricot kernels and the pineapple, and simmer over very low heat until the jam registers 220° on a candy thermometer.

With a slotted spoon, skim off and discard any foam from the surface. Then ladle the hot jam into hot sterilized jars or jelly glasses, following the directions for canning and sealing in the appendix.

## Beach-Plum Jelly *(New England)*

| To make 3 or 4 cups | and ⅓ green or underripe |
| 10 cups fresh beach plums, about | ½ cup water |
|    ⅔ of the plums fully ripened | 3 to 4 cups sugar |

Pick over the plums carefully, removing the stems and discarding any badly bruised fruit. Wash the plums in a colander under cold running water and drop them into an 8- to 10-quart enameled pot. Add the ½ cup of water and bring to a boil over high heat. Cover the pot tightly, reduce the heat to low and simmer for about 15 minutes, or until a plum can be mashed easily against the side of the pot with the back of a spoon.

Line a colander or sieve with 4 layers of damp cheesecloth and place it over a large enameled pot. The bottom of the colander or sieve should be suspended above the pot by at least 3 or 4 inches. Pour in the plums and, without disturbing them, allow the juice to drain through into the pot. (Do not squeeze the cloth or the finished jelly will be cloudy.)

When the juice has drained through completely, measure and return it to the first enameled pot. Discard the plums. Add ¾ cup of sugar for each cup of juice and bring to a boil over high heat, stirring until the sugar dissolves. Cook briskly, uncovered and undisturbed, until the jelly reaches a temperature of 220° (or 8° above the boiling point of water in your locality) on a jelly, candy or deep-frying thermometer.

Remove the pot from the heat and carefully skim off the surface foam with a large spoon. Ladle the jelly into hot sterilized jars or jelly glasses, following the directions for canning and sealing in the appendix.

NOTE: Beach-plum jelly is served as an accompaniment to meats and fowl as well as with hot toast or bread and butter.

## *Blackberry Jam* (Creole-Acadian)

To make about 5 cups

6 cups fresh ripe blackberries

½ cup water
4 cups sugar

Pick over the berries carefully, removing any stems and discarding fruit that is badly bruised or shows signs of mold. Do not discard any underripe berries; although tarter than ripe ones, they contain more pectin —the substance that jells the fruit.

Wash the blackberries briefly in a large sieve or colander set under cold running water and drop them into a heavy 4- to 6-quart enameled casserole. Add the water and sugar, and bring to a boil over high heat, stirring until the sugar dissolves. Reduce the heat to moderate and, stirring from time to time, cook uncovered until the jam reaches a temperature of 221° (or 9° above the boiling point of water in your locality) on a jelly, candy or deep-frying thermometer.

Remove the pan from the heat. With a large spoon, carefully skim off the foam from the surface and ladle the blackberry jam into hot sterilized jars. For canning and sealing directions see the appendix.

## Cranberry Sauce *(New England)*

To make about 1½ cups

| | |
|---|---|
| 2 cups (½ pound) firm fresh unblemished cranberries | ½ cup water |
| 1 cup sugar | 1 teaspoon finely grated fresh orange peel |

Wash the cranberries in a colander under cold running water. Combine the berries with the sugar and water in a small, heavy enameled or stainless-steel saucepan and, stirring frequently, bring them to a boil over high heat. Then reduce the heat to low and, still stirring from time to time, simmer uncovered for 4 or 5 minutes, until the skins of the cranberries begin to pop and the berries are tender. Do not overcook them to the point where they become mushy.

Remove the pan from the heat and stir in the grated orange peel. With a rubber spatula, scrape the entire contents of the pan into a 2-cup mold or small bowl. Refrigerate for 2 or 3 hours until the sauce is thoroughly chilled and firm to the touch.

To unmold and serve the sauce, run a thin-bladed knife around the sides of the mold or bowl to loosen it and dip the bottom briefly in hot water. Place a serving plate upside down over the mold and, grasping plate and mold firmly together, invert them. The cranberry sauce should slide out of the mold easily.

## Uncooked Cranberry Orange Relish *(New England)*

To make about 5 cups

| | |
|---|---|
| 1 pound (4 cups) firm fresh unblemished cranberries | 2 large thin-skinned oranges, preferably a seedless variety |
| | 2 cups sugar |

Wash the cranberries under cold running water and pat them dry with paper towels. Cut the oranges into quarters. (If the oranges have seeds, pick them out with the tip of a knife.) Then put the cranberries and the orange quarters (skins and all) through the coarsest blade of a food grinder into a deep glass or ceramic bowl. Add the sugar and mix well with a wooden spoon. Taste and add more sugar if desired.

Cover with plastic wrap and let the relish stand at room temperature for about 24 hours to develop flavor before serving. (Tightly covered, the relish can safely be refrigerated for 2 to 3 weeks.)

# Breads, Coffeecakes & Pancakes

Once your kitchen has been perfumed by a sweet yeast odor, once you have opened the oven door to discover a crusty, puffed-up loaf, and once you have tasted freshly baked bread you will probably decide the rewards of breadmaking warrant the effort involved. Moreover, the profusion of kitchen machines which mix and even knead dough in minutes can substantially reduce that effort.

Traditionally, Americans have been superb and innovative home bakers. In addition to such live ingredients as yeast and sourdough starter, they experimented with faster-working leaveners such as baking soda or powder or eggs to produce an almost endless—and mouth-watering—list of creations: spoon and corn breads from the South, Mormon johnneycake, Boston brown bread, San Francisco sourdough bread, griddle cakes, popovers, and fruit-and-nut breads and cranberry-studded muffins from New England. Americans became good bakers not just out of necessity, in the days when stores were poorly stocked or inaccessible, but because of the unprecedented abundance in this country of grains, butter and cane sugar.

Modern Americans can be innovators, too. Try baking more than one bread or batch of muffins on a rainy afternoon and freezing the extras. Or try spreading your stand-by sandwich fillings on Northwestern cheese bread, Boston brown or salt-rising bread from the Eastern Heartland. And you might surprise your family by turning any leftover white bread into *pain perdu,* the delicate, extraordinary Creole version of ordinary French toast.

To make one 9-inch loaf

1 package dry yeast
1 cup lukewarm milk
1½ tablespoons sugar
2½ to 3 cups all-purpose flour or
    bread flour

4 tablespoons soft butter
1 teaspoon salt

GLAZE
1 egg, lightly beaten with 1
    tablespoon milk

Sprinkle the yeast into a half cup of the lukewarm (110° to 115°) milk. Add 1 teaspoon of the sugar and stir until thoroughly dissolved. Place the mixture in a warm, draft-free place—such as an unlighted oven—for 5 to 8 minutes, or until the yeast has begun to bubble and almost doubled in volume.

Then pour it into a large mixing bowl, add the remaining ½ cup of milk and stir until the yeast is dissolved. With a large spoon, slowly beat into the mixture 1 cup of the flour and continue to beat vigorously until smooth. Still beating, add the butter, remaining sugar, salt and 1½ more cups of flour. Transfer the dough to a lightly floured surface and knead it by folding it end to end, then pressing it down, pushing it forward and folding it back for at least 10 minutes, sprinkling the dough every few minutes with small amounts of as much of the remaining flour as you need to prevent the dough from sticking to the board. When the dough is smooth and elastic, place it in a large, lightly buttered bowl. Dust it with a sprinkling of flour and cover the bowl loosely with a kitchen towel. Let the dough rise in a warm, draft-free place for 45 minutes to an hour, or until the dough doubles its bulk and springs back slowly when gently poked with a finger. Then punch the dough down again with one blow of your fist to reduce it to its original volume. Let it rise 30 to 40 minutes until it again doubles in bulk.

OPPOSITE
*America's versatile, hearty corn can turn into this luscious, crisp-crusted, cornbread, sliced piping hot and topped by butter.*

Preheat the oven to 375°. Lightly but thoroughly butter a 9-by-5-by-3-inch loaf pan. Shape the dough into a compact loaf, somewhat high and round in the center, and place it in the pan. Cover with a towel and let the dough rise in the same warm place (about 25 minutes) until it reaches the top of the pan. Thoroughly brush the top of the loaf with the egg and milk glaze. Bake in the lower third of the oven for 30 to 40 minutes, or until the loaf is golden brown and a toothpick inserted in its center comes out clean and dry. Invert the bread on to a cake rack and cool before slicing.

To make one 9-by-5-by-3-inch loaf

½ cup lukewarm water (110° to 115°)

1 package active dry yeast

1 teaspoon sugar

¼ cup dark molasses

½ cup lukewarm milk (110° to 115°)

2 to 2½ cups whole-wheat flour

1 cup unsifted all-purpose flour

1 teaspoon salt

4 tablespoons butter, cut into ½-inch bits and softened, plus 2 tablespoons butter, softened

1 egg lightly beaten with 1 tablespoon milk

Pour the lukewarm water into a small bowl and sprinkle in the yeast and sugar. Let the yeast and sugar rest for 2 or 3 minutes, then mix well. Set the bowl in a warm, draft-free place (such as an unlighted oven) for about 10 minutes, or until the yeast bubbles up and the mixture almost doubles in volume.

Pour the molasses into the milk and stir until well blended. Then place 2 cups of whole-wheat flour, the cup of all-purpose flour and the salt in a deep mixing bowl and make a well in the center. Pour in the yeast and the molasses-and-milk mixtures and, with a large wooden spoon, gradually incorporate the dry ingredients into the liquid ones. Stir until the mixture is smooth, then beat in the 4 tablespoons of butter bits, a few teaspoonfuls at a time. Continue to beat until the dough can be gathered into a medium-soft ball.

Place the ball on a lightly floured surface and knead, pushing the dough down with the heels of your hands, pressing it forward and folding it back on itself. As you knead, sprinkle whole-wheat flour over the ball by the tablespoonful, adding up to ½ cup flour if necessary to make a firm dough. Knead for about 10 minutes longer, until the dough is smooth and elastic.

With a pastry brush, spread 1 tablespoon of the softened butter evenly over the inside of a large bowl. Set the dough in the bowl and turn it about to butter the entire surface. Drape the bowl with a kitchen towel and set it aside in the draft-free place for 1 to 1½ hours, or until the dough doubles in volume.

Brush the remaining tablespoon of softened butter over the bottom and sides of a 9-by-5-by-3-inch loaf pan. Punch the dough down with a blow of your fist and, on a lightly floured surface, shape it into a loaf about 8 inches long and 4 inches wide. Place the dough in the buttered pan and set it in the draft-free place to rise again for about 45 minutes.

Preheat the oven to 450°. (If you have used the oven to let the bread rise, gently transfer the loaf to another warm place to rest while the oven heats.) Brush the top of the whole-wheat bread with the egg-and-milk mixture, then bake in the middle of the oven for 35 to 40 minutes, or until the loaf is golden brown. To test for doneness, turn the loaf out on a flat surface and rap the bottom sharply with your knuckles. The loaf should sound hollow; if not, slide it back into the pan and bake for 5 to 10 minutes longer.

Place the finished whole-wheat bread on a wire rack and let it cool before serving.

*A hot cranberry muffin, split in half, with dollops of butter, waits tantalizingly on a child's tin plate, a treat for any time of day.*

*Thousands of years before baking soda was discovered or commercial yeast became available, the ancient Egyptians made raised breads with sourdough, and sourdough "starters" have been bubbling away throughout the world ever since. In the United States, and particularly in the Far West, they impart a distinctive flavor and texture to waffles, pancakes and bread—most notably the great sourdough bread of San Francisco. Recipes for these foods and a pictorial guide to the preparation of sourdough bread are given on the following pages.*

*All these recipes must begin with the sourdough starter itself. Technically, the starter is a self-perpetuating leavening or fermenting agent composed of yeasts and bacteria, flour, water and sometimes sugar or other sweeteners. When added to a dough or batter, the starter makes the mixture rise. Part of the mixture is then set aside to become the starter for the next batch of dough or batter. Covered tightly and refrigerated, the starter may be stored for several weeks. If it is not used within that time, however, it must be freshened with additional flour and water (directions below). When used or freshened regularly, a starter keeps almost indefinitely—and its flavor improves with age.*

To make about 4 cups

| | |
|---|---|
| 3 cups all-purpose flour | 2½ cups lukewarm water (110° |
| 1 package active dry yeast | to 115°) |

Starting a day ahead, place the flour in a large glass mixing bowl. Make a well in the center and pour in the yeast and water. With a large spoon, gradually stir the flour into the yeast and water, continuing to stir until the ingredients are well combined. Then, with a whisk or a rotary or electric beater, beat vigorously until the mixture is completely smooth. Drape with a kitchen towel and set aside in a warm, draft-free spot (such as an unlighted oven) for 24 hours. If at the end of this time the starter has not bubbled, it must be discarded.

After you have used as much of the starter as you need, transfer the remaining starter to a glass jar or crock equipped with a tight-fitting lid. Covered and refrigerated, it can be stored for several weeks. If used regularly, it may keep indefinitely.

*This recipe was developed by amateur chef Joseph A. Flaherty, a resident of Port Washington, New York, but a regular visitor to California. Baking this bread is no casual undertaking. The first batch takes over 3 days fom start to finish, and successive batches require about 18 hours each.*

*For optimum results, the cook must improvise a counterpart to a baker's brick hearth oven by setting building bricks on the oven shelves; the cook should also make or purchase "proofing," or rising, trays, construct or improvise a proofing box in which the bread can rise, and purchase or make baker's "peels," or shovels, to transfer the bread to the oven. These devices are described more fully in the instructions below. The quantities of dough specified must be also weighed carefully on kitchen scales for best results.*

*This sourdough bread warrants the efforts expended. It is high in quality, and the loaves have the distinctive flavor, the springy texture, and the thick crisp crusts of their San Francisco prototype. This recipe may be doubled—if you have the strength to knead 6 pounds of dough.*

To make three 1-pound long loaves or two 1½-pound round loaves

BASIC SOURDOUGH BREAD STARTER
1 cup sourdough starter
¾ cup plus 2 tablespoons unsifted
hard-wheat bread flour,
preferably unbleached
1 teaspoon butter, softened

BASIC SOURDOUGH BREAD STARTER: Place the sourdough starter in a deep glass or ceramic mixing bowl, add 2 or 3 tablespoons of flour, and stir them together vigorously with a large wooden spoon. Repeat four or five more times until you have added ¾ cup of flour, and beat well after each addition. Continue to stir until the dough can be gathered into a stiff, though somewhat rough, ball.

Spread the remaining 2 tablespoons of flour on a breadboard, set the ball on top of it and knead—pressing the dough down, pushing it forward and folding it back on itself. Repeat for 10 minutes, until the dough is smooth and can be stretched about 3 inches without breaking.

Let the dough rest on the breadboard for about 5 minutes. Meanwhile, wash the mixing bowl, and with a pastry brush spread the inside with the 1 teaspoon of softened butter. Place the dough in the bowl and turn it about to butter the entire surface of the dough. Cover the bowl tightly with plastic wrap and set the dough aside in a warm (80°), draft-free place (such as an unlighted oven) for 8 hours. In this time the starter will double or even triple in volume and will be fully developed.

The bread starter will weigh about 11 ounces. It can be used immediately, or all or part of the starter can be punched down and stored in a tightly covered nonmetallic container in the refrigerator until the next batch of bread is to be baked. The starter can be held in this state in the refrigerator for up to one month, but do not freeze it. It should be freshened each time bread is baked and will last for years if freshened regularly.

SOURDOUGH STARTER SPONGE

| | |
|---|---|
| 4 ounces basic sourdough bread starter (*see above*) | 1 cup unsifted hard-wheat bread flour, preferably unbleached |
| ¼ cup warm water (90°) | 1 teaspoon butter, softened |

SOURDOUGH STARTER SPONGE: For the second, and each successive batch of sourdough bread, a starter "sponge" must be set the night before and allowed to ferment and develop for 8 to 10 hours. In baking, a sponge is rising dough; it gets its name from its cellular, "spongy" texture. In this instance, the sponge is a small amount of rising dough that is used as the base and leavening agent for the bread.

To prepare the sponge, cut off 4 ounces of the basic starter and stretch it with your hands five or six times. Break it into four small pieces and drop them into ¼ cup of warm (90°) water in a glass or ceramic mixing bowl. Add ¼ cup of flour and stir together vigorously with a large wooden spoon. Repeat until you have added ¾ cup of flour and beat well after each addition. Continue to stir the dough until it can be gathered into a stiff, somewhat rough, ball.

Spread 2 tablespoons of flour smoothly on a large breadboard. Set the ball on top of it and knead—pressing the dough down with the heels of your hands, pushing it forward 6 to 8 inches, and folding it back on itself. As you knead, gradually incorporate 2 tablespoons more flour as necessary, to prevent the dough from sticking to the board. Knead the dough for 5 to 10 minutes, until it is smooth and elastic enough for one edge to be stretched about 3 inches without breaking.

Let the dough rest on the breadboard for 5 minutes. Meanwhile, wash the mixing bowl, and with a pastry brush spread the inside with 1 teaspoon of softened butter. Place the dough in the bowl and turn it about to butter the entire surface. Cover the bowl tightly with plastic wrap and set it aside in a warm (80°), draft-free place for 8 to 10 hours.

The next morning, the sponge will have doubled or tripled in bulk. Mix the sourdough bread dough starting with this fully developed starter sponge. The starter sponge will weigh about 11 ounces.

SOURDOUGH BREAD DOUGH
5 ounces basic sourdough starter
   or starter sponge
2 cups warm water (90°)
7 cups unsifted hard-wheat bread
   flour, preferably unbleached

1 tablespoon salt
1 teaspoon butter, softened
¼ to ⅓ cup rice flour
2 to 3 tablespoons yellow cornmeal
1 egg white lightly beaten with
   2 tablespoons water

SOURDOUGH BREAD DOUGH: Cut off 5 ounces of fully developed basic sourdough bread starter or starter sponge. (Refrigerate the remaining starter or sponge in a tightly covered nonmetallic container to serve as starter for the next batch.) Pour 2 cups of warm (90°) water into a heavy 6-quart ceramic mixing bowl. Break the 5 ounces of starter or sponge into 12 small pieces, dropping them into the water as you proceed.

Stirring the mixture constantly with a large wooden spoon, slowly sprinkle in ½ cup of flour. Add 1 level tablespoon of salt. (Be precise; even a small amount of extra salt will severely inhibit the rising power of the sourdough.) Then add 5½ cups more flour, ½ cup at a time, mixing well with your hands after each addition. Continue to mix until the dough can be gathered into a rough, though somewhat sticky, ball. Spread 2 tablespoons of the remaining cup of flour on a breadboard and reserve the rest. Place the dough on the board and knead—pushing it down, pressing it forward 6 to 8 inches and folding it back on itself. As you knead, gradually incorporate flour from the reserved cup, sprinkling it over and under the dough by the tablespoonful and adding only as much as you need to make a nonsticky dough.

Continue kneading vigorously for at least 20 minutes, until the dough is smooth, satiny and elastic. This long kneading time is important to expand the gluten in the flour so that the loaves will hold their shape throughout the long proofing, or rising, process.

Let the dough rest for 5 minutes while you clean the bowl. Brush the bowl with 1 teaspoon of softened butter. Place the dough in the bowl and turn it about to butter the entire surface. Cover the bowl tightly with plastic wrap and set it in a warm (80°), draft-free place for one hour.

The sourdough will *not* rise significantly during this first hour. It should not increase much in volume at this point because natural sourdough yeast will not maintain its rising action through multiple proofings.

PREPARING THE OVEN: Arrange the racks of your oven so that one is about 4 inches from the bottom floor and a second about 4 inches from the top. Cover each rack with common building bricks with the flat side up—each rack should hold about 8 to 10 bricks. Set the oven regulator to 400° and preheat the bricks. It may take up to 3 hours for the bricks to reach this temperature. Bricks are essential to hold the oven temperature even and to give the loaves the intense, even heat necessary for them to attain the proper shape at the onset of the baking.

SHAPING AND PROOFING THE LOAVES: Return the dough to the bread-board and with a large sharp knife cut off 2 ounces and add them to the refrigerated starter to refresh it. Then cut the dough in half if you wish to make round loaves, or into thirds for long loaves. Weigh each piece. The halves should each weigh about 1½ pounds; the thirds should each weigh about 1 pound. Any extra dough should be added to the refrigerated starter; if there is too much for the container, discard the excess.

Shape each piece of dough into a smooth ball. Sprinkle 1 tablespoon of rice flour on the breadboard and set the balls of dough on it, cover them with plastic wrap, and let them rest for 15 minutes.

San Francisco sourdough bread is not baked in pans and tends to flatten and lose its shape unless properly formed and proofed. The long loaves are proofed on special divided trays. *( Metal proofing trays are available ready-made. )*

The round loaves are proofed on a breadboard large enough to hold them. Remember that they will expand as they rise, so allow ample space between the loaves. Before shaping the dough into loaves, spread a pastry cloth or a heavy linen towel over the appropriate proofing tray and sprinkle the cloth evenly with 2 to 3 tablespoons of rice flour.

Following the directions on pages 360 and 361, shape the balls of dough into cylindrical or round loaves. Arrange the loaves on the cloth-lined proofing trays and set them aside in a warm (80°), draft-free place next to a pan of warm water. Cover the trays and pan with an inverted cardboard box. High humidity is essential to proper proofing. Without it, the loaves may dry out or develop tough crusts.

*To control the temperature and humidity more exactly, the dough should be allowed to rise, or "proof," in a closed box with an interior temperature of 80° and a relative humidity of 90 per cent.*

The loaves must rise slowly to allow fermentation to develop the sour flavor so typical of sourdough bread. The proofing will take 3 to 4 hours at 80°. After 3½ hours, when the loaves have at least doubled in volume, poke a hole about ½ inch deep into the side of a loaf with your fingertip. If the dough is properly proofed, the loaf will slowly return to its original shape. (If the dough does not spring back, the loaves are overproofing and should be baked at once.)

BAKING THE BREAD: About 10 minutes before baking the bread, place a shallow pan on the hot floor of the oven, or, if the oven is electric, directly on top of the bottom heating coil. Pour boiling water into the pan and let the steam saturate the oven. Remove the proofing trays from the proofing box and let the loaves rest at room temperature for 5 minutes. Just before baking, increase the oven temperature to 425° and add more boiling water to the pan. Steam is essential for the baking.

Sprinkle a round baker's peel slightly larger than each round loaf with 1 tablespoon of the cornmeal. Slip both hands gently under one loaf and carefully lift it onto the peel. With a single-edge razor blade or the razor-edged device shown on page 362, cut four intersecting lines in a square pattern on top of each round loaf as shown.

Slide the peel into the oven across the bricks and quickly jerk it out from under the loaf. Sprinkle the peel again with 1 tablespoon of cornmeal and repeat the procedure with the second round loaf.

To transfer a long loaf from the proofing tray, you will need two peels, each 18 inches long and about 5 inches wide. Sprinkle one of the peels with 1 tablespoon of cornmeal and dust the other lightly with rice flour. Hold the peel covered with rice flour next to the loaf, as shown on page 148. Tip the loaf onto the peel by lifting one edge of the pastry cloth and then turn the loaf over onto the cornmeal-covered peel.

With a razor blade, cut four 3-inch-long overlapping diagonal slashes in the top of each loaf as shown on page 362. Slide the peel lengthwise into the oven directly over the bricks and quickly jerk it back out from under the loaf so that the bread bakes directly on the bricks. Repeat the procedure until all of the loaves are in the oven, sprinkling the peels with 1 tablespoon of cornmeal and 1 tablespoon of rice flour each time.

Bake the loaves for 15 minutes, then lower the oven temperature to 375° and continue baking for 15 minutes longer. Slide the loaves out of the oven on a peel, one at a time, and brush the tops lightly with the mixture of egg white and water. Bake the loaves for about 10 minutes longer, or until the crusts are crisp and a rich golden-brown color and the loaves sound hollow when thumped on the bottom. Use the peels to remove the bread from the oven and transfer the loaves to wire racks to cool.

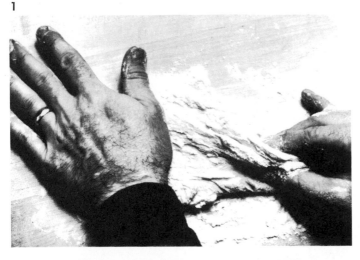

**TEXTURE BEGINS WITH THE BREAD STARTER**

*To expand the gluten in the flour, make the dough elastic and ensure a smooth-textured loaf, the sourdough bread starter must be well kneaded. (1) Holding an edge of the dough in one hand, press the dough flat and push it forward about 6 inches with the heel of your other hand. Then fold the dough back on itself. (2) Repeat for 10 minutes, until the dough can stretch 3 inches without breaking.*

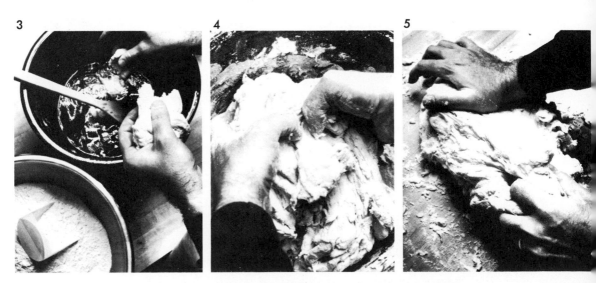

**KNEADING TO MAKE THE BREAD DOUGH STRONG AND LIGHT**

*After the starter doubles in volume, (3) pour warm water into a bowl and drop in the starter, a bit at a time. (4) Add salt and flour (see recipe for proportions) and mix with your hands until you can gather the dough into a ball. (5) Place the dough on a board and knead vigorously for 20 minutes.*

358

## A San Francisco Sourdough Bread
## You Can Make in Your Own Kitchen

*The ingredients for San Francisco sourdough bread are few: sourdough starter, hard-wheat bread flour (preferably unbleached), warm water and salt. A complete recipe for the bread appears in this chapter, but its success depends upon attention to detail. The starter must be active and bubbly. Only bread flour milled with hard wheat will produce a dough strong enough to keep its shape and encapsulate the gases that ensure a light-textured crumb. The water must be 90°: warmer water may kill the yeast in the starter; colder water will retard or prevent the growth of the yeast. Even the salt must be measured precisely—too much can slow or stop the rising process. Once mixed, the dough must be kneaded long and vigorously to develop elasticity. After it rises (or is proofed), the dough must be shaped carefully and the loaves treated gingerly. The pictures on these and the following pages will help you to master the techniques, from the first kneading to the finished loaf.*

*When the dough is fully kneaded, it will appear smooth and satiny. Place it in a buttered bowl, cover tightly and set the dough in a warm, draft-free place for an hour. Do not allow the dough to double in volume: overrising at this stage will exhaust the leavening power of the sourdough. Cut the dough in half if you plan to make round loaves (left), into thirds for long loaves. The cut surfaces will appear porous, as shown at left.*

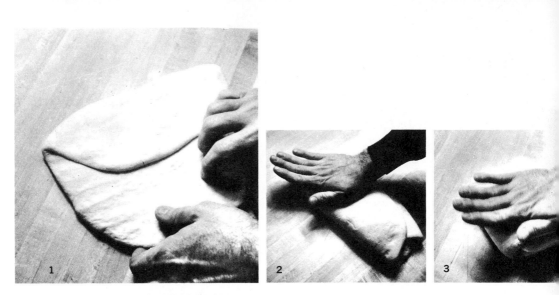

**FIRST STEPS IN SHAPING A SOURDOUGH LOAF**

*For each loaf, place a half or third of the dough on an unfloured surface and, with your hands, pound it into a flat round about ½ inch thick. (1) Fold down the top third of the round and pound it hard. (2) Then turn the bottom third up to overlap the top and pound again. (3) Fold both ends into the middle, overlapping them to make a square, and pound after each fold.*

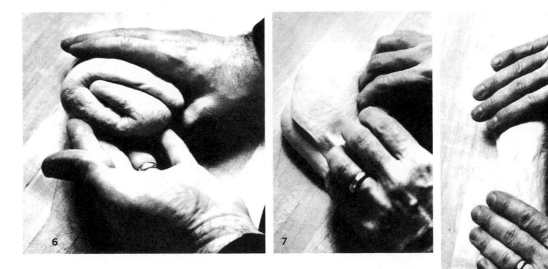

5

**SHAPING A ROUND SOURDOUGH LOAF**

*(4) Hold the square of dough seam side down and, with both hands, turn the ends under. (5) Smooth down the top and sides, and turn the dough between your hands for a minute or two, pressing firmly to form a tight, even ball with all the rough edges securely tucked beneath it. Place the loaf gently on a breadboard covered with a pastry cloth sprinkled with rice flour.*

**SHAPING A LONG SOURDOUGH LOAF**

*(6) Place the square of dough* (step 3, above) *on the board with one folded end toward you and (7), starting with the folded end, roll the square into a tight cyclinder. (8) Turn the dough seam side down and, with your hands in the center, roll it back and forth. Gradually move your hands to the ends to elongate the loaf. Repeat, pressing firmly to force out air bubbles, until (9) the loaf is about 17 inches long and 1½ inches in diameter and tapers at both ends.*

361

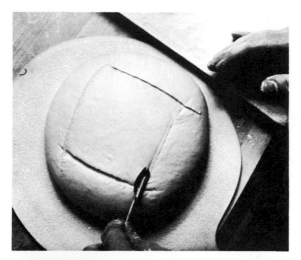

## BAKING ROUND LOAVES
*Pick up one loaf at a time, and set it on a round, cornmeal-covered baker's peel, or shovel. Cut four intersecting slits in the top and slide the loaf into the oven. After 30 minutes, brush each loaf with a mixture of egg white and water for the final baking.*

## BAKING LONG LOAVES
*To slide the loaves into the oven, you need two long baker's "peels," or shovels. Sprinkle one peel with rice flour, the other with cornmeal. Place the peel coated with rice flour at one side of a long loaf and lift the pastry cloth to turn the loaf over onto the peel. Set the meal-covered peel next to the loaf and tip the loaf upside down onto it. Slit the loaf with four 3-inch-long gashes, using a single-edged razor blade or a double-edged blade fitted onto the end of a popsicle stick. Slide the loaf into the oven. Bake for 30 minutes, brush with a mixture of egg white and water and bake 10 minutes more.*

To make 12 rolls

| | |
|---|---|
| 1 tablespoon sugar | 1 cup sourdough starter* |
| 1 package active dry yeast | 3½ to 4 cups all-purpose flour |
| 1¼ cups lukewarm water (110° to 115°) | 1 tablespoon butter, softened |

In a small, shallow bowl, sprinkle the sugar and yeast over ¼ cup of the lukewarm water. Let the mixture stand for 2 to 3 minutes, then stir once or twice and set the bowl in a warm, draft-free spot (such as an unlighted oven) for about 5 minutes, or until the mixture bubbles and almost doubles in volume.

Place the sourdough starter in a large glass or ceramic mixing bowl and pour in the yeast mixture. Add the remaining cup of lukewarm water and 1½ cups of the flour and stir with a large spoon until all of the ingredients are well combined. Then drape with a kitchen towel and set aside in the warm, draft-free place for about 2 hours, or until the mixture bubbles and doubles in volume.

Stir the mixture briefly with a large spoon. Remove 1 cup and refrigerate it in a tightly sealed glass jar or crock, to be used as your new sourdough starter. Or add it to any sourdough starter you may have left.

To the mixture remaining in the bowl gradually add 2 to 2½ cups of the remaining flour, beating vigorously after each addition and using only enough of the flour to make it firm enough to be gathered into a ball. On a heavily floured surface, knead the dough by pushing it down with the heels of your hands, pressing it forward, and folding it back on itself. Continue the kneading for about 10 minutes, or until the dough is smooth and elastic. Sprinkle it from time to time with a little flour to prevent it from sticking to the board.

Shape the dough into a ball and place it in a lightly buttered bowl. Drape with a towel and set aside in the warm, draft-free place for about 1 hour, or until the dough doubles in volume.

Preheat the oven to 375°. With a pastry brush, spread a large baking sheet with the tablespoon of softened butter. Punch the dough down with a single blow of your fist and with a large, sharp knife cut it into 12 equal parts. Shape the dough gently into balls and flatten them slightly with your hands. Place the balls about 2 inches apart on the prepared baking sheet. Bake in the center of the oven for 20 to 25 minutes, or until golden brown and crisp. Serve the rolls at once.

* *See index.*

## Sally Lunn *(South)*

To make one 10-inch loaf

| | |
|---|---|
| ¼ cup lukewarm water (110° to 115°) | ¾ cup lukewarm milk (110° to 115°) |
| 1 package active dry yeast | 3 eggs |
| 1 tablespoon plus ¼ cup sugar | 12 tablespoons butter, softened and |
| 4 to 4½ cups flour | cut into ½-inch bits, plus 2 |
| 2 teaspoons salt | tablespoons butter, softened |

Pour the lukewarm water into a small bowl and sprinkle the yeast and 1 tablespoon of the sugar over it. Let the mixture rest for 3 minutes, then mix. Set the bowl in a warm, draft-free place (such as an unlighted oven) for 10 minutes, or until the mixture almost doubles in volume.

Combine 4 cups of the flour, the remaining ¼ cup of sugar and the salt and sift them together into a deep bowl. Make a well in the center and into it pour the yeast, lukewarm milk and eggs. With a wooden spoon, gradually incorporate the dry ingredients into the liquid ones and stir until smooth. Beat in the 12 tablespoons of butter bits, a little at a time, and beat until the dough can be gathered into a compact ball. Place the dough on a lightly floured surface and knead by pushing it down with the heels of your hands, pressing it forward and folding it back on itself. As you knead, work in up to ½ cup more flour, sprinkling it over the dough and adding only enough to make a firm dough. Knead for about 15 minutes, or until the dough is smooth, shiny and elastic.

With a pastry brush, spread 1 tablespoon of softened butter over the inside of a large bowl. Drop in the dough and turn it about to butter the entire surface. Drape the bowl with a kitchen towel and place it in the draft-free place for about 30 minutes, or until it doubles in volume.

Brush the remaining tablespoon of softened butter over the bottom and sides of a 10-inch Turk's-head mold. Punch the dough down with a single blow of your fist. Then shape it into a ball and place it in the buttered mold. Drape with a towel and set aside in the draft-free place for about 1 hour, or until the loaf doubles in bulk.

Preheat the oven to 350°. Bake in the middle of the oven for 45 to 50 minutes, or until the bread is golden brown. Turn the bread out of the mold and rap the bottom with your fingertips. If it does not sound hollow, return it to the mold and bake for 5 to 10 minutes longer. Turn the bread out on a wire cake rack and serve warm or at room temperature.

NOTE: If you prefer, Sally Lunn may be baked in muffin tins. Prepare the dough as described above and let it rise once. Brush 1 tablespoon of butter evenly over the inside surfaces of 16 three-inch muffin tin cups. Then punch the dough down, divide it into 16 equal portions and shape each of these into a small ball. Place the balls in the buttered muffin cups, drape with a towel and set them aside in a draft-free place for about 45 minutes, or until they double in bulk. Bake in the middle of a preheated 350° oven for 40 to 45 minutes, or until golden brown. Turn the buns out on a wire cake rack and serve warm or at room temperature.

## Anadama Bread *(New England)*

To make 2 one-pound loaves

½ cup yellow cornmeal
4 tablespoons butter, cut into
   ½-inch bits, plus 4 teaspoons
   butter, softened
½ cup dark molasses

1½ teaspoons salt
½ cup lukewarm water (110° to
   115°) plus 2 cups water
1 package active dry yeast
4 to 5 cups flour

In a heavy 1- to 1½-quart saucepan, bring the 2 cups of water to a boil over high heat. Pour in the cornmeal in a slow, thin stream, stirring the mixture constantly with a wooden spoon so that the water continues to boil. Cook briskly for a minute or so, then remove the pan from the heat and beat in the 4 tablespoons of butter bits, the molasses and salt. Pour the cornmeal mixture into a deep bowl and cool to lukewarm. Meanwhile, pour the ½ cup of lukewarm water into a small bowl and sprinkle the yeast over it. Let the yeast rest for 2 or 3 minutes, then mix well. Set in a warm, draft-free place (such as an unlighted oven) for 10 minutes, or until the yeast bubbles up and the mixture almost doubles in volume. Add the yeast to the cornmeal mixture and mix well. Beat in about 4 cups of the flour, ½ cup at a time, and continue to beat until the dough can be gathered into a compact ball.

Place the ball on a lightly floured surface and knead, pushing the dough down with the heels of your hands, pressing it forward and folding it back on itself. As you knead, incorporate the remaining cup of flour, sprinkling it over the dough a few tablespoons at a time. Continue to knead for 10 minutes, or until the dough is smooth, shiny and elastic.

With a pastry brush, spread 2 teaspoons of the softened butter evenly over the inside of a large bowl. Place the dough in the bowl and turn the ball about to coat the entire surface. Drape the bowl with a kitchen towel and put it in the draft-free place for about 1½ hours, or until the dough doubles in volume.

Brush the remaining 2 teaspoons of softened butter over the bottoms and sides of two small (6½-by-2¾-by-2-inch) loaf pans. Punch the dough down with a single blow of your fist, knead for 2 or 3 minutes, then divide it in half. Pat and shape each half into a rectangular loaf and place it in a buttered pan. Put the loaves in the draft-free place for about 40 minutes longer, or until the dough rises to the tops of the pans.

Preheat the oven to 400°. Bake the bread in the middle of the oven for

1 hour, or until the crust is a light brown color and the loaves begin to shrink away from the sides of the pans. Turn the loaves out onto wire racks to cool to lukewarm or room temperature before serving.

## Mormon Rye Bread  (Far West)

To make one 9-by-5-by-3-inch loaf

1 cup lukewarm water (110° to 115°)
1 package active dry yeast
1 teaspoon granulated sugar
1 cup rye flour
2½ to 3 cups unsifted all-purpose flour

¼ cup dark brown sugar
1 teaspoon salt
¼ cup honey
½ cup vegetable shortening, cut into ½-inch bits and softened
2 tablespoons butter, softened
1 egg, beaten lightly with 1 tablespoon milk

Pour ¼ cup of the lukewarm water into a small bowl and sprinkle the yeast and granulated sugar over it. Let the yeast and sugar rest for 2 or 3 minutes, then mix well. Set in a warm, draft-free place (such as an un-lighted oven) for about 10 minutes, or until the yeast bubbles up and the mixture almost doubles in volume.

Place the rye flour, 2 cups of all-purpose flour, the brown sugar and salt in a deep mixing bowl and make a well in the center. Add the yeast mixture, the remaining ¾ cup of lukewarm water, the honey and vege-table-shortening bits. With a large spoon, gradually incorporate the dry ingredients into the liquid ones and continue to stir until the mixture is smooth and can be gathered into a medium-soft ball. If the dough be-comes too stiff to stir easily, mix it with your hands.

Transfer the ball to a lightly floured surface and knead, pushing the dough down with the heels of your hands, pressing it forward and fold-ing it back on itself. Incorporate up to 1 cup more all-purpose flour by the tablespoonful as you knead, adding only enough to make a smooth dough that is no longer sticky. Then continue kneading for about 10 min-utes, until the dough is smooth and elastic.

With a pastry brush, spread 1 tablespoon of the softened butter evenly inside a large bowl. Place the dough in the bowl and turn the ball about to butter the entire surface. Drape the bowl with a kitchen towel and set it aside in the warm, draft-free place for approximately 1½ hours, or until the dough doubles in volume.

Brush the remaining tablespoon of softened butter over the bottom and sides of a 9-by-5-by-3-inch loaf pan. Punch the dough down with a blow of your fist and, on a lightly floured surface, shape the dough into a loaf about 8 inches long and 4 inches wide. Place the loaf in the buttered pan and set it in the warm, draft-free place for about 45 minutes, or until it has doubled in volume.

Preheat the oven to 375°. (If you have used the oven to let the loaf rise, gently transfer it to another warm place to rest while the oven heats.) Brush the loaf with the egg-and-milk mixture and bake in the middle of the oven for 30 to 35 minutes, or until the top is golden brown. To test for doneness, turn the loaf out and rap the bottom sharply with your knuckles. The loaf should sound hollow; if not, return it to the pan and bake for 5 to 10 minutes longer. Place the Mormon rye bread on a wire rack and cool completely to room temperature before serving.

## *Dilly Bread* (Eastern Heartland)

To make one 9-by-5-by-3-inch loaf

| | |
|---|---|
| ¼ cup lukewarm water (110° to 115°) | ¼ teaspoon baking soda |
| 1 package active dry yeast | 1 teaspoon salt |
| 1 teaspoon plus 2 tablespoons sugar | 1 cup large-curd cottage cheese (8 ounces) |
| 1 tablespoon butter, cut into ¼-inch bits, plus 3 tablespoons butter, softened | 1 egg |
| | 2 teaspoons dill seed |
| 2 tablespoons finely chopped onions | 1 egg lightly beaten with 1 tablespoon milk |
| 2 to 2½ cups unsifted flour | Coarse (kosher) salt |

Pour the lukewarm water into a small bowl and add the yeast and 1 teaspoon of the sugar. Let the yeast and sugar rest for 2 or 3 minutes, then mix well. Set in a warm, draft-free place (such as an unlighted oven) for about 10 minutes, or until the yeast bubbles up and the mixture almost doubles in volume.

Meanwhile, melt the tablespoon of butter bits over moderate heat in a small skillet. When the foam begins to subside, add the onions and, stirring frequently, cook for 2 or 3 minutes, until they are soft but not brown. Set aside.

Combine 2 cups of the flour, the remaining 2 tablespoons of sugar, the baking soda and salt, and sift them together into a deep mixing bowl. Make a well in the center and scrape in the entire contents of the skillet. Add the yeast mixture, the cottage cheese, egg and dill seed, and gradually incorporate the dry ingredients into the liquid ones with a large wooden spoon. Continue to stir until the dough is smooth and can be gathered into a medium-soft ball.

Place the ball on a lightly floured surface and knead, pushing the dough down with the heels of your hands, pressing it forward and folding it back on itself. As you knead, sprinkle flour over the ball by the

367

tablespoonful, adding up to ½ cup more flour if necessary to make a firm dough. Knead for about 10 minutes longer, until the dough is smooth, shiny and elastic.

With a pastry brush, spread 1 tablespoon of the softened butter evenly over the inside of a large bowl. Set the ball of dough in the bowl and turn it about to butter the entire surface. Drape the bowl loosely with a kitchen towel and set it aside in the draft-free place for about 1 hour, or until it has doubled in volume.

Brush 1 tablespoon of the remaining softened butter over the bottom and sides of a 9-by-5-by-3-inch loaf pan. Punch the dough down with a blow of your fist and, on a lightly floured surface, shape it into a loaf about 8 inches long and 4 inches wide. Place the dough in the buttered pan and set it in the draft-free place to rise again for about 45 minutes.

Preheat the oven to 375°. (If you have used the oven to let the bread rise, gently transfer the loaf to another warm place to rest while the oven heats.) Brush the top of the bread with the egg-and-milk mixture, then bake in the middle of the oven for 30 to 35 minutes, or until the loaf is golden brown. To test for doneness, turn the loaf out on a flat surface and rap the bottom sharply with your knuckles. The loaf should sound hollow; if not, put it back in the pan and bake for 5 to 10 minutes longer.

Place the bread on a wire rack and brush the top with the remaining tablespoon of softened butter. Sprinkle lightly with coarse salt and let the bread cool before serving.


## Salt-rising Bread (Eastern Heartland)

To make two 9-by-5-by-3-inch loaves

| | |
|---|---|
| ½ cup stone-ground cornmeal | 1 tablespoon salt |
| 4 cups milk | 9 to 9½ cups unsifted flour |
| 5 tablespoons vegetable shortening, cut into ¼-inch bits | 2 tablespoons butter, softened |
| 1 tablespoon sugar | 1 egg lightly beaten with 1 tablespoon milk |

Starting a day ahead, measure the cornmeal into a heatproof bowl. Then heat 1 cup of the milk in a small saucepan until bubbles begin to form around the sides of the pan. Pour the milk over the cornmeal and stir to a smooth paste. Set the bowl in a warm draft-free place (such as an unlighted oven) overnight, or until the cornmeal mixture ferments and develops a strong cheeselike odor.

Place the bits of shortening, the sugar and salt in a mixing bowl 12 inches in diameter across the top. At the same time, pour water to a depth of 2 or 3 inches into a pot or saucepan 12 inches in diameter. The rim of the bowl should fit snugly over the rim of the pot; the pot must be deep enough so that the bottom of the bowl will be suspended above the water. Bring the water to a boil over high heat, then remove the pot from the stove and cover tightly to keep the water hot.

In a heavy 1- to 2-quart saucepan, heat the remaining 3 cups of milk until bubbles form around the sides of the pan. Pour the milk over the shortening and stir until the sugar and salt dissolve. Add 3½ cups of the flour and, when it is incorporated, stir in the cornmeal mixture.

Set the bowl over the pot of water and drape the top with a kitchen towel. Let the dough rise for about 2 hours, or until bubbles form on its surface. The water under the bowl must be kept at least lukewarm; check the pot occasionally and replenish with boiling water if necessary.

When the dough has fermented, remove the bowl from the pot. Stir in up to 6 cups more flour, 1 cup at a time, to make a firm ball. If the dough becomes difficult to stir, work in the remaining flour with your hands.

Place the dough on a lightly floured surface and knead it by pressing the dough down with the heels of your hands, pushing it forward and folding it back on itself. Repeat for about 20 minutes, until the dough is smooth and elastic.

With a pastry brush, spread the softened butter evenly over the bottom and sides of two 9-by-5-by-3-inch loaf pans. Divide the dough in half and shape each piece into a loaf about 8 inches long and 4 inches wide. Place the loaves in the buttered pans and set them aside in the draft-free place for 2 hours, or until the dough rises and the loaves double in bulk.

Preheat the oven to 400°. (If you have used the oven to let the bread rise, gently transfer the loaves to another warm place to rest while the oven heats.) Brush the tops of the loaves with the egg-and-milk mixture and bake in the middle of the oven for 10 minutes. Reduce the oven temperature to 350° and continue baking for 25 to 30 minutes longer, or until the bread is golden brown. To test for doneness, turn the loaves out on a flat surface and rap the bottoms sharply with your knuckles. The loaves should sound hollow; if not, slide them back into the pans and bake for 5 to 10 minutes more.

Place the bread on wire racks and let it cool before serving.

## Cheese Bread (Northwest)

To make one 8-inch round loaf

¼ cup lukewarm water (110° to 115°)
1 package active dry yeast
1 tablespoon sugar
2½ to 3½ cups flour
1 tablespoon salt
1 cup lukewarm milk (110° to 115°)

3 tablespoons butter, cut into ½-inch bits and softened, plus 2 tablespoons butter, softened
¾ cup freshly grated sharp Cheddar cheese
1 egg yolk
2 tablespoons heavy cream

Pour the lukewarm water into a small shallow bowl and sprinkle the yeast and sugar on top. Let the mixture stand for 2 or 3 minutes, then mix well. Set the bowl in a warm, draft-free place (such as an unlighted oven) for about 10 minutes, until the mixture almost doubles in bulk.

Combine 2½ cups of flour and the salt in a deep bowl and make a well in the center. Pour the yeast mixture and milk into the well and, with a large wooden spoon, gradually incorporate the dry ingredients into the liquid ones. Beat until the dough is smooth, then stir in the 3 tablespoons of butter bits.

Gather the dough into a ball and place it on a lightly floured surface. Knead the dough by pushing it down with the heels of your hands, pressing it forward, and folding it back on itself. Repeat for about 10 minutes, meanwhile sprinkling in up to 1 cup more flour, adding it by the tablespoonful and using only enough to make a smooth, elastic dough.

With a pastry brush, spread 1 tablespoon of the softened butter inside a deep bowl. Place the dough in the bowl and grease it on all sides by turning it about in the bowl. Drape loosely with a kitchen towel and set aside in the warm, draft-free place for about 45 minutes, or until the dough doubles in volume.

Brush the remaining tablespoon of softened butter over the bottom and sides of an 8-inch cake pan. Punch the dough down with a single blow of your fist, add the grated cheese and knead it in thoroughly. On a lightly floured surface, pat and shape the dough into a round loaf 7 or 8 inches in diameter. Place the loaf in the buttered pan and set it aside in the warm, draft-free spot for about 45 minutes longer, or until the dough has doubled in volume.

Preheat the oven to 400°. With a wire whisk, beat the egg yolk and cream together until well blended. Brush the egg-and-cream mixture over the loaf and bake in the middle of the oven for 20 minutes. Reduce the oven temperature to 350° and continue baking for another 15 to 20 minutes, or until the cheese bread is golden brown and sounds hollow when turned out and tapped sharply on the bottom with a finger. Let the bread cool on a wire rack and serve it at room temperature.

To make two 8-inch-round loaves

¾ cup sugar

⅓ cup lukewarm water (110° to 115°)

6 to 6½ cups flour

1 teaspoon salt

¼ cup lukewarm milk (110° to 115°) plus 2 tablespoons cold milk

8 eggs

14 tablespoons butter, cut into ½-inch bits, plus 4 teaspoons butter, softened

2 packages active dry yeast

Pour the lukewarm water and milk into a small bowl and sprinkle the yeast and a pinch of the sugar over them. Let the yeast and sugar stand for 2 or 3 minutes, then mix well. Set in a warm, draft-free place (such as an unlighted oven) for about 10 minutes, or until the yeast bubbles up and the mixture almost doubles in volume.

Place 5 cups of flour, the remaining sugar and the salt in a deep mixing bowl and make a well in the center. Pour the yeast into the well, add the eggs and, with a large wooden spoon, gradually incorporate the dry ingredients into the liquid ones. Stir until the mixture is smooth, then beat in the 14 tablespoons of butter bits, a few tablespoonfuls at a time. Continue to beat until the dough can be gathered into a compact ball.

Place the ball on a lightly floured surface and knead, pushing the dough down with the heels of your hands, pressing it forward and folding it back on itself. As you knead, incorporate up to 1½ cups more flour, sprinkling it over the dough a few tablespoonfuls at a time. Knead for 15 to 20 minutes, or until the dough is smooth, shiny and elastic.

With a pastry brush, spread 2 teaspoons of softened butter evenly over the inside of a large bowl. Set the dough in the bowl and turn it about to butter the entire surface. Drape the bowl with a towel and put it in the draft-free place for about 1 hour, or until the dough doubles in volume.

Brush the remaining two teaspoons of softened butter over a large baking sheet. Punch the dough down with a single blow of your fist and divide it into two equal portions. Pat and shape each portion into a round loaf about 7 inches in diameter and 2½ inches thick. Place the 2 loaves 2 inches apart on the buttered sheet, and drape them with a towel. Set the baking sheet aside in the draft-free place again for about 1 hour, or until the loaves double in volume.

Preheat the oven to 350°. Brush the top and sides of the loaves with the 2 tablespoons of cold milk. Bake in the middle of the oven for about 45 minutes, or until the bread is golden brown. Slide the loaves onto wire racks and let them cool to room temperature before serving.

## Mormon Johnnycake (Far West)

To make one 9-by-9-inch cake

| | |
|---|---|
| 1 tablespoon butter, softened, plus 2 tablespoons butter, melted and cooled | 2 tablespoons honey |
| | ½ cup unsifted flour |
| | 1 teaspoon baking soda |
| 2 eggs | 1 teaspoon salt |
| 2 cups buttermilk | 2 cups yellow cornmeal |

Preheat the oven to 425°. With a pastry brush, spread the tablespoon of softened butter evenly over the bottom and sides of a 9-by-9-by-2-inch baking dish. Set the dish aside.

In a deep mixing bowl, beat the eggs to a froth with a wire whisk. Beat in the buttermilk and honey, then add the flour, baking soda and salt. When the batter is smooth, beat in the cornmeal about ½ cup at a time. Stir in the 2 tablespoons of cooled melted butter and pour the batter into the buttered dish, spreading it evenly and smoothing the top with a rubber spatula.

Bake the johnnycake in the middle of the oven for about 20 minutes, or until the cake begins to pull away from the sides of the dish and the top is golden brown and crusty. Serve the Mormon johnnycake at once, directly from the baking dish.

## Leola's Cornbread (South)

To make one 9-inch loaf

| | |
|---|---|
| 1½ cups yellow cornmeal | 2 eggs |
| 1 cup all-purpose flour | 6 tablespoons melted and cooled butter |
| ⅓ cup sugar | 8 tablespoons melted and cooled vegetable shortening |
| 1 teaspoon salt | |
| 1 tablespoon baking powder | 1½ cups milk |

Preheat the oven to 400°. Sift into a mixing bowl the cornmeal, flour, sugar, salt and baking powder. Beat the eggs lightly, add the melted butter and shortening, and stir in the 1½ cups of milk. Pour into the bowl of dry ingredients and beat together for about a minute, or until smooth. Do not overbeat. Lightly butter an 8-by-12-inch shallow baking pan and pour in the batter. Bake in the center of the oven for about 30 minutes, or until the bread comes slightly away from the edge of the pan and is golden brown. Serve hot.

NOTE: If you wish you may bake the cornbread in a 9-by-5-by-3-inch loaf pan. Increase the baking time to 45 minutes.

To make 12 buns

| | |
|---|---|
| 1 package active dry yeast | ¼ teaspoon salt |
| Pinch sugar | 2 egg yolks |
| ½ cup lukewarm water (110° to 115°) | 1 teaspoon grated lemon rind |
| | 1 teaspoon cinnamon |
| 1 cup milk | ½ cup currants or raisins |
| 8 tablespoons melted butter (1 quarter-pound stick) | ½ cup water |
| | 1½ cups brown sugar, packed down |
| ½ cup sugar | 4 tablespoons butter |
| 3½ cups all-purpose flour | ½ cup coarsely chopped walnuts |

Sprinkle the yeast and a pinch of sugar into the lukewarm water. Let the mixture stand for 2 to 3 minutes, then stir it to dissolve the yeast. Set the container in a warm, draft-free place, such as an unlighted oven, for 5 to 8 minutes, or until the solution has begun to bubble and has almost doubled in volume.

Pour the milk into a heavy 1-quart saucepan and warm it over medium heat until bubbles form around the edge of the pan. Turn the heat to low and add 4 tablespoons of the butter and ¼ cup of the sugar. Stir constantly until the sugar dissolves, then cool to lukewarm and combine with the yeast mixture.

Sift the flour and salt into a deep mixing bowl. Make a well in the flour and pour into it the yeast and milk mixture, the egg yolks and the teaspoon of lemon rind. With your hands or a large wooden spoon, work the flour into the other ingredients until they become a medium-firm dough.

On a lightly floured surface, knead the dough by folding it end to end, then pressing it down and pushing it forward several times with the heel of your hand. Sprinkle the dough with a little extra flour whenever necessary to prevent it from sticking to the board. Repeat the kneading process until the dough becomes smooth and elastic. This will take about 10 minutes.

Shape the dough into a ball and put it in a large, lightly buttered bowl. Dust the top of the dough lightly with flour, cover with a kitchen towel and set in a warm, draft-free spot (again, an unlighted oven is ideal). In 45 minutes to an hour, the dough should double in bulk.

Punch the dough down with your fist, then transfer from the bowl to a lightly floured board and knead again briefly. Roll it out into a rectangle 12 inches long and ¼ inch thick. Brush the dough with 3 tablespoons of the remaining melted butter and sprinkle the combined ¼ cup of sugar, the cinnamon and currants or raisins over it evenly.

In a small, heavy saucepan, combine the ½ cup of water, the brown sugar and 4 tablespoons of butter. Stir until the sugar dissolves and bring to a boil over high heat. Reduce the heat to moderate and cook the syrup for about 10 minutes until it has the consistency and color of maple syrup.

Let the syrup cool slightly, then dribble half of it over the surface of the dough. With your hands, roll the dough into a tight cylinder about 2 inches in diameter and cut it crosswise into 1-inch rounds. Grease a round 10-inch cake pan with the remaining 1 tablespoon of melted butter. Pour into it the other half of the syrup and sprinkle it evenly with the chopped walnuts. Arrange the rounds, cut side down, in a circle around the edge of the pan; continue the pattern with the remaining rounds until the pan is full. Let them rise in a warm, draft-free place for about 25 minutes, or until they are double in bulk. Meanwhile, preheat the oven to 350°.

Bake the buns in the middle of the oven for about ½ hour. When the buns are golden brown and firm to the touch, remove them from the oven and invert them onto a cake rack. Separate the buns and serve warm or at room temperature.

## Snipdoodle

| To make one 12-inch cake | 4 teaspoons baking powder |
|---|---|
| 1 cup vegetable shortening | ½ teaspoon salt |
| 1⅓ cups sugar | 1⅓ cups milk |
| 2 eggs | ¼ cup sugar combined with 1 |
| 2⅔ cups flour | teaspoon cinnamon |

Preheat the oven to 350°. In a large mixing bowl, cream the vegetable shortening and the sugar by mashing and beating them together with a large spoon. When the mixture is light and fluffy, beat in the eggs, one at a time, thoroughly incorporating one before adding the other. Sift the flour, baking powder and salt together into another bowl, and beat ¼ cup of this into the egg mixture. Then beat in ¼ cup of the milk. Continue adding the flour and milk alternately in similar amounts, beating until the batter is smooth.

Lightly butter and flour an 8-by-12-inch shallow baking pan. Invert the pan and rap it on the edge of the table to knock out any excess flour. Pour in the batter and bake in the middle of the oven for 45 minutes, or until the cake comes slightly away from the edge of the pan and is firm to the touch. As a further test, a toothpick inserted in the center should come out dry and clean.

Sprinkle the top of the cake evenly with the cinnamon-sugar and cut the cake into 2-inch squares. With a metal spatula, transfer them from the pan to a cake plate and serve warm or at room temperature for breakfast or for tea.

## Popovers

| To make 8 | 1 cup all-purpose flour |
| | ¼ teaspoon salt |
| 2 eggs | 2 tablespoons melted vegetable |
| 1 cup milk | shortening |

Preheat the oven to 450°. In a large mixing bowl, beat the eggs with a rotary or electric beater for a few seconds until they froth. Still beating, pour in the milk, and then the flour, salt and a tablespoon of the melted shortening. Continue to beat until the mixture is smooth, but don't overbeat.

With a pastry brush, grease an 8-cup muffin tin or, preferably, heavy popover pans, with the remaining shortening. Pour enough batter into each cup to fill it about ⅔ of the way to the top. Bake in the center of the oven for 20 minutes. Then reduce the heat to 350° and bake 10 to 15 minutes longer, or until the popovers have puffed to their fullest height, and are golden brown and crusty. Serve at once.

NOTE: The popover batter may more easily be made in a blender if you have one. Simply combine all the ingredients in the blender container and whirl at high speed for 30 to 40 seconds, stopping the machine and scraping down the sides of the jar after the first 10 seconds. Bake as described above.

## Hush Puppies  *(South)*

| To make 18 to 20 | |
| ¼ cup flour | 2 eggs |
| 4 teaspoons double-acting baking | ¾ to 1 cup buttermilk |
|    powder | 1 tablespoon finely chopped onions |
| ½ teaspoon salt | 1 teaspoon finely chopped garlic |
| 1½ cups white cornmeal, | Lard or vegetable oil for deep |
|    preferably water-ground |    frying |

Combine the flour, baking powder and salt and sift them together into a deep bowl. Stir in the cornmeal, unsifted, then add the eggs, one at a time, and beat vigorously with a wooden spoon until the mixture is smooth. Pour in ¾ cup of the buttermilk and stir until it is completely absorbed. If the batter seems dense, add up to ¼ cup more buttermilk by the spoonful until the batter holds its shape in a spoon. Beat in the finely chopped onions and garlic.

Preheat the oven to its lowest setting. Line a large shallow baking dish with a double thickness of paper towels and place the baking dish in the middle of the oven.

In a deep fryer or large heavy saucepan, melt enough lard to fill the pan to a depth of 2 to 3 inches, or pour in vegetable oil to a depth of 2 to 3 inches. Heat the fat until it reaches a temperature of 375° on a deep-frying thermometer.

To shape each hush puppy, scoop up a rounded tablespoon of the batter and push it into the hot fat with another spoon. Deep-fry the hush puppies 4 or 5 at a time, turning them about frequently with a slotted spoon for about 3 minutes, or until they are golden brown. Transfer them to the lined baking dish to drain and keep them warm in the low oven while you deep-fry the rest.

Serve the hush puppies hot, accompanied by butter. Traditionally hush puppies accompany fried fish.

## Nahant Buns *(New England)*

| | |
|---|---|
| To make about 30 buns | ½ teaspoon baking soda |
| ½ cup lukewarm water (110° to 115°) | 1½ cups lukewarm milk (110° to 115°) |
| 2 packages active dry yeast | 8 tablespoons butter (1 quarter-pound stick), cut into ½-inch bits and softened, plus 5 teaspoons butter, softened, plus 4 tablespoons butter, melted |
| 1 teaspoon plus 1 cup sugar | |
| 4 to 5 cups flour | |
| 1 teaspoon ground nutmeg, preferably freshly grated | |

Pour the lukewarm water into a small bowl and sprinkle the yeast and 1 teaspoon of sugar over it. Let the yeast and sugar rest for 2 or 3 minutes, then mix well. Set in a warm, draft-free place (such as an unlighted oven) for about 10 minutes, or until the yeast bubbles up and the mixture almost doubles in volume.

Combine 4 cups of flour, the remaining cup of sugar, the nutmeg and soda and sift them into a deep mixing bowl. Make a well in the center, pour in the yeast and milk and, with a large wooden spoon, gradually incorporate the dry ingredients into the liquid ones. Stir until the mixture is smooth, then beat in the 8 tablespoons of butter bits, a tablespoonful at a time. Beat until the dough can be gathered into a medium-soft ball.

Place the ball on a lightly floured surface and knead, pushing the dough down with the heels of your hands, pressing it forward and folding it back on itself. As you knead, incorporate up to 1 cup more flour, sprinkling it over the ball by the tablespoonful until the dough is no longer sticky. Then continue to knead for about 10 minutes, or until the dough is smooth, shiny and elastic.

With a pastry brush, spread 2 teaspoons of softened butter evenly over the inside of a large bowl. Set the dough in the bowl and turn it about to butter the entire surface. Drape the bowl with a kitchen towel and put it in the draft-free place for 1 hour, or until the dough doubles in volume.

Brush the bottoms and sides of three 9-inch pie tins with the remaining 3 teaspoons of softened butter. Punch the dough down with a single blow of your fist and, on a lightly floured surface, roll it out into a rough rectangle about ¾ inch thick.

With a cookie cutter or the rim of a glass, cut the dough into 2-inch rounds, placing the rounds side by side in the buttered tins as you proceed. Gather the scraps into a ball, roll them out again and cut as many more 2-inch rounds as you can. Brush the tops of the buns with the melted butter and set them in a draft-free place to rise for about 15 minutes.

Preheat the oven to 400°. Bake the buns on the middle shelf of the oven for 15 to 20 minutes, or until they are golden brown. Serve Nahant buns hot, or transfer them to wire racks to cool before serving.

### *Mayo Farm's Squash Rolls* *(New England)*

To make about 30 rolls

| | |
|---|---|
| ½ pound acorn, Hubbard or butternut squash, peeled, seeded and cut into 2-inch chunks | 5 to 6 cups flour |
| | 1 teaspoon salt |
| | 1 cup lukewarm milk (110° to 115°) |
| ½ cup lukewarm water (110° to 115°) | |
| 2 packages active dry yeast | ½ cup plus 4 teaspoons butter, softened, plus 2 tablespoons butter, melted |
| ½ cup sugar | |

Pour water into the lower part of a steamer to within about 1 inch of the top pan. Bring the water to a boil, put the squash in the top pan and set it in place. Immediately cover the pan and steam over high heat for 30 minutes, or until the squash is tender.

(Lacking a steamer, you can improvise one by using a large pot equipped with a tightly-fitting cover, and a standing colander or a collapsible steaming basket on legs. Pour water into the pot to within about 1 inch of the perforated container and bring it to a boil. Place the squash in the basket or colander, set it in place, and cover the pot. Steam over high heat for about 30 minutes, or until the squash is soft.)

Purée the squash through a food mill or mash it smooth with a fork and set it aside. (There should be about ½ cup of purée.)

Pour the ½ cup of lukewarm water into a small bowl and add the yeast and a pinch of the sugar. Let the yeast and sugar rest for 2 or 3 minutes, then mix well. Set in a warm, draft-free place (such as an unlighted oven) for about 10 minutes, or until the yeast bubbles up and the mixture almost doubles in volume.

Combine 5 cups of the flour, the remaining sugar and the salt, sift them together into a deep mixing bowl and make a well in the center. Pour in the yeast mixture, add the squash purée, the milk and ½ cup of softened butter and, with a large wooden spoon, gradually beat the dry ingredients into the liquid ones. Continue to beat until the dough is smooth and can be gathered into a compact ball.

Place the ball on a lightly floured surface and knead, pushing the dough down with the heels of your hands, pressing it forward and folding it back on itself. As you knead, incorporate up to 1 cup more flour, sprinkling it over the ball by the tablespoonful until the dough is no longer moist and sticky. Then continue to knead for about 10 minutes, or until the dough is smooth, shiny and elastic.

With a pastry brush, spread 2 teaspoons of the softened butter evenly over the inside of a large bowl. Set the dough in the bowl and turn it about to butter the entire surface of the dough. Drape the bowl with a kitchen towel and put it in the draft-free place for about 1 hour to allow the dough to double in volume.

Brush the remaining 2 teaspoons of softened butter over the bottom and sides of two 9-inch cake pans. Punch the dough down with a single blow of your fist and, on a lightly floured surface, roll it out into a rough rectangle about 1 inch thick.

With a cookie cutter or the rim of a glass, cut the dough into 2½-inch rounds. Gather the scraps into a ball, roll them out as before and cut out as many more 2½-inch rounds as you can. With the blunt edge of a table knife, make a deep crease just off-center in each round, taking care not to cut all the way through. Fold the smaller part of the round over the larger part and press the edges together securely.

Arrange the rolls about ½ inch apart in the buttered cake pans and brush the tops with the melted butter. Set the rolls in the draft-free place to rise for about 15 minutes.

Meanwhile preheat the oven to 450°. Bake the rolls in the middle of the oven for 12 to 15 minutes, or until golden brown. Serve the rolls hot.

To make about 3 dozen rolls

¼ cup lukewarm water (110° to 115°)
1 package active dry yeast
6 teaspoons sugar
5 to 6 cups all-purpose flour
1 teaspoon salt

2 cups lukewarm milk (110° to 115°)
1 egg, lightly beaten
3 tablespoons unsalted butter,
  softened and cut into ½-inch
  bits, plus 4 teaspoons butter,
  softened, plus 4 tablespoons
  butter, melted

Pour the lukewarm water into a small bowl and sprinkle the yeast and 1 teaspoon of the sugar over it. Let the yeast and sugar rest for 2 or 3 minutes, then mix well. Set in a warm, draft-free place (such as an unlighted oven) for about 10 minutes, or until the yeast bubbles up and the mixture almost doubles in volume.

Place 4 cups of the flour, the remaining 5 teaspoons of sugar and the salt in a deep mixing bowl and make a well in the center. Pour the yeast mixture into the well, add the milk and egg and, with a large wooden spoon, gradually incorporate the dry ingredients into the liquid ones. Stir until the mixture is smooth, then beat in the 3 tablespoons of butter bits, a few teaspoonfuls at a time. Continue to beat until the dough can be gathered into a medium-soft ball.

Place the ball on a lightly floured surface and knead, pushing the dough down with the heels of your hands, pressing it forward and folding it back on itself. Knead for about 10 minutes meanwhile incorporating up to 2 cups more of flour, adding it by the tablespoonful until the dough is no longer sticky. Then continue to knead until the dough is smooth, shiny and elastic.

With a pastry brush, spread 2 teaspoons of the softened butter evenly over the inside of a large bowl. Set the dough in the bowl and turn it about to butter the entire surface. Drape the bowl with a kitchen towel and set it aside in the draft-free place for approximately 1 hour, or until the dough doubles in volume.

Brush the remaining 2 teaspoons of softened butter evenly over 2 large baking sheets. Punch the dough down with a blow of your fist and, on a lightly floured surface, roll it out into a rectangle about ¼ inch thick.

With a cookie cutter or the rim of a glass, cut the dough into 3-inch rounds. Gather the scraps into a ball, roll them out again and cut as many more 3-inch rounds as you can.

To shape each Parker House roll, make a deep crease just above the middle of the circle with the blunt edge of a table knife, being careful not to cut all the way through the dough. Fold the smaller side of the circle over the larger side and press down on the edges lightly. Arrange the rolls

379

about 1 inch apart on the buttered baking sheets, brush the tops with the melted butter, and set in a draft-free place to rise for about 15 minutes.

Preheat the oven to 450°. Bake the rolls on the middle shelf of the oven for 12 to 15 minutes, or until they are golden brown. Serve the rolls hot, or transfer them to wire racks to cool before serving.

## Philadelphia Cinnamon Buns

To make 14 buns

¼ cup lukewarm water (110° to 115°)
1 package active dry yeast
1 teaspoon plus ½ cup sugar
3 to 3½ cups unsifted flour
½ teaspoon salt
2 egg yolks

1 cup lukewarm milk (110° to 115°)
1 tablespoon butter, softened, plus 6 tablespoons butter, melted
1½ cups light brown sugar
½ cup light corn syrup
½ cup seedless raisins
2 teaspoons ground cinnamon

Pour the lukewarm water into a shallow bowl and sprinkle the yeast and 1 teaspoon of sugar over it. Let the mixture stand for 2 or 3 minutes, then stir well. Set the bowl in a warm, draft-free place (such as an unlighted oven) for about 5 minutes, or until the yeast bubbles up and the mixture almost doubles in volume.

Combine 3 cups of the flour, the remaining ½ cup of sugar and the salt in a deep mixing bowl, and make a well in the center. Add the yeast mixture, egg yolks and lukewarm milk. With a large spoon, slowly mix the ingredients together, then stir until the dough is smooth and can be gathered into a soft ball.

Place the ball on a lightly floured surface and knead, pushing the dough down with the heels of your hands, pressing it forward and folding it back on itself. As you knead, sprinkle flour over the ball by the tablespoonful, adding up to ½ cup more flour if necessary to make a firm dough. Continue to knead for about 10 minutes, or until the dough is smooth, shiny and elastic.

With a pastry brush, spread the tablespoon of softened butter evenly inside a deep mixing bowl. Place the ball in the bowl and turn it around to butter the entire surface of the dough. Drape the bowl loosely with a kitchen towel and put it in the draft-free place for about 1 hour, or until the dough doubles in bulk.

In a small bowl, mix ¾ cup of light brown sugar, 2 tablespoons of the melted butter, and the corn syrup to a smooth paste. Pour the mixture into two 9-inch cake pans, tipping the pans back and forth to spread it evenly. In another bowl, stir the remaining ¾ cup of light brown sugar, the raisins and cinnamon together until they are well blended. Set aside.

Punch the dough down with a blow of your fist and, on a lightly floured surface, roll it out into an 18-by-10-inch rectangle about ¼ inch thick. Brush the surface of the dough with 2 tablespoons of the melted butter and sprinkle it evenly with the sugar-and-raisin mixture.

Starting at one long side, roll the dough tightly into a cylinder about 18 inches long and 2½ inches in diameter. Then, with a sharp knife, cut the cylinder crosswise into 14 rounds about 1¼ inch thick and 2½ inches in diameter. Place one round, cut side up, in the center of each sugar-lined cake pan and arrange the remaining rounds in circles of six around each center round. Set the buns aside in the draft-free place for about 45 minutes, or until they double in volume.

Preheat the oven to 350°. (If you have used the oven to let the buns rise, gently transfer them to a warm place to rest while the oven heats.) Brush the tops of the buns with the remaining 2 tablespoons of melted butter and bake in the middle of the oven for about 25 minutes, or until they are golden brown.

Place a wire cake rack over each pan and, grasping rack and pan together firmly, quickly invert them. Let the cinnamon buns cool to lukewarm before serving them.

### *Buttermilk Soda Biscuits* (*Eastern Heartland*)

To make about 18 two-inch biscuits

| | |
|---|---|
| 1 tablespoon butter, softened, plus 4 tablespoons butter, melted and cooled | 1 tablespoon double-acting baking powder |
| 1¾ cups unsifted flour | ½ teaspoon baking soda |
| | 1 teaspoon salt |
| | ¾ cup buttermilk |

Preheat the oven to 450°. With a pastry brush, spread the tablespoon of softened butter evenly over a large baking sheet and set aside.

Combine the flour, baking powder, soda and salt, and sift them together into a deep bowl. Make a well in the center and pour in the cooled melted butter and the buttermilk. With a wooden spoon, gradually incorporate the dry ingredients into the liquid ones. Then stir until the dough is smooth, but do not beat or overmix or the biscuits will be heavy.

Gather the dough into a ball, place it on a lightly floured surface, and roll it out about ½ inch thick. With a biscuit cutter or the rim of a glass, cut the dough into 2-inch rounds. Gather the scraps together into a ball and roll out as before. Then cut as many more biscuits as you can.

Arrange the biscuits about 1 inch apart on the buttered baking sheet and bake in the middle of the oven for 10 to 12 minutes, or until the biscuits are golden brown. Serve at once.

## Spoon Bread  *(South)*

To serve 4 to 6

| | |
|---|---|
| 1 cup milk | 3 tablespoons butter |
| ½ cup yellow cornmeal | 3 egg yolks |
| ½ teaspoon salt | 3 egg whites |

Preheat the oven to 375°. Over moderate heat, in a 2-quart saucepan, heat the milk until small bubbles form around the side of the pan. Slowly pour in the cornmeal, stirring constantly, and cook without boiling until the mixture is thick and smooth. Add the salt and butter, and stir until the butter has been completely absorbed. Then remove from the heat. Add the egg yolks to the mixture one at a time, beating vigorously after each addition. Lightly butter a 6-by-8-by-2-inch baking dish. With a whisk or rotary beater, beat the egg whites in a large bowl until they form unwavering peaks on the beater when it is lifted out of the bowl. Mix a large spoonful of the whites into the cornmeal mixture, then, with a rubber spatula, gently but thoroughly fold in the rest. Pour into the baking dish, smooth the top with a spatula and bake the spoon bread in the center of the oven for 35 to 40 minutes, or until golden brown. Serve directly from the baking dish with a large serving spoon.

## Baking Powder Biscuits  *(South)*

To make about 10

| | |
|---|---|
| 2 teaspoons butter, softened plus 8 tablespoons butter, cut into ¼-inch bits | 2 teaspoons double-acting baking powder |
| 2 cups all-purpose flour | 1 teaspoon salt |
| | ⅔ cup milk |

Preheat the oven to 400°. With a pastry brush, spread the 2 teaspoons of softened butter evenly over a baking sheet. Set aside.

Combine the flour, baking powder and salt and sift them into a deep bowl. Add the 8 tablespoons of butter bits and rub the flour and fat together with your fingertips until they resemble flakes of coarse meal. Pour in the milk all at once and mix briefly with a wooden spoon, stirring just long enough to form a smooth soft dough that can be gathered into a compact ball. Do not overbeat.

Place the dough on a lightly floured surface and roll or pat it into a rough circle about ½-inch thick. With a biscuit cutter or the rim of a glass, cut the dough into 2½-inch rounds. Gather the scraps into a ball, pat or roll it out as before and cut as many more biscuits as you can.

Arrange the biscuits side by side on the buttered baking sheet and bake in the middle of the oven for about 20 minutes, or until they are a delicate golden brown. Serve at once.

ADDITIONAL INGREDIENTS FOR
CHEESE-AND-HERB BISCUITS
¼ cup freshly grated imported

Parmesan cheese
¼ cup finely cut fresh chives
¼ cup finely chopped fresh parsley

CHEESE-AND-HERB BISCUITS: Following precisely the directions for baking-powder biscuits, prepare the dough and gather it into a ball. While the dough is still in the bowl, knead into it the grated cheese, chives and parsley. Place the dough on a lightly floured surface, then roll, cut and bake the biscuits as described above.

## Beaten Biscuits *(South)*

*By tradition, the dough for these biscuits is actually beaten with a mallet, hammer or even an ax for anywhere from 20 to 40 minutes. However, putting the dough through a food grinder as described below is quicker and easier—and the biscuits themselves are enough like their beaten counterparts to please an old-time cook.*

To make about 2 dozen
1½-inch biscuits

1 teaspoon butter, softened
2 cups flour
1½ teaspoons sugar

1 teaspoon salt
2 tablespoons lard, cut into ¼-inch bits
¼ cup milk combined with ¼ cup
water

Preheat the oven to 400°. With a pastry brush, spread the softened butter evenly on a large baking sheet and set aside.

Combine the flour, sugar and salt, and sift them into a deep bowl. Drop in the lard and, with your fingers, rub the flour and fat together until they resemble flakes of coarse meal. Add the milk-and-water mixture, about 2 tablespoonfuls at a time, rubbing and kneading after each addition until the liquid is completely absorbed. Knead the dough vigorously in the bowl until it is smooth. Then put it through the coarsest blade of a food grinder four times, or until the dough is pliable and elastic.

To shape beaten biscuits the Maryland way, take a handful of the dough and squeeze your fingers into a fist, forcing the dough up between your thumb and forefinger. When it forms a ball about the size of a walnut, pinch it off and gently pat the dough into a flat round about ½ inch thick. To shape the biscuits as they do in Virginia, gather the dough into a ball and roll it out ½ inch thick on a lightly floured surface. With a biscuit cutter or the rim of a glass, cut the dough into 1½-inch rounds. Collect the scraps into a ball again, roll it out as before and cut as many more biscuits as you can.

Place the biscuits about 1 inch apart on the buttered baking sheet. Then prick the top of each one lightly with a three-tined fork to make a pattern of two or three parallel rows. Bake in the middle of the oven for about 20 minutes, or until the biscuits are a delicate golden color. Serve them at once with butter.

## Cream Biscuits  *(Northwest)*

To make about eight 2½-inch  biscuits

| | |
|---|---|
| 1 teaspoon butter, softened | powder |
| 1½ cups flour | ½ teaspoon salt |
| 2 teaspoons double-acting baking | 1 cup heavy cream, chilled |

Preheat the oven to 425°. With a pastry brush, spread the softened butter evenly on a large baking sheet. Combine the flour, baking powder and salt, and sift them together onto a plate or a strip of wax paper.

In a chilled bowl, beat the cream with a wire whisk or a rotary or electric beater until stiff enough to stand in soft peaks on the beater when it is lifted from the bowl. Sprinkle the flour mixture over the cream about ½ cup at a time and fold them together gently but thoroughly with a rubber spatula. Do not overfold.

Place the dough on a lightly floured surface and pat it into a rough rectangle about ½ inch thick. Then, with a cookie cutter or the rim of a glass, cut the dough into 2½-inch rounds. Gather the scraps gently into a ball, pat it flat, and cut as many more rounds as you can.

Arrange the biscuits about 1 inch apart on the buttered sheet and bake in the middle of the oven for 12 to 15 minutes, or until they are golden brown. Serve at once.

## Apple Muffins  *(Eastern Heartland)*

To make about 16 muffins

| | |
|---|---|
| 6 tablespoons butter, softened | 2 eggs |
| 2 cups unsifted flour | 1 cup sour cream |
| 4 teaspoons double-acting baking powder | 3 medium-sized firm ripe cooking apples, 2 apples peeled, cored and finely chopped (about 1 cup) and 1 apple cored and cut lengthwise into ⅛-inch-thick slices |
| ¼ teaspoon baking soda | |
| ½ teaspoon ground mace | |
| ½ teaspoon salt | |
| ¼ cup sugar | |

Preheat the oven to 425°. With a pastry brush, spread 2 tablespoons of softened butter evenly inside 16 muffin cups (each cup should be about 2½ inches across at the top). Combine the flour, baking powder, baking soda, mace and salt, and sift them together into a bowl. Set aside.

In a deep bowl, cream the remaining 4 tablespoons of butter and the sugar, beating and mashing them against the sides of the bowl with the back of a large spoon until the mixture is light and fluffy. Beat in the eggs, one at a time. Then add about 1 cup of the flour mixture and, when it is well incorporated, beat in ½ cup of the sour cream. Repeat, beating in the remaining flour and then the rest of the cream and stir until the batter is smooth. Stir in the chopped apples and spoon the batter into the muffin cups, filling each cup about halfway to the top. Insert a slice of apple, peel side up, partway into the top of each muffin.

Bake in the middle of the oven for 15 to 20 minutes, or until the muffins are brown and a cake tester or toothpick inserted in the centers comes out clean. Turn the muffins out of the tins and serve at once.

## Cranberry Muffins *(New England)*

To make a dozen 2½-inch muffins

| | |
|---|---|
| 1 tablespoon butter, softened, plus 4 tablespoons butter, melted and cooled | ¾ cup sugar |
| | 4 teaspoons double-acting baking powder |
| 1 cup firm fresh unblemished cranberries | ½ teaspoon salt |
| | 1 cup milk |
| 2¾ cups flour | 1 egg, lightly beaten |

Preheat the oven to 400°. With a pastry brush, spread the softened butter over the inside surfaces of a medium-sized 12-cup muffin tin (each cup should be about 2½ inches across at the top).

Wash the cranberries under cold running water and pat the berries dry with paper towels. Put them through the coarsest blade of a food grinder into a glass or ceramic bowl and set aside.

Combine the flour, sugar, baking powder and salt and sift into a deep mixing bowl. Stirring constantly with a large spoon, pour in the milk in a thin stream. When the milk is completely absorbed, stir in the egg and the 4 tablespoons of melted butter. Add the ground cranberries and continue to stir until all the ingredients are well combined.

Ladle about ⅓ cup of the batter into each of the muffin-tin cups, filling them about ⅔ full. Bake in the middle of the oven for 30 minutes, or until the muffins are puffed and brown on top, and a cake tester or toothpick inserted in the center comes out clean. Run a knife around the inside of each cup to loosen the muffins, then turn them out of the tin and serve at once, or cool to room temperature before serving.

## Blueberry Muffins *(New England)*

To make about twenty 2½-inch
    muffins
10 tablespoons butter, softened
2½ cups firm ripe blueberries
2 cups unsifted flour
2 teaspoons double-acting baking

powder
½ teaspoon salt
1 cup sugar
2 eggs
½ cup milk

Preheat the oven to 375°. With a pastry brush, spread 2 tablespoons of the softened butter evenly inside 20 muffin cups (each cup should be about 2½ inches across at the top).

Wash the blueberries in a sieve or colander set under cold running water, discarding the stems and any blemished berries. Spread the berries on paper towels and pat them completely dry with more paper towels. Place ½ cup of the berries in a small bowl and mash them to a smooth purée with the back of a fork. Drop the rest of the berries into another bowl, add 2 tablespoons of the flour and toss gently about with a spoon to coat the berries evenly. Set aside.

Combine the remaining flour, the baking powder and salt, and sift them together onto a sheet of wax paper.

In a deep bowl, cream the remaining 8 tablespoons of butter with the sugar, beating and mashing them against the sides of the bowl with the back of a large spoon until the mixture is light and fluffy. Beat in the eggs, one at a time.

Add about 1 cup of the flour mixture and, when it is well incorporated, beat in ¼ cup of the milk. Repeat, beating in the remaining flour mixture and then the rest of the milk, and continue to mix until the batter is smooth. Add the puréed berries, beat well, then add the reserved whole berries and gently fold them into the batter with a rubber spatula.

Spoon the batter into the buttered muffin cups, filling each cup about ¾ full. Bake in the middle of the oven for 20 to 25 minutes, or until a cake tester or toothpick inserted in the center of a muffin comes out clean. Turn the muffins out of the tins and serve at once.

## Boston Brown Bread

To make two 5½-by-3-inch
    cylindrical loaves
2 cups buttermilk
¾ cup dark molasses
¾ cup seedless raisins
1 cup rye flour

1 cup whole-wheat or graham flour
1 cup yellow cornmeal
¾ teaspoon baking soda
1 teaspoon salt
1 tablespoon butter, softened

In a deep bowl, beat the buttermilk and molasses together vigorously with a spoon. Stir in the raisins. Combine the rye flour, whole-wheat or graham flour, cornmeal, soda and salt and sift them into the buttermilk mixture 1 cup at a time, stirring well after each addition.

Thoroughly wash and dry two empty 2½-cup (No. 2) tin cans. Then, with a pastry brush, spread the softened butter over the bottom and sides of the cans. Pour the batter into the cans, dividing it evenly between them. The batter should fill each can to within about 1 inch of the top. Cover each can loosely with a circle of buttered wax paper and then with a larger circle of heavy-duty aluminum foil. The foil should be puffed like the top of a French chef's hat, allowing an inch of space above the top edge of the can so the batter can rise as it is steamed. Tie the wax paper and foil in place with kitchen string.

Stand the cans on a rack set in a large pot and pour in enough boiling water to come about ¾ of the way up the sides of the cans. Return the water to a boil over high heat, cover the pot tightly, and reduce the heat to low. Steam the bread for 2 hours and 15 minutes. Remove the foil and paper from the cans at once, and turn the bread out on a heated platter if you plan to serve it immediately. Or leave the bread in the cans with the foil and paper in place, and steam it for 10 to 15 minutes to reheat the loaves before you serve them. Steamed loaves, with covers in place, can safely be kept in the refrigerator for a week to 10 days.

NOTE: If rye and whole-wheat flours are not available at your grocery, you can find them in a health food store.

### Date, Pecan and Orange Bread *(Far West)*

To make one 9-by-5-by-3-inch loaf

| | |
|---|---|
| 5 tablespoons butter, softened | orange peel |
| 4 tablespoons plus 2 cups unsifted flour | 1 teaspoon double-acting baking powder |
| 8 ounces pitted dates, cut into small bits with kitchen scissors (about 1 cup) | 1 teaspoon baking soda |
| | 1 teaspoon salt |
| ½ cup finely chopped pecans | 1 cup sugar |
| 4 teaspoons finely chopped fresh | 1 egg |
| | 1 cup strained fresh orange juice |

Preheat the oven to 350°. With a pastry brush, spread 1 tablespoon of the softened butter over the bottom and sides of a 9-by-5-by-3-inch loaf pan. Add 2 tablespoons of the flour and tip the pan from side to side to distribute it evenly. Invert the pan and rap it sharply to remove excess flour.

Place the dates, pecans and orange peel in a bowl, add 2 tablespoons of flour, and toss together gently but thoroughly. Combine the remaining 2 cups of flour, the baking powder, soda and salt, and sift them together into a bowl. Set aside.

In a deep bowl, cream the remaining 4 tablespoons of butter and the sugar by beating and mashing them against the sides of the bowl with the back of a large spoon until the mixture is light and fluffy. Beat in the egg. Add about ½ cup of the flour mixture and, when it is incorporated, beat in ¼ cup of the orange juice. Repeat three times, alternating ½ cup of the flour with ¼ cup of orange juice and beating well after each addition. Stir in the reserved floured fruit and nuts.

Pour the batter into the prepared pan and bake in the middle of the oven for 50 to 60 minutes, or until a toothpick or cake tester inserted in the center comes out clean. Let the bread cool in the pan for 4 or 5 minutes, then turn it out on a wire rack to cool completely to room temperature before serving.

## Cranberry-Fruit-Nut Bread *(New England)*

To make one 9-by-5-inch loaf

| | |
|---|---|
| 1 teaspoon butter, softened, plus 6 tablespoons unsalted butter, softened and cut into ½-inch bits | ½ cup walnuts |
| | 1 cup sugar |
| | 1½ teaspoons double-acting baking powder |
| 1 teaspoon plus 2 cups all-purpose flour | ½ teaspoon baking soda |
| 2 cups (½ pound) firm fresh unblemished cranberries | ½ teaspoon salt |
| | 1 egg, lightly beaten |
| 1 medium-sized tart cooking apple, peeled, cored and cut into small chunks | 1 tablespoon finely grated fresh orange peel |
| | ½ cup strained fresh orange juice |

Preheat the oven to 350°. With a pastry brush, spread the teaspoon of softened butter evenly over the bottom and sides of a 9-by-5-inch loaf pan. Sprinkle 1 teaspoon of flour into the tin, tipping it to coat the bottom and sides evenly. Then invert the tin and rap it sharply on the table to remove any excess flour.

Wash the cranberries under cold running water and pat them dry with paper towels. Put the cranberries, apple and walnuts through the coarsest blade of a food grinder into a glass or ceramic bowl. Set aside.

Combine the 2 cups of flour, sugar, baking powder, baking soda and salt and sift into a deep bowl. Add the 6 tablespoons of butter bits and, with your fingertips, rub the fat and dry ingredients together until they look like flakes of coarse meal. Stir in the egg, orange peel and orange juice, then add the cranberry-apple-walnut mixture and continue to stir until the ingredients are thoroughly combined.

Spoon the batter into the buttered pan, spreading it and smoothing the top with a spatula. Bake in the middle of the oven for 1½ hours, or until the top is golden brown and a toothpick or cake tester inserted in the center of the loaf comes out clean. Turn the loaf out onto a wire cake rack to cool. Serve cranberry-fruit-nut bread while it is still warm or when it has cooled completely.

## *Sugar Doughnuts* (Eastern Heartland)

To make about 1½ dozen
  doughnuts and 2 to 3 dozen
  doughnut balls

4 to 5 cups unsifted flour
4 teaspoons double-acting baking
  powder
¼ teaspoon ground nutmeg
½ teaspoon salt
¾ cup milk

4 tablespoons butter, melted and
  cooled
1 teaspoon vanilla
3 eggs
1 cup granulated sugar
Vegetable oil for deep frying
2 cups confectioners' sugar, sifted

Combine 4 cups of the flour, the baking powder, nutmeg and salt, and sift them onto a plate or a sheet of wax paper. Pour the milk, cooled melted butter and vanilla into a measuring cup and mix well. Set aside.

In a deep bowl, beat the eggs and the granulated sugar with a wire whisk or a rotary or electric beater for 4 or 5 minutes, until the mixture falls in a slowly dissolving ribbon from the beater when it is lifted from the bowl. Add about 1 cup of the flour mixture and stir with a wooden spoon. When the flour is well incorporated, beat in about ¼ cup of the milk-and-butter mixture. Repeat three more times, alternating 1 cup of the flour with ¼ cup of the milk, and beating well after each addition. Add up to 1 cup more flour by the tablespoonful and continue to stir with the spoon, or knead with your hands, until the dough can be gathered into a compact ball. Cover the bowl with wax paper and refrigerate for at least 30 minutes.

Line two large baking sheets with wax paper. Cut off about one quarter of the dough and place it on a lightly floured surface. Flour a rolling pin and roll the dough out about ⅓ inch thick. If the dough sticks, dust a little flour over and under it.

With a 2¾-inch doughnut cutter, cut out as many doughnuts as you can. Using a wide metal spatula, transfer the doughnuts and their centers to the paper-lined pans. Refrigerate until ready to fry. Break off another quarter of the dough, roll it out, cut out more doughnuts and refrigerate as before. Repeat until all the dough has been used, but do not reroll the scraps or the doughnuts made from them may be tough. Instead use a 1-inch cutter to form balls out of the scraps.

Pour vegetable oil into a deep fryer or large heavy saucepan to a depth of 3 inches and heat the oil until it reaches a temperature of 375° on a deep-frying thermometer. Meanwhile place ½ cup of the confectioners' sugar in a paper bag and set it aside.

Deep-fry the doughnuts and balls 4 or 5 at a time, turning them about with a slotted spoon for 3 minutes, or until they are puffed and brown. Drain the doughnuts briefly on paper towels, then drop 2 at a time into the paper bag and shake to coat them with sugar. (Add sugar to the bag as needed.) Place the doughnuts on wire racks to cool while you fry and sugar the rest.

## Navajo Fry Bread *(Far West)*

To make three 8-inch round breads

2 cups unsifted flour
½ cup dry milk solids
2 teaspoons double-acting baking
    powder
½ teaspoon salt
2 tablespoons lard, cut into ½-inch
    bits, plus 1 pound lard for deep
    frying
½ cup ice water

Combine the flour, dry milk solids, baking powder and salt, and sift them into a deep bowl. Add the 2 tablespoons of lard bits and, with your fingertips, rub the flour and fat together until the mixture resembles flakes of coarse meal. Pour in the water and toss the ingredients together until the dough can be gathered into a ball. Drape the bowl with a kitchen towel and let the dough rest at room temperature for about 2 hours.

After the resting period, cut the dough into three equal pieces. Then, on a lightly floured surface, roll each piece into a rough circle about 8 inches in diameter and ¼ inch thick. With a small sharp knife, cut two 4- to 5-inch-long parallel slits completely through the dough down the center of each round, spacing the slits about 1 inch apart.

In a heavy 10-inch skillet, melt the remaining pound of lard over moderate heat until it is very hot but not smoking. The melted fat should be about 1 inch deep; add more lard if necessary. Fry the breads one at a time for about 2 minutes on each side, turning them once with tongs or a slotted spatula. The bread will puff slightly and become crisp and brown. Drain the Navajo fry bread on paper towels and serve warm.

To serve 4

| | |
|---|---|
| 5 eggs | peel |
| ½ cup granulated sugar | 8 half-inch-thick slices of day-old |
| 3 tablespoons brandy | French- or Italian-type bread |
| 2 tablespoons orange-flower water | 1 pound lard |
| 1 teaspoon finely grated fresh lemon | Confectioners' sugar |

In a large, deep bowl, beat the eggs and granulated sugar with a wire whisk or a rotary or electric beater until they are frothy and well combined. Beat in the brandy, orange-flower water and lemon peel, then add the bread slices and turn them about in the egg mixture to moisten them evenly. Let the bread soak at room temperature for at least 30 minutes.

In a heavy 12-inch skillet, melt the lard over moderate heat until it is very hot but not smoking. Fry the bread, three or four slices at a time, for 2 minutes on each side, turning the slices carefully with a wide metal spatula and regulating the heat so that they brown richly and evenly without burning. As they brown, transfer the bread slices to paper towels to drain.

Sprinkle the *pain perdu* with confectioners' sugar and serve at once, accompanied, if you like, by a pitcher of pure cane syrup.

To make 1 dozen 5-inch tortillas

| | |
|---|---|
| 2⅓ cups instant *masa harina* (corn flour) | 1 teaspoon salt |
| | 1 to 1½ cups cold water |

Combine the *masa harina* and salt in a deep bowl and, stirring the mixture constantly, pour in 1 cup of the water in a slow, thin stream. Then knead the mixture vigorously with your hands, adding up to ½ cup more water by the tablespoonful if necessary, until the dough becomes firm and no longer sticks to the fingers.

To shape the tortillas, divide the dough into 12 equal portions and roll each one between your palms into a ball the size of a walnut. Place one ball at a time between two 8-inch squares of wax paper, then flatten it into a 5- to 6-inch round in a tortilla press. Stack the tortillas on top of one another without removing the papers.

Preheat the oven to its lowest setting. Then heat an ungreased cast-iron griddle or a 7- to 8-inch cast-iron skillet over moderate heat until a drop of water flicked onto it splutters and evaporates instantly. Unwrap and fry one tortilla at a time for about 2 minutes on each side, turning it once with a spatula when the bottom becomes a delicate brown. Watch carefully and regulate the heat if the tortilla colors too quickly. As they brown, transfer the tortillas to a large platter. Wrap the tortillas in foil, four or five at a time, as you proceed, and keep them warm in the oven.

If you prefer, you may stack and wrap all of the tortillas together in paper towels, cover them with a damp cloth and finally with foil, then place them in the oven to keep warm for 2 to 3 hours.

To prepare tortillas days or weeks in advance, cook and cool them to room temperature. Stack them between pieces of wax paper and wrap the stack with foil. Tightly wrapped, the tortillas can safely be kept in the refrigerator for 2 or 3 days, or in the freezer for months. To rewarm the refrigerated tortillas, unwrap one at a time and heat it in an ungreased skillet for about 30 seconds, turning the tortilla frequently with tongs until it softens and is heated through. Frozen tortillas should be thoroughly defrosted before they are reheated.

## Griddle Cakes

| | |
|---|---|
| To make 18 to 20 pancakes | 1 teaspoon salt |
| | 3 eggs, lightly beaten |
| 2 cups all-purpose flour | 2 cups milk |
| 2 teaspoons baking powder | ¼ cup melted butter |
| 2 teaspoons sugar | ¼ cup vegetable oil |

Sift the flour, baking powder, sugar and salt together into a large mixing bowl. Make a well in the center of the flour and pour into it the eggs and milk. With a large spoon mix together only long enough to blend, then stir in the melted butter. Do not overmix; the pancakes will be lighter if the batter is not too smooth. Heat a griddle or heavy skillet over moderate heat until a drop of water flicked onto it evaporates instantly. Grease the griddle or skillet very lightly with a pastry brush dipped in oil; continue to grease when necessary. Pour the batter from a pitcher or small ladle into the hot pan to form pancakes 4 inches in diameter. Cook 2 to 3 minutes until small, scattered bubbles have formed—but have not broken—on the surface . Immediately turn with a spatula and cook for a minute until the other side of the pancake is golden brown. Stack on a heated plate and serve with melted butter and maple syrup.

NOTE: One cup of thoroughly drained, fresh, canned or thoroughly defrosted and drained frozen fruit may be added to the batter before frying.

## Cottage Cheese Pancakes *(Eastern Heartland)*

To make about 3 dozen 2-inch pancakes

1 cup creamed cottage cheese
  (8 ounces)
5 eggs, lightly beaten
½ cup unsifted flour

16 tablespoons butter (½ pound),
  melted and cooled
1 teaspoon vanilla extract
A pinch of salt

Preheat the oven to its lowest setting. Meanwhile, line a large baking sheet with paper towels and place it in the middle of the oven.

With the back of a spoon, rub the cottage cheese through a fine sieve into a deep mixing bowl. Beating constantly, pour in the eggs gradually and, when they are well incorporated, add the flour by the tablespoonful. Stir in 8 tablespoons of the cooled melted butter, the vanilla and salt.

Warm a large heavy griddle over moderate heat until a drop of water flicked onto it splutters and evaporates instantly. Grease the griddle lightly with a pastry brush dipped into the remaining 8 tablespoons of butter. Cook 5 or 6 pancakes at a time. To form each cake, pour about a tablespoon of the batter on the griddle, leaving enough space between them so that they can spread into 2-inch rounds. Fry them for 2 minutes on each side, or until they are golden and crisp around the edges.

As they brown, transfer the cakes to the paper-lined baking sheet and keep them warm in the oven while you fry the rest. Repeat the procedure, brushing the griddle with melted butter when necessary, until all the cottage-cheese pancakes are fried. Serve at once with jelly or jam.

## Lacy-edged Batty Cakes *(South)*

To make about 2 dozen

¾ cup white cornmeal, preferably
  water-ground
½ teaspoon double-acting baking
  powder
½ teaspoon baking soda

½ teaspoon salt
1 cup buttermilk
1 egg, lightly beaten
½ cup bacon fat, or substitute
  ¼ pound butter, softened

If you are using regular-ground cornmeal, combine it with the baking powder, soda and salt, and sift them together into a bowl. If you are using water-ground cornmeal, pour it into a bowl and stir in the baking powder, soda and salt. Pour in the buttermilk and beat vigorously with a spoon until it is completely absorbed. Then add the egg and continue to beat until the batter is smooth.

Heat a heavy griddle over high heat until a drop of water flicked onto it steams for a second and evaporates. With a pastry brush, grease the griddle lightly with the bacon fat or butter.

Pour about 1 tablespoon of batter onto the griddle for each batty cake. Fry 4 at a time for 2 to 3 minutes, until the cakes begin to bubble and the bottoms brown. Then turn them over with a spatula and brown the other side. Stack the finished cakes on a heated plate and drape foil over them to keep them warm while you fry the rest. Stir the batter before baking each batch of cakes and brush more bacon fat or butter on the griddle as necessary. Serve the batty cakes as soon as they are all cooked, as an accompaniment to turkey hash or like pancakes with butter and strained honey.

## Sourdough Waffles. *(Far West)*

| | |
|---|---|
| To make four 11-by-6-inch waffles | ¼ cup vegetable oil |
| 1 cup sourdough starter * | ½ cup dry milk solids |
| 2 cups warm water (90°) | 2 tablespoons sugar |
| 2½ cups unsifted flour | 1 teaspoon baking soda |
| 1 egg, lightly beaten | 1 teaspoon salt |

With a rubber spatula, scrape the starter into a deep ceramic or glass bowl. Give it a quick stir to recombine its ingredients, then add the warm water and stir the mixture to a paste. Stir in the flour, about ½ cup at a time. Cover the bowl tightly with plastic wrap and set the mixture aside in a warm, draft-free place (such as an unlighted oven) for 12 hours. (If the mixture has not bubbled at the end of this time, the starter was dead and the mixture must be discarded.) You should have about 4 cups of sourdough mixture.

Before preparing the waffles, ladle 1 cup of the mixture into a pint jar to serve as a starter for future sourdough cooking. Cover the jar tightly with its lid and refrigerate the starter until you are ready to use it. Unless the starter is used within 2 or 3 weeks, freshen it as described above.

With a wire whisk, beat the egg and vegetable oil into the 3 cups of sourdough mixture remaining in the bowl to form a sourdough batter. Combine the dry milk solids, sugar, baking soda and salt in a small sifter, sprinkle them directly over the batter and whisk all of the ingredients together gently but thoroughly.

Following the manufacturer's directions, preheat an 11-by-6-inch waffle iron to moderate. Pour 1½ cups of the batter into the center of the hot waffle iron, reduce the heat to moderately low and close the iron. Bake for 5 minutes, or until the steaming stops and the waffle is golden brown on both sides. (You can peek at the waffle to check it after 3 minutes, but do not open the cover earlier or the waffle may stick to the grid.)

* *See index.*

Serve the sourdough waffles at once, accompanied by butter and maple syrup, honey or jam.

### *Blueberry Coffee Ring*

To make 2 rings (serving 10 to 12)

YEAST DOUGH
¼ cup lukewarm water (110° to 115°)
1 package active dry yeast
1 teaspoon plus 3 tablespoons sugar
3 to 4 cups flour
½ teaspoon salt

¼ cup vegetable oil
¼ cup lukewarm milk (110° to 115°)
2 eggs
8 tablespoons butter, cut into ½-inch bits and softened, plus 3 tablespoons butter, softened

Pour the lukewarm water into a small shallow bowl and sprinkle the yeast and 1 teaspoon of the sugar on top. Let the mixture stand for 2 or 3 minutes, then mix well. Set the bowl in a warm, draft-free place (such as an unlighted oven) for 5 to 8 minutes, or until the mixture almost doubles in volume.

Combine 3 cups of the flour, the remaining 3 tablespoons of sugar and the salt in a deep bowl, and make a well in the center. Pour in the yeast mixture, vegetable oil, milk and eggs and, with a large spoon, gradually incorporate the dry ingredients into the liquid ones. Beat until smooth, then beat in the 8 tablespoons of butter bits.

Gather the dough into a ball and place it on a lightly floured surface. Knead it by pushing it down with the heels of your hands, pressing it forward, and folding it back on itself. Repeat for about 10 minutes, meanwhile sprinkling in up to 1 cup more flour, adding it by the tablespoonful and using only enough to make a smooth, elastic dough.

With a pastry brush, spread 1 tablespoon of the softened butter inside a deep bowl. Place the dough in the bowl and turn it about to grease all sides evenly. Drape loosely with a kitchen towel and set aside in the warm, draft-free place for about 45 minutes, or until the dough doubles in bulk. Meanwhile brush the remaining 2 tablespoons of butter evenly over two large baking sheets and set aside.

BLUEBERRY FILLING
2 cups firm ripe fresh blueberries
⅓ cup sugar

3 tablespoons cornstarch
2 tablespoons strained fresh lemon juice

While the dough is rising, prepare the blueberry filling in the following fashion: Combine the blueberries, ⅓ cup sugar, cornstarch and lemon juice in a 2- to 3-quart enameled or stainless-steel saucepan. Bring

395

to a simmer over moderate heat, stirring until the sugar dissolves. Still stirring from time to time, simmer uncovered over low heat for about 10 minutes longer, or until the mixture is thick enough to coat a spoon heavily. Remove the pan from the heat and let the blueberry filling cool.

Punch the dough down with a single blow of your fist and divide it in half. On a lightly floured surface, roll out one half of the dough into a rectangle about 16 inches long and 10 inches wide. Spread the top to within 2 inches of the edges with half of the blueberry filling and, starting at one of the 16-inch sides, roll the dough jelly-roll fashion into a cylinder. Crimp the ends of the cylinder tightly together with your fingers to seal them. Then place the cylinder on a buttered baking sheet and fold the ends together to make a horseshoe or ring. Roll, fill and shape the second half of the dough in the same manner, then set them both aside in a warm, draft-free place for about 45 minutes, or until they double in bulk.

LEMON TOPPING
¼ cup sugar
2 tablespoons milk

1 tablespoon finely grated fresh
   lemon peel

Preheat the oven to 350°. In a small bowl, stir the ¼ cup of sugar, the 2 tablespoons of milk and the lemon peel to a smooth paste. With a pastry brush, spread the lemon mixture over the top of the two coffee rings, dividing it equally between them. Bake in the middle of the oven for 20 minutes, or until the rings are golden brown. Serve hot, or cool to room temperature before serving.


## Blueberry Crumb Cake

To serve 10 to 12

9 tablespoons butter, softened, plus
   8 tablespoons butter, chilled and
   cut into ¼-inch bits
2 tablespoons plus 3¼ cups
   unsifted flour
2 cups sugar
1 teaspoon ground cinnamon
3 cups firm ripe blueberries

1 tablespoon double-acting baking
   powder
½ teaspoon ground nutmeg
¼ teaspoon ground cloves
1 teaspoon salt
3 eggs
¾ cup milk
2 cups heavy cream

Preheat the oven to 375°. With a pastry brush, spread 1 tablespoon of softened butter over the bottom and sides of a 13-by-9-by-3-inch baking dish. Add 2 tablespoons of the flour and tip the dish to spread it evenly. Invert the dish and rap the bottom sharply to remove excess flour.

Prepare the crumb topping by combining the 8 tablespoons of butter bits, ¾ cup of the flour, 1 cup of the sugar and the cinnamon in a deep bowl. Working quickly, rub the flour and fat together with your fingertips until the mixture resembles flakes of coarse meal. Set aside.

Wash the blueberries in a colander under cold running water. Remove the stems and discard any berries that are badly bruised. Spread the berries on paper towels and pat them completely dry with fresh towels.

Combine the remaining 2½ cups of flour, the baking powder, nutmeg, cloves and salt, and sift them together into a bowl.

In a deep bowl, cream the remaining 8 tablespoons of softened butter and 1 cup of sugar by beating and mashing them against the sides of the bowl with the back of a spoon until they are light and fluffy. Beat in the eggs, one at a time. Add about 1 cup of the sifted flour mixture and, when it is well incorporated, stir in ¼ cup of the milk. Repeat twice more, alternating 1 cup of the flour with ¼ cup of milk and beating well after each addition. Gently stir in the blueberries.

Pour the blueberry batter into the buttered-and-floured baking dish, spreading it evenly and smoothing the top with a rubber spatula. Then sprinkle the reserved crumb topping evenly over the cake.

Bake in the middle of the oven for 40 to 50 minutes, or until the top is crusty and a toothpick or cake tester inserted in the center of the cake comes out clean. Serve the blueberry crumb cake warm or at room temperature, and present the cream separately in a pitcher.

## Buttermilk Coffeecake (South)
BISHOP'S BREAD

| | |
|---|---|
| To make one 9-inch cake | 1 cup light brown sugar |
| 1 teaspoon unsalted butter, softened, plus 12 tablespoons unsalted butter, cut into bits | ⅔ cup buttermilk |
| | 1 egg, lightly beaten |
| 1 tablespoon plus 2 cups sifted all-purpose flour | ½ cup finely chopped pecans or almonds |
| 1½ teaspoons baking powder | 1 teaspoon ground cinnamon |
| | ½ cup currants |

Preheat the oven to 425°. With a pastry brush, brush the bottom and sides of a 9-inch layer-cake pan with the teaspoon of softened butter. Add 1 tablespoon of flour and tip the pan to distribute it evenly. Then invert the pan and rap it sharply to dislodge the excess flour.

In a large mixing bowl, combine the rest of the flour, the baking powder, brown sugar and butter bits, and rub them together with your fingertips until they look like fine crumbs. Set aside ½ cup of the mixture to be used for the topping.

Into the mixture remaining in the bowl gradually stir the buttermilk, egg, nuts, cinnamon and currants. When the ingredients are well combined and the batter is smooth, pour it into the pan and sprinkle the top evenly with the reserved crumb mixture. Bake the cake in the center of the oven for 15 minutes, then reduce the heat to 375°. Bake for an additional 20 to 25 minutes, or until a small knife inserted in the center comes out clean. Serve the coffeecake warm or at room temperature.

## Texas Stollen *(German-American)*
CINNAMON-AND-RAISIN COFFEE RING

To make one 12-inch ring

¼ cup lukewarm water (110° to 115°)
1 package active dry yeast
½ teaspoon plus 1½ cups sugar
4 to 4½ cups all-purpose flour
1 tablespoon salt
2 eggs
¾ cup lukewarm milk (110° to 115°)

8 tablespoons butter, cut into bits and softened, plus 8 tablespoons butter, softened
4 teaspoons cinnamon
1 cup seedless raisins
1 egg, lightly beaten with 1 tablespoon milk

Pour the lukewarm water into a small shallow bowl and sprinkle with the yeast and ½ teaspoon of the sugar. Let the mixture stand for 2 or 3 minutes, then stir to dissolve the yeast. Set the bowl in a warm, draft-free place (such as an unlighted oven) for 5 to 8 minutes, or until the mixture almost doubles in volume.

Combine 4 cups of the flour, ½ cup of the remaining sugar and the salt in a deep bowl, and make a well in the center. Pour in the yeast mixture, the 2 eggs, ¾ cup of lukewarm milk and the 8 tablespoons of softened butter bits and, with a large spoon, gradually incorporate the dry ingredients into the liquid.

Gather the dough into a ball and place it on a lightly floured surface. Knead the dough, pushing it down with the heels of your hands, pressing it forward, and folding it back on itself. Meanwhile, sprinkle in up to ½ cup more flour, adding it by the tablespoon until the dough no longer sticks to your hands. Continue to knead for 10 minutes, or until the dough is smooth and elastic.

With a pastry brush, spread 1 tablespoon of the softened butter inside a deep bowl. Place the dough in the bowl and turn it about to grease all sides evenly. Drape the bowl loosely with a kitchen towel and set it aside in the warm, draft-free place for about 45 minutes to 1 hour, or until the dough has doubled in volume. Punch it down with a single blow of your fist, and set it to rise again in the warm, draft-free place for another 30 to 45 minutes.

With a pastry brush, lightly coat a large baking sheet with 1 tablespoon of the softened butter and set it aside.

On a lightly floured surface, roll out the dough to a rectangle measuring 20 inches long and 15 inches wide. Spread the surface of the dough with the remaining 6 tablespoons of softened butter, then sprinkle it evenly with the remaining cup of sugar and the cinnamon. Scatter the raisins evenly over the top.

Starting at one of the 20-inch sides, roll up the dough, jelly-roll fashion, into a cylinder. Transfer the cylinder to the buttered baking sheet and bring together the ends of the dough to make a ring. With a sharp knife, cut two thirds of the way through the ring, from its outer edge inward, at 1-inch intervals, gently turning each cut pastry "leaf" to its right to reveal the filling. Drape the ring with a kitchen towel and set it aside in the warm, draft-free place for about 45 minutes to 1 hour, or until it doubles in volume.

Preheat the oven to 375°. With a pastry brush, coat the surface of the coffee ring with the egg-and-milk mixture and bake in the center of the oven for 25 to 30 minutes, or until it is golden brown.

FROSTING
2 cups confectioners' sugar
5 to 6 tablespoons cold water

While the coffee ring is baking, prepare the frosting. Place the confectioners' sugar in a large mixing bowl and, with a spoon, gradually beat in the water, a tablespoon at a time. Continue to beat until the frosting is smooth and has the consistency of heavy cream.

Transfer the coffee ring to a serving dish and, while it is still warm, spoon the frosting over the top, letting it run down the sides. Serve the *Stollen* at room temperature.

## Swedish Cherry Twist *(Northwest)*

To make one 16-inch twist

DOUGH
¼ cup lukewarm water (110° to 115°)
1 package active dry yeast
1 teaspoon plus ⅓ cup sugar
¾ cup lukewarm milk (110° to 115°)
6 tablespoons unsalted butter, softened
1 teapoon salt
1 egg, lightly beaten
3 to 3½ cups flour

DOUGH: Pour the water into a small bowl and sprinkle the yeast and 1 teaspoon of the sugar over it. Let stand for 2 or 3 minutes, then stir well. Set in a warm, draft-free place (such as an unlighted oven) for about 10 minutes, or until the yeast bubbles up and the mixture almost doubles in volume. Meanwhile, combine the milk and 4 tablespoons of the butter and, stirring occasionally, cook over moderate heat until the butter has melted and bubbles begin to form around the edges of the pan. Then pour the mixture into a deep bowl and set aside to cool to lukewarm.

Add the yeast mixture, the salt, the remaining ⅓ cup of sugar and the lightly beaten egg and, with a wooden spoon, stir until all the ingredients are well blended. Then add 3 cups of the flour, 1 cup at a time, and continue to stir until the dough can be gathered into a medium-soft ball.

Place the ball on a lightly floured surface and knead, pushing the dough down with the heels of your hands, pressing it forward and folding it back on itself. As you knead, incorporate as much of the remaining ½ cup of flour as is required to make a smooth, fairly dry dough. When the dough is shiny and elastic, reshape it into a ball. With a pastry brush, coat the inside of another large bowl with 1 tablespoon of the softened butter. Drop in the dough and turn it about to coat the entire ball with butter. Then drape the bowl with a towel and put it into the draft-free place for about 45 minutes, or until the dough doubles in volume. Meanwhile, brush a baking sheet with the remaining tablespoon of butter.

Punch the dough down with a single blow of your fist and place it on a lightly floured surface.

| TOPPING | chopped |
|---------|---------|
| 1 egg yolk, lightly beaten and combined with 1 teaspoon milk | ¼ cup sugar |
| ¼ cup blanched almonds, coarsely | 1 teaspoon ground cinnamon |
|  | 4 candied cherries, halved |

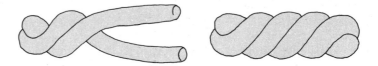

SHAPING AND TOPPING: Cut the dough in half and with your hands shape each half into a cylinder about 18 inches long and 1½ inches wide. Place the cylinders side by side on the baking sheet and pinch the tops together so that the cylinders form a narrow "V." Following the diagram above, shape the dough into a twist about 14 inches long. Set the twist aside to rise for 45 minutes, or until it doubles in bulk.

Preheat the oven to 375°. With a pastry brush, coat the twist with the combined egg yolk and milk, then mix the almonds, sugar and cinnamon, and sprinkle them over the top. Set the candied cherry halves in two rows along the length of the twist. Bake in the center of the oven for about 25 minutes, or until golden brown. Turn the cherry twist out on a wire rack to cool. Serve it warm or at room temperature.

# Desserts

Even in today's calorie-conscious society, dessert can play an important role in a meal. And, after all, a homemade dessert made with milk or cream, eggs, fruits and nuts can be nearly as nutritious as it is delicious. Everyday family desserts can be as simple as baked apples, prune whip or Southern lime sherbet (for which there are recipes below). A memorable dessert, however, will make any dinner festive. It should complement the dinner in color, texture and flavor. Follow a hearty dinner with one of the refreshing fruit desserts in this chapter—perhaps glazed oranges from the Far West, frozen cranberry mousse from New England, or Northwestern strawberry frango. Cap a light summer meal with rich, soul-satisfying strawberry shortcake, Creole-Acadian cherries jubilee or frozen nesselrode pudding enriched with raisins and chestnut purée, drenched in dark rum and decorated, in a spectacular example of caloric overkill, with rosettes of whipped cream. This may seem like a great deal of work for the postscript to a meal, but like most of the desserts in this chapter it can be prepared hours (even days) ahead of time.

The classic dessert to make at leisure for later serving is ice cream. Most Americans rate ice cream as their favorite dessert from childhood; following are recipes for old-fashioned vanilla and chocolate, as well as fruit- and candy-flavored varieties from the South and Far West. Most of these traditional ice creams are churned round and round in a freezer packed with rock salt and dry ice, but the wonderfully creamy rum-flavored Italian version of ice cream is a dessert you can beat up in a matter of minutes and preserve in your refrigerator freezer.

## Cold Orange Soufflé

To serve 6

2 envelopes unflavored gelatin

1 cup cold water

8 egg yolks

Two 6-ounce cans frozen orange juice
concentrate, thoroughly defrosted

but with no water added

8 egg whites

1 cup sugar

1 cup heavy cream, chilled

3 tablespoons sugar

½ cup heavy cream, whipped

Sprinkle the gelatin into the cup of cold water and let it soften for about 5 minutes. Meanwhile, with a whisk or a rotary or electric beater, beat the egg yolks until they are thick and lemon yellow. Beat in the softened gelatin.

Then cook the mixture in a small enameled or stainless-steel saucepan over moderate heat, stirring constantly, until it thickens enough to coat a spoon lightly. Do not let it come near a boil or it will curdle. Remove the pan from the heat and quickly stir in the defrosted orange juice. Transfer the mixture to a large mixing bowl and chill in the refrigerator for about ½ hour, or until it thickens to a syrupy consistency.

Beat the egg whites until they begin to froth, then pour in the sugar slowly and beat until the whites form unwavering peaks on the beater when it is lifted out of the bowl. In another bowl, whip the chilled cream until it holds its shape softly, then beat into it the 3 tablespoons of sugar. With a rubber spatula, fold the cream gently but thoroughly into the orange mixture (if it has set too firmly and formed lumps, beat gently with a whisk or rotary beater until smooth), then fold in the egg whites, folding until no streaks of white show. Tie a wax-paper collar around a 1½-quart soufflé dish. It should rise about 2 inches above the rim of the dish. Pour in the soufflé mixture up to the top of the collar, smooth the top with a spatula and chill in the refrigerator for at least 4 hours, or until firm. Carefully remove the collar and pipe decorative swirls or rosettes of whipped cream through a pastry bag on top of the soufflé.

## Maple Mousse (New England)

To serve 6 to 8

1 envelope plus 2 teaspoons
unflavored gelatin

½ cup cold water

1 cup pure maple syrup

4 egg yolks

½ cup brown sugar

4 egg whites

2 cups chilled heavy cream

Sprinkle the gelatin into the ½ cup of cold water and let it soften for about 5 minutes, then set the cup in a shallow pan of simmering water, and stir until the gelatin has dissolved and is clear. Combine with the maple syrup. In a large mixing bowl, beat the egg yolks with a whisk or a rotary or electric beater for 2 or 3 minutes until thick and lemon yellow. Beat into the yolks the maple syrup mixture and pour it into a small saucepan. Cook over moderate heat, stirring constantly, until the mixture thickens enough to coat the spoon heavily. Do not let it boil or the eggs will curdle. Remove from the heat, stir in the brown sugar and mix thoroughly. Transfer to a large bowl and cool to room temperature.

Meanwhile, beat the egg whites until they form unwavering peaks on the beater. In another bowl, whip the chilled cream until it holds its shape softly. With a rubber spatula, fold the cream gently but thoroughly into the maple syrup mixture, then fold in the egg whites, folding until streaks of white no longer show. Rinse a 1½-quart mold, preferably a charlotte mold, in cold water. Shake out the excess water and pour in the mousse mixture. Chill in the refrigerator for at least 4 hours, or until firm.

To unmold, run a knife around the inside edge of the mold, dip the bottom briefly in hot water and wipe it dry. Place a chilled platter on top of the mold, invert and rap it on the table. Chill until ready to serve.

### Frozen Cranberry Mousse  (New England)

To make about 2 quarts
8 egg yolks
1 cup bottled cranberry juice, or juice
   from drained cranberries plus
   enough bottled juice to make 1
   cup
Two 16-ounce cans whole cranberries

(about 4 cups), drained, or 4 cups
   freshly cooked cranberries, cooled
   and drained
1 tablespoon grenadine
4 egg whites
½ cup sugar
1 cup heavy cream, chilled

Beat the egg yolks with a whisk or a rotary or electric beater until they are thick and lemon yellow, then beat in the cranberry juice. Transfer the mixture to a small saucepan and cook over moderate heat, stirring constantly until it thickens enough to coat the spoon heavily. Under no circumstances allow this to boil or the eggs will curdle. Stir in the cranberries and grenadine, and pour into a bowl. Chill in the refrigerator for about ½ hour until it thickens slightly.

Beat the egg whites until they foam, then gradually beat in the sugar. Continue to beat until the whites form unwavering peaks on the beater when it is lifted out of the bowl. In another bowl whip the chilled cream until it holds its shape softly. With a rubber spatula, fold the cream gently but thoroughly into the thickened cranberry mixture, then fold in the egg whites, folding until streaks of white no longer show. Pour into refrigerator trays, or a 2-quart decorative mold or soufflé dish. Cover with foil and freeze until firm. The cranberry mousse may be served in scoops like ice cream, unmolded on a plate, or served directly from a soufflé dish.

To serve 8 to 10

| MERINGUE AND CUSTARD | 2 to 2¼ cups light cream |
| 5 egg whites | A 2-inch piece of vanilla bean |
| ½ cup plus ⅔ cup sugar | 5 egg yolks |

With a wire whisk or a rotary or electric beater, beat the egg whites. As soon as they are frothy, add ½ cup of the sugar. Then continue to beat until the meringue is stiff enough to stand in unwavering peaks on the beater when it is lifted from the bowl.

In a heavy 8- to 10-inch skillet, heat 2 cups of cream and the vanilla bean over low heat. When small bubbles begin to form around the sides of the pan, reduce the heat to the lowest point.

To form each "island" scoop up the meringue in one dessert spoon and invert another dessert spoon over it to shape the meringue into an oval. Slide the meringue off the spoon onto the surface of the simmering cream. Make similar ovals of the remaining meringue. Simmer the meringues uncovered for 2 minutes, turn them over gently with a slotted spoon and cook for 1 or 2 minutes longer, or until they are just firm to the touch. Do not overcook the meringues, or they might disintegrate. Transfer the meringues to a kitchen towel to drain and let them cool to room temperature.

Strain the cream through a fine sieve, measure it and add enough more cream to make 2 cups. Return the vanilla bean and set the cream aside.

Combine the egg yolks and ⅔ cup of sugar in a heavy 2- to 3-quart saucepan and beat them together with a wire whisk. Whisking the mixture constantly, pour in the cream in a slow, thin stream. Add the vanilla bean and place the pan over low heat. Stir gently with a spoon until the custard coats the spoon heavily. Do not let the custard come anywhere near a boil or it will curdle. Strain the custard through a fine sieve into a bowl, discarding the vanilla bean. Cool to room temperature, then refrigerate the custard for 3 to 4 hours to chill it thoroughly.

| CARAMEL | |
| ⅔ cup sugar | ⅓ cup water |

About half an hour before serving, prepare the caramel. Combine ⅔ cup of sugar and ⅓ cup of water in a small heavy pan and bring to a boil over high heat, stirring until the sugar dissolves. Boil the syrup over moderate heat, gently tipping the pan back and forth until the syrup turns a tealike brown. This may take 10 minutes or more. Immediately remove the pan from the heat and pour the caramel into a bowl.

Arrange the meringues on top of the custard and, when the caramel is lukewarm, dribble it over them with a small spoon. To serve, ladle the meringues onto individual dessert plates and spoon custard around them.

To serve 6

| | |
|---|---|
| 3 medium-sized firm ripe peaches | ¼ cup sugar |
| 1 cup heavy cream | 1 teaspoon vanilla extract |
| 1 cup milk | ¼ teaspoon ground nutmeg, |
| 3 eggs plus 2 egg yolks | preferably freshly grated |

Preheat the oven to 325°. Drop the peaches into enough boiling water to immerse them completely and boil briskly, uncovered, for 2 or 3 minutes. With a slotted spoon, transfer the peaches to a sieve or colander and run cold water over them. Peel the peaches with a small sharp knife, halve them and remove the pits. Place each peach half, cut side down, in a 6-ounce custard cup and set aside.

In a small heavy saucepan, warm the cream and milk over moderate heat until small bubbles appear around the sides of the pan. Remove the pan from the heat and cover to keep warm.

With a wire whisk or a rotary or electric beater, beat the eggs and additional egg yolks together in a bowl for 2 or 3 minutes. When they begin to thicken and cling to the beater, beat in the sugar. Then, beating the mixture constantly, pour in the warm cream-and-milk mixture in a slow, thin stream. Add the vanilla and pour the custard mixture over the peaches. Sprinkle the tops with the nutmeg.

Arrange the custard cups in a large shallow baking pan set in the middle of the oven. Pour enough boiling water into the pan to come about 1 inch up the sides of the cups. Bake for 30 to 40 minutes, or until a knife inserted in the custard comes out clean. Remove the cups from the baking pan, cool to room temperature, and serve at once. Or refrigerate and serve the peach custard chilled.

## *Nesselrode Pudding*

To serve 6

| | |
|---|---|
| ½ cup currants | 3 cups heavy cream |
| ¼ cup raisins | An 8¾-ounce can unsweetened |
| ½ cup dark rum | chestnut purée |
| 4 egg yolks | 1 teaspoon vanilla |
| 1 cup sugar | 1 teaspoon vegetable oil |

Soak the currants and raisins in the rum for at least 15 minutes, then drain and reserve the rum and the fruit separately. Beat the egg yolks with a whisk or a rotary or electric beater for about a minute, then beat in all but 3 tablespoons of the cup of sugar. Continue to beat until the yolks are thick and fall slowly back into the bowl in a ribbon when the beater is lifted up. Heat 2 cups of the cream in a small saucepan until small bubbles begin to form around the edge of the pan. Slowly beat the hot cream into the egg yolk mixture, then return to the pan. Cook over moderate heat, stirring constantly, until the mixture thickens enough to coat a spoon lightly. Do not let the mixture come near a boil or it will curdle. Remove from the heat and stir in the chestnut purée, rum, vanilla, currants and raisins. Chill for about ½ hour.

Whip the remaining cup of chilled cream until it thickens slightly, then add the reserved 3 tablespoons of sugar and whip until the cream forms firm peaks on the beater when it is lifted out of the bowl. Fold it into the Nesselrode mixture with a rubber spatula, making sure the two are well combined. Brush a 1½-quart mold, preferably a charlotte mold, with the teaspoon of oil. Invert to drain any excess oil, then fill the mold with the Nesselrode mixture. Cover the top of the mold securely with foil and freeze the pudding for at least 6 hours until firm.

To unmold, run a knife around the inside edge of the mold, dip the bottom briefly in hot water and wipe it dry. Place a chilled serving platter on top of the mold, invert and rap it once on the table to dislodge it.

GARNISH                     tablespoon confectioners' sugar
½ cup heavy cream whipped with 1      Candied chestnuts

Fit a pastry bag with a small star tip, fill the bag with the whipped cream, and pipe rosettes on the top and a decorative border around the bottom of the pudding. Place a small candied chestnut on each rosette.

## Syllabub (South)

*Syllabub was originally an English drink, closely related to eggnog. Its name is reputedly derived from wine that came from Sillery, in the Champagne region of France, and from "bub," which was Elizabethan English slang for a bubbly drink. Always made with wine, syllabub was considered by 18th- and 19th-Century American men to be a ladies' Christmas drink; they preferred the whiskey-based eggnog. In recent years syllabub has been served more frequently as a dessert, as described below. It may also be beaten very thick and used as a topping for fruits or cakes.*

To serve 8                    ¼ cup strained, fresh lemon juice
½ cup brandy               1 tablespoon finely grated fresh
½ cup pale dry sherry           lemon peel
½ cup superfine sugar          1 cup heavy cream

406

Combine the brandy, sherry, sugar, lemon juice and lemon peel in a large bowl. Mix well and set aside at room temperature for 15 to 20 minutes. Then stir in the cream and set aside for 15 minutes longer.

With a large wire whisk or a rotary beater, whip the mixture vigorously for about 1 minute until it begins to foam heavily on top. With a fine wire-mesh skimmer or slotted spoon, scoop the foam from the surface and place it gently in a wine or champagne glass. Beat the cream mixture for another minute or so, skim it as before and add the foam to the glass. Repeat until the glass is full; refrigerate it at once. Following this procedure, fill and immediately refrigerate 7 more glasses.

You may serve the syllabub at once or keep it in the refrigerator for as long as 12 hours. If you prefer to prepare this dessert well in advance, the glasses of syllabub can safely be kept in the freezer for 2 days.

## Baked Alaska

| | |
|---|---|
| To serve 6 to 8 | ½ cup all-purpose flour |
| 2 tablespoons soft butter | 1 cup orange marmalade or apricot |
| 4 egg whites |     preserves |
| Pinch of salt | 1 to 2 tablespoons orange juice |
| ¼ cup sugar |     (optional) |
| 4 egg yolks | 1 quart vanilla ice cream, slightly |
| ½ teaspoon vanilla |     softened |

Brush a tablespoon of soft butter over the bottom and sides of an 11-by-16-inch jelly-roll pan. Line the pan with a 22-inch strip of wax paper and let the extra paper extend over the ends of the pan. Brush the remaining butter over the paper and scatter a small handful of flour over it. Tip the pan from side to side to spread the flour evenly. Then turn the pan over and rap it sharply to dislodge the excess flour.

Preheat the oven to 400°. In a mixing bowl, beat the egg whites and salt until they form soft, wavering peaks. Add the sugar, two tablespoons at a time, and beat until the whites cling to the beater solidly when it is lifted out of the bowl. In another small bowl, beat the egg yolks for about a minute, then add the vanilla. Mix a large tablespoon of the whites into the yolks, then pour the mixture over the remaining egg whites. Fold together, adding the ½ cup flour, two tablespoons at a time.

Pour the batter into the jelly-roll pan and spread it out evenly. Bake in the middle of the oven for about 12 minutes, or until the cake draws slightly away from the sides of the pan, and a small knife inserted in its center comes out dry and clean. Turn the cake out on a sheet of wax paper, then gently peel off the top layer of paper. Let the cake cool and cut it in half crosswise. Spread one layer with the cup of marmalade or apricot preserves (if it is too thick to spread, thin it by beating into it 1 or 2 tablespoons of orange juice) and place the second layer on top. Mold the softened ice cream on a sheet of aluminum foil into a brick the length and width of the cake. Wrap in the foil and freeze until solid.

Pinch of salt
¾ cup superfine sugar

About 10 minutes before serving, make the meringue. First, preheat the broiler to its highest point. Then, beat the egg whites and salt until they form soft peaks. Still beating, slowly pour in the sugar, and continue to beat for about 5 minutes, or until the egg whites are stiff and glossy. Remove the ice cream from the freezer and place it on top of the cake on a flat, ovenproof baking dish. Mask the cake and ice cream on all sides with the meringue, shaping the top as decoratively as you like. Slide the cake under the broiler for 2 to 3 minutes, and watch it carefully; it burns easily. The meringue should turn a pale, golden brown in 2 to 3 minutes. Serve at once before the ice cream begins to melt.

## Strawberry Frango  (Northwest)

To serve 8 to 10
1 quart fresh strawberries, washed
   and hulled
1 cup milk

4 egg yolks
1 cup sugar
½ teaspoon vanilla extract
2 cups heavy cream, chilled

Crush the berries by mashing them against the sides of a bowl with a spoon and continue to mash until the berries are a smooth purée. Chill for at least 30 minutes.

Pour the milk into a heavy 2- to 3- quart enameled or stainless-steel saucepan and set it over moderate heat. When small bubbles form around the edges of the pan, immediately remove from the heat. Cover the pan and set the milk aside.

In a large mixing bowl, beat the egg yolks and sugar together with a whisk or a rotary or electric beater until they are thick enough to form a slowly dissolving ribbon when the beater is lifted from the bowl. Gradually pour in the milk, whisking all the while. Then beat in the vanilla extract and pour the mixture back into the saucepan. Stir over low heat until the custard thickens lightly; do not let it come to a boil or it will curdle. Pour into a mixing bowl and cool to room temperature. Then refrigerate for 30 minutes.

In a chilled mixing bowl, beat the heavy cream with a whisk or a rotary or electric beater until it forms firm peaks. Remove the custard from the refrigerator and, with a rubber spatula, fold in the berries and then the whipped cream. Spoon the mixture into a 2-quart mold and smooth the top with a spatula. Cover with plastic wrap or foil, and freeze for at least 6 hours, or until firm. In its frozen form the custard is known in the Northwest as a frango.

To serve 12

| | |
|---|---|
| 2½ cups heavy cream, chilled | (1 cup crumbs) |
| ½ cup confectioners' sugar | ¼ cup dark rum |
| A pinch of salt | 1½ teaspoons vanilla extract |
| 5 to 8 stale macaroons, crushed in a blender or wrapped in a towel and crushed with a rolling pin | ¼ cup sliced toasted almonds |
| | 6 candied cherries, cut in half |
| | (optional) |

Place a pleated paper liner in each of twelve 2- to 2½-inch muffin-tin cups and set aside. In a bowl, combine 1¼ cups of the heavy cream, the sugar, salt and macaroons and chill the mixture for 30 minutes.

In a large chilled mixing bowl, beat the remaining heavy cream with a whisk or a rotary or electric beater until it thickens and forms soft peaks. With a rubber spatula, fold in the macaroon mixture and the rum and vanilla extract. Fill the muffin-tin liners with the cream mixture. Sprinkle the tops evenly with the sliced almonds and, if you like, top with a candied cherry half. Freeze for at least 2 hours before serving.

## *San Antonio Fruit Ice Cream*

To make about 1½ quarts

| | |
|---|---|
| 1¼ cups strained fresh grapefruit juice | An 8½- to 9-ounce can pears, drained and coarsely chopped (about 1¼ cups) |
| ¾ cup strained fresh orange juice | |
| 3 tablespoons strained fresh lemon juice | ½ cup drained canned pineapple chunks |
| ½ to 1 cup sugar | 2 large ripe bananas, peeled and cut in chunks |
| A 1-pound 4-ounce can mangoes, drained and coarsely chopped (about 2½ cups) | 1 cup heavy cream |
| | 3 egg whites |

Pour the grapefruit, orange and lemon juice into a large mixing bowl, add ½ cup of sugar, and stir until it dissolves. Stir in the mangoes, pears, pineapple and bananas. Ladle 2 or 3 cups of the mixture into the jar of an electric blender and blend at high speed for 10 seconds. Turn off the machine, scrape down the sides of the jar with a rubber spatula, and blend again until the fruit is reduced to a purée. Scrape the purée into a bowl and blend the remaining fruit mixture in the same fashion.

Stir the heavy cream into the purée, taste and add up to ½ cup more sugar by the tablespoonful if desired. Then pour the mixture into three ice-cube trays from which the dividers have been removed, dividing it

409

evenly among them. Freeze for about 2 hours, or until the ice cream is slushy, stirring it every 30 minutes or so and scraping into it the ice particles that form around the edges of the trays.

In a deep bowl, beat the egg whites with a wire whisk or a rotary or electric beater until they are stiff enough to stand in unwavering peaks on the whisk or beater when it is lifted from the bowl. Working quickly, scrape the ice-cream mixture from the trays into a bowl with a rubber spatula. Scoop the egg whites over the ice cream and mix them together gently but thoroughly with a large spoon or table fork. Return the mixture to the trays, spreading it evenly and smoothing the tops with the spatula. Freeze for 2 or 3 hours longer, or until the ice cream is firm.

## Chocolate Ice Cream

To make about 2 quarts

| | |
|---|---|
| 1 quart heavy cream | chocolate, coarsely chopped |
| 8 ounces semisweet baking | 1 tablespoon vanilla extract |

In a heavy 2- to 3-quart saucepan, heat the cream over moderate heat until bubbles appear around the sides of the pan. Remove the pan from the heat, add the chocolate and stir until it is completely dissolved. Cool to room temperature, stir in the vanilla, and refrigerate the mixture until it is thoroughly chilled.

Pack a 2-quart ice-cream freezer with layers of finely crushed or cracked ice and coarse rock salt in the proportions recommended by the freezer manufacturer. Add cold water if the manufacturer advises it. Then ladle the ice cream into the ice-cream can and cover it.

If you have a hand ice-cream maker, fill it with the ice cream and let it stand for 3 or 4 minutes before beginning to turn the handle. It may take 15 minutes or more of turning for the ice cream to freeze, but do not stop turning at any time or the ice cream my be lumpy.

When the handle can barely be moved, the ice cream is ready to serve or to be molded. If you wish to keep it only for an hour or two, remove the lid and dasher. Scrape the ice cream off the dasher and pack it firmly in the container with a spoon. Cover securely, pour off any water in the bucket and repack the ice and salt solidly around it.

If you have an electric ice-cream maker, fill and cover the can, turn it on and let it churn for about 15 minutes, or until the motor slows or actually stops. Serve the ice cream immediately or follow the procedure above to keep it for an hour or so. Tightly covered, the ice cream may safely be kept in the freezer for several weeks.

To mold the ice cream, pack it tightly into ice-cream or other decorative molds. Fasten the hinges, set a lid on the mold, or cover it tightly with foil. Freeze for 3 or 4 hours, until the ice cream is very firm. Just before serving, wipe the outside of the ice-cream mold with a hot wet towel, open the hinges and carefully turn the ice cream out onto a serving plate. If you have used a conventional mold, dip the bottom briefly into hot water. Invert a serving plate over the mold, grasp plate and mold together firmly, and turn them over, letting the ice cream slide out.

## Peppermint Stick Candy Ice Cream *(South)*

To make 1½ quarts

6 ounces peppermint stick candy, 3 ounces pulverized in a blender or finely crushed with a rolling pin
and 3 ounces finely chopped
½ cup sugar
1 quart heavy cream
1½ teaspoons vanilla extract

Combine the pulverized peppermint stick candy, the sugar and 1 cup of the cream in a heavy 1½- to 2-quart saucepan. Then set the pan over low heat and stir until the sugar dissolves completely. Remove the pan from the heat and stir in the vanilla extract and the remaining 3 cups of cream. Refrigerate the cream mixture until it is thoroughly chilled.

Pack a 2-quart ice-cream freezer with layers of finely crushed or cracked ice and coarse rock salt in the proportions recommended by the manufacturers, adding cold water if the directions call for it.

If you have a hand ice-cream maker, fill it with the ice-cream mixture, and let it stand for 3 or 4 minutes. Then turn the handle, starting slowly at first, and crank continuously for a few minutes. Add the chopped peppermint stick candy and continue to crank for 10 minutes longer. Do not stop turning or the ice cream may be lumpy. When the handle can barely be moved, the ice cream is ready to serve. If you wish to keep it for an hour or two, remove the lid and dasher. Scrape the ice cream off the dasher and pack it firmly in the container. Cover securely, pour off any water in the bucket and repack the ice and salt solidly around it.

If you have an electric ice-cream maker, fill the can with the ice-cream mixture, cover the can, turn it on and let it churn for about 5 minutes. Add the chopped candy, cover again and continue to churn for 10 minutes longer, or until the motor slows or actually stops. Serve the ice cream immediately or follow the procedure above to keep it for an hour or two.

Lacking an ice-cream maker, pour the ice-cream mixture and chopped candy into three ice-cube trays without their dividers, spreading it evenly. Freeze for about 6 hours, stirring every 30 minutes or so and scraping into it the ice particles that form around the edges of the tray.

Tightly covered, the ice cream may safely be kept in the freezer for several weeks. Before serving, place it in the refrigerator for 20 or 30 minutes to let it soften slightly so that it can be easily served.

411

## Old-fashioned Vanilla Ice Cream

To make about 1½ quarts

| | |
|---|---|
| 4 cups heavy cream | ⅛ teaspoon salt |
| ¾ cup sugar | 1½-inch piece of vanilla bean |

In a heavy 1½- or 2-quart enameled or stainless-steel saucepan, heat 1 cup of the cream, the sugar, salt and the vanilla bean over low heat, stirring until the sugar is dissolved and the mixture is hot but has not come to a boil. Remove from heat and lift out the vanilla bean. Split the bean in half lengthwise and, with the tip of a small knife, scrape the seeds into the cream mixture. When the mixture has cooled somewhat, stir in the remaining 3 cups of cream.

Pack a 2-quart ice-cream freezer with layers of finely crushed or cracked ice and coarse rock salt in the proportions recommended by the freezer manufacturer, adding cold water if the directions call for it. Then pour or ladle the cream mixture into the ice-cream container and cover it. Let it stand for 3 or 4 minutes. Then turn the handle, starting slowly at first, and crank continuously until the handle can barely be moved. Wipe the lid carefully, remove it and lift out the dasher. Scrape the ice cream off the dasher into the container and pack down with a spoon. Cover the container securely. Drain off any water in the bucket and repack it with ice and salt. Replace the container and let it stand 2 or 3 hours before serving.

## Lime Sherbet  (South)

To make about 1 pint

| | |
|---|---|
| 2 tablespoons plus 2 cups cold water | 2 cups strained fresh lime juice |
| 1 teaspoon unflavored gelatin | ¼ teaspoon salt |
| 2 cups sugar | 2 drops green food coloring |
| | 2 egg whites |

Pour the 2 tablespoons of cold water into a small bowl and sprinkle the gelatin over it to soften.

Combine the remaining 2 cups of water and the sugar in a small heavy saucepan and boil over high heat for about 5 minutes, stirring until the sugar dissolves and the syrup becomes completely clear. Thoroughly stir in the gelatin, remove the pan from the heat, and add the lime juice, salt and food coloring. Pour into a bowl and cool to room temperature. Then pour the mixture into 2 ice-cube trays from which the dividers have been removed. Freeze for 1 to 1½ hours, or until solid particles begin to form on the bottom and sides of the tray. Beat the sherbet briskly with the flat of a fork and return it to the freezer for 1 to 1½ hours more.

With a wire whisk or a rotary or electric beater, beat the egg whites until stiff enough to stand in unwavering peaks on the beater when lifted from the bowl. With a rubber spatula, scrape the sherbet into a deep bowl. Scoop the egg whites over the sherbet and fold them together thoroughly, return the lime sherbet to the ice-cube trays, smooth the tops with a spatula and freeze for 2 or 3 hours longer until the finished sherbet has a fine snowy texture.

To serve, spoon the sherbet into parfait glasses or dessert dishes.

## Lemon-Orange Ice

To make 1½ pints

¾ pound large sugar cubes
3 medium navel oranges

2 cups water
¼ cup fresh lemon juice
Small bunch fresh mint

Rub about 10 sugar cubes over the skins of the whole oranges to saturate them with the orange oil. Then squeeze the oranges. If they do not produce 1 cup of juice, use another orange. In a 1½ or 2-quart saucepan, bring the water and all of the sugar cubes to a boil over high heat, stirring until the sugar dissolves. Timing from the moment when it begins to boil, let the mixture boil briskly, without stirring, for 5 minutes. Immediately remove the pan from the heat and cool the syrup to room temperature. Stir in the orange juice and lemon juice, and pour into 2 ice-cube trays. Freeze for 3 to 4 hours at least, beating the ice after a half hour to break up the solid particles that will form on the bottom and sides of the tray. Continue to beat every half hour until the ice has a fine and snowy texture. Serve on chilled dessert plates or in sherbet glasses and garnish with the mint.

## Lemon Sauce

To make about 2 cups

6 tablespoons butter, cut into ½-
   inch bits
⅔ cup sugar
½ cup water

⅓ cup strained fresh lemon juice
3 egg yolks
2 tablespoons freshly grated lemon
   peel

In a 2- to 3-quart enameled or stainless-steel saucepan, combine the butter, sugar, water, lemon juice and egg yolks. Stirring constantly with a large spoon, cook over the lowest possible heat until the mixture thickens enough to heavily coat the back of the spoon. Do not let the sauce come anywhere near a boil or it will curdle.

Pour the sauce into a bowl, stir in the lemon peel and let cool to room temperature. Lemon sauce can be served as an accompaniment to fruit salads or puddings or apple pandowdy.*

413

* See index.

*Durgin Park's Indian Pudding*  (*New England*)

___

To serve 6

| | |
|---|---|
| 1 teaspoon butter, softened, plus 4 tablespoons butter, cut into ½-inch bits | ½ cup dark molasses |
| | ¼ cup sugar |
| | ¼ teaspoon baking soda |
| 2 eggs | ¼ teaspoon salt |
| 6 cups milk | 1 cup yellow cornmeal |

Preheat the oven to 350°. With a pastry brush, spread the teaspoon of softened butter over the bottom and sides of a 2-quart soufflé or baking dish. Set aside.

In a heavy 4- to 5-quart saucepan, beat the eggs with a wire whisk until they are well mixed. Stirring constantly with the whisk, add 4 cups of the milk, the molasses, sugar, baking soda and salt. Then bring to a simmer over moderate heat, stirring until the molasses and sugar dissolve.

Pour in the cornmeal very slowly, making sure the simmering continues, and stirring constantly to keep the mixture smooth. Cook uncovered, stirring from time to time, until the pudding is thick enough to hold its shape solidly in a spoon. Beat in the 4 tablespoons of butter bits and remove the pan from the heat. Then pour in the remaining 2 cups of milk in a thin stream, beating constantly.

Pour the pudding into the buttered dish and bake in the middle of the oven for 1 hour. Reduce the oven temperature to 300° and continue baking for 4 hours longer, or until the pudding is very firm when prodded gently with a finger.

Serve the pudding at once, directly from the baking dish, or let it cool and serve at room temperature. Indian pudding may be accompanied by unsweetened whipped cream or vanilla ice cream, if you like.


*Bread Pudding with Whiskey Sauce*  (*Creole-Acadian*)

___

To serve 8 to 10

PUDDING

| | |
|---|---|
| 2 tablespoons butter, softened | 3 eggs |
| A 12-ounce loaf day-old French- or Italian-type white bread | 2 cups sugar |
| | ½ cup seedless raisins |
| 1 quart milk | 2 tablespoons vanilla extract |

Preheat the oven to 350°. With a pastry brush, spread the softened butter evenly over the bottom and sides of a 13-by-9-by-2-inch baking-serving dish. Set the dish aside.

Break the bread into chunks, dropping them into a bowl as you proceed, and pour milk over them. When the bread is softened, crumble it into small bits and let it continue to soak until all the milk is absorbed.

In a small bowl, beat 3 eggs and 2 cups of sugar together with a wire whisk or a rotary or electric beater until the mixture is smooth and thick. Stir in the raisins and vanilla extract, then pour the egg mixture over the bread crumbs and stir until all the ingredients are well combined.

Pour the bread pudding into the buttered dish, spreading it evenly and smoothing the top with a rubber spatula. Place the dish in a large shallow roasting pan set on the middle shelf of the oven and pour boiling water into the pan to a depth of about 1 inch. Bake for 1 hour, or until a knife inserted in the center of the pudding comes out clean.

SAUCE
8 tablespoons butter (1 quarter-
    pound stick), cut into ½-inch bits

1 cup sugar
1 egg
½ cup bourbon

Meanwhile, prepare the sauce in the following fashion: Melt the butter bits in the top of a double boiler set over hot, not boiling, water. Stir 1 cup of sugar and 1 egg together in a small bowl and add the mixture to the butter. Stir for 2 or 3 minutes, until the sugar dissolves completely and the egg is cooked, but do not let the sauce come anywhere near a boil or the egg will curdle. Remove the pan from the heat and let the sauce cool to room temperature before stirring in the bourbon.

Serve the bread pudding at once, directly from the baking dish, and present the whiskey sauce separately in a sauceboat or small bowl.

### Prune Whip with Custard Sauce

To serve 4

PRUNE WHIP
2 egg whites
½ teaspoon grated lemon rind

2 teaspoons lemon juice
⅓ cup sugar
½ cup strained prunes

Combine the egg whites, lemon rind, lemon juice and sugar in the top of a double boiler and cook over boiling water, beating with a rotary beater until the mixture fluffs up and holds its shape. Remove from the heat and fold in the strained prunes. (These can be the canned baby food or freshly made.)

CUSTARD SAUCE
1 tablespoon cornstarch
½ cup sugar

2 egg yolks, well beaten
1 cup hot milk
1 teaspoon vanilla extract

Mix the cornstarch and sugar, then stir them into the egg yolks. Pour the hot milk slowly into the egg mixture. Cook the custard in a double boiler until it is thick enough to coat a metal spoon. Stir in the vanilla extract, then chill and serve with the prune whip.

To serve 4 to 6

1 cup uncooked long-grain white rice, not the converted variety
¾ cup sugar
½ cup seedless raisins
½ teaspoon salt
4½ to 5 cups milk
2 egg yolks, lightly beaten
1 teaspoon finely grated fresh lemon peel
1 teaspoon vanilla extract

Combine the rice, sugar, raisins, salt and 4½ cups of milk in a heavy 3- to 4-quart saucepan. Bring the mixture to a boil over high heat, stirring until the sugar dissolves. Then reduce the heat to its lowest setting and cover the pan tightly. Simmer for 45 minutes, until the rice is soft and a grain can be easily mashed against the side of the pan with the back of a spoon. (Check the pan from time to time and, if the liquid seems to be cooking away, stir in up to ½ cup more milk by the tablespoonful.)

When the rice is fully cooked, ladle about 2 tablespoons of the hot liquid into the beaten egg yolks and mix well. Then, stirring the rice mixture constantly, pour in the egg yolks and cook gently over low heat for 2 to 3 minutes longer. Do not let the mixture come anywhere near a boil or it will curdle.

Remove the pan from the heat, stir in the lemon peel and vanilla, and pour the rice pudding into a serving bowl to cool to room temperature. Refrigerate the pudding for 1 or 2 hours, or until thoroughly chilled.

## *Yellow Rice with Cold Fruit and Curry Sauce* (*Northwest*)

To serve 6

FRUIT
1 pint (about 2 cups) fresh ripe strawberries
1 pint (about 3 cups) fresh ripe blueberries
1 pound (about 3 cups) fresh ripe sweet cherries
1 small ripe honeydew melon or cantaloupe
4 medium-sized firm ripe peaches
1 tablespoon fresh lemon juice

Pick over the strawberries, blueberries and cherries one at a time, removing any stems or caps and discarding any fruit that is badly bruised or shows signs of mold. If you like, pit the cherries. Wash the fruits separately in a sieve or colander under cold running water, then shake them dry and spread on paper towels to drain.

Cut the melon in half crosswise, and scoop out the seeds with a spoon. With a melon baller, shape the melon meat into balls.

With a small knife, peel the peaches and cut each of them lengthwise into quarters. Discard the stones. Drop the peach quarters into a small bowl, add the lemon juice to prevent discoloration, and turn the peaches about with a spoon until they are evenly coated. Then combine the strawberries, blueberries, cherries, melon balls and peach quarters in a serving bowl, cover with foil or plastic wrap and refrigerate until ready to serve.

YELLOW RICE
2 tablespoons butter
2 cups uncooked long-grain white rice (not the converted variety)

1 quart boiling water
¼ teaspoon finely crumbled saffron threads or ground saffron
8 whole toasted almonds

In a heavy 3- to 4-quart saucepan, melt the butter over moderate heat. When the foam begins to subside, add the rice and stir for 2 or 3 minutes, until the grains glisten with butter. Do not let the rice brown. Stir in the boiling water and saffron, and bring to a boil over high heat. Cover tightly, reduce the heat to low, and simmer for about 20 minutes, or until the rice is tender and has absorbed all the liquid in the pan.

CURRY SAUCE
1 cup dry white wine
2½ cups chicken stock, fresh or canned

2 tablespoons curry powder
2 tablespoons cornstarch
2 tablespoons cold water
¼ cup seedless raisins

While the rice is simmering, prepare the sauce in the following fashion: Combine the wine, chicken stock and curry powder in a small enameled or stainless-steel pan and, stirring frequently, bring to a boil over high heat. Reduce the heat to low and simmer for 2 or 3 minutes. In a small bowl or cup, stir the cornstarch and cold water together to make a smooth paste. Then, stirring the curry mixture constantly, pour in the cornstarch in a slow, thin stream and simmer until the sauce thickens lightly and is smooth. Stir in the raisins.

Spoon the rice into a 1-quart mold or deep bowl, packing it in firmly with the back of the spoon. Then place an inverted serving plate over the mold and, grasping plate and mold together firmly, turn them over. Rap the plate sharply on a table and the rice should slide out easily. Arrange the toasted almonds attractively on top of the rice. Pour the sauce into a bowl or sauceboat and serve it with the yellow rice and the fresh fruit.

*Upside-down Cranberry Pudding* (New England)

To serve 6
2 tablespoons butter, softened, plus 6 tablespoons butter, melted and cooled
1½ cups firm fresh unblemished cranberries

¼ cup coarsely chopped walnuts
⅓ cup plus ½ cup sugar
1 egg
½ cup flour
½ cup heavy cream, chilled

417

Preheat the oven to 325°. With a pastry brush, spread the 2 tablespoons of softened butter over the bottom and sides of an 8-inch pie tin. Wash the cranberries and pat them dry. Spread them evenly in the bottom of the buttered pan and sprinkle the berries with the chopped walnuts and ⅓ cup of the sugar.

In a mixing bowl, beat the egg and the remaining ½ cup of sugar together with a wire whisk or a rotary or electric beater, until the mixture thickens and clings to the beater. Beating constantly, add the flour, a few tablespoonfuls at a time. Then beat in the melted cooled butter and pour the batter over the cranberries and nuts. Bake in the middle of the oven for 45 minutes, or until the top is golden brown and a cake tester inserted in the center comes out clean. Cool the pudding to room temperature.

Meanwhile, in a chilled bowl, whip the cream with a whisk or a rotary or electric beater until it is stiff enough to stand in unwavering peaks on the beater when it is lifted from the bowl. Refrigerate covered with plastic wrap until ready to serve.

To unmold and serve the pudding, run a thin-bladed knife around the sides of the pan to loosen it. Place an inverted serving plate over the pudding and, grasping plate and pan together firmly, carefully turn them over. The pudding should slide out easily. Decorate the pudding as fancifully as you like by piping the whipped cream onto the top through a pastry bag fitted with a decorative tube, or simply spread the cream over the pudding and swirl it about with a small spatula.

## Cherry Cobbler

To serve 6

| | |
|---|---|
| 1 cup all-purpose flour | 2 tablespoons melted and cooled butter |
| 2 tablespoons sugar | ½ cup sugar |
| 1½ teaspoons baking powder | 2 one-pound cans pitted sour cherries, thoroughly drained, ¼ cup of juice reserved, or 2 pounds freshly cooked pitted cherries, with ¼ of their cooking liquid reserved |
| ½ teaspoon salt | |
| 2 tablespoons butter, chilled and cut into bits | |
| ⅔ cup heavy cream | 1 tablespoon arrowroot |

Preheat the oven to 425°. Sift the flour, 2 tablespoons of sugar, baking powder and salt together into a large mixing bowl. Add the chilled butter, and, with your fingertips, rub the dry ingredients and butter together until most of the lumps have disappeared and the mixture resembles coarse meal. Pour in the heavy cream and mix thoroughly until a soft dough is formed. Gather it into a compact ball and transfer it to a lightly floured board. Knead the dough for about a minute by folding it end to end and then pressing it down and pushing it forward several times with the heel of your hand. Now roll the dough out into a circle about ½ inch thick. With a 2½-inch cookie cutter, cut out 6 circles and set them aside. In a large mixing bowl, combine 1 tablespoon of the melted butter, sugar, the ¼ cup of cherry juice and arrowroot, and stir together until the arrowroot has dissolved. Add the cherries, stir again, then pour the entire contents of the bowl into a 6-by-8-by-2½-inch ovenproof baking dish. Spread the cherries out in the dish and arrange the circles of dough over them side by side. Brush the dough with the remaining 1 tablespoon of melted butter. Bake in the middle of the oven for 25 to 30 minutes, or until the biscuits are a golden brown. Serve warm or at room temperature directly from the dish.

## Ambrosia *(South)*

To serve 6

4 large seedless oranges, peeled
2 cups freshly shredded coconut, or

substitute 2 cups finely shredded
  packaged coconut
¼ cup sugar

With a small sharp knife, peel the oranges deeply enough to remove all of the white pith. Slice the oranges crosswise into ⅛-inch-thick rounds and place them in a large serving bowl. Add the shredded coconut and sugar and, with a large wooden spoon, toss together lightly but thoroughly. Cover the bowl with plastic wrap and refrigerate at least 2 hours before serving.

## Baked Apples

To serve 6

6 large apples, such as Rome
  Beauty, York Imperial or
  Jonathan
1 cup sugar

2 cups boiling water
1 cinnamon stick
½ cup currants or raisins
½ cup chopped walnuts

Preheat the oven to 375°. Core each of the apples to within ½ inch of its base and arrange them in a buttered baking dish just large enough to hold them comfortably.

Combine the sugar, water and cinnamon stick in a saucepan, stir to dissolve the sugar, then bring to a boil. Boil rapidly for about 8 minutes, or until the mixture becomes a thin syrup.

In a mixing bowl, combine the currants or raisins with the chopped walnuts and stuff the centers of the apples with the mixture. Remove the cinnamon stick from the syrup, pour the syrup over the apples and bake them in the middle of the oven for 40 minutes, or until they are soft to the touch but not falling apart.

Transfer the apples to individual serving dishes and pour the syrup remaining in the baking dish over them.

## Apple Jonathan *(Eastern Heartland)*

To serve 6 to 8

5 tablespoons butter, softened
1 cup flour
2 teaspoons double-acting baking
  powder
½ teaspoon salt
½ cup sugar
1 egg

¼ cup milk
6 medium-sized tart cooking apples
  (about 2 pounds), peeled, cored
  and cut lengthwise into ⅛-inch-
  thick slices
½ cup pure maple syrup
1 cup heavy cream

Preheat the oven to 400°. With a pastry brush, spread 1 tablespoon of the softened butter evenly over the bottom and sides of a shallow 3-quart baking dish. Combine the flour, baking powder and salt, and sift them together onto a plate or a sheet of wax paper.

In a deep bowl, cream the remaining 4 tablespoons of butter and the sugar, beating and mashing the mixture against the sides of the bowl with the back of a spoon until it is light and fluffy. Beat in the egg. Add about ½ cup of the flour mixture and, when it is well incorporated, stir in 2 tablespoons of the milk. Then beat in the remaining ½ cup of flour and the remaining 2 tablespoons of milk and stir until the batter is smooth.

Drop the apple slices into a bowl, pour in the maple syrup, and stir until the slices are coated on all sides. Spread the apple slices evenly in the bottom of the buttered baking dish and pour in the batter, smoothing the top with a rubber spatula.

Bake in the middle of the oven for 30 to 35 minutes, or until a cake tester or toothpick inserted in the topping comes out clean. Serve the apple Jonathan hot or at room temperature, spooning it out of the baking dish into individual dessert bowls. Present the cream separately in a pitcher.

OPPOSITE
*Hot bread pudding Creole style is a far cry from the bland nursery dessert of tradition. It is liberally laced just before serving with a rich, buttery whiskey sauce.*

## Strawberry Flummery *(Eastern Heartland)*

To serve 4 to 6

½ cup plus 2 tablespoons sugar
⅓ cup cornstarch
¼ teaspoon salt

3 cups milk
1 egg yolk, lightly beaten
1 teaspoon vanilla extract
1 pint firm ripe strawberries

420

Combine ½ cup of the sugar, the cornstarch and salt in a heavy 2- to 3-quart saucepan and, stirring the mixture constantly with a wire whisk, pour in the milk in a slow, thin stream. Whisking constantly, cook over

moderate heat until the mixture comes to a boil and thickens heavily. Reduce the heat to its lowest setting.

Ladle several tablespoonfuls of the liquid into the beaten egg yolk, mix well and, still whisking, gradually pour the yolk into the simmering liquid. Simmer for 3 or 4 minutes longer to cook the egg yolk through, but do not let the mixture come anywhere near a boil.

Remove the pan from the heat and stir in the vanilla. Cool to room temperature, then pour the flummery into a serving bowl. Cover with wax paper and refrigerate for at least 2 hours, or until the flummery is thoroughly chilled.

Just before serving, pick over the strawberries, removing the hulls and discarding any blemished berries. Wash the strawberries briefly in a sieve or colander set under cold running water. Spread the berries on paper towels and pat them completely dry with fresh towels. Cut each berry in half lengthwise. Place the halves in a bowl, add the remaining 2 tablespoons of sugar, and toss gently together with a wooden spoon to coat the berries evenly. Arrange the strawberries attractively on top of the flummery and serve at once.

## Rhubarb Ring with Strawberries  *(Northwest)*

To serve 6

| | |
|---|---|
| 1 tablespoon vegetable oil | 2 envelopes unflavored gelatin |
| 2 pounds fresh rhubarb, trimmed, washed and cut into ½-inch pieces (about 4 cups) | 1 cup heavy cream, chilled |
| | 1 tablespoon rum |
| 1 cup plus 1 tablespoon sugar | 2 cups fresh ripe strawberries, hulled |
| 1½ cups water | Confectioners' sugar |

Brush the tablespoon of oil evenly over the inside surfaces of a 1-quart ring mold, and wipe away all excess with a paper towel.

Combine the rhubarb, 1 cup of the sugar and 1 cup of the water in a 2- to 3-quart enameled or stainless-steel saucepan and bring to a boil over high heat, stirring until the sugar dissolves. Reduce the heat to low and simmer partially covered for about 10 minutes, or until the rhubarb is tender but still intact.

Meanwhile, sprinkle the 2 envelopes of gelatin into the remaining ½ cup of water and let it soften for 4 or 5 minutes. Add the gelatin to the rhubarb mixture and stir until it dissolves completely. Then pour the mixture into the oiled ring mold, spreading it and smoothing the top with a spoon or rubber spatula. Cool to room temperature, cover the mold with foil or plastic wrap, then refrigerate for at least 3 hours, or until it is firm to the touch.

422

Just before serving, pour the cream into a large chilled bowl. Whip with a wire whisk or a rotary or electric beater until the cream is stiff enough to stand in firm, unwavering peaks on the beater when it is lifted from the bowl. Beat in the remaining tablespoon of sugar and the rum, and taste for sweetness.

To unmold and serve the rhubarb ring, run a thin knife around the sides of the mold and dip the bottom briefly into hot water. Place an inverted serving plate on top of the mold and, grasping plate and mold together firmly, turn them over. Rap the plate on a table and the rhubarb ring should slide out easily. Arrange a row of strawberries around the ring and mound the rest of the berries in the center of the mold. Sprinkle the berries with confectioners' sugar. Serve the whipped cream separately from a small bowl.

### Glazed Oranges  (Far West)

| | |
|---|---|
| To serve 6 | A 2-inch cinnamon stick and 10 |
| 6 navel or Temple oranges | whole cloves, wrapped together |
| 1 cup dry white wine | in cheesecloth |
| 2 tablespoons red wine vinegar | 2 tablespoons Grand Marnier or |
| ¾ cup sugar | other orange liqueur (optional) |

With a small sharp knife, remove the skin from two of the oranges without cutting into the bitter white pith beneath it. Cut the peel into strips about ⅛ inch wide, drop them into enough boiling water to cover them completely and cook briskly for about 2 minutes. With a slotted spoon, transfer the strips to paper towels to drain.

Cut the white outer pith and membrane from the two skinned oranges, using short sawing motions. Then cut away and discard the peel, pith and all the white outside membrane from the remaining four oranges.

Combine the wine, vinegar, sugar, and the cheesecloth-wrapped cinnamon and cloves in a 3- to 4-quart enameled or stainless-steel saucepan and bring to a boil over high heat, stirring until the sugar dissolves. Add the oranges and the strips of orange peel, and turn them about with a spoon to coat them evenly with the syrup. Reduce the heat to low, then simmer uncovered for 15 minutes, turning the oranges over frequently.

With a slotted spoon, transfer the oranges and peel to a deep bowl. Pick out and discard the cheesecloth bag of spices and taste the syrup for sweetness. If you like, you may add 1 or 2 tablespoons of orange liqueur to the syrup. Pour the syrup over the oranges and cool to room temperature. Cover the bowl tightly with foil or plastic wrap and refrigerate the oranges for at least 2 hours to chill them thoroughly before serving.

Syllabub is a frothy Southern sweet adapted from a 16th Century English tipple. In the old recipe, a cow was milked directly into a bowl of wine to create a bubbly drink. In the modern version, brandy and sherry are flavored with sugar and lemon, then thickened with heavy cream and beaten briefly. The froth that forms is scooped into a glass with a skimmer.

To serve 4

A 1-pound can pitted sweet Bing
   cherries, drained, with all their
   liquid reserved
1 tablespoon cornstarch mixed with

1 tablespoon cold water
¼ cup kirsch liqueur
¼ cup maraschino liqueur
1 pint vanilla ice cream

Pour the cherry liquid into a small saucepan and bring it to a simmer over moderate heat. Stirring constantly, add the cornstarch-and-water mixture and cook until the sauce comes to a boil, thickens lightly and is smooth. Remove the pan from the heat and let the sauce cool to room temperature, then cover tightly and set it aside.

Prepare and assemble the cherries jubilee at the dinner table, when you are ready to serve them. Light an alcohol burner or table-top stove and set a 12-inch copper *flambé* or *crêpe suzette* pan over the flame. Arrange the cherry sauce, cherries, kirsch and maraschino conveniently beside the pan. Place a scoop of ice cream in each of four chilled individual dessert bowls and set them to one side.

Drop the cherries into the *flambé* pan and stir until they are heated. Carefully pour the kirsch and maraschino into the pan, step back from the table and let the liqueurs warm for a few seconds. They may burst into flame spontaneously. If not, ignite them with a match.

Gently slide the pan back and forth over the heat until the flames die, basting the cherries all the while with the liqueurs. Then stir in the cherry sauce and cook briefly to heat it through.

Ladle the cherries and sauce over the ice cream and serve at once.

## *Strawberry Shortcake*

To make 6 small shortcakes

4 cups all-purpose flour
6 tablespoons sugar
5 teaspoons baking powder
2 teaspoons salt
12 tablespoons butter (1½ quarter-

pound sticks) chilled and cut into
   bits
1½ cups heavy cream
6 teaspoons melted and cooled butter
2 pints of fresh, ripe strawberries
1½ teaspoons sugar
1 pint heavy cream for topping

Preheat the oven to 450°. Sift the flour, sugar, baking powder and salt together into a large mixing bowl. Add the butter, and, with your fingertips, rub the dry ingredients and butter together until most of the lumps disappear and the mixture resembles coarse meal. Pour in the heavy cream

425

and, with your hands or a large spoon, mix thoroughly until a soft dough is formed. Gather it into a compact ball and transfer it to a lightly floured board. Knead the dough for about a minute by folding it end to end and pressing it down and pushing it forward several times with the heel of your hand. Then roll the dough out into a circle about 1 inch thick. With a 3-inch cookie cutter, cut out 6 circles. Cut the remaining dough into six 2½-inch circles. (If there isn't enough dough, gather the scraps together, knead briefly and roll out again.) Arrange the 3-inch circles on a lightly buttered cookie sheet. Brush each with a teaspoon of melted butter, then top with the smaller circle. Bake in the middle of the oven for 12 to 15 minutes until firm to the touch and golden brown.

Meanwhile, chop half the strawberries coarsely, reserving the most attractive ones for the top. Separate the shortcakes. Spread a layer of chopped strawberries on the bottom circles, sprinkle with sugar and gently place the smaller circles on top. Garnish with the whole strawberries. Strawberry shortcake is traditionally served with heavy cream.

## Bananas Foster *(Creole-Acadian)*

To serve 4

1 pint vanilla ice cream
8 tablespoons butter, cut into
    ½-inch bits
½ cup brown sugar

4 firm ripe bananas, peeled and cut
    lengthwise into halves
½ teaspoon ground cinnamon
½ cup banana liqueur
1 cup rum

OPPOSITE
*Bananas Foster is a spectacular but easily assembled dessert. The bananas are peeled and halved, then cooked at the table in a brown-sugar syrup. In a final blaze of glory they are flamed with banana liqueur and rum and served over vanilla ice cream.*

Prepare and assemble the bananas Foster at the dinner table when you are ready to serve them. Light an alcohol burner or table-top stove and set a 12-inch copper *flambé* or crêpe-suzette pan over the flame. Arrange all the ingredients conveniently beside the pan. Place a scoop of ice cream on each of four chilled individual dessert plates and set them to one side.

Combine the butter and brown sugar in the *flambé* pan and stir until the mixture becomes a smooth syrup. Add the bananas and baste them with the syrup for 3 or 4 minutes, then sprinkle in the cinnamon.

Carefully pour in the banana liqueur and rum, and let the liquors warm for a few seconds. They may burst into flame spontaneously. If not, ignite them with a match. Slide the pan back and forth until the flames die, basting the bananas all the while. Place two banana halves around each scoop of ice cream, spoon the sauce over the top and serve at once.

## Blueberry Grunt *(New England)*

To serve 6

| | |
|---|---|
| 2 cups firm ripe blueberries | ¼ teaspoon salt |
| 1 cup all-purpose flour | ½ cup light cream |
| 2 teaspoons double-acting baking | ½ cup sugar |
|    powder | 1 cup water |
| | 1 cup heavy cream |

Wash the blueberries in a colander set under cold running water, discarding any stems or blemished berries. Drain thoroughly and place the berries in a 2- to 3-quart enameled or stainless-steel saucepan.

To make the batter for the dumplings, combine the flour, baking powder and salt and sift them into a deep mixing bowl. Pour in the light cream and stir briskly until the batter is smooth.

Add the sugar and water to the blueberries and bring to a boil over high heat. Boil for 1 minute, then drop the batter into the pan by the tablespoonful, spacing the dumplings about 1 inch apart. Reduce the heat to low, cover tightly and simmer undisturbed for 20 minutes. When done the dumplings will be puffed and a small skewer or toothpick inserted in the center of one will come out clean.

To serve, transfer the dumplings with a slotted spoon to 6 heated individual dessert bowls and pour the blueberry sauce around them. Present the heavy cream separately in a pitcher, or whip the cream until stiff and serve it in a small bowl.

## Olga's Flan *(Puerto Rican-American)*
CARAMEL CUSTARD

To serve 8 to 10

| | |
|---|---|
| 3½ cups sugar | ½ teaspoon salt |
| Two 13-ounce cans evaporated milk | 1 tablespoon vanilla extract |
| | 8 eggs |

To line an ovenproof mold—which should hold 2 to 2½ quarts and be at least 2 inches deep—with caramel, it is necessary to work very quickly, or the caramel will harden. Because the temperature of the hot caramel will be over 300°, handle the mold with extreme caution.

Place 1½ cups of the sugar in a small heavy saucepan or skillet and set over high heat. Stir constantly until the sugar completely dissolves, then reduce the heat to moderate and cook briskly without stirring for about 10 minutes, or until the syrup turns a rich golden tealike brown. As soon as the syrup reaches this color, remove the pan from the heat and carefully pour the caramel syrup in a thin stream into the mold. Tip and swirl the mold from side to side to coat the bottom as evenly as possible. Set the mold aside.

Preheat the oven to 325°. In a 1- to 1½-quart saucepan, bring the evaporated milk almost to a boil over moderate heat. Remove from the heat and stir in the salt and vanilla extract.

With a wire whisk or a rotary or electric beater, beat the eggs together in a large mixing bowl until well blended, then add the remaining 2 cups of sugar gradually. Continue to beat until the mixture is thick and pale yellow. Stirring constantly, pour in the hot milk mixture in a slow, thin stream. Then strain the contents of the bowl through a fine sieve directly into the caramel-lined mold.

Place the mold in a large shallow baking pan, and set the pan on the middle shelf of the oven. Pour enough boiling water into the baking pan to come halfway up the sides of the mold. Bake the custard—lowering the oven temperature if the water in the pan begins to simmer—for 1½ hours, or until a thin knife inserted in the center of the custard comes out dry and clean. Remove the mold from the pan, cool to room temperature, then refrigerate the custard in the mold for at least 2 hours, or until it is thoroughly chilled.

To unmold the custard, run a sharp knife around the sides and dip the bottom of the mold briefly in hot water. Wipe the outside of the mold dry, place a chilled serving plate upside down over the mold and, grasping both the plate and mold firmly together with both hands, quickly turn them over. Rap the plate on a table and the custard should slide easily out of the mold. Serve cold.

# Pies & Pastries

"As American as apple pie" is a familiar expression, but not a very precise one. Americans make many kinds of apple pie: shallow- and deep-dish, single- and double-crusted. Puréed apples are used as well as slices, cinnamon flavors some and maple sugar others. The likeliest candidate for the classic version is the two-crusted pie described on the following pages, filled to overflowing with slices of Greening apples, lightly spiced with cinnamon, allspice and nutmeg, sweetened with sugar and then made a bit tart with lemon juice. But in Marlborough pie, one of the earliest New England versions, a single-crust pie, or tart is filled with lemony applesauce and custard, then topped with mounds of whipped cream. Still another New England version produces individual fried pies.

Popular as apple pie may be, in any version, it is certainly not the only fruit-filled American pie. In fact, much of the nation's rich bounty finds its way into pie shells: blueberries, pecans and sweet potatoes from the South; pumpkins and cranberries from New England; sour cherries, blackberries and rhubarb from the Northwest. Although fruit pies dominate American pastry-making, the most devastatingly rich pies of all have no fruit: bourbon-and-caramel-custard and black-bottom pies from the South, and Boston cream and maple-walnut pies from New England.

Pastry dough can also be deep fried. Italian-Americans wrap circles around metal *cannoli* tubes, then fill the crisp shells with a succulent mixture of ricotta cheese and candied fruit.

Happily, pastry dough can be made at any time and refrigerated before rolling for as long as two days. Or it can be wrapped in airtight plastic bags, frozen, then defrosted in the refrigerator. Alternatively, the pastry may be rolled and shaped, and the unbaked pie shells frozen, then defrosted, before filling and baking.

430

To make one 9-inch pastry shell or
  piecrust top

NONSWEET SHORT-CRUST PASTRY
6 tablespoons unsalted butter,
  chilled and cut into ¼-inch bits
2 tablespoons lard, chilled and cut

into ¼-inch bits
1½ cups unsifted flour
1 teaspoon salt
3 to 4 tablespoons ice water

SWEET SHORT-CRUST PASTRY
6 tablespoons unsalted butter,
  chilled and cut into ¼-inch bits
2 tablespoons lard, chilled and cut
  into ¼-inch bits
1½ cups unsifted flour
¼ teaspoon salt
1 tablespoon sugar
3 to 4 tablespoons ice water

TO PREPARE THE PASTRY DOUGH: In a large, chilled bowl, combine the butter and lard bits, the flour and salt. (Add 1 tablespoon of sugar, if you are making a sweet pastry.) With your fingertips, rub the flour and fat together until the mixture looks like flakes of coarse meal.

Pour 3 tablespoons of ice water over the mixture all at once, toss together lightly and gather the dough into a ball. If the dough crumbles, add up to 1 tablespoon more ice water by drops until the particles adhere. Dust the pastry dough with a little flour and wrap it in wax paper. Refrigerate for at least 1 hour before using.

TO MAKE AN UNFILLED PIE SHELL: Spread 1 tablespoon of softened butter over the bottom and sides of a 9-inch pie pan with a pastry brush.

On a lightly floured surface, pat the chilled short-crust pastry dough into a rough circle about 1 inch thick. Dust a little flour over and under it, and roll it out from the center to within an inch of the far edge of the circle. Lift the dough and turn it clockwise about 2 inches; roll again from the center to within an inch or so of the far edge. Repeat—lifting, turning, rolling—until the circle is about ⅛ inch thick and 13 to 14 inches in diameter. If the dough sticks to the board or table, lift it gently with a metal spatula and sprinkle a little flour under it. Drape the dough over the rolling pin, lift it up, and unroll it slackly over the buttered pie pan. Gently press the dough into the bottom and sides of the pan, taking care not to stretch it. With a pair of scissors, cut off the excess dough from the edges, leaving a 1-inch overhang all around the outside rim. Tuck the overhang under the edge all around and crimp it with your fingers or the tines of a fork.

TO MAKE A PARTIALLY BAKED PIE SHELL: Preheat the oven to 400°. Roll out the short-crust pastry dough as described above and fit it into a buttered 9-inch pie pan. To prevent the pie shell from buckling as it bakes, spread a piece of buttered aluminum foil across the pan and press it gently

431

into the bottom and against the sides of the pie shell. Bake in the middle of the oven for 10 minutes, then remove the foil. Bake for another 2 or 3 minutes, or until the pastry is a very delicate golden color. Remove the pie shell from the oven and cool to room temperature before filling.

TO MAKE A FULLY BAKED PIE SHELL: Preheat the oven to 400°. Roll out the short-crust pastry dough as described above and fit it into a buttered 9-inch pan. To prevent the pie shell from buckling as it bakes, spread a piece of buttered aluminum foil across the pan and press it gently into the bottom and against the sides of the pie shell. Bake in the middle of the oven for 10 minutes, then remove the foil. Bake for 4 or 5 minutes longer, or until the pastry is lightly browned. Remove the pie shell from the oven and cool to room temperature before filling.

## Apple Pie

To make one 9-inch pie

2½ cups all-purpose flour
8 tablespoons chilled vegetable
   shortening or lard
4 tablespoons chilled butter, cut in
¼-inch pieces
¼ teaspoon salt
6 tablespoons ice water
1 tablespoon melted and cooled
   butter

In a large mixing bowl, combine the flour, vegetable shortening or lard, butter and salt. Working quickly, use your fingertips to rub the flour and fat together until they look like flakes of coarse meal. Pour the ice water over the mixture, toss together, and press and knead gently with your hands until the dough can be gathered into a compact ball. Dust very lightly with flour, wrap in wax paper and chill for at least ½ hour.

Lightly butter a 9-inch pie plate and divide the ball of dough in half. On a floured surface, roll out half of the ball into a circle about ⅛ inch thick and 13 to 14 inches in diameter. Lift it up on the rolling pin and unroll it over the pie plate. Be sure to leave enough slack in the middle of the pastry to enable you to line the plate without pulling or stretching the dough. Trim the excess pastry with a sharp knife, so that the pastry is even with the outer rim of the pie plate. Preheat the oven to 375°.

FILLING
¾ cup granulated sugar
1 teaspoon cinnamon
¼ teaspoon allspice
¼ teaspoon nutmeg
1 tablespoon flour
6 cups of peeled, cored and sliced
   Greening apples, about ⅛-inch
   thick (1¾ to 2 pounds)
1 tablespoon lemon juice
2 tablespoons butter, cut in small
   pieces

For the filling, combine the sugar, cinnamon, allspice, nutmeg and flour in a large mixing bowl. Add the apples and the lemon juice, and toss together gently but thoroughly. Fill the pie shell with the apple mixture, mounding it somewhat higher in the center. Although the apple filling may appear quite high, it will shrink considerably during the baking. Dot the top of the filling with the 2 tablespoons of butter.

For the upper crust, roll out the remaining half of the dough into a circle the same size and thickness as the bottom crust. Lift it up on the rolling pin and drape it gently over the filling. With a scissors, trim the top crust to within ¼ inch of the pie plate. Tuck the overhanging ¼ inch under the edge of the bottom crust all around the rim and then press down with the tines of a fork to seal the two crusts securely. Brush the pastry evenly with the melted butter and cut two small gashes in the center of the top crust to allow the steam to escape. Bake the pie in the middle of the oven for 40 minutes, or until the crust is golden brown. Serve warm or at room temperature with vanilla ice cream or heavy cream.

## Fried Apple Pies *(New England)*

To make about 30 small pies

PASTRY DOUGH

2 cups all-purpose flour
1 tablespoon sugar
1 teaspoon double-acting baking
   powder
2 tablespoons butter, chilled and cut

into ¼-inch bits
2 tablespoons lard, chilled and cut
   into ¼-inch bits
1 egg, lightly beaten
½ cup milk

Combine the flour, 1 tablespoon of sugar and the baking powder and sift them into a deep bowl. Drop in the butter bits and the lard and, with your fingertips, rub the flour and fat together until they resemble flakes of coarse meal. Add the egg and milk and beat vigorously with a wooden spoon until the dough is smooth and can be gathered into a compact ball. Refrigerate for at least 30 minutes before using.

APPLE FILLING

2 tablespoons butter
5 medium-sized tart cooking apples,
   peeled, cored and coarsely

chopped (about 1¾ cups)
¼ cup sugar
⅛ teaspoon ground cinnamon

Meanwhile, prepare the apple filling in the following fashion: Melt 2 tablespoons of butter over moderate heat in a heavy 1½- to 2-quart saucepan. Add the apples and turn them about with a spoon to coat the pieces evenly. Reduce the heat to low, and simmer partially covered for 15 to 20 minutes, or until the apples are soft. With a rubber spatula, scrape the entire contents of the pan into a bowl, and mash the apples to a smooth purée with the back of a fork. Stir in the sugar and cinnamon and set the mixture aside to cool to room temperature.

Vegetable oil for deep frying          Confectioners' sugar

Preheat the oven to its lowest setting. Line a large baking sheet with a double thickness of paper towels and place it in the middle of the oven.

Pour vegetable oil into a deep fryer or large, heavy saucepan to a depth of 3 inches and heat the oil to 385° on a deep-frying thermometer.

On a lightly floured surface, roll out the chilled dough until it is no more than ⅛ inch thick. With a cookie cutter or the rim of a glass, cut the dough into 4-inch rounds. Gather the scraps together, roll them out as before and cut as many more rounds as possible.

To make each pie, place about 1½ teaspoons of the apple filling in the center of each round of dough. Dip a pastry brush in cold water and lightly moisten the edges. Then fold the round in half and crimp the edges securely together with the tines of a table fork.

Deep-fry the pies 3 or 4 at a time, turning them occasionally with a slotted spoon, for 8 to 10 minutes, or until they are golden brown on all sides. As they brown, transfer the pies to the lined pan and keep them warm in the oven while you fry the rest.

To serve, arrange the fried pies attractively on a heated platter and sprinkle them lightly with confectioners' sugar.


## Blackberry-and-Apple Pie (Northwest)

To serve 6 to 8

3 medium-sized tart cooking apples (about 1 pound), peeled, cored and cut into ¼-inch thick slices

3 pints ripe blackberries (about 2¼ pounds), washed and thoroughly drained

½ cup plus 3 tablespoons sugar

Short-crust pastry

2 tablespoons butter, melted

1 tablespoon superfine sugar (below)

Preheat the oven to 425°. In a heavy 8- to 10-inch skillet, combine the apples, 3 tablespoons of the sugar and the butter, and cook uncovered over moderate heat, stirring frequently, for 5 minutes, or until the apples are tender but not falling apart. Remove the pan from the heat and let the apples cool to room temperature.

Pack the blackberries snugly into the bottom of a round, deep pie dish about 7½ inches in diameter and 2½ inches deep, preferably a dish with a ½-inch-wide rim. Sprinkle the berries with ¼ to ½ cup sugar, depending on taste, and spread the cooled apple slices evenly over the top.

On a lightly floured surface, roll the pastry into a rough circle at least

10 inches in diameter and ⅛ inch thick. From the edge cut two strips about 12 inches long and ½ inch wide. Moisten the edge of the pie dish with a pastry brush or your finger dipped in cold water and lay the strips of pastry around it, overlapping the ends to secure them and pressing the strips firmly against the edge of the dish. Moisten the tops of the strips, then drape the remaining pastry over the rolling pin and unroll it over the dish. Press it gently in place. With scissors or a knife trim the pastry to within ½ inch of the dish and fold the border into a roll around the rim. Press the tines of a fork all around the edges of the pastry to secure it to the dish. With a small, sharp knife, cut three 1-inch-long parallel slits about ½ inch apart in the center of the pie. Brush the top lightly with cold water and sprinkle it evenly with 1 tablespoon of superfine sugar. Bake in the middle of the oven for 25 minutes, or until the crust is golden brown. Serve the pie at once, directly from its baking dish, or let it cool to room temperature. Blackberry-and-apple pie is traditionally accompanied by custard sauce or heavy cream.

CUSTARD SAUCE

| To make about 1½ cups sauce | 1 tablespoon sugar |
|---|---|
| 1½ cups milk | 1 egg yolk |
| 2 teaspoons cornstarch | ½ teaspoon vanilla extract |

In a heavy 1- to 1½-quart saucepan, combine ¼ cup of the milk and the cornstarch, and stir with a whisk until the cornstarch is dissolved. Add the remaining 1¼ cups of milk and the sugar, and cook over moderate heat, stirring, until the sauce thickens and comes to a boil. In a small bowl break up the egg yolk with a fork and stir in 2 or 3 tablespoons of the sauce. Then whisk the mixture back into the remaining sauce. Bring to a boil again and boil for 1 minute, stirring constantly. Remove the pan from the heat and add the vanilla. Custard sauce is served hot with blackberry-and-apple pie.

## Marlborough Pie (New England)

To make one 9-inch pie

| | |
|---|---|
| 1 tablespoon butter, softened | 4 eggs |
| Short-crust pastry for an 8- to 9-inch pie shell | 2 egg yolks |
| | 2 tablespoons strained fresh lemon juice |
| 6 medium-sized tart cooking apples, peeled, cored and coarsely chopped | 1 tablespoon finely grated fresh lemon peel |
| 1½ cups sugar | 1 cup heavy cream, chilled |

With a pastry brush, spread the butter evenly over the bottom and sides of a 9-inch pie tin.

Following the directions for a baked unfilled pie shell, roll the dough into a circle about ⅛ inch thick and at least 12 inches in diameter. Drape the dough over the rolling pin, lift it up and unroll it slackly over the buttered pie tin. Gently press the dough against the sides of the tin and trim off the excess dough with a small knife, leaving a 1-inch overhang all around the rim. Turn the overhang underneath the edge of the circle and secure the dough to the rim by crimping it with your fingers or the tines of a fork. Chill for 1 hour.

Preheat the oven to 400°. Spread a sheet of buttered aluminum foil over the tin and press it gently against the dough to support the sides of the pastry as it bakes. Bake in the middle of the oven for 10 minutes. Then discard the foil and, with the point of a small skewer or knife, gently prick the pastry in the places where it has puffed up. Bake the pastry for 15 minutes longer, or until it begins to brown. Set it aside to cool, and reduce the oven temperature to 350°.

Meanwhile, in a 2- to 3-quart enameled or stainless-steel saucepan, bring the apples and sugar to a simmer over moderate heat, stirring until the sugar dissolves. Reduce the heat to low and simmer, partially covered, for about 15 minutes, or until a chunk of apple can be easily mashed against the side of the pan with a spoon. If the mixture seems too fluid, stir it over high heat for a few minutes to evaporate the excess liquid. Purée the apples through a food mill or, with the back of a spoon, rub them through a fine sieve into a bowl. There should be about 2 cups of sauce.

In a deep bowl, beat the eggs and egg yolks with a wire whisk or a rotary or electric beater for 3 or 4 minutes. When the eggs thicken and cling to the beater, add the applesauce, lemon juice and lemon peel and fold them together gently but thoroughly. Pour the apple mixture into the pastry shell and bake in the middle of the oven for about 45 minutes, or until a knife inserted in the center comes out clean.

Let the Marlborough pie cool to room temperature. Just before serving, pour the cream into a chilled bowl. With a whisk or a rotary or electric beater, whip the cream until it is stiff enough to stand in unwavering peaks on the beater when it is lifted from the bowl. When serving the pie present the cream separately in a chilled serving bowl or sauceboat.

To make one 9-inch pie

2 pints fresh whole blueberries, washed and thoroughly drained (5 cups)

1 cup sugar.

1 cup water

1 teaspoon grated lemon rind

3 tablespoons cornstarch

A 9-inch fully baked pastry shell, cooled

1 cup heavy cream

2 teaspoons confectioners' sugar

In a 1- to 1½-quart enameled or stainless-steel saucepan, combine 1 cup of the blueberries, the sugar, water, lemon rind and cornstarch. Bring to a boil over high heat, then reduce the heat and, stirring almost constantly, cook for 5 to 10 minutes, until the sauce is thick and glossy. Remove from the heat and, with a rubber spatula, transfer the mixture to a small bowl to cool to lukewarm.

Spread the remaining 4 cups of blueberries out in a single layer on paper towels and pat them thoroughly dry with additional towels. Then spoon them into the pastry shell and mound the berries slightly in the center. When the sauce has cooled sufficiently, pour it into the shell.

With a whisk or a rotary or electric beater, whip the heavy cream in a cold mixing bowl until the cream begins to thicken. Then beat in the confectioners' sugar and continue to beat until the cream is stiff enough to form firm peaks on the beater when it is lifted from the bowl. Spoon the whipped cream into a pastry bag fitted with a plain or decorative tip and pipe a border around the edge of the pie. Or spoon the cream over the pie and swirl the top attractively with a spatula. Serve the pie at once.

## *Apricot Chiffon Pie*

To make one 9-inch pie

A 9-inch pastry shell

1 cup canned or cooked apricots

1 tablespoon gelatin

¼ cup cold water

½ cup apricot juice

½ cup sugar

¼ teaspoon salt

2 tablespoons lemon juice

1 cup heavy cream

Bake the pastry shell and while it is cooling make the filling. Purée the apricots. Soak the gelatin in the cold water for 5 minutes, until it has softened. In a saucepan, heat the apricot juice, then add the gelatin, sugar, salt, lemon juice and puréed apricots. Mix well, then allow to cool. Whip ¾ cup of the cream. When the apricot mixture begins to congeal, fold in the whipped cream, then pour the filling into the pastry shell. Chill thoroughly. Before serving, whip the remaining cream and spread it on top of the pie.

To make one 9-inch pie

PASTRY
1¼ cups all-purpose flour
4 tablespoons chilled vegetable

shortening or lard
2 tablespoons chilled butter, cut in
¼ inch pieces
⅛ teaspoon salt
3 tablespoons ice water

In a large mixing bowl, combine the flour, vegetable shortening or lard, butter and salt. Working quickly, use your fingertips to rub the flour and fat together until they look like flakes of coarse meal. Pour 3 tablespoons of ice water over the mixture, toss together, and press and knead gently with your hands until the dough can be gathered into a compact ball. Dust very lightly with flour, wrap in wax paper and chill the dough for at least ½ hour.

Lightly butter a 9-inch pie plate. On a floured surface, roll the dough out into a circle about ⅛ inch thick and 13 to 14 inches in diameter. Lift it up on the rolling pin and unroll it over the pie plate, leaving enough slack in the middle of the pastry to enable you to line the plate without pulling or stretching the dough. Trim the excess pastry with a sharp knife to within ½ inch of the pie plate and fold the extra ½ inch to make a double thickness all around the rim of the plate. With the tines of a fork or your fingers, press the pastry down around the rim.

Preheat the oven to 400°. To prevent the unfilled pastry from buckling as it bakes, either set another pie plate, lightly buttered on the underside, into the pastry shell, or line it with a sheet of lightly buttered foil. In either case, do not prick the pastry or the filling will run out when it is added later.

Bake the shell in the center of the oven for 10 minutes, remove the pie plate or foil, then turn the oven down to 350° for 10 minutes more, or until the pastry has lightly browned. Let the shell cool while you make the filling.

FILLING
½ cup granulated sugar
5 tablespoons flour
¼ teaspoon salt
3 egg yolks
2 cups milk
2 tablespoons butter, cut into ½

inch pieces
½ teaspoon vanilla
2 tablespoons dark rum
1½ cups chilled heavy cream
3 large, ripe bananas, peeled and
sliced into ¼-inch rounds

Sift the sugar, flour and salt into a large mixing bowl. With a large spoon, beat in the egg yolks one at a time. Heat the milk and 2 tablespoons of butter in a small saucepan until the butter melts and small bubbles form around the edge of the pan. Slowly, pour it into the mixing bowl, stirring constantly with a whisk. Add the vanilla and rum, and return the mixture to the saucepan. Bring almost to a boil, reduce the heat to low and simmer, stirring until it thickens to a smooth, heavy custard. Let it cool to lukewarm. Meanwhile, beat ½ cup of the cream with a whisk or rotary or electric beater until it forms firm peaks on the beater when it is lifted out of the bowl. With a rubber spatula, gently but thoroughly fold it into the custard. Spread ¼ inch of custard on the bottom of the pie shell and arrange a layer of bananas on top of it. Continue alternating a layer of custard with one of bananas, ending with a top layer of bananas. Beat the remaining cream until stiff, and either pipe it on top of the pie through a pastry bag fitted with a plain or decorative tip or spread it on with a spatula in decorative swirls. Chill for at least an hour before serving.

## Boston Cream Pie

To serve 8

CAKE

| | |
|---|---|
| 2 teaspoons plus 6 tablespoons butter, softened | ¼ teaspoon salt |
| 2 tablespoons all-purpose flour | ¾ cup sugar |
| 1½ cups cake flour (not self-rising) | 2 eggs |
| 2 teaspoons double-acting baking powder | 1 teaspoon vanilla extract |
| | ½ cup milk |

CAKE: Preheat the oven to 375°. With a pastry brush, spread 2 teaspoons of softened butter over the bottom and sides of two 9-inch pie tins. Sprinkle the all-purpose flour onto the tins and tip them from side to side to spread the flour evenly. Then invert the tins and rap the bottoms sharply to remove the excess flour. Combine the cake flour, baking powder and ¼ teaspoon of salt and sift them onto a plate or wax paper.

In a deep bowl, cream the 6 tablespoons of softened butter and ¾ cup of sugar together, beating them against the sides of the bowl with the back of a large spoon until they are light and fluffy. Beat in two eggs, one at a time, and 1 teaspoon of vanilla. Then, beating constantly, sprinkle in about ½ cup of the cake-flour mixture and, when it is incorporated, add 2 or 3 tablespoonfuls of the milk. Repeat two more times, adding ½ cup of the flour alternately with 2 or 3 tablespoons of the milk, and continue to beat until the batter is smooth.

Pour the batter into the tins, dividing it equally and smoothing it with a spatula. Bake in the middle of the oven for about 15 minutes, or until the cakes begin to shrink away from the sides of the tin and the center springs back immediately when prodded gently with a finger. Turn the cakes out on wire racks to cool to room temperature.

CUSTARD FILLING
½ cup light cream
½ cup milk
¼ cup sugar

A pinch of salt
4 teaspoons cornstarch
2 eggs, lightly beaten
½ teaspoon vanilla extract

CUSTARD FILLING: In a heavy 2- to 3-quart saucepan, warm ½ cup of cream and ¼ cup of milk over moderate heat. When bubbles begin to form around the edges of the pan, add the ¼ cup of sugar and a pinch of salt and stir until the sugar has dissolved. Remove the pan from the heat and cover to keep the filling warm.

Combine the remaining ¼ cup of milk and the cornstarch in a bowl and stir with a wire whisk until smooth. Whisk in the two beaten eggs and then, stirring the mixture constantly, pour in the cream-and-milk mixture in a slow, thin stream. Return the contents of the bowl to the saucepan and, stirring all the while, cook over low heat until the custard thickens heavily and is smooth. Once it thickens, remove it from the heat; overcooking will make it lumpy. Add ½ teaspoon of vanilla, and let the custard cool to room temperature.

Place one layer of the cake, upside down, on a serving plate and, with a metal spatula, spread the top evenly with the cooled custard. Carefully set the second layer, also upside down, on top of the custard.

CHOCOLATE FROSTING
3 one-ounce squares semi-sweet
    chocolate, cut into small bits
2 tablespoons butter

¼ cup light cream
½ cup confectioners' sugar, sifted
½ teaspoon vanilla extract

CHOCOLATE FROSTING: In a small, heavy saucepan, stir the chocolate bits and 2 tablespoons of butter over low heat to melt them completely. Remove from the heat and, stirring the mixture constantly, pour in ¼ cup of cream in a thin stream. When the mixture is smooth, sift the confectioners' sugar over the top and beat vigorously for a minute or two. Stir in ½ teaspoon of vanilla. Then pour the frosting evenly over the cake, allowing it to flow down the sides of the layers.

NOTE: A simpler, but equally traditional, version of Boston cream pie is filled with raspberry jam and topped with confectioners' sugar. Melt ½ cup of jam over low heat, rub it through a fine sieve, then spread it smoothly over the bottom cake layer. Set the top layer in place and sprinkle it lightly with ¼ cup of sifted confectioners' sugar.

## Deep-Dish Peach Pie with Cream-Cheese Crust

To serve 6
8 tablespoons butter (1 quarter-
    pound stick), softened
8 tablespoons cream cheese, softened

1¼ cups all-purpose flour
2 tablespoons sugar
¼ teaspoon salt
2 tablespoons heavy cream

In a large mixing bowl, cream the butter and cheese by beating them together with a large spoon until smooth and fluffy. Sift the combined flour, sugar and salt into the mixture, add the cream and, with your hands or a large spoon, mix thoroughly until the dough can be gathered into a compact ball. Dust lightly with flour, wrap in wax paper and refrigerate while you prepare the filling.

FILLING

1½ pounds fresh peaches (8 to 10 medium-sized peaches)

1 tablespoon flour

2 tablespoons brown sugar

3 tablespoons melted butter

2 teaspoons vanilla

1 egg yolk, lightly beaten with 2 teaspoons cold water

1 teaspoon sugar

Preheat the oven to 350°. To peel the peaches easily, drop them into a pan of boiling water. Scoop them out after about 30 seconds, and while they are still warm, remove their skins with a small, sharp knife. Cut the peaches in half, discard the pits and slice thinly.

Combine the peaches, flour, brown sugar, melted butter and vanilla in a large bowl, and with a large spoon mix them together gently but thoroughly. With a rubber spatula, scrape the entire contents of the bowl into an 8-inch-square baking dish about 2½ inches deep. Spread the peaches out evenly. On a lightly floured surface, roll the pastry into a 10- to 11-inch square. Lift it up on the rolling pin and gently drape it over the top of the dish. Crimp the edges of the pastry to secure it around the outside of the dish and brush the pastry evenly with the egg-yolk-water mixture, then sprinkle with the sugar. Cut 2 small slits in the top of the pie to allow steam to escape and bake in the middle of the oven for 35 to 40 minutes, or until the crust is golden brown. Serve directly from the dish.

## Pumpkin Pie *(New England)*

To make one 9-inch pie

1¼ cups all-purpose flour

4 tablespoons chilled vegetable shortening or lard

2 tablespoons chilled butter, cut in ¼-inch pieces

⅛ teaspoon salt

3 tablespoons ice water

In a large mixing bowl, combine the flour, vegetable shortening or lard, butter and salt. Use your fingertips to rub the flour and fat together until they look like flakes of coarse meal. Pour the ice water over the mixture, toss together, and press and knead gently with your hands, only until the dough can be gathered into a compact ball. Dust very lightly with flour, wrap in wax paper and chill for at least ½ hour.

Lightly butter a 9-inch pie plate. On a floured surface, roll the dough out into a circle about ⅛ inch thick and 13 to 14 inches in diameter. Lift it up on the rolling pin and unroll it over the pie plate, leaving enough

441

slack in the middle of the pastry to enable you to line the plate without pulling or stretching the dough. Trim the excess pastry with a sharp knife to within ½ inch of the pie plate and fold the extra ½ inch under to make a double thickness all around the rim of the plate. With the tines of a fork or with your fingers, press the pastry down around the rim. Preheat the oven to 350°.

FILLING

½ cup heavy cream
½ cup milk
¾ cup dark brown sugar
1 teaspoon cinnamon
⅛ teaspoon ground cloves

½ teaspoon ground ginger
3 eggs, lightly beaten
2 tablespoons applejack
1½ cups puréed pumpkin, freshly
    cooked or canned

In a large mixing bowl, combine the cream, milk, brown sugar, cinnamon, cloves and ginger. Stir thoroughly, then add the lightly beaten eggs and the applejack. Stir in the 1½ cups of puréed pumpkin. Carefully pour the filling into the pie shell. Bake for 40 to 50 minutes in the center of the oven until the filling is firm and the center of the pie barely quivers when the pie pan is gently moved back and forth. Serve warm or at room temperature with vanilla ice cream or stiffly whipped cream.

## Key Lime Pie  (South)

*Originally Key lime pie was made with a pastry crust—and traditional cooks insist it should still be. (For that version, use a fully baked short-crust pastry pie shell.)  Inasmuch as the pie is at its best when refrigerated and served very cold, a graham-cracker crust—which survives chilling nicely—has been popular, even in Key West, since the mid-19th Century.*

To make one 9-inch pie

GRAHAM CRACKER CRUST

6 ounces graham crackers,
    pulverized in a blender or
    wrapped in a towel and finely

crushed with a rolling pin (¾
    cup)
6 tablespoons unsalted butter,
    melted

Combine the graham-cracker crumbs and the melted butter in a 9-inch pie tin and rub them between your fingers until the crumbs are evenly moistened. Spread the crumbs loosely, place a second 9-inch pie tin on top and press down firmly to distribute the crumbs evenly over the bottom and sides of the lower tin. Remove the second pan and, with your fingers, smooth the top edges of the crust. Refrigerate until ready to fill.

PIE

6 egg yolks
Two 14-ounce cans sweetened
    condensed milk

1 cup strained fresh Key lime juice,
    or substitute other fresh lime
    juice
1 cup heavy cream, chilled

In a deep bowl, beat the egg yolks with a wire whisk or a rotary or electric beater for 4 or 5 minutes, or until they are very thick. Beat in the sweetened condensed milk and the lime juice. Pour the mixture into the pie shell and smooth the top with a rubber spatula. Cover with foil or plastic wrap and refrigerate the pie for at least 4 hours, or until the filling is firm to the touch.

Just before serving, whip the cream with a wire whisk or a rotary or electric beater until it is stiff enough to stand in unwavering peaks on the beater when it is lifted from the bowl. Spread the cream over the pie, smoothing it and creating decorative swirls on the top with a small metal spatula. Serve at once.

## Sour-Cherry Pie *(Northwest)*

To make one 9-inch double-crust pie

1 tablespoon unsalted butter,
   softened, plus 2 tablespoons
   unsalted butter, cut into ¼-inch
   bits
Short-crust pastry for a double-crust
   pie

6 cups pitted sour cherries (from
   about 3¾ pounds)
¼ cup quick-cooking tapioca
1 cup sugar
1½ tablespoons strained fresh
   lemon juice
¼ teaspoon almond extract

With a pastry brush, spread the tablespoon of softened butter over the bottom and sides of a 9-inch pie tin. Make twice the recipe for a pie shell, divide it in half, and chill for at least one hour.

On a lightly floured surface, roll half of the dough into a rough circle about ⅛ inch thick and 12 to 13 inches in diameter. Drape the dough over the rolling pin, lift it up, and unroll it slackly over the pie tin. Gently press the dough into the bottom and sides of the tin. With a pair of scissors, cut off the excess dough from the edges, leaving a 1-inch overhang all around the outside rim. Refrigerate while you prepare the filling.

Combine the sour cherries, tapioca, sugar, lemon juice and almond extract in a large bowl, and toss together gently but thoroughly. Let the mixture rest uncovered and at room temperature for about 10 minutes. Then spoon the contents of the bowl into the unbaked pie shell and, with a rubber spatula, spread out the cherries as evenly as possible. Dot the top of the filling with the butter bits.

Preheat the oven to 450°. For the upper crust, roll the remaining half of the dough into a circle about ⅛ inch thick and 12 to 13 inches in diameter. With a pastry brush dipped in cold water, lightly moisten the outside edge of the pastry shell. Drape the dough over the rolling pin, lift it up and unroll it over the pie. Trim off the excess pastry from around the rim with scissors, then crimp the top and bottom pastry together firmly

443

with your fingertips or press them with the tines of a fork. Cut a 1-inch hole in the center of the top of the pie. Bake in the center of the oven for 10 minutes, then lower the heat to 350° and bake another 40 to 45 minutes, or until the top is golden brown.

## Fresh Strawberry Pie  *(Northwest)*

To make one 9-inch pie

6 cups (1½ quarts) firm ripe strawberries, preferably wild strawberries

A 9-inch short-crust pastry pie shell, baked and cooled

½ cup sugar

3 tablespoons cornstarch

2 tablespoons cold water

1 tablespoon strained fresh lemon juice

1 cup heavy cream, chilled

Pick over the berries carefully, removing the stems and hulls and discarding any fruit that is badly bruised or shows signs of mold. Wash in a sieve or colander under cold running water, then spread on paper towels to drain. Pat the berries completely dry. Place half of them in the cooled baked pie shell and set aside.

Chop the remaining berries fine and combine them with the sugar in a 2- to 3-quart enameled or stainless-steel saucepan. Stirring from time to time, bring the berries to a simmer over moderate heat. In a small bowl, mix the cornstarch, cold water and lemon juice together to make a smooth paste. Then, stirring constantly, pour the paste into the berry mixture and continue to cook for 2 or 3 minutes, until the mixture thickens enough to hold its shape lightly in the spoon. Purée through a fine sieve set over a bowl, pressing down hard on the berries before discarding the seeds. Taste and add more sugar or lemon juice if desired. Pour the purée over the berries in the pie shell, spreading it evenly with a rubber spatula. Drape the pie lightly with aluminum foil or wax paper and refrigerate for at least 2 hours.

Just before serving, whip the cream in a chilled bowl with a wire whisk or a rotary or electric beater. When it is stiff enough to stand in unwavering peaks on the beater, scoop it over the pie and spread it out with a spatula. Make decorative swirls in the cream with the tip of the spatula and serve at once. Alternatively, you may serve the cream separately, permitting each diner to add as much as he wants to his portion.

## The Publick House's Cranberry Chiffon Pie  *(New England)*

To serve 8

CRUST

2½ cups pecans, pulverized in an

electric blender or with a nutgrinder

7 tablespoons sugar

4 tablespoons butter, melted and cooled

First prepare the crust in the following fashion: Combine the pulverized pecans and 7 tablespoons of sugar in a deep bowl and stir until they are well mixed. Sprinkle the melted butter over them and stir until the butter is completely absorbed. Scatter the mixture into a pie tin 9½ inches across at the top and 2 inches deep. With your fingers or the back of a spoon, press the crust firmly and evenly against the bottom and sides of the tin. Refrigerate for at least 30 minutes.

Preheat the oven to 350°. Bake the crust in the middle of the oven for 10 minutes, or until it browns lightly and is firm to the touch. Remove the tin from the oven and let the crust cool to room temperature.

FILLING

| | |
|---|---|
| 2 cups bottled cranberry juice | 3 egg whites |
| 1 envelope unflavored gelatin | ½ teaspoon salt |
| ¾ cup firm fresh unblemished cranberries | 2 cups heavy cream, chilled |
| ¾ cup sugar | 2 tablespoons confectioners' sugar |
| | 14 pecan halves |

Meanwhile, prepare the filling. Pour ¼ cup of the cranberry juice into a heatproof measuring cup and sprinkle it with the gelatin. When the gelatin has softened for 2 or 3 minutes, set the cup in a small skillet of simmering water and cook over low heat, stirring constantly, until the gelatin dissolves. Remove the skillet from the heat but leave the cup in the water to keep the gelatin fluid and warm.

Wash the cranberries under cold running water, drop them into a small enameled or stainless-steel saucepan. Add the remaining 1¾ cups of cranberry juice and the ½ cup of sugar and bring to a boil over high heat, stirring constantly until the sugar dissolves. Reduce the heat to low and, still stirring from time to time, simmer uncovered for 4 or 5 minutes, until the skins of the berries just begin to pop and the berries are tender. Remove the pan from the heat, add the gelatin and stir until dissolved. Then drain the entire mixture through a fine sieve into a large glass or ceramic bowl. Measure the liquid and, if necessary, add enough cranberry juice to make 1½ cups. Set the liquid aside to cool.

Select the 12 or 15 best-shaped whole, cooked cranberries, pat them dry with paper towels and reserve them for use as a garnish. Pat the remaining berries dry and chop them as fine as possible with a knife.

When the cranberry liquid begins to thicken and is somewhat syrupy, beat the egg whites and salt with a whisk or a rotary or electric beater until they are frothy. Sprinkle the remaining ¼ cup of sugar over them and continue to beat until the egg whites stand in soft peaks on the beater when it is lifted from the bowl.

In a deep chilled bowl, whip ½ cup of the cream with a whisk or a rotary or electric beater until it is firm and stands in unwavering peaks in the bowl. Scoop the egg whites over the cream and, with a rubber spatula, fold them together gently but thoroughly, using an over-under cutting motion rather than stirring.

Pour the egg white-and-cream mixture over the thickened cranberry syrup and fold with the spatula until no trace of white remains. Gently fold in the chopped cranberries, distributing them as evenly as possible. Pour the mixture into the cooled pie crust and refrigerate for at least 3 hours, or until the chiffon is firm to the touch.

Just before serving, whip the remaining cream and the confectioners' sugar with a whisk or a rotary or electric beater until the mixture forms unwavering peaks on the beater when it is lifted from the bowl. Spread the whipped cream over the entire surface of the pie, smoothing it with a spatula. Arrange the reserved whole cranberries and the pecan halves attractively on top and serve at once.


## Rhubarb Custard Pie *(Northwest)*

To make one 9-inch pie

3 eggs
1 cup sugar
½ cup milk
1 pound fresh rhubarb, trimmed,
washed and cut into ⅓-inch dice
(2 cups)
A 9-inch short-crust pastry pie shell, partially baked and cooled to room temperature

Preheat the oven to 350°. With a wire whisk or a rotary or electric beater, beat the eggs and sugar together in a deep bowl for 4 or 5 minutes, or until the mixture is thick enough to fall from the beater in a slowly dissolving ribbon when it is lifted from the bowl. Then add the milk and beat until it is thoroughly absorbed.

Spread the rhubarb evenly in the cooled, partially baked pie shell and pour the egg-and-milk mixture over it. Bake in the middle of the oven for 20 to 30 minutes, or until the custard is firm and a knife inserted in the center comes out clean.

Cool the pie to room temperature before serving it.


## Lemon Chess Pie *(South)*

To make one 9-inch pie

5 egg yolks
¾ cup sugar
1 tablespoon cornmeal
1 tablespoon heavy cream
1 tablespoon unsalted butter, softened
2 teaspoons grated lemon rind
¼ cup strained fresh lemon juice
A 9-inch short-crust pastry shell, unbaked and refrigerated

Preheat the oven to 350°. In a large mixing bowl, beat the egg yolks and sugar together with a whisk or a rotary or electric beater. When the mixture thickens and clings to the beater, beat in the cornmeal, cream, butter, lemon rind and lemon juice with a wooden spoon. Pour the filling into the pie shell and bake in the center of the oven for 45 minutes, or until the filling has set. Cool to room temperature.

LEMON CHESS TARTLETS: If you prefer, you can make eight individual tartlets rather than one pie. Roll out the dough as described on page 431. and, with a 4½-inch cookie cutter or glass, cut out eight circles. Fit the circles into eight 3½-inch tartlet shells and refrigerate while you make the filling. Double the ingredients given for the filling and prepare as described above. Divide the filling evenly among the shells and bake in the center of the oven for 30 minutes. Cool to room temperature.

## Maple-Walnut Pie *(New England)*

To make one 9-inch pie

4 eggs
2 cups pure maple syrup
2 tablespoons butter, melted and
　cooled

2 teaspoons cider vinegar
A 9-inch short-crust pastry pie
　shell, fully baked and cooled
¼ cup coarsely chopped walnuts

Preheat the oven to 400°. With a wire whisk or a rotary or electric beater, beat the eggs for 2 or 3 minutes until they begin to thicken and cling to the beater. Beating constantly, pour in the syrup in a slow, thin stream. Then beat in the cooled, melted butter and the vinegar.

Pour the maple filling into the baked and cooled pie shell and bake in the middle of the oven for 35 to 40 minutes, or until the top is delicately browned. (The filling may appear somewhat undercooked and soft, but it will become firm as it cools.) Remove the pie from the oven and let it cool to room temperature. Sprinkle the walnuts in a circle around the edge of the pie before serving.

## Pecan Pie *(South)*

To make one 9-inch pie

1¼ cups all-purpose flour
4 tablespoons chilled vegetable
　shortening or lard

2 tablespoons chilled butter, cut in
　¼-inch pieces
⅛ teaspoon salt
3 tablespoons ice water

Preheat the oven to 400°. In a large mixing bowl, combine the flour, vegetable shortening or lard, butter and salt. Use your fingertips to rub the flour and fat together until they look like flakes of coarse meal. Pour the

447

ice water over the mixture, toss together, and press and knead gently with your hands only until the dough can be gathered into a compact ball. Dust very lightly with flour, wrap in wax paper and chill for at least ½ hour. Lightly butter a 9-inch pie plate. On a floured surface, roll the dough out into a circle about ⅛ inch thick and 13 to 14 inches in diameter. Lift it up on the rolling pin and unroll it over the pie plate, leaving enough slack in the middle of the pastry to enable you to line the plate without pulling or stretching the dough. Trim the excess pastry to within ½ inch of the rim of the pie plate and fold the extra ½ inch under to make a double thickness all around the rim. With the tines of a fork or with your fingers, press the pastry down around the rim.

To prevent the unfilled pastry from buckling as it bakes, either set another pie plate lightly buttered on the underside into the pastry shell or line it with a sheet of lightly buttered foil. In either case do not prick the pastry, or the filling will run out when it is added later. Bake the shell in the middle of the oven for 8 minutes, then remove the pan or foil and let the shell cool while you make the filling.

| FILLING | 2 tablespoons melted butter |
| --- | --- |
| 4 eggs | 1 teaspoon vanilla |
| 2 cups dark corn syrup | 1½ cups pecans |

With a wire whisk or rotary beater, beat the eggs in a mixing bowl for about 30 seconds. Then slowly pour in the syrup and continue to beat until they are well combined. Beat in the melted butter and vanilla, and stir in the pecans. Carefully pour the filling into the pie shell. Bake in the middle of the oven for 35 to 40 minutes, or until the filling is firm. Serve the pie warm or cooled to room temperature.

## Sweet-Potato Pie  (South)

| To make one 9-inch pie | 2 teaspoons finely grated fresh |
| --- | --- |
| 4 medium-sized sweet potatoes, peeled and quartered | lemon peel |
| | 1 teaspoon vanilla extract |
| 4 tablespoons butter, softened | ¼ teaspoon ground nutmeg, preferably freshly grated |
| ¾ cup dark-brown sugar | |
| 3 eggs, lightly beaten | ½ teaspoon salt |
| ⅓ cup light corn syrup | A 9-inch short crust pastry pie shell, |
| ⅓ cup milk | fully baked and cooled |

Preheat the oven to 425°. Drop the quartered sweet potatoes into enough boiling water to immerse them completely and boil briskly, uncovered, until they are tender and show no resistance when they are pierced with the point of a small skewer or knife. Drain off the water, return the pan to low heat and slide it back and forth for a minute or so to dry the potatoes completely.

Rub the sweet potatoes through a fine sieve with the back of a spoon or purée them through a food mill. Set the puréed potatoes aside to cool to room temperature.

In a deep bowl, cream the butter and brown sugar together by beating and mashing them against the sides of the bowl with the back of a wooden spoon until they are light and fluffy. Beat in the cooled puréed sweet potatoes and, when they are completely incorporated, add the eggs one at a time, beating well after each addition. Add the light corn syrup, milk, grated lemon peel, vanilla, grated nutmeg and salt and continue to beat until the filling is smooth.

Pour the sweet-potato filling into the fully baked pie shell, spreading it evenly with a rubber spatula. Bake in the middle of the oven for 10 minutes. Then reduce the oven temperature to 325° and bake the pie for 35 minutes longer, or until a knife inserted in the center comes out clean.

Serve the sweet-potato pie warm or at room temperature.

## Black Bottom Pie *(South)*

To make one 9-inch pie

CRUST

24 ginger snaps, pulverized in a blender or wrapped in a towel and finely crushed with a rolling pin (about 1⅓ cups)

4 tablespoons butter, melted

Preheat the oven to 375°. To prepare the crust, combine the pulverized gingersnaps and melted butter in a 9-inch pie tin and stir until all the crumbs are moistened. Spread the crumb mixture in the bottom of the tin. Place another 9-inch pie tin over the crumbs and press it down firmly to spread the crust mixture evenly in the bottom and sides of the first tin. Remove the second tin and smooth the top edges of the crust with your fingers. Bake in the middle of the oven for 8 to 10 minutes, or until the crust is delicately colored. Set aside and cool to room temperature.

CUSTARD

¼ cup cold water

1 tablespoon unflavored gelatin

1¾ cups milk

4 egg yolks

½ cup sugar

1 tablespoon cornstarch

A pinch of salt

Meanwhile, prepare the custard and chocolate layer in the following fashion: Pour the cold water into a small heatproof bowl and sprinkle the gelatin over it. When the gelatin has softened for 2 or 3 minutes, set the bowl in a skillet of simmering water and, stirring constantly, cook over low heat until the gelatin dissolves completely. Remove the skillet from the heat, but leave the bowl in the water to keep the gelatin fluid.

449

In a heavy 2- to 3-quart saucepan, heat the milk until small bubbles begin to form around the edges of the pan. Remove from the heat and cover to keep warm. With a wire whisk or a rotary or electric beater, beat the egg yolks, ½ cup of sugar, cornstarch and a pinch of salt for 3 to 4 minutes, or until the yolks thicken slightly. Beating constantly, pour in the hot milk in a thin stream, then pour the mixture into the saucepan.

Place the pan over low heat and, stirring constantly and deeply with a wooden spoon, simmer for 10 to 12 minutes, or until the custard is thick enough to coat the spoon lightly. Do not allow the mixture to come anywhere near the boiling point or it may curdle. Remove the pan from the heat and stir in the dissolved gelatin.

CHOCOLATE LAYER
3 one-ounce squares semisweet chocolate
1 teaspoon vanilla extract

Melt the 3 ounces of chocolate in a small heavy pan over low heat, stirring constantly. Measure 1 cup of the custard into a bowl and set the rest aside. Stirring the custard in the bowl constantly, slowly pour in the melted chocolate and, when it is completely incorporated, add the vanilla. Pour the chocolate-layer mixture into the cooled pie shell, spreading it and smoothing the top with a rubber spatula. Refrigerate for at least 1 hour, or until the chocolate layer is firm to the touch.

RUM LAYER
4 egg whites
⅛ teaspoon cream of tartar
⅓ cup sugar
1 tablespoon rum

With a whisk or beater, beat the egg whites and cream of tartar together until they begin to thicken. Add the sugar and continue to beat until the whites are stiff enough to form unwavering peaks on the beater when it is lifted out of the bowl. Set the reserved custard into a larger pan half filled with ice and cold water. Stir it with a metal spoon until it thickens enough to flow sluggishly off the spoon. Remove from the ice. With a rubber spatula, stir the rum and 2 or 3 tablespoons of the egg whites into the custard. Scoop the remaining egg whites over the custard and, with the spatula, fold them together gently but thoroughly. Pour the mixture gently into the pie, and smooth with the spatula. Refrigerate for 2 hours, or until the top layer is firm to the touch.

TOPPING
1 cup heavy cream, chilled
2 tablespoons confectioners' sugar
¼ ounce semisweet chocolate

Just before serving, prepare the topping. In a chilled bowl, whip the heavy cream with a wire whisk or a rotary or electric beater until firm enough to stand in unwavering peaks on the beater when it is lifted from the bowl. Beat in the confectioners' sugar, then spread over the top of the pie with a rubber spatula. Using the finest side of a hand-grater, grate the remaining chocolate evenly over the cream. Serve at once.

To make one 9-inch pie

1 cup unsifted flour
½ cup light brown sugar
¼ cup vegetable shortening, cut
    into ¼-inch bits
1 teaspoon baking soda

1 cup boiling water
⅔ cup light corn syrup
⅓ cup dark molasses
A 9-inch unbaked short-crust sweet
    pastry shell

Preheat the oven to 375°. To prepare the crumb topping, combine the flour, brown sugar and shortening in a bowl and rub them together with your fingertips until the mixture resembles coarse meal.

In a deep bowl, dissolve the soda in the boiling water. Then add the corn syrup and molasses, and stir to blend well. Pour the mixture into the unbaked pie shell and sprinkle the crumbs evenly over the top.

Bake the shoofly pie in the middle of the oven for 10 minutes. Reduce the oven temperature to 350° and continue baking for about 25 minutes longer, or until the filling is set and does not quiver when the pie pan is gently shaken from side to side. Do not overbake or the filling will become too dry. Cool the pie to room temperature before serving, and accompany it if you like with sweetened whipped cream or scoops of vanilla ice cream.

To make one 9-inch pie

1½ cups heavy cream
1½ cups milk
1 cup sugar
5 egg yolks
¼ cup bourbon

1 teaspoon vanilla extract
A 9-inch short-crust pastry shell,
    partially baked and cooled
¼ teaspoon nutmeg, preferably
    freshly grated

Preheat the oven to 450°. In a heavy 1- to 1½-quart saucepan, warm the cream and milk over moderate heat, stirring occasionally, until small bubbles appear around the edges of the pan. Cover the pan and set aside off the heat.

Caramelize the sugar in a small heavy saucepan by stirring it over moderate heat until it melts and turns a light golden brown. Stirring the sugar constantly with a wooden spoon, pour in the warm cream-and-milk mixture in a thin stream. Continue to stir until the caramel has thoroughly dissolved. Set aside off the heat.

With a whisk or a rotary or electric beater, beat the egg yolks in a large mixing bowl until they are well blended, then, stirring constantly, slowly

451

pour in the caramel-and-cream mixture, the bourbon and the vanilla extract. Strain the mixture through a fine sieve directly into the baked, cooled pie shell. Sprinkle the top evenly with nutmeg and place the pie in the center of the oven. Lower the heat at once to 350°, and bake the pie about 30 minutes, until the filling is about to set. (The filling may appear somewhat undercooked, but it will become firm as it cools.) Remove the pie from the oven and let it cool to room temperature.

## Mincemeat Pie  *(New England)*

To make one 9-inch pie

| | |
|---|---|
| 1 tablespoon butter, softened | 2 medium-sized tart cooking apples, |
| Short-crust pastry | peeled, cored and cut into ¼- |
| 2½ cups *Grandma Howland's* | inch dice (about 1½ cups) |
| *mincemeat* (*see below*), | 1 egg, lightly beaten with 2 |
| thoroughly drained | tablespoons milk |

Preheat the oven to 350°. With a pastry brush, spread the butter evenly over the bottom and sides of a 9-inch pie tin. Double the recipe for short-crust pastry, roll out half the pastry dough and line the pie tin with it. Combine the mincemeat and apples in a bowl and mix well. Then spoon them into the pastry shell, spreading the mixture evenly with a spatula.

On a lightly floured surface, roll out the remaining pastry dough into a circle about ⅛ inch thick and 12 inches in diameter. With a pastry brush dipped in cold water, lightly moisten the outside edge of the pastry shell. Drape the dough over the rolling pin, lift it up and unroll it over the pie. Trim off the excess dough with scissors or a small knife, then crimp the top and bottom pastry together firmly with your fingers or the tines of a fork. Cut a 1-inch hole in the center of the top crust.

Brush the surface of the pie with the egg-milk mixture and bake in the middle of the oven for 1¼ hours, or until the crust is golden brown. Serve mincemeat pie hot or cooled to room temperature.

GRANDMA HOWLAND'S MINCEMEAT

To make about 5 quarts

A 2-pound fresh beef tongue
2 pounds lean fresh beef brisket, preferably first cut, trimmed of all fat
1 pound fresh beef suet, finely chopped (about 4 cups)
2 pounds dried currants (about 6 cups)
2 pounds seedless raisins (about 6 cups)
1 cup coarsely chopped dried figs
8 ounces finely diced candied citron (about 1 cup)
4 ounces finely diced candied orange peel (about ½ cup)
4 ounces finely diced candied lemon peel (about ½ cup)
3 tablespoons coarsely grated fresh lemon peel
½ teaspoon ground cinnamon
½ teaspoon ground nutmeg, preferably freshly grated
½ teaspoon ground cloves
1 teaspoon freshly ground black pepper
1 teaspoon salt
3 cups dry sherry
2 cups cognac
1 cup sweet cider

Place the beef tongue and brisket in a heavy 6- to 8-quart casserole and pour in enough water to cover it by at least 2 inches. Bring to a boil over high heat, meanwhile skimming off the foam and scum as they rise to the surface. Reduce the heat to low and simmer partially covered for about 3 hours, or until the meats are tender and show no resistance when pierced deeply with the prongs of a long-handled fork. Add more boiling water to the casserole if necessary; the meats should be covered with water throughout the cooking period.

Transfer the tongue and brisket to a platter and discard the cooking liquid. While the tongue is still hot, skin it with a small, sharp knife, cutting away and discarding all the fat, bones and gristle at its base. Chop the tongue and brisket into small chunks and put them through the coarsest blade of a food grinder.

In a 6- to 8-quart earthenware crock or bowl, combine the suet, currants, raisins, figs, citron, candied orange and lemon peel, fresh lemon peel, cinnamon, nutmeg, cloves, pepper and salt. Mix them well with a wooden spoon, then stir in the ground tongue and brisket. Pour in the sherry, cognac and cider and continue to stir until the ingredients are thoroughly moistened.

Cover the bowl or pot and set the mincemeat aside in a cool place (not the refrigerator) for at least 2 weeks before using it. Check every 3 or 4 days. As the liquid is absorbed, replenish it with additional sherry, cognac or cider, stirring in about ½ cup at a time.

Mincemeat can be safely kept indefinitely in a cool place, in sterilized, covered containers.

*Cannoli*  (*Italian-American*)
PASTRY TUBES FILLED WITH RICOTTA

To serve 16

CANNOLI
2 cups all-purpose flour
½ teaspoon salt

2 tablespoons sugar
2 eggs
4 to 6 tablespoons white wine

Place the flour, salt and sugar in a large mixing bowl and make a well in the center. Drop in the eggs and 4 tablespoons of the white wine and, with a large wooden spoon, gradually incorporate the dry ingredients into the liquid. Continue to beat the mixture, adding up to 2 more tablespoons of wine if necessary, until you have a medium-firm dough that can be gathered into a ball. Set the dough aside to rest for 30 minutes.

FILLING
4 cups (2 pounds) ricotta cheese
1 tablespoon vanilla extract
1½ cups confectioners' sugar
½ cup finely chopped citron
½ cup finely chopped candied
  orange peel

1 egg white, beaten
Vegetable oil for deep frying

1 ounce semisweet chocolate, grated
2 tablespoons finely chopped
  pistachio nuts
Confectioners' sugar

Meanwhile, prepare the filling: With a large spoon, rub the ricotta through a fine sieve set over a large bowl. Beat in the vanilla extract, the 1½ cups of confectioners' sugar, the citron and the orange peel, and continue to beat until the mixture is smooth. Set aside.

Transfer the dough to a lightly floured surface and, with a rolling pin, roll it into an 18-inch circle about ⅟₁₆ inch thick. With a 3½-inch cookie cutter, cut out 16 circles; if necessary, gather the scraps into a ball, roll them out again and cut out the additional circles. With the rolling pin, gently roll each circle into an oval shape about 4 inches long. Wrap the pastry ovals around metal *cannoli* forms, overlapping the edges in the center. With a pastry brush, seal the edges with the beaten egg white.

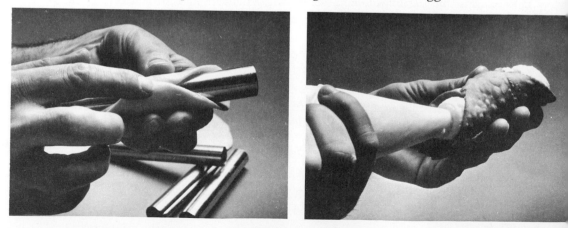

Fill a deep fryer or deep heavy saucepan with vegetable oil to a depth of 2 or 3 inches and set over moderately high heat until the oil reaches a temperature of 350° on a deep-frying thermometer. Fry two or three *cannoli* at a time for 2 to 3 minutes, turning them several times with tongs, until they are golden. With the tongs, transfer them to paper towels to drain. When the *cannoli* have cooled enough to handle, slip the pastry off the forms. Repeat, shaping and frying the remaining pastry ovals.

Put the ricotta filling into a pastry bag fitted with a plain tube equipped with a ½-inch opening and squeeze the filling into the cooled *cannoli* shells, letting it mound on the open sides. Set the filled *cannoli* on a serving tray and sprinkle the exposed filling with the grated chocolate and nuts. Just before serving, dust with confectioners' sugar.

## *Croquignoles* (Creole-Acadian)
### DEEP-FRIED PASTRIES

To make about 3 dozen round or
　　triangular pastries

| | |
|---|---|
| | 3 eggs |
| 2 cups unsifted flour | ½ cup sugar |
| 1 teaspoon double-acting baking | 1 tablespoon butter, melted and |
| 　powder | 　cooled |
| ½ teaspoon ground nutmeg, | 1 tablespoon vanilla extract |
| 　preferably freshly grated | Vegetable oil for deep frying |
| ½ teaspoon salt | Confectioners' sugar |

Combine the flour, baking powder, nutmeg and salt, sift them together into a bowl, and set aside.

In a deep mixing bowl, beat the eggs with a wire whisk until they are light and frothy. With a wooden spoon, beat in the sugar, the cooled melted butter and the vanilla extract and, when all the ingredients are thoroughly incorporated, beat in the flour mixture, about ½ cup at a time. Divide the dough into two equal portions.

To shape the dough into rounds, roll out one portion into a rough rectangle about ⅛ inch thick. With a cookie cutter or the rim of a glass, cut the dough into 3-inch rounds. Gather the scraps into a ball, roll them out as before and cut as many more rounds as you can. With a sharp knife, cut two parallel slashes about 2 inches long and ½ inch apart in the center of each round.

To shape the dough into triangles, roll out one portion into a circle about 12 inches in diameter and ⅛ inch thick. With a pastry wheel or sharp knife, divide the circle into 16 equal pie-shaped wedges. Cut a 3-inch slash lengthwise down the center of each wedge.

Pour vegetable oil into a deep fryer or large heavy saucepan to a depth of 2 or 3 inches and heat the oil until it reaches a temperature of 360° on a deep-frying thermometer.

Fry the *croquignoles,* two or three at a time, turning them about with a slotted spoon for 4 minutes, or until they are golden brown and crisp. As they are deep-fried, transfer them to paper towels to drain.

Serve the *croquignoles* warm, or cooled to room temperature. Just before serving, sprinkle them lightly with confectioners' sugar.

# Cakes

Cake is ceremonial. Whether served as the grand finale of a dinner, brought out as the *pièce de resistance* at a birthday party, or made the centerpiece at a tea party or champagne reception, a cake bespeaks time, thought and care—seemingly, too much time and care. But if, for example, the tantalizingly rich layers of three-layer chocolate cake (for which a recipe follows) were baked on a rainy afternoon and frozen, it would take less than ten minutes to make a chocolate sour-cream frosting and then assemble the cake. Even a glorious Southern coconut cake, filled with lemon custard, topped with white icing and delicious freshly grated coconut, can be made in easy stages in advance.

Baking a cake, of course, requires precise attention to details. Of primary importance is the accurate measuring of ingredients. Too many sautéed onions will rarely spoil a stew, but too much flour will definitely weigh down a cake. The size of the cake pan, too, is critical: if it is too small, the batter will rise too high and spill over; if too large, the batter will spread out and produce a too-thin layer. Lastly, the oven heat must be true and constant: check the thermostat from time to time.

To make one 3-layer cake

CAKE

| | |
|---|---|
| 2 tablespoons plus ½ pound unsalted butter, softened | ¼ teaspoon salt |
| 2 tablespoons plus 3 cups cake flour | 1 cup milk |
| 1 tablespoon double-acting baking powder | 1 teaspoon almond extract |
| | 1½ cups sugar |
| | 5 egg whites |

NOTE: Before making the cake, see the frosting section opposite for instructions regarding the soaking of dried fruits and nuts.

CAKE: Preheat the oven to 350°. With a pastry brush, spread 2 tablespoons of the softened butter on the bottom and sides of three 9-inch layer-cake pans. Divide 2 tablespoons of the flour among the three pans and tip the pans from side to side to distribute the flour evenly. Then invert each pan and rap it sharply to remove the excess flour.

Combine the remaining flour, baking powder and salt, and sift them together into a bowl. Stir the milk and almond extract together in a small bowl and set aside.

In a large deep bowl, cream the remaining butter and the sugar together by beating them against the sides of the bowl with the back of a wooden spoon until the mixture is light and fluffy. Beat in about 1 cup of the flour mixture and, when it is well incorporated, beat in ⅓ cup of the milk-and-almond-extract mixture. Repeat twice more, alternating the flour and milk mixtures, and continue to beat until the batter is smooth.

With a wire whisk or a rotary or electric beater, beat the 5 egg whites in a large bowl until they are firm enough to stand in stiff peaks on the beater when it is lifted out of the bowl. Stir a few tablespoons of the whites into the batter, then scoop the batter over the whites and fold together gently but thoroughly with a rubber spatula.

Pour the batter into the pans, dividing it equally among them and smoothing the tops with the spatula. Bake in the middle of the oven for 25 to 30 minutes, until the tops of the cakes are pale gold and they have begun to shrink away from the sides of the pans. Turn the cake layers out onto the wire racks to cool to room temperature.

FRUIT AND NUT FROSTING

| | |
|---|---|
| 2 cups seedless raisins, finely chopped | 4 egg whites |
| 2 cups walnuts, finely chopped | ¼ teaspoon cream of tartar |
| 12 figs, pitted and finely chopped | 3 cups sugar |
| 1 cup sherry | 1 cup water |
| | 1 tablespoon light corn syrup |

FROSTING: At least 3 hours before you plan to make the filling, place the raisins, walnuts and figs in a bowl. Pour in the sherry and soak the mixture at room temperature, tossing frequently with a wooden spoon.

With a wire whisk or a rotary or electric beater, beat the 4 egg whites and cream of tartar in a deep bowl until they are firm enough to stand in stiff peaks on the beater when it is lifted from the bowl.

Quickly combine the sugar, water and corn syrup in a heavy 1- to 1½-quart enameled or stainless-steel saucepan and, stirring frequently, cook over moderate heat until the sugar dissolves. Raise the heat and continue to cook uncovered and undisturbed until the syrup reaches 238° on a candy thermometer, or until a few drops spooned into ice water immediately form a soft ball.

Beating the reserved egg whites constantly, pour in the hot syrup in a slow, thin stream, and continue to beat until the filling is smooth, thick and cool.

Place the raisins, nuts and figs in a fine sieve and drain them. Discard the soaking liquid. Stir the fruit and nuts into the frosting.

TO ASSEMBLE: Set one cake layer upside down on an inverted cake pan and, with a metal spatula or knife, spread about ½ cup of the frosting evenly over the surface of the cake. Carefully put the second cake layer in place right side up, and spread with another ½ cup of the frosting. Top with the third cake layer right side up and coat the top and sides of the cake with the remaining frosting. Carefully slide the cake onto a serving plate and serve. Or, if you prefer, cover loosely with wax paper or aluminum foil and set aside at room temperature for as long as 2 days; frosting will keep the cake moist.

## Cheesecake

| | |
|---|---|
| To make one 9-inch cheesecake | 2 tablespoons sugar |
| | ½ teaspoon cinnamon |
| 1 six-ounce box Graham crackers, | 6 tablespoons unsalted butter, melted |
| finely crumbled (¾ cup) | 2 tablespoons soft butter |

In a mixing bowl, with a large spoon combine the finely crumbled Graham crackers, the sugar and cinnamon. Stir the melted butter into the cracker crumbs until they are well saturated. With a pastry brush, heavily butter a 9-inch, 3-inch-deep springform pan with the 2 tablespoons of soft butter. With your fingers, pat an even layer of the cracker-crumb mixture on the bottom and sides of the pan to form a shell. Refrigerate while you make the filling.

*A rich chocolate cake is an easily made and immensely popular dessert. The delicious frosting is a simple mixture of melted chocolate and sour cream.*

CHEESECAKE FILLING

3 eight-ounce packages cream cheese, softened
1¼ cups sugar
6 egg yolks
1 pint sour cream
3 tablespoons all-purpose flour
2 teaspoons vanilla
1 tablespoon lemon juice
1 tablespoon finely grated lemon rind
6 egg whites
2 tablespoons confectioners' sugar

Preheat the oven to 350°. Cream the softened cheese by beating it with a spoon in a mixing bowl until it is smooth. Then gradually beat in the sugar. Beat in the egg yolks one at a time, and continue to beat until all the ingredients are well combined. Stir in the sour cream, flour, vanilla, lemon juice and lemon rind.

With a large whisk or rotary beater, beat the egg whites, preferably in an unlined copper bowl, until they are stiff enough to form unwavering peaks on the beater when it is lifted out of the bowl. With a rubber spatula fold the egg whites gently but thoroughly into the cream cheese mixture until no streaks of white show, but be careful not to overfold.

Pour the filling into the pan, spreading it out evenly with a rubber spatula. Bake in the middle of the oven for 1 hour. Then turn off the oven, and with the oven door open, let the cake rest on the oven shelf for 15 minutes. Remove and let cool to room temperature. Before serving, remove the sides of the pan and sprinkle the cake with confectioners' sugar.

To make one 9-inch cake

### COOKIE CRUST

| | |
|---|---|
| 1 cup all-purpose flour | 1 egg yolk |
| ¼ cup sugar | 8 tablespoons (1 quarter-pound |
| 1 teaspoon finely grated lemon rind | stick) unsalted butter, chilled and |
| ¼ teaspoon vanilla extract | cut into ¼-inch bits |

COOKIE CRUST: Place 1 cup of flour, ¼ cup of sugar, 1 teaspoon grated lemon rind, ¼ teaspoon of vanilla extract, 1 egg yolk and 8 tablespoons of butter in a large mixing bowl. With your fingertips, rub the ingredients together until they are well combined and can be gathered into a ball. Dust with a little flour, wrap in wax paper, and refrigerate for at least 1 hour. Preheat the oven to 400°.

Place the chilled dough in an ungreased 9-inch springform pan. With your hands, pat and spread the dough evenly over the bottom and about 2 inches up the sides of the pan. Bake in the center of the oven for 10 minutes, then remove and set aside to cool to room temperature.

### CHEESE FILLING

| | |
|---|---|
| 1¼ pounds cream cheese, softened | 1 teaspoon finely grated orange rind |
| ¾ cup sugar | ½ teaspoon vanilla extract |
| 1½ tablespoons all-purpose flour | 3 eggs plus 1 egg yolk |
| 1 teaspoon finely grated lemon rind | 2 tablespoons heavy cream |

FILLING: Lower the oven temperature to 250°. Place the cream cheese in a large mixing bowl and beat vigorously with a wooden spoon until it is creamy and smooth. Beat in ¾ cup of sugar a few tablespoons at a time and, when it is well incorporated, beat in 1½ tablespoons of flour, 1 teaspoon of lemon rind, the orange rind, ½ teaspoon of vanilla extract, the eggs and egg yolk, and the heavy cream. Pour the filling into the cooled cookie crust and bake in the center of the oven for 1 hour, then remove from the oven and set aside to cool in the pan.

### STRAWBERRY TOPPING

| | |
|---|---|
| 1 quart fresh strawberries | ¼ cup cold water |
| ½ cup sugar | Dash of salt |
| 4 teaspoons cornstarch dissolved in | Dash of red food coloring |
| | (optional) |

STRAWBERRY TOPPING: Wash and hull the strawberries and place them, 1 cup at a time, in a fine sieve set over a bowl. With the back of a wooden spoon, press just enough berries through the sieve to get ¾ cup of purée. Set the purée aside. With the cake still in the pan, arrange the remaining whole berries, stem side down, over the top of the cake.

Beat ½ cup of sugar, the cornstarch-and-water mixture and the salt into the puréed berries, and pour the mixture into a 1- to 1½-quart enameled or stainless-steel saucepan. Bring to a boil over high heat, stirring frequently, then boil the syrup undisturbed for 2 minutes. Remove from the heat and, if you prefer a deeper red color, stir in a drop or two of red food coloring. Spoon the hot glaze over the whole berries and refrigerate the cheesecake for at least 3 hours before serving.

## Marble Spice Cake

To make one 9½-inch cake

| | |
|---|---|
| 1 tablespoon butter, softened | 2 tablespoons flour |

Preheat the oven to 350°. With a pastry brush, spread 1 tablespoon of softened butter over the bottom and sides of a tube cake pan 9½ inches in diameter and 3¾ inches deep. Add 2 tablespoons of flour and tip the pan from side to side to coat it evenly. Then invert the pan and rap the bottom sharply to remove the excess flour.

SPICE CAKE

| | |
|---|---|
| 2 cups cake flour, sifted before measuring | ¼ teaspoon salt |
| 1 teaspoon baking soda | 8 tablespoons vegetable shortening |
| 1½ teaspoons ground cinnamon | 1 cup dark-brown sugar, firmly packed |
| ½ teaspoon ground cloves | 4 egg yolks |
| ½ teaspoon ground nutmeg | ½ cup dark molasses |
| | 1 cup buttermilk |

For the spice cake, combine the 2 cups of cake flour, the baking soda, cinnamon, cloves, nutmeg and ¼ teaspoon of salt, and sift them into a bowl. In another bowl, cream the vegetable shortening and brown sugar together, beating and mashing them against the sides of the bowl with the back of a spoon until they are light and fluffy. Beat in the egg yolks, one at a time, and then the molasses. Stir in about ½ cup of the flour mixture and, when it is well incorporated, add ¼ cup of the buttermilk. Repeat three more times, alternately adding ½ cup of the flour mixture and ¼ cup of the buttermilk, and continue to beat until the batter is smooth. Set aside.

WHITE CAKE

| | |
|---|---|
| 2½ cups cake flour, sifted before measuring | 8 tablespoons butter, softened |
| 2 teaspoons double-acting baking powder | 1 cup sugar |
| | ¾ cup milk |
| ¼ teaspoon salt | 1 teaspoon vanilla extract |
| | 4 egg whites |

For the white cake, combine the 2½ cups of cake flour, the baking powder and ¼ teaspoon of salt, and sift them into a bowl. In another bowl, cream the 8 tablespoons of softened butter and the sugar together, beating and mashing them against the sides of the bowl with the back of a spoon until they are light and fluffy. Stir in about ½ cup of the flour mixture and, when it is well incorporated, add 2 or 3 tablespoons of the milk. Repeat three more times, alternately adding ½ cup of the flour mixture and 2 or 3 tablespoons of milk, and continue to beat until the batter is smooth. Stir in the vanilla.

With a wire whisk or a rotary or electric beater, beat the egg whites until they are stiff enough to stand in firm, unwavering peaks on the beater when it is lifted from the bowl. Pour the egg whites over the white-cake batter and, with a rubber spatula, fold them together gently.

To create a marbleized effect with the two cake batters, scoop about ¼ cup of each of them into two ladles or small liquid measuring cups. Alternately place ¼ cup of the dark batter and ¼ cup of the light batter next to each other all around the bottom of the pan. Fill the ladles or cups again and make a second layer placing dark on light and light on dark. Repeat, alternating dark and light batters in each layer, until all the batter is used.

Bake in the middle of the oven for 50 to 60 minutes, or until a toothpick or cake tester inserted into the center of the cake comes out clean. Let the cake cool in the pan for about 10 minutes, then turn it out onto a wire rack to cool to room temperature.

FROSTING (optional)

6 one-ounce squares semisweet chocolate, coarsely chopped
3 tablespoons butter, cut into ½-inch bits
⅓ cup light cream
½ teaspoon vanilla extract
½ teaspoon ground cinnamon
½ cup confectioners' sugar

Meanwhile, if you want chocolate cream frosting, prepare it in the following fashion: In a small, heavy saucepan, melt the chocolate and 3 tablespoons of butter bits over low heat, stirring constantly to prevent the chocolate from burning. Add the light cream, vanilla and cinnamon, and stir until the mixture is smooth. Remove the pan from the heat and sift in the confectioners' sugar a few tablespoonfuls at a time, beating well after each addition. Stirring from time to time, let the frosting cool until it thickens enough to be easily spread. Then frost the top and sides of the cake with a metal spatula or table knife.

*California grapefruit, the "aristocrat of the breakfast table," also shines at dinner in fruit-flavored cake swathed in a cream-cheese icing.*

## Applesauce Cake *(Eastern Heartland)*

To make one 9-inch tube cake

APPLESAUCE

3 medium-sized tart cooking apples,
    cored and coarsely chopped
½ cup sugar

2 tablespoons water
2 teaspoons strained fresh lemon
    juice

Combine the apples, ½ cup of sugar, water and lemon juice in a small saucepan and bring to a boil over moderate heat. Reduce the heat to its lowest setting, cover tightly and simmer for 15 to 20 minutes, or until the apples can be easily mashed with the back of a fork. Purée the applesauce through a food mill set over a bowl, or rub it through a fine sieve with the back of a spoon. Then return the purée to the pan and, stirring frequently, cook briskly until the applesauce is thick enough to hold its shape almost solidly in a spoon. Measure 1 cup of the applesauce and set it aside to cool to room temperature.

CAKE
9 tablespoons butter, softened
2 tablespoons plus 2 cups cake flour,
    not the self-rising variety
1 tablespoon unsweetened cocoa
1 teaspoon baking soda
1 teaspoon ground cinnamon
½ teaspoon ground cloves
½ teaspoon salt
1 cup light brown sugar
2 eggs
1 cup coarsely chopped walnuts
½ cup coarsely chopped dates
½ cup seedless raisins

Preheat the oven to 350°. With a pastry brush, spread 1 tablespoon of the softened butter over the bottom and sides of a 9-inch tube pan. Add 2 tablespoons of the flour and tip the pan from side to side to spread it evenly. Then invert the pan and rap the bottom sharply to remove the excess flour. Combine the remaining 2 cups of flour, the cocoa, baking soda, cinnamon, cloves and salt, and sift them together into a bowl or onto a sheet of wax paper. Set aside.

In a deep bowl, cream the remaining 8 tablespoons of softened butter and 1 cup of brown sugar by beating and mashing them against the sides of the bowl with the back of a large spoon until the mixture is light and fluffy. Beat in the eggs, one at a time. Add about ½ cup of the flour-and-cocoa mixture and, when it is thoroughly incorporated, beat in about ¼ cup of the cooled applesauce. Repeat three more times, alternating ½ cup of the flour-and-cocoa mixture with ¼ cup of applesauce and beating well after each addition. When the batter is smooth, stir in the chopped walnuts, the dates and the raisins.

Pour the batter into the tube pan, spreading it and smoothing the top with a rubber spatula. Bake in the middle of the oven for 50 to 60 minutes, or until a cake tester or toothpick inserted in the center comes out clean. Turn the cake out on a rack to cool to room temperature.

BROWN SUGAR ICING
2 cups light brown sugar
8 tablespoons butter, cut into
½-inch bits
½ cup heavy cream
1 teaspoon vanilla extract

To prepare the icing, combine 2 cups of brown sugar, 8 tablespoons of butter bits and the cream in a 2- to 3-quart saucepan. Bring to a boil over high heat, stirring until the sugar dissolves. Then cook briskly, uncovered and undisturbed, until the syrup reaches a temperature of 240° on a candy thermometer, or until about ⅛ teaspoon of syrup dropped into ice water immediately forms a soft ball.

Pour the hot syrup into a mixing bowl, add the vanilla, and beat vigorously with a wooden spoon until the mixture is light and creamy. Quickly spread the warm icing on the top and sides of the cake with a metal spatula. If the frosting becomes too stiff as you proceed, dip the spatula into hot water.

## Houston Gingerbread

To make a 13-by-9-inch cake

9 tablespoons butter, softened
2 tablespoons plus 2 cups unsifted flour
1 tablespoon unsweetened cocoa
2 teaspoons baking soda
2 teaspoons ground cinnamon

1½ teaspoons ground ginger
¼ teaspoon ground nutmeg
1 cup sugar
2 egg yolks
1 cup dark molasses
1 cup buttermilk
2 egg whites

Preheat the oven to 350°. With a pastry brush, spread 1 tablespoon of the softened butter over the bottom and sides of a 13-by-9-by-2-inch baking pan. Add 2 tablespoons of the flour and tip the pan from side to side to distribute it evenly. Invert the pan and rap the bottom sharply to remove the excess flour.

Combine the remaining 2 cups of flour, the cocoa, baking soda, cinnamon, ginger and nutmeg, and sift them into a bowl. Set aside.

In a deep bowl, cream the remaining 8 tablespoons of softened butter and the sugar together by beating and mashing them against the sides of the bowl with the back of a large spoon until the mixture is light and fluffy. Beat in the egg yolks, one at a time, and add the molasses. Add about ½ cup of the flour mixture and, when it is well incorporated, beat in about ¼ cup of the buttermilk. Repeat three times, alternating ½ cup of the flour mixture with ¼ cup of the buttermilk and beating the batter well after each addition.

With a wire whisk or a rotary or electric beater, beat the egg whites until they are stiff enough to stand in unwavering peaks on the beater when it is lifted from the bowl. With a rubber spatula, scoop the whites over the batter and fold them together gently but thoroughly.

Pour the batter into the prepared pan, spreading it evenly and smoothing the top with the spatula. Bake in the middle of the oven for about 25 minutes, or until a toothpick or cake tester inserted in the center comes out clean. Remove the gingerbread from the oven and let it cool completely to room temperature before cutting and serving it.

## Poundcake

To make one 9-by-5-by-3-inch loaf

2 teaspoons plus ½ pound unsalted butter, softened
2 tablespoons plus 2½ cups all-purpose flour

1¼ cups sugar
6 large eggs
1 tablespoon grated lemon rind
2 teaspoons vanilla extract

Preheat the oven to 350°. With a pastry brush, spread 2 teaspoons of the softened butter evenly over the bottom and sides of a 9-by-5-by-3-inch loaf pan. Sprinkle the butter with 2 tablespoons of the flour and tip the pan from side to side to spread it evenly; then invert the pan and rap it sharply to remove the excess flour.

In a deep bowl, cream the remaining butter and the sugar together by mashing and beating them against the sides of the bowl with the back of a spoon until they are light and fluffy. Beat in the eggs, one at a time, then beat in the lemon rind and vanilla.

With a wooden spoon beat in the remaining flour, 1 cup at a time. When the flour is thoroughly incorporated and the batter is smooth, pour it into the prepared loaf pan, smoothing the top with a spatula. Bake in the center of the oven for 1 hour and 20 minutes, or until the cake begins to shrink away from the sides of the pan. Turn the cake out onto a wire rack and let it cool to room temperature.

Poundcake may be served in a variety of ways: alone, with whipped cream or ice cream, or as a breakfast cake with butter.

## Whipped-Cream Cake (Northwest)

To make one 8-inch layer cake

| | |
|---|---|
| 2 tablespoons butter, softened | ½ teaspoon salt |
| 2 tablespoons plus 2¼ cups cake flour, not the self-rising variety | 3½ cups heavy cream, chilled |
| 1½ cups sugar | ½ teaspoon vanilla extract |
| 2 teaspoons double-acting baking powder | ½ teaspoon almond extract |
| | 3 eggs |
| | 1 pint (about 2 cups) fresh ripe strawberries |

Preheat the oven to 350°. With a pastry brush, spread the softened butter over the bottom and sides of two 8-by-1½-inch round cake pans. Add 1 tablespoon of flour to each pan, then tip the pans from side to side to spread the flour evenly. Invert the pans one at a time and rap the bottom sharply to remove the excess flour. Set aside.

Combine the remaining flour, the sugar, baking powder and salt, and sift them together onto a plate or a sheet of wax paper. Set aside. In a chilled bowl, beat 1½ cups of the cream with a wire whisk or a rotary or electric beater until stiff enough to stand in firm peaks on the beater when it is lifted from the bowl. Beat in the vanilla and almond extracts.

With the same unwashed beater, beat the eggs in a deep bowl for 4 or 5 minutes, until they are thick enough to fall in a slowly dissolving ribbon from the lifted beater. With a rubber spatula scoop the whipped cream over the eggs and fold them together using an over-under cutting motion rather than a stirring motion. Sprinkle the reserved flour-and-sugar mixture over the batter about 1 cup at a time, and fold it in gently but thoroughly.

Pour the batter into the buttered-and-floured cake pans, dividing it evenly between them and smoothing the top with the spatula. Bake in the middle of the oven for about 30 minutes, or until a toothpick or cake tester inserted in the middle of the cake comes out clean. Turn the layers out on wire racks to cool.

Meanwhile, pick over the strawberries, remove the stems or caps and discard any fruit that is badly bruised or shows signs of mold. Wash the berries in a sieve or colander under cold running water, drain, then spread them on paper towels and pat them completely dry. Set the 12 best strawberries aside to garnish the cake and chop the rest coarsely.

Just before serving, beat the remaining 2 cups of cream in a chilled bowl with a wire whisk or a rotary or electric beater. When the cream is stiff enough to stand in unwavering peaks, place one cooled cake layer on a serving plate and spread it evenly with half of the whipped cream. Scatter the chopped strawberries over it, and set the second cake layer on top. Spread the remaining whipped cream over the cake and decorate the top with the reserved whole berries. Serve at once.

## Wellesley Fudge Cake (New England)

To serve 8 to 10

CAKE

| | |
|---|---|
| 3 teaspoons plus 8 tablespoons butter, softened | powder |
| | ½ teaspoon salt |
| 2 tablespoons plus 1 cup all-purpose flour | 2 cups milk |
| | 2 teaspoons vanilla extract |
| 1 cup unsweetened cocoa | 2 cups sugar |
| 4 teaspoons double-acting baking | 4 egg yolks |
| | 4 egg whites |

Preheat the oven to 350°. With a pastry brush, spread 3 teaspoons of softened butter evenly over the bottom and sides of three 9-inch cake pans. Sprinkle the butter with 2 tablespoons of flour and tip the pans from side to side to spread it evenly; then invert the pans and rap them sharply to remove the excess flour. Combine the remaining cup of flour, the cocoa, baking powder and ½ teaspoon of salt and sift them into a bowl. Stir the milk and 2 teaspoons of vanilla in a measuring cup. Set aside.

In a deep bowl, mix the remaining 8 tablespoons of softened butter and the sugar together until they are thoroughly combined. Beat in the egg yolks, one at a time. Then add ½ cup of the flour-and-cocoa mixture and, when it is well incorporated, ½ cup of the milk-and-vanilla mixture. Repeat three more times, adding ½ cup of the flour mixture alternately with ½ cup of the milk mixture, and continue to beat until the batter is completely smooth.

With a wire whisk or a rotary or electric beater, beat the egg whites until they are firm enough to stand in soft peaks on the beater when it is lifted from the bowl. Stir a few tablespoonfuls of the egg whites into the batter, then scoop the remaining batter over the egg whites and fold them together gently but thoroughly with a rubber spatula.

Pour the batter into the floured and buttered pans, dividing it equally between them and smoothing the tops with the spatula. Bake in the middle of the oven for about 30 minutes, or until the cakes begin to shrink away from the sides of the pans and the tops spring back immediately when prodded gently with a finger. Turn the cake layers out onto wire racks to cool to room temperature.

CHOCOLATE FROSTING
12 one-ounce squares semi-sweet
   chocolate, coarsely chopped
¾ cup sour cream
1 teaspoon vanilla extract
A pinch of salt

When the cake has cooled, prepare the frosting in the following fashion: Drop the chocolate into the top of a double boiler set over simmering, not boiling, water. Stir until the chocolate melts, then remove from the heat and beat in the sour cream, 1 teaspoon of vanilla and a pinch of salt.

Set one cake layer upside down on an inverted cake pan and, with a metal spatula or knife, spread about ½ cup of the frosting over it. Carefully put the second cake layer in place, right side up, and coat the top and sides with the remaining frosting. Slide the cake onto a serving plate.

*Three-Layer Chocolate Cake*

To make one 9-inch cake

Six 1-ounce squares of unsweetened
   chocolate
12 tablespoons unsalted butter
   (1½ quarter-pound sticks),
   softened

2¼ cups sugar
4 eggs
1 teaspoon vanilla
2 cups all-purpose flour
1½ level teaspoons baking powder
¼ teaspoon salt
1½ cups milk

Preheat the oven to 375°. Break the chocolate into small pieces, place in a small saucepan and melt over moderate heat, stirring constantly with a spoon. Do not let it boil. Cool to room temperature. In a large mixing bowl, cream the butter and sugar together by mashing and beating it with a large spoon until it is light and fluffy. Beat in the eggs, one at a time, then beat in the melted chocolate and vanilla. Sift the flour, baking powder and salt together into another bowl. Beat ¼ cup of the dry ingredients into the chocolate mixture, then beat in ¼ cup of milk. Continue adding the flour and milk alternately in similar amounts, beating until the batter is smooth.

Butter and flour three 9½-inch circular cake pans. Invert the pans and rap them on the edge of the table to knock out any excess flour. Divide the batter equally among the three pans and bake them in the center of the oven for 15 to 20 minutes, or until the cakes come slightly away from the edge of the pan and are firm to the touch. A knife inserted in the center of the cakes should come out dry and clean. Turn the cakes out on cake racks to cool.

Spread the top of each cake with about ¼ inch of the chocolate sour-cream frosting and place the layers one on top of another on a cake plate. With a long metal spatula or knife, thoroughly coat the sides of the cakes with the remaining frosting, and add more frosting to the top of the cake if you wish. Decorate the top with the halved walnuts.

CHOCOLATE SOUR-CREAM FROSTING
Three 6-ounce packages semisweet chocolate bits

¼ teaspoon salt
1½ cups sour cream
12 to 15 shelled walnut halves

CHOCOLATE SOUR-CREAM FROSTING: In the top of a double boiler, melt the chocolate over boiling water. With a whisk or spoon, stir into it the salt and the sour cream. Ice the cake while the frosting is still slightly warm.

## German's Chocolate Cake with Coconut Frosting

To make a 3-layer 9-inch cake

CAKE
3 tablespoons plus ½ pound butter, softened
6 tablespoons all-purpose flour
½ cup water
6 ounces (1½ bars) German's sweet chocolate, broken into ½-inch bits
2½ cups cake flour (not the self-rising variety), sifted before measuring
1 teaspoon baking soda
½ teaspoon salt
1¾ cups sugar
4 egg yolks
1½ teaspoons vanilla extract
1 cup buttermilk
4 egg whites

First prepare the cake in the following manner: Preheat the oven to 350°. With a pastry brush spread 3 tablespoons of the softened butter evenly over the bottom and sides of three 9-inch layer-cake pans. Add 2 tablespoons of the all-purpose flour to each pan and tip the pans from side to side to distribute the flour evenly. Invert the pans and rap the bottoms sharply to remove the excess flour. Set them aside.

Bring the water to a boil in a small saucepan and drop in the 6 ounces of chocolate bits. Stirring constantly, cook over low heat until the chocolate melts and the mixture is smooth. Remove the pan from the heat and let the chocolate mixture cool to room temperature.

Combine the cake flour, baking soda and salt, sift them into a bowl, and set the bowl aside.

In a deep bowl, cream the remaining ½ pound of softened butter and 1¾ cups of sugar together by beating and mashing them against the sides of the bowl with the back of a spoon until the mixture is light and fluffy. Beat in 4 egg yolks one at a time, and add 1½ teaspoons of vanilla.

Stirring the batter constantly, pour in the chocolate mixture in a slow, thin stream and continue to beat until the batter is smooth. Add about ½ cup of the cake-flour mixture and, when it is well incorporated, beat in ¼ cup of the buttermilk. Repeat three times, alternating about ½ cup of the flour mixture with ¼ cup of buttermilk and beating the batter well after each addition.

With a wire whisk or a rotary or electric beater, beat the egg whites until they are stiff enough to stand in unwavering peaks on the beater when it is lifted from the bowl. With a rubber spatula, scoop the egg whites over the batter and fold them together gently but thoroughly.

Pour the batter into the prepared pans, dividing it equally among them and smoothing the tops with the spatula. Bake in the middle of the oven for about 35 minutes, or until a toothpick or cake tester inserted in the centers comes out clean. Let the cakes cool in the pans for about 5 minutes, then turn them out on wire racks to cool completely to room temperature.

COCONUT-NUT FROSTING
4 egg yolks
1 cup sugar
1 cup evaporated milk
12 tablespoons butter, cut into
½-inch bits and softened

2 ounces (½ bar) German's sweet chocolate, coarsely grated
1 teaspoon vanilla extract
A 4-ounce can sweetened shredded coconut (1⅓ cups)
1 cup coarsely chopped pecans

Meanwhile, prepare the frosting. With a wire whisk, beat 4 egg yolks and 1 cup of sugar together in a heavy 2- to 3-quart saucepan for 1 or 2 minutes. When the mixture is smooth and light, whisk in the evaporated milk. Add 12 tablespoons of softened butter bits and 2 ounces of grated chocolate, and set the pan over low heat. Stirring constantly with a large metal spoon, cook the mixture for 5 to 10 minutes, or until it is smooth and thick enough to cling lightly to the spoon. Do not let the mixture come anywhere near a boil or the egg yolks will curdle. Remove the pan from the heat and stir in 1 teaspoon of vanilla, the coconut and pecans.

Let the frosting cool to room temperature. Then refrigerate it for about 1 hour, stirring every 15 minutes, until the frosting holds its shape almost solidly in the spoon.

Place one layer of the cooled cake upside down on a serving plate and, with a metal spatula, spread the top with about one third of the frosting. Set the second layer in place, frost it, and add the third cake layer. Frost the top of the cake with all the remaining frosting (since the frosting is fragile, do not attempt to spread it on the sides of the cake).

Serve at once or refrigerate the cake until you are ready to serve it.

## Coconut Cake with Lemon Filling  (South)

To make one 9-inch 4-layer cake

CAKE

| | |
|---|---|
| 2 tablespoons butter, softened | 8 egg yolks |
| 2 tablespoons plus 2 cups flour, sifted before measuring | 2 cups sugar |
| | ¼ cup strained fresh lemon juice |
| 1 teaspoon double-acting baking powder | 2 teaspoons finely grated fresh lemon peel |
| ⅛ teaspoon salt | 8 egg whites |

Preheat the oven to 350°. With a pastry brush, spread the 2 tablespoons of softened butter over the bottom and sides of two 9-inch layer-cake pans. Add 1 tablespoon of flour to each pan and, one at a time, tip the pans from side to side to distribute the flour evenly. Then invert each pan and rap it sharply to remove the excess flour.

Combine the 2 cups of sifted flour, the teaspoon of baking powder and ⅛ teaspoon of salt and sift them together on a plate or on a sheet of wax paper. Set aside.

In a deep bowl, beat the egg yolks and 2 cups of sugar with a wire whisk or a rotary or electric beater for 4 to 5 minutes, or until the mixture is thick enough to fall back on itself in a slowly dissolving ribbon when the beater is lifted from the bowl. Beat in the ¼ cup lemon juice and 2 teaspoons lemon peel. Then add the flour mixture, about ½ cup at a time, beating well after each addition.

With a whisk or a rotary or electric beater, beat the 8 egg whites in another bowl until they are stiff enough to stand in unwavering peaks on the beater when it is lifted up out of the bowl. Scoop the egg whites over the batter and, with a rubber spatula, fold them gently but thoroughly together until no trace of white shows.

Pour the batter into the buttered and floured pans, dividing it equally between them and smoothing the tops with the spatula. Bake in the middle of the oven for about 20 minutes, or until a toothpick or cake tester inserted in the center of the cake comes out clean and dry. Let the cakes cool in the pans for about 5 minutes, then turn them out on wire racks to cool to room temperature.

**FILLING**
1½ cups sugar
¼ cup cornstarch
⅛ teaspoon salt
2 eggs, lightly beaten
2 tablespoons butter, cut into
¼-inch bits
2 tablespoons finely grated fresh
lemon peel
⅔ cup strained fresh lemon juice
1 cup water

Meanwhile, prepare the filling in the following fashion: Combine the 1½ cups sugar, the cornstarch, ⅛ teaspoon salt and the 2 beaten eggs in a heavy 1½- to 2-quart saucepan and mix well with a wire whisk or wooden spoon. Stir in the butter bits, 2 tablespoons lemon peel, ⅔ cup lemon juice and 1 cup water and, when all the ingredients are well blended, set the pan over high heat.

Stirring the filling mixture constantly, bring to a boil over high heat. Immediately reduce the heat to low and continue to stir until the filling is smooth and thick enough to coat the spoon heavily. Scrape the filling into a bowl with a rubber spatula, and let it cool to room temperature.

**COCONUT ICING**
4 egg whites
½ cup confectioners' sugar
1 teaspoon vanilla extract
1½ cups white corn syrup
2 cups freshly grated, peeled
coconut meat

When the cake and filling are cool, prepare the icing: With a wire whisk or a rotary or electric beater, beat the 4 egg whites until they are stiff enough to stand in soft peaks on the uplifted beater. Sprinkle them with the confectioners' sugar and vanilla and continue to beat until the egg whites are stiff and glossy.

In a small saucepan, bring the corn syrup to a boil over high heat and cook briskly until it reaches a temperature of 239° on a candy thermometer, or until a drop spooned into ice water immediately forms a soft ball. Beating the egg white mixture constantly with a wooden spoon, pour in the corn syrup in a slow, thin stream and continue to beat until the icing is smooth, thick and cool.

To assemble, cut each cake in half horizontally, thus creating four thin layers. Place one layer, cut side up, on an inverted cake or pie tin and, with a small metal spatula, spread about ⅓ of the lemon filling over it. Put another cake layer on top, spread with filling, and cover it with the third layer. Spread this layer with the remaining filling, and place the fourth layer on top.

Smooth the icing over the top and sides of the cake with the spatula. Then sprinkle the coconut generously on the top and, with your fingers, pat it into the sides of the cake. Carefully transfer the coconut cake to a serving plate and serve at once. If the cake must wait, drape waxed paper around the top and sides to keep the icing moist.

In Key West and other parts of the Deep South coconut cake is traditionally served at Christmastime.

# Grapefruit Cake with Cream-Cheese Icing *(Far West)*

To make a 2-layer 9-inch cake

CAKE

2 tablespoons butter, softened

2 tablespoons all-purpose flour

2 cups cake flour (not the self-rising variety), sifted before measuring

2 teaspoons double-acting baking powder

½ teaspoon salt

⅓ cup strained fresh grapefruit juice

⅓ cup vegetable oil

¼ cup water

4 egg whites

⅛ teaspoon cream of tartar

4 egg yolks

1 cup granulated sugar

1 tablespoon finely grated fresh grapefruit peel

Preheat the oven to 350°. With a pastry brush, spread the softened butter over the bottom and sides of two 9-inch layer-cake pans. Add 1 tablespoon of all-purpose flour to each pan and tip it from side to side to distribute the flour evenly. Invert the pans and rap them sharply to remove the excess flour.

Combine the cake flour, baking powder and salt, and sift them together into a bowl. Pour the grapefruit juice, vegetable oil and water into a glass measuring cup. Set aside.

With a wire whisk or a rotary or electric beater, beat the egg whites and cream of tartar until the whites are stiff enough to stand in unwavering peaks on the beater when it is lifted from the bowl. Set aside.

In a separate bowl but with the same beater, beat the egg yolks and granulated sugar together for 4 to 5 minutes, or until the mixture is thick. Beat in about ½ cup of the flour mixture and, when it is thoroughly incorporated, add about ¼ cup of the juice-and-oil mixture. Repeat three times, alternating ½ cup of the flour with ¼ cup of the juice and oil and beating the batter well after each addition. Stir in 1 tablespoon of grated grapefruit peel.

With a rubber spatula scoop the egg whites over the batter and fold them together gently but thoroughly. Pour the batter into the prepared pans, dividing it evenly between them and smoothing the tops with the spatula. Bake the cakes in the middle of the oven for about 25 minutes, or until a toothpick or cake tester inserted in the centers comes out clean. Let the cakes cool in the pans for 4 or 5 minutes, then turn them out onto wire racks to cool to room temperature.

CREAM-CHEESE ICING

1 large firm grapefruit

2 eight-ounce packages cream cheese, cut into ½-inch bits and softened

1 cup confectioners' sugar

2 tablespoons finely grated fresh grapefruit peel

½ teaspoon vanilla extract

Meanwhile, prepare the cream-cheese icing in the following fashion: Wash the grapefruit and pat it dry with paper towels. With a small sharp knife, remove the skin without cutting into the bitter white pith beneath it. Cut the peel into strips about ⅛ inch wide and set them aside.

To section the grapefruit, cut the white outer pith and membrane away, using short sawing motions. Then cut along both sides of each membrane division to the core of the grapefruit. As each section is freed, carefully lift it out and set it aside on paper towels to drain.

In a deep bowl, cream the cream cheese and confectioners' sugar together by beating and mashing them against the sides of the bowl with the back of a large spoon until the mixture is light and fluffy. Beat in the grated grapefruit peel and vanilla extract.

When the cake is cool, place one layer upside down on an inverted cake pan. With a metal spatula, spread about ½ cup of the cream-cheese icing over this layer and put the top layer in place. Reserve ½ cup of the icing to make roses, as shown in the photographs on pages 96 and 97. Then spread the remaining icing evenly over the top and sides of the cake and decorate the sides with the reserved strips of grapefruit peel. Arrange the grapefruit sections and icing roses attractively on top and refrigerate the cake until ready to serve.

## Pear Upside-down Cake (Eastern Heartland)

To make one 9-inch cake

| | |
|---|---|
| 1 tablespoon butter, softened, plus 14 tablespoons butter, melted | 1 teaspoon ground ginger |
| | ¼ teaspoon ground cloves |
| | 1 teaspoon salt |
| 1 cup light brown sugar | ½ cup dark molasses |
| 3 medium-sized firm ripe pears | ½ cup honey |
| 2½ cups unsifted flour | ¾ cup hot water |
| 1½ teaspoons baking soda | 1 egg |
| 1 teaspoon ground cinnamon | ½ cup sugar |

Preheat the oven to 350°. With a pastry brush, spread the tablespoon of softened butter evenly on the sides of a 9-inch springform cake pan. Then stir 6 tablespoons of the melted butter and the brown sugar together and pat the mixture smoothly over the bottom of the pan.

Peel the pears with a small sharp knife and cut them in half lengthwise. Scoop out the cores with a small spoon. Then arrange the pear halves in one layer in a heavy 10- to 12-inch skillet and add enough water to cover them by 1 inch. Bring to a boil over high heat, reduce the heat to low, and simmer uncovered for 5 to 10 minutes, until the pears show only slight resistance when pierced with the point of a sharp knife.

With a slotted spoon arrange the pears, cored side down, on a wire rack to drain. To flatten each pear, cut a round slice about ¼ inch thick off the curved side of each half. Place one of the round slices, cut side down, in the center of the sugar-coated pan. Arrange the trimmed halves, core side up, around the round slice so that their stem ends face the center and the pears radiate from it like the spokes of a wheel. Chop the remaining round slices of pear coarsely and set them aside.

Combine the flour, baking soda, cinnamon, ginger, cloves and salt, and sift them together into a bowl. Combine the molasses, honey and hot water in a small bowl and mix together thoroughly.

In a deep bowl, beat the egg and sugar with a large spoon or a wire whisk. Stir in the remaining 8 tablespoons of melted butter. Add about 1 cup of the flour mixture and, when it is thoroughly incorporated, beat in about ½ cup of the molasses-and-honey mixture. Repeat twice, alternating 1 cup of the flour mixture with ½ cup of the molasses-and-honey mixture, and beating well after each addition. Gently stir in the reserved chopped pears and dribble the batter slowly into the pear-lined pan.

Bake in the middle of the oven for about 1½ hours, or until the topping is golden and a toothpick or cake tester inserted in the center comes out clean. Let the cake cool in the pan for about 5 minutes.

To unmold and serve the cake, place an inverted serving plate over the top of the pan. Grasping plate and pan together firmly, turn them over. Rap the plate on a table and the cake should slide out easily. Remove the sides of the pan and serve the cake warm or at room temperature.

## Fig Cake *(Creole-Acadian)*

To make one 10-inch tube cake

9 tablespoons butter, softened
2 tablespoons plus 2½ cups
    unsifted flour
1 teaspoon baking soda
1 teaspoon double-acting baking
    powder
1 teaspoon ground cinnamon
1 teaspoon ground nutmeg,
    preferably freshly grated

½ teaspoon salt
4 one-pound cans figs, drained,
    patted dry with paper towels and
    finely chopped
1 cup sugar
3 eggs
1 cup milk
1 tablespoon cider vinegar
1 teaspoon vanilla extract

Preheat the oven to 350°. With a pastry brush, spread 1 tablespoon of the softened butter over the bottom and sides of a 10-inch tube cake pan. Add 2 tablespoons of the flour and tip the pan from side to side to distribute the flour evenly. Then invert the pan and rap the bottom sharply to remove the excess flour.

Sift the remaining 2½ cups of flour and the baking soda, baking powder, cinnamon, nutmeg and salt together into a bowl. Place the figs in another bowl, stir in about ½ cup of the flour mixture, and set aside.

In a deep bowl, cream the remaining 8 tablespoons of softened butter and the sugar together by beating and mashing them against the sides of the bowl with the back of a spoon until the mixture is light and fluffy. Beat in the eggs, one at a time. Add ½ cup of the remaining flour mixture and, when it is well incorporated, beat in ¼ cup of the milk. Repeat three more times, alternating ½ cup of the flour mixture with ¼ cup of the milk and beating well after each addition. Stir in the vinegar and vanilla extract. Then, with a rubber spatula, gently fold the reserved floured figs into the batter.

Pour the batter into the prepared tube pan, spreading it evenly and smoothing the top with the spatula. Bake in the middle of the oven for about 1 hour, or until a toothpick or cake tester inserted into the center of the cake comes out clean.

Let the fig cake cool in the pan for about 10 minutes before turning it out on a wire rack to cool completely to room temperature. Wrap the cake tightly in foil and let it rest at room temperature for at least 24 hours before serving.

## *Gâteau de Sirop* (Creole-Acadian)
SYRUP CAKE

To make one 9-inch square cake

9 tablespoons butter, softened
2 tablespoons plus 2½ cups
   unsifted flour
1½ teaspoons double-acting
   baking powder
½ teaspoon baking soda
1 teaspoon ground ginger
1 teaspoon ground cinnamon
¼ teaspoon ground nutmeg,
   preferably freshly grated

¼ teaspoon ground cloves
½ teaspoon salt
½ cup coarsely chopped pecans
½ cup seedless raisins
1 cup pure cane syrup or substitute
   ⅔ cup dark corn syrup mixed
   with ⅓ cup dark molasses
1 cup boiling water
½ cup sugar
2 eggs

Preheat the oven to 350°. With a pastry brush, spread 1 tablespoon of the softened butter over the bottom and sides of a 9-by-9-by-2-inch baking pan. Add 1 tablespoon of the flour and tip the pan from side to side to distribute it evenly. Invert the pan and rap the bottom sharply to remove the excess flour.

Combine 2½ cups of the flour, the baking powder, baking soda, ginger, cinnamon, nutmeg, cloves and salt, and sift them together into a mixing bowl. In a separate bowl, mix the remaining tablespoon of flour with the chopped pecans and raisins. Pour the syrup and boiling water into another bowl and mix the liquids well.

In a deep bowl, cream the remaining 8 tablespoons of softened butter and the sugar together by beating and mashing them against the sides of the bowl with the back of a large spoon until the mixture is light and fluffy. Beat in the eggs, one at a time.

Add about ⅔ cup of flour-and-spice mixture and, when it is well incorporated, beat in ½ cup of the syrup mixture. Repeat three more times, alternating about ⅔ cup of the flour-and-spice mixture with ½ cup of the syrup mixture, and beating well after each addition. Add the floured pecans and the raisins and, with a rubber spatula, fold them in gently but thoroughly.

Pour the batter into the prepared pan, spreading it evenly and smoothing the top with the spatula. Bake the syrup cake in the middle of the oven for 50 to 60 minutes, or until a toothpick or cake tester inserted in the center comes out clean.

Cool and serve the syrup cake from the pan or, if you prefer, turn it out on a wire rack to cool and serve the cake from a plate.

## Lane Cake (South)

To make one 3-layer cake

CAKE

| | |
|---|---|
| 1 tablespoon plus ½ pound unsalted butter, softened | powder |
| | A pinch of salt |
| 3 tablespoons plus 2½ cups all-purpose flour | ¾ cup milk |
| | 1 teaspoon vanilla extract |
| 2 teaspoons double-acting baking | 1½ cups sugar |
| | 8 egg whites |

CAKE: Preheat the oven to 350°. With a pastry brush, spread 1 tablespoon of the softened butter evenly over the bottom and sides of three 9-inch cake pans. Add 1 tablespoon of the flour to each pan and tip the pans from side to side to spread the flour evenly; then invert the pans and rap them sharply to remove the excess flour.

Combine the remaining 2½ cups of flour, the baking powder and salt, and sift them into a bowl. Stir the milk and vanilla extract together and set aside.

In a deep bowl, cream the remaining butter and the sugar together by beating and mashing them against the sides of the bowl with the back of a spoon until the mixture is light and fluffy. Beat in about 1 cup of the flour mixture and, when it is well incorporated, ¼ cup of the vanilla-flavored milk. Repeat twice more, alternating 1 cup of the flour mixture and ¼ cup of the milk each time. Continue to beat until the batter is completely smooth.

With a wire whisk or a rotary or electric beater, beat the 8 egg whites in a large bowl until they are firm enough to stand in soft peaks on the beater when it is lifted from the bowl. Stir a few tablespoons of the egg whites into the batter, then scoop the remaining batter over the whites and fold them together gently but thoroughly with a rubber spatula.

Pour the batter into the prepared pans, dividing it equally among them and smoothing the tops with the spatula. Bake in the middle of the oven for about 25 minutes, or until the cakes begin to shrink away from the sides of the pans and the tops spring back immediately when prodded gently with a finger. Turn the cakes out onto wire racks and let them cool to room temperature.

FILLING
8 egg yolks
1 cup sugar
A pinch of salt
1 cup brandy
8 tablespoons (1 quarter-pound stick) butter, melted and cooled

1 cup seedless raisins, finely chopped
¾ cup freshly grated coconut, or substitute ¾ cup shredded packaged coconut
1 cup finely chopped pecans
1 teaspoon vanilla extract

FILLING: In a deep bowl, beat the egg yolks, sugar and salt with a wire whisk or a rotary or electric beater for 3 or 4 minutes, or until the yolks form a slowly dissolving ribbon when the beater is lifted from the bowl. Whisking constantly, pour in the brandy in a slow, thin stream, then whisk in the melted butter. When thoroughly blended, transfer the mixture to a 1- to 1½-quart enameled or stainless-steel saucepan. Cook over low heat, stirring constantly, until the filling has thickened enough to coat a spoon lightly. Do not let the mixture come near a boil or it will curdle. Stir in the raisins, coconut, pecans and vanilla, and set the filling aside to cool to room temperature. Then cover with plastic wrap and refrigerate until ready to use.

BOILED ICING
2 egg whites
A pinch of salt

2 cups sugar
2 tablespoons light corn syrup
⅔ cup cold water

BOILED ICING: In a large mixing bowl, beat the egg whites and salt with a wire whisk or a rotary or electric beater until the whites are firm enough to stand in soft peaks when the beater is lifted from the bowl.

Combine the sugar, corn syrup and cold water in a heavy 1- to 1½-quart saucepan and, stirring frequently, cook over moderate heat until the sugar dissolves. Raise the heat to high and boil uncovered and undisturbed until the syrup reaches 240° on a candy thermometer. Remove the saucepan from the heat.

Beating constantly, pour the hot syrup over the beaten egg whites in a slow, thin stream, and continue to beat until the boiled icing is smooth, thick and cool.

TO ASSEMBLE: Set one cake layer on an inverted cake pan and, with a metal spatula or knife, spread about ¾ cup of the filling over it. Carefully set the second cake layer in place and spread with the remaining filling. Top with the third cake layer, and coat the top and sides with the boiled icing. Slide the cake onto a serving plate and serve. Or, if you prefer, cover loosely with wax paper or aluminum foil and set aside at room temperature for as long as two days; the filling will keep the cake moist.

## White Fruit Cake  (South)

To make one 6-pound cake

14 tablespoons butter, softened
3 cups flour
2 teaspoons double-acting baking powder
½ teaspoon ground nutmeg, preferably freshly grated
¾ teaspoon salt
2 cups golden raisins
¾ cup finely slivered candied lemon peel (about 6 ounces)
¾ cup finely slivered candied orange peel (about 6 ounces)
¾ cup finely slivered candied pineapple (about 6 ounces)
¾ cup finely chopped candied citron (about 6 ounces)
1 cup sugar
1¼ cups bourbon
1½ cups slivered blanched almonds (about 6 ounces)
8 egg whites

Preheat the oven to 250°. With a pastry brush, spread 1 tablespoon of the softened butter over the bottom and sides of a 9-by-3-inch spring-form tube cake pan. Coat two strips of wax paper with another tablespoon of the butter and fit the strips around the tube and the sides of the pan, with the greased surfaces toward the center. Set aside.

Combine the flour, baking powder, nutmeg and salt and sift them together into a deep bowl. Add the raisins, lemon peel, orange peel, pineapple and citron, and toss the fruit about with a spoon until the pieces are evenly coated.

In another deep bowl, cream the remaining 12 tablespoons of butter and the sugar together, beating and mashing them against the sides of the bowl with the back of a large wooden spoon until the mixture is light and fluffy. Stir in the flour-and-fruit mixture a cup or so at a time. Then add ¾ cup of the bourbon and, when it is completely incorporated, stir in the slivered almonds.

With a wire whisk or a rotary or electric beater, beat the egg whites until they are stiff enough to stand in unwavering peaks on the beater when it is lifted from the bowl. Scoop the egg whites over the batter and, with a rubber spatula, fold them together gently but thoroughly.

Pour the batter into the paper-lined pan, filling it about three quarters full, and smooth the top with the spatula. Bake in the middle of the oven for 2½ to 3 hours, or until a toothpick or cake tester inserted in the center of the cake comes out clean.

Let the cake cool overnight before removing the sides of the spring-form. Then slip it off the bottom of the pan and carefully peel away the paper. Place the cake on a serving plate and sprinkle it evenly with the remaining ½ cup of bourbon. Wrap in cheesecloth and set the cake aside at room temperature for at least 24 hours before serving. Securely wrapped in foil or plastic, it can be kept for several months, and its flavor will improve with age.

## *Bûche de Noël* (New England)
### YULE-LOG CAKE ROLL

| | |
|---|---|
| 2 tablespoons butter, softened, plus 8 tablespoons unsalted butter, softened and cut into ½-inch bits | 1 cup sugar |
| | ½ teaspoon vanilla extract |
| | 4 egg yolks |
| | 3 tablespoons cold water |
| 2 tablespoons plus 1 cup flour | ¾ cup crab-apple jelly |
| 4 teaspoons cornstarch | ¾ cup pure maple syrup |
| 1¼ teaspoons double-acting baking powder | 1 ounce unsweetened baking chocolate, coarsely grated |
| ¼ teaspoon salt | Candied cherries |
| 6 egg whites | Candied green citron |

Preheat the oven to 350°. Brush 1 tablespoon of softened butter over the bottom and sides of a 10½-by-15½-inch jelly-roll pan. Line the pan with a 20-inch strip of wax paper and let the extra paper extend over the ends. Brush 1 tablespoon of softened butter on the paper and sprinkle it with 2 tablespoons of flour, tipping the pan from side to side. Turn the pan over and rap it sharply to remove the excess flour. Combine the 1 cup of flour, cornstarch, baking powder and salt and sift them onto a plate.

With a wire whisk or a rotary or electric beater, beat 4 of the egg whites until they begin to thicken. Slowly add ½ cup of the sugar, beating continuously until the whites are stiff enough to form unwavering peaks on the beater when it is lifted from the bowl. Beat in the vanilla.

In another bowl and with the unwashed whisk or beater, beat the egg yolks, the remaining ½ cup of sugar and the water together. When the yolk mixture thickens enough to fall from the beater in a slowly dissolving ribbon, beat in the sifted flour mixture a few tablespoons at a time. Make sure each addition is completely incorporated before beating in more. Stir ½ cup of the beaten egg whites into the yolk mixture, then scoop it over the whites and fold the two together gently but thoroughly.

Pour the batter into the lined pan and spread it evenly into the corners with a spatula. Bake in the middle of the oven for 20 minutes, or until the sides of the cake have begun to shrink away from the pan and the cake springs back instantly when pressed lightly with a fingertip.

Carefully turn the cake out on wax paper, peel the layer of paper from the top, and let it rest for 5 minutes, then spread the surface with crab-apple jelly. Starting at one long edge, roll the cake into a cylinder. Cut a 1-inch-thick slice from each end of the cake and trim each slice into a round about 1½ inches in diameter. Set the cake aside to cool.

To prepare the icing, bring the maple syrup to a boil over moderate heat in a 3- to 4-quart saucepan. Cook uncovered and undisturbed, regulating the heat to prevent the syrup from boiling over. When the syrup reaches a temperature of 238° on a candy thermometer, or when a drop spooned into ice water immediately forms a soft but compact mass, remove the pan from the heat. Add the chocolate and stir to dissolve it.

In a large bowl, beat the two remaining egg whites with a wire whisk or a rotary or electric beater until they are stiff enough to stand in unwavering peaks on the beater when it is lifted from the bowl. Beating the egg whites constantly, pour in the maple syrup-and-chocolate mixture in a slow, thin stream and continue to beat until the mixture has cooled to room temperature. Then beat in the butter bits a few pieces at a time.

When the icing is smooth and thick, spread most of it over the top, sides and ends of the cake roll with a metal spatula or knife. With fork tines, make irregular lines the length of the roll to give the icing a bark-like look and the cake the appearance of a log. Ice one side and the edges of the reserved rounds and set one on top of the log and the other on a side to resemble knotholes. Decorate the cake with holly berries made from the cherries and with leaf shapes cut from the citron.

## Apple Pandowdy *(New England)*

To serve 8

| | |
|---|---|
| 1 teaspoon butter, softened | peeled, cored and cut lengthwise |
| ⅓ cup plus 2 tablespoons sugar | into ½-inch-thick slices (about |
| ¼ cup dark molasses | 6 cups) |
| 1 tablespoon ground cinnamon | 2 cups flour |
| ¼ teaspoon ground cloves | 2½ teaspoons double-acting |
| ¼ teaspoon ground nutmeg, | baking powder |
| preferably freshly grated | ¼ teaspoon salt |
| 9 medium-sized tart cooking apples | 1 cup heavy cream |

Preheat the oven to 350°. With a pastry brush, spread the butter evenly over the bottom and sides of a 10-by-6-by-2-inch baking dish. Place ⅓ cup of sugar, the molasses, cinnamon, cloves and nutmeg in a large bowl and mix well. Add the apple slices and turn them about with a spoon to coat them evenly with the sugar mixture.

Combine the flour, the remaining 2 tablespoons of sugar, the baking powder and salt and sift them into a bowl. Make a well in the center, pour in the cream and, with a large spoon, slowly mix the ingredients together. When the mixture becomes a smooth dough, knead it for a few minutes with your hands until it can be gathered into a compact ball.

Place the dough on a lightly floured surface and again knead it briefly. Then roll it out into a rough rectangle about 12 inches long, 8 inches wide and ¼ inch thick.

Spread the apple mixture evenly in the buttered dish. Drape the dough over the rolling pin, lift it up and carefully unroll it over the dish. With a pair of scissors, cut off the excess dough from the edges, leaving a ½-inch overhang all around the outside rim to allow for shrinkage as the crust bakes. Bake in the middle of the oven for 45 minutes, or until the crust is puffed and golden brown.

Serve the apple pandowdy while it is still warm, accompanied if you like by a pitcher of heavy cream or by lemon sauce.*

# Small Cakes & Cookies

Generations of American schoolchildren celebrate their arrival home from school each day with a snack of milk and cookies—and many of their parents treat themselves to a midnight snack of milk and cookies. Probably the universal favorite for the cookie jar and refrigerator raid is the ubiquitous Toll House cookie in which crunchy nuts and chocolate chips are twirled in a butter-rich batter. Close behind in popularity are walnut-flecked chocolate brownies and crisp, golden-brown oatmeal cookies. Recipes for these American classics follow, along with directions for making other candidates for the cookie jar: ginger cookies and Spritz cookies from the Northwest; lollies from the Far West; lemon bars and coconut cupcakes.

Not all cookies are for snacking, though; some cookies are more appropriate with after-dinner coffee than with lunchbox sandwiches. Among these are the airy almond-flavored Portuguese-American meringues known as *suspiros* (sighs); the Creole-Acadian pecan lace cookies; walnut crescents from the Eastern Heartland; fig squares from the Far West —all are decidedly adult in their appeal.

To make 16 brownies

2 squares unsweetened chocolate
½ cup butter
1 cup sugar
2 eggs

½ cup all-purpose flour
½ teaspoon baking powder
½ teaspoon salt
1 teaspoon vanilla
1 cup coarsely chopped walnuts

Preheat the oven to 350°. Melt the chocolate in a small heavy saucepan over low heat, stirring constantly, but do not let it come to a boil. Set it aside to cool slightly. Meanwhile, in a mixing bowl cream the butter and sugar together by beating them with a large spoon until the mixture is light and fluffy. Beat in the eggs, one at a time, and then the cooled chocolate. Sift the flour, baking powder and salt together into the mixture, and beat for 10 or 15 seconds, or until the ingredients are well combined. Stir in the vanilla and walnuts. Lightly butter an 8-inch-square baking pan. Pour in the batter and bake the brownies in the center of the oven for 30 to 35 minutes, or until a small knife inserted in the center comes out clean. Cool for about 10 minutes, then cut into 2-inch squares.

To make 16 brownies

4 tablespoons butter
1 cup dark brown sugar
1 egg

1 teaspoon vanilla
½ cup all-purpose flour
1 teaspoon baking powder
½ teaspoon salt
½ cup coarsely chopped walnuts

Preheat the oven to 350°. Line an 8-inch-square baking pan with lightly buttered wax paper. Over low heat, melt the 4 tablespoons of butter in a small saucepan and add the brown sugar. Stir constantly until the sugar dissolves, then pour the mixture into a medium-sized mixing bowl. Cool until tepid. Beat in the egg and vanilla, and when they are thoroughly incorporated beat in the flour, baking powder and salt, first sifted together. Gently fold in the chopped walnuts and pour the batter into the baking pan. Bake in the center of the oven for about 25 minutes until the cake is firm to the touch and a small knife inserted in the center comes out clean. Let the cake cool for about 10 minutes, then cut it into 2-inch squares.

485

## Harwich Hermits *(New England)*

To make about 3 dozen 2-inch
squares

9 tablespoons butter, softened
1 tablespoon plus 2 cups all-purpose
flour
1½ teaspoons double-acting
baking powder
1 teaspoon ground cinnamon
½ teaspoon ground cloves
¼ teaspoon ground nutmeg,
preferably freshly grated
¼ teaspoon ground mace
⅛ teaspoon ground allspice
½ teaspoon salt
1 cup coarsely chopped seedless raisins
½ cup sugar
2 eggs
½ cup dark molasses
½ cup coarsely chopped walnuts

Preheat the oven to 350°. With a pastry brush, spread 1 tablespoon of softened butter evenly over the bottom and sides of a 13-by-8-inch baking pan. Sprinkle 1 tablespoon of the flour over the butter and tip the pan from side to side to spread it evenly. Invert the pan and rap the bottom sharply to remove the excess flour.

Combine the remaining 2 cups of flour, the baking powder, cinnamon, cloves, nutmeg, mace, allspice and salt and sift them onto a long sheet of wax paper. Place the raisins in a bowl, add 2 or 3 tablespoonfuls of the flour-and-spice mixture and toss together gently but thoroughly.

In a deep bowl, cream the remaining 8 tablespoons of softened butter and the sugar, beating and mashing them against the sides of the bowl with the back of a spoon until they are light and fluffy. Beat in the eggs, one at a time, and then add the molasses. Stir in the flour-and-spice mixture by the ½ cupful, and continue to beat until the batter is smooth. Fold in the reserved raisins and the walnuts.

Pour the batter into the floured, buttered pan, spreading it evenly and smoothing the top with a rubber spatula. Bake in the middle of the oven for about 15 minutes, or until a toothpick or cake tester inserted in the center comes out clean. Cool to room temperature in the baking dish and just before serving, cut the Harwich hermits into 2-inch squares.

## Fig Squares *(Far West)*

To make about 4 dozen

1 tablespoon butter, softened
2 tablespoons plus ¾ cup unsifted
flour
1 teaspoon double-acting baking
powder
¼ teaspoon ground cloves
¼ teaspoon ground cinnamon
¼ teaspoon salt
3 eggs
1 cup sugar
1 teaspoon vanilla extract
2 cups finely chopped dried figs
(about 16 ounces)
1 cup finely chopped walnuts
Confectioners' sugar

Preheat the oven to 325°. With a pastry brush, spread the softened butter over the bottom and sides of a 13-by-9-by-2-inch baking pan. Add 2 tablespoons of the flour and tip the pan from side to side to distribute it evenly. Then invert the pan and rap the bottom sharply to remove the excess flour. Combine the remaining ¾ cup of flour, the baking powder, cloves, cinnamon and salt, and sift them together into a bowl. Set aside.

In a deep bowl, beat the eggs with a wire whisk or a rotary or electric beater until they are smooth. Add the sugar and the flour mixture, about ½ cup at a time, beating well after each addition. Stir in the vanilla extract, figs and nuts.

Pour the batter into the prepared pan and smooth the top with a rubber spatula. Bake in the middle of the oven for about 25 minutes, or until the top is delicately browned and firm to the touch. Remove the pan from the oven and let the baked fig cake cool to room temperature. With a sharp knife, cut the cake into individual 1½-inch squares. Sift a little confectioners' sugar evenly over the squares.

## Lemon Bars

To make about 32 two-by-one-inch bars

9 tablespoons butter, softened
1¼ cups confectioners' sugar
1 cup plus 2 tablespoons unsifted flour
1 cup granulated sugar
½ teaspoon double-acting baking powder
2 eggs
4 to 5 tablespoons strained fresh lemon juice
2 teaspoons finely grated fresh lemon peel

First prepare the base in the following manner: Preheat the oven to 350°. With a pastry brush, spread 1 tablespoon of the softened butter evenly over the bottom of an 8-inch square cake pan. Set it aside.

In a deep bowl, cream the remaining 8 tablespoons of butter and ¼ cup of the confectioners' sugar together by beating and mashing them against the sides of the bowl with the back of a large spoon until the mixture is light and fluffy. Beat in 1 cup of the flour ½ cup at a time. Place the mixture in the buttered pan and, with your fingers, pat it smooth. Bake in the middle of the oven for 15 minutes, or until the cookie base is delicately colored and firm to the touch.

Meanwhile, combine the granulated sugar, the remaining 2 tablespoons of flour and the baking powder, and sift them into a bowl. Add the eggs and beat vigorously with a spoon until the mixture is smooth. Stir in 2 tablespoons of the lemon juice and the 2 teaspoons of lemon peel.

When the cookie base has baked its allotted time, pour the egg batter over it and smooth the top with the back of the spoon. Continue baking for about 25 minutes longer, or until the top is golden brown and firm. Remove the pan from the oven and let cool to room temperature.

To prepare the icing: Combine the remaining cup of confectioners' sugar and 2 tablespoons of lemon juice in a bowl and mix well. If the icing is stiff, stir in up to 1 tablespoon more lemon juice by the teaspoonful until the icing becomes creamy enough to spread. With a rubber spatula, scoop the icing onto the cooled lemon-bar cake and spread it evenly over the top.

Set the lemon-bar cake aside for about 15 minutes, until the icing hardens, then cut the cake into 2-by-1-inch bars. Drape foil or wax paper over the pan and let the lemon bars rest at room temperature for about a day before serving them. The three layers—cookie base, lemon topping and icing—will blend with one another and give the lemon bars the chewy, somewhat sticky consistency of gumdrops.

## Coconut Cupcakes

| | |
|---|---|
| To make about 30 cupcakes | 8 egg yolks |
| 4 tablespoons butter, softened | 2 egg whites |
| 1 cup sugar | 1 cup all-purpose flour |
| 1 teaspoon orange flower water | 1 cup freshly grated, or |
| ¼ teaspoon ground cloves | 1 cup packaged flaked, coconut |
| ¼ teaspoon ground cinnamon | 3 tablespoons melted butter |

Preheat the oven to 350°. In a large mixing bowl, beat the 4 tablespoons of butter, sugar, orange flower water, cloves and cinnamon together with a large spoon, mashing and beating against the side of the bowl until the mixture is light and fluffy. Beat in the egg yolks one at a time and then the egg whites, beating vigorously until the batter is smooth. Add the flour, ¼ cup at a time, and continue to beat until all the flour has been absorbed. Then stir in the coconut. With a pastry brush, liberally coat the insides of two 12-cup muffin tins with melted butter. Pour enough batter into each cup to fill it about halfway.

Place the filled muffin tins in one or two large shallow baking pans and pour in enough boiling water to reach at least halfway up the side of the tins. Bake the cupcakes in the middle of the oven for 40 minutes, until they are slightly brown on top. Let them cool to room temperature, then run a small, sharp knife around the inside rim of each muffin tin, invert the pans, and turn the cupcakes out on a rack to cool.

## Spritz Cookies (Northwest)

| | |
|---|---|
| To make about 4 dozen pressed cookies | 2 egg yolks |
| 1 cup butter, softened | 1 teaspoon almond extract |
| 1 cup sugar | 2½ cups flour |

Preheat the oven to 350°. In a deep bowl, cream the butter and sugar together by beating and mashing them against the sides of the bowl with the back of a large spoon until they are light and fluffy. Beat in the egg yolks and, when they are well incorporated, add the almond extract. Sift the flour into the mixture about ½ cup at a time, beating the dough well after each addition.

Place the dough in a pastry bag or cookie press fitted with a medium-sized star tip. Pipe the dough out onto ungreased baking sheets, forming rings about 1½ inches in diameter or "S" shapes or crescents about 2 inches long, spaced about 1 inch apart.

Bake in the middle of the oven for about 10 minutes, or until the cookies are firm and delicately browned. With a wide metal spatula, transfer them immediately to wire racks to cool. The cookies can be stored for several weeks in tightly sealed jars or tins.

## Creole Macaroons

To make about 40 three-inch round
    cookies
2 tablespoons butter, softened
4 egg yolks
2 cups sugar
¼ cup finely grated fresh orange
    peel

1 cup (4 ounces) finely ground
    blanched almonds
1 cup whole-wheat flour
4 egg whites
2½ cups (12 ounces) slivered
    blanched almonds

Preheat the oven to 350°. With a pastry brush, spread the softened butter evenly over two large baking sheets. Set the sheets aside.

In a deep bowl, stir the egg yolks and sugar together with a wooden spoon. When they are well mixed, beat in the orange peel and add the ground almonds and the whole-wheat flour, about ½ cup at a time. Continue to stir to make a smooth, thick pastelike dough.

With a wire whisk or a rotary or electric beater, beat the egg whites until they are stiff enough to stand in unwavering peaks on the whisk or beater when it is lifted out of the bowl. Using a rubber spatula, fold in the slivered almonds, then scoop the egg-white mixture over the dough and fold the dough and mixture together gently but thoroughly.

To shape each macaroon, brush your hands with flour, break off a tablespoonful of the dough and gently roll it between your palms into a ball about 1½ inches in diameter. Arrange the balls 2 inches apart on the buttered baking sheets to allow them to spread into 3-inch rounds.

Bake the macaroons in the middle of the oven for 10 to 12 minutes, or until the edges are delicately browned. With a large metal spatula, transfer the cookies to wire racks to cool before serving. In a tightly covered jar or tin, Creole macaroons can safely be kept for about a week.

## Toll House Cookies (New England)

To make 24 cookies

8 tablespoons (1 quarter-pound stick)
  softened butter
6 tablespoons granulated sugar
6 tablespoons dark brown sugar
½ teaspoon salt
½ teaspoon vanilla

¼ teaspoon cold water
1 egg
½ teaspoon baking soda
1 cup all-purpose flour
1 six-ounce package semisweet
  chocolate bits
¾ cup coarsely chopped pecans
1 tablespoon soft butter

Preheat the oven to 375°. In a large mixing bowl, combine the butter, white and brown sugar, salt, vanilla and water, and beat them together with a large spoon until the mixture is light and fluffy. Beat in the egg and baking soda and when they are well combined add the flour, beating it in ¼ cup at a time. Then, gently but thoroughly fold in the chocolate bits and nuts.

With a pastry brush coat a cookie sheet evenly with the tablespoon of soft butter. Drop the cookie batter onto the sheet a tablespoon at a time, leaving about 1½ inches between the cookies. Gently pat down the tops of each cookie with a spatula, but don't flatten them entirely. Bake in the middle of the oven for about 12 minutes, or until the cookies are firm to the touch and lightly brown. Cool on a cake rack.

## Oatmeal Cookies

To make 24 cookies
1 cup all-purpose flour
½ teaspoon baking powder
½ teaspoon salt
8 tablespoons (1 quarter-pound stick)
  unsalted butter, softened

¾ cup dark brown sugar
¼ cup granulated sugar
1 egg
1 teaspoon vanilla
1 tablespoon milk
1¼ cups uncooked oatmeal

Preheat the oven to 350° and lightly butter two 11-by-17-inch baking sheets. Sift the flour, baking powder and salt together into a mixing bowl. Cream the butter, the brown sugar and the granulated sugar together by mashing them against the side of another mixing bowl with a wooden spoon. Stir in the egg, the vanilla extract and the milk, continuing to stir until the mixture is smooth. Beat in the flour mixture, a little at a time, then add the oatmeal, stirring until the mixture is well blended. Drop the batter by the tablespoonful onto the baking sheets, leaving space between for the cookies to expand. Bake for 12 minutes, or until the cookies are lightly browned on top.

To make about thirty 1½-inch
round drop cookies

⅛ teaspoon ground cardamom

10 tablespoons butter, softened
1⅓ cups flour
½ teaspoon baking soda

½ cup sugar
1 egg
¼ cup whole filberts, shelled

Preheat the oven to 350°. With a pastry brush, spread 2 tablespoons of the softened butter evenly over two large baking sheets. Combine the flour, baking soda and cardamom, and sift them together onto a plate or a piece of wax paper. Set aside.

In a deep bowl, cream the remaining 8 tablespoons of butter and the sugar together, beating and mashing them against the side of the bowl with the back of a spoon until the mixture is light and fluffy. Beat in the egg and, when it is thoroughly incorporated, add the flour mixture about ½ cup at a time, beating well after each addition.

To shape each dream, scoop up about 1 tablespoon of the dough, then pat and roll it into a ball about 1 inch in diameter. Arrange the cookies 2 inches apart on the buttered baking sheets and press a whole filbert gently but firmly into the center of each one. Bake in the middle of the oven for about 10 minutes, or until the cookies are firm to the touch and a delicate golden-brown color.

Immediately transfer the cookies to wire cake racks with a metal spatula to cool to room temperature. The dreams can be kept safely in tightly covered jars or tins for several weeks.

## *Rugala* *(Jewish-American)*
### CREAM-CHEESE COOKIES WITH RAISINS AND NUTS

To make about 4 dozen
DOUGH
½ pound cream cheese, softened

½ pound unsalted butter, softened
2 cups all-purpose flour

In a large mixing bowl, cream the cheese and butter together by beating them against the sides of the bowl with a wooden spoon until the mixture is light and fluffy. Beat in the flour, about ½ cup at a time, and continue to beat until the dough is smooth and can be gathered into a ball. Wrap the dough in wax paper and refrigerate for at least 1 hour.

FILLING
½ cup sugar
1 teaspoon cinnamon

½ cup seedless raisins
¾ cup finely chopped walnuts

491

Meanwhile, prepare the filling by combining the sugar, cinnamon, raisins and nuts in a large mixing bowl.

Preheat the oven to 350°. Place the dough between two sheets of wax paper and roll it out to a large rough circle about ⅟₁₆ inch thick. Peel off the top sheet and, using a 9-inch cake pan as a guide, cut out two 9-inch circles of dough. Gather the scraps into a ball, wrap it in wax paper, and refrigerate.

Working with one circle of dough at a time, start at the center of the circle and, with a small sharp knife or pastry wheel, cut the dough as you would a pie, into 16 narrow wedges. Sprinkle the filling evenly over the dough, and cover with another sheet of wax paper. With a rolling pin, press down on the wax paper so that the filling adheres to the dough. Peel off the top sheet of wax paper and, with the aid of a small knife, roll up the triangles. Tuck under the pointed end of each cookie and place the cookies on a cookie sheet. Repeat with the other circle of dough, and similarly roll out, fill and shape the refrigerated dough scraps.

Bake the cookies in the center of the oven for 15 to 18 minutes, until they are pale gold, then transfer to wire racks to cool.

## Ginger Cookies

To make about 5 dozen rolled cookies

| | |
|---|---|
| 2 cups flour | 1 cup dark-brown sugar |
| 1½ teaspoons baking soda | ⅓ cup dark molasses |
| 1 tablespoon ground ginger | ¼ teaspoon lemon extract |
| ½ teaspoon ground cloves | ⅓ cup heavy cream |
| ½ teaspoon ground mace | ½ cup finely chopped crystallized |
| 6 tablespoons butter, softened | ginger |

Combine the flour, baking soda, ginger, cloves and mace, and sift them onto a plate or a sheet of wax paper. In a deep bowl, cream 4 tablespoons of the butter with the brown sugar, beating and mashing them against the sides of the bowl with the back of a spoon until they are light and fluffy. Mix in the molasses and the lemon extract.

Beat in about ½ cup of the flour mixture and, when it is thoroughly incorporated, add 1 or 2 tablespoons of the cream. Repeat three more times, alternating ½ cup of the flour with 1 or 2 tablespoons of the cream and beating well after each addition. Then stir in the chopped crystallized ginger, and shape the dough into a ball, then cut it in half. Wrap in wax paper and refrigerate for at least 8 hours, or overnight, until the dough is completely chilled.

Preheat the oven to 375°. With a pastry brush, spread 1 tablespoon of softened butter over two large baking sheets.

On a lightly floured surface, roll half of the dough into a rough rectangle about ⅛ inch thick. With a round or decorative cutter or the rim of a glass, cut the dough into individual cookies and arrange these about 1 inch apart on the buttered baking sheets. Gather the scraps of dough into a ball, roll it out as before and cut as many more cookies as you can.

Bake in the middle of the oven for about 8 minutes, or until the ginger cookies are crisp around the edges. With a metal spatula transfer them to wire racks to cool.

Let the baking sheets cool to room temperature, then brush them with the remaining tablespoon of softened butter. Roll out the remaining half of the dough and cut it as before. Arrange the cookies on the baking sheets and bake for 8 minutes, or until crisp. Cool them on wire racks. In tightly covered jars or tins, the ginger cookies can safely be kept for two or three weeks.

## *Moravian Sand Tarts* (*Eastern Heartland*)

To make about 8 dozen medium-sized cookies

| | |
|---|---|
| 3½ cups flour, sifted before measuring | 2⅓ cups sugar |
| 2 teaspoons double-acting baking powder | 3 eggs |
| | 1 teaspoon vanilla extract |
| 1 teaspoon salt | 2 teaspoons ground cinnamon |
| ½ pound plus 4 tablespoons butter, softened | 1 cup very finely chopped walnuts |
| | ½ cup milk |

Combine the flour, baking powder and salt, and sift them together onto a plate or a sheet of wax paper.

In a deep bowl, cream ½ pound of the softened butter with 2 cups of the sugar, beating and mashing the mixture against the sides of the bowl with the back of a spoon until it is light and fluffy. Beat in the eggs, one at a time and, when they are well incorporated, stir in the flour mixture by the cupful. Add the vanilla and continue to beat until the dough is smooth. Cover with wax paper or plastic wrap and refrigerate the dough for at least 8 hours, or overnight.

Preheat the oven to 350°. With a pastry brush, spread 1 tablespoon of the remaining softened butter evenly over two large baking sheets. Mix the remaining ⅓ cup of sugar, the cinnamon and nuts together and set them aside.

Cut off about one quarter of the dough and shape it into a ball. (Return the rest to the refrigerator.) On a lightly floured surface, roll the ball of dough out into a rough circle about ⅛ inch thick. Cut the dough into any shapes you like, using a star, heart or other decorative cookie cutter. Gather the scraps together into a ball and roll out as before. Then cut as many more cookies as you can. Brush the tops of the cookies lightly with milk and sprinkle them with a little of the sugar-and-nut mixture.

With a wide metal spatula, arrange the sand tarts about 1 inch apart on the baking sheets. Bake in the middle of the oven for 8 to 10 minutes, or until the cookies are crisp around the edges and the tops feel firm when prodded gently with a finger. With the spatula, transfer the sand tarts to wire racks to cool.

Let the baking sheets cool completely, then repeat the entire procedure three more times—using 1 tablespoon of the softened butter to grease the pans for each batch of cookies and rolling and baking one quarter of the dough at a time. In a tightly covered jar or box, the Moravian sand tarts can safely be kept for 2 or 3 weeks.

## Lollies *(Far West)*

| | |
|---|---|
| To make about 4 dozen 1½-inch square cookies | ½ teaspoon double-acting baking powder |
| 9 tablespoons butter, softened | ½ teaspoon vanilla extract |
| 1½ cups dark brown sugar | 1 cup finely chopped pecans |
| 1 cup unsifted flour | 1 cup canned shredded coconut |
| 2 eggs | |

First prepare the cookie base in the following manner: Preheat the oven to 375°. With a pastry brush, spread 1 tablespoon of the softened butter evenly over the bottom of a 13-by-9-by-2-inch cake pan and set it aside.

In a deep bowl, cream the remaining 8 tablespoons of butter and ½ cup of the dark brown sugar together by beating and mashing them against the sides of the bowl with the back of a large spoon until the mixture is light and fluffy. Beat in the flour ½ cup at a time. Place the mixture in the buttered pan and, with your fingers, pat it smooth. Bake in the middle of the oven for 15 minutes, or until the cookie base is delicately colored and firm to the touch.

Meanwhile, beat the eggs, baking powder and vanilla extract together lightly with a wire whisk or a fork. Add the remaining cup of brown sugar and mix well, then stir in the pecans and coconut.

When the cookie base has baked its allotted time, pour the egg batter over it and smooth the top with the back of a spoon. Continue baking for 15 minutes longer, or until the top is golden brown and firm. Remove the pan from the oven and let the cake cool completely to room temperature, then cut it into 1½-inch squares for serving.

To make about thirty 2½-inch-
  long sticks

1 tablespoon plus ½ pound
  unsalted butter, softened
¼ cup granulated sugar
¼ teaspoon salt

2 cups unsifted flour
2 teaspoons vanilla extract
1 cup finely chopped walnuts or
  filberts
1 cup confectioners' sugar

Preheat the oven to 350°. With a pastry brush, spread the tablespoon of softened butter evenly over a large baking sheet and set it aside.

In a deep bowl, cream the remaining ½ pound of the softened butter with the granulated sugar by beating and mashing them against the sides of the bowl with the back of a large spoon until light and fluffy. Sprinkle the salt over the flour and add the flour mixture to the butter ½ cup at a time, beating after each addition. Beat in the vanilla and chopped nuts.

To shape each *bâton,* cut off a heaping tablespoon of the dough and roll it with your hands into a cylinder about 2½ inches long and ½ inch in diameter. Arrange the *bâtons* 1 inch apart on the buttered baking sheet and bake them in the middle of the oven for 10 to 12 minutes, or until they are a delicate golden color.

With a wide metal spatula, transfer the *bâtons* to wire racks. When they are completely cool, roll each cookie in the confectioners' sugar to coat it evenly on all sides. In a tightly covered jar or tin, *bâtons de noisettes* can safely be kept for several weeks.

## Walnut Crescents

To make about 4 dozen cookies

2 tablespoons butter, softened, plus
  ½ pound butter, chilled and cut
  into ¼-inch bits, plus 3
  tablespoons butter, melted
¾ cup light brown sugar
1½ teaspoons ground cinnamon

¾ cup finely chopped walnuts
1 cup (8 ounces) creamed cottage
  cheese
2 cups flour, sifted before
  measuring
1 egg yolk, lightly beaten with 2
  tablespoons cold water

Preheat the oven to 400°. With a pastry brush, spread the 2 tablespoons of softened butter evenly over two large baking sheets. Combine the brown sugar and cinnamon and sift them together into a bowl. Add the chopped nuts and mix well. Set aside.

Place the cottage cheese and ½ pound of the butter bits in a deep bowl and mash them together with a large spoon. Add the flour, stir briefly, then rub the flour and fat between your fingers until they are well blended and the dough can be gathered into a ball. Cut the dough into three equal parts and shape each part into balls.

To shape the cookies, place one ball of dough on a lightly floured surface and roll it out into a circle about 10 inches in diameter and ⅛ inch thick. Brush the circle with 1 tablespoon of the melted butter and sprinkle the top evenly with ½ cup of the brown-sugar-and-walnut mixture. Using a small sharp knife or a pastry wheel, cut the circle into quarters, then into eighths, and finally into 16 wedges. Starting from the wide outside edge, roll up each wedge and shape the roll into a crescent. Arrange the crescents 1 inch apart on the baking sheet, then roll and shape each of the remaining balls of dough in a similar fashion.

With the pastry brush, coat the top and sides of each crescent lightly with the egg-yolk-and-water mixture. Bake in the middle of the oven for 12 to 15 minutes, or until the crescents are golden brown. Then transfer them to wire racks to cool before serving. In a tightly covered jar, the walnut crescents can safely be kept for 2 or 3 weeks.

## Pecan Lace Cookies *(Creole-Acadian)*

To make about 30 four-inch round cookies

| | |
|---|---|
| 6 tablespoons butter, softened | A pinch of salt |
| 4 tablespoons plus ½ cup unsifted flour | 2 cups sugar |
| 1 teaspoon double-acting baking powder | 2 eggs, well beaten |
| | 1 teaspoon vanilla extract |
| | 2 cups coarsely chopped pecans |

Preheat the oven to 400°. With a pastry brush, spread 2 tablespoons of the softened butter over two large baking sheets. Sprinkle each baking sheet with 1 tablespoon of the flour and tip the pan from side to side to distribute the flour evenly. Invert the baking sheet and rap it sharply to remove the excess flour. Combine ½ cup of the flour, the baking powder and the salt, and sift them together into a bowl. Set aside.

In a deep bowl, cream 2 tablespoons of softened butter by beating and mashing it against the sides of the bowl with the back of a spoon until it is light and fluffy. Add the sugar, beat in the eggs and the vanilla extract, and stir the flour mixture into the batter. Then add the pecans.

Drop the batter by the heaping teaspoonful onto the prepared baking sheets, spacing the cookies about 3 inches apart. Bake in the middle of the oven for 5 minutes, or until the cookies have spread into lacelike 4-inch rounds and have turned golden brown. Let the cookies cool for a minute or so, then transfer them to wire racks to cool completely.

Let the baking sheets cool completely, then coat them with the remaining 2 tablespoons of softened butter and 2 tablespoons of flour, and bake the remaining cookies in the preheated oven. In a tightly covered jar or box, the cookies can safely be kept for a week or so.

## Suspiros *(Portuguese-American)*

To make about 4 dozen cookies

| | |
|---|---|
| 1 tablespoon butter, softened | ½ teaspoon strained fresh lemon |
| 3 egg whites |    juice |
| ¾ cup sugar | 1 teaspoon grated lemon rind |
| ⅛ teaspoon vanilla extract | 1 cup slivered blanched almonds |

Preheat the oven to 250°. With a pastry brush or paper towel, lightly coat two cookie sheets with the tablespoon of softened butter. Set the cookie sheets aside.

In a large mixing bowl (preferably one of unlined copper), beat the egg whites with a whisk or a rotary or electric beater until they froth. Gradually beat in the sugar and vanilla extract, and continue to beat until the whites are stiff enough to form firm unwavering peaks on the beater when it is lifted out of the bowl. With a rubber spatula, using an over-and-under rather than a stirring motion, gently but thoroughly fold in the lemon juice, lemon rind and almonds.

Drop the meringue by the teaspoon onto the buttered cookie sheets, letting it mound naturally and leaving at least 1 inch between each mound. Bake in the center of the oven for 40 minutes, then transfer the cookies to wire racks to cool to room temperature.

## Pecan Drops *(Far West)*

To make about 2 dozen cookies

| | |
|---|---|
| 1 tablespoon butter, softened | 1 cup light brown sugar, sifted |
| 1 egg white | 1½ cups pecan halves (about 6 |
| |    ounces) |

Preheat the oven to 250°. With a pastry brush, spread the softened butter evenly over two large baking sheets and set them aside.

With a wire whisk or a rotary or electric beater, beat the egg white until it is stiff enough to form soft peaks on the whisk or beater when it is lifted from the bowl. Beat in the brown sugar about ¼ cup at a time, and continue to beat until the meringue mixture is very stiff and no longer glossy. With a rubber spatula, gently fold in the pecan halves.

497

To form each pecan drop, scoop up 1 tablespoonful of the meringue mixture and, with the aid of another spoon, slide it in a small mound onto the buttered baking sheets. Arrange the pecan drops about 1 inch apart to allow them to spread slightly. Bake in the middle of the oven for about 30 minutes, or until the pecan drops have lost all their sheen and are a pale biscuit color. With a spatula, transfer them to a cake rack to cool before serving.

# *Candy & Nuts*

Candymaking was once a delightful pastime for adults and children alike. And taffy pulls and fudge parties can still be wonderful family activities, serving as well as sweet introductions to the art of cooking. More sophisticated candies like French-Canadian penuche, Southern bourbon balls and Creole pecan pralines and almond nougats make marvelous party fare. Or they can be gaily boxed and wrapped as holiday gifts. Alas, a dreary rainy day is not the best time for candymaking. The high humidity will require longer cooking, and produce less predictable results.

Success in candymaking depends not only on weather but on the temperatures at which the sugar forms crystals. The easiest and most accurate guide is a professional candy thermometer. To use it properly, test its accuracy by placing it in a pan of water and bringing the water to a boil. The temperature should read 212°F: If not, adjust the degrees called for in the recipe accordingly. Warm the thermometer before inserting it in the hot candy mixture, and do not let the bulb touch the bottom of the pan. Read the temperature at eye level, and clean the thermometer after each use by soaking it in warm water.

## Peanut Brittle *(South)*

To make about 1¾ pounds

| | |
|---|---|
| 2 teaspoons unsalted butter, softened, plus 2 tablespoons unsalted butter, cut into bits | ⅔ cup cold water |
| 1½ cups sugar | 2 cups lightly salted toasted Spanish peanuts, unpeeled |
| ⅔ cup light corn syrup | 1 teaspoon strained fresh lemon juice |

With a pastry brush, lightly coat a 15-inch-long cookie sheet or jelly-roll pan with the 2 teaspoons of softened butter.

Combine the sugar, corn syrup and water in a heavy 1½- to 2-quart enameled or stainless-steel saucepan. Stirring constantly, cook over moderate heat until the sugar dissolves. Raise the heat and bring the syrup to a boil. Continue to boil uncovered until the syrup reaches a temperature of 300° on a candy thermometer, meanwhile brushing down the crystals that form on the sides of the pan with a pastry brush lightly moistened with cold water.

Remove the pan from the heat and, with a wooden spoon, quickly stir in the nuts, butter bits and lemon juice. Pour the mixture at once onto the cookie sheet or jelly-roll pan and set aside at room temperature for about 30 minutes, until the candy hardens. Break the peanut brittle into irregularly shaped pieces and serve at once, or wrap in plastic bags and store in a covered container.

## Candied Cranberries *(New England)*

To make about 2 cups

| | |
|---|---|
| | 4 cups sugar |
| 2 cups firm fresh unblemished cranberries | 1 cup water |
| | A pinch of cream of tartar |

Wash the cranberries under cold running water and pat them completely dry with paper towels. With a trussing needle or a small skewer, pierce each berry completely through. Set the berries aside.

In a 2- to 3-quart enameled or stainless-steel saucepan, combine 3 cups of the sugar, the water and the cream of tartar. Stirring constantly, cook over moderate heat until the sugar dissolves. Raise the heat, let the syrup come to a boil, and cook briskly, uncovered and undisturbed, for about 5 minutes more, or until the syrup reaches a temperature of 220° on a candy thermometer. Remove the pan from the heat and gently stir the cranberries into the syrup, turning them about with a spoon until the berries are evenly coated. Set aside at room temperature for at least 12 hours, preferably overnight.

Stirring gently, bring the cranberries and syrup to a simmer over moderate heat. Then drain the berries in a sieve or colander set over a bowl and return the syrup to the saucepan.

Bring the syrup to a boil over high heat and cook briskly, uncovered and undisturbed, until it reaches a temperature of 250° on a candy thermometer, or until a few drops spooned into water immediately form a firm but still slightly pliable ball.

Remove the pan from the heat, drop the berries into the syrup, and stir gently until they are thoroughly coated and glistening. With a slotted spoon, arrange the berries in one layer on a long strip of wax paper. (Discard the remaining syrup.) Let the berries cool to lukewarm; if pools of syrup collect around any of the berries, carefully move the berries to a clean part of the paper.

Two or three at a time, roll the berries in the remaining cup of sugar and transfer them to fresh wax paper. Cool the berries completely to room temperature before serving.

## *Almond Nougat* (Creole-Acadian)

To make about eighty 1¼-inch squares

| | |
|---|---|
| 1½ cups coarsely chopped almonds (about ½ pound) | 1¾ cups light corn syrup |
| | 3 egg whites |
| 1 tablespoon butter, softened, plus 2 tablespoons butter, cut into ½-inch bits | ⅓ cup water |
| | ¾ cup confectioners' sugar |
| | 1 teaspoon vanilla extract |
| 2½ cups granulated sugar | ½ teaspoon salt |

Preheat the oven to 350°. Spread the almonds in one layer in a shallow baking dish and, stirring occasionally, toast them in the middle of the oven for about 5 minutes, or until they are delicately browned. Remove the dish from the oven and set the almonds aside. With a pastry brush, spread the tablespoon of softened butter evenly over a large baking sheet. Set the baking sheet aside.

Combine ½ cup of the granulated sugar and 1 cup of the corn syrup in a heavy 2- to 3-quart saucepan and stir over moderate heat until the sugar dissolves. Raise the heat and boil briskly, uncovered and undisturbed, until the syrup reaches a temperature of 248° on a candy thermometer, or until a few drops spooned into ice water immediately forms a firm but still slightly pliable ball.

Watch the syrup carefully and when it begins to bubble and rise in the pan, reduce the heat for a few moments. When sugar crystals appear inside the pan, brush them back into the syrup with a natural-bristle (not nylon) pastry brush that has been lightly moistened with water.

Meanwhile, in the large bowl of a stationary electric beater, beat the egg whites at medium speed until they are stiff enough to stand in soft peaks on the beater when it is lifted out of the bowl.

Beating constantly at medium speed, pour in the syrup in a slow, thin stream and continue to beat for 4 to 5 minutes, or until the mixture is thick and begins to stiffen. Turn off the machine and let the candy mixture stand at room temperature while you prepare a second batch of syrup.

In a heavy 3- to 4-quart saucepan, combine the remaining 2 cups of granulated sugar, the remaining ¾ cup of corn syrup and the water, and stir over moderate heat until the sugar dissolves. Raise the heat and boil briskly, uncovered and undisturbed, until the syrup reaches a temperature of 272° on a candy thermometer, or until a drop spooned into ice water immediately separates into hard, but not brittle, threads. Watch the syrup carefully and adjust the heat when necessary.

Beating constantly at medium speed, pour the second batch of syrup into the egg-white-and-syrup mixture in a slow, thin stream. Continue to beat for about 10 minutes longer, or until the candy becomes opaque and creamy, then beat in the 2 tablespoons of butter bits and the confectioners' sugar, vanilla extract and salt. With a wooden spoon, stir in the reserved toasted almonds.

Working quickly, spread the nougat mixture in the buttered baking dish. Pat it to a thickness of about ¾ inch with the palms of your hands and smooth the top with a rolling pin. When the nougat cools to room temperature, cover it with wax paper and set it aside in a cool place (not the refrigerator) for at least 12 hours.

Cut the nougat into 1¼-inch squares and serve at once. Or packet each piece in a square of foil or plastic wrap and store the nougat in a tightly covered jar or tin until ready to serve.

## Pecan Pralines (Creole-Acadian)

To make about 2 dozen 2½-inch round candies

| | |
|---|---|
| ⅓ cup light brown sugar | 2 tablespoons butter, softened |
| ⅛ teaspoon salt | ¼ cup light cream or evaporated |
| 1 teaspoon vanilla extract | milk |
| 2 cups (about ½ pound) coarsely | 2 cups granulated sugar |
| chopped pecans | ½ cup water |

With a pastry brush, spread the softened butter on the bottom of two large baking sheets or jelly-roll pans. Set them aside.

Warm the light cream or evaporated milk over low heat in a small saucepan. When bubbles begin to form around the edges of the pan, remove the pan from the heat and cover it tightly to keep the cream or evaporated milk warm.

Combine the granulated sugar and water in a 10-inch cast-iron or enameled-iron skillet about 2 inches deep and bring to a boil over high heat, stirring until the sugar dissolves. Reduce the heat to moderate and, gripping a pot holder in each hand, tip the pan back and forth gently until the syrup turns a rich, golden brown. This may take 10 minutes or more.

As soon as the syrup reaches the correct color, remove the skillet from the heat and, with a wooden spoon, stir in the brown sugar and salt. Stirring constantly, pour in the warm cream or evaporated milk in a slow, thin stream. Add the vanilla extract, and then stir in the pecans.

To form each praline, ladle about 4 teaspoons of the pecan mixture onto a buttered baking sheet. As you proceed, space the pralines about 3 inches apart to allow room for them to spread into 2½-inch rounds. When the pralines have cooled to room temperature, transfer them to a serving plate with a wide metal spatula.

NOTE: To make benne pralines, substitute ½ cup of sesame (or benne) seeds for the 2 cups of pecans. Before warming the cream or milk, place the seeds in a heavy ungreased 8-inch skillet and, stirring constantly, toast them over moderate heat for about 5 minutes, or until they are a delicate golden color. Then prepare the pralines as described above, adding the benne seeds after the vanilla extract is incorporated into the candy.

## *Spiced Mixed Nuts*

To make about 1 pound

| | |
|---|---|
| 1 tablespoon butter, softened | ½ teaspoon salt |
| ¾ cup sugar | 1 egg white, lightly beaten |
| 1 teaspoon ground cinnamon | 2 tablespoons cold water |
| ½ teaspoon ground cloves | 1 cup whole blanched unsalted |
| ¼ teaspoon ground nutmeg |   almonds |
| ¼ teaspoon ground ginger | 1 cup unsalted broken black walnuts |
| ¼ teaspoon ground allspice | ½ cup whole unsalted filberts |

Preheat the oven to 275°. With a pastry brush, spread the tablespoon of softened butter over a large baking sheet. Combine the sugar, cinnamon, cloves, nutmeg, ginger, allspice and salt in a small bowl and mix well. Add the egg white and water and stir until the mixture is a smooth paste. With a table fork, stir in about ½ cup of the nuts and, when they are evenly coated, transfer one at a time to the baking sheet. Coat the remaining nuts by the half cupful and arrange on the sheet in one layer.

Bake the nuts in the middle of the oven for 45 minutes, or until the spice coating is crisp and golden brown. Cool to room temperature and store the spiced mixed nuts in a tightly covered jar until ready to serve.

To make 1½ pounds

2 to 3 tablespoons butter, softened,
   plus 4 tablespoons butter, cut into
   ½-inch bits
2 cups dark molasses
1 cup granulated sugar
½ cup dark brown sugar, packed

down
¾ cup water
2 teaspoons distilled white vinegar
⅛ teaspoon baking soda
¼ teaspoon salt
2 or 3 drops oil of peppermint
   (optional)

With a pastry brush, spread 1 tablespoon of the softened butter evenly on the bottom and sides of a large shallow baking pan. Set aside.

Combine the molasses, granulated sugar, brown sugar and water in a heavy 6- to 8-quart enameled casserole and cook over high heat, stirring constantly until the molasses and sugar dissolve. Reduce the heat to moderate and boil uncovered and undisturbed until the syrup reaches a temperature of 200° on a candy thermometer. Regulate the heat to prevent the syrup from foaming up and boiling over the sides of the pan.

Stirring deeply and constantly with a wooden spoon to prevent the syrup from burning, continue to boil until it reaches a temperature of 250° on a candy thermometer or until a few drops spooned into ice water immediately form a firm but still slightly pliable ball.

Remove the pan from the heat and beat in the 4 tablespoons of butter bits, the vinegar, soda, salt and, if you like, a few drops of oil of peppermint. Pour the candy into the buttered pan and set it aside for about 10 minutes to cool slightly.

While the taffy is still warm and pliable, coat your hands with a tablespoon or so of the remaining softened butter and pinch off about one fourth of the candy. Grasp the piece of candy with both hands and pull it into a ropelike strand about 1 inch thick. Fold the rope together into thirds and stretch it out again. Working quickly, repeat the pulling and folding until the taffy lightens to a pale brown color and begins to stiffen. Stretch the taffy into a rope and, with kitchen scissors, cut it into 1-inch lengths. Butter your hands again, pinch off another fourth of the candy, and repeat the entire procedure until all the taffy has been pulled.

Serve at once. Or wrap each piece of taffy in a 5-inch square of wax paper, twisting the ends tightly, and store in a covered container.

## *Maple-Walnut Fudge Balls* (New England)

To make about 36 one-inch balls
1 teaspoon butter, softened
1 pound maple sugar
1 cup sugar

1 cup heavy cream
½ teaspoon cream of tartar
1 cup walnuts, pulverized in a
   blender or with a nut grinder

With a pastry brush, spread the softened butter evenly over the bottom and sides of an 8-by-6-by-2-inch baking dish.

If the maple sugar is moist, grate it on the finest side of a stand-up hand grater. If it is dry, grate it with a nut grinder. (There should be about 2 cups, packed, of grated maple sugar.) Combine the maple sugar, white sugar, cream and cream of tartar in a heavy 3- to 4-quart saucepan. Bring to a boil over high heat, stirring until the sugar dissolves. Reduce the heat and boil slowly, uncovered and undisturbed, until the syrup reaches a temperature of 240° on a candy thermometer, or until a few drops spooned into ice water immediately form a soft ball.

Pour the fudge into the buttered dish, cool to room temperature, then chill in the refrigerator for at least 3 hours. Transfer the fudge to a deep bowl and, with an electric beater or wooden spoon, beat it until light and creamy. Pinch off about 1 tablespoon of the fudge and roll it between the palms of your hands until it forms a ball about 1 inch in diameter. Roll it gently in the pulverized walnuts and when the entire surface is lightly coated set it aside on a platter. Refrigerate until ready to serve.

## Bourbon Balls  *(South)*

To make about 60 one-inch candies

| | |
|---|---|
| 8 one-ounce squares semisweet chocolate, coarsely chopped | pin (about 3 cups) |
| 60 vanilla wafers, pulverized in a blender or wrapped in a towel and finely crushed with a rolling | 1 cup finely chopped pecans |
| | 1⅔ cups sugar |
| | ½ cup bourbon |
| | ¼ cup light corn syrup |

In a small heavy skillet, melt the chocolate over low heat, stirring almost constantly to prevent the bottom from scorching. Remove the pan from the heat and let the chocolate cool to lukewarm.

Combine the pulverized vanilla wafers, pecans and ⅔ cup of sugar in a deep bowl. Pour in the chocolate, bourbon and corn syrup and stir vigorously with a wooden spoon until the ingredients are well combined.

To shape each bourbon ball, scoop up about a tablespoon of the mixture and pat it into a ball about 1 inch in diameter. Roll the balls in the remaining cup of sugar and, when they are lightly coated on all sides, place them in a wide-mouthed 1-quart jar equipped with a securely fitting lid. Cut two rounds from a double thickness of paper towels to fit inside the lid of the jar. Moisten the paper rounds with a little additional bourbon and press them tightly into the lid.

Seal the jar with the paper-lined lid and set the bourbon balls aside at room temperature for 3 or 4 days before serving. Tightly covered, the bourbon balls can safely be kept for 3 to 4 weeks.

To make about 30 one-inch squares

2 cups light brown sugar, firmly
    packed
2 cups white sugar

2 cups light cream
1 teaspoon butter, softened
½ teaspoon vanilla extract

Combine the brown sugar, white sugar and cream in a heavy 3- to 4-quart saucepan and stir over moderate heat until the sugar dissolves. Raise the heat and boil briskly, uncovered and undisturbed, until the candy reaches a temperature of 238° on a candy thermometer, or until a few drops spooned into ice water immediately form a soft but compact ball. Watch the candy carefully and when it begins to bubble up in the pan, reduce the heat for a few moments. If sugar crystals appear around the inside of the pan, brush them back into the candy with a natural bristled (not nylon) pastry brush that has been lightly moistened with water.

Remove the pan from the heat and let the candy cool for about 5 minutes. Meanwhile, with a dry pastry brush, spread the softened butter evenly over the bottom and sides of an 8-by-6-by-2-inch baking dish.

When the candy has cooled slightly, beat it with a wooden spoon until it is thick enough to hold its shape almost solidly in the spoon. Beat in the vanilla, then pour the *sucre à la crème* into the buttered dish, spreading it and smoothing the top with the spoon or a spatula. Cool to room temperature, then cut the candy into 1-inch squares.

# *Appendix*

## *Tips on Outdoor Cooking*

Cooking foods over coals gives them a unique, smoky flavor. Of the three common fuels —nonresinous wood, charcoal and briquets— the latter are the cleanest, most dependable and easiest to work with.

If you are using a grill or brazier, as most outdoor cooks do, first line the box or bowl with heavy aluminum foil to catch the drippings. Then, make a fire base about an inch deep of gravel or one of the commercial fire bases. Use enough to provide an ample level surface for the fire.

The easiest way to start a fire is with an electric fire starter, but if you do not have one, use starter fluid.

Most cooks make larger fires than they need. In a small portable grill, you may begin with one or two dozen briquets. If you need to add fuel later, lay the fresh fuel around the burning coals and rake it in as it ignites. The fire will be ready about half an hour after it has been lit, or when all briquets are ignited and a little white ash begins to show.

Before starting to cook, spread the coals evenly with a poker, creating a flat surface slightly larger than that of the food to be cooked. Start the cooking with the meat as high as possible above the coals and bring it closer as the fire cools. (If your grill is not adjustable, regulate the heat by spreading the coals or sprinkling them with a little water.)

## *Grilling (Broiling)*

Relatively low temperatures are best for all cooking over coals, but the fire should be hotter for broiling than for spit roasting. An instant response thermometer is helpful for checking the internal temperature, or doneness of meats.

BEEF, PORK AND LAMB: Any meat that can be fried, oven- or pan-broiled can be broiled on an outdoor grill.

POULTRY: Small broiling chickens should be split and the backbones removed to make them flat. Larger ones should be cut into pieces. Small chickens will cook in 30 minutes, larger ones in 50 minutes. Ducklings, halved or quartered, should be broiled 45 to 60 minutes. Any fowl should be turned occasionally.

SEAFOOD: Fish should be cooked in a grill basket for easy flipping. Whole fish weighing 5 to 6 pounds can be grilled in 20 to 45 minutes. They are done when the internal temperature reaches 150°. Small fish may be wrapped in a double thickness of aluminum foil and roasted in the coals. They will be done in 15 to 20 minutes. Fish steaks will cook on a grill in 7 to 15 minutes. Fillets will be done in 5 to 7 minutes.

Charcoal-broiled lobsters are delicious. A 1¼-pound one will take about 12 to 14 minutes. Split the lobster after it is done, remove the stomach and fill with butter.

Oysters grilled in the shell have a unique, smoky flavor; cook them until the shells pop open.

Shrimp to be broiled should be dipped in oil or butter, or marinated for a couple of hours. They will cook in 3 to 5 minutes.

FRUITS AND VEGETABLES: Whole apples may be wrapped in foil and baked in the edge of the coals, or they may be cored and filled with sugar, cinnamon and butter before they are wrapped and cooked in the same way. They will be done in about 30 minutes in either case.

To cook corn on the cob, pull back the husks, remove the silk, put the husks back in place and tie them with a string. Then soak them in water for at least 30 minutes so they will be tender and moist. Corn will roast on a grill in 10 to 15 minutes over a hot fire.

Potatoes in their skins will roast in about 45 minutes buried in the coals.

KABOBS: Food cooked on skewers is usually cut into 1½- to 2-inch cubes. It may be beef, pork, lamb, veal, fish, shellfish, poultry, fruits or vegetables, alone or in any of several combinations.

The skewers may be ready-made ones of metal or bamboo, or they may be improvised from wire or green twigs.

String meat cubes close together to cook them rare—farther apart if you want them well done. Meat kabobs will cook in 10 to 16 minutes.

## Rotisserie or Spit Roasting

Cooking roasts, whole poultry or game birds over coals requires a rotisserie or hand-turned spit and a meat thermometer. Most outdoor roasting today is done on electrically turned rotisseries.

For roasts to cook properly on a rotisserie, they must be perfectly balanced on the rod and should turn easily with it. The rod must pass as nearly as possible through the center of gravity of the meat. If the meat is not balanced the spit will turn jerkily and its motor may even stop. Therefore, it is advisable to buy roasts that are boned, rolled and tied.

The thermometer should be inserted at a slight angle so that the tip is in the center of the roast but not resting in fat or against the rod or a bone.

Before starting to cook anything on a rotisserie, make a trough of aluminum foil about 3 or 4 inches wide and the length of the spit. Position the trough underneath the spit to catch the drippings, thus preventing flareups from burning fat. Bank the coals around the trough.

Only the leaner and tenderer cuts of meat should be cooked on a rotisserie. Here are some suggested cuts, approximate cooking times for the weights given and the temperatures the thermometer should reach.

BEEF: Rib-eye or Delmonico, 4 to 6 pounds: rare, 20-22 minutes per pound, 135°; medium, 22 to 24 minutes per pound, 145°.
Sirloin tip, 3½ to 4 pounds: rare to medium, 35 to 40 minutes per pound, 135°-145°.
Rolled rib, 5 to 7 pounds: rare, 18 to 20 minutes per pound, 135°; medium, 30 to 35 minutes per pound, 145°.

PORK: Boned rolled shoulder, 4 to 5 pounds: 20 to 22 minutes per pound.
Loin roll, 3 to 5 pounds: 20 to 25 minutes per pound.
Leg, boned, 7 to 10 pounds: 20 to 25 minutes per pound.
Fresh ham, 10 to 12 pounds: 20 to 25 minutes per pound.
(All pork roasts should reach a temperature of 170°.)

LAMB: Rolled leg, 4 to 5 pounds: 18 to 22 minutes per pound, 140°.
Shoulder roll, 3 to 5 pounds: 18 to 22 minutes per pound, 140°.

POULTRY: Chicken, 3 to 5 pounds: 20 minutes per pound, 165°.
Duckling, 4 to 5 pounds: 18 minutes per pound, 165°.
Goose, 12 to 15 pounds: 12 to 15 minutes per pound, 160°.
Turkey, 12 to 15 pounds: 18 to 20 minutes per pound, 160°.

FISH: Whole fish, 5 to 6 pounds: 20 to 45 minutes, 150°.
A small whole fish cooks in 15 minutes.

## Marinades and Bastes

A marinade is a liquid mixture in which food is soaked before it is cooked. It usually contains wine, vinegar or lemon juice to tenderize the flesh.

A baste is brushed or sprinkled on the food while it is cooking. It is designed to add a distinctive flavor on the outside and to moisten the food. Most marinades can be converted to bastes by adding oil to them.

Some meats, poultry and fish to be cooked over coal should first be marinated. Some should be basted as they cook. Others do not need marinades or bastes. Avoid indiscriminate use of "barbecue" sauces that do nothing but disguise natural flavors. An all-purpose marinade and baste, one that may be used with any meat, game or poultry, can be made by combining equal parts of dry Italian or French vermouth and olive oil.

For less tender cuts of beef and for game, combine 2 cups of red wine, ¼ cup of vinegar or lemon juice, 1 sliced onion, ¼ cup each of chopped onion and carrot, a few peppercorns and an herb bouquet consisting of bay, parsley and thyme. (Add one cup of oil to make a baste.)

For poultry, shellfish, beef or pork, combine equal parts of soy sauce, sherry or whiskey and oil. This may be seasoned with garlic.

To make a highly seasoned barbecue sauce for meat and poultry, combine one 8-ounce can of tomato sauce, 1 teaspoon each of dry mustard, sugar and salt, 1 tablespoon each of Worcestershire sauce and vinegar, ½ cup of red wine, 1 clove of finely chopped garlic. Add Tabasco to taste. Simmer 10 minutes and strain. For a baste, add ½ cup of oil.

To make pepper barbecue sauce for steaks, chops and hamburgers, combine one 8-ounce can of tomato juice with ¼ cup each of olive oil, chopped green pepper and chopped green onion. Add 3 cloves of finely chopped garlic, 1 tablespoon or more of chili powder and salt to taste. Simmer 10 minutes and strain. For a baste, add ½ cup of oil.

# Extra Mileage for Lard and Oil

After it has been used for deep frying, lard or vegetable oil may be cooled and strained through a fine sieve lined with a double thickness of dampened cheesecloth, then refrigerated in a tightly covered, labeled can or jar. Preserved in this fashion, the fat may be stored for several weeks and re-used two or three times.

# How to Handle Hot Chilies

Hot chilies are cousins to the familiar green bell peppers, but they require special handling. Their volatile oils may make your skin tingle and your eyes burn. While working with the chilies, wear rubber gloves if you can and be careful not to touch your face. To prepare chilies, rinse them clean under cold running water. (Hot water may cause fumes to rise from dried chilies, and even these fumes can irritate your nose and eyes.) Cut or break off the stems if you wish to leave the seeds (the hottest parts of chilies) in the pods. If a chili is to be seeded, pull out the stem and the seeds with your gloved fingers. In most cases the ribs inside are thin, but if they seem thick and fleshy you may cut them out with a small sharp knife. Follow the instructions in the recipes for slicing or chopping chilies. After handling hot chilies it is essential that you wash your hands and gloves thoroughly with soap and water.

# How to Clean and Fillet Fish

Landing an elusive fish is not the last of a sport fisherman's problems. Unless a friendly fishmonger is nearby, the fisherman must clean his catch, a job that often entails boning the fish and may also require skinning it, as shown in the drawings.

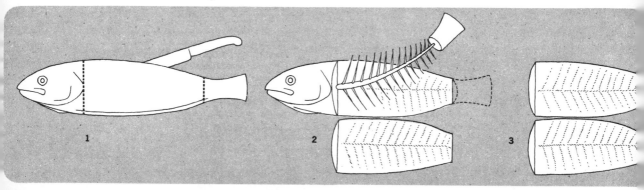

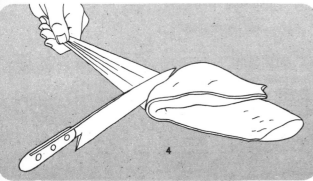

### FILLETING AND SKINNING A RAW FISH

Slit the fish open along the belly and gut it. Wash the fish inside and out under cold running water. With a large sharp knife, cut off the fins, head and bony plates below the gills (1). Starting at the head end, cut along the back (2) and free the flesh from the skeleton (3). Turn the fish over and repeat the procedure, starting from the tail. Discard tail and skeleton. Some fish, such as largemouth bass and catfish, must be skinned after being filleted. Insert the knife between the skin and flesh at the tail end (4). Holding the skin with one hand, cut and push the flesh away from it with the edge and side of the knife blade.

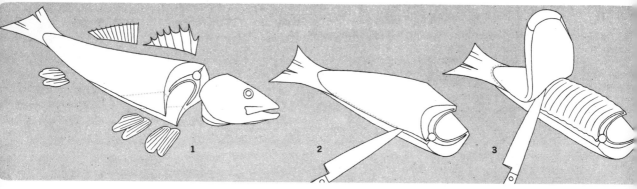

### FILLETING A COOKED TROUT

With the trout laid flat on a plate, use a knife to free the top fillet from the rest of the body by cutting through to the skeleton behind the gills, just above the tail and along the back (1). Lift the freed fillet and turn it skin side down (2). Pick up the tail and carefully cut and lift the skeleton and the head away from the bottom fillet. Discard the bones—and enjoy your two fresh fillets of trout (3).

# Techniques for Home Canning

To ensure consistent results in home canning, use standard canning jars or jelly glasses with matching lids. Examine each jar or glass carefully and discard those with loose covers and those with cracked or chipped edges. An airtight seal is essential to prevent food spoilage.

Wash the jars, glasses, lids and rubber rings in hot soapy water and rinse them in scalding water. Place them in a large deep pot and pour in enough hot water to cover them completely. Bring to a boil over high heat, then turn off the heat while you finish cooking the food that you plan to can. The jars or glasses must be hot when they are filled. (If you have a dishwasher with a sanitizing cycle, simply run the jars, glasses, lids and rings through the cycle, using your usual dishwashing powder, and leave them in the closed machine until you are ready to can.)

To prepare for sealing the glasses, grate a 4-ounce bar of paraffin into the top of a double boiler (preferably one with a pouring spout), and melt the paraffin over hot water. Paraffin is highly flammable; melting it in a sauce pan over direct heat is dangerous.

When the food is ready for canning, lift the jars or glasses from the pot or dishwasher with tongs and stand them upright on a level surface. Leave the lids and rings in the pot (or dishwasher) until you are ready to use them. Fill and seal the jars one at a time, filling each jar to within $\frac{1}{8}$ inch of the top or each glass to within $\frac{1}{2}$ inch of the top. Each jar should be sealed quickly and tightly with its ring and lid. (If there is not enough food to fill the last jar or glass completely, do not attempt to seal it. Refrigerate and use within the next week.)

The jelly glasses also should be sealed at once. Pour a single thin layer of hot paraffin over the surface of the jelly, making sure it covers the jelly completely and touches the glass on all sides. If air bubbles appear on the paraffin, prick them immediately with the tip of a knife. Let the glasses rest until the paraffin cools and hardens, then cover with metal lids.

If a recipe calls for finishing the preserving process with a water bath, place the filled and sealed jars side by side on a rack in a canner or other deep large pot. Pour in enough hot (not boiling) water to cover the jars by at least 1 inch, securely cover the pot with its lid, and bring to a boil over moderate heat. Boil for the time recommended in the particular recipe. Then, with tongs, remove the jars from the pot and let them cool at room temperature for about 12 hours. Test the seal by pressing the center of each lid with your forefinger. If the inner lid remains in place, unscrew the outer ring, leaving the seal intact. Store the jar upright in a cool, dry, dark spot. If the lid moves at all, the jar is not properly sealed; in that event, refrigerate and serve the food within a week.

For additional information on canning, see "How to Make Jellies, Jams and Preserves at Home," USDA Home and Garden Bulletin No. 56, and "Making Pickles and Relishes at Home," USDA Home and Garden Bulletin No. 92. These bulletins cost 15 cents each and can be ordered from the Superintendent of Documents, U.S. Government Printing Office, Washington, D.C. 20402.

# Recipes by Region

Most of the recipes in this book are identified by region or by their ethnic heritage. Those that are not identified have, over the years, escaped from their regional confines to become American favorites. The listings below group the recipes by their geographical regions. In addition, there is a listing of those dishes from "the melting pot" that have retained their ethnic characters and have not yet entered the mainstream of American cooking.

CREOLE-ACADIAN
Shrimp-stuffed artichokes
*Daube glacé*
Oysters Rockefeller
Stuffed crabs

Creole vinaigrette sauce
Cold shrimp and tomato bisque
Crab, shrimp and okra gumbo
Crawfish bisque

Eggs Sardou
Creamed eggs Chartres
Creole shrimp omelets

Shrimp-and-crab-stuffed flounder
Broiled Spanish mackerel
Pompano *en papillote*
Speckled trout amandine
Shellfish boil
Boiled crawfish
Shrimp and ham jambalaya
Shrimp Creole

Louisiana chicken
Chicken Rochambeau
Pigeon casserole

Ham-stuffed eggplants
*Chaurice*
Veal rolls and olives
Veal stew
Grillades and grits

Dirty rice
Red beans and rice
Stewed corn and tomatoes
Leeks vinaigrette
Creole tomatoes

Blackberry jam

*Pain perdu*

Bread pudding with whiskey
  sauce

Bananas Foster
Cherries Jubilee
*Croquignoles*
Fig cake
*Gâteau de sirop*
Creole macaroons
*Bâtons de Noisettes*
Pecan lace cookies
Almond nougats
Pecan pralines

NORTHWEST
Shad-roe pâté

King crab salad ring
Green bean salad
Oriental salad

Dungeness crab bisque
Pacific oyster stew

Corn and clam soufflé
Molded salmon with cucumber
  sauce
Trout in aspic

Individual turkey hash ovals
Roast leg of venison
Venison mincemeat
Pheasant and apples with
  sour-cream sauce
Wild-rice-stuffed quail
Grouse with brandied-orange
  stuffing

Stuffed spareribs
Swedish pot roast
Swiss steak
Meatloaf with bacon
Veal steaks with apple rings
Veal stew with dumplings

Wild rice with mushrooms and
  almonds
Basque potatoes

Spinach ring with cheese sauce
Tomato-cheese pie

Plum ketchup
Pear honey
Apricot and pineapple jam

Sourdough rolls
Cheese bread
Cream biscuits
Swedish cherry twist

Strawberry frango
Yellow rice with cold fruit and
  curry sauce
Rhubarb custard pie
Rhubarb ring with strawberries
Blackberry and apple pie
Sour-cherry pie
Strawberry pie
Whipped cream cake
Spritz cookies
Dreams

NEW ENGLAND
Mussel, herb and caper spread
Pickled mussels

Senator Lodge's bean soup
Clam chowder
Corn chowder
Fish chowder
Nantucket scallop chowder
Dunvegan Welsh rabbit

Codfish balls
Deviled finnan haddie
Scrod broiled in lemon butter
Fried Ipswich clams
Steamed clams
Boiled lobster
Locke Ober's Lobster Savannah

*Moules marinière*
Fried scallops Portuguese style
Skewered sea scallops

Vermont chicken pie
Roast turkey with oyster stuffing

New England boiled dinner
Joe Booker stew
Red flannel hash
Braised stuffed shoulder of lamb
Boiled lamb with caper sauce
Squibnocket lamb stew
Somerset Club lamb kidneys

Boston baked beans
Harvard beets
Corn pudding
Corn oysters
Summer succotash
Squash soufflé
Maple-baked acorn squash

Green tomato relish
Beach-plum jelly
Cranberry sauce
Uncooked cranberry-orange relish

Anadama bread
Portuguese sweetbread
Nahant buns
Mayo Farm squash rolls
Parker House rolls
Cranberry muffins
Blueberry muffins
Boston brown bread
Cranberry fruit-and-nut bread

Maple mousse
Frozen cranberry mousse
Durgin Park's Indian pudding
Cranberry upside-down pudding
Blueberry grunt
Fried apple pies
Marlborough pie
Boston cream pie
Pumpkin pie
Cranberry chiffon pie
Maple walnut pie
Mincemeat pie
Wellesley fudge cake
Yule log
Apple pandowdy
Harwich hermits

Toll House cookies
Maple-walnut fudge balls
Candied cranberries
Penuche

SOUTH
Pickled shrimp
Shrimp paste
Beer cheese

Southern chicken salad
Country-style potato salad

Virginia peanut soup
Black bean soup
Shrimp-and-oyster gumbo
Seafood gumbo

Egg croquettes
Kentucky scramble
Eggs Derby
Grits and cheddar cheese
  casserole
Southern fried fish
Red snapper citrus
Maryland deviled crab
Crab cakes
Fried soft-shell crabs
Shrimp pilau

Oven-fried chicken
Southern-fried chicken with gravy
Brunswick stew
Chicken liver casserole with
  mushrooms
Roast turkey with cornbread
  stuffing
Barbecued quail

Baked ham with brown-sugar
  glaze
Baked bourbon-glazed ham
Country ham stuffed with greens
Ham hocks and black-eyed peas
Homesteaders ham loaf
Barbecued spareribs
Spiced beef round
Kentucky burgoo

Southern dry rice
Hominy grits soufflé
Plantation string beans
Hopping John
Kentucky minted carrots
Boiled greens

Sweet potatoes in orange baskets
Sherried yams with pecans

Mixed vegetable pickles
Pickled watermelon rind
Summer fruit conserve
Citrus marmalade

Sally Lunn
Leola's cornbread
Hush puppies
Spoon bread
Baking powder biscuits
Beaten biscuits
Lacy-edged batty cakes
Buttermilk coffee cake

Peppermint stick ice cream
Lime sherbet
Syllabub
Ambrosia
Black bottom pie
Pecan pie
Key lime pie
Bourbon and caramel custard pie
Lemon cheese pie
Sweet-potato pie
Lady Baltimore cake
Coconut cake with lemon filling
Lane cake
White fruit cake
Bourbon balls
Peanut brittle

FAR WEST
Crab-olive spread
*Chili con queso*
*Guacamole*
*Tostaditas*

Crab Louis
Palace Court salad
Caviar-potato salad
Yoghurt-honey dressing
Strawberry and sour cream
  dressing
Poppy seed dressing

Spiced meatball soup
Mormon split pea soup
Bowl of the Wife of Kit Carson

San Francisco fried trout
Cioppino

Lemon chicken
Grapefruit duck
Hearst Ranch squab

Broiled ham steak with
 cantaloupe
Texas chili con carne
Beef tacos
*Carne Santa Fe*
Vineyard leg of lamb
Lamb chops with pine nuts
Lamb and broccoli St. Francis

Pinto beans
Refried beans
Celery Victor
Eggplant and banana casserole
Okra and tomatoes

Trappers' fruit
Ginger fruit kabobs

Sourdough starter
San Francisco sourdough bread
Mormon rye bread
Mormon Johnnycake
Date, pecan and orange bread
Navajo fry bread
Corn tortillas
Sourdough waffles

San Antonio fruit ice cream
Glazed oranges
Houston gingerbread
Grapefruit cake
Fig squares
Lollies
Pecan drops

## EASTERN HEARTLAND
John Clancy's broiled clams

Waldorf salad
Shaker salad

Consommé Bellevue
Philadelphia pepper pot
Chicken-corn soup
Shaker herb soup
Clam bisque
Manhattan clam chowder

Broiled bluefish fillets
Mushroom-stuffed halibut steaks
Barbecued stuffed Coho salmon

Poached salmon steaks with
 *mousseline* sauce
Shad roe on bed of sorrel
Planked shad with potatoes
 *duchesse*

Batter-fried chicken
Stewed chicken with parsley
 dumplings
Chicken potpie
Chicken breasts and ham with
 sherried sauce
Roast duck with apricot-rice
 stuffing
Broiled Long Island duckling

Barbecued venison chops
Roast pheasant with filbert
 stuffing
Stuffed fresh ham
Smoked ham and apple stew with
 dumplings
Smoked pork chops and lentils
Flank steak with meat stuffing
Beef potpie
Pasties, Michigan style
Deviled short ribs
Sweetbreads *en coquille*
Martha Washington's leg of lamb

Homemade egg noddles
Broccoli purée
Batter-fried mushrooms
Fresh asparagus with lemon
 cream sauce
Fresh spinach and herbs
Pennsylvania-fried tomatoes

Chowchow
Bread-and-butter pickles
Apple butter

Whole-wheat bread
Dilly bread
Salt-rising bread
Philadelphia cinnamon buns
Buttermilk soda biscuits
Sticky buns
Apple muffins
Sugar doughnuts
Cottage cheese pancakes

Floating Island
Apples Jonathan

Strawberry flummery
Shoofly pie
Applesauce cake
Pear upside-down cake
Moravian sand tarts

## MELTING POT
Cheese-stuffed mushrooms
 (*Italian*)
Vegetables with hot
 butter-and-anchovy dip
 (*Italian*)
Sicilian pizza (*Italian*)
Melon and prosciutto (*Italian*)

Spring salad (*Jewish*)
Louis Pappas' Greek salad
 (*Greek*)
Bulghur salad (*Armenian*)

Cold borscht (*Jewish*)
Chicken soup with matzo balls
 (*Jewish*)
Minestrone (*Italian*)
Cream of leek soup (*Romanian*)

*Tortilla de Patatas (Basque)*
Egg foo yung (*Chinese*)
Blintzes (*Jewish*)

Rolled stuffed fish fillets
 (*Ukrainian*)
Fish teriyaki (*Japanese*)
Shrimp tempura *(Japanese)* )
Red snapper with vegetable sauce
 (*Greek*)
Shrimp chow mein (*Chinese*)

Chicken *alla cacciatore (Italian)*
Chicken chop suey (*Chinese*)
Chicken and shrimp casserole
 (*Basque*)
Roast chicken stuffed with chicken
 livers (*Polish*)
Chicken Tetrazzini (*Italian*)
Trader Vic's Pineapple Chicken
 (*Hawaiian*)

Herb-stuffed pork chops
 (*Ukrainian*)
Home-cured corn beef (*Jewish*)
Beef Stroganoff (*Russian*)
Sweet-and-sour stuffed cabbage
 rolls (*Jewish*)
Beef tongue in sweet-and-sour
 sauce (*Jewish*)

Veal *parmigiana (Italian)*
Veal *paprikash (Hungarian)*

Noodle pudding with apples,
  raisins and apricots (*Jewish*)
Green noodles with red clam
  sauce (*Italian*)
Spaghetti with meatballs in
  tomato sauce (*Italian*)

Baked lasagna (*Italian*)
Spaetzle (*Hungarian*)
Kasha varnishkes (*Jewish*)
Barley-and-mushroom casserole
  (*Czech*)
Gnocchi (*Italian*)

Deep-fried mixed vegetables
  (*Italian*)

Texas stollen (*German*)
Biscuit tortoni (*Italian*)
Cannoli (*Italian*)
Lindy's cheesecake (*Jewish*)
*Rugala (Jewish)*
*Suspiros (Portuguese)*
Olga's flan (*Puerto Rican*)

# Regional Menus

Although you can sample recipes in this book individually—a soup Sunday, a dessert Monday, a fish dish Tuesday—the most exciting way to experiment with this food is to concoct whole menus based on the cookery of one region or another. The foods of a region, based as they are on a common culinary background, tend to complement each other. And the selection of recipes in this book includes so many dishes from each region (the listing begins on page 512) that you can easily assemble regional menus, such as the ones on the following pages, for everything from casual brunches to elegant dinners. The New England recipes alone include 8 appetizers and soups, 19 fish, poultry and meat main dishes; 9 breads; 7 vegetables; 20 desserts. That repetoire provides the inspiration for an after-ski winter supper, a summer seashore dinner, a Thanksgiving dinner and a weekend brunch.

In these menus, dishes are designed to complement one another in flavor, texture and color—factors you should keep in mind when planning your own variations. Some other guidelines to remember are to precede or follow a rich dish with a light one, to avoid repeating a main ingredient such as shrimp or tomatoes in two courses, and to contrast strongly-seasoned foods with bland-flavored ones. Most important from the cook's standpoint, menus should be planned so that they can be prepared by one person working alone —except for occasional help from a cooperative family. Be sure to read over all of the recipes for a menu before you start to make it so that you can anticipate how long each dish will take to prepare and cook.

## CREOLE-ACADIAN MENUS

A NEW ORLEANS DINNER PARTY
*Daube glacé*

Pompano *en papillote*
French bread
Leeks vinaigrette

Bananas Foster
Pecan pralines

A BAYOU DINNER
Boiled crawfish

Shrimp and ham jambalaya
French bread

*Gâteau de sirop*

A WEEKEND BRUNCH
Oysters Rockefeller

Grillade and grits
Creole tomatoes

Cherries Jubilee

### A FAMILY SUPPER

Crawfish bisque

Ham-stuffed eggplants
Dirty rice

Pecan lace cookies

## NORTHWESTERN MENUS

### A PACIFIC LUNCH

Shad-roe pâté

King crab salad ring
Cream biscuits

Rhubarb ring with strawberries

### A FAMILY LUNCH

Corn and clam soufflé
Green bean salad
Sourdough rolls

Blackberry and apple pie

### A FIELD AND STREAM DINNER

Trout in aspic

Roast leg of venison
Spinach ring with cheese sauce
Wild rice with mushrooms and
   almonds

Sour-cherry pie

### A WINTER SUPPER

Pacific oyster stew

Stuffed spareribs
Tomato-cheese pie

Whipped cream cake

## SOUTHERN MENUS

### A DERBY DAY BUFFET BREAKFAST

Eggs Derby
Baked bourbon-glazed ham
Sweet potatoes in orange baskets

Spoon bread
Baking powder biscuits

Ambrosia

### A WEEKEND BRUNCH

Shrimp paste
Beaten biscuits

Maryland deviled crab
Buttermilk coffeecake
Citrus marmalade

Syllabub

### A SOUL FOOD DINNER

Oven-fried chicken
Ham hocks and black-eyed peas
Boiled greens
Hush puppies

Sweet-potato pie

### A SUMMER LUNCH

Virginia peanut soup

Southern chicken salad
Sally Lunn buns

Peppermint stick ice cream
Iced tea with fresh mint

## NEW ENGLAND MENUS

### AN AFTER-SKI SUPPER

Corn chowder

New England boiled dinner
Green salad

Durgin Park's Indian pudding

### A THANKSGIVING DINNER

Mussel, herb and caper spread

Roast turkey with oyster stuffing
Maple-baked acorn squash
Harvard beets
Parker House rolls
Cranberry sauce

Pumpkin pie
Cranberry chiffon pie
Mincemeat pie

### A SUMMER SEASHORE DINNER

Nantucket scallop chowder

Steamed clams
Boiled lobster
Boiled corn-on-the-cob
Mayo Farm squash rolls

Blueberry grunt

### A WEEKEND BRUNCH

Fresh fruit

Deviled finnan haddie
Portuguese sweetbread
Cranberry muffins
Beach-plum jelly

Maple mousse

## FAR WESTERN MENUS

### A TEX-MEX BUFFET

*Guacamole*
*Chili con queso*
*Tostaditas*

Texas chile con carne
Pinto beans
Corn tortillas

San Antonio fruit ice cream
Houston gingerbread

### A SAN FRANCISCO LUNCH

Steak tartare balls

Cioppino
Sourdough bread

Grapefruit cake

### A WINTER DINNER

Mormon split pea soup
Navaho fry bread

Carne Santa Fe
Okra and tomatoes

Lollies

A SUMMER DINNER

Crab-olive spread (with crackers)

Lemon chicken
Caviar-potato salad

Glazed oranges

## EASTERN HEARTLAND MENUS

A PENNSYLVANIA DUTCH DINNER

Chicken-corn soup

Stuffed fresh ham
Pennsylvania-fried tomatoes
Salt-rising bread
Apple butter
Bread-and-butter pickles

Shoofly pie

A LONG ISLAND DINNER

John Clancy's broiled clams

Roast duck with apricot-rice
  stuffing
Batter-fried mushrooms
Broccoli purée

Pear upside-down cake

A PHILADELPHIA DINNER

Consommé Bellevue

Chicken breasts and ham with
  sherried cream sauce
Green salad
Buttermilk soda biscuits

Floating Island

A SHAKER SUPPER

Shaker herb soup

Flank steak with meat stuffing
Fresh spinach and herbs

Strawberry flummery

## ALL-AMERICAN MENUS

A WEEKEND BRUNCH

Baked apples

Dilled salmon soufflé
Popovers
Rhubarb marmalade

Frozen Nesselrode pudding

A FOURTH OF JULY PARTY

Cheese balls
Scallops remoulade

Barbecued swordfish
Sautéed potato balls
Zucchini in cheese sauce

Strawberry shortcake

A SUMMER SUPPER

Cold split pea soup with mint

Grilled hamburgers
Spinach salad
Tomato aspic

Deep dish peach pie
Old-fashioned vanilla ice cream

A WINTER DINNER

Vegetables with red caviar dip

Roast beef
Stuffed baked potatoes with sour
  cream
Buttermilk fried onions
Green salad with blue-cheese
  dressing

Three-layer chocolate cake

## MELTING POT MENUS

A BUFFET SUPPER

Vegetables with hot-butter-and-
  anchovy dip

Veal *paprikash*
Spaetzle
Deep-fried mixed vegetables

Biscuit tortoni

A WEEKEND BRUNCH

Melon and proscuitto
*Tortilla de Patatas*
Texas stollen

*Suspiros*

A SUMMER LUNCH

Cold borscht

Louis Pappas' Greek Salad

Cannoli

A WINTER DINNER

Cream of leek soup

Red snapper with vegetable sauce
Kasha varnishkes

Lindy's cheesecake

# *Metric Equivalents*

Within a decade, the United States, now following a system of ounces, pounds, spoons and cups, will "go metric" like ninety percent of the world. It will take a while for American cooks to accustom themselves to liters, grams and kilograms, but the metric system will have the advantage of being universal and convenient: it is based on units of ten. Below are three tables which should help you make the adjustment as painlessly as possible if you are faced with measuring ingredients in unfamiliar weights and measures.

## WEIGHTS

| OUNCES AND POUNDS | METRIC EQUIVALENTS |
|---|---|
| 1/4 ounce | 7 grams |
| 1/3 ounce | 10 grams |
| 1/2 ounce | 14 grams |
| 1 ounce | 28 grams |
| 1 3/4 ounces | 50 grams |
| 2 ounces | 57 grams |
| 2 2/3 ounces | 75 grams |
| 3 ounces | 85 grams |
| 3 1/2 ounces | 100 grams |
| 4 ounces (1/4 pound) | 114 grams |
| 6 ounces | 170 grams |
| 8 ounces (1/2 pound) | 227 grams |
| 9 ounces | 250 grams |
| 16 ounces (1 pound) | 464 grams |
| 1.1 pounds | 500 grams |
| 2.2. pounds | 1,000 grams (1 kilogram) |

## TEMPERATURES

| C° (*Centigrade or Celsius*) | F° (*Farenheit*) |
|---|---|
| 0 | 32 (water freezes) |
| 10 | 50 |
| 20 | 68 |
| 30 | 86 |
| 60 | 140 |
| 95 | 203 (water simmers) |
| 100 | 212 (water boils) |
| 107.2 | 225 (very slow oven) |
| 120 | 245 |
| 130 | 266 |
| 149 | 300 (slow oven) |
| 177 | 350 (moderate oven) |
| 205 | 400 (hot oven) |
| 260 | 500 (very hot oven) |

## LIQUID MEASURES

| SPOONS AND CUPS | OUNCES AND QUARTS | METRIC EQUIVALENTS |
|---|---|---|
| 1 tsp. | 1/6 ounce | 5 milliliters (5 grams) |
| 2 tsp. | 1/3 ounce | 10 milliliters (10 grams) |
| 3 tsp. (1 Tbs.) | 1/2 ounce | 15 milliliters (15 grams) |
| 3 1/3 Tbs. | 1 3/4 ounces | 1/2 deciliter (50 milliliters) |
| 1/3 cup | 2 2/3 ounces | 1 deciliter less 1 1/3 Tbs. |
| 1/3 cup plus 1 Tbs. | 3 1/2 ounces | 1 deciliter (100 milliliters) |
| 1 cup | 8 ounces | 1/4 liter less 1 1/4 Tbs. |
| 1 cup plus 1 1/4 Tbs. | 8.45 ounces | 1/4 liter |
| 2 cups | 1 pint (16 oz.) | 1/2 liter less 2 1/2 Tbs. |
| 2 cups plus 2 1/2 Tbs. | 17 ounces | 1/2 liter |
| 4 cups | 1 quart | 1 liter less 1 deciliter |
| 4 1/3 cups | 1 quart 2 ounces | 1 liter (1,000 milliliters) |

# Index